A STANDARD GUIDE TO
PURE-BRED
DOGS

A STANDARD GUIDE TO
PURE-BRED
DOGS

Compiled and Edited by Harry Glover

McGRAW-HILL BOOK COMPANY
NEW YORK · ST. LOUIS · SAN FRANCISCO · TORONTO

To G.T. without whose help and encouragement
none of this would have been possible

Created, designed and produced by Trewin
Copplestone Publishing Ltd, London

Phototypeset in Great Britain
by Filmtype Services Limited, Scarborough
Printed in Italy by New Interlitho Spa, Milan

Published in the United States by McGraw-Hill
Book Company, 1978

Library of Congress Cataloging in Publication Data
Main entry under title:
A Standard guide to pure-bred dogs.
Includes index.
    1. Dogs—Standards.   2. Dog breeds.
    I. Glover, Harry.
SF425.2.S7 1977   636.7'1   77-27890
ISBN 0–07–023501–5

The Standards are reproduced with the
permission of the American Kennel Club

The co-operation of other Kennel Clubs throughout
the world is gratefully acknowledged

Colour photographs were contributed by Sally Ann
Thompson and most of the black-and-white
photographs by Sally Ann Thompson and Marc
Buzzini.

The Publishers thank the following for permission to reproduce copyright photographs:
Aftenposten, Oslo, 433 bottom, 447 left. *The American Kennel Club,* 40, 62 top, 110, 130 top, 268. *Australian News
and Information Service,* 416. *Marc Buzzini,* 417 bottom, 418, 420 bottom, 421 bottom, 422, 425, 427 top, 431, 432
right, 433 top, 434, 435, 436 top, 437, 438 right, 440 top & centre, 441 right, 444 right, 445 left, 447 top & bottom,
448, 451 right, 453, 454 right, 455, 456 left, 457, 460 centre. *Camera Press,* 62 bottom, 112. *Danish Kennel Club,* 454
left, 460 top. *Finnish Kennel Club,* 419 centre, 429 centre, 436 top, 444 left. *Fujifotos, Tokyo,* 166, 424, 428, 432 left,
458. *Harry Glover,* 7 centre & bottom, 10 bottom, 17 left, back cover, top centre. *Hungarian Kennel Club,* 460 top.
Mrs W. H. Mills-de Hoog, 38. *The Mansell Collection,* 8 centre & bottom, 9 top & bottom. *Diane Pearce,* 104, 146
bottom, 174, 188 top, 191, 251, 275 top, 338, 357, 376, 440 bottom, 441 top, 445 right. *Photoresearchers Inc.,* 60, 65,
110 bottom, 130 bottom, 243, 245, 443. *Polish Kennel Club,* 438 top. *Popperfoto Ltd.,* 6 top. *Radio Times Hulton
Picture Library,* 5, 12 bottom. *Anne Roslin-Williams,* 80, 86, 91, 136, 146 top, 280, 298, 341 right, 359, 417 top, 420
centre, 427 bottom, 429 top & bottom, 442, 443, 451 left, 459, 460 bottom. *Sally Anne Thompson,* 2, 3, 6 centre &
bottom, 7 top, 8 top, 89, 93, 96, 98, 101, 102, 106, 107, 113, 116, 117, 119, 120, 122, 124, 126 top & bottom, 128,
132, 134, 138, 139, 140, 142, 143, 148, 149, 150, 151, 153, 156, 157, 159, 161, 164, 168, 171, 173, 177, 180, 182, 184,
185, 187, 188 bottom, 193, 195, 196, 199, 200, 201, 202, 203, 204, 206, 207, 210, 212, 213, 215, 218, 220, 221,
222, 224, 226, 227, 229, 230, 233, 234, 236, 237, 238, 239, 241, 242, 245, 254, 255, 256, 261, 264, 266, 270, 272, 274,
275 bottom, 276, 278, 282, 284, 286, 287, 288, 290, 295, 301, 302, 304, 305, 307, 308, 311, 313, 315, 318, 319, 321,
323, 325, 327, 329, 332, 334, 336, 339, 340, 341 left, 342, 344, 345, 347, 349, 350, 352, 354, 358, 361, 362, 363, 365,
367, 369, 370, 371, 373, 374, 378, 380, 381, 384, 386, 388, 390, 391, 394, 396, 398, 400, 402, 403, 404, 406, 408, 410,
413, 419 top & bottom, 420 top, 422, 426, 430, 449, 452, 456 right, front cover, back cover (except top ceqtre).

INTRODUCTION

Positive evidence of how man and dog first became associated cannot precisely be established. There are many hypotheses, any of which would make an interesting story. There is early evidence for example in the palaeolithic cave paintings of France and northern Spain and in the paintings and sculptured friezes of Ancient Egypt and Mesopotamia of the dog existing as a domestic animal, but in fact the association must have existed even earlier than that. What evidence we have suggests that early man shared his cave dwellings with dogs. Early cave sites and midden excavations in northern Europe have disclosed remains of canines that clearly lived close to man, though for what exact purpose we do not know. They may have been fellow hunters, joining early man in the chase of game for food. They could possibly have been just scavengers living in close contact with primitive tribes as an easier method of obtaining food than catching it themselves, or they could perhaps have been camp guards. It is likely that they combined any of these, or even all three roles.

The most popular theory concerning the origin of the domestic dog is that it descended from the wolf, or at least one of the wolves, for even they vary from continent to continent. The opponents of that theory, however, point to the vast differences between the various breeds of dog that we have today and maintain that these deny a common ancestry in one animal. Others suggest that several different forms of wild dog, some probably long extinct, played their part in introducing the wide variety of dogs that we now possess and some weight is lent to that theory by the number of wild dogs still in existence, from the Dingo of Australia to the wild dogs of the continent of Africa.

It is not difficult to speculate about how man and dog first became partners. It could have been among the nomadic tribes of Europe, who moved from place to place as the game which was their staple diet moved to avoid the winter snows, or it might have occurred on the continent of America or in the Far East. The association could indeed have developed more or less simultaneously in many parts of the world. It is easy enough to visualise early hunters returning from the chase with whelps of wild dogs or wolves which they would give to their young to keep them quiet and out of the way. At that primitive stage, sentiment would hardly have been likely to have entered into the relationship, and there would have been no thought of dogs as playthings. The whelps would just have been added to the tribe as one of its possessions.

Wolves and wild dogs are very territorially minded, with tribal customs of their own, and the value of these wild animals as guards around the camp or cave would quickly have been realised, and the step from that to

---

Below: A scene from an Egyptian fresco at Thebes—an early example of the dog as a domestic animal.

duties as hunters would have been a very short one. Bones of dogs found in Scandinavia prove that dogs and men lived together at least 10,000 years ago and it is likely that the relationship goes back much further. The cave paintings at Altamira (about 12,000 BC) and Lascaux (15,000–10,000 BC) contain representations of dogs, but these are conceived in a generalised way, the dogs being dog-like but with no distinctive features. Subsequent evidence from Ancient Egypt show various dogs of recognizable types, as do the hunting reliefs from Nineveth (7th century BC), where mastiff-like creatures accompany the royal hunt.

By the time of the New Kingdom in Egypt (circa 1570 BC), there were clearly several different breeds of dog in existence, or at least there were sufficient variations to suggest that selective breeding was capable of producing different breeds. Dogs are shown with straight tails or curly tails, with prick ears or pendant ears and with spotted or plain coats. Most of them were hunting dogs or battle dogs and are depicted performing the task for which they had been selected. The heavy, mastiff type of animal is shown in war scenes and the longer-legged sort taking part in the chase. This has led to modern enthusiasts for different breeds laying claim to various paintings or sculptures from the past to prove the antiquity of their own favourite breed. It becomes a little ironical however, when two or more enthusiasts claim the same illustration as proof of ancient ancestry for their own particular choice!

From that time onward, there is little doubt that the many varieties of dog were produced by man's insatiable desire to improve on nature. It is difficult when looking, for example, at a Great Dane and a Pomeranian standing adjacent to one another in the ring, to accept the possibility of a common ancestor. One weighs around five pounds, the other something like thirty times as much, one is eight inches tall, the other thirty. One is small and fluffy, the other huge and smooth-coated, yet somewhere back in time they must have shared common origins. From our knowledge of early man's interest in the dog we can be sure that in the highly sophisticated civilizations of Egypt and the Far East, there were people who spent their time, energy and ingenuity producing animals that had the differences emphasised and fixed. Certainly as civilization spread almost every nation would try to influence the natural development in many species not least in their domesticated dogs, dividing and sub-dividing until the different breeds would be numbered in their hundreds as they are today.

It has been a slow process. Many breeds have emerged and as many have disappeared, and the develop-

Top: The wild dog of Australia, the Dingo. Other wild dogs are still in existence, particularly in Africa.
Centre: Many of the skills learned by the domestic dog are a development of survival instincts.
Bottom: The dog is amenable to command to a degree not often found in other domesticated animals.

Top: Many of the small dogs from China and Japan were bred purely as toy dogs, at a time when dogs from other parts of the world were going through a very primitive stage in their history.
Centre: A Boar hunt. In the Middle East, sport rather than the arts was considered a suitable pastime for a young man, and this led to the development of a whole race of running dogs, for example the Persian Greyhound, the Saluki and the Afghan.
Bottom: In Spain and Italy particularly, the 'chase' occupied much of a gentleman's time.

ment still goes on. In Britain the Old English White Terrier has gone, as has the Lancashire Heeler, or almost, and other breeds only survived because of the dedication and enthusiasm of a small number of breeders. At the same time the Boxer, the Dobermann and the Norwich Terrier have appeared along with a large number of other breeds and variations.

The domestic dog shares many of the characteristics of the wild members of his race. He will turn round several times before settling down in his bed, will mark his territory by leg-lifting on the local trees and gateposts. He is intelligent, but at the same time has a certain fierceness, and will howl at the moon like the wolf and jackal. Kept in numbers, the domestic dog will establish a 'pecking order' by fighting for supremacy, and the group will thus find itself with a leader as the wolf pack does. There are, however, certain characteristics that are more sophisticated in the domestic dog. The limited vocal noise that the wolf makes has been enlarged and today's domestic dog can express himself much more widely. Any owner can tell by the tone of a bark what it is that has disturbed his dog, and the tone varies from the welcoming back for the children to the hard noise what warns of approaching strangers.

Through his association with man, the domestic dog has developed a whole range of noises with which to express his feelings. He has even been known to mimic, and in one extreme case was taught to say at least two words. He employs many of the movements of submissiveness that can be seen in the wolf and the wild dog when greeting his master, obviously accepting him as the pack leader, but he has added the rather frantic tail wagging, which is not the habit of the wild canines.

Many of the skills learned by the domestic dogg are a development and a sophistication of instincts associated with survival. It is natural for members of the canine race to carry things around in their mouths, and when feeding their young, to transport food to the family lair in this manner. This habit has been used by man as a basis for training a dog to retrieve, which appears to be a clever trick on the part of gundogs, but merely exploits the instinct to pick things up and return with them. The guarding of a territory, instinctive in the wild dogs to preserve the supply of food for the family and to protect it from marauders, develops

easily into guarding a home occupied by humans whom he regards as members of his family. The dog's intelligence has made it a simple matter for man to associate certain actions with certain words, and the result is that the dog is amenable to command to a degree that is not often found in other domesticated animals.

As the relationship between man and dog developed, dogs were bred for different functions, and this in itself led not only to the evolution of new breeds, but to a natural grouping of those breeds according to the work that they were to do. Naturally enough this development took place at different speeds in different countries, with the result that some breeds appear in different groups in different countries. The independent growth of civilizations and the lack of communication in the early days led to this, and the apparent anomalies have become so much a part of the history of the dogs of a particular nation that they are difficult to regularise internationally. A typical example of this is the Pomeranian, which appears in Scandinavia as a Spitz breed, in Spain as a companion dog, and in the rest of the world as a toy, in Sweden being shown alongside the Chow Chow, in Spain with the Dalmatian, and in the rest of the world with the Chihuahuas. The manner in which people lived, their relative safety from attack by wild animals or neighbouring tribes, their pursuits and their sports differed widely. In the Far East, where the cultural centres were the emperors' courts, and where women of the household whilst subservient, wielded considerable power, the companion dog became a very important members of the family. The result was that many of the small dogs from China and Japan were bred purely as toy dogs at a time when dogs in other parts of the world were going through a very primitive stage in their history. The Pekingese and the Pug are certainly ancient breeds.

In the Middle East, where the culture was based more on a system of sheikdoms, and where sport rather than the arts was considered a suitable pastime for a young man and where the women took little part in anything apart from the running of the household, coursing dogs were more important. This led to the development of a whole race of running dogs, the Saluki, the Afghan Hound and the Persian Greyhound for example. As with the toys dogs of the Far East, they were much prized and cared for, and their breeding and performance was a matter of considerable pride. In Egypt and the Mediterranian countries generally the dog was not so prized, which is remarkable as he had at one time been an object of worship. There has been some controversy over whether the

Top: Pointer trials. The Pointer is bred for sport in the field, and should look and act the part.
Centre: A hunting-relief of Mastiff-like creatures from the Mound of Kuyunjik, Nineveh.
Bottom: A section from the Bayeux Tapestry, showing Harold hunting. At that time the courts in Britain had a profound influence on dog breeding.

*Top: Tsu-Tsi, Dowager Empress of China with her pet.
Companion dogs were popular at the Imperial Court.
Bottom: A statue of the Egyptian dog or jackal God
Anubis, from the Vatican Museum, Rome.*

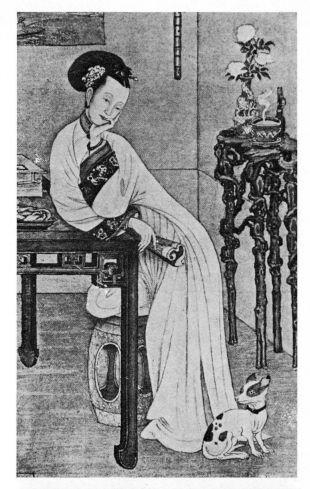

God Anubis was in fact a dog or a Jackal, but whichever happens to be the truth the creature was undoubtedly a member of the canine race.

The Western World developed more slowly. At the
time of Confucius China was already well developed
whilst in Britain many of the cultural activities were in
the hands of the Cistercian monks, and America was
still peopled by warring tribes. Britain was divided and
in a constant state of war between the various families.
The Scots were crossing the border from time to time
on their raids, the White Rose and the Red had not
sorted out their own particular problem, and the
Welsh were somewhat unsettled. This meant that the
sort of dog that was needed was a large fearsome animal
not only capable of guarding a castle, but of emerging
from it to go to war when needed. Such a dog was
actually bred in Britain, the ancient Mastiff type,
which, collared with steel spikes went to war every bit
as much as did the man and his horse.

In France and Southern Europe the gentlemen had
yet another idea of what constituted sport, and in Spain
and Italy particularly 'the chase' occupied much of
a gentleman's time. The influence of the running dog
from the Middle East was felt, but was the invention
of gunpowder there was a great change, and a whole
new race of dogs was developed to help the huntsman
with his gun to find and retrieve game. In Spain there
grew up a race of small dogs used to spring game from
coverts, and larger dogs to help discover the whereabouts of animals taking cover, the Pointers. In France
whilst this form of sport was popular enough, the
ancient sport of scent hunting remained important so
that in that country there was yet another race of dogs
bred to use their noses rather than their eyes—pack-
hounds of differing appearance and size yet all with
this well-developed ability to hunt game by its scent.

The difference between races of dogs—it is important at this stage not to use the word 'breed' as the idea
was not to produce finely bred animals whose value
lay in their appearance, but in their ability to perform
the duty for which they were intended—varied with
the game that was indigenous in their country. A much
smaller dog was needed to chase and catch the hare of
Europe than the antelope of Afghanistan, and a much
stronger dog to subdue the wild boar of Germany than
the red deer of Scotland. This led to a fairly early
grouping of dogs on a national basis as well as on a
'use' basis; France produced more scent-hunting dogs,
Spain more gundogs, and the middle European
countries more of the heavy types. It was not in fact
until the advent of dog shows that more concise grouping was arrived at, and even then, with the shows being
small events held in the yard of a hostelry, subdivision
was not needed.

One of the problems associated with research into the history of the dog is that he was so much taken for granted that he rarely gets a mention. He is depicted in drawings, paintings and tapestry, but rarely written about. The battle scenes of the Bayeux Tapestry show dogs, and the early forest laws of the time of William the Conquerer lay down regulations concerning who might and might not own dogs of certain types, but it was not until much later that anyone wrote about dogs as dogs. In the late 15th century Dame Juliana Berners in her book of hunting lists 'divers manners of hounds'.

The courts of Britain had a profound influence on dog breeding at this time. They followed the French in fashion, even adopted the language, and undoubtedly followed their sporting habits. The dog was either something used to take part, and a very active part indeed, in the hunting of game, and was thus tough, hard kept and probably expendable, or was an animal that was the favourite of the ladies of the court, soft and probably overfed, and deeply mourned when it died. There was at that time none of the semi-professional attitude towards dog breeding that is typical of today, and pride in a dog was either pride in performance or the affected pleasure of having a child substitute with none of the attendant responsibilities.

Today's grouping of dogs into a number of fairly similar types, either by appearance or performance has really come about as a matter of convenience. As the numbers of dogs grew under the modern system of registration and shows, it became necessary to sub-divide. The process is going on to this day as the Kennel Club in Great Britain has only quite recently divided the Non-Sporting dogs other than the Toys, into the Utility and the Working groups. This pattern has not been followed by other countries, and in many there are far more groups than there are in Britain and the United States of America. Basically the smaller subdivisions are more logical even though perhaps less practical, and the division has been dictated by other factors than registration or exhibition, and it might therefore be easier to consider the various groupings along Scandinavian lines, where the division is more fundamentally to do with purpose.

The invention of gunpowder changed the whole pattern of hunting. Prior to that it was almost entirely a case of chasing game, of driving it into nets, or of treeing, digging or trapping it, and the type of dog needed was fitted to one or the other of those methods. With the advent of the gun, however, game could be dispatched at greater distance and with more certainty, though the advocates of the crossbow might quarrel with that assumption. For the purpose a whole new

Top: English Setters, shown here at a trial.
Centre: The Bloodhound, like most scent hunting dogs, is heavily built, for stamina rather than speed.
Bottom: A foxhound by the nineteenth century painter Archer, from Vero Shaw's Book of the Dog, *1881.*
Right: Borzois—from Russia, 'huge and silky'.

race of dogs was needed, dogs that could locate game, that could indicate where it was, and others that could cause it to move, either along the ground in the case of fur, or into the air in the case of feather. Others were needed to recover the game when it had been killed, and even specialists that would retrieve over water.

Within the group of gundogs, came even further divisions. The names Springer, Cocker, Retriever, Setter and Pointer indicate the tasks that these various dogs performed, though there is more than one Springer and a number of Retrievers, some developed in Britain, and others overseas particularly in Spain, Germany and Italy. Old illustrations in such books as The Sportsman's Repository show dogs that are half-way between Spaniel and Setter, and from around the beginning of the 19th century the changes and developments can be followed in words and pictures. Fortunately it was the habit when a gentleman of substance had his portrait painted for posterity, for him to have his dogs included, so that we have more than a fair idea —always allowing for artistic licence—of the appearance of the dogs years ago.

With the spread of wealth, hunting, which was at one time the prerogative of the wealthy landowner, has now become the leisure pursuit of thousands, particularly in America, where the opening of the hunting season sees a great number of men who would normally be seated at their desks, heading for the hills with gun and dog. In Britain too, people of all walks of life now shoot, and have done so for many years, which has meant a tremendous upsurge in the popularity of the gundogs.

Another natural division is the group of dogs that hunt by scent. In many parts of the world they are included in the Hound Group, but they are a natural subdivision as they are built differently and have the gift of a highly developed sense of smell. They do not have the powerful angulation of the running dogs, the group known in some countries as the sight hounds, and they are more heavily built, for stamina rather than speed. Hunting with packs of hounds has been in existence for centuries, particularly in France, where there are still breeds of dog descended from such packs that are not generally known in other countries, such as the Ariegeois and the Bleu de Gascogne, whose names indicate that they originated in small areas of France where they were bred in packs.

In Britain hunting with packs of hounds has always been popular, and now there are probably something over four hundred packs in the country. They too vary from area to area, but there has been a good deal of interchange of drafts of hounds from one pack to another to improve strains, and it is now improbable that anyone can say at a glance where a particular

Top: Wire-haired Dachshunds, supreme as pets.
Centre: Mastiffs, formidable protectors of property.
Bottom: Mosaic pavement from Pompeii, 'Beware of the Dog'—a British idea that impressed the Romans.

hound comes from, though this was once possible. Beagling too is popular, and there are packs of Basset Hounds. Even such unlikely dogs as Sealyhams at one time hunted in packs. In the United States too, pack hunting is extremely popular, and it is almost certain the the number of packs and hounds outnumber by far those in any other country in the world. Careful importation and the expertise that the American people have in the art of livestock breeding have resulted in there being a large number of hounds used in different ways, some still in packs, but some, like the Coonhound used individually.

Unlike the gundogs, the scent hunting group as a whole, with the possible exception of the Beagle and the Basset have never attained popularity as a pet and housedog, as they have certain temperament problems, are somewhat wilful and not easy to train. To any member of this group the scent overrules everything else, and the natural inclination of the dogs to follow their noses does create problems. The other great exception is of course the Dachshund, as whilst it is a scent hunting dog, and is at times used in a pack, it occupies a very special place in the affections of all dog people as being supreme as a pet and a housedog. It could be that its size, and the years that have gone by since it was regularly hunted have blunted its instincts to a certain extent, making it more amenable to domestic restraints than some of the others.

One of the most ancient uses of the dog, was as a guard, which leads to the next type, the Mastiff Group. The Scandinavians do not devote a whole group to these dogs, but they are a natural subdivision widespread all over Europe and even in the Far East. Even before man settled down to till the soil and grow crops, when he was nomadic and moved around and followed his food. The dog must have been a valuable member of the tribe, being territorially minded, attached to the family and seeing the members of it as pack leaders. In his still semi-wild state he would have been a formidable protector of property against the incursions of other tribes and predatory animals.

This guarding instinct was handed down, and in no group more formidably than in the Mastiffs. There is early record of them in places as far apart as Tibet (there is still a Chinese Fighting Dog), and Spain, where there is a Mastin Espanol, and they were all typified by their size. They are large and heavy dogs, and their fierceness, until modern breeding eliminated this, often made them unhandleable. Even to this day examples do occur that cannot be approched, though this is exceptional. When the Romans invaded Britain they found these large heavy dogs which were used as guards and fighting dogs, which impressed them so much that they took some of them back to Rome, where they played their part in the rather sanguine affairs that the Romans called sport.

Modern selective breeding has produced a number of variations on the traditional Mastiff. For example such dogs as the Boxer and the Bulldog are develop-

ments of the original theme, the Boxer being a very modern creation and the other, the Bulldog dating back to the 17th century. During the Second World War the Mastiff virtually disappeared from Britain, and this ancient British dog was only saved from extinction because some had been exported to the United States from where specimens were generously exported back to Britain.

The use of the dog as a worker came fairly late in the development of the race, and has been brought into its present heights in comparatively recent years. There is a history of guarding and herding dogs in many countries, often using what are apparently quite unusual animals, and often the herding dog had to serve in other capacities. A dog like the Afghan Hound for instance was not only a coursing dog, but was also used as a guard, particularly at night, and there is even a suggestion that he too was used for rounding up livestock. The type of herding dog required varied considerably with the sort of terrain they worked in and on the flocks they had to work. This produced mountain dogs such as the Pyrenean, and plains dogs like the Tervueren.

The hills of Scotland and Wales produced a race of dogs which were brilliant herders, the Collies. The original Collie bore little resemblance to the modern show Collie, and was probably more like the Bearded Collie as we know it today, but the work that it did has been continued through various breeds, and the most recent one recognised, the Border Collie is world renowned for its intelligence and hard work. Much of the sheep herding that now goes on throughout the world would have been impossible without the working sheepdog in some form or another, and although the Border Collie is not by any means the only working sheepdog, it forms the bulk of the dogs that are used today in most countries for this work.

Sheepdog trials are an important part of country life, and few of the larger agricultural shows are without these trials as part of the programme in many of the sheep areas of most countries. Whilst the dogs used in say Australia are of many different breeds, working collies and Sheepdogs have been imported to improve the stock and to take part in trials there. The International Sheepdog Society has records of pedigrees of dogs and their performances going back further than those of the Kennel Club of Great Britain, and their requirements for such registration are even stricter than other bodies, the emphasis being on the capability of the animal as a worker only and has nothing to do with appearance.

Britain is the home of the Terrier, and of all the dogs listed in this Group, all but one or two have their origins there. The working terrier has always played a part in the hunting of a pack of hounds, and it was a familiar sight to see small dogs capable of going to ground to turn out the fox, accompanying the hunt, either on foot, or if the journey was likely to be a lengthy one, in special panniers carried by the hunts-

men for the purpose. While the noble families had their sport running deer to death and coursing hares and other animals, the working man also had his sport, carried on under much more humble conditions and with none of the ceremony of the chase.

The Terrier was siezed upon as the particular friend of the British working man, and in most of the industrial areas, almost every home would have its Terrier. In the North they were Borders, or one of the Scottish breeds, in the Midlands they would be the Old English White Terrier or a version of the Staffordshire or Manchester Terrier. They were kept as vermin killers, and at the beginning of the 19th century they are mentioned as an essential part of a farmer's livestock for keeping down rats. The name is said to come from the word 'terra' as they were originally intended for unearthing the fox, but they attracted a much wider public by their spirit and sheer dogginess, and became a very important collection of breeds in the latter part of the 19th and the beginning of this century.

Their popularity unfortunately declined over the years, and in most countries their registrations and appearances at shows are getting smaller each year. One or two, the West Highland White and the Staffordshire Bull Terrier have retained their popularity, but for the most part the members of the Group are not so numerous. One of the great countries for Terriers was Ireland, and they had several native terriers, mostly the larger ones that typified a great deal of what was considered the Irish temperament by some people, being sporty, quick, and always prepared to take care of themselves.

From early times there have been dogs that hunted by sight and ran down their prey, for the most part killing the game once it was caught. In Scandinavia these are known as the Vinthundar, 'Wind Hounds' which is a very descriptive name for the Group. They are all the extremely fast, long-legged dogs that have been evolved for the purpose of catching game by running them down rather than by the sheer persistence of the scent-hunting dogs.

In the Far East they were the much prized elegant hounds kept by tribes for sport and for replenishing the larder, the Saluki and the Afghan Hound; in Britain the Greyhound, which is one of Britain's oldest breeds of dog. In Mediterranean countries they were smooth and large, in the colder countries such as Scotland they were rough and large, and in Russia huge and silky. The variations were enormous, but they were all long in the leg, capable of tremendous speed, and had a touch of the killer instinct.

In recent years the members of the Hound Group have largely been denied their right to course, as modern conditions do not lend themselves to this sport. Indeed recently in Britain coursing has come

Top and centre: Norwich Terriers, at work and at play—sporting dogs for working men.
Bottom: The Afghan, once much prized in the East.

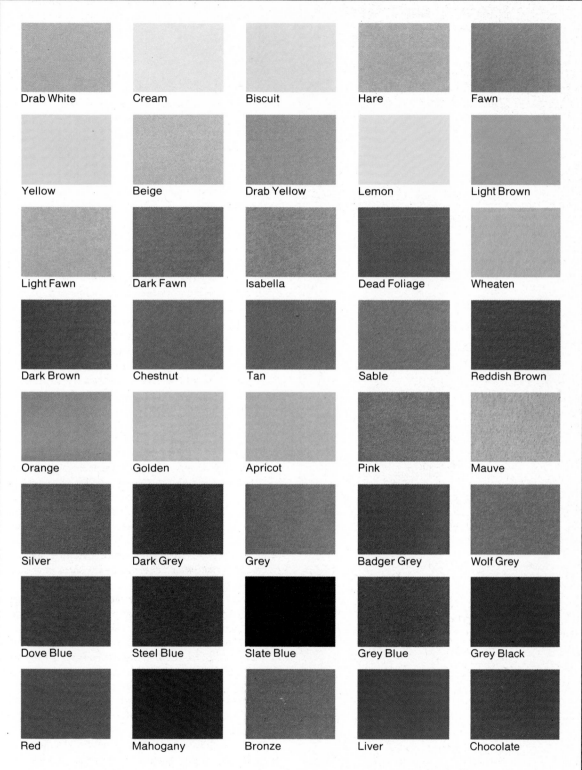

Drab White	Cream	Biscuit	Hare	Fawn
Yellow	Beige	Drab Yellow	Lemon	Light Brown
Light Fawn	Dark Fawn	Isabella	Dead Foliage	Wheaten
Dark Brown	Chestnut	Tan	Sable	Reddish Brown
Orange	Golden	Apricot	Pink	Mauve
Silver	Dark Grey	Grey	Badger Grey	Wolf Grey
Dove Blue	Steel Blue	Slate Blue	Grey Blue	Grey Black
Red	Mahogany	Bronze	Liver	Chocolate

One of the problems constantly encountered in describing coat colour in dogs, is that a word does not adequately describe a colour. There are, for example, so many reds that to say of a certain dog that it is red, probably conveys little of the actual colour of the dog. This chart lists all the major colour names used to describe dogs' coats, and in each case shows the colour.

into disfavour to such an extent that it is likely to cease altogether. Fortunately, however, the breeds that comprise the Group have wonderful temperament and make superb housedogs, and also, the sport of Greyhound racing, which began in America, spread to the rest of the world, and became particularly popular in Britain, has guaranteed the continuance of this particular breed. In recent years other breeds have been tried on the track against the time when coursing became illegal, and have proved themselves to some extent. Oddly enough, Italian Greyhound racing has become popular in Sweden, where the breed is included in this Group, despite the fact that it appears as a toy dog almost everywhere else, and where the proving of a breed for the work that it is supposed to do is an essential part of the philosophy of the sport of dog showing.

For many centuries man has enjoyed the companionship of animals, and pets have become not only part of the everyday life of most families, but have at the same time become big business. There is hardly a household anywhere in the world that does not have its pet or pets, from the domestic cat to the budgerigar and from the goldfish to the alligator and it is natural enough that from man's associationship with the dog should grow up one of the closest relationships between animals and humans. In much the same way as the first dogs were almost incidentally adopted as part of the primitive tribe, so in later years the runts from working and sporting dogs would be adopted as pets by the children and womenfolk of a much more civilized culture.

The result has been a whole number of breeds which are included in the Toy Group. They are mostly typified by their lack of size, their charm and their companionable nature. They are almost all of them too, related to dogs from other groups, the Spaniels, the Terriers and the Running Dogs all having relatives in the group easily recognised as descendants from the original breeds. Constant companionship,

however, has changed their temperament, and environment has played its part, so that whilst an Italian Greyhound will still chase small birds and will kill and eat them given the chance, he is still very much at home on a silk cushion or a counterpane.

Some of the members of the Toy Group have their origins in the courts of Spain and Italy or the Far East. Paintings and drawings of members of the Italian courts show Toy dogs easily recognised for what they are, and the history of the Pekingese is well documented in stories of the early imperial courts of China. There have over the years been attempts to miniaturise breeds in order to produce more small dogs that could be included in the Group, but most of them fortunately have failed, as the Group is well established and has sufficient variety as it stands. New breeds are still being popularised however and appearing for the first time in the showrings of the world. The Lowchen is a typical example of this, as is the Bichon Frise, breeds that went quietly along in their own countries until they were discovered and exploited by the rest of the world.

There is no doubt at all that as the years go by new breeds will be evolved. There is no reason to suppose that man's ingenuity will rest with the Boxer and the Dobermann. There will be other attempts to produce a 'manmade' dog either for a purpose or simply as a challenge. It is not a difficult exercise. Dogs reproduce their kind comparatively quickly, and any determined effort to produce a dog of a given size, colour, proportions and temperament is almost certain to succeed. Such efforts are already being made in many countries, and provided that those who are conducting the experiments have the resources and the patience, any list of breeds of dog will be outdated within a few years.

Left: 'Scotch Deerhounds' from Vero Shaw's Book of the Dog *1881 — long-legged, rough and large.*
Below left: Toy dogs, print by Burton Barber, 1881.
Below right: Italian Greyhounds at play.

NOTE

Group Numbering

In most countries, the Groups of breeds into which dogs are arranged, are numbered. The Groups are known by these numbers as well as by their names, and this numbering is given equal importance with the naming. In Italy for instance the catalogue of a show will be arranged in Group number order. In Belgium the programme of events will indicate which Groups are being judged on a given day, and a judge, when invited to officiate will be informed of the number of the Group in which the breed or breeds that he is to judge, appears. In Australia, where breed standards are often printed in a hard-back edition, the Groups are arranged in number order. In the USA the Groups of breeds are numbered but the numbering is not considered as important as it is in some European countries.

In Britain, none of this happens. Each Group does have a number, but after appearing on the cover of the pamphlet in which the standards are printed, it is never seen again. Catalogues of shows, reports, programmes and invitations to judges, just give the Group its name, and never its number. Thus, in Britain, there is no set order for the Groups.

Standards

The pages which give the official standards also show line illustrations and variations which are our additions and in no way part of the official standard.

The line drawings accompanying the standards have been specially drawn by the author, Harry Glover.

CONTENTS

** Dogs not granted championship status by the AKC*

PART TWO:
Breeds recognised by the Fédération Cynologique Internationale (FCI)

PART THREE:
Other Pedigree Breeds

PART FOUR:
Old and Extinct Breeds

PART ONE:
Breeds recognised by the American Kennel Club and the Kennel Club of Great Britain

The United States of America and Great Britain have always led the rest of the world in drawing the attention of the public to pure-bred dogs. Both countries have very powerful and well-organised Kennel Clubs founded many years ago, and both have as their purpose the encouragement of the breeding, exhibiting and general promotion of the pedigree dog. The original purpose of the American Kennel Club was clearly stated in the very early days of that organisation as 'promoting and safeguarding the industry of pure-bred dogs', whilst that of the Kennel Club in Great Britain is laid down in its rule number 1, 'promoting the improvement of Dogs, Dog Shows, Field Trials, Working Trials and Obedience Tests'.

In America, shows were held as early as 1878 when the first benched show was held in Chicago, and field trials go back even further, to 1874. At that time several clubs were compiling stud books. By the 1880s these various activities had been brought under a centralised control, and by the 1890s forty-one breeds had been recognised, a number that has now grown to one hundred and thirty-three. In Britain a similar picture was emerging. The first organised dog show was held in Newcastle-upon-Tyne in June, 1859, and the number gradually grew, until, by the early 1870s it was obvious that some form of controlling body was needed. The Member of Parliament for one of the Midland constituencies, living at Ettington, called together a body of twelve gentlemen to a meeting in London on 4 April 1873, and thus the Kennel Club was founded. Since then these organisations on either side of the Atlantic have followed very similar courses; the detailed programme may have varied, but the original intentions have remained the same.

In Britain, the Kennel Club is an elected body of people who have devoted a great deal of time to pursuing objects similar to those of the club itself through breeding, exhibiting and the training of dogs. The representation of the world of pedigree dogs in Britain as a whole is through three breed councils composed of those with interests in a specific championship show, a breed or breeds of dogs, or an area of the country. They act in an advisory capacity, putting forward recommendations to the Kennel Club Committee and generally acting as a link with those interested in dogs throughout the country. The arrangement in America is slightly different, as the main organisation itself consists of delegates from clubs throughout the United States, which elects a board of directors that is the central core of canine administration.

The control of the world of the pedigree dog by both Kennel Clubs, and indeed by all Kennel Clubs, is evidenced in many and diverse ways. Shows are approved, judges appointed, venues agreed upon and regulations laid down to cover most eventualities. This control is, however, probably more clearly shown in the establishment of standards for the various breeds. In this book will be found the approved standards of all those breeds recognised by both Kennel Clubs, and it is interesting to consider how these were established. The standard of a breed develops with the breed from the date of its first recognition and is constantly under review.   As and when a breed club is formed to look after the interests of a particular breed, one of its first functions is to write a standard description of the breed, outlining its main features in a readily comprehensible manner, and to a now accepted formula, and stating those faults which need to be prevented or eliminated. These standards are the guidelines for every judge and it is part of his duty to familiarise himself with the standards before taking up the appointment.

There are variations in the standards between the two countries, and the main ones are described in this book. In most cases, either country accepts the standard of the country of origin, but local conditions dictate certain differences, as do fashion and breeders' preferences. Some breeds in the United States of America are shown, for instance, with cropped ears, whilst this, being illegal in Great Britain, is unacceptable in the show ring. Occasionally the names are different, and in a number of cases breeds are placed in different groups. This can sometimes lead to confusion, and it is part of the purpose of this book to clarify the position by drawing attention to these differences.

GROUP I:
SPORTING DOGS

Large Munsterlander

Pointer

German Shorthaired Pointer

German Wirehaired Pointer

Curly-coated Retriever

Chesapeake Bay Retriever

Flat-coated Retriever

Labrador Retriever

Golden Retriever

Gordon Setter

English Setter

Irish Setter

Brittany Spaniel

American Water Spaniel

Clumber Spaniel

Cocker Spaniel

English Cocker Spaniel

English Springer Spaniel

Field Spaniel

Welsh Springer Spaniel

Irish Water Spaniel

Sussex Spaniel

Vizsla

Weimaraner

Wirehaired Pointing Griffon

GROUP I: SPORTING DOGS

The capture of wild animals has been achieved in a variety of ways over the centuries, from the setting of primitive pit traps to today's sophisticated sport of driving game to guns hidden in butts. Animals have been speared, snared, shot with arrows, driven into nets, hauled down by fast dogs, lassoed, tripped by bolas, or even just dug out of the ground, and for many of these methods dogs have been evolved to assist the hunter. With the advent of the sporting gun, the hunting of game became a much more intricate business as the game had to be found before it was scared off by the hunter, and had to be collected when the gun had brought it down. For this purpose a whole Group of dogs was developed, many of which had specific duties in the field, and some were developed as all-purpose gundogs. They all, however, had one thing in common, they existed to help the sportsman armed with a gun when he was out in the field in search of game.

Within the Group there are further divisions according to the specific purposes for which the dog is used. There are those that locate the game, those that put it up so that the sportsman can get a shot at it, and those that retrieve it when it falls. It is, however, not quite as simple as that, as there are other breeds that work under special conditions. There are those that are experts in water, and there is also considerable overlap between duties, some breeds performing at least two tasks well, and others that will perform all the work that a gundog is expected to do. The situation is further complicated by the fact that whilst some of the gundog breeds are normally the property, and under the control of, the man who has the gun, others are kept by gamekeepers, and others by breeders who run their dogs at field trials, and attend shoots, for the purpose of training and using their dogs.

The breeds that locate the game are the Pointers and Setters, and their task is to work in front of the guns when game is being walked up, locating it before it can be seen by the sportsman, and indicating exactly where it is. The Pointers do this by what is called coming to the point, which means that they stand rigidly often with one foot in mid-stride ready to take a further cautious step if it is needed. They carry their tails out in a rigid straight line and the whole dog can thus be used as the sights on a gun to discover the squatting bird or hare. Two such dogs often work together at some distance from one another, which permits the guns to use them as co-ordinates, to discover not only the direction of the game but also its distance. Stories of the powers of these dogs are plentiful.

The Setters perform a similar task, but on discovering the whereabouts of the game do not necessarily stand at the point but sink down, as their name suggests.

The second sub-group is the Spaniels, whose task it is to move the game, either by putting it up in the case of a bird, or forcing it to run in the case of ground game. Spaniels hunt vigorously in front of the guns, but never so far in front as to disturb the game out of gunshot range. They are trained to work within range, to cover the ground by running backwards and forwards, quartering as much ground as possible and using their remarkable noses to put up any game that is lying hidden in the area. They vary a great deal in size and agility, and thus in the speed at which they work, and the sportsman chooses the breed which best suits the country over which he will be hunting and the species of game likely to be encountered.

The third category is those breeds that retrieve the game once it has been killed. These are mostly the larger and stronger dogs, capable of making their way quickly and efficiently through the roughest and most difficult cover. They have wonderful scenting powers, and the ability to mark fallen game, so that a brilliant Retriever can be trusted to watch birds fall, remember where they have come to ground, and fetch them in turn with very little assistance or direction from the gun or the gamekeeper.

Finally there are one or two breeds that have been evolved purely as all-purpose gundogs, dogs that will perform most of the tasks normally undertaken by the three main sub-groups, and one or two specialists such as the Irish Water Spaniel, developed for use in lake and estuary country where protection against wet and cold are essential. When sportsmen are gathered together there is always discussion as to which breed makes the best all-purpose gundog, but like everything else in the world of dogs, this must remain a matter of opinion. What is fact and not conjecture, is that the whole of this group, by virtue of its long association with man and generations of training to obey commands, contains some of the most intelligent and companionable dogs of the whole canine race.

LARGE MUNSTERLANDER

NATIONAL GROUPING		
	Name	Number
AKC	—	–
KC(GB)	—	–
FCI	Gundogs	7

This dog was evolved by a reversal of the more common practice of miniaturisation. The Small Munsterlander was developed at the beginning of this century from old breeds of long-haired hunting dogs common in Westphalia, and as with most breeds that were bred down to size, some large ones were inevitably produced. After a considerable battle the Large Munsterlander Club which had been formed by the supporters of the larger dogs managed to persuade the German Kennel Club to accept the larger dog as a separate breed.

He rapidly gained popularity, and has a number of supporters among the show goers of Germany and Holland where his qualities are appreciated more than they are so far in the rest of the world. In recent years there have been some importations into Britain and since 1971 when the first registrations took place numbers have increased at a remarkable rate, and now he is appearing at most of the major shows. In 1976 thirteen were exhibited in the variety classes under the author as judge at Crufts, and there is no doubt that he will be one of the next breeds to achieve championship status. He is a large, but not heavy dog, having the elegance of the Setters combined with the strength of the Retrievers, and is always black and white in colour. He is a lively dog, and is said to be very spirited and active in the field.

OFFICIAL STANDARD

Characteristics
The Large Munsterlander is a multi-purpose gun-dog, ideal for the rough shooter. He has an excellent nose, staying power, and works equally well on land and in water. A keen worker, easily taught, loyal, affectionate and trustworthy.

General appearance
Alert and energetic, with a strong muscular body, having good movement with drive.

Head and skull
Well proportioned to the body, elongated. Skull sufficiently broad, slightly rounded, with no pronounced occiput. Strong jaw muscles, well formed black nose, wide soft nostrils, slight rise from the nasal bone to the forehead but no pronounced stop. Lips slightly rounded, and well-fitting.

Eyes
Intelligent, medium size, dark brown, not deep set or protruding. No haw showing.

Ears
Broad and set high, lying flat and close to the head, with a rounded tip. Hair on the ears should be long, extending beyond the tip.

Mouth
Strong and sound, with well developed teeth, faultless scissor bite and molars meeting exactly.

Neck
Strong muscular, slightly arched, joining the shoulder and chest smoothly.

Forequarters
Chest, wide and with good depth of brisket. Shoulders laid well back, forelegs straight, pasterns strong.

Body
Firm strong back, short coupled. slightly higher at the shoulder, sloping smoothly towards the croup and tail. Wide well muscled loin. Wide croup. Ribs well sprung, deep and reaching well up to the loins. Taut abdomen, slightly tucked up.

Hindquarters
Hips broad. Well muscled thighs, well turned stifles, hocks well let down. Dew claws should be removed.

Feet
Tight, moderately rounded and well-knuckled with dense hair between the toes; well padded. Nails black and strong.

Gait
Free, long striding springy gait.

Tail
Well set on, in line with the back. Base thick, tapering evenly towards the tip, well feathered. It should be carried horizontally or curved slightly upwards. Docking optional, 1 to 2 cms.

Coat
Hair long and dense, but not curly or coarse. Well feathered on front and hind legs and on tail, more so in dogs than in bitches. The hair must lie short and smooth on the head.

Colour
Head solid black, white blaze, snip or star allowed. Body white with black patches, flecked, ticked, or combination of these.

Weight and size
Height: Dogs approximately 24 inches. Bitches approximately 23 inches. Weight: Dogs approximately 55 to 65 pounds. Bitches approximately 55 pounds.

Faults
Any departure from the foregoing points should be considered a fault and the seriousness of the fault should be in exact proportion to its degree.

Note
Male animals should have two apparently normal testicles fully descended into the scrotum.

AKC VARIATION TO STANDARD
This dog is not granted championship status by the AKC or the KC(GB). The above standards are the interim standards of the KC(GB).

POINTER

Towards the end of the 17th century and for some time afterwards, the old flintlock gun which took some time to load and to get into position, dictated what type of dog was needed. He had to find the game, indicate its whereabouts, and keep it under observation, until the sportsman was in a position to take a shot. For this purpose the Pointer was developed. There is some difference of opinion as to whether this particular dog was developed first in Spain, in Britain or in other European countries, but there is little doubt that he owes his origin to a mixture of Foxhound, Greyhound and probably Bloodhound. He needed a superb nose, speed over the ground and absolute steadiness, and those breeds were the most likely ones to produce these qualities. It could well be that the development took place simultaneously in several European countries.

The first Pointers of any sort appeared in Britain midway through the 17th century, which was some years before the shooting of birds in flight was a common practice. They were used at this time to locate hares, which were then coursed by the much faster Greyhounds which did not have the ability to locate the game as the Pointers did. By the end of the 17th century the shooting of game on the wing was in vogue and the Pointer began to come into its own. The old-fashioned Pointer still proved for a long time to lack drive and dash, and up to the end of the 19th

NATIONAL GROUPING		
	Name	Number
AKC	Sporting Dogs	1
KC(GB)	Gundog	2
FCI	Companion Dogs	8

century the Foxhound cross was still being resorted to to impart these qualities into the over-cautious Pointer of that time. During that century too the Pointer was repeatedly crossed with various Setters with the idea of improving temperament, as the residue of Greyhound blood together with the Foxhound produced a dog that was over-fierce and had natural killing instincts which needed to be eradicated.

By the middle of the 19th century, the old fashioned Spanish type of Pointer had been left entirely behind and the English Pointer was being accepted as the model of pace, stamina and nerve. By this time sportsmen were shooting with weapons which were self-loaded, and were working their dogs themselves rather than having highly organised teams of beaters, and the sort of dog that could be taken out by one man for a few hours shooting was required. The Pointer was trained to work as one of a pair, and the theory, indeed the practice was for two of these dogs to back one another up to confirm the presence of game and to give a cross-reference as to its exact position. The degree to which they could be thus trained was phenomenal, and endless stories are told of the remarkable performance of individual dogs. This was confirmed by thousands of spectators who witnessed the Pointer that finished in the final six at Crufts some years ago, which for reasons which only it knew, made a superb fix on one of the television cameras.

The modern Pointer is one of the most handsome of the Sporting Dogs. There is nothing glamorous about him, he has no glowing coat or picturesque colour, but his outline is the epitome of the working gundog at its best, and his conformation is there for everyone to see. He is an upstanding dog with deep chest, straight bone and very lovely body proportions, which, when he is well-muscled up gives him the appearance of a blood horse in full training. He is a show dog with a record of major wins all over the world, and his approach to the show business makes him a delight to handle. His natural ability to freeze in one position and to hold the pose for considerable lengths of time is one of the features of the Sporting Dogs' ring. He is, moreover, not a difficult dog to prepare as he has a short smooth coat that can be given a fine sheen with a little work with a hound glove. Few people look upon the Pointer as a pet, but those who do maintain that he makes a responsive companion and housedog.

OFFICIAL STANDARD

General appearance

The Pointer is bred primarily for sport afield; he should unmistakably look and act the part. The ideal specimen gives the immediate impression of compact power and agile grace; the head noble, proudly carried; the expression intelligent and alert; the muscular body bespeaking both staying power and dash. He is an animal whose every movement shows him to be a wide-awake, hard-driving hunting dog possessing stamina, courage, and the desire to go. And in his expression are the loyalty and devotion of a true friend of man.

Temperament

The Pointer's even temperament and alert good sense make him a congenial companion both in the field and in the home. He should be dignified and should never show timidity toward man or dog.

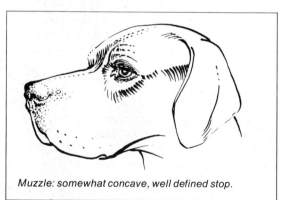

Muzzle: somewhat concave, well defined stop.

Head

The skull of medium width, approximately as wide as the length of the muzzle, resulting in an impression of length rather than width. Slight furrow between the eyes, cheeks cleanly chiseled. There should be a pronounced stop. From this point forward the muzzle is of good length, with the nasal bone so formed that the nose is slightly higher at the tip than the muzzle at the stop. Parallel planes of the skull and muzzle are equally acceptable. The muzzle should be deep without pendulous flews. Jaws ending square and level, should bite evenly or as scissors. Nostrils well developed and wide open. *Ears:* set on at eye level. When hanging naturally, they should reach just below the lower jaw, close to the head, with little or no folding. They should be somewhat pointed at the tip—never round—and soft and thin in leather. *Eyes:* of ample size, rounded and intense. The eye color should be dark in contrast with the color of the markings, the darker the better.

Neck

Long, dry, muscular and slightly arched, springing cleanly from the shoulders.

Shoulders

Long, thin, and sloping. The top of blades close together.

Front

Elbows well let down, directly under the withers and truly parallel so as to work just clear of the body. Forelegs straight and with oval bone. Knee joint never to knuckle over. Pasterns of moderate length, perceptibly finer in bone than the leg, and slightly slanting. Chest, deep

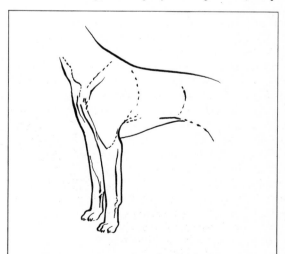

Forequarters: shoulders long and sloping. Forelegs: straight and firm.

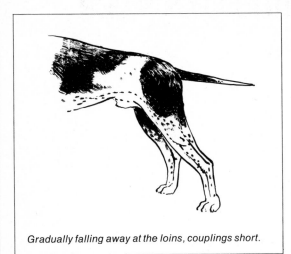

Gradually falling away at the loins, couplings short.

rather than wide, must not hinder free action of forelegs. The breastbone bold, without being unduly prominent. The ribs well sprung, descending as low as the elbow-point.

Back
Strong and solid with only a slight rise from croup to top of shoulders. Loin of moderate length, powerful and slightly arched. Croup falling only slightly to base of tail. Tuck-up should be apparent, but not exaggerated.

Tail
Heavier at the root, tapering to a fine point. Length no greater than to hock. A tail longer than this or docked must be penalized. Carried without curl, and not more than 20 degrees above the line of the back; never carried between the legs.

Hindquarters
Muscular and powerful with great propelling leverage. Thighs long and well developed. Stifles well bent. The hocks clean; the legs straight as viewed from behind. Decided angulation is the mark of power and endurance.

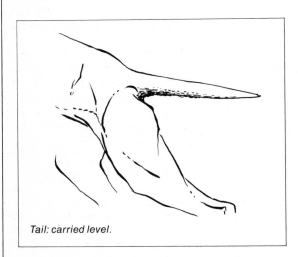

Tail: carried level.

Feet
Oval, with long, closely-set, arched toes, well-padded, and deep. Cat-foot is a fault. Dewclaws on the forelegs may be removed.

Coat
Short, dense, smooth with a sheen.

Color
Liver, lemon, black, orange; either in combination with white or solid-colored. A good Pointer cannot be a bad color. In the darker colors, the nose should be black or brown; in the lighter shades it may be lighter or flesh-colored.

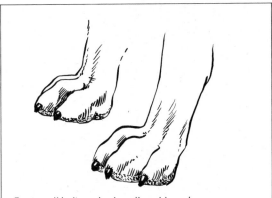

Feet: well knit, arched, well cushioned.

Gait
Smooth, frictionless, with a powerful hindquarters' drive. The head should be carried high, the nostrils wide, the tail moving from side to side rhythmically with the pace, giving the impression of a well-balanced, strongly-built hunting dog capable of top speed combined with great stamina. Hackney gait must be faulted.

Balance and size
Balance and over-all symmetry are more important in the Pointer than size. A smooth, balanced dog is to be more desired than a dog with strongly contrasting good points and faults. Hound or terrier characteristics are most undesirable. Because a sporting dog must have both endurance and power, great variations in size are undesirable, the desirable height and weight being within the following limits:

Height and weight
Dogs: 25 to 28 inches; bitches: 23 to 26 inches. Dogs: 55 to 75 pounds; bitches: 45 to 65 pounds.

Approved by the AKC 12 November 1968

KC(GB) VARIATION TO STANDARD
Mouth: not over or undershot. *Eyes:* same distance from occiput as from nostrils. *Size:* dogs 25 to 27 inches; bitches 24 to 26 inches.

GERMAN SHORTHAIRED POINTER

NATIONAL GROUPING		
	Name	Number
AKC	Sporting Dogs	1
KC(GB)	Gundog	2
FCI	Gundogs	7

Supporters of almost all gundog breeds will from time to time attempt to convince everyone else that theirs is in fact the best all-round gundog. If there is one breed that has most of the qualities to claim this title, it is without doubt the German Shorthaired Pointer. He is a good pointing dog, a natural retriever on land and water, and an excellent worker with birds. This paragon of all the gundog virtues started off as his name suggests in Germany, being produced from a German pointing dog which was itself probably developed from the old Spanish Pointer. Other blood was introduced from local German hunting dogs of which there were a good many all over Germany and which were used by the German *försteren*. These various *hunde* were descended from the hounds that were popular in France, mostly long in the leg and something of the running type, but with very good noses.

The breed was in existence in the 17th century, though it was probably not the very standardised form that exists today. It was with the establishment of the stud book of the Shorthair Club in 1870 when records started, that it was possible to produce a standard of breed points and abilities. It was this latter which remained uppermost in the minds of the German breeders for many years. The hounds from which the breed descended were not notably obedient and the Spanish Pointer blood did not give the absolute steadiness to command that was desired. The German breeders resorted to the introduction of the English Pointer to establish the classical work that was needed, and by selective breeding for obedience, finally around the turn of the century produced what they wanted, a good-looking dog, with a stylish manner of working and the obedience that was required for an all-round gundog.

The German Shorthaired Pointer was recognised in the United States of America in 1930, and some years later the first field trial for the breed was held. This use of the dog in the field has remained a very strong point with German Shorthair Pointer people and trials are now held regularly in many countries. The Shorthair is, however, in the view of many people the ideal one-dog-man's dog. There are large numbers of the breed, beautiful dogs that will never see the inside of a show ring, but will spend their lives doing what they were bred for and leading a very happy life whilst doing it—out with the gun in all weathers. For this purpose he is ideally built, being strongly made with a very robust body, strong limbs and a waterproof coat. He is very tractable, willing, and agile, powerful in performance over all sorts of country and in water, and has tremendous powers of endurance. His nose is excellent and he works just as well at night as he does during the daylight hours, the most severe conditions of snow and ice never deterring him.

As a show dog the German Shorthaired Pointer is excellent, being beautifully behaved, a little suspicious of strangers but very steady with other dogs. He stands well, and is among the soundest of the gundogs, being bred from running hound stock and having the same sort of conformation. As his qualities are becoming recognised his numbers are steadily increasing and over the thirty years since World War II he has become a regular feature of our shows. His temperament is just what is expected of a gundog. He has a high degree of intelligence, and the ability to work out the solutions to problems himself and not to depend on purely repetitive training. He makes a very good watchdog and companion around the house.

OFFICIAL STANDARD

General appearance

The over-all picture which is created in the observer's eye should be that of an aristocratic, well-balanced, symmetrical animal with conformation indicating power, endurance and agility and a look of intelligence and animation. The dog should be neither unduly small nor conspicuously large. It should rather give the impression of medium size, but be like the proper hunter, 'with a short back, but standing over plenty of ground.' Tall, leggy individuals seldom possess endurance or sound movement.

Dogs which are ponderous or unbalanced because of excess substance should be definitely rejected. The first impression should be that of a keenness which denotes full enthusiasm for work without indication of nervous or flighty character. Movement should be alertly co-ordinated without waste motion. Grace of outline, clean-cut head, sloping shoulders, deep breast, powerful back, strong quarters, good bone composition, adequate muscle, well-carried tail and taut coat, all of which should combine to produce a look of nobility and an indication of anatomical structure essential to correct gait which must indicate a heritage of purposefully conducted breeding.

Head

Clean-cut, neither too light nor too heavy, in proper proportion to the body. Skull should be reasonably broad, arched on side and slightly round on top. Scissura (median line between the eyes at the forehead) not too deep, occipital bone not as conspicuous as in the case of the Pointer. The foreface should rise gradually from nose to forehead—not resembling the Roman nose. This is more strongly pronounced in the dog than in the bitch, as befitting his sex. The chops should fall away from the somewhat projecting nose. Lips should be full and deep, never flewy. The chops should not fall over too much, but form a proper fold in the angle. The jaw should be

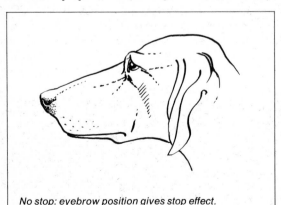

No stop: eyebrow position gives stop effect.

powerful and the muscles well developed. The line to the forehead should rise gradually and should never possess a definite stop as in the case of the Pointer, but rather a stop-effect when viewed from the side, due to the position of the eyebrows. The muzzle should be sufficiently long to enable the dog to seize properly and to facilitate his carrying game a long time. A pointed muzzle is not desirable. The entire head should never give the impression of tapering to a point. The depth should be in the right proportion to the length, both in the muzzle and in the skull proper. *Ears:* ears should be broad and set fairly high, lie flat and never hang away from the head. Placement should be above eye level. The ears, when laid in front without being pulled, should about meet the lip angle. In the case of heavier dogs, they should be correspondingly longer. *Eyes:* the eyes should be of medium size, full of intelligence and expressive, good-humored, and yet radiating energy, neither protruding nor sunk. The eyelids should close well. The best color is a dark shade of brown. Light yellow, china or wall (bird of prey) eyes are not desirable. *Nose:* brown, the larger the better; nostrils well opened and broad. Flesh-colored and spotted noses are not desirable. *Teeth:* the teeth should be strong and healthy. The molars should intermesh properly. Incisors should fit close in a true scissors bite. Jaws should be neither overshot nor under-shot.

Neck

Of adequate length to permit the jaws reaching game to be retrieved, sloping downwards on beautifully curving lines. The nape should be rather muscular, becoming gradually larger towards the shoulders. Moderate hound-like throatiness permitted.

Breast and thorax

The breast in general should give the impression of depth rather than breadth; for all that, it should be in correct proportion to the other parts of the body with fair depth of chest. The ribs forming the thorax should be well-curved and not flat; they should not be absolutely round or barrel-shaped. Ribs that are entirely round prevent the necessary expansion of the chest when taking breath. The back ribs should reach well down. The circumference of the breast immediately behind the elbows should be smaller than that of the breast about a hands-breadth behind elbows, so that the upper arm has room for movement.

Back and loins

Back should be short, strong and straight with slight rise from root of tail to withers. Excessively long or hog-backed should be penalized. Loin strong, of moderate length and slightly arched. Tuck-up should be apparent.

Assembly of back members

The hips should be broad with hip sockets wide apart and fall slightly toward the tail in a graceful curve. Thighs strong and well muscled. Stifles well bent. Hock joints should be well angulated with strong, straight bone structure from hock to pad. Angulation of both stifle and hock joints should be such as to combine maximum combination of both drive and traction. Hocks should turn neither in nor out.

Assembly of front members

The shoulders should be sloping, movable, well covered with muscle. The shoulder blades should lie flat. The upper arm (also called the cross bar, *i.e.* the bones between the shoulder and elbow joints) should be as long as possible, standing away somewhat from the trunk so that the straight and closely muscled legs, when viewed from in front, should appear to be parallel. Elbows which stand away from the body, or are pressed right into same, indicate toes turning inwards or outwards, which should be regarded as faults. Pasterns should be strong, short and nearly vertical.

Feet
Should be compact, close-knit and round to spoon-shaped. The toes sufficiently arched and heavily nailed. The pad should be strong and hard.

Coat and skin
The skin should look close and tight. The hair should be short and thick and feel tough and hard to the hand; it is somewhat longer on the underside of the tail and the back edge of the haunches. It is softer, thinner and shorter on the ears and the head.

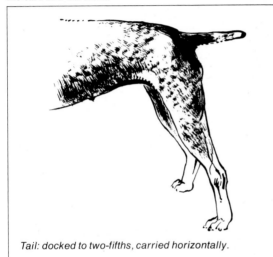
Tail: docked to two-fifths, carried horizontally.

Tail
Is set high and firm, and must be docked, leaving approximately two-fifths of length. The tail hangs down when the dog is quiet, is held horizontally when he is walking, never turned over the back or considerably bent, but violently wagged when he is on the search.

Bones
Thin and fine bones are by no means desirable in a dog which should be able to work over any and every country and should possess strength. The main importance accordingly is laid not so much on the size as being in proper proportion to the body. Dogs with coarse bones are handicapped in agility of movement and speed.

GROUP 1: SPORTING DOGS
Desirable weight and height
Dogs 55 to 70 pounds.
23 to 25 inches.
Bitches 45 to 60 pounds.
21 to 23 inches at the shoulders.

Color
Solid liver, liver and white spotted, liver and white spotted and ticked, liver and white ticked, liver roan. Any colors other than liver and white (gray white) are not permitted.

Symmetry and field quality are most essential. A dog well balanced in all points is preferable to one with oustanding good qualities and defects. A smooth, lithe gait is most desirable.

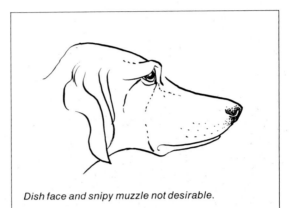
Dish face and snipy muzzle not desirable.

FAULTS
Bone structure too clumsy or too light; head too large; too many wrinkles in forehead; dish-faced; snipy muzzle; ears too long, pointy or fleshy; flesh-colored nose; eyes too light, too round or too closely set together; excessive throatiness; cowhocks; feet or elbows turned inward or outward; down on pasterns; loose shoulders; sway-back; black coat or tri-colored, any colors except liver or some combination of liver and white.

Approved by the AKC 7 May 1946

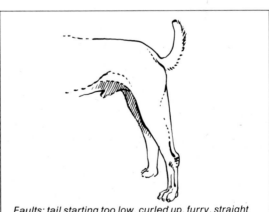
Faults: tail starting too low, curled up, furry, straight hindlegs, feet turned out.

KC(GB) VARIATION TO STANDARD
Faults: sway-back; cone shaped skull or occiput too prominent. Eyelids not closing properly. Wrinkles in neck. Soft sunken or splayed toes. Straight hindlegs. Tail starting too low; undocked; too thick; curled up or too furry.

GERMAN WIREHAIRED POINTER

NATIONAL GROUPING		
	Name	Number
AKC	Sporting Dogs	I
KC(GB)	—	—
FCI	Gundogs	7

In an attempt to produce an all purpose gundog, German fanciers turned to the Pointer type as a promising basis on which to build. Pointers of several sorts were being bred in a good many European countries more or less at the same time, and most of them were retrievers as well. The more sophisticated type of hunting that was to develop later when each type of gundog was used for a specialised purpose, had not yet become fashionable.

There were a number of basic breeds of gundog in Europe, and several of them were other than smooth coated. There were the Braques, probably descended from the now extinct Griffon de Bresse in France, the Spinone of Italy, still in existence as a separate breed, the Poodle Pointer of Germany and the various long and rough-coated gundogs in Britain. Breeders in Germany, having established as their aim the production of a Wirehaired Pointer had a number of breeds to choose from. Beginning with the Short-haired Pointer which was already in existence, they probably used several breeds to develop the one we know as the German Wirehaired Pointer.

Shooting in Germany has always been something of a mixed experience. The country is such that it is possible to switch from pheasant to hare and from duck to buck all in the space of a few hours, and a hardy well-coated dog with enthusiasm, endurance and an adaptability to all sorts of game was needed. In the Wirehaired Pointer just such a dog was produced. Using the best of the existing Pointer blood and intro-ducing that of the Foxhound, the Poodle and the English Pointer the breeders developed a dog that would do all the work of most of the other gundogs, and was staunch enough to stand up to a strenuous day across the roughest country. By the turn of the century the breed was well established, and a club had been formed, the Drahthaar Club. In a few short years he had become such a popular dog that he ousted most of the other gundogs in Germany. He arrived in the United States of America in 1920 and was soon seen as the ideal answer to the all-round gundog. He has only recently been introduced into Britain where a surfeit of very popular gundogs has probably prevented him from becoming better known, as he is still only shown among the rare breeds.

The German Wirehaired Pointer is, like his near relation the German Shorthaired, a very sturdy and energetic dog. He always gives the impression of enjoying hard work, an enthusiasm that he shares with the *Jäger* with whom he frequently works, as there are few more enthusiastic Sportsmen than the professional German hunter. His coat is one of his most important features and one on which a great deal of emphasis has been placed by the German Club. It lies flat but is long enough and strong enough to protect the body when he is forcing his way through thorn and bramble, and the whiskers around the nose and eyes protects those parts of the dog from injury.

His modern history as a show dog is short as he was accepted for registration for championship in the United States only in 1959, and is insufficiently well-established yet to have made his mark at the highest level. He is, however, a very attractive dog in the ring, his size, outline and colouring making him strikingly different, and there is every chance that he will become a popular show dog. He is intelligent and friendly, and whilst he is not effusive, he stands handling in the ring very well, and can be as good a house dog and com-panion as any other dog in the Sporting Group.

OFFICIAL STANDARD

The German Wirehaired Pointer is a dog that is essentially Pointer in type, of sturdy build, lively manner, and an intelligent, determined expression. In disposition the dog has been described as energetic, rather aloof but not unfriendly.

Head

The *head* is moderately long, the *skull* broad, the occipital bone not too prominent. The *stop* is medium, the *muzzle* fairly long with nasal bone straight and broad, the *lips* a trifle pendulous but close and bearded. The *nose* is dark brown with nostrils wide open, and the *teeth* are strong with scissors bite. The *ears*, rounded but not too broad, hang close to the sides of the head. *Eyes* are brown, medium in size, oval in contour, bright and clear and overhung with bushy eyebrows. Yellow eyes are not desirable. The *neck* is of medium length, slightly arched and devoid of dewlap; in fact, the skin throughout is notably tight to the body.

Head: stop medium, lips close and bearded.

Body and tail

The body is a little longer than it is high, as ten is to nine, with the back short, straight and strong, the entire back line showing a perceptible slope down from withers to croup. The chest is deep and capacious, the ribs well sprung, loins taut and slender, the tuck-up apparent. Hips are broad, with croup nicely rounded and the tail docked, approximately two-fifths of original length.

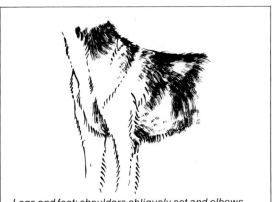

Legs and feet: shoulders obliquely set and elbows close.

Legs and feet: hind legs moderately angulated, agile.

Legs and feet

Forelegs are straight, with shoulders obliquely set and elbows close. The thighs are strong and muscular. The hind legs are moderately angulated at stifle and hock and as viewed from behind, parallel to each other. Round in outline, the feet are webbed, high arched with toes close, their pads thick and hard, and their nails strong and quite heavy. Leg bones are flat rather than round, and strong, but not so heavy or coarse as to militate against the dog's natural agility.

Coat

The coat is weather-resisting and to some extent water-repellent. The undercoat is dense enough in winter to insulate against the cold but so thin in summer as to be almost invisible. The distinctive outer coat is straight, harsh, wiry and rather flat-lying, from one and one-half to two inches in length; it is long enough to protect against the punishment of rough cover but not so long as to hide the outline. On the lower legs it is shorter and between the toes of softer texture. On the skull it is naturally short and close fitting, while over the shoulders and around the tail it is very dense and heavy. The tail is nicely coated, particularly on the underside, but devoid of feather. These dogs have bushy eyebrows of strong, straight hair and beards and whiskers of medium length.

A short smooth coat, a soft woolly coat, or an excessively long coat is to be severely penalized.

Color

The coat is liver and white, usually either liver and white spotted, liver roan, liver and white spotted with ticking and roaning or sometimes solid liver. The nose is dark brown. The head is brown, sometimes with a white blaze, the ears brown. Any black in the coat is to be severely penalized. Spotted and flesh-colored noses are undesirable and are to be penalized.

Size

Height of dogs should be from 24 to 26 inches at the withers, bitches smaller but not under 22 inches.

Approved by the AKC 7 February 1959

KC(GB) VARIATION TO STANDARD
This dog is not granted championship status by the KC(GB).

CHESAPEAKE BAY RETRIEVER

NATIONAL GROUPING		
	Name	Number
AKC	Sporting Dogs	I
KC(GB)	—	—
FCI	Gundogs	8

The history of this rather unusual dog is clearly recorded and there is no need to delve into vague references and ancient manuscripts. In 1807 an English ship was wrecked off the coast of Maryland and everyone on board was rescued by the American ship *Canton*. Among the rescued were two puppies, a red dog and a black bitch which were presumed to be Newfoundlands as there was a certain export of these dogs going on at the time. The two were presented to the gentleman who gave hospitality to the rescued sailors and were found to have retrieving ability. As was usual at that time their fame as gundogs spread and they were outcrossed to other dogs being used as sporting dogs in the area, and by 1885 the type had become fixed. Renowned for his powers of retrieving in the cold waters of Chesapeake Bay the dog soon took his name from that stretch of water.

Since that time his sterling qualities as a retriever, especially in water, where he is used extensively to duck, and will retrieve literally hundreds of duck in one day, have endeared him to the waterfowler, and he is now an invaluable ally for the sportsman addicted to that form of shooting. Oddly enough he has never quite achieved the popularity at shows or at field trials that his great ability might warrant. This is probably because he is a rather unglamorous dog, not having the appeal of the Labrador Retriever nor the picturesque qualities of some of the more colourful gundogs, and it is colour which really distinguishes him from all others. He is very much a working animal with no pretence to the more accepted forms of beauty. His appearance is rugged and no attempt has been made over the years to change him into anything else.

He is described as having a coat that varies from dead grass to wet sedge in colour, the actual tone fading in summer to look like the colour of the dead and shedding coat of the buffalo. It is this coat which is one of the major features of the breed and every effort is being made to retain it, as not only the colour, but also the texture is important. He is used for hunting under the most adverse weather conditions and the natural oiliness of the outer coat and the dense undercoat permit him to swim for long periods in very cold water and remove most of it with one brisk shake when returning to land. He is a well-proportioned dog with a balanced look about him, strong bone and good musculation.

His steadiness to hand makes him a comparatively easy dog to show as he does not suffer normally from nervousness though he can be a little reserved like some of the other gundogs. The breed has made little progress as a show dog outside the United States of America, and is rarely seen at any except the major shows. He is a willing, alert and intelligent dog, very friendly and attached to those that he knows, and always ready to work. They probably make better house dogs than they do kennel dogs, as they are hard and tend to be loners, objecting if other dogs intrude on their territory.

OFFICIAL STANDARD

Head
Skull broad and round with medium stop, nose medium short-muzzle, pointed but not sharp. Lips thin, not pendulous. Ears small, set well up on head, hanging loosely and of medium leather. Eyes medium large, very clear, of yellowish color and wide apart.

Neck
Of medium length with a strong muscular appearance, tapering to shoulders.

Shoulder, chest and body
Shoulders, sloping and should have full liberty of action with plenty of power without any restrictions of movement. Chest strong, deep and wide. Barrel round and deep. Body of medium length, neither cobby nor roached,

but rather approaching hollowness, flanks well tucked up.

Back quarters and stifles
Back quarters should be as high or a trifle higher than the shoulders. They should show fully as much power as the forequarters. There should be no tendency to weakness in either fore or hindquarters. Hindquarters should be especially powerful to supply the driving power for swimming. Back should be short, well-coupled and powerful. Good hindquarters are essential.

Legs, elbows, hocks and feet
Legs should be medium length and straight, showing good bone and muscle, with well-webbed hare feet of good size. The toes well rounded and close, pasterns slightly bent and both pasterns and hocks medium length—the straighter the legs the better. Dewclaws, if any, must be removed from the hind legs. Dewclaws on the forelegs may be removed. A dog with dewclaws on the hind legs must be disqualified.

Stern
Tail should be medium length—varying from: dogs, 12 to 15 inches, and bitches from 11 to 14 inches; medium heavy at base, moderate feathering on stern and tail permissible.

Coat and texture
Coat should be thick and short, nowhere over 1½ inches long, with a dense fine woolly undercoat. Hair on face and legs should be very short and straight with tendency to wave on the shoulders, neck, back and loins only. The curly coat or coat with a tendency to curl not permissible.

Color
Any color varying from a dark brown to a faded tan or deadgrass. Deadgrass takes in any shade of deadgrass, varying from a tan to a dull straw color. White spot on breast and toes permissible, but the smaller the spot the better, solid color being preferred.

Weight
Dogs, 65 to 75 pounds; bitches, 55 to 65 pounds. *Height:* Dogs, 23 to 26 inches; bitches, 21 to 24 inches.

Symmetry and quality
The Chesapeake dog should show a bright and happy disposition and an intelligent expression, with general outlines impressive and denoting a good worker. The dog should be well proportioned, a dog with a good coat and well balanced in other points being preferable to the dog excelling in some but weak in others.

The texture of the dog's coat is very important, as the dog is used for hunting under all sorts of adverse weather conditions, often working in ice and snow. The oil in the harsh outer coat and woolly undercoat is of extreme value in preventing the cold water from reaching the dog's skin and aids in quick drying. A Chesapeake's coat should resist the water in the same way that a duck's feathers do. When he leaves the water and shakes himself, his coat should not hold the water at all, being merely moist. Color and coat are extremely important, as the

dog is used for duck hunting. The color must be as nearly that of his surroundings as possible and with the fact that dogs are exposed to all kinds of adverse weather conditions, often working in ice and snow, the color of coat and its texture must be given every consideration when judging on the bench or in the ring.

Courage, willingness to work, alertness, nose intelligence, love of water, general quality, and, most of all, disposition, should be given primary consideration in the selection and breeding of the Chesapeake Bay dog.

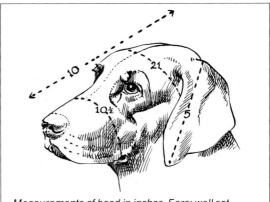

Measurements of head in inches. Ears: well set, hanging loosely.

APPROXIMATE MEASUREMENTS (in inches)
Length head, nose to occiput (9½ to 10). Girth at ears (20 to 21). Muzzle below eyes (10 to 10½). Length of ears (4½ to 5). Width between eyes (2½ to 2¾). Girth neck close to shoulder (20 to 22). Girth of chest to elbows (35 to 36). Girth at flank (24 to 25). Length from occiput to tail base (34 to 35). Girth forearms at shoulders (10 to 10½). Girth upper thigh (19 to 20). From root to root of ear, over skull (5 to 6). Occiput to top shoulder blades (9 to 9½). From elbow to elbow over the shoulders (25 to 26).

DISQUALIFICATIONS
Black or liver colored. Dewclaws on hind legs. White on any part of body, except breast, belly or spots on feet. Feathering on tail or legs over 1¾ inches long. Undershot, overshot or any deformity. Coat curly or tendency to curl all over body. Specimens unworthy or lacking in breed characteristics.

Approved by the AKC 9 July 1963

POSITIVE SCALE OF POINTS
Head, incl. lips, ears and eyes (16). Neck (4). Shoulders and body (12). Back quarters and stifles (12). Elbows, legs and feet (12). Color (4). Stern and tail (10). Coat and texture (18). General conformation (12). *Total (100).*

Note: the question of coat and general type of balance takes precedence over any scoring table which could be drawn up.

KC(GB) VARIATION TO STANDARD
This dog is not granted championship status by the KC(GB).

CURLY-COATED RETRIEVER

There existed in Europe some centuries ago a dog known as the Water Dog. He was about the size of a large Spaniel, was mostly black in colour with some white markings, and was covered with close curls. He is presumed by many people to have been the ancestor of the Poodle, and bore a strong resemblance to that other dog that enjoys working in water, the Irish Water Spaniel. There is little doubt that this old breed was also responsible for the Curly-coated Retriever. In fact one old writer carried out an experiment by crossing a Poodle with a Labrador and produced something very like a rather poor Curly-coated Retriever, which led him to the conclusion that through the German Pudel, the old Water Dog had a good deal to do with the ancestry of this breed. At one time the Poodle was shown in curly-coat or at least in cords, which are merely curls left to cling together, and even today, a pet poodle kept in fairly

NATIONAL GROUPING		
	Name	Number
AKC	Sporting Dogs	1
KC(GB)	Gundog	2
FCI	Gundogs	8

short coat will invariably develop curls.

The Curly-coated Retriever is said to have been crossed with the Poodle until well into the 19th century. This could be done without in any way undermining the ability of the breed in the field, as the Poodle was originally a hunting dog, and even today can be trained to perform well in the field. The curly-coated were at one time one of the more popular of the gundogs and it is interesting that Vero Shaw in 1881 stated that they were beginning to lose ground to the Wavy-coated Retriever, with no mention of today's most popular breeds in the retrieving family. The first were exhibited in 1860 at Birmingham, England, and before very long they were being exported to many countries where their capabilities were recognised. New Zealand and Australia took to them and soon after 1900 they began to make their appearance in the United States of America. In spite of his particular qualities as a water dog, he failed to make the progress in either the show ring or the field that some of the other breeds did, and he is now almost relegated to the status of a minority breed in the Gundog Group in Britain.

His principal physical characteristic, his coat, is the one thing that breeders are particularly enthusiastic about preserving. Early writers described the coat in detailed terms, and insisted that each lock should be tightly curled and that they should be close together, anything in the nature of an open coat to be severely penalised. The breed club, first formed in 1896 and reformed in 1933 produced a standard for the breed which re-emphasised this point. This thick curly coat enables him to work through the thickest and most punishing coverts and to spend considerable time in water, where the air trapped forms a good insulation against both wet and cold. He is a strong dog with a depth of chest and tremendously strong hindquarters. His performance in the field makes him a great favourite with gamekeepers in spite of the fact that he has the reputation of being somewhat harder than the other retrievers.

He presents few problems as a show dog, though the search for the perfect coat is constant, a good many tricks of the trade being used to improve and prepare coats. One old expert on the breed was in the habit of stopping at the nearest stretch of fresh water on the way to a show and giving his dogs a swim, allowing them to dry out naturally and trying to disturb the curls as little as possible before entering the ring. He is easily trained, either for the ring or the field, and makes an excellent guard and house dog.

OFFICIAL STANDARD

General appearance
A strong smart upstanding dog, showing activity, endurance and intelligence.

Head
Long and well proportioned, skull not too flat, jaws long and strong but not inclined to snipiness, nose black, in the black coated variety, with wide nostrils. Teeth strong and level. *Eyes:* black or brown, but not yellow, rather large but not too prominent. *Ears:* rather small, set on low, lying close to the head, and covered with short curls.

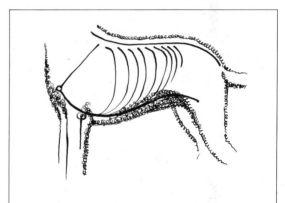

Body: well sprung. Ribs: good depth of brisket, little tuck up.

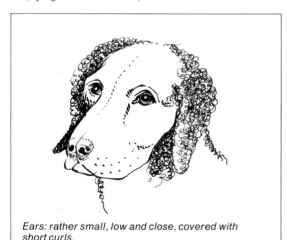

Ears: rather small, low and close, covered with short curls.

Coat
Should be one mass of crisp curls all over. A slightly more open coat not to be severely penalized, but a saddle back or patch of uncurled hair behind the shoulder should be penalized, and a prominent white patch on breast is undesirable, but a few white hairs allowed in an otherwise good dog. Color, black or liver.

Shoulders, chest, body and loins
Shoulders should be very deep, muscular and obliquely placed. Chest, not too wide, but decidedly deep. Body, rather short, muscular and well ribbed up. Loin, powerful, deep and firm to the grasp.

Legs and feet
Legs should be of moderate length, forelegs straight and set well under the body. Quarters strong and muscular, hocks low to the ground with moderate bend to stifle and hock. Feet round and compact with well-arched toes.

Tail
Should be moderately short, carried fairly straight and covered with curls, slightly tapering towards the point.

KC(GB) VARIATION TO STANDARD
Faults: wide skull, light eyes, curled tail and bad movement.

FLAT-COATED RETRIEVER

NATIONAL GROUPING		
	Name	Number
AKC	Sporting Dogs	I
KC(GB)	Gundog	2
FCI	Gundogs	8

In some ways the Flat-coated Retriever has a strange history, as he was produced from two breeds, the Labrador and the Newfoundland, both of which had their origins in the United States. Yet while he remained virtually unknown in that country he made a name for himself and became quite popular in Britain. The first evidence of the breed is of a dog named Wyndham that was shown at the Birmingham Show in 1860, where he caused something of a sensation. He was new to the dog breeders of Britain in spite of the fact that there was a tremendous interest in Retrievers in general at that time even though their numbers were small. He was christened the Wavy-coated Retriever and the name Flat-coated came later, when it was thought that a wavy coat was not the best for the work that he did in water, something at which he was very adept. It is fairly certain that there had been others before Wyndham, as it was very unlikely that he should be a single one of his type, and much more likely that some experimental breeding had been going on for several generations.

It is fairly certain that the Gordon Setter and the Irish Setter were used later, as the breed had become more elegant and less heavily built than it once was and the coat quality has developed into the fine flat texture that is now so much a feature of the breed. He is an admirable water dog, and this particular quality endeared him to gundog people, as he combined most of the other qualities of the retriever with a constitution that rendered him almost impervious to the effects of long immersion. Later still his popularity was assured when one of the greatest dog men of all time, S.E. Shirley, founder of the British Kennel Club and its Chairman from 1873 until 1899 when he became President, took an interest in the breed and bred, exhibited and worked some of the finest of those times. His portrait hanging in the Board Room of the Kennel Club in London, depicts him with a Flat-coated Retriever.

The breed went into something of a decline as a show dog during the First World War, but was kept alive by the efforts of gamekeepers, many of whom looked upon the Flat-coated Retriever as the finest of all the gundogs. The Flat-coated Retriever Association however did much to revive the breed after 1923 when the club was formed, and since that time representatives of the breed have been seen in ever increasing numbers at the major shows, just on one hundred being exhibited at Crufts in 1977. Fortunately for the working qualities of the breed, they are also being taken up increasingly by those interested in field work.

He is a strong dog, less weighty for his size than the Labrador Retriever, but sturdier than the Irish Setter, and he is remarkably intelligent. His coat, which is his outstanding characteristic is close-lying and dense, and whilst the favourite colour is black, some liver specimens are seen now though they were frowned upon in the early days of the breed. He is a fine show-dog, his intelligent response to environment and circumstances allowing him to deal with the attentions of a judge and the physical contact with people and other dogs with the calm that is part of his nature. His coat, glowing in the sunshine makes him an ideal dog for showing out of doors, where he looks at his best. Temperamentally he is very steady, responsive to attention, and makes a remarkably good guard, as he is very territorially minded.

OFFICIAL STANDARD

General appearance
A bright, active dog of medium size (weighing from 60 to 70 pounds) with an intelligent expression, showing power without lumber and raciness without weediness.

Ears: small, well set on.

Head
This should be long and nicely molded. The skull flat and moderately broad. There should be a depression or stop between the eyes, slight and in no way accentuated, so as to avoid giving either a down or a dish-faced appearance. The nose of good size with open nostrils. The eyes, of medium size, should be dark brown or hazel, with a very intelligent expression (a round prominent eye is a disfigurement), and they should not be obliquely placed.

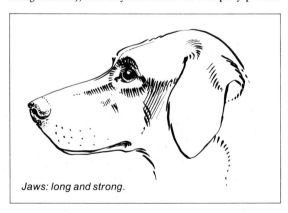

Jaws: long and strong.

The jaws should be long and strong, with a capacity of carrying a hare or pheasant. The ears small and well set on close to the side of the head.

Neck, shoulders and chest
The head should be well set in the neck, which latter should be long and free from throatiness, symmetrically set and obliquely placed in shoulders, running well into the back to allow of easily seeking for the trail. The chest should be deep and fairly broad, with a well defined brisket, on which the elbows should work cleanly and evenly. The fore ribs should be fairly flat showing a

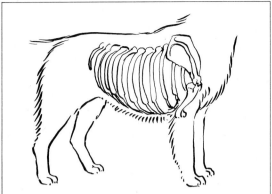

Body: fore-ribs fairly flat, gradual spring in centre of body.

gradual spring and well arched in the center of the body but rather lighter towards the quarters. Open couplings are to be ruthlessly condemned.

Back and quarters
The back should be short, square and well ribbed up, with muscular quarters. The stern short, straight and well set on, carried gaily but never much above the level of the back.

Legs and feet
These are of the greatest importance. The forelegs should be perfectly straight, with bone of good quality carried right down to the feet which should be round and strong. The stifle should not be too straight or too bent and the dog must neither be cowhocked nor move too wide behind; in fact, he must stand and move true all round on legs and feet, with toes close and well arched, the soles being thick and strong. When the dog is in full coat the limbs should be well feathered.

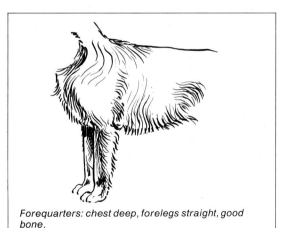

Forequarters: chest deep, forelegs straight, good bone.

Coat
Should be dense, of fine quality and texture, flat as possible.

Color
Black or liver.

GOLDEN RETRIEVER

NATIONAL GROUPING		
	Name	Number
AKC	Sporting Dogs	1
KC(GB)	Gundog	2
FCI	Gundogs	8

Scotland has many native breeds, most of them belonging to the Terrier Group. There are many Scots who would like to lay claim to the Golden Retriever too, but it was in fact more of an accident of geography that resulted in much of the early development of this breed taking place North of the Border. Retrievers in general became popular in Britain during the early part of the 19th century, when, with the growth of wildfowling as a sport, there came the demand for dogs that would work as collectors of game under extreme conditions of wet and cold. The less heavy form of Newfoundland, known at that time as the St. John's Newfoundland had found its way over to Britain from the other side of the Atlantic, and its ability as a water dog was soon realised. This breed was crossed with Setters and Spaniels and produced large strong, intelligent dogs with an affinity to water, the will to work and a soft mouth.

It happened that the early work on the breed was carried out by Lord Tweedmouth. The legend of his having bought a troop of performing Russian dogs from a circus, was exploded by other members of his family. In more recent records it was made clear that the first member of the race was in fact a mutation from Flat-coated Retriever stock, a dog named Nous. He was mated to a small English Retriever, and the line had started. The Tweedmouth dogs were carefully outcrossed to further water-spaniels and some of the Flat-coated Retrievers then known as Wavy-coats, and by the beginning of the 19th century the type and colour was fixed. These yellow Retrievers were recognised as Flat-coats until 1913, when they were registered as a separate variety, called at first Yellow or Golden Retrievers, and eventually Golden Retrievers. The modernity of the breed is best indicated by the fact that in Robert Leighton's very comprehensive work of 1907, it does not get a mention.

Their growth in popularity since those early days has been one of the phenomena of the dog world. In fifty years the number registered in Britain has grown from virtually nothing, to something approaching ten thousand each year, making them one of the most prolific breeds in the Gundog Group. It is not now unusual for them to outnumber both Cockers and Labrador Retrievers at some of the major shows, and one or two quite outstanding dogs have won major honours in recent years.

The Golden Retriever's working qualities are still much exploited and he is seen regularly at field trials, takes part in obedience work and even makes a successful guide dog for the blind. His intelligence is extraordinary and he is one of the few dogs that can work out a problem for himself rather than merely acting on instruction or as the result of repetitive training. As a show dog he has few peers, as he is one of the quietest and best behaved dogs in existence, behaving always in a gentlemanly fashion, at the same time cheerful and never dull. His coat lends itself to preparation and grooming and the minimum amount of shaping and control. His relaxed and quiet behaviour makes it possible to transport several in a car without fuss, and to bench them with confidence.

He is a gentle, sensitive, always responsive dog and is very good with children. His obedience is renowned and his lack of vice recognised throughout the world of dogs. He makes a first class guard and companion.

OFFICIAL STANDARD

General appearance

A symmetrical, powerful, active dog, sound and well put together, not clumsy or long in the leg, displaying a kindly expression and possessing a personality that is eager, alert and self-confident. Primarily a hunting dog, he should be shown in hard working condition. Over-all appearance, balance, gait and purpose to be given more emphasis that any of his component parts.

Size

Dogs 23 to 24 inches in height at withers; females 21½ to 22½ inches. Length from breastbone to buttocks slightly greater than height at withers in ratio of 12:11. Weight for dogs 65 to 75 pounds; bitches 60 to 70 pounds.

Head

Broad in skull, slightly arched laterally and longitudinally without prominence of frontal or occipital bones. Good stop. Foreface deep and wide, nearly as long as skull. Muzzle, when viewed in profile, slightly deeper at stop than at tip; when viewed from above, slightly wider at stop than at tip. No heaviness in flews. Removal of whiskers for show purposes optional. *Eyes:* friendly and intelligent, medium large with dark rims, set well apart and reasonably deep in sockets. Color preferably dark brown, never lighter than color of coat. No white or haw visible when looking straight ahead. *Teeth:* scissors bite with lower incisors touching inside of upper incisors. *Nose:* black or dark brown, though lighter shade in cold weather not serious. Dudley nose (pink without pigmentation) to be faulted. *Ears:* Rather short, hanging flat against head with rounded tips slightly below jaw. Forward edge attached well behind and just above eye with rear edge slightly below eye. Low, houndlike earset to be faulted.

Neck

Medium long, sloping well back into shoulders, giving sturdy muscular appearance with untrimmed natural ruff. No throatiness.

Body

Well balanced, short-coupled, deep through the heart. Chest at least as wide as a man's hand, including thumb. Brisket extends to elbows. Ribs long and well sprung but not barrel shaped, extending well to rear of body. Loin short, muscular, wide and deep, with very little tuck-up. Topline level from withers to croup, whether standing or moving. Croup slopes gently. Slabsidedness, narrow chest, lack of depth in brisket, excessive tuck-up, roach or sway back to be faulted.

Forequarters

Forequarters well co-ordinated with hindquarters and capable of free movement. Shoulder blades wide, long and muscular, showing angulation with upper arm of approximately 90 degrees. Legs straight with good bone. Pastern short and strong, sloping slightly forward with no suggestion of weakness.

Hindquarters

Well-bent stifles (angulation between femur and pelvis approximately 90 degrees) with hocks well let down. Legs straight when viewed from rear. Cowhocks and sickle hocks to be faulted.

Feet

Medium size, round and compact with thick pads. Excess hair may be trimmed to show natural size and contour. Open or splayed feet to be faulted.

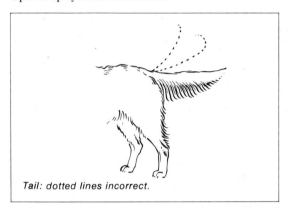

Tail: dotted lines incorrect.

Tail

Well set on, neither too high nor too low, following natural line of croup. Length extends to hock. Carried with merry action with some upward curve but never curled over back nor between legs.

Coat and color

Dense and water-repellent with good undercoat. Texture not as hard as that of a shorthaired dog, nor silky as that of a setter. Lies flat against body and may be straight or wavy. Moderate feathering on back of forelegs and heavier feathering on front of neck, back of thighs and underside of tail. Feathering may be lighter than rest of coat. Color lustrous golden of various shades. A few white hairs on chest permissible but not desirable. Further white markings to be faulted.

Gait

When trotting, gait is free, smooth, powerful and well co-ordinated. Viewed from front or rear, legs turn neither in nor out, nor do feet cross or interfere with each other. Increased speed causes tendency of feet to converge toward center line of gravity.

DISQUALIFICATIONS

Deviation in height of more than one inch from standard either way. Undershot or overshot bite. This condition not to be confused with misalignment of teeth. Trichiasis (abnormal position or direction of the eyelashes).

Approved by the AKC 10 September 1963

KC(GB) VARIATION TO STANDARD

Weight and size: dogs 70 to 80 pounds and 22 to 24 inches at shoulders. Bitches 60 to 70 pounds and 20 to 22 inches at shoulders.

LABRADOR RETRIEVER

Few dogs earn their names from a casual remark in a letter. They draw on their country of origin, or the work that they do, or even on the names of those who first bred them. The Labrador Retriever owes his name to a letter written by the Earl of Malmesbury in 1887 in which, in speaking of these dogs he said that he always called his 'Labradors'. The name had the right sort of ring about it and it was adopted for the breed.

Newfoundland was much visited by fishermen and travellers in the early part of the 19th century, and one reported on a small breed of water dog that he had seen there, short-haired, usually black and trained as a retriever by wildfowlers. The Earl of Malmesbury is said to have seen one of these brought over to Britain and found it so attractive that he imported some. The breed gradually died out in Newfoundland where it was virtually taxed out of existence as local fishermen would not pay a heavy dog tax, but it flourished in Britain where its qualities were recognised.

The Labrador Retriever undoubtedly played a part in the development of the at one-time much more popular Flat-coated Retriever, and it is remarkable that he remained a true type as a good deal of inter-breeding must have taken place. It is interesting in this context to note that in the early part of this century, one well known writer was saying he doubted that the Labrador would ever be appreciated by the rank and file and become popular as a show dog. How surprised he would be now to see him one of the best known dogs in the world. Hexham near the Scottish border was the first Show to schedule the breed, and the Crystal

NATIONAL GROUPING		
	Name	Number
AKC	Sporting Dogs	1
KC(GB)	Gundog	2
FCI	Gundogs	8

Palace, and Crufts soon followed. It is not, however, merely in the show ring that the popularity of the Labrador has grown. He is regularly seen at gundog trials as well as being popular with gamekeepers for day to day work with game, but it is still as a water dog and a wildfowler's companion that he is best known.

At one time almost all Labradors were black, but the yellows have now overtaken the other colours in popularity, and a few chocolates are now appearing in the ring. There was some controversy about which colour was the best for field work, some preferring the blacks which they felt were better workers in water, others the yellows as they were generally more easily seen at work. In fact there is probably little to choose between them, and temperament and ability are more important considerations. The Labrador Retriever must be one of the best all round dogs in the world. In addition to his value as a field dog, and his tremendous popularity as a show dog, he has achieved fame in other directions. He proved a valuable dog in war time, being an excellent mine detector, capable of locating mines by scent even when they were buried at considerable depths. He is a fine police dog, being easily trained in criminal work and as a specialist for sniffing out drugs. In addition most of the dogs trained as guide dogs for the blind are now Labrador bitches.

As a show dog he has attained prominence in recent years over most of the other members of the group, and the number of registrations in the breed in most countries is the highest among the gundogs. He is one of those breeds that in Britain cannot become a full champion until they have received working certificates, and the title of Show Champion has been introduced to cover those that gain certificates but do not qualify. He is a good dog in the ring, being very steady and cheerful, enjoying the company of other dogs and the noise of the crowd. He is not difficult to keep in condition provided that he is given enough exercise to prevent him putting on weight. His temperament is almost ideal, as he is attached to people and places, adopts a sufficiently possessive attitude to property to make a good guard, and is very good with children.

OFFICIAL STANDARD

General appearance

The general appearance of the Labrador should be that of a strongly built, short-coupled, very active dog. He should be fairly wide over the loins, and strong and muscular in the hindquarters. The coat should be close, short, dense and free from feather.

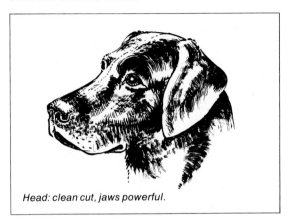

Head: clean cut, jaws powerful.

Head

The skull should be wide, giving brain room; there should be a slight stop, *i.e.* the brow should be slightly pronounced, so that the skull is not absolutely in a straight line with the nose. The head should be clean-cut and free from fleshy cheeks. The jaws should be long and powerful and free from snipiness; the nose should be wide and the nostrils well developed. Teeth should be strong and regular, with a level mouth. The ears should hang moderately close to the head, rather far back, should be set somewhat low and not be large and heavy. The eyes should be of a medium size, expressing great intelligence and good temper, and can be brown, yellow or black, but brown or black is preferred.

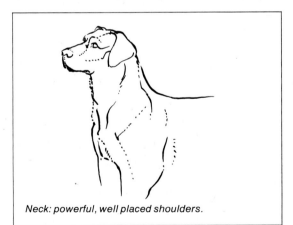

Neck: powerful, well placed shoulders.

Neck and chest

The neck should be medium length, powerful and not throaty. The shoulders should be long and sloping. The chest must be of good width and depth, the ribs well sprung and the loins wide and strong, stifles well turned,

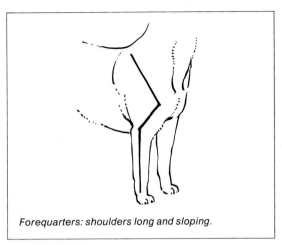

Forequarters: shoulders long and sloping.

and the hindquarters well developed and of great power.

Legs and feet

The legs must be straight from the shoulder to ground, and the feet compact with toes well arched, and pads well developed; the hocks should be well bent, and the dog must neither be cowhocked nor be too wide behind; in fact, he must stand and move true all round on legs and feet. Legs should be of medium length, showing good bone and muscle, but not so short as to be out of balance with rest of body. In fact, a dog well balanced in all points is preferable to one with outstanding good qualities and defects.

Tail

The tail is a distinctive feature of the breed; it should be very thick towards the base, gradually tapering towards the tip, of medium length, should be free from any feathering, and should be clothed thickly all round with the Labrador's short, thick, dense coat, thus giving that peculiar 'rounded' appearance which has been described as the 'otter' tail. The tail may be carried gaily but should not curl over the back.

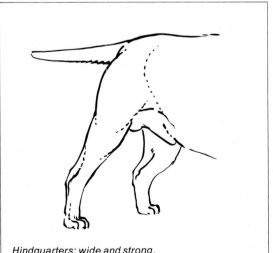

Hindquarters: wide and strong.

Coat

The coat is another very distinctive feature; it should be short, very dense and without wave, and should give a fairly hard feeling to the hand.

Color

The colors are black, yellow, or chocolate and are evaluated as follows:

(a) *Blacks:* all black, with a small white spot on chest permissible. Eyes to be of medium size, expressing intelligence and good temper, preferably brown or hazel, although black or yellow is permissible.

(b) *Yellows:* Yellows may vary in color from fox-red to light cream with variations in the shading of the coat on ears, the underparts of the dog, or beneath the tail. A small white spot on chest is permissible. Eye coloring and expression should be the same as that of the blacks, with black or dark brown eye rims. The nose should also be black or dark brown, although 'fading' to pink in winter weather is not serious. A 'Dudley' nose (pink without pigmentation), should be penalized.

(c) *Chocolates:* shades ranging from light sedge to chocolate. A small white spot on chest is permissible. Eyes to be light brown to clear yellow. Nose and eye-rim pigmentation dark brown or liver colored. 'Fading' to pink in winter weather not serious. 'Dudley' nose should be penalized.

Movement

Movement should be free and effortless. The forelegs should be strong, straight and true, and correctly placed. Watching a dog move towards one, there should be no signs of elbows being out in front, but neatly held to the body with legs not too close together, and moving straight forward without pacing or weaving. Upon viewing the dog from the rear, one should get the impression that the hind legs, which should be well muscled and not cow-hocked, move as nearly parallel as possible, with hocks doing their full share of work and flexing well, thus giving the appearance of power and strength.

Approximate weights of dogs and bitches in working condition

Dogs: 60 to 75 pounds; bitches: 55 to 70 pounds.

Height at shoulders

Dogs: $22\frac{1}{2}$ to $24\frac{1}{2}$ inches; bitches: $21\frac{1}{2}$ to $23\frac{1}{2}$ inches.

Approved by the AKC 9 April 1957

KC(GB) VARIATION TO STANDARD

Head: jaws should be medium length. *Size:* dogs 22 to $22\frac{1}{2}$ inches; bitches $21\frac{1}{2}$ to 22 inches. *Faults:* under or overshot mouth; no undercoat; bad action feathering; snipiness on the head; large or heavy ears; cow-hocked; tail curled over back.

ENGLISH SETTER

Even before the days of the shotgun, some of the dogs used to locate the prey were trained to sit when they found the game by nose and eye, and became known as 'sitting' or 'setting' dogs. The English Setter has developed from these dogs. He is essentially European, developed mainly for work on moors or in stubble or roots where his task is to remain motionless when he has located game to give the sportsman the opportunity to see it and dispatch it. His origins probably lie in the Spaniel and the Old Spanish Pointer, and engravings of the Springer and the Setter of 1820 show two dogs with marked similarities. The Springer is lighter and longer in the leg than the modern Spaniel, and the Setter is heavier and shorter than the Setter of today. As their colour and markings are the same they look rather like two examples of the same breed.

The major credit for the development of the modern English Setter undoubtedly belongs to Mr. Edward Laverack who in 1825 obtained a pair from the Rev. Harrison and inbred them until he had fixed the type that he wanted. In 1874 a pair of these dogs was imported into the United States and formed the foundations of the Llewellin line which became the main strain in that country. The Laverack line was so important in the early days of the breed that they were known as Laverack Setters, whilst the Llewellin strain was given

NATIONAL GROUPING		
	Name	Number
AKC	Sporting Dogs	1
KC(GB)	Gundog	2
FCI	Gundogs	8

equal prominence and Setter breeders spoke of the two strains almost as if they were separate breeds. The three breeds of Setters, the English, the Irish and the Gordon, almost certainly descended from the same parent stock, but it is remarkable how the popularity of the three breeds has varied. The Irish Setter having gone through a period of doldrums is now one of the most popular of breeds, the Gordon Setter has never achieved a great deal of popularity, whilst the English Setter has made steady progress over the years.

He is one of the dogs that most typifies the English country scene, and many people have an image of the English gentleman, dressed in tweeds, gun under his arm and English Setter by his side, firmly fixed in their minds as part of an idyllic English scene. This is not surprising as he is a very English dog in character. He is gentle and quiet, less exuberant than some of the other gundogs, and with a mild and sweet disposition. He is elegant in appearance yet strongly built with the look of the outdoors about him: he is in fact more hardy and sturdy than his appearance might suggest. The first show of the breed was held in Newcastle-upon-Tyne in 1859 and since that time he has made steady progress as a show dog, culminating in the great win of Supreme Best in Show by Ch. Silbury Soames of Madavale at Crufts in 1964. His elegance of outline, lovely coat and beautiful head make him a superb show dog, and his steadiness in the ring, makes him an easy dog to show. The breed matures late, however, and puppies look very unimpressive alongside some of the faster maturing breeds such as the Terriers, which tends to make them competitive only among other members of their own breed. He is quiet and usually relaxed, well-mannered and most affectionate, and can be completely trusted with children. He settles down to domestic life very easily, and although when out walking he will cover considerable ground enjoying every scent on the air, he is easily trained to return.

51

OFFICIAL STANDARD

Head

Long and lean, with a well-defined stop. The skull oval from ear to ear, of medium width, giving brain room but with no suggestion of coarseness, with but little difference between the width at base of skull and at brows and with a moderately defined occipital protuberance. Brows should be at a sharp angle from the muzzle. Muzzle should be long and square, of width in harmony with the skull, without any fullness under the eyes and straight from eyes to tip of the nose. A dish-face or Roman nose objectionable. The lips square and fairly pendant. Nose should be black or dark liver in color, except in white,

Head: long, well-defined stop.

lemon and white, orange and white, or liver and white dogs, when it may be of lighter color. Nostrils should be wide apart and large in the openings. Jaws should be of equal length. Overshot or undershot jaw objectionable. Ears should be carried close to the head, well back and set low, of moderate length, slightly rounded at the ends, and covered with silky hair. Eyes should be bright, mild, intelligent and dark brown in color.

Neck

The neck should be long and lean, arched at the crest, and not too throaty.

Shoulders

Shoulders should be formed to permit perfect freedom of action to the forelegs. Shoulder blades should be long, wide, sloping moderately well back and standing fairly close together at the top.

Chest

Chest between shoulder blades should be of good depth but not of excessive width.

Ribs

Ribs, back of the shoulders, should spring gradually to the middle of the body and then taper to the back ribs, which should be of good depth.

Back

Back should be strong at its junction with the loin and should be straight or sloping upward very slightly to the top of the shoulder, the whole forming a graceful outline of medium length, without sway or drop. Loins should be strong, moderate in length, slightly arched, but not to the extent of being roached or wheel-backed. Hipbones should be wide apart without too sudden drop to the root of the tail.

Forelegs

The arms should be flat and muscular, with bone fully developed and muscles hard and devoid of flabbiness; of good length from the point of the shoulder to the elbow, and set at such an angle as will bring the legs fairly under the dog. Elbows should have no tendency to turn either in or out. The pastern should be short, strong and nearly round with the slope from the pastern joint to the foot deviating very slightly forward from the perpendicular.

Hind legs

The hind legs should have wide, muscular thighs with well developed lower thighs. Stifles should be well bent and strong. Hocks should be wide and flat. The hind pastern or metatarsus should be short, strong and nearly round.

Feet

Feet should be closely set and strong, pads well developed and tough, toes well arched and protected with short, thick hair.

Tail

Tail should be straight and taper to a fine point, with only sufficient length to reach the hocks, or less. The feather

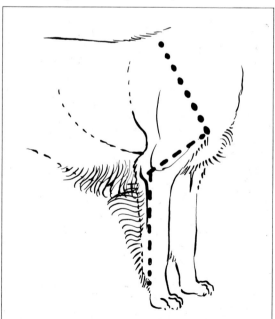

Forequarters: shoulders well set back. Brisket: good depth. Forearm: big, very muscular.

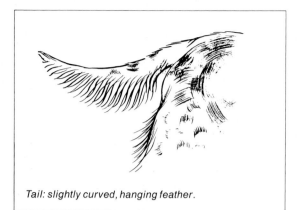

Tail: slightly curved, hanging feather.

must be straight and silky, falling loosely in a fringe and tapering to the point when the tail is raised. There must be no bushiness. The tail should not curl sideways or above the level of the back.

Coat

Coat should be flat and of good length, without curl; not soft or woolly. The feather on the legs should be moderately thin and regular.

Height

Dogs about 25 inches; bitches about 24 inches.

Colors

Black, white and tan; black and white; blue belton; lemon and white; lemon belton; orange and white; orange belton; liver and white; liver belton; and solid white. *Markings:* dogs without heavy patches of color on the body, but flecked all over preferred.

Symmetry

The harmony of all parts to be considered. Symmetrical dogs will have level backs or be very slightly higher at the shoulders than at the hips. Balance, harmony of proportion, and an appearance of breeding and quality to be looked for, and coarseness avoided.

Movement and carriage

An easy, free and graceful movement, suggesting rapidity and endurance. A lively tail and a high carriage of head. Stiltiness, clumsiness or a lumbering gait are objectionable.

SCALE OF POINTS
Head (20): skull (5), ears (5), eyes (5), muzzle (5). Body (27): neck (5), chest and shoulders (12), back, loin and ribs (10). *Running Gear (23):* forelegs (5), hips, thighs and hind legs (12), feet (6). Coat (8): length and texture (5), color and marking (3). Tail (5): length and carriage (5). *General Appearance and Action (17):* symmetry, style and movement (12), size (5). *Total (100).*

Approved by the AKC 8 May 1951

KC(GB) VARIATION TO STANDARD

Head: moderately defined occipital protuberance. *Weight and size:* dogs 60 to 66 pounds and $25\frac{1}{2}$ to 27 inches. *Faults:* course lumpy shoulders; short foreface; tapering to nose; lack of 'stop'; light or obliquely set eyes; high ear placement; loose elbows from bad shoulder placement; flat ribs; too long loin; wide feet; weak pasterns; straight stifles; narrow quarters; gay 'flag'; lightness of bone; mouth undershot or overshot; lacking freedom of action.

GORDON SETTER

NATIONAL GROUPING		
	Name	Number
AKC	Sporting Dogs	1
KC(GB)	Gundog	2
FCI	Gundogs	8

Speed in a gundog, and particularly in a Setter, is not all important and this is exemplified in the Gordon Setter, the most heavily built of the three British Setter breeds. In the case of the Gordon, steadiness and brain power have replaced flashiness and he will work on steadily all day, rarely if ever making a mistake. He was developed as the others were by selective breeding from crossing the old fashioned Spaniel with other breeds and was largely a colour separation in the first instance. He was known as the Gordon Setter in his early days as he came to the attention of sportsmen largely through the efforts of the fourth Duke of Gordon, who kept a large kennel of the breed in the latter part of the 18th century. Oddly enough at the turn of the 19th century, he became known as the Black and Tan Setter, as the strain originally kept by the Gordon Castle Kennels was black, tan and white. It was somewhat clumsy and heavy in appearance, and by that time, with the introduction of Irish blood, a more elegant and fashionable dog was being bred.

When Kennel Club registrations started, the name Gordon Setter was restored, and the formation of a club and the establishment of a standard for the breed ensured its preservation. By 1842 the breed had arrived in the United States of America and by careful further importations from both Britain and Scandinavia the breed has become well established. In recent years the breed went into something of a decline as a show dog, and the numbers of registrations in Britain fell well below the hundred though he still remained popular as a working dog. There is now something of a recovery and the numbers are climbing steadily. It is as a gundog, working in the field that the Gordon Setter has really made his mark, and the efforts of the Gordon Setter Club of America to foster the breed and to organise field trials have done much to preserve those qualities.

It is one of his characteristics that he is ever willing complete attachment to one person makes him at times shy of strangers. He is intelligent and extremely loyal to the members of the family, taking great pleasure in being a member of a household, and is to work, and this has made him a great favourite with the one-dog sportsman who finds him a tireless and co-operative companion. The Gordon Setter breeders and owners have never allowed the sharp division between the show dog and the field dog to develop as it has in so many of the gundog breeds, and most of the dogs are as good in the field as they are on the bench. He is the heavyweight of the Setter trio, is sturdier looking and has a stronger body with a fairly heavy head. He is dignified and even noble in his bearing, and his look is that of a strong dog with stamina rather than a racy type.

He looks well in the ring as his colour is quite dramatic, and the glow that comes on the coat of a healthy dog makes him look quite glamorous when he is mature and well feathered. He suffers from the rather gangling awkward look of the others when a puppy, and he needs understanding for promise rather than polish in his early stages. He is steady though sometimes rather reserved in the ring, and his friendly to those he knows without being effusive.

OFFICIAL STANDARD

General appearance

The Gordon Setter is a good sized, sturdily built, black and tan dog, well muscled, with plenty of bone and substance, but active, upstanding, and stylish, appearing capable of doing a full day's work in the field. He has a strong, rather short back, with well-sprung ribs and a short tail. The head is fairly heavy and finely chiseled. His bearing is intelligent, noble, and dignified, showing no signs of shyness or viciousness. Clear colors and straight or slightly waved coat are correct. He suggests strength and stamina rather than extreme speed. Symmetry and quality are most essential. A dog well-balanced in all points is preferable to one with outstanding good qualities and defects. A smooth, free movement, with high head carriage, is typical.

Size

Shoulder height for dogs, 24 to 27 inches. For bitches, 23 to 26 inches.

Weight

Dogs, 55 to 80 pounds; bitches, 45 to 70 pounds. Animals that appear to be over or under the prescribed weight limits are to be judged on the basis of conformation and condition. Extremely thin or fat dogs should be discouraged on the basis that under- or overweight hampers the true working ability of the Gordon Setter. The weight-to-height ratio makes him heavier than other setters.

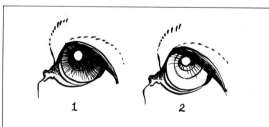

Eyes: (1) dark and bright, (2) too light.

Head

The head is deep, rather than broad, with plenty of brain room; a nicely rounded, good-sized skull, broadest between the ears. The head should have a clearly indicated stop. Below and above the eyes should be lean, and the cheek as narrow as the leanness of the head allows. The muzzle is fairly long and not pointed, either as seen from above or from the side. The flews should not be pendulous. The nose should be broad, with open nostrils and black in color. The muzzle is the same length as the skull from occiput to stop, and the top of the muzzle is parallel to the line of the skull extended. The lip line from the nose to the flews shows a sharp, well-defined, square contour. *Eyes:* of fair size, neither too deep-set, nor too bulging, dark brown, bright, and wise. The shape is oval rather than round. The lids should be tight. *Ears:* set low on the head approximately on line with the eye, fairly large and thin, well folded and carried close to the head. *Teeth:* the teeth should be strong and white, and preferably should meet in front in a scissors bite, with the upper incisors slightly forward of the lower incisors. A level bit is not to be considered a fault. Pitted teeth from distemper or allied infections should not be penalized.

Neck

Long, lean, arched to the head, and without throatiness.

Shoulders

Should be fine at the points, and lying well back, giving a moderately sloping topline. The tops of the shoulder blades should be close together. When viewed from behind, the neck appears to fit into the shoulders in smooth, flat, lines that gradually widen from neck to shoulder.

Chest

Deep and not too broad in front; the ribs well sprung, leaving plenty of lung room. The chest should reach to the elbows. A pronounced forechest should be in evidence.

Body

The body should be short from shoulder to hips, and the distance from the forechest to the back of the thigh should approximately equal the height from the ground to the withers. The loins should be short and broad and not arched. The croup is nearly flat, with only a slight slope to the tailhead.

Forequarters

The legs should be big-boned, straight, and not bowed, with elbows free and not turned in or out. The angle formed by the shoulder blade and upper arm bone should be approximately 90 degrees when the dog is standing so that the foreleg is perpendicular to the ground. The pasterns should be straight.

Hindquarters

The hind legs from hip to hock should be long, flat, and muscular; from hock to heel, short and strong. The stifle and hock joints are well bent and not turned either in or out. When the dog is standing with the hock perpendicular to the ground, the thigh bone should hang downward parallel to an imaginary line drawn upwards from the hock.

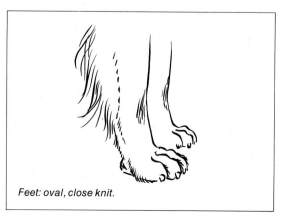

Feet: oval, close knit.

Feet

The feet should be formed by close-knit, well-arched toes with plenty of hair between; with full toe pads and deep heel cushions. Feet should not be turned in or out. Feet should be catlike in shape.

Tail

Short and should not reach below the hocks, carried horizontal or nearly so; thick at the root and finishing in a fine point. The feather which starts near the root of the tail should be slightly waved or straight, having triangular appearance, growing shorter uniformly toward the end. The placement of the tail is important for correct carriage. If the croup is nearly flat, the tail must emerge nearly on the same plane as the croup to allow for horizontal carriage. When the angle of the tail bends too sharply at the first coccygeal bone, the tail will be carried too gaily or will droop. The tail placement should be judged in its relationship to the structure of the croup.

Temperament

The Gordon Setter should be alert, gay, interested, and aggressive. He should be fearless and willing, intelligent and capable. He should be loyal and affectionate, and strong-minded enough to stand the rigors of training.

Gait

The action of the Gordon Setter is a bold, strong, driving, free-swinging gait. The head is carried up and the tail 'flags' constantly while the dog is in motion. When viewed from the front, the forefeet move up and down in straight lines so that the shoulder, elbow, and pastern joints are approximately in line with each other. When viewed from the rear, the hock, stifle, and hip joints are approximately in line. Thus the dog moves in a straight pattern forward without throwing the feet in or out. When viewed from the side, the forefeet are seen to lift up and reach forward to compensate for the driving hindquarters. The hindquarters reach well forward and stretch far back, enabling the stride to be long and the drive powerful. The over-all appearance of the moving dog is one of smooth-flowing, well-balanced rhythm, in which the action is pleasing to the eye, effortless, economical and harmonious.

Coat

Should be soft and shining, straight or slightly waved, but not curly, with long hair on ears, under stomach and on chest, on back of the fore- and hind legs, and on the tail.

Color and markings

Black with tan markings, either of rich chestnut or mahogany color. Black pencilling is allowed on the toes. The borderline between black and tan colors should be clearly defined. There should not be any tan hairs mixed in the black. The tan markings should be located as follows: (1) two clear spots over the eyes and not over three quarters of an inch in diameter; (2) on the sides of the muzzle. The tan should not reach to the top of the muzzle, but resembles a stripe around the end of the muzzle from one side to the other; (3) on the throat; (4) two large clear spots on the chest; (5) on the inside of the hind legs showing down the front of the stifle and

Tan markings over eyes and on side of muzzle.

broadening out to the outside of the hind legs from the hock to the toes. It must not completely eliminate the black on the back of the hind legs; (6) on the forelegs from the carpus, or a little above, downward to the toes; (7) around the vent; (8) a white spot on the chest is allowed, but the smaller the better. Predominantly tan, red, or buff dogs which do not have the typical pattern of markings of a Gordon Setter are ineligible for showing and undesirable for breeding.

DISQUALIFICATION
Predominantly tan, red, or buff dogs which do not have the typical pattern of markings of a Gordon Setter.

Approved by the AKC 13 November 1962

SCALE OF POINTS
While not a part of the official breed standard, may be helpful in placing proper emphasis upon qualities desired in the physical make-up of the breed.

Head and neck, incl. ears and eyes (10). Body (15). Shoulders, forelegs, forefeet (10). Hind legs and feet (10). Tail (5). Coat (8). Color and markings (5). Temperament (10). Size, general appearance (15). Gait (12). *Total (100).*

KC(GB) VARIATION TO STANDARD

Mouth: must be even and not over or undershot. *Faults: general impression:* unintelligent appearance. Bloodhound type with heavy, big head and ears and clumsy body; the collie type with pointed muzzle and curved tail. *Head:* pointed, snipy, down or upturned muzzle, too small or large mouth. *Eyes:* too light in colour, too deep set or too prominent. *Ears:* set too high, or unusually broad or heavy. *Neck:* thick and short. *Shoulders and back:* irregularly formed. *Chest:* too broad. *Legs and Feet:* crooked legs. Out turned elbows. Toes scattered, flat footed. *Tail:* too long, badly carried or hooked at the end. *Coat:* curly like wool, not shining. *Colour:* yellow, or straw-coloured tan, or without clearly defined lines between different colours. White feet. Too much white on chest. In the black there should be no tan hairs.

IRISH SETTER

NATIONAL GROUPING		
	Name	Number
AKC	Sporting Dogs	1
KC(GB)	Gundog	2
FCI	Gundogs	8

The dog that has raced ahead of the other Setters in popularity is the Irish Setter. His glamour, his association, however tenuous, with the world of field sports and his gay exuberant temperament have endeared him to vast numbers of people throughout the world. His history is fairly obscure, but there is little doubt that he started, as the other Setters did, by careful selective breeding from a number of Spaniels and other Setter types, with perhaps a little Pointer blood thrown in. Suggestions that he began as a cross between the Irish Water Spaniel and the Irish Terrier are pure guesswork as there is no evidence to support the idea. He is known as the Irish Red Setter to many people, who look upon him as a solid all-red dog, but in fact his Irish ancestors were largely red and white and rarely self-coloured.

The solid red dog first appeared in Ireland in the 19th century, and the Earl of Enniskillen had nothing but all-red dogs in his kennels. At the Dublin Show of 1874 there were more classes for red and white setters than for the pure red, and only in 1876 were they classified as merely Irish Setters, when the distinction by colour disappeared. In modern times the only colour that is generally accepted is solid rich chestnut though on both sides of the Atlantic small inconspicuous white markings are not considered a serious fault. The breed is essentially a sporting one, and the fact that the Irish Setter is more suitable to the conditions that exist in Ireland has probably more to do with the way in which the breed has progressed there than any consideration of appearance. In the early days of importation into the United States of America it was his capabilities as a shooting dog that endeared him to so many people and ensured his popularity. In the early days, as now, he was looked upon as a dog that could perform well in the field and look equally well on the bench.

He has the reputation of being flighty and unreliable, but this is almost certainly due to the fact that being such a colourful and glamorous dog he appealed to a great number of people as a pet, and thus got into the wrong hands from the breeders' point of view. There is little doubt that he is a gay and excitable character, and probably needs more careful and consistent training than do some of the other gundogs. However, when he is trained he is a fast and tireless worker in the field, and a steady and reliable companion. In recent years he has achieved great success in the show ring, the number of registrations having quadrupled in most countries, and at most major shows, when a class of the breed is being judged, the ring is full of these striking glossy red dogs.

He is an ideal show dog. He looks the part, is highly intelligent and appreciative of an audience, can be trained to stand and perform with decorum in the ring whatever he happens to be like outside it, is extrovert and an exhibitionist. He enjoys being prepared for show, and his glowing silky coat with the feathering flowing in the breeze on a fully mature dog, pays well for constant brushing, as it contains natural oils and needs no artificial aids. He is a gay dog, full of spirit and usually has a very positive personality. He makes a good family pet and house guard, but it is his value as a shooting dog that really persuades people to own him. He usually develops late, and his training takes more time than does that of some other breeds, but once trained he is very obedient and is a dog of whose appearance any shooting man can be proud.

OFFICIAL STANDARD

General appearance

The Irish Setter is an active, aristocratic bird-dog, rich red in color, substantial yet elegant in build. Standing over two feet tall at the shoulder, the dog has a straight, fine, glossy coat, longer on ears, chest, tail, and back of legs. Afield he is a swift-moving hunter; at home, a sweet-natured, trainable companion. His is a rollicking personality.

Head

Long and lean, its length at least double the width between the ears. The brow is raised, showing a distinct stop midway between the tip of nose and the well-defined occiput (rear point of skull). Thus the nearly level line from occiput to brow is set a little above, and parallel to, the straight and equal line from eye to nose. The skull is oval when viewed from above or front; very slightly domed when viewed in profile. Beauty of head is emphasized by delicate chiseling along the muzzle, around and below the eyes, and along the cheeks. Muzzle moderately deep, nostrils wide, jaws of nearly equal length. Upper lips fairly square but not pendulous, the underline of the jaws being almost parallel with the top line of the muzzle. The teeth meet in a scissors bite in which the upper incisors fit closely over the lower, or they may meet evenly. *Nose:* black or chocolate. *Eyes:* somewhat almond-shaped, of medium size, placed rather well apart; neither deep-set nor bulging. Color, dark to medium brown. Expression soft yet alert. *Ears:* set well back and low, not above level

Ears: feather on upper portion, long and silky.

of eye. Leather thin, hanging in a neat fold close to the head, and nearly long enough to reach the nose.

Neck

Moderately long, strong but not thick, and slightly arched; free from throatiness and fitting smoothly into the shoulders.

Body

Sufficiently long to permit a straight and free stride. Shoulder blades long, wide, sloping well back, fairly close together at the top, and joined in front to long upper arms angled to bring the elbows slightly rearward along the brisket. Chest deep, reaching approximately to the elbows; rather narrow in front. Ribs well sprung. Loins of moderate length, muscular and slightly arched. Top line of body from withers to tail slopes slightly downward without sharp drop at the croup. Hindquarters should be wide and powerful with broad, well-developed thighs.

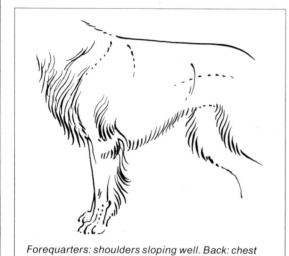

Forequarters: shoulders sloping well. Back: chest deep.

Legs and feet

All legs sturdy, with plenty of bone, and strong, nearly straight pastern. Feet rather small, very firm, toes arched and close. Forelegs straight and sinewy, the elbows moving freely. Hind legs long and muscular from hip to hock, short and nearly perpendicular from hock to ground; well angulated at stifle and hock joints, which, like the elbows, incline neither in nor out.

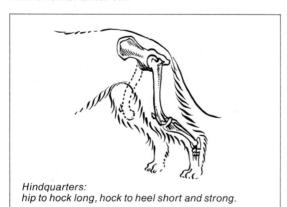

Hindquarters:
hip to hock long, hock to heel short and strong.

Tail

Strong at root, tapering to fine point, about long enough to reach the hock. Carriage straight or curving slightly upward, nearly level with the back.

Tail: low set, tapering, carried level.

Coat

Short and fine on head, forelegs, and tips of ears; on all other parts, of moderate length and flat. Feathering long and silky on ears; on back of forelegs and thighs long and fine, with a pleasing fringe of hair on belly and brisket extending on to the chest. Feet well feathered between the toes. Fringe on tail moderately long and tapering. All coat and feathering as straight and free as possible from curl or wave.

Color

Mahogany or rich chestnut red, with no trace of black. A small amount of white on chest, throat, or toes, or a narrow centered streak on skull, is not to be penalized.

Size

There is no disqualification as to size. The make and fit of all parts and their over-all balance in the animal are rated more important. Twenty-seven inches at the withers and a show weight of about 70 pounds is considered ideal for a dog; the bitch 25 inches, 60 pounds. Variance beyond an inch up or down to be discouraged.

Gait

At the trot the gait is big, very lively, graceful and efficient. The head is held high. The hindquarters drive smoothly and with great power. The forelegs reach well ahead as if to pull in the ground, without giving the appearance of a hackney gait. The dog runs as he stands: straight. Seen from the front or rear, the forelegs, as well as the hind legs below the hock joint, move prependicularly to the ground, with some tendency toward a single track as speed increases. But a crossing or weaving of the legs, front or back, is objectionable.

Balance

At his best, the lines of the Irish Setter so satisfy in over-all balance that artists have termed him the most beautiful of all dogs. The correct specimen always exhibits balance whether standing or in motion. Each part of the dog flows and fits smoothly into its neighbouring parts without calling attention to itself.

Approved by the AKC 14 June 1960

KC(GB) VARIATION TO STANDARD
Mouth: not over or undershot.

AMERICAN WATER SPANIEL

NATIONAL GROUPING		
	Name	Number
AKC	Sporting Dogs	I
KC(GB)	—	—
FCI	—	—

There is so much similarity between the American Water Spaniel and the Irish Water Spaniel that the idea that the American version developed from an early Irish emigrant is inescapable. He is smaller by a couple of inches than his Irish cousin, is the same colour, and is covered with the same dense curly coat. He differs in the head, and has a plumed tail rather than the partly bare tail of the Irish breed.

There is a possibility that he goes back to the old Water Dog that was the ancestor of many of the curly-coated breeds of gundogs in Europe. The Pilgrim Fathers settled in Massachusetts Bay in 1620, along with their families, possessions, and of course their dogs, which could well have been water dogs. At the time there were three varieties of Water Spaniel in Ireland, the Tweed Water Spaniel, the Northern Water Spaniel and the Southern Water Spaniel. By the 19th century two of these had disappeared, but it is interesting to note that at the beginning of this century there were still old sportsmen in Ireland who spoke of the Northern Irish Water Spaniels as about twenty inches high and like bad specimens of liver-coloured Retrievers.

It is obviously possible that these rather different dogs could have found their way to the United States during the intervening couple of centuries and have formed the foundation of the present American Water Spaniel. Prior to 1940, when the breed was recognised by the American Kennel Club, he had been essentially a working gundog, and his virtues in that capacity had been much admired. Fortunately he is one of those dogs that has stood the challenge of the show bench without losing any of his prowess. As a retriever he is superb, and it is said that he will watch and mark a number of fallen birds, and then on command go out and retrieve them all in turn, which makes him a very good one-man dog. He is said to have a soft mouth, high intelligence and to be powerful in the water. His coat, as with the Irish Water Spaniel and the Curly-coated Retriever, traps air and remains almost waterproof, as well as protecting him when working through the thick undergrowth. There is very little information about his performance as a show dog, and he is virtually unknown outside the United States. He is, however, reputed to be a very friendly companion and house dog, and in common with so many others in the Group, he is an excellent watchdog and guard.

OFFICIAL STANDARD

General appearance
Medium in size, of sturdy typical spaniel character, curly coat, an active muscular dog, with emphasis placed on proper size and conformation, correct head properties, texture of coat and color. Of amicable disposition; demeanor indicates intelligence, strength and endurance.

Head
Moderate in length, skull rather broad and full, stop moderately defined, but not too pronounced. Forehead covered with short smooth hair and without tuft or topknot. Muzzle of medium length, square and with no inclination to snipiness, jaws strong and of good length, and neither undershot nor overshot, teeth straight and well shaped. Nose sufficiently wide and with well-developed nostrils to insure good scenting power. *Faults:* very flat skull, narrow across the top, long, slender or snipy muzzle.

Eyes
Hazel, brown or of dark tone to harmonize with coat; set well apart. Expression alert, attractive, intelligent. *Fault:* yellow eyes to disqualify.

Ears
Lobular, long and wide, not set too high on head, but

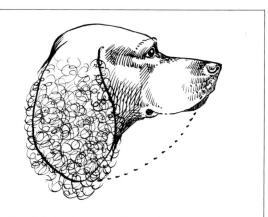

Ears: lobular, long and wide, leather extends to end of nose.

Tail
Moderate in length, curved in a slightly rocker shape, carried slightly below level of back; tapered and covered with hair to tip, action lively. *Faults:* rat or shaved tail.

Coat
The coat chould be closely curled or have marcel effect and should be of sufficient density to be of protection against weather, water or punishing cover, yet not coarse. Legs should have medium short, curly feather. *Faults:* coat too straight, soft, fine or tightly kinked.

Color
Solid liver or dark chocolate, a little white on toes or chest permissible.

Height
15 to 18 inches at the shoulder.

slightly above the eyeline. Leather extending to end of nose and well covered with close curls.

Neck
Round and of medium length, strong and muscular, free of throatiness, set to carry head with dignity, but arch not accentuated.

Body structure
Well developed, sturdily constructed but not too compactly coupled. General outline is a symmetrical relationship of parts. Shoulders sloping, clean and muscular. Strong loins, lightly arched, and well furnished, deep brisket but not excessively broad. Well-sprung ribs. Legs of medium length and well boned, but not so short as to handicap for field work.

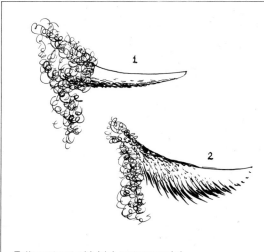

Tail: contrast with Irish water spaniel (1) incorrect, (2) correct.

Weight
Dogs: 28 to 45 pounds; bitches: 25 to 40 pounds.

DISQUALIFICATION
Yellow eyes.

Legs and feet: hocks well let down.

Legs and feet
Forelegs powerful and reasonably straight. Hind legs firm with suitably bent stifles and strong hocks well let down. Feet to harmonize with size of dog. Toes closely grouped and well padded. *Fault:* Cowhocks.

KC(GB) VARIATION TO STANDARD
This dog is not granted championship status by the KC(GB).

BRITTANY SPANIEL

NATIONAL GROUPING		
	Name	Number
AKC	Sporting Dogs	I
KC(GB)	—	—
FCI	Gundogs	7

Great Britain has so many gundogs that it claims as native to the country, though originally in fact none of them were, that gundogs from other countries have failed until recent years to gain a foothold there. The Brittany Spaniel is a typical example of this. He has been popular in Europe for centuries, has become well-established in the United States of America, but is never seen in Britain. He is one of the early French gundogs well established in France and especially in the North as his name would suggest. His ancestors almost certainly came from Spain along with those of many other gundogs, and though many of them finished up in Britain others remained in Europe and have developed along very different lines.

The height of the Brittany Spaniel at the shoulders suggests the Setter rather than the Spaniel, and in general conformation he looks more like the popular conception of one of that family rather than the shorter-legged types that have become popular in Britain. It could well be that it is something to do with the work that by tradition he has had to do, that he has evolved in this way, whilst the Cockers and the Sussex and other British breeds have grown ever shorter in the leg. Even the French, who designed him, do not claim that he is a very good looking dog, but say that he works so well that appearance is relatively unimportant. This has been appreciated in the United States more than anywhere else in the world, and since the breed was first imported into the country its popularity has grown to such an extent that it has become one of the important bird dog breeds there.

The first mention of the tailless Spaniel dates back to about a century ago in Pontou, and resulted from a cross between an imported lemon and white dog and a bitch belonging to an old hunter in the district. A race of dogs resulted that were noted for their work in the field, but by the turn of the century the breed had declined and was revived largely by the efforts of a M. Arthur Enaud. An American club was formed when the breed was first imported into the United States, but declined during the Second World War, to be reformed as the American Brittany Club in 1942. The standard for the breed was then agreed, and the club expressed as one of its aims the desire that the working qualities of the breed should not be subservient to its show career. In this they have succeeded, for the dog has remained an excellent worker, while it has also achieved great success on the bench.

His height, and the favourite colour of deep orange and white make him very striking and easily recognised. He is compact but at the same time leggy and very agile, a strong runner, and at home in the water. He has proved himself as an all-round gundog, being easily trained as a retriever as well as a finder of game. His intelligence is unquestionable, and he reacts to human company in a delightfully friendly fashion.

OFFICIAL STANDARD

General appearance

A compact, closely-knit dog of medium size, a leggy spaniel having the appearance, as well as the agility, of a great ground coverer. Strong, vigorous, energetic and quick of movement. Not too light in bone, yet never heavy-boned and cumbersome. Ruggedness, without clumsiness, is a characteristic of the breed. So leggy is he that his height at the withers is the same as the length of his body. He has no tail, or at most, not more than 4 inches.

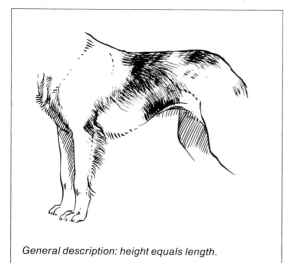

General description: height equals length.

Weight

Should weigh between 30 and 40 pounds.

Height

$17\frac{1}{2}$ to $20\frac{1}{2}$ inches—measured from the ground at the highest point of the shoulders. Any Brittany Spaniel measuring under $17\frac{1}{2}$ inches or over $20\frac{1}{2}$ inches shall be disqualified from bench-show competition.

Coat

Hair dense, flat or wavy, never curly. Not as fine as in other spaniel breeds, and never silky. Furnishings not profuse. The ears should carry little fringe. Neither the front nor hind legs should carry heavy featherings. *Note:* long, curly, or silky hair is a fault. Any tendency toward excessive feathering should be severely penalized, as undesirable in a sporting dog which must face burrs and heavy cover.

Skin

Fine and fairly loose. (A loose skin rolls with briars and sticks, thus diminishing punctures or tearing. But a skin so loose as to form pouches is undesirable.)

Color

Dark orange and white, or liver and white. Some ticking is desirable, but not so much as to produce belton patterns. Roan patterns or factors of orange or liver shade are permissible. The orange or liver are found in standard parti-color, or piebald patterns. Washed out or faded colors are not desirable. Tri-colors (liver and white with some orange markings) are to be severely faulted. Any black in the coat, or a nose so dark in color as to appear black, shall disqualify.

Skull

Medium length (approximately $4\frac{3}{4}$ inches). Rounded, very slightly wedge-shaped, but evenly made. Width, not quite as wide as the length (about $4\frac{3}{8}$ inches) and never so broad as to appear coarse, or so narrow as to appear racy. Well-defined, but gently sloping stop effect. Median line rather indistinct. The occipital crest only apparent to the touch. Lateral walls well rounded. The Brittany should never be 'apple-headed' and he should never have an indented stop. (All measurements of skull are for a $19\frac{1}{2}$-inch dog.)

Muzzle

Medium length, about two thirds the length of the skull, measuring the muzzle from the tip to the stop, and the skull from the occipital crest to the stop between the eyes. Muzzle should taper gradually in both horizontal and vertical dimensions as it approaches the nostrils. Neither a Roman nose nor a concave curve (dish-face) is desirable. Never broad, heavy, or snipy.

Nose

Nostrils well open to permit deep breathing of air and adequate scenting while at top speed. Tight nostrils should be penalized. Never shiny. Color, fawn, tan, light shades of brown or deep pink. A black nose is a disqualification. A two-tone or butterfly nose should be severely penalized.

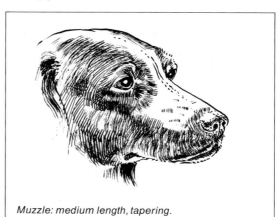

Muzzle: medium length, tapering.

Eyes

Well set in head. Well protected from briars by a heavy, expressive eyebrow. A prominent, full or pop eye should be heavily penalized. It is a serious fault in a hunting dog that must face briars. Skull well chiseled under the eyes, so that the lower lid is not pulled back to form a pocket or haw for catching seeds, dirt and weed dust. Judges should check by forcing head down to see if lid falls away from the eye. Preference should be for darker-colored eyes, though lighter shades of amber should not be penalized. Light and mean-looking eyes to be heavily penalized.

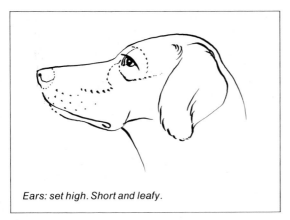

Ears: set high. Short and leafy.

Ears
Set high, above the level of the eyes. Short and leafy, rather than pendulous, reaching about half the length of the muzzle. Should lie flat and close to the head, with the tip rounded very slightly. Ears well covered with dense, but relatively short hair, and with little fringe.

Lips
Tight to the muzzle, with the upper lip overlapping the lower jaw only sufficiently to cover under lip. Lips dry so that feathers do not stick. Drooling to receive a heavy penalty. Flews to be penalized.

Teeth
Well-joined incisors. Posterior edge of upper incisors in contact with anterior edge of lower incisors, thus giving a true scissors bite. Overshot or undershot jaw to be penalized heavily.

Neck
Medium length. Not quite permitting the dog to place his nose on the ground without bending his legs. Free from throatiness, though not a serious fault unless accompanied by dewlaps. Strong, without giving the impression of being overmuscled. Well set into sloping shoulders. Never concave or ewe-necked.

Body length
Approximately the same as the height when measured at the withers. Body length is measured from the point of the forechest to the rear of the haunches. A long body should be heavily penalized.

Withers
Shoulder blades should not protrude much. Not too widely set apart with perhaps two thumbs' width or less between the blades. At the withers, the Brittany is slightly higher than at the rump.

Shoulders
Sloping and muscular. Blade and upper arm should form nearly a 90-degree angle when measured from the posterior point of the blade at the withers to the junction of the blade and upper arm, and thence to the point of the elbow nearest the ribs. Straight shoulders do not permit sufficient reach.

Back
Short and straight. Slight slope from highest point of withers to the root of the tail. Never hollow, saddle, sway, or roach-backed. Slight drop from hips to root of tail. Distance from last rib to upper thigh short, about three to four finger widths.

Chest
Deep, reaching the level of the elbow. Neither so wide nor so rounded as to disturb the placement of the shoulder bones and elbows, which causes a paddling movement, and often causes soreness from elbow striking ribs. Ribs well sprung, but adequate heart room provided by depth as well as width. Narrow or slab-sided chests are a fault.

Flanks
Rounded. Fairly full. Not extremely tucked up, nor yet flabby and falling. Loins short and strong. Narrow and weak loins are a fault. In motion the loin should not sway sideways, giving a zigzag motion to the back, wasting energy.

Hindquarters
Broad, strong and muscular, with powerful thighs and well-bent stifles, giving a hip set well into the loin and the marked angulation necessary for a powerful drive when in motion. Fat and falling hindquarters are a fault.

Tail
Naturally tailless, or not over four inches long. (A tail substantially more than 4 inches in length shall disqualify.) Natural or docked. Set on high, actually an extension of the spine at about the same level.

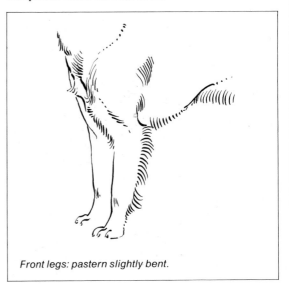

Front legs: pastern slightly bent.

Front legs
Viewed from the front, perpendicular, but not set too wide as in the case of a dog loaded in shoulder. Elbows and feet turning neither in nor out. Viewed from the side, practically perpendicular to the pastern. Pastern slightly bent to give cushion to stride. Not so straight as in terriers. Falling pasterns, however, are a serious fault. Leg bones

clean, graceful, but not too fine. An extremely heavy bone is as much a fault as spindly legs. One must look for substance and suppleness. Height to the elbows should approximately equal distance from elbow to withers.

Thighs: well feathered. Hocks: perpendicular.

Hind legs

Stifles well bent. The stifle generally is the term used for knee joint. If the angle made by the upper and lower leg bones is too straight, the dog quite generally lacks drive, since his hind legs cannot drive as far forward at each stride as is desirable. However, the stifle should not be bent as to throw the hock joint far out behind the dog. Since factors not easily seen by the eye may give the dog his proper drive, a Brittany should not be condemned for straight stifle until the judge has checked the dog in motion from the side. When at a trot, the Brittany's hind foot should step into or beyond the print left by the front foot. The stifle joint should not turn out making a cow-hock. The cowhock moves the foot out to the side, thus driving out of line, and losing reach at each stride. Thighs well feathered, but not profusely, halfway to the hock. Hocks, that is, the back pasterns, should be moderately short, pointing neither in nor out; perpendicular when viewed from the side. They should be firm when shaken by the judge.

Feet

Should be strong, proportionately smaller than other spaniels, with close-fitting, well-arched toes and thick pads. The Brittany is not 'up on his toes.' Toes not heavily feathered. Flat feet, splayed feet, paper feet, etc., are to be heavily penalized. An ideal foot is halfway between the hare- and cat-foot.

A guide to the judge: the points below indicate only relative values. To be also taken into consideration are type, gait, soundness, spirit, optimum height, body length and general proportions.

SCALE OF POINTS
Head (25). Body (35). Running gear (40). *Total (100).*

DISQUALIFICATIONS
Any Brittany Spaniel measuring under $17\frac{1}{2}$ inches or over $20\frac{1}{2}$ inches. Any black in the coat or a nose so dark in color as to appear black. A tail substantially more than 4 inches in length.

Approved by the AKC 13 September 1966

KC(GB) VARIATION TO STANDARD
This dog is not granted championship status by the KC(GB).

CLUMBER SPANIEL

NATIONAL GROUPING		
	Name	Number
AKC	Sporting Dogs	1
KC(GB)	Gundog	2
FCI	Gundogs	8

The Spaniel Group of breeds is one of the most numerous and varied in the world of dogs. The division between the Toy Spaniels and the Sporting Spaniels is itself confusing, and the large number of different breeds listed among the sporting members of the Group, the Cocker, Springer and Field for instance, named after the work they are bred to do creates even more problems. There is one breed, however, the Clumber Spaniel that is distinctive not only in appearance, but in name, as it takes its title from a place. Research has so far failed to disclose the origin of the breed beyond the time when the Duc de Noailles presented some of his dogs to the second Duke of Newcastle from whose estate, Clumber Park, the breed took its name. It is probable that the early ancestor of the breed was the old Alpine Spaniel which was crossed with an early form of Basset and even with the Bloodhound, giving it its short legs and heavy head. From Clumber Park the breed spread to surrounding estates and families, and soon became known as a shooting dog.

One of the earliest records of the breed is in a portrait of the second Duke of Newcastle by Francis Wheatley, R.A. at Clumber Park, in which he is depicted seated on a shooting pony with Colonel Litchfield, Mansell, who was his head keeper, and three Spaniels which were believed to have been three of the original draft. The portrait was painted in 1788, almost a hundred years before the breed was first shown in Britain, and before they arrived in the United States of America. It is interesting that whilst the other breeds of Spaniels have changed considerably over the years, the heavyweight of the family has changed hardly at all. The abundance of game in the 18th and 19th centuries meant that a fast-moving Spaniel was not needed, and the better nose, greater efficiency and persistence of the Clumber was more appreciated.

He does in fact have a wonderful nose, considered by many sportsmen the best in the family. He has too, a natural inclination to hunt, tremendous perseverance and stamina, and in spite of his massive build, is considerably agile. He is easily trained, being quieter than some of the other Spaniels, and is very biddable. He also makes a good retriever, and is thus one of the better all-round gundogs. Whilst retaining his popularity among sportsmen, he has never achieved a great deal of fame on the bench since his early days. Although his massive frame and large intelligent looking head give him the look of the aristocratic dog, he has rarely in recent years had major awards at shows. Very few are now registered, under a hundred each year in Britain, and he is hardly seen outside that country and the United States of America. He is not an easy dog to show, as he is somewhat independent in the ring, having the sort of intelligence that causes him to see little point in standing around indoors when he could be hunting through the local countryside. His colour and size, however, make him very spectacular and he is always much admired by spectators, and there is an indication that he is in for something of a revival within the next few years.

He is friendly, affectionate in fact, and makes a very good country companion though he is a little cumbersome indoors.

OFFICIAL STANDARD

General appearance and size
General appearance, a long, low heavy-looking dog, of a very thoughtful expression, betokening great intelligence. Should have the appearance of great power. Sedate in all movements, but not clumsy. Weight of dogs averaging between 55 and 65 pounds; bitches from 35 to 50 pounds.

Head
Head large and massive in all its dimensions; round above eyes, flat on top, with a furrow running from between the eyes upon the center. A marked stop and large occipital protuberance. Jaw long, broad and deep. Lips of upper jaw overhung. Muzzle not square, but at the same time powerful-looking. Nostrils large, open and flesh-colored, sometimes cherry-colored. *Eyes:* Eyes large, soft, deep-set and showing haw. Hazel in color, not too pale, with

Head and skull: large, square, massive.

dignified and intelligent expression. *Ears:* ears long and broad at the top, turned over on the front edge; vine-shaped: close to the head; set on low and feathered only on the front edge, and there but slightly. Hair short and silky, without the slightest approach to wave or curl.

Neck and shoulders
Neck long, thick and powerful, free from dewlap, with a large ruff. Shoulders immensely strong and muscular, giving a heavy appearance in front.

Body
Long, low and well ribbed up. The chest is wide and deep, the back long, broad, and level, with very slight arch over the loin.

Legs and feet
Forelegs short, straight, and very heavy in bone; elbows close. Hind legs only slightly less heavily boned than the forelegs. They are moderately angulated, with hocks well let down. Quarters well developed and muscular. No feather above the hocks, but thick hair on the back of the legs just above the feet. Feet large, compact, and well filled with hair between the toes.

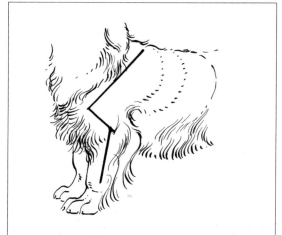

Forequarters: shoulders strong sloping, muscular.

Coat and feathers
Coat silky and straight, not too long, extremely dense; feather long and abundant.

Color and markings
Color, lemon and white, and orange and white. Fewer markings on body the better. Perfection of markings, solid lemon or orange ears, evenly marked head and eyes, muzzle and legs ticked.

Stern
Stern set on a level and carried low.

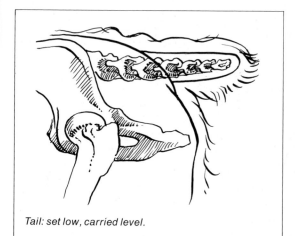

Tail: set low, carried level.

SCALE OF POINTS
General appearance and size (10). Head (15). Eyes (5). Ears (10). Neck and shoulders (15). Body and quarters (20). Legs and feet (10). Coat and feather (10). Color and marking (5). *Total (100).*

Approved by the AKC 6 February 1960

KC(GB) VARIATION TO STANDARD
Weight: dogs 55 to 70 pounds; bitches 45 to 60 pounds.

COCKER SPANIEL

NATIONAL GROUPING		
	Name	Number
AKC	Sporting Dogs	1
KC(GB)	Gundog	2
FCI	Gundogs	8

A further division in the Spaniel family resulted from the importation of the smaller Spaniels into the United States of America, where they developed along quite different lines from those in Britain. This has led to a certain amount of confusion, as whilst the English Cocker Spaniel is known as the Cocker Spaniel in Britain, the dog known in the United States as the Cocker Spaniel is called the American Cocker Spaniel in other countries. The English Cocker Spaniel Club of America which was formed in 1935 aimed to discourage interbreeding between the two types and in 1946 the English Cocker as distinct from the American Cocker was finally recognised. Meanwhile in Britain the English Cocker Spaniel was developing, and the American Cocker was not seen on the British show bench until well into the 1960s.

The type developed in the United States is smaller than the British variety, fourteen to fifteen inches as against sixteen to seventeen, and proportionately less heavy. The demands of field work in the United States are different from those in Britain. Birds are on the whole smaller, and quail, which are one of the favourite small game birds in the one country are virtually unknown in the other. In Britain the Cocker is expected to carry pheasant and hare, a task that would prove beyond many of the Cockers on this side of the Atlantic. Unregistered in Britain until 1968, he has made rapid strides since then, and is fast becoming one of the more popular of the Spaniel family. Apart from the English Cocker and the English Springer he has already overtaken all the other Spaniels and is competing hard even with those, one hundred and sixty-four entries having been made at the Birmingham Show in 1976.

He works in the field by quartering the ground in front of the guns, hunting and putting up game, which he does quickly and efficiently. When the game is flushed he stands still or drops whilst the animal is shot, and then goes in to retrieve on command. This takes a little training, as whilst a Cocker hunts naturally, and will do it all the time, the freezing on a shot is something that is not natural to him and the habit of running in and thus interfering with possible subsequent shots, has to be trained out. Fortunately, he is an easily trained little dog, very biddable and anxious to please. He is a successful showdog, as like his English counterpart, he has natural good manners and an inbuilt willingness to obey commands.

He has the same coat problem as the English dog, and indeed it was only after some heart-searching and an injunction to judges that the British objection to too much coat was finally overcome. Now he is shown with a somewhat reduced volume of coat though still with considerably more than the English Cocker. He poses well in the ring, and covers a great deal of ground for so small a dog stretching out his long neck to produce a very spectacular outline. When moving he goes with such drive that on a dry day he will leave a cloud of dust behind him. Within the last few years there have been one or two dogs that have won at the major shows in Britain, and there is no doubt that this, allied to the fact that he has qualified at field trials, has ensured his future in Britain as a popular gundog.

He is one of the most friendly and affectionate little dogs. One of the features of his character is that he behaves well with children, and is now being shown regularly by youngsters in junior handling classes.

OFFICIAL STANDARD

General appearance
The Cocker Spaniel is the smallest member of the Sporting Group. He has a sturdy, compact body and a cleanly chiseled and refined head, with the overall dog in complete balance and of ideal size. He stands well up at the shoulder on straight forelegs with a topline sloping slightly toward strong, muscular quarters. He is a dog capable of considerable speed, combined with great endurance. Above all he must be free and merry, sound, well balanced throughout, and in action show a keen inclination to work; equable in temperament with no suggestion of timidity.

Head and skull: well-developed and rounded.

Head
To attain a well-proportioned head, which must be in balance with the rest of the dog, it embodies the following:

Skull
Rounded but not exaggerated with no tendency toward flatness; the eyebrows are clearly defined with a pronounced stop. The bony structure beneath the eyes is well chiseled with no prominence in the cheeks.

Muzzle
Broad and deep, with square, even jaws. The upper lip is full and of sufficient depth to cover the lower jaw. To be in correct balance, the distance from the stop to the tip of the nose is one half the distance from the stop up over the crown to the base of the skull.

Teeth
Strong and sound, not too small, and meet in a scissors bite.

Nose
Of sufficient size to balance the muzzle and foreface, with well-developed nostrils typical of a sporting dog. It is black in color in the blacks and black and tans. In other colors it may be brown, liver or black, the darker the better. The color of the nose harmonizes with the color of the eye rim.

Eyes
Eyeballs are round and full and look directly forward. The shape of the eye rims gives a slightly almond-shaped appearance; the eye is not weak or goggled. The color of the iris is dark brown and in general the darker the better. The expression is intelligent, alert, soft and appealing.

Ears
Lobular, long, of fine leather, well feathered, and placed no higher than a line to the lower part of the eye.

Neck and shoulders
The neck is sufficiently long to allow the nose to reach the ground easily, muscular and free from pendulous 'throatiness'. It rises strongly from the shoulders and arches slightly as it tapers to join the head. The shoulders are well laid back forming an angle with the upper arm of approximately 90 degrees which permits the dog to move his forelegs in an easy manner with considerable forward reach. Shoulders are clean-cut and slopint without protrusion and so set that the upper points of the withers are at an angle which permits a wide spring of rib.

Body
The body is short, compact and firmly knit together, giving an impression of strength. The distance from the highest point of the shoulder blades to the ground is fifteen per cent or approximately two inches more than the length from this point to the set-on of the tail. Back is strong and sloping evenly and slightly downward from the shoulders to the set-on of the docked tail. Hips are wide and quarters well rounded and muscular. The chest

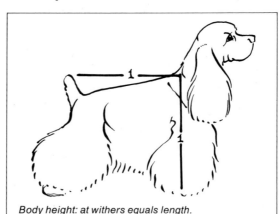

Body height: at withers equals length.

is deep, its lowest point no higher than the elbows, its front sufficiently wide for adequate heart and lung space, yet not so wide as to interfere with the straightforward movement of the forelegs. Ribs are deep and well sprung. The Cocker Spaniel never appears long and low.

Tail
The docked tail is set on and carried on a line with the topline of the back, or slightly higher; never straight up like a terrier and never so low as to indicate timidity. When the dog is in motion the tail action is merry.

Legs and feet
Forelegs are parallel, straight, strongly boned and muscular and set close to the body well under the scapulae. When viewed from the side with the forelegs vertical, the elbow is directly below the highest point of the shoulder blade. The pasterns are short and strong. The hind legs are strongly boned and muscled with good angulation at the stifle and powerful, clearly defined thighs. The stifle joint is strong and there is no slippage of it in motion or when standing. The hocks are strong, well let down, and when viewed from behind, the hind legs are parallel when in motion and at rest. *Feet:* compact, large, round and firm with horny pads; they turn neither in nor out. Dewclaws on hind legs and forelegs may be removed.

Coat
On the head, short and fine; on the body, medium length, with enough undercoating to give protection. The ears, chest, abdomen and legs are well feathered, but not so excessively as to hide the Cocker Spaniel's true lines and movement or affect his appearance and function as a sporting dog. The *texture* is most important. The coat is silky, flat or slightly wavy, and of a texture which permits easy care. Excessive or curly or cottony textured coat is to be penalized.

Color and markings
Black variety is jet black; shadings of brown or liver in the sheen of the coat is not desirable. A small amount of white on the chest and throat is to be penalized, and white in any other location shall disqualify.

Any solid color other than black shall be a uniform shade. Lighter coloring of the feathering is permissible. A small amount of white on the chest and throat is to be penalized, and white in any other location shall disqualify.

Black and Tans, shown under the variety of *any solid color other than black*, have definite tan markings on a jet black body. The tan markings are distinct and plainly visible and the color of the tan may be from the lightest cream to the darkest red color. The amount of tan markings is restricted to ten per cent or less of the color of the specimen; tan markings in excess of ten per cent shall disqualify. Tan markings which are not readily visible in the ring or the absence of tan markings in any of the specified locations shall disqualify. The markings shall be located as follows:
(1) A clear spot over each eye.
(2) On the sides of the muzzle and on the cheeks.
(3) On the undersides of the ears.
(4) On all feet and legs.
(5) Under the tail.
(6) On the chest, optional, presence or absence not penalized.
Tan on the muzzle which extends upward, over and joins, shall be penalized. A small amount of white on the chest and throat is to be penalized, and white in any other location shall disqualify.

Parti-color variety: two or more definite colors appearing in clearly defined markings, distinctly distributed over the body, are essential. Primary color which is ninety per cent or more shall disqualify; secondary color or colors which are limited solely to one location shall disqualify. Roans are classified as Parti-colors and may be of any of the usual roaning patterns. Tri-colors are any of the above colors combined with tan markings. It is preferable that the tan markings be located in the same pattern as for Black and Tans.

Movement
The Cocker Spaniel, though the smallest of the sporting dogs, possesses a typical sporting dog gait. Prerequisite to good movement is balance between the front and rear assemblies. He drives with his strong, powerful rear quarters and is properly constructed in the shoulders and forelegs so that he can reach forward without constriction in a full stride to counterbalance the driving force from the rear. Above all, his gait is co-ordinated, smooth and effortless. The dog must cover ground with his action and excessive animation should never be mistaken for proper gait.

Height
The ideal height at the withers for an adult dog is 15 inches and for an adult bitch 14 inches. Height may vary one-half inch above or below this ideal. A dog whose height exceeds $15\frac{1}{2}$ inches or a bitch whose height exceeds $14\frac{1}{2}$ inches shall be disqualified. An adult dog whose height is less than $14\frac{1}{2}$ inches or an adult bitch whose height is less than $13\frac{1}{2}$ inches shall be penalized.
Note: height is determined by a line perpendicular to the ground from the top of the shoulder blades, the dog standing naturally with its forelegs and the lower hind legs parallel to the line of measurement.

DISQUALIFICATIONS
Color and markings: blacks—white markings except on chest and throat. Solid colors other than black—white markings except on chest and throat. Black and tans—tan markings in excess of ten per cent; tan markings not readily visible in the ring, or the absence of tan markings in any of the specified locations; white markings except on chest and throat. Parti-colors—ninety per cent or more of primary color; secondary color or colors limited solely to one location. Height: dogs over $15\frac{1}{2}$ inches; bitches over $14\frac{1}{2}$ inches.

Approved by the AKC 12 December 1972

KC(GB) VARIATION TO STANDARD
Colour: in all solid colours small amount of white on chest and throat allowed but white in any other location penalised. *Black and Tan:* tan markings in excess of 10% shall be penalised. *Parti-colours:* primary colour which is 90% or more should be penalised. *Height:* a dog whose height exceeds $15\frac{1}{2}$ inches or a bitch whose height exceeds $14\frac{1}{2}$ inches should be penalised. An adult dog whose height is less than $14\frac{1}{2}$ inches or an adult bitch whose height is less than $13\frac{1}{2}$ inches should be penalised.

ENGLISH COCKER SPANIEL

NATIONAL GROUPING		
	Name	Number
AKC	Sporting Dogs	1
KC(GB)	Gundog	2
FCI	Gundogs	8

The family of Spaniels is one of the largest of the canine race, and certainly one of the oldest. They date back as a Group to the 14th century when they are described as consisting of two sorts, the Land Spaniel and the Water Spaniel. Water Spaniels existed as a separate breed in Britain until well into the 20th century and were shown as small, curly-coated parti-coloured dogs with classes of their own. The Land Spaniels became further divided and whilst some of them became Toys, the others became workers in the field, the smallest of these being called 'Cockers'. There is little dispute about how he got his name. Edwards, writing in 1801 divides the smaller Land Spaniels into two groups, the 'starters' and the 'cockers', the former being used to spring the game when falconry was a popular sport, and the latter to hunt the woodcock for which they were specially trained.

The division into clearly defined breeds took some time, but gradually a distinctive race of dogs emerged, largely in the South West of Britain and in Wales. At first, and indeed well into this century, they had to give pride of place in popular esteem to other Spaniels such as the Sussex and the Field, but they rapidly overtook the other breeds, and by the mid-thirties had become Britain's most popular dog, a position that was held for many years. At first most English Cockers were self-coloured, and mainly black, and it was only with the development of the other colours and the roans and black and whites that popularity finally came.

He is highly intelligent, sensitive and affectionate, becoming firmly attached to one family and making a most attractive little house dog. He is amusing, as so many of the Spaniels are, and it is in this respect that his relationship with the Toy Spaniels becomes obvious. This relationship is closer than might at first be suspected, and a team of Toys such as English Toy Spaniels will still hunt, and the larger ones have been known to be trained to retrieve game. The English Cocker is a sturdy little dog, hardy, not susceptible to illness, and will live quite happily in kennels, though his favourite place is indoors by a warm fire.

As a show dog he is supreme, and has a long list of major wins to his credit. H. S. Lloyd did much to popularise the breed with his win at Crufts, and his Ware strain remains world famous. He is not the easiest of dogs to prepare for the ring, as whilst his coat appears trouble free, there is always a tendency for him to grow an amount of strong curly coat which is difficult to remove, indicative of his ancestry among the strong-coated Water Spaniels of many years ago. Left in the rough with an uncared-for coat he looks very untidy.

He loves country walks and plenty of exercise, and is never happier than when hunting along a hedgerow scenting out small game or chasing a rabbit. He is adaptable, perfectly at home in a farmyard or city apartment, in the back of a car or sitting on his owner's knee; and his personal qualities are undoubtedly the reason for his remarkable popularity.

OFFICIAL STANDARD

General appearance

The English Cocker Spaniel is an attractive, active, merry sporting dog; with short body and strong limbs, standing well up at the withers. His movements are alive with energy; his gait powerful and frictionless. He is alert at all times, and the carriage of head and incessant action of his tail while at work give the impression that here is a dog that is not only bred for hunting, but really enjoys it. He is well balanced, strongly built, full of quality and is capable of top speed combined with great stamina. His head imparts an individual stamp peculiar to him alone and has that brainy appearance expressive of the highest intelligence; and is in perfect proportion to his body. His muzzle is a most distinctive feature, being of correct conformation and in proportion to his skull.

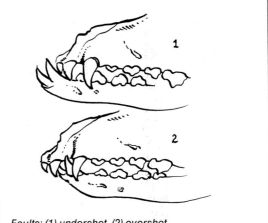

Faults: (1) undershot, (2) overshot.

Good square muzzle, skull well developed, neither fine nor coarse.

Character

The character of the English Cocker is of extreme importance. His love and faithfulness to his master and household, his alertness and courage are characteristic. He is noted for his intelligence and merry disposition; not quarrelsome; and is a responsive and willing worker both in the field and as a companion.

Head

The skull and forehead should be well developed with no suggestion of coarseness, arched and slightly flattened on top when viewed both from the stop to the end of the skull as well as from ear to ear, and cleanly chiseled under the eyes. The proportion of the head desirable is approximately one half for the muzzle and one half for the skull. The muzzle should be square with a definite stop where it blends into the skull and in proportion with the width of the skull. As the English Cocker is primarily a sporting -dog, the muzzle and jaws must be of sufficient strength and size to carry game; and the length of the muzzle should provide room for the development of the olfactory nerve to insure good scenting qualities, which require that the nose be wide and well developed. Nostrils black in color except in reds, livers, parti-colors and roans of the ligher shades, where brown is permissible, but black preferred. Lips should be square, full and free from flews. Teeth should be even and set squarely. *Faults:* muzzle too short or snipy. Jaw overshot or undershot. Lips snipy or pendulous. Skull too flat or too rounded, cheeky or coarse. Stop insufficient or exaggerated.

Eyes

The eyes should be of medium size, full and slightly oval shaped; set squarely in skull and wide apart. Eyes must be dark brown except in livers and light parti-colors where hazel is permissible, but the darker the better. The general expression should be intelligent, alert, bright and merry. *Faults:* light, round or protruding eyes. Conspicuous haw.

Ears

Lobular; set low and close to the head; leather fine and extending at least to the nose, well covered with long, silky, straight or slightly wavy hair. *Faults:* set or carried too high; too wide at the top; insufficient feathering; positive curls or ringlets.

Neck

Long, clean and muscular; arched towards the head; set cleanly into sloping shoulders. *Faults:* short; thick, with dewlap or excessive throatiness.

Body

Close coupled, compact and firmly knit, giving the impression of great strength without heaviness. Depth of brisket should reach to the elbow, sloping gradually upward to the loin. Ribs should spring gradually to middle of body, tapering to back ribs which should be of good depth and extend well back. *Faults:* too long and lacking depth; insufficient spring of rib; barrel rib.

Shoulders and chest

Shoulders sloping and fine; chest deep and well developed but not too wide and round to interfere with the free action of the forelegs. *Faults:* straight or loaded shoulders.

Back and loin

Back short and strong. Length of back from withers to tail-set should approximate height from ground to withers. Height of the dog at the withers should be greater than the height of the hip joint, providing a gradual slope between these points. Loin short and powerful, slightly arched. *Faults:* too low at withers; long, sway-back or roach back; flat or narrow loin; exaggerated tuck-up.

Forelegs

Straight and strong with bone nearly equal in size from elbow to heel; elbows set close to the body with free action from shoulders; pasterns short, straight, and strong. *Faults:* shoulders loose; elbows turned in or out; legs bowed or set too close or too wide apart; knees knuckled over; light bone.

Tail: set on slightly lower than back, line carried level.

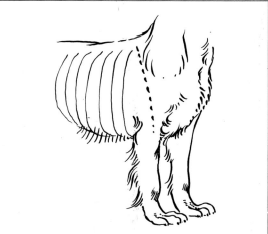

Faults: straight shoulder, weak pasterns, light bone, flat ribs.

Feet

Size in proportion to the legs; firm, round and catlike with thick pads and strong toes. *Faults:* too large, too small; spreading or splayed.

Hindquarters

The hips should be rounded; thighs broad; well developed and muscular, giving abundance of propelling power. Stifles strong and well bent. Hock to pad moderately short, strong and well let down. *Faults:* excessive angulation; lightness of bone; stifle too short; hocks too long or turned in or out.

Tail

Set on to conform with the topline of the back. Merry in action. *Faults:* set too low; habitually carried too high; too short or too long.

Color

Various. In self colors a white shirt frill is undesirable. In parti-colors, the coloring must be broken on the body and be evenly distributed. No large portion of any one color should exist. White should be shown on the saddle.

A dog of any solid color with white feet and chest is not a parti-color. In roans it is desirable that the white hair should be distributed over the body, the more evenly the better. Roans come in various colors: blue, liver, red, orange and lemon. In black and tans the coat should be black; tan spots over the eyes, tan on the sides of the muzzle, on the throat and chest, on forelegs from the knees to the toes and on the hind legs on the inside of the legs, also on the stifle and extending from the hock to the toes. *Faults:* white feet are undesirable in any specimen of self color.

Coat

On head, short and fine; on body, flat or slightly wavy and silky in texture. Should be of medium length with enough undercoating to give protection. The English Cocker should be well feathered but not so profusely as to hide the true lines or interfere with his field work. *Faults:* lack of coat; too soft, curly or wiry. Excessive trimming to change the natural appearance and coat should be discouraged.

Height

Ideal heights at withers: Dogs, 16 to 17 inches; bitches, 15 to 16 inches. Deviations to be severely penalized but not disqualified.

Weight

The most desirable weights: Dogs, 28 to 34 pounds; bitches, 26 to 32 pounds. Proper physical conformation and balance should be considered more important than weight alone.

Approved by the AKC 13 September 1955

KC(GB) VARIATION TO STANDARD

Coat: never wiry or wavy. *Height: at withers:* dogs $15\frac{1}{2}$ to 16 inches; bitches 15 to $15\frac{1}{2}$ inches. *Weight:* 28 to 32 pounds. *Faults:* light bone; unsound movement, weak hocks, small beady eyes; uncertain or aggressive temperament.

ENGLISH SPRINGER SPANIEL

NATIONAL GROUPING		
	Name	Number
AKC	Sporting Dogs	1
KC(GB)	Gundog	2
FCI	Gundogs	8

When the Spaniel family divided into the Water Spaniels and the Land Spaniels, the latter further divided into Toys and Working, and the Working Spaniels were allocated different tasks in the field. The smaller ones became the Cockers and the larger and taller ones became the Springers. Their task was to range further than some of the others in the family and to flush or 'spring' the game. He was originally known as the Norfolk Spaniel, though that county can lay no claim to his origins other than the fact that the Duke of Norfolk kept a kennels of the breed. He came from some of the early imported Spaniel stock that produced the other members of the family and helped to produce the Setters, but was not recognised in Britain as a separate breed until 1902. The Sporting Spaniel Society was responsible for christening him, as they decided to drop the name Norfolk Spaniel and revert to the much older name of Springer, looking after this long legged member of the family partly as a protest at what was going on to make the Field Spaniel so ridiculous a dog. They were determined that the Springer should remain as a sporting Spaniel.

Unfortunately the Springer Spaniel is one of the gundogs that has become sharply divided between the working and the show type, so that a modern show Springer will often stand higher than the twenty inches laid down in the standard, and is a tall rather narrow dog, on the other hand the type most favoured for field work is considerably smaller and is a stockier type with a far less exaggerated head. There are show dogs that perform well in trials, but they are the exception, and there are few dogs of the field type that would win in the show rings of today. In 1924 the English Springer Spaniel Field Trial Association was formed in the United States of America and has as its aim the production of dogs for both the field and the bench, and it could well be that as a result of their efforts greater unity can be achieved in the breed.

He is probably the best dog for the sportsman who wants one dog only, to live in the house, and to do all the work in the field that a single gun requires. He will not point, nor would one expect that he should, but he will do just about everything else. He hunts further and faster than any of the other Spaniels, is an excellent retriever, and a first-class water dog, apparently impervious to wet and cold conditions and a tireless worker in the field with great tenacity and endurance.

As a show dog he is tremendously successful, being adaptable to any sort of condition, shows equally well indoors or outside, is friendly and free from vice in the ring and on the bench, and appears to enjoy being the centre of attention. He is a happy dog, full of character, and always appears interested in what is going on around him. He is easily prepared for show, the minimum amount of straightening up of coat being all that is required, and he enjoys exercise to such an extent that keeping him in fit muscular show condition presents no problems. His temperament is excellent as he is very friendly, even affectionate with those that he knows, and though normally quiet, makes a very good guard.

OFFICIAL STANDARD

General appearance and type

The English Springer Spaniel is a medium-size sporting dog with a neat, compact body, and a docked tail. His coat is moderately long, glossy, usually liver and white or black and white, with feathering on his legs, ears, chest and brisket. His pendulous ears, soft gentle expression, sturdy build and friendly wagging tail proclaim him unmistakably a member of the ancient family of spaniels. He is above all a well proportioned dog, free from exaggeration, nicely balanced in every part. His carriage is proud and upstanding, body deep, legs strong and muscular with enough length to carry him with ease. His short level back, well developed thighs, good shoulders, excellent feet, suggest power, endurance, agility. Taken as a whole he looks the part of a dog that can go and keep going under difficult hunting conditions, and moreover he enjoys what he is doing. At his best he is endowed with style, symmetry, balance, enthusiasm and is every inch a sporting dog of distinct spaniel character, combining beauty and utility. *To be penalized:* those lacking true English Springer type in conformation, expression, or behavior.

Temperament

The typical Springer is friendly, eager to please, quick to learn, willing to obey. In the show ring he should exhibit poise, attentiveness, tractability, and should permit himself to be examined by the judge without resentment or cringing. *To be penalised:* excessive timidity, with due allowance for puppies and novice exhibits. But no dog to receive a ribbon if he behaves in a vicious manner toward handler or judge. Aggressiveness toward other dogs in the ring not to be construed as viciousness.

Size and proportion

The Springer is built to cover rough ground with agility and reasonable speed. He should be kept to medium size— neither too small nor too large and heavy to do the work for which he is intended. The ideal shoulder height for dogs is 20 inches; for bitches, 19 inches. Length of topline (the distance from top of the shoulders to the root of the tail) should be approximately equal to the dog's shoulder height—never longer than his height—and not appreciably less. The dog too long in body, especially when long in loin, tires easily and lacks the compact outline characteristic of the breed. Equally undesirable is the dog too short in body for the length of his legs, a condition that destroys his balance and restricts the gait.

Weight

Weight is dependent on the dog's other dimensions: a 20-inch dog, well proportioned, in good condition should weigh about 49-55 pounds. The resulting appearance is a well-knit, sturdy dog with good but not too heavy bone, in no way coarse or ponderous. *To be penalized:* over-heavy specimens, cloddy in build. Leggy individuals, too tall for their length and substance. Oversize or undersize specimens (those more than one inch under or over the breed ideal).

Color and coat

Color may be liver or black with white markings; liver and white (or black and white) with tan markings; blue or liver roan; or predominantly white with tan, black or liver markings. On ears, chest, legs and belly the Springer is nicely furnished with a fringe of feathering (of moderate heaviness). On his head, front or forelegs, and below hocks on front of hind legs, the hair is short and fine. The body coat is flat or wavy, of medium length, sufficiently dense to be water-proof, weather-proof and thorn-proof. The texture fine and the hair should have the clean, glossy, live appearance indicative of good health. It is legitimate to trim about head, feet, ears; to remove dead hair; to thin and shorten excess feathering particularly from the hocks to the feet and elsewhere as required to give a smart, clean appearance. *To be penalized:* Rough, curly coat. Over-trimming especially of the body coat. Any chopped, barbered or artificial effect. Excessive feathering that destroys the clean outline desirable in a sporting dog. Off colors such as lemon, red or orange not to place.

Head

The head is impressive without being heavy. Its beauty lies in a combination of strength and refinement. It is important that the size and proportion be in balance with the rest of the dog. Viewed in profile the head should appear approximately the same length as the neck and should blend with the body in substance. The skull (upper head) to be of medium length, fairly broad, flat on top, slightly rounded at the sides and back. The occiput bone inconspicuous, rounded rather than peaked or angular. The foreface (head in front of the eyes) approximately the same length as the skull, and in harmony as to width and general character. Looking down on the head the muzzle to appear to be about one half the width of the skull. As the skull rises from the foreface it makes a brow or 'stop,' divided by a groove or fluting between the eyes. This groove continues upward and gradually disappears as it reaches the middle of the forehead. The

Head: skull medium length, and fairly broad and rounded.

amount of 'stop' can best be described as moderate. It must not be a pronounced feature as in the Clumber Spaniel. Rather it is a subtle rise where the muzzle blends into the upper head, further emphasized by the groove and by the position and shape of the eyebrows which should be well-developed. The stop, eyebrow and the chiseling of the bony structure around the eye sockets contribute to the Springer's beautiful and characteristic expression.

Viewed in profile the topline of the skull and the muzzle lie in two approximately parallel planes. The nasal bone should be straight, with no inclination downward toward the tip of the nose which gives a downfaced look so undesirable in this breed. Neither should the nasal bone be concave resulting in a 'dish-faced' profile; nor convex giving the dog a Roman nose. The jaws to be of sufficient length to allow the dog to carry game easily; fairly square, lean, strong, and even, (neither undershot nor overshot). The upper lip to come down full and rather square to cover the line of the lower jaw, but lips not to be pendulous nor exaggerated. The nostrils, well opened and broad, liver color or black depending on the color of the coat. Flesh-colored ('Dudley noses') or spotted ('butterfly noses') are undesirable. The cheeks to be flat, (not rounded, full or thick) with nice chiseling under the eyes. *To be penalized:* oval, pointed or heavy skull. Cheeks prominently rounded, thick and protruding. Too much or too little stop. Over heavy muzzle. Muzzle too short, too thick, too narrow. Pendulous slobbery lips. Under- or over-shot jaws—a very serious fault, to be heavily penalized.

Teeth

The teeth should be strong, clean, not too small; and when the mouth is closed the teeth should meet in an even bite or a close scissors bite (the lower incisors touching the inside of the upper incisors). *To be penalized:* any deviation from above description. One or two teeth slightly out of line not to be considered a serious fault, but irregularities due to faulty jaw formation to be severely penalized.

Eyes

More than any other feature the eyes contribute to the Springer's appeal. Color, placement, size influence expression and attractiveness. The eyes to be of medium size, neither small, round, full and prominent, nor bold and hard in expression. Set rather well apart and fairly deep in their sockets. The color of the iris to harmonize with the color of the coat, preferably a good dark hazel in the liver dogs and black or deep brown in the black and white specimens. The expression to be alert, kindly, trusting. The lids, tight with little or no haw showing. *To be penalized:* eyes yellow or brassy in color or noticeably lighter than the coat. Sharp expression indicating unfriendly or suspicious nature. Loose droopy lids. Prominent haw (the third eyelid or membrane in the inside corner of the eye).

Ears

The correct ear-set is on a level with the line of the eye; on the side of the skull and not too far back. The flaps to be long and fairly wide, hanging close to the cheeks, with no tendency to stand up or out. The leather, thin, approximately long enough to reach the tip of the nose. *To be penalized:* short round ears. Ears set too high or too low or too far back on the head.

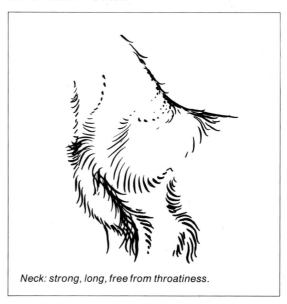

Neck: strong, long, free from throatiness.

Neck

The neck to be moderately long, muscular, slightly arched at the crest, gradually blending into sloping shoulders. Not noticeably upright, nor coming into the body at an abrupt angle. *To be penalized:* short neck, often the sequence to steep shoulders. Concave neck, sometimes called ewe neck or upside down neck (the opposite of arched). Excessive throatiness.

Body

The body to be well coupled, strong, compact; the chest deep but not so wide or round as to interfere with the action of the front legs; the brisket sufficiently developed to reach to the level of the elbows. The ribs fairly long, springing gradually to the middle of the body then tapering as they approach the end of the ribbed section. The back (section between the withers and loin) to be straight and strong, with no tendency to dip or roach. The loins to be strong, short; a slight arch over loins and hip bones. Hips nicely rounded, blending smoothly into hind legs. The resulting topline slopes *very gently* from withers to tail—the line from withers to back descending without a sharp drop; the back practically level; arch over hips somewhat lower than the withers; croup sloping gently to base of tail; tail carried to follow the natural line of the body. The bottom line, starting on a level with the elbows, to continue backward with almost no up-curve until reaching the end of the ribbed section, then a more noticeable up-curve to the flank, but not enough to make the dog appear small waisted or 'tucked up.' *To be penalized:* body too shallow, indicating lack of brisket. Ribs too flat sometimes due to immaturity. Ribs too round (barrel-shaped), hampering the gait. Swayback (dip in back), indicating weakness or lack of muscular development, particularly to be seen when dog is in action and viewed from the side. Roach back (too much arch over loin and extending forward into middle section). Croup falling away too sharply; or croup too high—unsightly faults, detrimental to outline and good movement. Topline sloping sharply, indicating steep withers (straight shoulder placement) and a too low tail-set.

Tail
The Springer's tail is an index both to his temperament and his conformation. Merry tail action is characteristic. The proper set is somewhat low following the natural line of the croup. The carriage should be nearly horizontal, slightly elevated when dog is excited. Carried straight up is untypical of the breed. The tail should not be docked too short and should be well fringed with wavy feather. It is legitimate to shape and shorten the feathering but enough should be left to blend with the dog's other furnishings. *To be penalized:* tail habitually upright. Tail set too high or too low. Clamped down tail (indicating timidity or undependable temperament, even less to be desired than the tail carried too gaily).

Forequarters
Efficient movement in front calls for proper shoulders. The blades sloping back to form an angle with the forearm of approximately 90 degrees which permits the dog to swing his forelegs forward in an easy manner. Shoulders (fairly close together at the tips) to lie flat and mold smoothly into the contour of the body. The forelegs to be straight with the same degree of size to the foot. The bone, strong, slightly flattened, not too heavy or round. The knee, straight, almost flat; the pasterns short, strong; elbows close to the body with free action from the shoulders. *To be penalized:* shoulders set at a steep angle limiting the stride. Loaded shoulders (the blades standing out from the body by overdevelopment of the muscles). Loose elbows, crooked legs. Bone too light or too coarse and heavy. Weak pasterns that let down the feet at a pronounced angle.

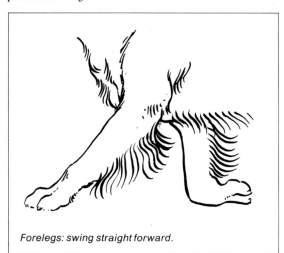
Forelegs: swing straight forward.

Hindquarters
The Springer should be shown in hard muscular condition, well developed in hips and thighs and the whole rear assembly should suggest strength and driving power. The hip joints to be set rather wide apart and the hips nicely rounded. The thighs broad and muscular; the stifle joint strong and moderately bent. The hock joint somewhat rounded, not small and sharp in contour, and moderately angulated. Leg from hock joint to foot pad, short and strong with good bone structure. When viewed from the rear the hocks to be parallel whether the dog is standing or in motion. *To be penalized:* too little or too much angulation. Narrow, undeveloped thighs. Hocks too short or too long (a proportion of $\frac{1}{3}$ the distance from hip joint to foot is ideal). Flabby muscles. Weakness of joints.

Feet
The feet to be round, or slightly oval, compact, well arched, medium size with thick pads, well feathered between the toes. Excess hair to be removed to show the natural shape and size of the foot. *To be penalized:* thin, open or splayed feet (flat with spreading toes). Hare foot (long, rather narrow foot).

Movement
In judging the Springer there should be emphasis on proper movement, which is the final test of a dog's conformation and soundness. Prerequisite to good movement is balance of the front and rear assemblies. The two must match in angulation and muscular development if the gait is to be smooth and effortless. Good shoulders laid back at an angle that permits a long stride are just as essential as the excellent rear quarters that provide the driving power. When viewed from the front, the dog's legs should appear to swing forward in a free and easy manner, with no tendency for the feet to cross over or interfere with each other. Viewed from the rear, the hocks should drive well under the body following on a line with the forelegs, the rear legs parallel, neither too widely nor too closely spaced. Seen from the side, the Springer should exhibit a good, long forward stride, without high-stepping or wasted motion. *To be penalized:* short choppy stride, mincing steps with up and down movement, hopping. Moving with forefeet wide, giving roll or swing to body. Weaving or crossing of fore or hind feet. Cowhocks—hocks turning in toward each other.

In judging the English Springer Spaniel, the over-all picture is a primary consideration. It is urged that the judge look for type which includes general appearance, outline and temperament and also for soundness, especially as seen when the dog is in motion. Inasmuch as the dog with a smooth easy gait must be reasonably sound and well balanced he is to be highly regarded in the show ring; however, not to the extent of forgiving him for not looking like an English Springer Spaniel. A quite untypical dog, leggy, foreign in head and expression, may move well. But he should not be placed over a good all-round specimen that has a minor fault in movement. It should be remembered that the English Springer Spaniel is first and foremost a sporting dog of the spaniel family and he must look and behave and move in character.

Approved by the AKC 12 June 1956

FIELD SPANIEL

NATIONAL GROUPING		
	Name	Number
AKC	Sporting Dogs	1
KC(GB)	Gundog	2
FCI	Gundogs	8

This is one of those breeds that has suffered the vicissitudes of fortune as the result of man's attempts to conform to fashion rather than considering the work that a gundog was expected to perform. At the turn of the century extremes of selective breeding had produced a race of dogs that looked rather like very heavily built short-legged long-coated Daschshunds. The standard of that time described the breed as long and very low with immensely boned short legs, which was described by Colonel Claude Cane in Robert Leighton's book of 1907 as an "absurd craze". The Field Spaniel is one of the older forms of the small Land Spaniel, developed by crossing the Cocker and Springer types, and producing a dog which was in its early days sharply divided into the blacks and the coloureds. At first the blacks were the more important, so much so that they were called Black Spaniels, and it was some time later that the coloured dogs achieved some status.

The craze for a low outline and shorter and shorter legs produced a dog that was useless in the field, and after considerable vogue during the early part of the century, the breed went into such a decline that by the middle sixties the number of registrations at the British Kennel Club had shrunk to single figures. In 1879 a dog named Kaffir, a Black Spaniel, looked almost exactly like a modern Field Spaniel, judging from the engraving in Vero Shaw's book of 1881, and it was only in between times that the gross exaggeration took place which almost killed the breed. Fortunately there have always been a few enthusiasts interested in preserving old breeds, and old Spaniel breeds in particular, and it is to them that we owe the fact that the Field Spaniel has survived at all. Now, the breed is again on the increase, and by the judicious use of Cocker crosses either openly or otherwise, a type has evolved which looks like a working Spaniel, yet in its better form is unlike any of the others.

He is stronger, larger and nowadays longer in the leg and more active than the Cocker, and he has a particular manner of working through roots and heavy going, where his ability to spring from the ground and leap from tussock to tussock is of particular value. He has a good nose, can be trained to retrieve, and is a willing and tireless worker. Like all the other members of the family he is a friendly dog, attaches himself to families and households, and makes a good pet and housedog.

OFFICIAL STANDARD

General appearance
That a well-balanced, noble, upstanding sporting dog; built for activity and endurance. A grand combination of beauty and utility, and bespeaking of unusual docility and instinct.

Head
Should be quite characteristic of this grand sporting dog, as that of the Bulldog, or the Bloodhound; its very stamp and countenance should at once convey the conviction of high breeding, character and nobility; skull well developed, with a distinctly elevated occipital tuberosity, which, above all, gives the character alluded to; not too wide across the muzzle, long and lean, never snipy or squarely cut, and in profile curving gradually from nose to throat; lean beneath the eyes—a thickness here gives coarseness to the whole head. The great length of muzzle gives surface for the free development of the olfactory nerve, and thus secures the highest possible scenting powers.

Nose
Well developed, with good open nostrils.

Eyes
Not too full, but not small, receding or overhung, color

dark hazel or brown, or nearly black, according to the color of the dog. Grave in expression and showing no haw.

Head and skull: long and lean, neither snipy nor square.

Ears

Moderately long and wide, sufficiently clad with nice setterlike feather and set low. They should fall in graceful folds, the lower parts curling inwards and backwards.

Neck

Long, strong and muscular, so as to enable the dog to retrieve his game without undue fatigue.

Body

Should be of moderate length, well ribbed up to a good strong loin, straight or slightly arched, never slack.

Shoulders and chest

Former long, sloping and well set back, thus giving great activity and speed; latter deep and well developed, but not too round and wide.

Back and loin

Very strong and muscular.

Hindquarters

Strong and muscular. The stifles should be moderately bent, and not twisted either in or out.

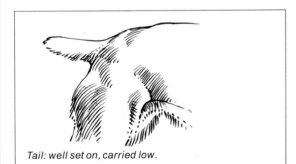

Tail: well set on, carried low.

Stern

Well set on and carried low, if possible below the level of the back, in a straight line or with a slight downward inclination, never elevated above the back, and in action always kept low, nicely fringed with wavy feather of silky texture.

Forelegs

Should be of fairly good length, with straight, clean, flat bone, and nicely feathered. Immense bone is no longer desirable.

Feet

Not too small; round, with short soft hair between the toes; good, strong pads.

Coat

Flat or slightly waved, and never curled. Sufficiently dense to resist the weather, and not too short. Silky in texture, glossy and refined in nature, with neither duffleness on the one hand, nor curl or wiriness on the other. On the chest, under belly and behind the legs, there should be abundant feather, but never too much, especially below the hocks, and that of the right sort, *viz.* setterlike. The hindquarters should be similarly adorned.

Coat: abundant setter-like feather under chest and behind legs.

Color

Black, liver, golden liver, mahogany red, or roan; or any one of these colors with tan over the eyes and on the cheeks, feet, and pasterns. Other colors, such as black and white, liver and white, red or orange and white, while not disqualifying, will be considered less desirable since the Field Spaniel should be clearly distinguished from the Springer Spaniel.

Height

About 18 inches to shoulder.

Weight

From about 35 to 50 pounds.

SCALE OF POINTS
Head and jaw (15). Eyes (5). Ears (5). Neck (5). Body (10). Forelegs (10). Hind legs (10). Feet (10). Stern (10). Coat and feather (10). General appearance (10). *Total (100)*.

Approved by th AKC 14 July 1959

IRISH WATER SPANIEL

NATIONAL GROUPING		
	Name	Number
AKC	Sporting Dogs	1
KC(GB)	Gundog	2
FCI	Gundogs	8

This member of the Spaniel family is very different from all the others, being considerably larger and having a closely curled coat of one colour. There are said to have been two distinct varieties of this breed in Ireland in the early days, the Northern Water Spaniel and the Southern Water Spaniel with somewhere along the line a possible third known as the Tweed Water Spaniel which disappeared somewhere around the middle of the 19th century. The Northern dog was sometimes described as the "Old Brown Irish Retriever" which confuses the issue even further, and fortunately there is now only one Irish Water Spaniel. A certain Mr. Justin McCarthy claimed to have invented the breed in about 1850, but what is more likely is that he acquired specimens of a variety that fitted the description of what he required and interbred them until he had perfected the strain. There is little doubt that the breed owes its origins to the old European Water Dog, which was a Spaniel type, and which was also the ancestor of the Poodle.

It was not until 1862 that the breed attracted attention in the British show ring, when classes were put on at the Birmingham Show, and from that time onwards he became fairly popular, some very good specimens being exhibited between 1880 and 1890. From then to the turn of the century the breed declined and by the middle of this century the registration figures had dropped to an alarming extent and there was even a danger that the breed might not survive. Survive it did, however, and there is now once more an upsurge in interest and the numbers are steadily increasing. There is no member of the Spaniel family with a more distinctive appearance than the Irish Water Spaniel. He has been described as the clown of the Spaniels, which is no reflection on his intelligence or his behaviour, as in these respects he is anything but. It is merely that his appearance is very unusual with his rather strange shape, his closely curled coat and his somewhat ridiculous tail which starts off looking like a tail and fades away to almost nothing. The Irish Water Spaniel is a first-class water dog as his name would suggest, and is particularly suited to working in his native country of marshes and bogland. He can, and does, work as any other of the Spaniel family, hunting, putting up game, and retrieving, but it is his work with snipe and as a wildfowler that has earned him his reputation. He has a very good nose indeed, a virtually waterproof coat, and tremendous strength and powers of endurance. He is courageous, as indeed any dog needs to be to work tidal waters after duck in the middle of the winter, as he will in the treacherous estuaries of the rivers of Northern Ireland and Scotland. He is highly intelligent and adaptable, easily trained and a great sporting companion.

As a show dog he is only just recovering some of the ground that he lost after the First World War and through to the Second, and more are now seen at shows than have been for some years. He is not an ideal show dog, as his coat is something of a problem. To retain the close curls special care and attention is needed, and some exhibitors maintain that the only way of preserving the quality of the coat at its best is to allow the dog to go for a swim in fresh water just before a show, never bathing in between shows. As the coat is particularly oily which is part of its waterproof character, the result is a dog that often smells like a dog. He makes a very faithful and attentive companion, who enjoys country walks, and is an excellent gundog for the one-dog man.

OFFICIAL STANDARD

General appearance
That of a smart, upstanding, strongly built but not leggy dog, combining great intelligence and the rugged endurance with a bold, dashing eagerness of temperament.

Head
Skull rather large and high in dome with prominent occiput; muzzle square and rather long with deep mouth opening and lips fine in texture. Teeth strong and level. The nose should be large with open nostrils, and liver in color. The head should be cleanly chiseled, not cheeky, and should not present a short wedge-shaped appearance. Hair on face should be short and smooth.

Topknot
Topknot, a characteristic of the true breed, should consist of long loose curls growing down into a well-defined peak between the eyes and should not be in the form of a wig; i.e. growing straight across.

Eyes
Medium in size and set almost flush, without eyebrows. Color of eyes hazel, preferably of dark shade. Expression of the eyes should be keenly alert, intelligent, direct and quizzical.

Ears
Long, lobular, set low with leathers reaching to about the end of the nose when extended forward. The ears should be abundantly covered with curls becoming longer toward the tips and extending two or more inches below the ends of the leathers.

Neck
The neck should be long, arching, strong and muscular, smoothly set into sloping shoulders.

Shoulders and chest
Shoulders should be sloping and clean; chest deep but not too wide between the legs. The entire front should give the impression of strength without heaviness.

Body, ribs and loins
Body should be of medium length, with ribs well sprung, pear-shaped at the brisket, and rounder toward the hind quarters. Ribs should be carried well back. Loins should be short, wide and muscular. The body should not present a tucked-up appearance.

Hindquarters
The hindquarters should be as high as or a trifle higher than the shoulders and should be very powerful and muscular with well-developed upper and second thighs. Hips should be wide; stifles should not be too straight; and hocks low-set and moderately bent. Tail should be set on low enough to give a rather rounded appearance to the hindquarters and should be carried nearly level with the back. Sound hindquarters are of great importance to provide swimming power and drive.

Forelegs and feet
Forelegs medium in length, well boned, straight and muscular with elbows close set. Both fore and hind feet should be large, thick and somewhat spreading, well clothed with hair both over and between the toes, but free from superfluous feather.

Tail
The so-called 'rat tail' is a striking characteristic of the breed. At the root it is thick and covered for 2 or 3 inches with short curls. It tapers to a fine point at the end, and from the root-curls is covered with short, smooth hair so as to look as if the tail had been clipped. The tail should not be long enough to reach the hock joint.

Coat
Proper coat is of vital importance. The neck, back and sides should be densely covered with tight crisp ringlets entirely free from wooliness. Underneath the ribs the hair should be longer. The hair on lower throat should be short. The forelegs should be covered all around with abundant hair falling in curls or waves, but shorter in front than behind. The hind legs should also be abundantly covered by hair falling in curls or waves, but the hair should be short on the front of the legs below the hocks.

Color
Solid liver; white on chest objectionable.

Height and weight
Dogs: 22 to 24 inches; bitches: 21 to 23 inches. Dogs: 55 to 65 pounds; bitches: 45 to 58 pounds.

Gait
Should be square, true, precise and not slurring.

SCALE OF POINTS
Head (20): skull and topknot (6), ears (4), eyes (4), muzzle and nose (6). Body (17): neck (5), chest, shoulders, back, loin and ribs (12). *Driving Gear (23):* feet, hips, thighs, stifles and continuity of hindquarter muscles (14), feet, legs, elbows and muscles of forequarters (9). Coat (20): tightness, denseness of curl and general texture (16), color (4). Tail (5): general appearance and 'set on', length and carriage (5). *General Conformation and Action (15):* symmetry, style, gait, weight and size (15). *Total (100).*

Approved by the AKC 11 June 1940

KC(GB) VARIATION TO STANDARD
Height: to shoulders: dogs 21 to 23 inches; bitches 20 to 22 inches.

SUSSEX SPANIEL

NATIONAL GROUPING		
	Name	Number
AKC	Sporting Dogs	1
KC(GB)	Gundog	2
FCI	Gundogs	8

This particular member of the Spaniel family is one of the oldest, yet it is difficult to understand why he should have evolved as he has, since he has few of the qualities associated with the working Spaniel, being slower and shorter on the leg than many of the others. The Sportsman's Repository of 1820 speaks of the Spaniels of Sussex as good working dogs and in the same pages mentions the fact that the Toy Spaniels will hunt though they are too small to work all day, being described as delicate and small or 'carpet' Spaniels with exquisite noses that will hunt truly and pleasantly. The juxtaposition of these two pieces of information indicates that at that time although the different breeds of Spaniel were still dividing, there was a race of Spaniels peculiar to Sussex.

One of the principal characteristics of the breed is the rich golden liver colour with the hairs shading to gold at the tips. This colour is said to have originated with one bitch belonging to Dr. Watts which came from the then famous kennels of Mr. Fuller at Rosehill Park. This kennel produced the Rosehill line which on the death of Mr. Fuller in 1847 would have disappeared but for his head keeper who retained a dog and a bitch which kept the strain going. From that time the breed declined, and it was only the efforts of a group of enthusiasts in the 1870s that preserved the breed. Mr. Phineas Bullock who around that time owned the strongest kennel of Field Spaniels, was also successfully showing Sussex, but there is some doubt about the parentage of his big winners as they were believed to be bred from Field Spaniels.

Colonel Claude Cane writing in the early part of this century said that he found the breed difficult, as the bitches did not breed freely, the puppies were rather delicate and difficult to rear, and laid this down to excessive inbreeding, which he claimed was almost unavoidable as there were so few specimens left at that time. The same situation almost exists today, as

in Britain only a handful are registered each year. Fortunately they are beginning to find their way into other countries and it will be possible in the future to re-import outcrosses from lines bred in places far distant from their native Sussex. During the early years of this century it was the habit for field trial judges to penalise a Spaniel that gave tongue. Most Sussex Spaniels give tongue when on a scent, and the deep melodious tone of the Sussex is a very pleasing sound and useful in some forms of hunting, especially on fur in heavy undergrowth as the sportsman gets early warning of game.

Owing to his build, the Sussex is a comparatively slow worker, but very conscientious and persevering, being particularly good in heavy coverts, where his strength at a low level and his abundant flat coat enable him to do considerable work without excessive tiring and with no damage to himself. He is a handsome dog and his colour so distinctive that he is much admired in the show ring. He is however rare, and seldom does one make much impression at the higher level at a large show. He shows well enough, as he is a placid individual, easily trained to behave well, and with the sort of temperament that allows him to enjoy the environment of a show without being too demonstrative about it. He is a soft and affectionate companion, makes a very good house dog.

OFFICIAL STANDARD

General appearance
Rather massive and muscular, but with free movements and nice tail action, denoting a cheerful and tractable disposition.

Head
The skull should be moderately long and also wide, with an indention in the middle and a full stop, brows fairly heavy; occiput full, but not pointed, the whole giving an appearance of heaviness without dullness. *Eyes:* hazel color, fairly large, soft and languishing, not showing the haw overmuch. *Nose:* the muzzle should be about three inches long, square, and the lips somewhat pendulous. The nostrils well developed and liver color. *Ears:* thick, fairly large and lobe shaped; set moderately low, but relatively not so low as in the black Field Spaniel; carried close to the head and furnished with soft, wavy hair.

Neck
Is rather short, strong and slightly arched, but not carrying the head much above the level of the back. There should not be much throatiness about the skin, but well-marked frill in the coat.

Chest and shoulders
The chest is round, especially behind the shoulders, deep and wide giving a good girth. The shoulders should be oblique.

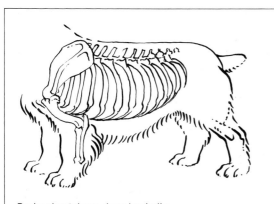
Body: chest deep, deep back ribs.

Back and back rib
The back and loin is long and should be very muscular, both in width and depth; for this development the back ribs must be deep. The whole body is characterized as low, long and level.

Legs and feet
The arms and thighs must be bony as well as muscular, knees and hocks large and strong; pasterns very short and bony, feet large and round, and with short hair between the toes. The legs should be very short and strong, with great bone, and may show a slight bend in the forearm, and be moderately well feathered. The hind legs should

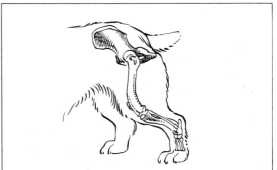
Hindquarters: thighs strongly boned, not too much bend.

not appear to be shorter than the forelegs, nor be too much bent at the hocks. They should be well feathered above the hocks but should not have much hair below that point. The hind legs are short from the hock to the ground, and wide apart.

Tail
Should be docked from 5 to 7 inches, set low, and not carried above the level of the back, thickly covered with moderately long feather.

Coat
Body coat abundant, flat or slightly waved, with no tendency to curl, moderately well feathered on legs and stern, but clean below the hocks.

Color
Rich golden liver; this is a certain sign of the purity of the breed, dark liver or puce denoting unmistakably a recent cross with the black or other variety of Field Spaniel.

Weight
From 35 to 45 pounds.

POSITIVE POINTS
Head (10). Eyes (5). Nose (5). Ears (10). Neck (5). Chest and shoulders (5). Back and back ribs (10). Legs and feet (10). Tail (5). Coat (5). Color (15) General appearance (15). *Total (100).*

NEGATIVE POINTS
Light eyes (5). Narrow head (10). Weak muzzle (10). Curled ears or set on high (5). Curled coat (15). Carriage of stern (5). Topknot (10). White on chest (5). Color, too light ot too dark (15). Legginess or light of bone (5). Shortness of body or flat sided (5). General appearance—sour or crouching (10). *Total (100).*

Approved by the AKC 14 July 1959

KC(GB) VARIATION TO STANDARD
General appearance: movement is a decided roll. *Neck:* long. *Coat:* ample undercoat for weather resistance. *Weight and size:* dogs 45 pounds; bitches 40 pounds. Height 15 to 16 inches.

WELSH SPRINGER SPANIEL

NATIONAL GROUPING		
	Name	Number
AKC	Sporting Dogs	I
KC(GB)	Gundog	2
FCI	Gundogs	8

To the unitiated there appears very little difference between the English and the Welsh Springer, but in fact the differences are quite marked. He is a smaller dog to start with, has shorter ears, and never varies from the dark rich red and white colour. His head too is usually smaller and finer than his English counterpart. He is however a Springer, or as the Welsh sometimes prefer to call him, a 'starter' and there is no doubt that the two breeds share a common origin, though the people of Wales claim that he has been a separate breed for hundreds of years, which would place him before the English Springer. When the claims for the antiquity of the breed were first put forward they were contested by those who maintained that he was merely a cross between the Springer and probably the Clumber which gave him his colour. The fact that he was not officially recognised as a separate breed until 1902 supports the theory that he is a recently developed breed.

There is some evidence that a small Spaniel, somewhere in size between a Cocker and a Springer had been in use as a gundog in Wales for some considerable time before the Welsh Springer emerged. However, when the first really good dogs were shown, around the 1890s, the Welsh exhibitors admitted that they were better than anything previously seen, which suggests that until then these indigenous Spaniels had been a fairly nondescript collection. In 1902 the breed was recognised and a standard produced, with the result that this active little worker was on his way. He is still principally known in Wales, but has now been exported to many other countries of the world, where his ability to withstand extremes of climate has enabled him to become established both as a working dog and on the show bench. His popularity has steadily increased in recent years and registration figures are growing all the time, but it has only been quite recently that one has won really high honours at a major show in Britain.

The Welsh Springer is an active hard-working dog, well suited to the mountainous country of his native Wales, where he will meet with in any one day the extremes of gorse covered hills and mountain torrents, boggy valleys and rocky gorges. He is smaller and more lightly built than the English Springer, with finer bone and a more silky coat, but this does not prevent him from being an excellent water dog, though it would be unwise to subject him to a hard day's work as a wildfowler during the winter. He can be used on all forms of game, and unless he is well-trained, can become somewhat too active, going off on excursions of his own. He is a good hunter and springer of game and can be trained to retrieve more than adequately.

He did have one or two common faults at one time which held him back as a major winner at big shows, but these have been bred out by careful selection, and he is now a very fine sound dog with few faults and no vices. He is easy to show as he trains well and is then steady and fearless in the ring. His preparation is minimal, and he is easily kept fit and in hard condition as he loves exercise and will run all day. His temperament is pleasant as is that of most of the Spaniels, and though at one time some of them were nervous, he is now generally a fairly bold and friendly dog that makes a good pet and housedog as well as a fine sporting companion.

OFFICIAL STANDARD

The 'Welsh Spaniel' or 'Springer' is also known and referred to in Wales as a 'Starter.' He is of very ancient and pure origin, and is a distinct variety which has been bred and preserved purely for working purposes.

General appearance

A symmetrical, compact, strong, merry, very active dog; not stilty, obviously built for endurance and activity.

Head and skull: moderate length, clear stop, well chiselled.

Head

Skull: proportionate, of moderate length, slightly domed, clearly defined stop, well chiseled below the eyes. *Muzzle:* medium length, straight, fairly square; the nostrils well developed and flesh colored or dark. *Jaw:* strong, neither undershot nor overshot. *Eyes:* hazel or dark, medium size, not prominent, nor sunken, nor showing haw. *Ears:* set moderately low and hanging close to the cheeks, comparatively small and gradually narrowing towards the tip, covered with nice setterlike feathering. A short chubby head is objectionable.

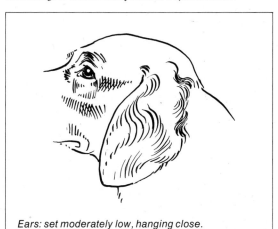

Ears: set moderately low, hanging close.

Neck and shoulders

Neck: Long and muscular, clean in throat, neatly set into long and sloping shoulders. *Forelegs:* medium length,

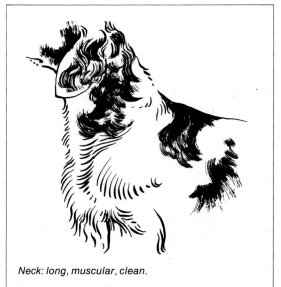

Neck: long, muscular, clean.

straight, well boned, moderately feathered.

Body

Not long; strong and muscular with deep brisket, well sprung ribs; length of body should be proportionate to length of leg, and very well balanced; with muscular loin slightly arched and well coupled up. *Quarters:* strong and muscular, wide and fully developed with deep second thighs. *Hind legs:* hocks well let down; stifles moderately bent (neither twisted in nor out), moderately feathered. *Feet:* round with thick pads. *Stern:* well set on and low, never carried above the level of the back; lightly feathered and with lively action.

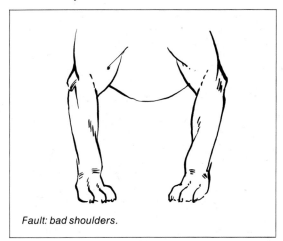

Fault: bad shoulders.

Coat

Straight or flat and thick, of a nice silky texture, never wiry nor wavy. A curly coat is most objectionable. *Color:* dark rich red and white.

KC(GB) VARIATION TO STANDARD

Height: to shoulders, not to exceed: dogs 19 inches; bitches 18 inches.

VIZSLA

Hungary has produced several quite remarkable breeds, notable in that they differ greatly from anything known anywhere else in the world. The Puli and the Komondor are two typical examples. This is probably explained by the fact that the country has acted as something of an ecological bridge across Asia and Europe. The Magyars who penetrated into Europe some thousand years ago brought with them their customs, their peoples and undoubtedly their dogs. Not all the dogs of Hungary, however, are as strange as the Puli. The Vizsla is one that more nearly fits the Western World's idea of what a dog should look like, and it is this, together with other valuable qualities that has made it the increasingly popular dog that it is. Writers on the subject of falcony in the middle ages described a dog that was certainly the Vizsla type.

The plains of Hungary, largely agricultural, and rich in game were the perfect place in which to develop a gun dog with more than average all round ability, a dog that would work equally well with fur or feather, one that was fast, clever and with the sort of nose that would permit him to discover game in the thick ground cover of crops and high grasslands. The Vizsla was the answer, and he flourished under these conditions. The period between the wars was a difficult time for the Vizsla owners and breeders in Hungary, and by the beginning of the Second World War, the breed had almost disappeared. A small number of enthusiasts, however, refused to allow it to become extinct and kept the breed alive. World War II brought in its wake the Russian occupation of the country, and those who fled to Austria, as many did, took their dogs with them. Others went to Italy and Germany, and the breed not only became more widely dispersed, but, what was more important for its continuance, became more widely known.

By 1960 the breed was admitted to the American Kennel Club register, and since that date has climbed the popularity list until it is now well established. Britain was a little slower in recognising the qualities of this very attractive and indeed important breed, but in recent years more and more are being seen at shows, and now that challenge certificates are being offered in the breed it will increase.

He is described in the official Hungarian standard as a medium sized hunting type dog of noble appearance and lean musculation, a description which fits him admirably, as he is an aristocratic and distinguished looking dog, robust but lightly built with a long strong muscular neck and a lean elegant head. His solid colour, rusty gold or dark yellow makes him quite outstanding among his fellow gundogs and his powerful, light and graceful movement helps to make him popular with spectators at shows. It is, however, as a gundog that he is at his best, and in competition with other pointing breeds he has always held his own. His short coat and clean habits, with his quiet and steady temperament make him an excellent housedog.

OFFICIAL STANDARD

General appearance
That of a medium-sized hunting dog of quite distinguished appearance. Robust but rather lightly built, his short coat is an attractive rusty-gold, and his tail is docked. He is a dog of power and drive in the field, and a tractable and affectionate companion in the home.

Head
Lean but muscular. The skull is moderately wide between the ears, with a median line down the forehead. Stop moderate. The muzzle is a trifle longer than the skull and, although tapering, is well squared at its end. Jaws strong, with well-developed white teeth meeting in a scissors bite. The lips cover the jaws completely but they are neither loose nor pendulous. Nostrils slightly open, the nose

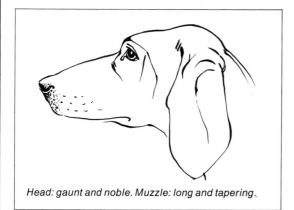

Head: gaunt and noble. Muzzle: long and tapering.

brown. A black or slate-gray nose is objectionable.

Ears
Thin, silky, and proportionately long, with rounded-leather ends; set fairly low and hanging close to the cheeks.

Eyes
Medium in size and depth of setting, their surrounding tissue covering the whites, and the iris or color portion harmonizing with the shade of the coat. A yellow eye is objectionable.

Neck
Strong, smooth, and muscular; moderately long, arched, and devoid of dewlap. It broadens nicely into shoulders which are well laid back.

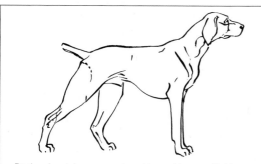

Body: chest deep, prominent breast bone, slight tuck up.

Body
Strong and well proportioned. The back is short, the withers high, and the topline slightly rounded over the loin to the set-on of the tail. Chest moderately broad and deep, and reaching down to the elbows. Ribs well sprung, and underline exhibiting a slight tuck-up beneath the loin.

Legs and feet
Forelegs straight, strong, and muscular, with elbows close. The hind legs have well-developed thighs, with moderate angulation at stifles and hocks. Too much angulation at the hocks is as faulty as too little. The hocks which are well let down, are equidistant from each other from the hock joint to the ground. Cowhocks are faulty. Feet are cat-like, round and compact, with toes close. Nails are brown and short; pads thick and tough. Dew-claws, if any, to be removed. Hare feet are objectionable.

Tail
Set just below the level of the back, thicker at the root, and docked one third off.

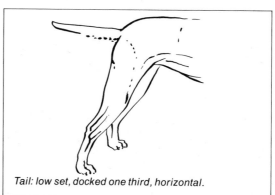

Tail: low set, docked one third, horizontal.

Coat
Short, smooth, dense, and close-lying, without woolly undercoat.

Color
Solid. Rusty gold or rather dark sandy yellow in different shades, with darker shades preferred. Dark brown and pale yellow are undesirable. Small white spots on chest or feet are not faulted.

Temperament
That of the natural hunter endowed with a good nose and above-average ability to take training. Lively, gentle-mannered, and demonstratively affectionate. Fearless, and with well-developed protective instinct.

Gait
Far-reaching, light-footed, graceful, smooth.

Size
Dogs: 22 to 24 inches; bitches: 21 to 23 inches at the highest point of the shoulders. Any dog measuring over or under these limits shall be considered faulty, the seriousness of the fault depending on the extent of the deviation. Any dog that measures more than 2 inches over or under these limits shall be disqualified.

DISQUALIFICATION
Deviation in height of more than 2 inches from standard either way.

Approved by the AKC 10 December 1963

KC(GB) VARIATION TO STANDARD
Body: croup should be well muscled. *Tail:* should be held horizontally whilst moving. *Weight and size:* optimum weight 48½ to 66 pounds. Height at withers: dogs 22½ to 25 inches; bitches 21 to 23 inches.

WEIMARANER

The number and variety of gundogs emanating from Germany is considerable. It has always been a hunting country, with a wealth of game, both small animals and birds, and a considerable population of deer and boar. Most of the breeds have found their way into other countries including the United States of America, and the one that did so early in its history and with spectacular success is the Weimaraner. He is not an ancient dog, dating back to the 19th century when he was produced from several indigenous German breeds by careful selective breeding. It is almost certain that at least one of the early scent hounds played some part in his ancestry, probably one of the pack hounds of France. In his early days he was known as the Weimar Pointer and is referred to as such in a few lines in Leighton's book of 1907, which may indicate that the Spanish Pointer which is a fairly early breed was used to produce him.

NATIONAL GROUPING		
	Name	Number
AKC	Sporting Dogs	I
KC(GB)	–	–
FCI	Gundogs	7

The court of Weimar, which was a great sportsman's court in the early 19th century, sponsored the production of the breed in an attempt to design the perfect all-round gundog, one that would not only hunt the smaller game but would cope with the bigger animals found in the forests of the republic. The result was a big strong fine dog with wonderful nose and great tracking abilities. In the early days the breed was very jealously guarded, matings being carefully considered for the best bloodlines, and litters being ruthlessly culled to produce only the best specimens. The breeders were reluctant to sell, and it was almost impossible for anyone from another country to acquire one of these dogs. In 1929 an American dog breeder, Howard Knight became a member of the German Weimaraner Club, and was permitted to own a couple which he brought back, founded the breed, helped form a club and became its first President.

From that time onwards the breed found considerable favour with American sportsmen, who found in him the answer to the problem of the all-round gundog. There has been for many years a great deal of personal hunting in America. One or two sportsmen with dogs of their own, kept at home, would spend short periods of time in the country enjoying their favourite sport, and in the Weimaraner they found the ideal dog. He was much later finding favour in Britain, not arriving there until the 1950s, but since then he has made great progress. Nicknamed the 'grey ghost' because of his distinctive colour, he soon became popular as a family dog as well as a worker in the field and a show dog, and in the past ten years his numbers have quadrupled.

He is a fine show dog, easily trained and responsive. He has few vices, is easily prepared for the ring, as all that is required is some work with a hound glove to bring out the natural gloss of his short coat, and is reasonably quiet on the bench. He makes a good companion and housedog, and it is this particular quality that has endeared him to so many sportsmen who do not have to face up to the problem of having a shooting dog that is not allowed in the family home.

OFFICIAL STANDARD

General appearance
A medium-sized gray dog, with fine aristocratic features. He should present a picture of grace, speed, stamina, alertness and balance. Above all, the dog's conformation must indicate the ability to work with great speed and endurance in the field.

Height
Height at the withers: dogs, 25 to 27 inches; bitches, 23 to 25 inches. One inch over or under the specified height of each sex is allowable but should be penalized. Dogs measuring less than 24 inches or more than 28 inches and bitches measuring less than 22 inches or more than 26 inches shall be disqualified.

Head
Moderately long and aristocratic, with moderate stop and slight median line extending back over the forehead. Rather prominent occipital bone and trumpets well set back, beginning at the back of the eye sockets. Measure-

Head and skull: moderately long and aristocratic, powerful jaw.

ment from tip of nose to stop equal that from stop to occipital bone. The flews should be straight, delicate at the nostrils. Skin drawn tightly. Neck clean-cut and moderately long. Expression kind, keen and intelligent. *Ears:* long and lobular, slightly folded and set high. The ear when drawn snugly alongside the jaw should end approximately 2 inches from the point of the nose. *Eyes:* In shades of light amber, gray or blue-gray, set well enough apart to indicate good disposition and intelligence. When dilated under excitement the eyes may appear almost black. *Teeth:* well set, strong and even; well-developed and proportionate to jaw with correct scissors bite, the upper teeth protruding slightly over the lower teeth but not more than $\frac{1}{16}$ of an inch. Complete dentition is greatly to be desired. *Nose:* gray. *Lips and gums:* pinkish flesh shades.

Body
The back should be moderate in length, set in a straight line, strong, and should slope slightly from the withers. The chest should be well developed and deep with shoulders well laid back. Ribs well sprung and long. Abdomen firmly held; moderately tucked-up flank. The brisket should extend to the elbow.

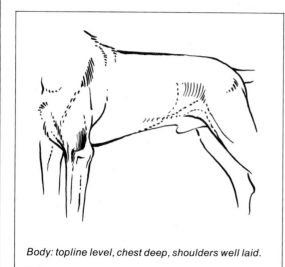

Body: topline level, chest deep, shoulders well laid.

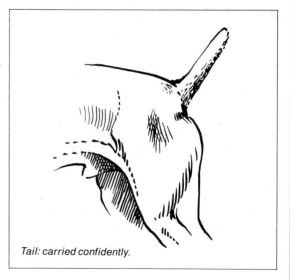

Tail: carried confidently.

Coat and color

Short, smooth and sleek, solid color, in shades of mouse-gray to silver-gray, usually blending to lighter shades on the head and ears. A small white marking on the chest is permitted, but should be penalized on any other portion of the body. White spots resulting from injury should not be penalized. A distinctly long coat is a disqualification. A distinctly blue or black coat is a disqualification.

Forelegs

Straight and strong, with the measurement from the elbow to the ground approximately equaling the distance from the elbow to the top of the withers.

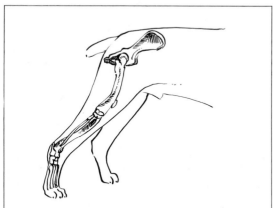

Hindquarters: moderately angulated, hock joint well let down.

Hindquarters

Well-angulated stifles and straight hocks. Musculation well developed.

Feet

Firm and compact, webbed, toes well arched, pads closed and thick, nail short and gray or amber in color. *Dewclaws:* should be removed.

Tail

Docked. At maturity it should measure approximately 6 inches with a tendency to be light rather than heavy and should be carried in a manner expressing confidence and sound temperament. A non-docked tail shall be penalized.

Gait

The gait should be effortless and should indicate smooth co-ordination. When seen from the rear, the hind feet should be parallel to the front feet. When viewed from the side, the topline should remain strong and level.

Temperament

The temperament should be friendly, fearless, alert and obedient.

FAULTS

Minor faults: tail too short or too long. Pink nose.

Major faults: doggy bitches. Bitchy dogs. Improper muscular condition. Badly affected teeth. More than four teeth missing. Back too long or too short. Faulty coat. Neck too short, thick or throaty. Low-set tail. Elbows in or out. Feet east and west. Poor gait. Poor feet. Cowhocks. Faulty backs, either roached or sway. Badly overshot, or undershot bite. Snipy muzzle. Short ears.

Very serious faults: white, other than a spot on the chest. Eyes other than gray, blue-gray or light amber. Black mottled mouth. Non-docked tail. Dogs exhibiting strong fear, shyness or extreme nervousness.

DISQUALIFICATIONS

Deviation in height of more than one inch from standard either way. A distinctly long coat. A distinctly blue or black coat.

Approved by the AKC 14 December 1971

KC(GB) VARIATION TO STANDARD

Although given an interim standard, this dog has not yet been granted championship status by the KC(GB). *Coat:* in long-haired Weimaraner coat should be from 1 to 2 inches long on body and somewhat longer on neck. Tail and backs of limbs should be feathered. *Size:* height at withers: dogs 24 to 27 inches; bitches 22 to 25 inches.

WIREHAIRED POINTING GRIFFON

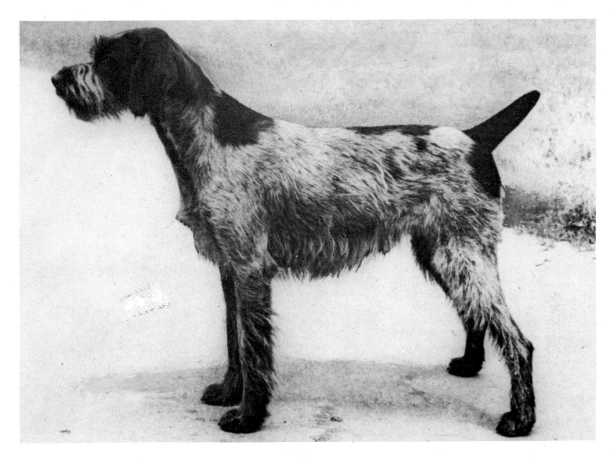

There are some breeds whose history, either because it has been carefully chronicled from very early times as in the case of the Pekingese, or because it is of fairly recent origin, is known in some detail. The Wirehaired Pointing Griffon is one of these. Prior to 1874 the breed did not exist, and it was the decision in that year by Mr. Korthals of Haarlem to produce a new breed that started it. At first the breed was known as the Korthals Griffon, and although the breed is completely unknown now in Britain, it is interesting to note that Mr. Korthals had a fine team, some of which were exhibited in Britain. In fact classes were put on for the breed by the Kennel Club at a show held at Barn Elms in Jubilee Year. On another occasion Mr. Korthals gained the prize for the best sporting dog in the show owned by a foreigner, with one of his Griffons at the Agricultural Hall in London.

When Mr. Korthals began to collect the dogs with which to conduct his experiments, he purchased a Griffon bitch and proceeded to add to his team short-coated, rough-coated and even smooth breeds of sporting dogs, and all of these are known by name. One litter produced three specimens, Moustache, Querida and Lina that are generally accepted as the

NATIONAL GROUPING		
	Name	Number
AKC	Sporting Dogs	I
KC(GB)	—	—
FCI	Gundogs	7

original ancestors of all the best lines in the breed. Although the breed developed in Holland as the result of work done by a Dutchman, the origins must be accepted as French, as the basic stock from which they were all bred, came in fact from France and the major part of the breeding programme was carried out there. Young Korthals left home and moved to Germany where he continued with his experiments to produce the breed that he was aiming for, and became a well known figure around the field trials, and other sporting activities connected with dogs, in many of the countries of Europe.

The progress of the breed from its early days is well-recorded, but the actual breeds of dog employed remain in some doubt, as Eduard Korthals had fixed ideas of what he wished the breed to be like when he had produced it, and was more interested in the appearance and performance of the dogs that he used than in their breed. He is said to have used French, German and Belgian dogs as various crosses, and in those countries at the end of the 19th century there was a wealth of gundog breeds to choose from. He probably used a mixture of Boulet, Barbet and Griffon and possibly even the Spinone. By the beginning of this century he had fixed the breed, and photographs of dogs in 1907 are remarkably like those of today.

As a working dog he has the reputation of being slow but thorough, and of being intelligent and easily trained. He is shorter on the leg than some of the gundogs, and thus lacks a little elegance. His rough harsh coat, almost bristly, gives him a somewhat unkempt appearance which some find unattractive. He is, however, a strong and vigorous dog, capable of working under extreme conditions. His temperament and intelligence make him a pleasant companion and guard, and there is no reason to suppose that he would be anything other than a very good housedog.

OFFICIAL STANDARD

General appearance
The Wirehaired Griffon is a dog of medium size, fairly short-backed, rather a little low on his legs. He is strongly limbed, everything about him indicating strength and vigor. His coat is harsh like the bristles of a wild boar and his appearance, notwithstanding his short coat, is as unkempt as that of the long-haired Griffon, but on the other hand he has a very intelligent air.

Head
Long, furnished with a harsh coat, forming a mustache and eyebrows, skull long and narrow, muzzle square. *Eyes:* large, open, full of expression, iris yellow or light brown. *Ears:* of medium size, flat or sometimes slightly curled, set rather high, very lightly furnished with hair. *Nose:* always brown.

Hind legs: long thighs.

Head: ears medium sized, set rather high.

Neck
Rather long, no dewlap.

Shoulders
Long, sloping.

Ribs
Slightly rounded.

Forelegs
Very straight, muscular, furnished with rather short wire hair.

Hind legs
Furnished with rather short stiff hair, and thighs long and well developed.

Feet
Round, firm and well formed.

Tail
Carried straight or gaily, furnished with a hard coat without plume, generally cut to a third of its length.

Coat
Hard, dry, stiff, never curly, the undercoat downy.

Color
Steel gray with chestnut splashes, gray white with chestnut splashes, chestnut, dirty white mixed with chestnut, never black.

Height
$21\frac{1}{2}$ to $23\frac{1}{2}$ inches for dogs, and $19\frac{1}{2}$ to $21\frac{1}{2}$ inches for bitches.

KC(GB) VARIATION TO STANDARD
This dog is not granted championship status by the KC(GB).

GROUP II: HOUNDS

Afghan Hound

Basenji

Basset Hound

Black and Tan Coonhound

Bloodhound

Beagle

Scottish Deerhound

Dachshund

Miniature Dachshund

Norwegian Elkhound

English Foxhound

Borzoi

Finnish Spitz

American Foxhound

Greyhound

Harrier

Irish Wolfhound

Ibizan Hound

Otter Hound

Pharaoh Hound

Whippet

Saluki

Rhodesian Ridgeback

GROUP II: HOUNDS

Long before the invention of the gun, man hunted animals for food and for sport. Even when the bow and arrow had been developed into an efficient hunting weapon, it was virtually useless in certain terrains. In heavy woodland where it is possible to approach close enough without being seen by the quarry, the bow and arrow served, but in open areas the game had to be run down either by sheer speed or steady persistence and stamina. Many breeds of dog evolved for chasing game hundreds and thousands of years ago, which means that the Hound Group has among its breeds some of the oldest in the world.

The Group is large and very diverse including breeds that sight and then run down their game, those that hunt by scent, others that chase, corner the game and bay to call up the hunter, and specialised breeds for hunting large and ferocious animals. There is also a sub-group of smaller dogs that has been developed to go to ground and keep the quarry entertained until it has been dug out. Although the breeds in the Group have for the most part the same sort of temperament, that drives them on to hunt and kill, there is very little overlap of purpose.

The first sub-group, those that hunt by catching and killing their quarry, includes not only some of the most ancient breeds, but also the greatest variety of sizes; from the Irish Wolfhound whose task it was originally to hunt the wolf, wild deer and boar, to the Whippet, one of the youngest breeds, whose quarry is the humble rabbit. They are all built to the same general pattern, with long legs, long necks and very deep briskets, which makes them among the most efficient runners in the animal world. Amongst the oldest breeds are the Saluki and the Afghan Hound which are recorded in ancient Persian manuscripts.

The second category, the ones that hunt by scent, includes most of the pack-hunting dogs, whose task it was to outrun the quarry by sheer persistence and stamina, chasing it until it collapsed through sheer exhaustion or decided to turn and face its pursuers. These dogs are built on heavier lines, with strong legs, deep chests and a very different form of head from the faster breeds. They have large muzzles and noses to allow a greater intake of breath and scent, and are not as streamlined. They are capable of following a scent hours and in some cases days after their quarry has gone.

There is another smaller category which hunts by scent, but which instead of going in to kill when the quarry is cornered, is trained to surround the game, and give tongue, keeping the animal at bay until the hunter arrives to dispatch it. Mostly they hunt the larger animals such as the moose and elk, and the Elkhound is a typical example. Others such as the Black and Tan Coonhound have been evolved to corner their quarry in a tree and give tongue in the same way.

The collection of small low-to-ground Hounds, the Dachshunds, occupies a special position in the Group. The work of the Dachshunds could be described as a mixture of that of the Hounds and the Terriers, in that they hunt by scent, and when their quarry, usually a fox or badger goes to ground, it is their duty to follow it down and engage it until both they and the quarry can be dug out by the hunter. There are in addition one or two specialists in the Group, the Otter Hound for instance which is able to scent in water, and the Bloodhound which has the finest scenting powers in the whole canine race but does not kill. There is in addition one breed which will tackle the fiercest game including the big cats, the Rhodesian Ridgeback, which has been known to handle a leopard.

Most dogs in the Hound Group become attached to people, largely because they have enjoyed civilisation for centuries. They have for the most part a well-controlled killer instinct, but many of them have a streak of independence which, under certain circumstances will make them disobedient.

AFGHAN HOUND

In those countries spreading eastwards from the Mediterranean, through Persia and across the north of the land mass of India, coursing has always been the 'sport of kings', or at least ever since tribes had leaders and rulers. In those areas a breed of running dogs developed, varying slightly from country to country, and even from the valleys to the hills. They were called in general terms Eastern Greyhounds, but were given specific names based on the countries or areas of origin. In that area which includes Afghanistan this particular type of dog developed as an extremely fast animal with great stamina, and with a coat to withstand the extreme cold of the hills in which it lived. Early attempts to acquire these dogs from tribesmen failed as they were highly prized and as closely kept as were horses and hawks, and it was in conjunction with both of these that the Afghan Hound was originally used.

Those who first brought these dogs to the West gave them the collective name Afghan Hound, and that name is now applied to a breed that has become popular throughout the world, with a common standard of points, and an accepted appearance. The old tribal names have disappeared in spite of attempts by some people to resurrect them.

The purpose of the dog was to chase game until it became exhausted, and until the sportsman could come up with it and dispatch it. The pattern of the chase was for a hawk to be loosed when an antelope was sighted, to swoop on the head of the animal and delay it so that the Afghan Hound could catch up and detain it until the hunter arrived. The hawks were trained by being flown at stuffed animal heads, and the Afghan Hound was trained to run in on the spot where the hawk swooped. To this day an Afghan Hound will often be seen watching the flight of a bird very closely, and even following it if he happens to be running free.

There is no more glamorous dog in the world than the Afghan Hound. It has a long silky coat, which can be of any colour or mixture of colours, and which grows to a remarkable length. In movement or in a breeze the coat flows beautifully around the contours of the dog, and owners spend considerable time grooming, even when the dog is not being prepared for exhibition, as the result is so rewarding.

As a show dog the Afghan has achieved tremendous popularity and numbers throughout the world, both of registrations and dogs on exhibition, now rival many of the one-time more popular breeds. Increased interest in the dog was due partly to the fact that the worlds of fashion, stage and screen, and professional photography realised the visual potential of so beautiful an animal, and it appeared in the company of beautiful women all over the world.

Temperamentally the dog has certain difficulties. It is a natural pursuer of anything that runs, is very difficult to recall when once it has embarked on a chase, and will kill whatever it happens to catch provided that it is not too big. It is not amenable to discipline, and needs a great deal of exercise, but once these elements are accepted, it has qualities that few other dogs have, and a distinct Eastern personality very different from the dogs of the Western world.

OFFICIAL STANDARD

General appearance

The Afghan Hound is an artisocrat, his whole appearance one of dignity and aloofness with no trace of plainness or coarseness. He has a straight front, proudly carried head, eyes gazing into the distance as if in memory of ages past. The striking characteristics of the breed—

Long topknot.

exotic, or 'Eastern', expression, long silky topknot, peculiar coat pattern, very prominent hipbones, large feet, and the impression of a somewhat exaggerated bend in the stifle due to profuse trouserings—stand out clearly, giving the Afghan Hound the appearance of what he is, a king of dogs, that has held true to tradition throughout the ages.

Head

The head is of good length, showing much refinement, the skull evenly balanced with the foreface. There is a

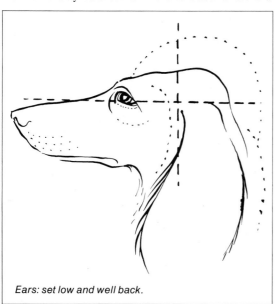

Ears: set low and well back.

slight prominence of the nasal bone structure causing a slightly Roman appearance, the center line running up over the foreface with little or no stop, falling away in front of the eyes so there is an absolutely clear outlook with no interference; the underjaw showing great strength, the jaws long and punishing; the mouth level, meaning that the teeth from the upper jaw and lower jaw match evenly, neither overshot nor undershot. This is a difficult mouth to breed. A scissors bite is even more punishing and can be more easily bred into a dog than a level mouth, and a dog having a scissors bite, where the lower teeth slip inside and rest against the teeth of the upper jaw, should not be penalized. The occipital bone is very prominent. The head is surmounted by a topknot of long silky hair. *Ears:* the ears are long, set approximately on level with outer corners of the eyes, the leather of the ear reaching nearly to the end of the dog's nose, and covered with long silky hair. *Eyes:* the eyes are almond-shaped (almost triangular), never full or bulgy, and are dark in color. *Nose:* nose is of good size, black in color. *Faults:* coarseness; snipiness; overshot or undershot; eyes round or bulgy or light in color; exaggerated Roman nose; head not surmounted with topknot.

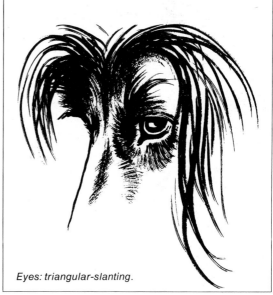

Eyes: triangular-slanting.

Neck

The neck is of good length, strong and arched, running in a curve to the shoulders which are long and sloping and well laid back. *Faults:* neck too short or too thick; a ewe neck; a goose neck; a neck lacking in substance.

Body

The back line appearing practically level from the shoulders to the loin. Strong and powerful loin and slightly arched, falling away toward the stern, with the hipbones very pronounced; well ribbed and tucked up in flanks. The height at the shoulders equals the distance from the chest to the buttocks; the brisket well let down, and of medium width. *Faults:* roach back, sway-back, goose rump, slack loin; lack of prominence of hipbones; too much width of brisket, causing interference with elbows.

Tail.

length; the toes arched, and covered with long thick hair; hindquarters powerful and well muscled, with great length between hip and hock; hocks are well let down; good angulation of both stifle and hock; slightly bowed from hock to crotch. *Faults:* front or back feet thrown outward or inward; pads of feet not thick enough; or feet too small; or any other evidence of weakness in feet; weak or broken down pasterns; too straight in stifle; too long in hock.

Coat
Hindquarters, flanks, ribs, forequarters, and legs well covered with thick, silky hair, very fine in texture; ears and all four feet well feathered; from in front of the shoulders; and also backwards from the shoulders along the saddle from the flanks and the ribs upwards, the hair is short and close, forming a smooth back in mature dogs—this is a traditional characteristic of the Afghan Hound. The Afghan Hound should be shown in its natural state; the coat is not clipped or trimmed; the head is surmounted (in the full sense of the word) with a topknot of long, silky hair—that is also an outstanding characteristic of the Afghan Hound. Showing of short hair on cuffs on either front or back legs is permissible. *Fault:* lack of short-haired saddle in mature dogs.

Tail
Tail set not too high on the body, having a ring, or a curve on the end; should never be curled over, or rest on the back, or be carried sideways; and should never be bushy.

Legs
Forelegs are straight and strong with great length between elbow and pastern; elbows well held in; forefeet large in both length and width; toes well arched; feet covered with long thick hair; fine in texture; pasterns long and straight; pads of feet unusually large and well down on the ground. Shoulders have plenty of angulation so that the legs are well set underneath the dog. Too much straightness of shoulder causes the dog to break down in the pasterns, and this is a serious fault. All four feet of the Afghan Hound are in line with the body, turning neither in nor out. The hind feet are broad and of good

Height
Dogs, 27 inches, plus or minus one inch; bitches, 25 inches, plus or minus one inch.

Weight
Dogs, about 60 pounds; bitches, about 50 pounds.

Color
All colors are permissible, but color or color combinations are pleasing; white markings, especially on the head, are undesirable.

Gait
When running free, the Afghan Hound moves at a gallop, showing great elasticity and spring in his smooth, powerful stride. When on a loose lead, the Afghan can trot at a fast pace; stepping along, he has the appearance of placing the hind feet directly in the foot prints of the front feet, both thrown straight ahead. Moving with head and tail high, the whole appearance of the Afghan Hound is one of great style and beauty.

Temperament
Aloof and dignified, yet gay. *Faults:* sharpness or shyness.

Approved by the AKC 14 September 1948

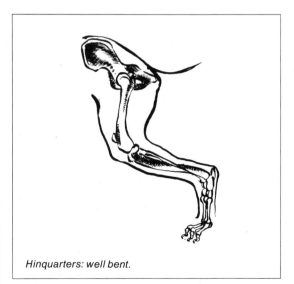

Hinquarters: well bent.

KC(GB) VARIATION TO STANDARD
Faults: weak underjaw. Skull too wide or foreface too short. Back too long or too short.

BASENJI

The prick-eared ring-tailed dogs so often depicted on friezes in ancient Egyptian tombs, have been claimed as the ancestors of a good many breeds, but the strongest claim almost certainly belongs to the Basenji, a breed of dog that has survived on the African continent. It was in the second half of the 19th century that these unusual native dogs began to be commented upon by explorers. They were unusual in that they were small, whereas most hunting dogs are large; that they were of a uniform colour, whilst most native dogs are so mixed that their colour varies considerably; and they did not bark, but merely made a low ululating noise unlike that of any other dog.

The Basenji was used by the natives of the Congo as a pack hunting dog, often wearing a bell to help in location, and controlled by a huntsman sometimes by voice, but even with a whistle in an almost European manner. The pack was used to drive game in to a net, and was so essential a part of the life of a tribe that the

NATIONAL GROUPING		
	Name	Number
AKC	Hound	II
KC(GB)	Hounds	I
FCI	Small Hounds	6

individual dogs were much prized and well cared for.

The first evidence of importation is in 1895 and one was first shown at Crufts in 1937 as an African Bush Dog or Congo Terrier. At the same time there was a pair in the Paris Zoo. Little further interest was displayed in the breed until six were imported but unfortunately failed to survive the effects of inoculation against distemper. The final efforts in the mid-thirties were more successful, and the breed became established from stock from Southern Sudan. The numbers have steadily increased since that time, and

the Basenji is now a popular little dog.

It combines the qualities of being attached to people and places, with many of the instincts of the hunting dog, and is appreciated by those who are enthusiastic about the breed as a good housedog.

Physically the animal is very attractive, being well-proportioned, having a pleasing expression, slightly quizzical because of the wrinkling between the ears, and with a short silky coat that is pleasant to the touch. It is a friendly dog, and centuries of attachment to the human race have given the Basenji an attitude towards people that is a strange mixture of self-confidence and dependence.

As a show dog the Basenji is much admired for its colour, the reds glowing in the sunlight and the parti-coloured being flashy and showy. It is, however, the showmanship of the dog that most appeals. He will stand like a statue for a considerable time in the ring, and when he moves he does so with all the athleticism of a much bigger dog, flowing round the ring with tremendous style and panache.

The personality of the Basenji is not the easiest to live with if you happen to be another dog. They are very good indeed with people, but have the ingrained habit of the pack dog of scrapping with one another. A pack needs a leader, and leadership is established only by individual combat between contenders. Once the pecking order has been established, and until such time as the leader grows weak or old and loses his place, then generally things are fairly settled. Those Basenji owners who have a number of dogs, either separate them, or allow them to establish their own pecking order.

OFFICIAL STANDARD

General appearance
The Basenji is a small, lightly built, short backed dog, giving the impression of being high on the leg compared to its length. The wrinkled head must be proudly carried, and the whole demeanor should be one of poise and alertness.

Characteristics
The Basenji should not bark, but is not mute. The wrinkled forehead and the swift, tireless running gait

Ears: small pointed erect.

(resembling a racehorse trotting full out) are typical of the breed.

Head and skull
The skull is flat, well chiseled and of medium width, tapering towards the eyes. The foreface should taper from eye to muzzle and should be shorter than the skull. Muzzle, neither coarse, nor snipy but with rounded cushions. Wrinkles should appear upon the forehead, and be fine and profuse. Side wrinkles are desirable, but should never be exaggerated into dewlap. *Nose:* black greatly desired. A pinkish tinge should penalize an otherwise first class specimen, but it should be discouraged in breeding. *Eyes:* dark hazel, almond shaped, obliquely set and far

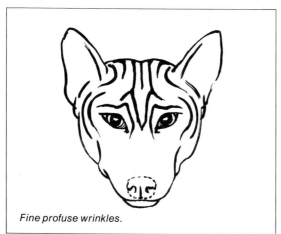

Fine profuse wrinkles.

seeing. *Ears:* small, pointed and erect, of fine texture, set well forward on top of head. *Mouth:* teeth must be level with scissors bite.

Neck
Of good length, well crested and slightly full at base of throat. It should be well set into flat, laid back shoulders.

Forequarters
The chest should be deep and of medium width. The legs straight with clean fine bone, long forearm and well defined sinews. Pasterns should be of good length, straight and flexible.

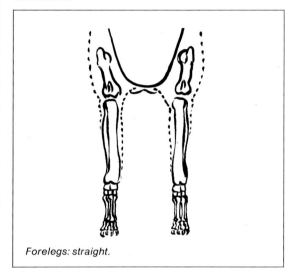

Forelegs: straight.

Body
The body should be short and the back level. The ribs well sprung, with plenty of heart room, deep brisket, short coupled, and ending in a definite waist.

Hindquarters
Should be strong and muscular, with hocks well let down, turned neither in nor out, with long second thighs.

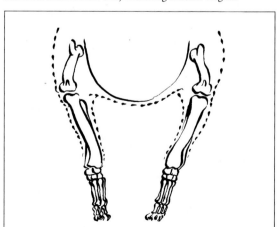

Faults: wide chest, out at elbows, short legs, toeing in.

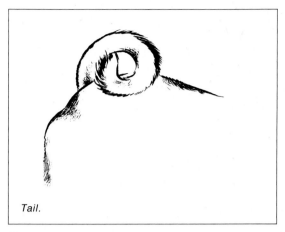

Tail.

Feet
Small, narrow and compact, with well-arched toes.

Tail
Should be set on top and curled tightly over to either side.

Coat
Short and silky. Skin very pliant.

Color
Chestnut red (the deeper the better) or pure black, or black and tan, all with white feet, chest and tail tip. White legs, white blaze and white collar optional.

Weight
Bitches 22 pounds approximately. Dogs 24 pounds approximately.

Size
Bitches 16 inches and dogs 17 inches from the ground to the top of the shoulder. Bitches 16 inches and dogs 17 inches from the front of the chest to the farthest point of the hindquarters.

FAULTS

Coarse skull or muzzle. Domed or peaked skull. Dewlap. Round eyes. Low set ears. Overshot or undershot mouths. Wide chest. Wide behind. Heavy bone. Creams, shaded or off colors, other than those defined above, should be heavily penalized.

Approved by the AKC 8 June 1954

KC(GB) VARIATION TO STANDARD
Feet: deep pads, short nails. *Tail:* should be set high with a posterior curve of buttock extending beyond root of tail giving reachy appearance to hindquarters. Tail curls tightly over spine and lies closely to thigh with single or double curl. *Weight:* bitches 21 pounds. *Faults:* cheekiness; light eyes; ears too large. Barrel ribs; shelly brisket. Short in leg; out at elbow; toeing in. Cowhocks; low set or straight tail; thin flat open feet; long or heavy coat. Poor temperament.

BASSET HOUND

Prior to the Revolution in France, hunting was an elaborate business, almost a ritual. There were a number of scent Hounds that were regularly hunted in packs by the nobles, and the breeding was as carefully carried out as any modern breeding plan. During the Revolution, hunting was neglected and the packs were dispersed along with the possessions and wealth of the court, and they came into the hands of peasants who used them to help support their families by adding game to a fairly sparse diet.

After the Revolution interest in hunting was revived, but in a different form and using firearms rather than the purer method of merely running the game down. The less wealthy took to hunting on foot and for this purpose they needed a slower dog, still with a wonderful nose, heavy and strong to cope with the conditions under which they worked, but with shorter legs than the traditional pack Hounds of the past. For this purpose the Basset Hound was developed.

Four different versions of the short-legged Hound were produced, the Basset Artésien Normand, the Basset Bleu de Gascogne, the Basset Griffon Vendéen and the Basset Fauve de Bretagne. The Artésien Normand was the one that most nearly resembled the Basset Hound as we know it today throughout the world, being smooth-coated, somewhat similar in head, and roughly the same size and proportions. Everett Millais is presumed by many to be the 'father'

of the modern Basset Hound, as it was he who claimed to have made the first importation from France, though this has been disputed. Certainly he was showing his famous dog 'Model' in 1875, and was deeply involved in early breeding experiments.

Unfortunately numbers in the early days were small, and some of the stock became very inbred and weak until further importations were made. Since those early days the breed has gone from strength to strength, and as the result of tremendous publicity it is one of the most popular breeds of the Hound Group. This is not surprising as the Basset has a most appealing personality, and not just because of his somewhat unusual appearance. He is a sturdy representative of the race, is as friendly as almost all scent-hunting Hounds are, and exceptionally good with children.

He is somewhat wilful, and difficult. He has remarkable scenting powers, will follow a trail that is hours old, and as a result, so thoroughly enjoys what he considers to be his purpose in life that he tends to forget that civilisation has caught up with him and that he is supposed to be an obedient family dog. He makes a first class house dog providing that he can get enough exercise to keep down his weight.

As a show dog the Basset has reached heights that would not at one time have been considered possible. Registration figures have climbed in most countries and there are few climates from temperate North America to tropical Ceylon where this magnificent Hound does not flourish, and where, from time to time, he does not command attention and respect in the show ring. He is amenable, behaves well, and his noble head and distinctive tail carriage always create a favourable impression in competition with other breeds.

OFFICIAL STANDARD

General appearance

The Bassett Hound possesses in marked degree those characteristics which equip it admirably to follow a trail over and through difficult terrain. It is a short-legged dog, heavier in bone, size considered, than any other breed of dog, and while its movement is deliberate, it is in no sense clumsy. In temperament it is mild, never sharp or timid. It is capable of great endurance in the field and is extreme in its devotion.

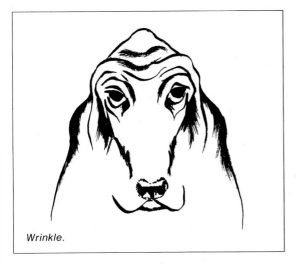

Wrinkle.

Head

The head is large and well proportioned. Its length from occiput to muzzle is greater than the width at the brow. In over-all appearance the head is of medium width. The *skull* is well domed, showing a pronounced occipital protuberance. A broad flat skull is a fault. The length from nose to stop is approximately the length from stop to occiput. The sides are flat and free from cheek bumps. Viewed in profile the top lines of the muzzle and skull are straight and lie in parallel planes, with a moderately defined stop. The skin over the whole of the head is loose, falling in distinct wrinkles over the brow when

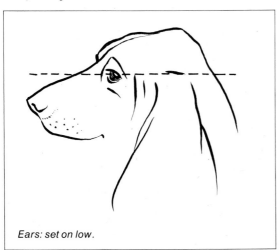

Ears: set on low.

the head is lowered. A dry head and tight skin are faults. The *muzzle* is deep, heavy, and free from snipiness. The *nose* is darkly pigmented, preferably black, with large wide-open nostrils. A deep liver-colored nose conforming to the coloring of the head is permissible but not desirable. The *teeth* are large, sound, and regular, meeting in either a scissors or an even bite. A bite either overshot or undershot is a serious fault. The *lips* are darkly pigmented and are pendulous, falling squarely in front and, toward the back, in loose hanging flews. The *dewlap* is very pronounced. The *neck* is powerful, of good length, and well arched. The *eyes* are soft, sad, and slightly sunken, showing a prominent haw, and in color are brown, dark brown preferred. A somewhat lighter-colored eye conforming to the general coloring of the dog is acceptable but not desirable. Very light or protruding eyes are faults. The *ears* are extremely long, low set, and when drawn forward, fold well over the end of the nose. They are velvety in texture, hanging in loose folds with the ends curling slightly inward. They are set far back on the head at the base of the skull and, in repose, appear to be set on the neck. A high set or flat ear is a serious fault.

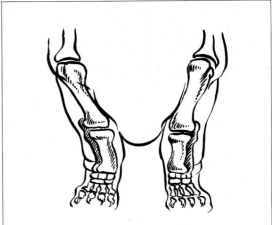

Forelegs: short, powerful and with great bone.

Forequarters

The *chest* is deep and full with prominent sternum showing clearly in front of the legs. The *shoulders* and elbows are set close against the sides of the chest. The distance from the deepest point of the chest to the ground, while it must be adequate to allow free movement when working in the field, is not to be more than one-third the total height at the withers of an adult Basset. The shoulders are well laid back and powerful. Steepness in shoulder, fiddle fronts, and elbows that are out, are serious faults. The *forelegs* are short, powerful, heavy in bone, with wrinkled skin. Knuckling over of the front legs is a diqualification. The *paw* is massive, very heavy with tough heavy pads, well rounded and with both feet inclined equally a trifle outward, balancing the width of the shoulders. Feet down at the pastern are a serious fault. The *toes* are neither pinched together nor splayed, with the weight of the forepart of the body borne evenly on each. The dew-claws may be removed.

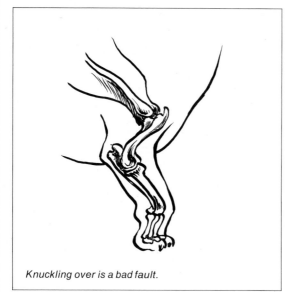

Knuckling over is a bad fault.

Body
The rib structure is long, smooth, and extends well back. The ribs are well sprung, allowing adequate room for heart and lungs. Flatsidedness and flanged ribs are faults. The topline is straight, level, and free from any tendency to sag or roach, which are faults.

Hindquarters
The hindquarters are very full and well rounded, and are approximately equal to the shoulders in width. They must not appear slack or light in relation to the over-all depth of the body. The dog stands firmly on its hind legs showing a well-let-down stifle with no tendency toward a crouching stance. Viewed from behind, the hind legs are parallel, with the hocks turning neither in nor out. Cowhocks or bowed legs are serious faults. The hind feet point straight ahead. Steep, poorly angulated hindquarters are a serious fault. The dewclaws, if any, may be removed.

Tail
The tail is not to be docked, and is set in continuation of the spine with but slight curvature, and carried gaily in hound fashion. The hair on the underside of the tail is coarse.

Size
The height should not exceed 14 inches. Height over 15 inches at the highest point of the shoulder blades is a disqualification.

Gait
The Basset Hound moves in a smooth, powerful, and effortless manner. Being a scenting dog with short legs, it holds its nose low to the ground. Its gait is absolutely true with perfect co-ordination between the front and hind legs, and it moves in a straight line with hind feet following in line with the front feet, the hocks well bent with no stiffness of action. The front legs do not paddle, weave, or overlap, and the elbows must lie close to the body. Going away, the hind legs are parallel.

Coat
The coat is hard, smooth, and short, with sufficient density to be of use in all weather. The skin is loose and elastic. A distinctly long coat is a disqualification.

Color
Any recognized hound color is acceptable and the distribution of color and markings is of no importance.

DISQUALIFICATIONS
Height of more than 15 inches at the highest point of the shoulder blades. Knuckled over front legs. Distinctly long coat.

Approved by the AKC 14 January 1964

KC(GB) VARIATION TO STANDARD
Feet: well knuckled up. *Tail:* is never curling or gay. *Height:* 13 to 15 inches. *Faults:* lack of balance (undue exaggeration of any point). Lack of typical Basset appearance.

BEAGLE

NATIONAL GROUPING		
	Name	Number
AKC	Hounds	II
KC(GB)	Hound	I
FCI	Small Hounds	6

The highly organised hunt on horseback with large packs of Hounds and a number of hunt staff has become a regional feature of many countries, and being centred around large estates and country houses carried great social weight. However, a need was found for the smaller organisation, attached to schools and colleges or army regiments, which did not have the staff, accommodation or financial resources to maintain a large pack.

The Beagle filled this purpose admirably, and since the 16th century packs of these smaller Hounds have been in existence. They probably started out as small Foxhounds or Harriers, and it is likely that Terrier and even Spaniel blood was introduced to decrease the size whilst retaining the spirit and scenting powers of the larger Hounds. What was wanted was a smaller Hound, shorter in the leg, but not so cumbersome as the Basset, light, easily housed, and not with the rather voracious appetite of the Foxhound. The result is that a very popular small dog has been produced, but that a sport has survived which might otherwise have disappeared.

There are many Beagle packs throughout the world, and every country that enjoys the sport, has organisations to control hunting interests. Associations of Masters of Harriers and Beagles in Great Britain and Ireland, the National Beagle Club of the United States of America are typical examples, and the sport is well established even though it has achieved less publicity than foxhunting.

The breeding of the Beagle down to size continued until a race of Hounds that were under ten inches high at the shoulder became fixed, bred true to type and size, and became known as the Pocket Beagle. This very small Hound was popular up to the First World War, and was exhibited and hunted. They seem to have disappeared after that, though an attempt is being made to reintroduce them.

There was also at one time a rough or hard-coated variety. The rough-coat seems to have disappeared in favour of the popular smooth-coat of today's Hounds.

The popularity of the Beagle as a show dog has become such that in most countries it vies with the most numerous of the Hound Group. It was for a while, the most popular show dog in the United States of America. There are few more attractive sights than a ring full of these small Hounds, all behaving beautifully, and in their rich variety of colours. The Beagle is easily handled even by the youngest child, and is a great favourite with children in the children's handling classes.

The Beagle is a most attractive dog, completely friendly, very attached to particular members of the family, and wonderfully playful. He is, however, somewhat wilful, like so many of the Hounds, and will from time to time go off on his own business from which it is difficult to divert him. One of the most humorous of sights is an owner trying to attract the attention of his Beagle which is fast disappearing, nose in the air, and apparently completely oblivious to all blandishments.

OFFICIAL STANDARD

General appearance
A miniature Foxhound, solid and big for his inches, with the wear-and-tear look of the hound that can last in the chase and follow his quarry to the death.

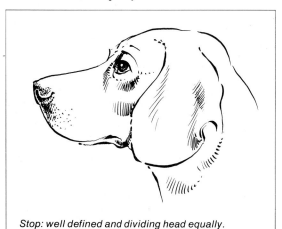

Stop: well defined and dividing head equally.

Head
The skull should be fairly long, slightly domed at occiput, with cranium broad and full. *Ears:* ears set on moderately low, long, reaching when drawn out nearly, if not quite, to the end of the nose; fine in texture, fairly broad—with almost entire absence of erectile power—setting close to the head, with the forward edge slightly inturning to the

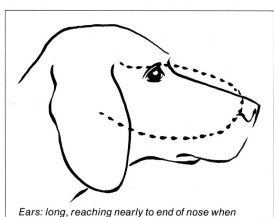

Ears: long, reaching nearly to end of nose when drawn out.

cheek—rounded at tip. *Eyes:* eyes large, set well apart—soft and houndlike—expression gentle and pleading; of a brown or hazel color. *Muzzle:* muzzle of medium length—straight and square-cut—the stop moderately defined. *Jaws:* level. Lips free from flews; nostrils large and open. *Defects:* a very flat skull, narrow across the top; excess of dome, eyes small, sharp and terrierlike, or prominent and protruding; muzzle long, snipy or cut away decidedly below the eyes, or very short. Roman-nosed, or upturned, giving a dish-face expression. Ears short, set on high or with a tendency to rise above the point of origin.

Body
Neck and throat—neck rising free and light from the shoulders strong in substance yet not loaded, of medium length. The throat clean and free from folds of skin; a slight wrinkle below the angle of the jaw, however, may be allowable. *Defects:* a thick, short, cloddy neck carried on a line with the top of the shoulders. Throat showing dewlap and folds of skin to a degree termed 'throatiness'.

Shoulders and chest
Shoulders sloping—clean, muscular, not heavy or loaded—conveying the idea of freedom of action with activity and strength. Chest deep and broad, but not broad enough to interfere with the free play of the shoulders. *Defects:* straight, upright shoulders. Chest disproportionately wide or with lack of depth.

Back, loin and ribs
Back short, muscular and strong. Loin broad and slightly arched, and the ribs well sprung, giving abundance of lung room. *Defects:* very long or swayed or roached back. Flat, narrow loin. Flat ribs.

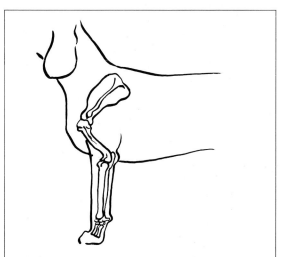

Forelegs: well under, height to elbow half height to withers.

Forelegs and feet
Forelegs: straight, with plenty of bone in proportion to size of the hound. Pasterns short and straight. *Feet:* close, round and firm. Pad full and hard. *Defects:* out at elbows. Knees knuckled over forward, or bent backward. Forelegs crooked or Dachshundlike. Feet long, open or spreading.

Hips, thighs, hind legs and feet
Hips and thighs strong and well muscled, giving abundance of propelling power. Stifles strong and well let down. Hocks firm, symmetrical and moderately bent. Feet close and firm. *Defects:* cowhocks, or straight hocks. Lack of muscle and propelling power. Open feet.

Tail
Set moderately high; carried gaily, but not turned for-

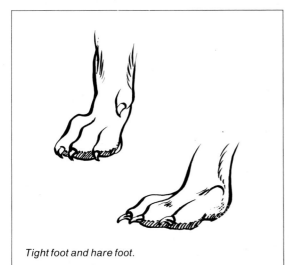

Tight foot and hare foot.

ward over the back; with slight curve; short as compared with size of the hound; with brush. *Defects:* A long tail. Teapot curve or inclined forward from the root. Rat tail with the absence of brush.

Coat

A close, hard, hound coat of medium length. *Defects:* a short, thin coat, or of a soft quality.

Color

Any true hound color.

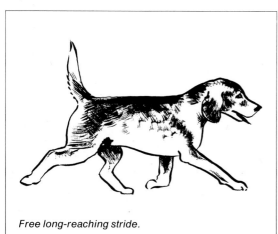

Free long-reaching stride.

Varieties

There shall be two varieties: thirteen inch—which shall be for hounds not exceeding 13 inches in height. Fifteen inch—which shall be for hounds over 13 but not exceeding 15 inches in height.

DISQUALIFICATION

Any hound measuring more than 15 inches shall be disqualified.

Packs of Beagles

Levelness of pack: The first thing in a pack to be considered is that they present a unified appearance. The hounds must be as near to the same height, weight, conformation and color as possible.

Individual merit of the hounds: is the individual bench-show quality of the hounds. A very level and sporty pack can be gotten together and not a single hound be a good Beagle. This is to be avoided.

Manners: The hounds must all work gaily and cheerfully, with flags up—obeying all commands cheerfully. They should be broken to heel up, kennel up, follow promptly and stand. Cringing, sulking, lying down to be avoided. Also, a pack must not work as though in terror of master and whips. In Beagle packs it is recommended that the whip be used as little as possible.

Appointments: master and whips should be dressed alike, the master or huntsman to carry horn—the whips and master to carry light thong whips. One whip should carry extra couplings on shoulder strap.

RECOMMENDATIONS FOR SHOW LIVERY

Black velvet cap, white stock, green coat, white breeches or knickerbockers, green or black stockings, white spats, black or dark brown shoes. Vest and gloves optional. Ladies should turn out exactly the same except for a white skirt instead of white breeches.

Approved by the AKC 10 September 1957

SCALE OF POINTS

Head (25): skull 5, ears 10, eyes 5, muzzle 5. *Body (35):* neck 5, chest and shoulders 15, back, loin and ribs 15. *Running Gear (40):* forelegs 10, hips, thighs and hind legs 10, feet 10, coat 5, stern 5. *Total (100).*

Packs of Beagles

SCORE OF POINTS FOR JUDGING

Hounds: general levelness of pack 40, individual merit of hounds 30, manners 20, appointments 10. *Total (100).*

KC(GB) VARIATION TO STANDARD

Head: stop well defined and dividing length between occiput and tip of nose as equally as possible. Lips well flewed. Teeth strongly developed. Scissor bite. *Forelegs:* height to elbow about half hound's height at withers. *Feet:* well knuckled up. Not hare-footed. Nails short. *Colour:* not liver. Tip of stern white. *Height:* 13 to 16 inches from ground to withers.

BLACK AND TAN COONHOUND

NATIONAL GROUPING		
	Name	Number
AKC	Hounds	II
KC(GB)	—	–
FCI	—	–

The Black and Tan Coonhound, which is peculiar to the United States of America, is one of the newest breeds to be admitted to the American Kennel Club register, only in fact in 1945. It is, however, not only a much older breed than that in America, but is also considerably older in ancestry. It has been suggested that it descends from the Talbot of Britain, through the Bloodhound and Foxhound, but there are other possibilities. The Kerry Beagle is one, as there was certainly some importation of dogs from Ireland into the United States of America, and the small Foxhound of the Ring of Kerry could well lay claim, as it is essentially black and tan. There are breeds in France too, and even in Sweden, where the Hamiltonstövare could have played some part in the early formation of the Coonhound. There were other Coonhounds that were not black and tan, but that particular colour belongs to the line which proved most proficient at the task of hunting the raccoon and the opossum, with the result that the other colours have remained in the background.

The Coonhound is no mere hunting dog in that although he will trail by scent more normal game, he has been specifically bred to hunt the raccoon and opossum which are climbing animals. He has been trained over the years to trail these animals, often by night, as they are both nocturnal in their habits and, when he finally gets them treed, to give voice until the huntsman comes along and dispatches the quarry. Raccoon and opossum hunting is a highly organised sport in the United States of America and Canada, with much of the planning of the activity being in the hands of the United Kennel Club of America rather than the American Kennel Club. The UKCA began the registration of the various types of Coonhounds much earlier than the date of acceptance of the Black and Tan Coonhound by the American Kennel Club,

and hundreds of licensed hunting trials take place annually. The United Kennel Club also holds shows of these hunting dogs in much the same way as the various hunts in Britain hold Hound and Terrier shows in many parts of the country.

The various types of Coonhound resemble breeds of dogs in other countries and it is easy to tell from where they stemmed. The Bluetick, for instance, resembles the Grand Bleu de Gascogne from France, and the Redbone is very close to the red Bloodhound.

The Black and Tan is a powerful, agile and alert dog, with an aggressive and eager expression. Emphasis has at all times been placed on his working qualities even when he is appearing on the show bench. His movement is one of his strong points. He has been evolved to cover the ground very fast even during the hours of darkness, so that he needs a long, powerful rhythmic stride. Black and Tans need, and indeed enjoy a great deal of exercise, and like most of the scent hunting dogs they have a friendly attitude towards humans.

OFFICIAL STANDARD

General appearance

The Black and Tan Coonhound is first and fundamentally a working dog, capable of withstanding the rigors of winter, the heat of summer, and the difficult terrain over which he is called upon to work. Judges are asked by the club sponsoring the breed to place great emphasis upon these facts when evaluating the merits of the dog. The general impression should be that of power, agility, and alertness. His expression should be alert, friendly, eager, and aggressive. He should immediately impress one with his ability to cover the ground with powerful rhythmic strides.

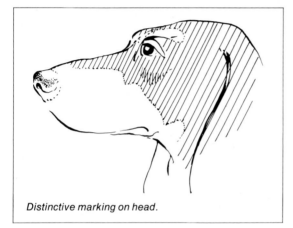

Distinctive marking on head.

Head

The head should be cleanly modeled, with medium stop occurring midway between occiput bone and nose. The head should measure from 9 to 10 inches in dogs and from 8 to 9 inches in bitches. Viewed from the profile, the line of the skull is on a practically parallel plane to the foreface or muzzle. The *skin* should be devoid of folds or excess dewlap. The *flews* should be well developed with typical hound appearance. *Nostrils* well open and always black. *Skull* should tend toward oval outline. *Eyes* should

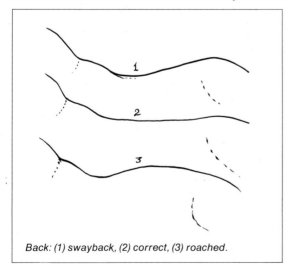

Back: (1) swayback, (2) correct, (3) roached.

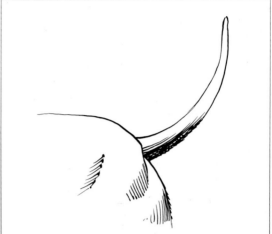

Tail: base below level of back line, carried free.

be from hazel to dark brown in color, almost round and not deeply set. The *ears* should be low set and well back. They should hang in graceful folds giving the dog a majestic appearance. In length they should extend well beyond the tip of the nose. *Teeth* should fit evenly with slightly scissors bite.

Body

Neck, shoulders, and *chest:* the neck should be muscular, sloping, medium length, extending into powerfully

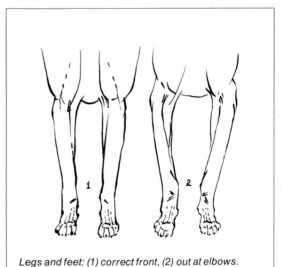

Legs and feet: (1) correct front, (2) out at elbows.

constructed shoulders and deep chest. The dog should possess full, round, well-sprung ribs, avoiding flat-sidedness. *Back and tail:* the back should be level, powerful and strong, with a visible slope from withers to rump. Tail should be strong, with base slightly below level of back line, carried free, and when in action at approximately right angles to back. *Legs and feet:* the forelegs should be straight, with elbows well let down, turning neither in nor out; pasterns strong and erect. Feet should be catlike with compact, well-arched toes and thick strong pads. *Hindquarters:* quarters should be well boned and muscled. From hip to hock long and sinewy, hock to pad short and strong. Stifles and hock well bent and not inclining either in or out. When standing on a level surface the hind feet should set back from under the body, and leg from pad to hock be at right angles to the ground when viewed both from profile and the rear. The stride of the Black and Tan Coonhound should be easy and graceful with plenty of reach in front and drive behind.

Coat and color
The coat should be short but dense to withstand rough going. As the name implies, the color should be coal black, with rich tan markings above eyes, on sides of muzzle, chest, legs and breeching with black pencil markings on toes.

Size
Measured at the shoulder: dogs, 25 to 27 inches; bitches, 23 to 25 inches. Height should be in proportion to general conformation so that dog appears neither leggy nor close to the ground. Dogs oversized should not be penalized when general soundness and proportion are in favor.

Judges should penalize the following defects:
Undersize, elbows out at shoulder, lack of angulation in hindquarters, splay feet, sway- or roach back, flatsidedness, lack of depth in chest, yellow or light eyes, shyness and nervousness.

Faults
Dewclaws; white on chest or other parts of body is highly undesirable and if it exceeds $1\frac{1}{2}$ inches in diameter should be disqualified.

DISQUALIFICATION
White on chest or other parts of the body if it exceeds $1\frac{1}{2}$ inches in diameter.

Approved by the AKC 10 July 1945

KC(GB) VARIATION TO STANDARD
This dog is not granted championship status by the KC(GB).

BLOODHOUND

The Bloodhound is an excellent example of mankind's persistence in the search for perfection. Competition between the big estates or the courts of many countries as to who could produce the Hound that could follow the longest or the oldest trail has always been keen. In this work the Bloodhound is supreme, being capable of following a scent for long distances, even when that scent has been laid days before.

The Bloodhound undoubtedly owes its origins to France, along with so many of the scent hunting breeds. The most popular theory is that his ancestor was the St. Hubert Hound, an all black breed supposed to have been brought from the Holy Land, though this, like the reputation that the breed gained at one time for its fierceness, is probably a myth. The fact remains that in France the Bloodhound as we know it is still known as the Chien de Saint Hubert.

Owing to the use of the Bloodhound in the fiction of the early part of this century, the dog gained an evil reputation which was ill-fitted to it, as it is the most friendly of creatures. Its association with the capture

NATIONAL GROUPING		
	Name	Number
AKC	Hounds	II
KC(GB)	Hound	I
FCI	Large Hounds	5

of runaway slaves and the putting down of uprisings with the cruelty involved, did not help the Bloodhound's reputation. The hound has been used extensively for tracking possible criminals, and is still called upon by police forces for that purpose from time to time. The fact remains, however, that when the quarry is finally apprehended, the Bloodhound is more likely to lick him than devour him as some novelists would have had us believe.

The Bloodhound is the biggest and the strongest of the scent hunting Hounds, and when on a trail, it needs a very fit person at the other end of a long leash to keep pace with him. He is forceful and positive when tracking, and it takes a great deal to break him off his intended course. His scenting powers are formidable, and this trait is used by owners who run trials for the breed in competition with one another in order to retain this essential quality.

As a showdog the Bloodhound has not achieved a great deal of popularity, as he is a big dog that is not easily transported in numbers to a show, is heavy and not easily handled. One needs to be something of an enthusiast to enjoy showing the breed. In the ring however he is a noble dog, upstanding when he is behaving. He moves up and down the ring with a long,

loose, swinging stride that is very deceptive in the manner with which it covers the ground at a remarkable speed.

The Bloodhound is one of the most friendly dogs, wonderful with children on which it tends to fawn, sometimes to the embarrassment of the child, for a kiss from a Bloodhound can be a damp affair. For his size he has a moderate appetite, and is not difficult to feed, though he needs more than average care to keep him in good health, and more exercise than some people are prepared to take themselves.

OFFICIAL STANDARD

General appearance
The Bloodhound possesses, in a most marked degree, every point and characteristic of those dogs which hunt together by scent (Sagaces). He is very powerful, and stands over more ground than is usual with hounds of other breeds. The skin is thin to the touch and extremely loose, this being more especially noticeable about the head and neck, where it hangs in deep folds.

Height
The mean average height of adult dogs is 26 inches, and of adult bitches 24 inches. Dogs usually vary from 25 to 27 inches, and bitches from 23 to 25 inches; but, in either case, the greater height is to be preferred, provided that character and quality are also combined.

Weight
The mean average weight of adult dogs, in fair condition, is 90 pounds, and of adult bitches 80 pounds. Dogs attain the weight of 110 pounds, bitches 100 pounds. The greater weights are to be preferred, provided (as in the case of height) that quality and proportion are also combined.

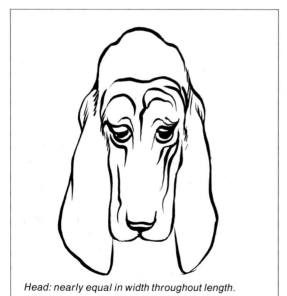
Head: nearly equal in width throughout length.

Expression
The expression is noble and dignified, and characterized by solemnity, wisdom, and power.

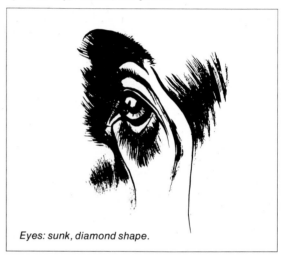
Eyes: sunk, diamond shape.

Temperament
In temperament he is extremely affectionate, neither quarrelsome with companions nor with other dogs. His nature is somewhat shy, and equally sensitive to kindness or correction by his master.

Head
The head is narrow in proportion to its length, and long in proportion to the body, tapering but slightly from the temples to the end of the muzzle, thus (when viewed from above and in front) having the appearance of being flattened at the sides and of being nearly equal in width throughout its entire length. In profile the upper outline of the skull is nearly in the same plane as that of the foreface. The length from end of nose to stop (midway between the eyes) should be not less than that from stop to back of occipital protuberance (peak). The entire length of head from the posterior part of the occipital protuberance to the end of the muzzle should be 12 inches, or more, in dogs, and 11 inches, or more, in bitches. *Skull:* the skull is long and narrow, with the occipital peak very pronounced. The brows are not prominent, although, owing to the deep-set eyes, they may have that appearance. *Foreface:* the foreface is long, deep, and of even width throughout, with square outline

Ears: lower part curling inwards and backwards.

when seen in profile. *Eyes:* the eyes are deeply sunk in the orbits, the lids assuming a lozenge or diamond shape, in consequence of the lower lids being dragged down and everted by the heavy flews. The eyes correspond with the general tone of color of the animal, varying from deep hazel to yellow. The hazel color is, however, to be preferred, although very seldom seen in red-and-tan hounds. *Ears:* the ears are thin and soft to the touch, extremely long, set very low, and fall in graceful folds, the lower parts curling inward and backward. *Wrinkle:* the head is furnished with an amount of loose skin, which in nearly every position appears superabundant, but more particularly so when the head is carried low; the skin then falls into loose, pendulous ridges and folds, especially over the forehead and sides of the face. *Nostrils:* the nostrils are large and open. *Lips, flews and dewlap:* in front the lips fall squarely, making a right angle with the

Furnished with loose skin.

upper line of the foreface; whilst behind they form deep, hanging flews, and, being continued into the pendant folds of loose skin about the neck, constitute the dewlap, which is very pronounced. These characters are found, though in a less degree, in the bitch.

Neck, shoulders and chest
The neck is long, the shoulders muscular and well sloped backwards; the ribs are well sprung; and the chest well let down between the forelegs, forming a deep keel.

Legs and feet
The forelegs are straight and large in bone, with elbows squarely set; the feet strong and well knuckled up; the thighs and second thighs (gaskins) are very muscular; the hocks well bent and let down and squarely set.

Back and loin
The back and loins are strong, the latter deep and slightly

Tail: carried scimitar fashion.

arched. *Stern:* the stern is long and tapering, and set on rather high, with a moderate amount of hair underneath.

Gait
The gait is elastic, swinging and free, the stern being carried high, but not too much curled over the back.

Color
The colors are black and tan, red and tan, and tawny; the darker colors being sometimes interspersed with lighter or badger-colored hair, and sometimes flecked with white. A small amount of white is permissible on chest, feet, and tip of stern.

KC(GB) VARIATION TO STANDARD
Eyes: Free from interference from eyelashes.

BORZOI

NATIONAL GROUPING		
	Name	Number
AKC	Hounds	II
KC(GB)	Hound	I
FCI	Coursing Dogs	10

There are breeds of dog that hunt in packs and follow the quarry by sight rather than by scent, in fact in some countries the whole group is known as the Sight Hounds. These breeds are usually distinguishable by their length of leg and neck and their greater elegance. In some countries the courts preferred this type of hunting as it was more spectacular than scent hunting where the pack, the quarry and the kill were often out of sight of the followers. The coursing hounds provided a view from sighting to kill that had all the elements of speed, colour and tragedy that give spice and excitement to the sport.

The Emperors of Russia developed in the Borzoi the most glamorous of all the sight hounds, though owners of other running dogs will disagree. They are the tallest, the most slender and graceful and among the most colourful of the Levriers. Known at one time as the Russian Wolfhound, they were bred in packs with different characteristics, much as Foxhounds were bred elsewhere, but in the present-day Borzoi these differences have disappeared. Some of the old stories about the fierceness and untrustworthiness of the Borzoi that emanated from Russia did little to increase the popularity of the breed.

The first Borzoi specimens appeared in the show rings outside Russia in the late 19th century and created something of a sensation, particularly as shortly afterwards a number were presented by the then Czar to Queen Alexandra. As always when any royal household takes an interest in a breed, a degree of popular enthusiasm follows. This graceful hound quickly gained favour, and was soon seen at most of the major shows in both the United States of America and in Great Britain.

The Borzoi as we know it today might be claimed, by those who favour the Greyhound for coursing, to be too narrow in front to carry out the work for which it was originally intended, but that is one of the penalties paid by a breed when it becomes fashionable. The modern Borzoi can run, as it has proved when it has been tried on the running track and in pursuit of the live hare, but it would not compare for toughness with its ancestors that ran wild wolves to ground.

As a show dog this magnificent hound has few peers. Its long silky, often wavy or curly coat repays attention more than does that of other breeds, and as white often predominates, the total effect is most striking. Add to that the fact that it is often the tallest hound in the ring, and almost certainly one of the most graceful, and we have a dog that immediately commands attention both among dog people and the general public. The Borzoi is one of the most graceful of movers in the show ring, carrying himself with great pride, and using his hind legs with a slightly mincing gait.

A Borzoi is far from being the perfect house pet. It is true that one will look most decorative lying on a Turkish rug in front of an Adam fireplace, but the same dog would be completely out of place in a small modern apartment. He needs a good deal of exercise to keep him fit, and that exercise must include a certain amount of free running and playing. Without this, a Borzoi becomes unfit, probably overweight, and grows somewhat neurotic and unhappy.

OFFICIAL STANDARD

General appearance
The Borzoi was originally bred for the coursing of wild game on more or less open terrain, relying on sight rather than scent. To accomplish this purpose, the Borzoi needed particular structural qualities to chase, catch and hold his quarry. Special emphasis is placed on sound running gear, strong neck and jaws, courage and agility, combined with proper condition. The Borzoi should always possess unmistakable elegance, with flowing lines, graceful in motion or repose. Dogs, masculine without coarseness; bitches, feminine and refined.

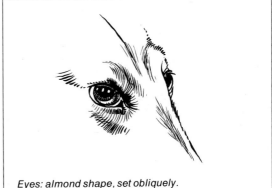

Eyes: almond shape, set obliquely.

Neck
Clean, free from throatiness; slightly arched, very powerful and well set on.

Shoulders
Sloping, fine at the withers and free from coarseness or lumber.

Chest
Rather narrow, with great depth of brisket.

Ribs
Only slightly sprung, but very deep, giving room for heart and lung play.

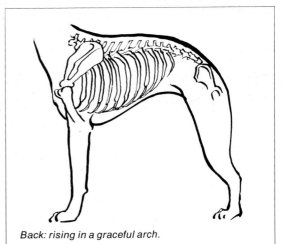

Back: rising in a graceful arch.

Head
Skull slightly domed, long and narrow, with scarcely any perceptible stop, inclined to be Roman-nosed. Jaws long, powerful and deep, somewhat finer in bitches but not snipy. Teeth strong and clean with either an even or a scissors bite. Missing teeth should be penalized. Nose large and black.

Ears
Small and fine in quality, lying back on the neck when in respose with the tips when thrown back almost touching behind occiput; raised when at attention.

Eyes
Set somewhat obliquely, dark in color, intelligent but rather soft in expression; never round, full nor staring, nor light in color; eye rims dark; inner corner midway between tip of nose and occiput.

Back
Rising a little at the loins in a graceful curve.

Loins
Extremely muscular, but rather tucked up, owing to the great depth of chest and comparative shortness of back and ribs.

Forelegs
Bones straight and somewhat flattened like blades, with the narrower edge forward. The elbows have free play and are turned neither in nor out. Pasterns strong.

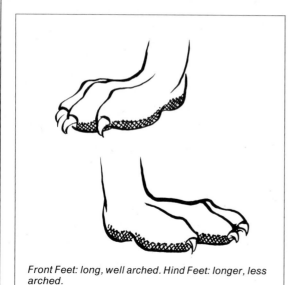

Front Feet: long, well arched. Hind Feet: longer, less arched.

Feet

Hare-shaped, with well-arched knuckles, toes close and well padded.

Hindquarters

Long, very muscular and powerful with well bent stifles; somewhat wider than the forequarters; strong first and second thighs; hocks clean and well let down; legs parallel when viewed from the rear.

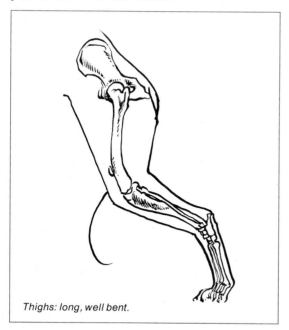

Thighs: long, well bent.

Dewclaws

Dewclaws, if any, on the hind legs are generally removed; dewclaws on the forelegs may be removed.

Tail

Long, set on and carried low in a graceful curve.

Coat

Long, silky (not woolly), either flat, wavy or rather curly. On the head, ears and front of legs it should be short and smooth; on the neck the frill should be profuse and rather curly. Feather on hindquarters and tail, long and profuse, less so on chest and back of forelegs.

Color

Any color, or combination of colors, is acceptable.

Size

Mature dogs should be at least 28 inches at the withers and mature bitches at least 26 inches at the withers. Dogs and bitches below these respective limits should be severely penalized; dogs and bitches above the respective limits should not be penalized as long as extra size is not acquired at the expense of symmetry, speed and staying quality. Range in weight for dogs from 75 to 105 pounds and for bitches from 15 to 20 pounds less.

Gait

Front legs must reach well out in front with pasterns strong and springy. Hackneyed motion with mincing gait is not desired nor is weaving and crossing. However, while the hind legs are wider apart than the front, the feet tend to move closer to the center line when the dog moves at a fast trot. When viewed from the side there should be a noticeable drive with a ground-covering stride from well-angulated stifles and hocks. The over-all appearance in motion should be that of effortless power, endurance, speed, agility, smoothness and grace.

FAULTS

The foregoing description is that of the ideal Borzoi. Any deviation from the above described dog must be penalized to the extent of the deviation keeping in mind the importance of the contribution of the various features toward the basic original purpose of the breed.

Approved by the AKC 13 June 1972

KC(GB) VARIATION TO STANDARD

Nose: not pink or brown. *Mouth:* neither pig jawed nor undershot. *Body:* well sprung flexible ribs. *Feet:* hind-feet harelike. *Height:* dogs from 29 inches upwards; bitches from 27 inches at shoulder.

DACHSHUND

Smooth-haired Dachshund

The question of which variety of the Dachshund is the oldest and the original type is a matter of some discussion wherever Dachshund people get together. Each will claim the distinction for his own particular favourite, and there is some evidence to support all claims. In Germany, however, which is the native country of the breed, there is no doubt which is the most popular variety. The dogs most commonly seen on the streets of Germany are the Boxer, the German Shepherd Dog, the Doberman Pinscher and the Dachshund, and by far the largest proportion of these Smooth-haired Dachshunds.

The Dachshund, and at that time this meant the Smooth-haired Dachshund, became known outside Germany around the middle of the 19th century and soon attracted attention because of his somewhat quaint conformation and his sporting instincts. At that time other countries were accustomed to a dog of what were considered to be more 'normal' proportions. The Terriers and the Gundogs, and even the Toy Dogs were more or less square dogs. To other than German eyes the long bodied Dachshund appeared to be a very strange beast indeed. Nevertheless he

NATIONAL GROUPING		
	Name	Number
AKC	Hounds	II
KC(GB)	Hound	I
FCI	Dachshunds	4

soon became quite popular and his numbers increased as he won his way into the hearts of the dog-loving public of other countries.

During the First World War the Dachshund's popularity went into a decline as anti-German feeling grew, and this most attractive little dog was denigrated in cartoons, stories and even by catcalls in the streets. After the war, the Dachshund returned to popularity on a scale even greater than before, and by the 1950's he was among the most popular dogs in the world.

The Smooth-haired Dachshund has many advantages over other dogs. In the first place he combines the qualities of a hunting dog with those of a family pet and favourite. He is sporting and affectionate, cheerful and friendly yet very protective, and makes a magnificent house guard. Being a small dog he is easily housed and fed, though he is somewhat greedy

119

as a general rule, and with little exercise and feeding that is too rich, he can rapidly become overweight and suffer the spine trouble that affects the breed, and this variety particularly. Properly kept, fed and exercised he remains a very fit, active and sporting dog living to a good age in perfect health.

The show rings of the world have been enriched by the addition of the Dachshund, and of the Smooth-haired particularly, as he is an extremely graceful dog in spite of his lack of height, with a long neck, sweeping lines and proud carriage. His coat too helps, as the smooth quality repays attention, and this little dog can literally be polished to enter the ring. He needs no lotions or special preparations to give his coat this glow, if he is healthy, all that is needed is a good rubbing with a hound glove and he will shine like satin. His colours are attractive, the self-reds and black and tans particularly, and a ring full of Dachshunds in the sunshine is a delightful sight.

His temperament is most attractive. He becomes attached to one person or family very quickly, remains faithful and protective to the members of the family, and succeeds in being affectionate without fawning. Yet all the time he retains much of the instinct of a sporting dog and will enjoy a rabbit chase over the fields and through the thickest undergrowth.

Wirehaired Dachshund

At first sight there seemed to be no need for yet another variety of Dachshund, the smooth coated and the long coated varieties were already in existence, and in those countries outside Germany in two sizes. But they had snags. The smooth coated variety, which is presumed by many to be the earliest form, has a short dense and smooth coat. It is supposed at the same time to be strong, but proved insufficient protection when hunting through gorse and brambles. The longhaired variety on the other hand, whilst having more protection, did tend to lose coat, as do most of the long coated hunting dogs, when hunted through very rough

going. It was felt that an even stronger coated dog was needed, with a harsh outer coat as protection from damage, and a dense softer undercoat to keep out the weather. The heavy beard and longer coat around the head came as a bonus.

The first wirehaired versions appeared in Germany towards the end of the 19th century, and were almost certainly the result of crossing the smooth coated variety with one or other of the wirehaired dogs of Germany, probably the Schnauzer. This produced the coat, but increased the leg length so that further crosses were needed to bring this back down again without destroying the quality of the coat. The breed used could well have been the Czesky Terrier from Bohemia, itself a cross between Sealyham and Scottish Terriers, or the Dandie Dinmont. The variety was not known outside Germany until well into this century, but then it soon became quite popular through its ability to work, combined with its temperament which is very like that of the best of the hounds.

It is a keen little dog with an inbuilt desire to hunt, having good scenting powers, a certain obstinacy which gives it persistence, and great courage and stamina. It is a hardy dog, does not suffer from some of the ailments associated with other small varieties, and is a willing and obedient companion.

As a show dog he has never quite achieved the popularity of the other varieties, largely perhaps because of the variation in coat quality that occurred until recent years. The variety has always been fairly low down in the registration figures, but this may well change, as the type is now more fixed, and the inter-breeding that has gone on for a great number of years has now virtually ceased with the result that the overall appearance of the variety is more regular. One or two quite notable dogs that have won the highest honours,

OFFICIAL STANDARD

General appearance

Low to ground, short-legged, long-bodied, but with compact figure and robust muscular development; with bold and confident carriage of the head and intelligent facial expression. In spite of his shortness of leg, in comparison with his length of trunk, he should appear neither crippled, awkward, cramped in his capacity for movement, nor slim and weasel-like. He should be clever, lively, and courageous to the point of rashness, persevering in his work both above and below ground; with all the senses well developed. His build and disposition

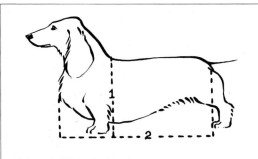

Height: half length of body.

qualify him especially for hunting game below ground. Added to this, his hunting spirit, good nose, loud tongue, and small size, render him especially suited for beating the bush. His figure and his fine nose give him an especial advantage over most other breeds of sporting dogs for trailing.

Head

Viewed from above or from the side, it should taper uniformly to the tip of the nose, and should be clean-cut. The skull is only slightly arched, and should slope gradually without stop (the less stop the more typical) into the finely-formed slightly-arched muzzle (ram's nose). The bridge bones over the eyes should be strongly prominent. The nasal cartilage and tip of the nose are long and narrow; lips tightly stretched, well covering the lower jaw, but neither deep nor pointed; corner of the mouth not very marked. Nostrils well open. Jaws opening wide and hinged

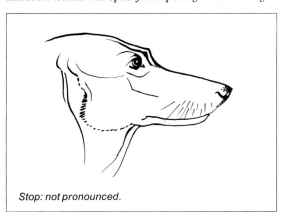

Stop: not pronounced.

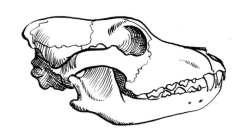

Mouth: extending back, teeth strong, lower teeth inside upper.

well back of the eyes, with strongly developed bones and teeth. *Teeth:* powerful canine teeth should fit closely together, and the outer side of the lower incisors should tightly touch the inner side of the upper. (Scissors bite.) *Eyes:* medium size, oval, situated at the sides, with a clean, energetic, though pleasant expression; not piercing. Color, lustrous dark reddish-brown to brownish-black for all coats and colors. Wall eyes in the case of dapple dogs are not a very bad fault, but are also not desirable. *Ears:* should be set near the top of the head, and not too far forward, long but not too long, beautifully rounded, not narrow, pointed, or folded. Their carriage should be animated, and the forward edge should just touch the cheek. *Neck:* fairly long, muscular, clean-cut, not showing any dewlap on the throat, slightly arched in the nape, extending in a graceful line into the shoulders, carried proudly but not stiffly.

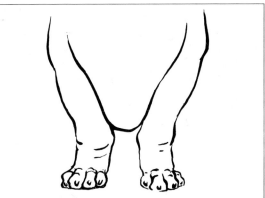

Lower arm: short, slightly inclined inwards.

Front

To endure the arduous exertion underground, the front must be correspondingly muscular, compact, deep, long and broad. Forequarters in detail: *Shoulder Blade:* long, broad, obliquely and firmly placed upon the fully developed thorax, furnished with hard and plastic muscles. *Upper Arm:* of the same length as the shoulder blade, and at right angles to the latter, strong of bone and hard of muscle, lying close to the ribs, capable of free movement. *Forearm:* this is short in comparison to other breeds, slightly turned inwards; supplied with hard but plastic muscles on the front and outside, with tightly stretched tendons on the inside and at the back. *Joint*

particularly in Britain, have kept interest in the dog alive.

As a house dog there can hardly be any breed of dog more attractive. He is small, compact, takes up very little space and is easy to feed. He is generally rather quiet and unobtrusive about the house. He has too a slightly quizzical expression which makes him attractive to those who like something a little different. He is, moreover, quick and alert as are many of the hounds, and makes an excellent guard and watchdog.

Longhaired Dachshund

There are almost as many styles of hunting with dogs as there are nations that hunt. Sport with dogs varies from laying a pack of hounds on a line to hunt in unison, to chasing one animal with one dog, and from coursing an antelope across the plains, to trying to catch rats under someone's garden shed. For every different form of the hunt, a different dog is needed. The dog that can catch a deer has legs that are too long to allow it to go underground, and a dog that has been built to travel slowly across the fields is incapable of catching a hare.

The forests of Germany have for centuries been the haunt of badgers and foxes, and as the country is completely unsuitable for running these animals down on horseback, some other form of control is needed. The sport of hunting them down to their lairs, sending in dogs to pin them there or pull them out and destroy them, or even digging them out was devised for this purpose. A small, short legged dog with great spirit, the ability to fight in very confined spaces, and the lung room to allow it to breathe under extremely difficult conditions was needed.

The small dog that German sportsmen developed for the purpose was called the Teckel, and it is from this animal that the six varieties of Dachshund that we now know have descended. The original dog was almost certainly the short-coated or smooth variety, and for many years it was this dog that was the most popular; but by careful introduction of other breeds, three varieties of coat and two sizes of each have been

developed. The basic Teckel was a shorter smooth coated dog with longer legs than are now fashionable, and it is probable that Spaniel blood was introduced to give the long coat, and selective breeding has produced the shorter legs and longer bodies that are now seen in our show dogs.

The Longhaired Dachshund is certainly the most glamorous of the family. Often red in colour, he has something of the appearance of a miniature Irish Setter, as he has the same sort of glow on his long silky coat, and his well developed fringes and tail hair give him similar visual appeal. To those who admire him he has lost something of the grotesque character seen in others of the family, whose extremely short legs and long body have a disproportion that many people find very strange, especially those who have not experienced the charm of these little dogs.

As a show dog the Longhaired Dachshund is at the bottom of the poll compared with the remainder of the family, fewer of them being registered and shown that most of the others with the exception perhaps of the Wirehaired variety. This is surprising as some of those that have been shown achieved great success in the hands of enthusiasts and won at major shows.

These little dogs vary tremendously in temperament between one coat or one size and the other, which gives credence to the suggestion that the variations have been brought about by the introduction of blood from other breeds. The Longhaired Dachshund is on the whole less bold, and rather more reserved than the others, though this rarely reaches a stage of nervousness or fear. They are playful enough among friends, and very good with one another and with other dogs, though they are somewhat diffident with strangers and strange animals. There are few breeds that make better housedogs than the Dachshunds, and the Longhaired is no exception. He is a good guard, very territorially minded, makes defensive sounds more in keeping with a much bigger dog, and will defend his own property and family as well as almost any other breed. He is moreover a dog that needs only moderate exercise, and does not have a large appetite which makes him very suitable for modern living conditions.

Miniature Smoothhaired Dachshund

The Teckel was used for several different types of hunting in Germany. When it left that country it was given the name Dachshund which implied that it hunted badgers. However, the Teckel was used for chasing other game, and was even sometimes used in packs as a scent dog very much as a Foxhound. He was used on fox and hare, though attacking and dealing with the badger is supposed to have been his primary purpose in life. To this day a Teckel owner in Germany will proudly show photographs of the aftermath of

Faulty outline: roach back, weak loins, excessively drawn up flanks.

between forearm and foot (wrists): these are closer together than the shoulder joints, so that the front does not appear absolutely straight. *Paws:* full, broad in front, and a trifle inclined outwards; compact, with well-arched toes and tough pads. *Toes:* there are five of these, though only four are in use. They should be close together, with a pronounced arch; provided on top with strong nails, and underneath with tough toe-pads. Dewclaws may be removed.

Trunk

The whole trunk should in general be long and fully muscled. The back, with sloping shoulders, and short, rigid pelvis, should lie in the straightest possible line between the withers and the very slightly arched loins, these latter being short, rigid, and broad. *Chest:* the breastbone should be strong, and so prominent in front

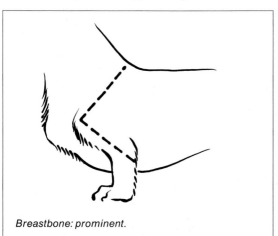

Breastbone: prominent.

that on either side a depression (dimple) appears. When viewed from the front, the thorax should appear oval, and should extend downward to the mid-point of the forearm. The enclosing structure of ribs should appear full and oval, and when viewed from above or from the side, full-volumed, so as to allow by its ample capacity, complete development of heart and lungs. Well ribbed up, and gradually merging into the line of the abdomen. If the length is correct, and also the anatomy of the shoulder and

upper arm, the front leg when viewed in profile should cover the lowest point of the breast line. *Abdomen:* slightly drawn up.

Hindquarters

The hindquarters viewed from behind should be of completely equal width. *Croup:* long, round, full, robustly muscled, but plastic, only slightly sinking toward the tail. *Pelvic bones:* not too short, rather strongly developed, and moderately sloping. *Thigh bone:* robust and of good length, set at right angles to the pelvic bones. *Hind legs:* robust and well-muscled, with well-rounded buttocks. *Knee joint:* broad and strong. *Calf bone:* in comparison with other breeds, short; it should be perpendicular to the thigh bone, and firmly muscled. *The bones at the base of the foot (tarsus)* should present a flat appearance, with a strongly prominent hock and a broad

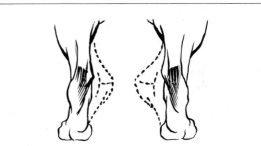

Legs: straight from behind (dotted line, incorrect cow-hocks).

tendon of Achilles. *The central foot bones (metatarsus)* should be long, movable toward the calf bone, slightly bent toward the front, but perpendicular (as viewed from behind). *Hind paws:* four compactly closed and beautifully arched toes, as in the case of the front paws. The whole foot should be posed equally on the ball and not merely on the toes; nails short. *Tail:* set in continuation of the spine, extending without very pronounced curvature, and should not be carried too gaily.

Note—inasmuch as the Dachshund is a hunting dog, scars from honorable wounds shall not be considered a fault.

SPECIAL CHARACTERISTICS OF THE THREE COAT-VARIETIES
The Dachshund is bred with three varieties of coats: (1) Shorthaired (or *Smooth*); (2) Wirehaired; (3) Longhaired. All three varieties should conform to the characteristics already specified. The longhaired and shorthaired are old, well-fixed varieties, but into the wirehaired Dachshund, the blood of other breeds has been purposely introduced; nevertheless, in breeding him, the greatest stress must be placed upon conformity to the general Dachshund type. The following specifications are applicable separately to the three coat-varieties, respectively:

(1) SHORTHAIRED (or SMOOTH) DACHSHUND
Hair
Short, thick, smooth and shining; no bald patches. Special faults are: Too fine or thin hair, leathery ears, bald patches, too coarse or too thick hair in general.

such an underground hunt with the quarry laid out and the Teckels standing proudly by.

Originally the Dachshund was divided by weight in Germany, and the smallest weight, up to twelve pounds, was designated the Toy, which probably gives some clue to the fact that it was not intended that this very small dog should be used to badger. That is not to say that given the opportunity he would not. Even the smallest are very sporting and always ready to hunt anything that moves, especially anything that is covered in fur, even the neighbour's cat.

Outside Germany the Miniature Smoothhaired Dachshund has changed from the rather short heavily built little dog with large ribs and bowed legs, to something much more slender, with a longer neck and straighter legs. The German Teckel owner will rather scornfully say that he doubts very much if this type of dog would go to ground even to the rabbits for which he uses them. The original German version had to conform to a limited measurement round the chest rather than the weight by which we distinguish them, and probably originated by breeding from the small members of a litter from normal sized Dachshunds. Others were probably produced by introducing other breeds of smooth-coated toy dogs.

This particular variety has all the sporting qualities of other Dachshunds, but has additional attributes. He is very self-assured, is lively, gay and dominating, and he is built like a hound. He is very strong and hardy for his size, capable of great exertion for so small a dog, and is determined and persistent in the chase.

It is his air of self-importance which makes him such an excellent show dog. In the ring he is a proud little dog, carrying himself with the complete confi-

dence that he can handle any situation that arises. The result is that the Miniature Smoothhaired Dachshund figures largely among the major awards at shows all over the world, and gains favour with ringsiders as well as with judges everywhere. This keeps him at the top of Dachshund registrations.

This popularity is not surprising and is not limited to the show world, as his temperament is most attractive. He is an affectionate little dog, quick and lively, intelligent and amusing in his antics, and always very sporting and ready for a game, which endears him to children. He is in addition very suited to modern life, fitting into the smallest space, being easily groomed and fed, and needing only the sort of exercise that can be obtained in games round the garden.

Miniature Wirehaired Dachshund

It is probable that the smaller version of the Wirehaired Daschshund was in existence some time before the standard type. Germany divided the sizes some-

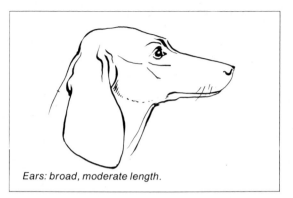

Ears: broad, moderate length.

Tail

Gradually tapered to a point, well but not too richly haired, long, sleek bristles on the underside are considered a patch of strong-growing hair, not a fault. A brush tail is a fault, as is also a partly or wholly hairless tail.

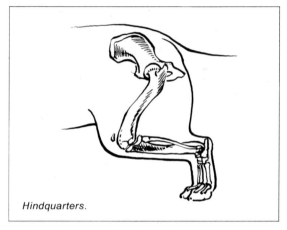

Hindquarters.

Color of hair, nose and nails

One-colored dachshund: this group includes red (often called tan), red-yellow, yellow, and brindle, with or without a shading of interspersed black hairs. Nevertheless a clean color is preferable, and red is to be considered more desirable than red-yellow or yellow. Dogs strongly shaded with interspersed black hairs belong to this class, and not to the other color groups. A small white spot is admissible, but not desirable. Nose and nails—Black; brown is admissible, but not desirable.

Two-colored dachshund: these comprise deep black, chocolate, gray (blue), and white; each with tan markings over the eyes, on the sides of the jaw and underlip, on the inner edge of the ear, front, breast, inside and behind the front legs, on the paws and around the anus, and from there to about one-third to one-half of the length of the tail on the under side. The most common two-colored Dachshund is usually called black-and-tan. A small white spot is admissible but not desirable. Absence, undue prominence or extreme lightness of tan markings is undesirable. Nose and nails—In the case of black dogs, black; for chocolate, brown (the darker the better); for gray (blue) or white dogs, gray or even flesh color, but the last named color is not desirable; in the case of white dogs, black nose and nails are to be preferred.

Dappled dachshund: the color of the dappled Dachshund is a clear brownish or grayish color, or even a white ground, with dark irregular patches of dark-gray, brown, red-yellow or black (large areas of one color not desirable). It is desirable that neither the light nor the dark color should predominate. Nose and nails—As for one- and two-colored dachshund.

(2) WIREHAIRED DACHSHUND

The general appearance is the same as that of the short-haired, but without being long in the legs, it is permissible for the body to be somewhat higher off the ground.

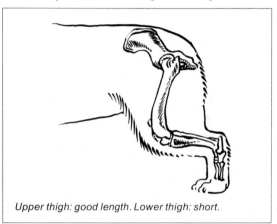

Upper thigh: good length. Lower thigh: short.

Hair

With the exception of jaw, eyebrows, and ears, the whole body is covered with a perfectly uniform tight, short, thick, rough, hard coat, but with finer, shorter hairs (undercoat) everywhere distributed between the coarser hairs, resembling the coat of the German Wirehaired Pointer. There should be a beard on the chin. The eyebrows are bushy. On the ears the hair is shorter than on the body; almost smooth, but in any case conforming to the rest of the coat. The general arrangement of the hair should be such that the wirehaired Dachshund, when

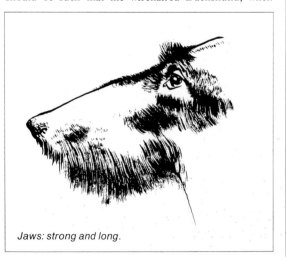

Jaws: strong and long.

what differently from other countries and the early Rabbit Dachshund was probably produced in the wirehaired form for the reasons given in the history of the Wirehaired Dachshund, practical reasons which had nothing to do with appearance. Oddly enough, however, it was the last of the six varieties to be recognised in Britain, having been given championship status as recently as 1959.

Miniature Longhaired Dachshund

Miniaturisation by selective breeding has always been one of man's ambitions, whether he happens to be interested in roses, horses, or dogs, and in many breeds of dog there is a miniature version that closely follows in type and detail the larger relation. Some claim that the standard Longhaired Dachshund developed from the oldest form of the Teckel. Certainly its history parallels that of the smooth variety from early days, and it could well be that the development was a natural division rather than an artificial one, as in many breeds

a long coat is found as a sub-variety of the basic animal. The willingness to hunt, the intelligence and amenity to discipline of the Miniature Longhaired Dachshund, allied to its sensitive nose and the protection that its coat affords add to the belief that it is an early variety.

The Miniature Longhaired Dachshund has most of the qualities of the larger variety and it is reasonable to assume that he is just a smaller version of the same dog. In Germany, the country of origin of the Dachshund, division by size has always been accepted in the show ring; and in the field the smaller dogs have often been preferred.

Judging from old photographs, the long coat of some years ago had little of the silky glowing quality that we know today. It was often broken, and rough rather than long, and these little dogs looked rather ragged as a result. In recent years, by carefully selecting the stock from which future generations were bred, the coat has become a particular feature of the variety, and the dogs are now really attractive. In Germany three colour types were encouraged, the One Coloured, the Two Coloured which was a mixture of any one of two or three colours and tan, and the Dappled which is a splashing of dark irregular spots of grey, brown, tan or black on a background of silvery grey.

The Miniature Longhaired Dachshund is one of

the most popular of the six varieties of the breed, it is easily transported, very rewarding to prepare for exhibition and usually gives a very sparkling performance in the ring. He is a sharp little dog, positive in his actions, moves with a certain amount of pride, and can be trained easily to stand perfectly still. He is always a great favourite with those at the ringside, and in competition with the other varieties often carries off the major awards.

The character of the breed is that of a big dog in a small compass, the standard allows a maximum weight of not more than eleven pounds. He is a proud animal, fully aware of the fact that he is much admired, and can dominate a household if he is given the opportunity. With human beings, and particularly with children he is well-mannered and very friendly, which leads to one of his problems. The Miniature Longhaired Dachshund is a sporting dog, a hunter and a hound, but his size and his behaviour often lead people to treat him as a toy, which could eventually lead to the deterioration of the breed.

seen from a distance should resemble the smooth-haired. Any sort of soft hair in the coat is faulty, whether short or long, or wherever found on the body; the same is true of long, curly, or wavy hair, or hair that sticks out irregularly in all directions; a flag tail is also objectionable.

Tail

Robust, as thickly haired as possible, gradually coming to a point, and without a tuft.

Color of hair, nose and nails

All colors are admissible. White patches on the chest, though allowable, are not desirable.

(3) LONGHAIRED DACHSHUND
The distinctive characteristic differentiating this coat from the short-haired, or smooth-haired Dachshund is alone the rather long silky hair.

Hair

The soft, sleek, glistening, often slightly wavy hair should be longer under the neck, on the underside of the body, and especially on the ears and behind the legs, becoming there a pronounced feather; the hair should attain its greatest length on the underside of the tail. The hair should fall beyond the lower edge of the ear. Short hair on the ear, so-called 'leather' ears, is not desirable. Too luxurious a coat causes the longhaired Dachshund to seem coarse, and masks the type. The coat should remind one of the Irish Setter, and should give the dog an elegant appearance. Too thick hair on the paws, so-called 'mops', is inelegant, and renders the animal unfit for use. It is faulty for the dog to have equally long hair over all the body, if the coat is too curly, or too scrubby, or if a flag tail or overhanging hair on the ears are lacking; or if there is a very pronounced parting on the back, or a vigorous growth between the toes.

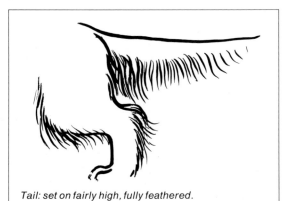
Tail: set on fairly high, fully feathered.

Tail

Carried gracefully in prolongation of the spine; the hair attains here its greatest length and forms a veritable flag.

Color of hair, nose and nails

Exactly as for the smooth-haired Dachshund, except that the red-with-black (heavily sabled) color is permissible and is formally classed as a red.

MINIATURE DACHSHUNDS
Note: Miniature Dachshunds are bred in all three coats. Within the limits imposed, symmetrical adherence to the general Dachshund conformation, combined with smallness, and mental and physical vitality, should be the outstanding characteristics of Miniature Dachshunds. They have not been given separate classification but are a division of the Open Class for 'under 10 pounds, and 12 months old or over.'

GENERAL FAULTS
Serious faults
Over- or undershot jaws, knuckling over, very loose shoulders.

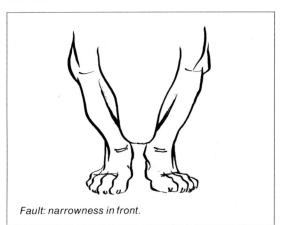
Fault: narrowness in front.

Secondary faults: a weak, long-legged, or dragging figure; body hanging between the shoulders; sluggish, clumsy, or waddling gait; toes turned inwards or too obliquely outwards; splayed paws; sunken back, roach (or carp) back; croup higher than withers; short-ribbed or too weak chest; excessively drawn-up flanks like those of a Greyhound; narrow, poorly-muscled hindquarters; weak loins; bad angulation in front or hindquarters; cowhocks; bowed legs; wall eyes, except for dappled dogs; bad coat.

Minor faults: ears wrongly set, sticking out, narrow or folded; too marked a stop; too pointed or weak a jaw; pincer teeth; too wide or too short a head; goggle eyes, wall eyes in the case of dappled dogs, insufficiently dark eyes in the case of all other coat-colors; dewlaps; short neck; swan neck; too fine or too thin hair; absence of, or too profuse or too light tan markings in the case of two-colored dogs.

Approved by the AKC 12 January 1971

KC(GB) VARIATION TO STANDARD

All six varieties are given separate championship status by the KC(GB). *Long-haired: Tail:* set on fairly high, not too long, tapering and without too marked curve. Not carried too high. Fully feathered. *Wire-haired: Tail:* continues line of the spine; is slightly curved, must not be carried too gaily or reach ground when at rest. *Weight and size:* dogs 20 to 22 pounds; bitches 18 to 20 pounds.

FINNISH SPITZ

NATIONAL GROUPING		
	Name	Number
AKC	—	—
KC(GB)	Hound	I
FCI	Small Hounds	6

Dogs do not recognise national boundaries, and although there has always been a tendency to associate a certain breed with a certain country, there were inevitably areas where bloods and varieties crossed borders. This has led to certain dogs evolving from a mixture of strains. The Finnish Spitz is a typical example of this. This little dog, apart from its colour, which is distinctive, is undoubtedly a mixture of the Spitz types from the Scandinavian countries and certain Russian dogs. The Elkhounds of Norway have always been of more slender build than the Jämthund, and there existed bird hunting dogs in the northern area of the Baltic which were of a similar type to the

Finnish Spitz. The Laika too of Russia is a bird-hunting dog so that between the two the evolution of a type such as the Finnish Spitz was almost certain to take place.

The breed was first officially recognised in the latter part of the 19th century and the type became fixed. It was at the turn of this century that the Finnish Spitz was introduced into Britain though it was not until much later that it made any impression on the show scene.

The Spitz is an active, sometimes noisy little dog with a most alert expression and keen look about him. His stand-off stiff coat with a distinct mane especially on the males, allied with his rich bright orange or red colour, gives him a very distinctive appearance. As a show dog he has never achieved great success though one or two enthusiasts have persevered with the breed.

The Finnish Spitz is a friendly little dog as so many of the hunting dogs are. Centuries of dependence on man, and man's dependence on the dog have built up a trusting relationship. Their high-pitched voice and well developed protective instinct make them particularly good guard dogs.

OFFICIAL STANDARD

Characteristics
The Finnish Spitz characteristics are eagerness to hunt, courage and fidelity.

General appearance
Body almost square. Bearing bold. The whole appearance, and particularly eyes, ears and tail, indicates liveliness.

Head and skull
Medium sized and clean cut, forehead slightly arched, stop pronounced. Muzzle narrow and clean cut, seen from above and from the sides evenly tapering. Nose pitch black. Lips tightly closed and thin.

Eyes
Medium sized, lively, preferably dark.

Head: tapering muzzle, pronounced stop.

Ears
Cocked, sharply pointed, fine in texture, exceedingly mobile.

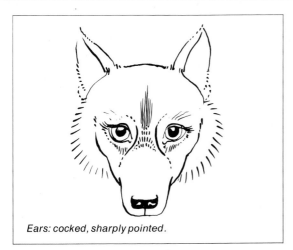

Ears: cocked, sharply pointed.

Neck
Muscular, in males it looks rather short, due to the thick coat, in bitches medium long.

Forequarters
Strong and straight.

Body
Back, straight and strong. Chest, deep. Belly, slightly drawn up.

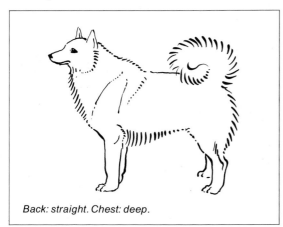

Back: straight. Chest: deep.

Hindquarters
Strong, hocks comparatively straight.

Feet
Preferably roundish.

Tail
Curves vigorously from its root in an arch, forward, downward and backward, then pressing down against the thigh, with its tip extending to the middle part of the thigh. Extended, the tail vertebrae usually reaches to the hock joint.

Coat
On head and legs, except their back sides, short and close-lying, on the body longish, semi-erect or erect, on the neck and back stiffer. The outer coat on the shoulders, particularly in males, considerably longer and coarser. On the back of the thighs the hair is long and dense, also on the tail. Undercoat short, soft, dense, light in colour.

Colour
On the back reddish-brown or yellowish-red, preferably bright. The hairs on innersides of the ears, cheeks, under the muzzle, on the breast, abdomen, inside the legs, at the back of thighs, under the tail are of a lighter shade. White markings on feet and a narrow white stripe on the breast can be permitted also some black hairs on the lips and sparse separate hairs with black points along the back.

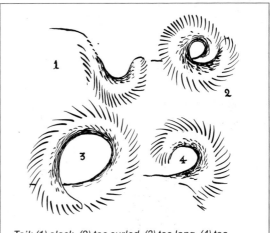

Tail: (1) slack, (2) too curled, (3) too long, (4) too short.

Weight and size
Height at withers and length of body in males $17\frac{1}{2}$ inches, 20 inches; in bitches $15\frac{1}{2}$ inches, 18 inches.

Faults
Fleshy head, coarse muzzle, ears pointing forward at a sharp angle or their tips pointing outwards or towards one another, ears curving backwards or with slack points or with long hairs inside. Yellow or wall-eyes, elbows turned inwards, too weak pastern, slack tail or too excessively curled tail, long, soft or too short, close wavy or curly coat, dirty colour particularly distinctly defined differences between the colours, disfiguring dewclaws.

Note
Male animals should have two apparently normal testicles fully descended into the scrotum.

AKC VARIATION TO STANDARD
The dog is not granted championship status by the AKC. The above standards are those of the KC(GB).

AMERICAN FOXHOUND

NATIONAL GROUPING		
	Name	Number
AKC	Hounds	II
KC(GB)	—	–
FCI	Large Hounds	5

Hunting has always been a popular sport in the United States of America, and even in the face of increasing urbanisation, the country is so huge that large tracts of it remain unspoilt and rich in game even today. The history of fox hunting goes back almost as far as the history of America to the days of the first settlements. In 1650 Robert Brooke took his pack of hounds with him when he sailed to the Crown Colony and the descendants of these remained in the family for three hundred years or more and formed the basis of the American Foxhound of today. Further importations took place in the middle to late 18th century, some from Britain and others from France. In the early 19th century the Gloucester Foxhunting Club imported some of the best English hounds and then followed further importations from France and Ireland, the latter lending weight to the idea that the Black and Tan Coonhound may have descended from the Kerry Beagle.

The Foxhound in the United States is used for four different purposes and for these four rather different types of Hound are needed. There is the field trial Hound which is run competitively at trials where speed is important. There is the hunting of the fox with the gun, where a slower Hound with a good voice is needed. Trail Hounds or Drag Hounds which are raced on a drag, much as the Fell Hounds of Cumberland are run, are different again, and here speed alone counts. Finally, there is pack hunting where the type is very much the same as in the English Foxhound, where a combination of some speed, great jumping power, a good voice and willingness to hunt in a pack, is needed. As in Britain, Hounds have varied considerably from one area to another, but whilst in that country packs have tended to stick to their own type, in the United States of America there has been a move towards greater standardisation.

In Britain Foxhounds are rarely shown, except at Hound shows such as Peterborough, the registration being largely in the hands of the Masters of Foxhounds Association whose stud books go back to the beginning of the 19th century. It is many years now since one was shown at a Kennel Club Show in Britain, and the last group of registrations took place in 1967 when four were registered with the Kennel Club. In the United States things are somewhat different, and the American Foxhound is recognised as a show dog. He is a biggish dog, twenty-two to twenty-five inches, very powerfully built and muscular with a close hard hound coat, and very friendly. Hunts still continue the habit of puppy walking, putting young Hounds out to be reared in the locality of the kennels by hunt supporters, where they live as members of the family, and become as attached and affectionate as any other breed of dog. However, like many other Hounds, they do have a streak of independence and wilfulness, and can become disobedient in later life.

OFFICIAL STANDARD

Head

Skull: should be fairly long, slightly domed at occiput, with cranium broad and full. *Ears:* ears set on moderately low, long, reaching when drawn out nearly, if not quite, to the tip of the nose; fine in texture, fairly broad, with almost entire absence of erectile power—setting close to the head with the forward edge slightly inturning to the cheek—round at tip. *Eyes:* eyes large, set well apart—soft and houndlike—expression gentle and pleading; of a brown or hazel color. *Muzzle:* muzzle of fair length—straight and square-cut—the stop moderately defined. *Defects:* a very flat skull, narrow across the top; excess of dome; eyes small, sharp and terrierlike, or prominent and protruding; muzzle long and snipy, cut away decidedly below the eyes, or very short. Roman-nosed, or upturned giving a dish-face expression. Ears short, set on high, or with a tendency to rise above the point of origin.

Skull: slightly domed. Muzzle: fair length, square cut.

Body

Neck and throat: neck rising free and light from the shoulders, strong in substance yet not loaded, of medium length. The throat clean and free from folds of skin, a slight wrinkle below the angle of the jaw, however, is allowable. *Defects:* a thick, short, cloddy neck carried on a line with the top of the shoulders. Throat showing dewlap and folds of skin to a degree termed 'throatiness.'

Shoulders, chest and ribs

Shoulders sloping—clean, muscular, not heavy or loaded —conveying the idea of freedom of action with activity and strength. Chest should be deep for lung space, narrower in proportion to depth than the English hound— 28 inches (*girth*) in a 23-inch hound being good. Well-sprung ribs—back ribs should extend well back—a three-inch flank allowing springiness. *Back and loins:* back moderately long, muscular and strong. Loins broad and slightly arched. *Defects:* very long or swayed or roached back. Flat, narrow loins.

Forelegs and feet

Forelegs: straight, with fair amount of bone. Pasterns short and straight. *Feet:* foxlike. Pad full and hard. Well-arched toes. Strong nails. *Defects:* straight, upright

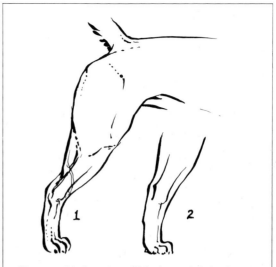

(1) correct hindquarters, (2) faulty straight hocks.

shoulders, chest disproportionately wide or with lack of depth. Flat ribs. Out at elbow. Knees knuckled over forward, or bent backward. Forelegs crooked. Feet long, open or spreading.

Hips, thighs, hind legs and feet

Hips and thighs, strong and muscled, giving abundance of propelling power. Stifles strong and well let down. Hocks firm, symmetrical and moderately bent. Feet close and firm. *Defects:* cowhocks, or straight hocks. Lack of muscle and propelling power. Open feet.

Tail

Set moderately high; carried gaily, but not turned forward over the back; with slight curve; with very slight brush. *Defects:* a long tail, Teapot curve or inclined forward from the root. Rat tail, entire absence of brush.

Coat

A close, hard, hound coat of medium length. *Defects:* a short thin coat, or of a soft quality.

Height

Dogs should not be under 22 or over 25 inches. Bitches should not be under 21 or over 24 inches measured across the back at the point of the withers, the hound standing in a natural position with his feet well under him.

Color

Any color.

Head (20): skull 5, ears 5, eyes 5, muzzle 5. *Body (35):* neck 5, chest and shoulders 15, back, loins and ribs 15. *Running Gear (35):* forelegs 10, hips, thighs and hind legs 10, feet 15. *Coat and Tail (10):* coat 5, tail 5. *Total (100).*

KC(GB) VARIATION TO STANDARD

This dog is not granted championship status by the KC(GB).

ENGLISH FOXHOUND

NATIONAL GROUPING		
	Name	Number
AKC	Hounds	II
KC(GB)	Hound	I
FCI	Large Hounds	5

The whole history of sport with dogs is tied up with the hunting of game, with the exception of the breeds that were vermin killers, and those that were used to hunt the fox. While in the view of some people, the fox belongs among the vermin, it has nevertheless been accorded some status as it has long been associated with the sport of horse riding. Few breeds have their history so well documented as the Foxhound. Whilst other breeds depended on the showbench and registration with Kennel Clubs for their records, the Foxhound had its development written down in the history of the various hunts which were spread all over Europe and the United States of America. Even so, the early history of the breed is as much a matter of debate as many other breeds.

As early as 1631 Gervase Markham was writing that 'the best parts of the country bred large hounds, the woodlands and mountains of Cheshire and Lancashire the middle-sized hounds and,' as he so delightfully put it, 'other champaigne countreys the light nimble, swift and slender dog'. The light Northern Foxhound is thought to have resulted from the crossing of the old Northern Hound and the Greyhound. Whatever the origins and the differences, the fact remains that very early in the history of Britain and America the Foxhound became well established as the number of packs increased. A complete list of all packs in England alone in 1880, reveals that there were one hundred and forty in existence with an average of some fifty couples per pack which gives an astounding total of seven thousand Hounds.

The Masters of Foxhounds Association has been in existence longer than the British Kennel Club. Stud books have been carefully kept and it is possible even now to trace the ancestry of the modern Hounds further back than that of any other breed. Hunting became fashionable, with the result that no difficulty was encountered in keeping packs or staffing them as they were supported by wealthy families.

The Foxhound is a friendly creature, calm and almost affectionate. It is one of the sights of the countryside during the winter months to see well-wrapped children making a fuss of the Hounds at a meet, and being fussed over in return. He is a big, squarely built dog with the sort of conformation and build that give him strength and stamina as well as the ability to jump and to crash through thick undergrowth. A pack must be capable of spending the whole day in the field from early morning to late at night, and of running several foxes during that time.

Unfortunately they have never been popular as a showdog, apart from their regular appearance at specific shows arranged for Foxhounds. This is a pity, as they are handsome dogs, very spectacular, and with physical qualities that could well allow them to outshine many of the breeds more frequently shown.

OFFICIAL STANDARD

Head
Should be of full size, but by no means heavy. Brow pronounced, but not high or sharp. There should be a good length and breadth, sufficient to give in a dog hound a girth in front of the ears of fully 16 inches. The nose should be long (4½ inches) and wide, with open nostrils. Ears set on low and lying close to the cheeks. Most English hounds are 'rounded' which means that about 1½ inches is taken off the end of the ear. The teeth must meet squarely, either a *pig-mouth* (overshot) or undershot being a disqualification.

Neck
Must be long and clean, without the slightest throatiness, not less than 10 inches from cranium to shoulder. It should taper nicely from shoulders to head, and the upper outline should be slightly convex.

The Shoulders
Should be long and well clothed with muscle, without being heavy, especially at the points. They must be well sloped, and the true arm between the front and the elbow must be long and muscular, but free from fat or lumber. *Chest and back ribs:* The chest should girth over 31 inches in a 24-inch hound, and the back ribs must be very deep.

Back and loin
Must both be very muscular, running into each other without any contraction between them. The couples must be wide, even to raggedness, and the topline of the back should be absolutely level, the *stern* well set on and carried gaily but not in any case curved *over* the back like a squirrel's tail. The end should taper to a point and there should be a fringe of hair below. The *hindquarters* or propellers are required to be very strong, and as endurance is of even greater consequence than speed, straight stifles are preferred to those much bent as in a Greyhound. *Elbows* set quite straight, and neither turned in nor out are a *sine qua non*. They must be well let down by means of the long true arm above mentioned.

Legs and feet
Every Master of Foxhounds insists on legs as straight as a post, and as strong; size of bone at the ankle being especially regarded as all important. The desire for straightness had a tendency to produce knuckling-over, which at one time was countenanced, but in recent years this defect has been eradicated by careful breeding and intelligent adjudication, and one sees very little of this trouble in the best modern Foxhounds. The bone cannot be too large, and the feet in all cases should be round and catlike, with well-developed knuckles and strong horn, which last is of the greatest importance.

Color and coat
Not regarded as very important, so long as the former is a good 'hound color,' and the latter is short, dense, hard, and glossy. Hound colors are black, tan, and white, or any combination of these three, also the various 'pies' compounded of white and the color of the hare and badger,

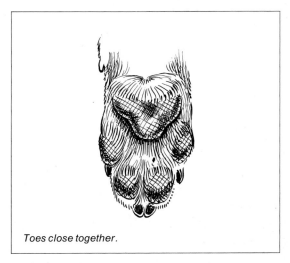

Toes close together.

or yellow, or tan. The *symmetry* of the Foxhound is of the greatest importance, and what is known as 'quality' is highly regarded by all good judges.

Approved by the AKC 1935

KC(GB) VARIATION TO STANDARD
Head and skull: skull broad. *Neck:* long, but not thick. A short-necked hound is deficient in pace. *Forequarters:* shoulders should show quality and no lumber. A shoulder with excessive amount of fleshy conformation will prevent hound from running up or down hill at top pace. Legs full of bone right down to feet, and not tapering off in any way. *Body:* girth should be deep with plenty of heart room. Back broad, and a hound should be well ribbed up; but there should be a fair space between end of ribs and commencement of hindquarters, otherwise hound will be deficient in stride and therefore lack pace. *Hindquarters:* full, and of great muscular proportions. Hocks should be well let down, and bone of hindlegs (as in forelegs) should continue all way down to foot, and not become light under pastern. *Feet:* Toes should be close together, and not open. *Tail:* should be well put on at end of good quarters, and quarters should in no way end abruptly and be of type that hound-men term 'chopped off behind.' A curly stern, although unsightly, will not be detrimental to hound's hunting qualities.

GREYHOUND

NATIONAL GROUPING		
	Name	Number
AKC	Hounds	II
KC(GB)	Hound	I
FCI	Coursing Dogs	10

By studying old photographs and prints it can be seen that the modern dog of many breeds, is very different from his forebears. The modern Bulldog looks little like that of a hundred years ago, and the Fox Terrier, especially a Wire Fox Terrier of the turn of the century looks very different from today's. The Greyhound on the other hand has hardly changed at all. Even the name of the dog has its roots in early British history. Today old running-dog men especially in the north of Britain will talk of a 'Greu' which comes from the Saxon word for a running dog. In common with some other breeds, the Greyhound was denied to the commoner at one time in order to prevent him from poaching game and thus spoiling the sport of the wealthier classes. Mention of the dog was made in the time of King Canute, and prior to the signing of the Magna Carta, the destruction of a Greyhound was an extremely serious crime.

Juliana Berners in the 15th century 'Book of St. Albans' describes the Greyhound in detail in a doggerel which has been repeated so often that it is now hackneyed. In the 16th century the coursing of buck by Greyhounds was a regular sport, the buck being driven into an area where they could be watched in comfort by spectators. The buck were pulled down by Greyhounds having been given what was called 'fair law' which means that they had a start. In recent years the Greyhound has been developed along three quite distinct lines, the show dog which is bigger and narrower; the coursing dog which is handier and more agile; and the track Greyhound which was evolved for racing to the artificial hare in the United States and later in Britain; the finest dogs for this purpose being bred in Ireland.

From the earliest days of dog shows the Greyhound has been a popular dog for exhibition, and as the records of the coursing Hounds have been kept in the Greyhound Stud Book since about 1880, so the details of the show Greyhound have been kept, even to their measurements. We even know that a dog named Lauderdale, whelped in 1869 and successfully shown from 1873 to 1880 weighed sixty-seven pounds, so detailed are the records.

The Greyhound has a wonderful temperament, friendly, refined, as gentle with children as he is affectionate with adults. It is remarkable that he has not become more popular as a house pet. His size is against him, though he curls up into a remarkably small space, and is quite wonderfully trainable. The Greyhound is one of the few breeds that takes quite naturally to the lead, obeys commands usually without demur, and is easily handled by a child. It is being well behaved that makes him such a magnificent show dog. He stands like a statue in the ring, and a parade of these magnificent Hounds in their varied colours, with their coats shining in the sunshine at an outdoor show is a fine sight. In spite of his natural killer instinct, he is among the most sympathetic and even sentimental of dogs, as those who have adopted a Greyhound that has been retired from the track would agree.

OFFICIAL STANDARD

Head
Long and narrow, fairly wide between the ears, scarcely perceptible stop, little or no development of nasal sinuses, good length of muzzle, which should be powerful without coarseness. Teeth very strong and even in front.

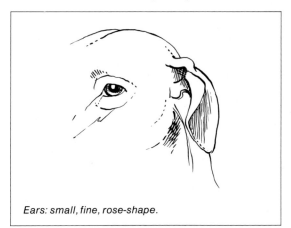

Ears: small, fine, rose-shape.

Ears
Small and fine in texture, thrown back and folded, except when excited, when they are semipricked.

Eyes
Dark, bright, intelligent, indicating spirit.

Neck
Long, muscular, without throatiness, slightly arched, and widening gradually into the shoulder.

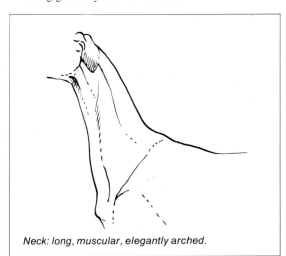

Neck: long, muscular, elegantly arched.

Shoulders
Placed as obliquely as possible, muscular without being loaded.

Forelegs
Perfectly straight, set well into the shoulders, neither turned in nor out, pasterns strong.

Chest
Deep, and as wide as consistent with speed, fairly well-sprung ribs.

Back
Muscular and broad.

Loins
Good depth of muscle, well arched, well cut up in the flanks.

Hindquarters
Long, very muscular and powerful, wide and well let down, well-bent stifles. Hocks well bent and rather close to ground, wide but straight fore and aft.

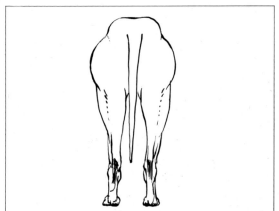

Hocks: inclining neither outwards nor inwards.

Feet
Hard and close, rather more hare than cat-feet, well knuckled up with good strong claws.

Tail
Long, fine and tapering with a slight upward curve.

Coat
Short, smooth and firm in texture.

Color
Immaterial.

Weight
Dogs: 65 to 70 pounds; bitches: 60 to 65 pounds.

KC(GB) VARIATION TO STANDARD
Head: long, moderate width. *Colour:* black, white, red, blue, fawn, fallow, brindle, or any of the colours broken with white. *Height:* dogs 28 to 30 inches; bitches 27 to 28 inches.

HARRIER

With the exception of Australasia, the hare has a cosmopolitan distribution, being found from the Arctic Circle to the Southern Hemisphere. It has in addition been a favourite food throughout the world since history began, and the hunting of it in one form or another has been in existence for thousands of years. In the Far East, as in many other parts of the world, this consisted of coursing which resulted in the development of breeds that were fast and clever enough to catch him. Certainly hare hunting did go on in ancient Greece with dogs other than those which caught them by sheer speed. The hare was finally caught in a net rather than being run down, and as food rather than sport was the purpose, this is probably excusable.

Though the Harrier looks very much like a small Foxhound, he is a separate breed and should not be confused. There are indications that at one time the tendency was to take small Foxhounds from packs and

NATIONAL GROUPING		
	Name	Number
AKC	Hounds	II
KC(GB)	—	—
FCI	Small Hounds	6

by selective breeding of the smaller specimens, to produce a line of so-called Harriers. The Association of Masters of Harriers however did all possible to prevent this practice, and kept their own stud books of pure bred Hounds.

The first pack of Harriers in Britain was the Penistone pack which was established by Sir Elias de Midhope in 1260. This pack existed for some five hundred years, the Masters being the Wilsons of Broomhead Hall. The pack no longer exists, but it is interesting to note that the hunting of the hare on foot is still popular in the area, and a pack of Beagles still meets regularly there. This hunting of the hare on foot was what led to the popularity of the Harrier as a pack hound as it was not everyone who could, or who wished to ride a horse. Many of the early packs were scratch packs, individual Hounds being owned privately and meeting to hunt, which brought the whole sport within reach of the less wealthy. In the United States of America the Harrier has been known as long as any of the other scent hunting Hounds and has been used for hunting since colonial times. In more recent years he proved a favourite with the drag hunt where his slower pace was found more suitable.

As with the Foxhound there has been no attempt to establish the Harrier as a show dog in Britain. He is never seen on the bench, which is unfortunate, as he is one of the oldest breeds in the country, and now has very little place as a pack hunting Hound. In the United States, however, he is accepted and shown. He is a solidly built little dog, handy in size, well constructed and muscular, and both hardy and active. Those who have had a Foxhound in the house when puppy walking will say how attractive this type of dog can be as a companion, and there is no reason why at some future date the Harrier should not prove as popular as the Beagle.

OFFICIAL STANDARD

The points of the modern Harrier are very similar to those of the English Foxhound. The Harrier, however, is smaller than the English Foxhound and the most popular size is 19 to 21 inches. They should be active, well balanced and full of strength and quality, with shoulders sloping into the muscles of the back, clean and not loaded on the withers or point.

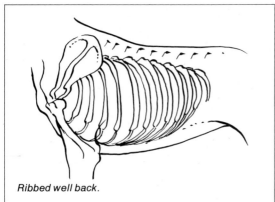

Ribbed well back.

The back level and muscular, and not dipping behind the withers or arching over the loin. The elbow's point set well away from the ribs, running parallel with the body and not turning outwards. Deep, well-sprung ribs, running well back, with plenty of heart room, and a deep chest.

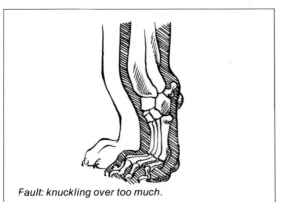

Fault: knuckling over too much.

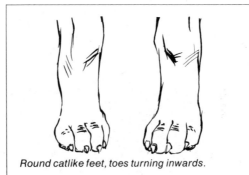

Round catlike feet, toes turning inwards.

Good straight legs with plenty of bone running well down to the toes, but not overburdened, inclined to knuckle over very slightly but not exaggerated in the slightest degree. Round catlike feet, and close toes turning inwards. Hind legs and hocks stand square, with a good sweep and muscular thigh to take the weight off the body.

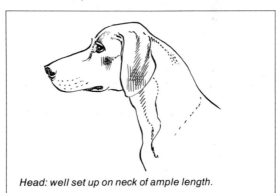

Head: well set up on neck of ample length.

The head should be of a medium size with good bold forehead, and plenty of expression; head must be well set up on a neck of ample length, and not heavy; stern should be set well up, long and well controlled.

KC(GB) VARIATION TO STANDARD
This dog is not granted championship status by the KC(GB).

IBIZAN HOUND

NATIONAL GROUPING		
	Name	Number
AKC	—	—
KC(GB)	Hound	1
FCI	Coursing Dogs	10

This dog is probably the one breed with justifiable claims to great antiquity. Its origins lie in the area of the Mediterranean and particularly in the islands off the coast of Spain, and it is true that ancient drawings and paintings of hunting dogs dating back to Egyptian times depict a type of Hound to which the modern Ibizan Hound bears a remarkable resemblance. A near relative, the Pharaoh Hound can possibly lay equal claim, but the varied colour of the Ibizan is frequently shown in ancient decorations. He was bred as a hunting dog, working by scent as well as sight, though his conformation, the length of his leg and his undoubted speed make it more than likely that he is primarily a sight Hound. Though he was known centuries ago on the islands of Ibiza, Formentera, Majorca and Minorca, he was regularly used on the mainland of the Spanish Peninsula. He is described at the beginning of this century as the Podengo, and was being used for coursing rabbit and hare, but in Andalusia and Estremadura he is said to have been used to catch stag and bear, and to have made an excellent gundog.

In more recent times he has become a popular dog in Spain and in many other countries in southern Europe, being seen frequently at all the major shows in considerable numbers, and being used as a coursing dog. A small number of breeders have worked hard to maintain the breed over the past couple of decades. It says a good deal for their efforts that the breed that we see today has remained almost exactly like the dogs of centuries ago, when the temptation must have been from time to time to introduce the blood of other running dogs such as the Greyhound or the Saluki to improve speed and performance. They have, however, concentrated on the typical dog of the islands and have succeeded in retaining the erect ears, one of the main characteristics of the dog.

He is a tall Hound, standing around twenty-six inches at the shoulder and very much the running type, with flat sides and long legs. He is less elegant than the Greyhound, and has strong bone, rather larger feet and more bulky joints. His head too is not so long and narrow as some of the other running dogs. He is seen in two coats, the one short and smooth, and the other longer and rather hard. The longer coated variety is rarely seen outside Spain though at shows in Europe it is fairly common. He makes a good show dog though he is sometimes a little restless and impatient. His size and colour make him quite striking, and his preparation is minimal, involving the simplest of cleaning and attention to nails and teeth. He is one of those dogs that looks well as a team, and when a number of them are seen together, standing level, with keen expression and alert ears, they prove very competitive.

His temperament is typical of many of the other running dogs, quiet and steady when relaxed, and very keen when aroused. If he has one fault as a show dog it is that at times he is a little hard in temperament, and can prove somewhat intractable. Although he has the wilfulness of many of the other Hounds, and a streak of independence, he does, however, become very attached to his owner, and is affectionate and faithful.

OFFICIAL STANDARD

Characteristics
A tireless controlled hunter. Retrieves to hand, very kind, rather cautious with strangers, has the ability to jump great heights without take-off run. An agile hound.

General appearance
Tall, narrow, finely built, large erect ears.

Head and Skull
Fine, long, flat skull with prominent occipital bone. Stop not well defined, slightly convex muzzle, the length of which from the eyes to the tip of the nose should be equal to the length from the eyes to the occiput. Nose flesh coloured, should protrude beyond the teeth, jaw very strong and lean.

Eyes
Clear amber, expressive. Almond shaped; not prominent, large or round.

Ears
Large, thin, stiff, highly mobile, erect when dog is alert, in a continuous line with the arch of the neck when viewed in profile; base set on level with the eyes.

Mouth
Perfectly even white teeth; scissor bite; thin lips with no dew-lap.

Neck
Very lean, long, muscular and slightly arched.

Forequarters
Rather steep short shoulder blade, long straight legs, erect pasterns of good length.

Body
Level back sloping slightly from the pinbones to the rump. Long, flat ribcage. Short coupled with well tucked up waist, breast bone very prominent. Depth measured between the bottom of the ribcage and elbow $2\frac{1}{2}$ inches to 3 inches.

Hindquarters
Long, strong, straight and lean, no great angulation, long second thigh, turning neither in nor out.

Feet
Well arched toes, thick pads, light coloured claws. Front feet may turn slightly outwards. Dew claws should not be removed in front. No hind dew claws.

Gait
A suspended trot, which is a long far reaching stride, with a slight hover before placing the foot to the ground.

Tail
Long, thin, low set, reaching well below the hock, when passed between the legs and round the flank should reach the spine; may be carried high when excited but not curled within itself or low over the back.

Coat
Either smooth or rough always hard, close, dense. Longer under the tail and at the back of the legs. Hunting scars should not be penalised.

Colour
White, Chestnut or Lion solid color, or any combination of these.

Weight and size
The Standard in the country of origin varies between 22 inches and 29 inches, but balance is the overriding factor.

Faults
Any departure from the foregoing, the degree of the departure stipulating the seriousness of the fault.

Note
Male animals should have two apparently normal testicles fully descended into the scrotum.

AKC VARIATION TO STANDARD
This dog is not granted championship status by the AKC. The above standards are those of the KC(GB).

IRISH WOLFHOUND

Throughout history dogs have been the subjects of myth and legend, either as in the case of the Lion Dog of China romantic little stories accounting for the character of the Pekingese, or, as in the case of much larger animals living in a country that thrives on legend as Ireland has always done, tales of huge ravening beasts that were capable of giant feats of strength. The Irish Wolfhound gave ample opportunity for such stories, as he is one of the largest dogs in the world, certainly the tallest, and though he is nowadays one of the gentlest of dogs, it could well be that he was not always so. Finn, the hero of one Irish legend had as his companion a dog named Bran which was gifted with magical properties including a deadly poisonous claw and the ability to foretell the future. He was described as a huge black dog, but others such as the one given to Finn by the princess of Iruath were said to be multi-coloured, this one was wearing a gold chain and had the gift of producing gold and silver from its mouth.

Leaving legend behind, however, there is no doubt that large hunting dogs comparable with the modern Irish Wolfhound did exist in Ireland some centuries ago. They were used for the hunting of the Irish wolf and the Irish elk, an exceptionally large version of this member of the deer family said to have stood some six feet at the shoulder. The Romans appreciated him and are said to have imported specimens and used them in arena battles, though there is indication that these were heavier dogs more on the lines of the Mastiff. Bewick in 1792 writes 'The Irish Greyhound is the largest of the dog kind, and its appearance the most beautiful'. By the end of the 19th century the breed had almost disappeared, and there was a good deal of discussion as to whether it should, or even could, be saved. Fortunately, largely by the efforts of one man, the breed was revived. Even though there will always be discussion as to whether this was done by proper means or by the use of crosses, we have been left with one of the greatest and noblest members of the canine race.

The Irish Wolfhound is a huge, impressive, calm and graceful Hound with a most intelligent and understanding expression. He is still very much the running and hunting dog, built for power and speed, though he has come a long way from the apparently rougher more cumbersome animal used for chasing and pulling down wolves in the early days of Irish history.

As a show dog he has few peers, especially in his own group, where his sheer size and magnificence always make him outstanding. There have been one or two kennels in recent years that have campaigned the breed at shows until they have attained world wide recognition, and the numbers have grown steadily as a result. They now appear at shows in almost every country, and some fine dogs have been exported though few these days from Ireland itself.

The temperament of this great dog is wonderful. Gentle and quiet, he is completely friendly and trusting with everyone and even with his own kind, which cannot be said of all breeds. He makes a wonderful guard, his sheer size being sufficient to daunt most intruders, and his bark, when he does give voice, echoes like thunder around the landscape. In spite of his bulk, he is a favourite house dog as his manners and general behaviour are quite impeccable.

OFFICIAL STANDARD

General appearance

Of great size and commanding appearance, the Irish Wolfhound is remarkable in combining power and swiftness with keen sight. The largest and tallest of the galloping hounds, in general type he is a rough-coated, Greyhoundlike breed; very muscular, strong though gracefully built; movements easy and active; head and neck carried high, the tail carried with an upward sweep with a slight curve towards the extremity. The minimum height and weight of dogs should be 32 inches and 120 pounds; of bitches, 30 inches and 105 pounds; these to apply only to hounds over 18 months of age. Anything below this should be debarred from competition. Great size, including height at shoulder and proportionate length of body, is the desideratum to be aimed at, and it is desired to firmly establish a race that shall average from 32 to 34 inches in dogs, showing the requisite power, activity, courage and symmetry.

Head: long, little stop.

Head

Long, the frontal bones of the forehead very slightly raised and very little indentation between the eyes. *Skull* not too broad. *Muzzle* long and moderately pointed. *Ears* small and Greyhoundlike in carriage.

Neck

Rather long, very strong and muscular, well arched, without dewlap or loose skin about the throat.

Chest

Very deep. Breast, wide.

Back

Rather long than short. Loins arched.

Tail

Long and slightly curved, of moderate thickness, and well covered with hair.

Belly

Well drawn up.

Coat: rough and hardy.

Forequarters

Shoulders, muscular, giving breadth of chest, set sloping. Elbows well under, neither turned inwards nor outwards.

Leg

Forearm muscular, and the whole leg strong and quite straight.

Hindquarters

Muscular thighs and second thigh long and strong as in the Greyhound, and hocks well let down and turning neither in nor out.

Feet

Moderately large and round, neither turned inward nor outwards. Toes, well arched and closed. Nails, very strong and curved.

Feet: moderately large and round, well arched.

Hair

Rough and hard on body, legs and head; especially wiry and long over eyes and under jaw.

Color and markings

The recognized colors are gray, brindle, red, black, pure white, fawn, or any other color that appears in the Deerhound.

FAULTS

Too light or heavy a head, too highly arched frontal bone;

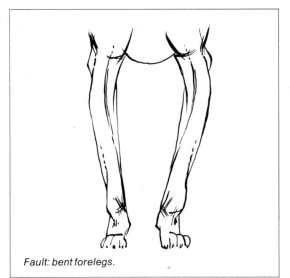

Fault: bent forelegs.

4. Head, long and level, carried high.
5. Forelegs, heavily boned, quite straight; elbows well set under.
6. Thighs long and muscular; second thighs, well muscled, stifles nicely bent.
7. Coat, rough and hard, specially wiry and long over eyes and under jaw.
8. Body, long, well ribbed up, with ribs well sprung, and great breadth across hips.
9. Loins arched, belly well drawn up.
10. Ears, small, with Greyhoundlike carriage.
11. Feet, moderately large and round; toes, close, well arched.
12. Neck, long, well arched and very strong.
13. Chest, very deep, moderately broad.
14. Shoulders, muscular, set sloping.
15. Tail, long and slightly curved.
16. Eyes, dark.

Note: the above in no way alters the 'Standard of Excellence,' which must in all cases be rigidly adhered to; they simply give the various points in order of merit. If in any case they appear at variance with Standard of Excellence, it is the latter which is correct.

Approved by the AKC 12 September 1950

large ears and hanging flat to the face; short neck; full dewlap; too narrow or too broad a chest; sunken or hollow or quite straight back; bent forelegs; overbent fetlocks; twisted feet; spreading toes; too curly a tail; weak hindquarters and a general want of muscle; too short in body. Lips or nose liver-colored or lacking pigmentation.

1. *Typical.* The Irish Wolfhound is a rough-coated Greyhoundlike breed, the tallest of the coursing hounds and remarkable in combining power and swiftness.
2. *Great size* and commanding appearance.
3. Movements easy and active.

KC(GB) VARIATION TO STANDARD

Height and weight: (minimum) dogs 31 inches and 120 pounds; bitches 28 inches and 90 pounds.

NORWEGIAN ELKHOUND

The native deer of Scandinavia is the Elk, a very large and powerful creature indeed, with a menacing head of horns and a weight approaching a thousand pounds. There are few dogs capable of tackling such an animal and pulling it down, though the wolf, hunting in a pack and careless of losses did so when wolves were indigenous to the same country as this large deer. The Elk provided a very welcome addition to food stocks in countries where the winter was long and hard and where the keeping of domestic cattle was far from easy. They had to be hunted through fairly thick forests, often when snow lay on the ground, and through tangled undergrowth that would have dismayed a small weak dog. For the purpose the Scandinavians evolved a number of dogs of very similar build and characteristics, strong, active, with a good voice and a thick coat to protect them against the severe weather.

The basis was a Spitz type of dog that had existed in Scandinavia for centuries, and which is typical of the dogs of the frozen areas of Northern Europe and Asia.

NATIONAL GROUPING		
	Name	Number
AKC	Hounds	II
KC(GB)	Hound	I
FCI	Large Hounds	5

The Finnish Spitz and the Samoyed are other examples. In Scandinavia there still exists a much larger version of the Elkhound called the Jamthund or Swedish Elkhound, recognised in Sweden but not elsewhere, and there are at least two other variations still in existence. The dog was originally developed as a hunter, but its other qualities have quickly been recognised and appreciated in most countries, where it makes an excellent guard and housedog. It retains the hunting instinct, and undoubtedly would enjoy a day in the woods, though whether in its smaller form it would still hunt and bay the Elk is another matter.

The coat of the Elkhound is one of its special features, being thick, abundant, coarse and weather resistant, and the extra length of hair around the neck gives it a most distinctive appearance. The dog is one of the stoutest breeds for its size, being very strong in the leg and with great stamina, quite capable of living out of doors in the coldest weathers, and extremely energetic.

As a showdog he has achieved a degree of popularity that does not compare with his Spitz cousins the Samoyed and the Chow Chow, but he has a following because of his tremendous comportment in the ring. The Norwegian Elkhound is easily trained to stand like a statue even when in close proximity to his fellows,

and while on occasions one will give tongue, on the whole when the Elkhounds are being shown things are fairly calm and quiet. There are certain problems in keeping him in good trim as from time to time he sheds his coat, and until this has grown again he loses a great deal of his glamour.

He is a friendly dog, very intelligent and alert, and with a good personality, never being dull and listless and always good company. His voice, which has a bell-like quality, handed down from his forebears who used it in the forests to disclose the whereabouts of the game, is a great deterrent to intruders.

OFFICIAL STANDARD

General appearance

The Norwegian Elkhound is a hardy gray hunting dog. In appearance, a typical northern dog of medium size and substance, square in profile, close coupled and balanced in proportions. The head is broad with prick ears, and the tail is tightly curled and carried over the back. The distinctive gray coat is dense and smooth-lying. In temperament, the Norwegian Elkhound is bold and energetic, an effective guardian yet normally friendly, with great dignity and independence of character. As a hunter, the Norwegian Elkhound has the courage, agility and stamina to hold moose and other big game at bay by barking and dodging attack, and the endurance to track for long hours in all weather over rough and varied terrain. In the show ring, presentation in a natural, unaltered condition is essential.

Head: broad between the ears, slightly arched nose, not pointed.

Head

Broad at the ears, wedge-shaped, strong, and dry (without loose skin). Viewed from the side, the forehead and back of the skull are only slightly arched; the stop not large, yet clearly defined. The bridge of the nose is straight, parallel to and about the same length as the skull. The muzzle is thickest at the base and, seen from above or from the side, tapers evenly without being pointed. Lips are tightly closed and teeth meet in a scissors bite.

Ears

Set high, firm and erect, yet very mobile. Comparatively small; slightly taller than their width at the base with pointed (not rounded) tips. When the dog is alert, the orifices turn forward and the outer edges are vertical.

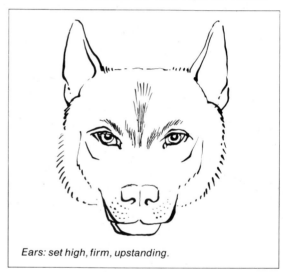

Ears: set high, firm, upstanding.

Eyes

Very dark brown, medium in size, oval, not protruding.

Neck

Of medium length, muscular, well set up with a slight arch and with no loose skin on the throat.

Body

Square in profile and close coupled. Distance from brisket to ground appears to be half the height at the withers. Distance from forechest to rump equals the height at the withers. Chest deep and moderately broad; brisket level with points of elbows; and ribs well sprung. Loin short and wide with very little tuck-up. The back is straight and strong from its high point at the withers to the root of the tail.

Forequarters

Shoulders sloping with elbows closely set on. Legs well under body and medium in length; substantial, but not coarse, in bone. Seen from the front, the legs appear

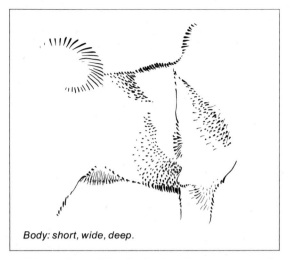

Body: short, wide, deep.

straight and parallel. Single dewclaws are normally present.

Hindquarters

Moderate angulation at stifle and hock. Thighs are broad and well-muscled. Seen from behind, legs are straight, strong and without dewclaws.

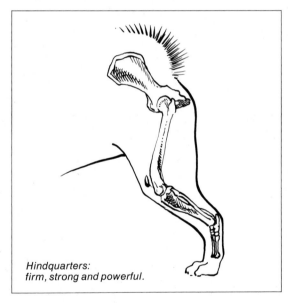

Hindquarters: firm, strong and powerful.

Feet

Paws comparatively small, slightly oval with tightly-closed toes and thick pads. Pasterns are strong and only slightly bent. Feet turn neither in nor out.

Tail

Set high, tightly curled, and carried over the centerline of the back. It is thickly and closely haired, without brush, natural and untrimmed.

Coat

Thick, hard, weather-resisting and smooth-lying; made up of soft, dense, woolly undercoat and coarse, straight covering hairs. Short and even on head, ears, and front of legs; longest on back of neck, buttocks and underside of tail. The coat is not altered by trimming, clipping or artificial treatment. Trimming of whiskers is optional.

Color

Gray, medium preferred, variations in shade determined by the length of black tips and quantity of guard hairs. Undercoat is clear light silver as are legs, stomach, buttocks, and underside of tail. The gray body color is darkest on the saddle, lighter on the chest, mane and distinctive harness mark (a band of longer guard hairs from shoulder to elbow). The muzzle, ears, and tail tip are black. The black of the muzzle shades to lighter gray over the forehead and skull. Yellow or brown shading, white patches, indistinct or irregular markings, 'sooty' coloring on the lower legs and light circle around the eyes are undesirable. Any overall color other than gray as described above, such as red, brown, solid black, white or other solid color, disqualifies.

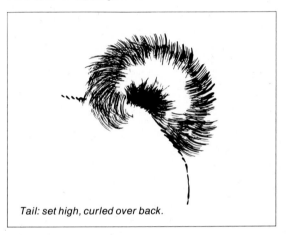

Tail: set high, curled over back.

Gait

Normal for an active dog constructed for agility and endurance. At a trot the stride is even and effortless; the back remains level. As the speed of the trot increases, front and rear legs converge equally in straight lines toward a center line beneath the body so that the pads appear to follow in the same tracks (single-track). Front and rear quarters are well balanced in angulation and muscular development.

Size

The height at the withers for dogs is $20\frac{1}{2}$ inches, for bitches $19\frac{1}{2}$ inches. Weight for dogs about 55 pounds; for bitches about 48 pounds.

DISQUALIFICATIONS
Any overall color other than gray as described above, such as red, brown, solid black, white or other solid color.

Approved by the AKC 13 February 1973

KC(GB) VARIATION TO STANDARD

The dog is known simply as the Elkhound in GB. *Weight:* dogs 50 pounds; bitches 43 pounds.

OTTER HOUND

NATIONAL GROUPING		
	Name	Number
AKC	Hounds	II
KC(GB)	—	—
FCI	Small Hounds	6

The first mention of the Otter Hound as a specific type of dog comes from the records left by William Twici the huntsman of a pack during the time of Edward II in the 14th century, who writes that they were a rough sort of dog between a Hound and a Terrier. To understand that description better one needs to remember that the Hound to which he was referring was probably something like the Southern Hound, an early form of Foxhound, and the Terrier would be fairly non-descript. Otter hunting never became as popular as fox hunting, largely because in the first place it is a wetter and more uncomfortable pursuit, and secondly because it lacks the glamorous trappings of the fox hunt. During the second half of the 19th century, however, there were upwards of twenty packs in Britain, most of these in the South West and in Wales where the otter was plentiful, and indeed still is.

The origins of the breed are obscure. The Southern Hound and the Harrier have been credited, the Water Spaniel and even the Bulldog have been said by some writers to have played a part in its makeup, but the idea that the breed originated in France is much more credible. A comparison between a painting of the head of a young Griffon de Bresse by Rosa Bonheur in the Wallace Collection and a head study by George Earl of an Otter Hound called Swimmer at the turn of the century, reveals a remarkable similarity, whilst a photograph of M. Henri Baillet's pack of Griffons Vendéens and Griffons Nivernais of the same period could well be a photograph of a pack of Otterhounds. It was at about the same time, the beginning of this century that the Otterhound first made his appearance in the United States, and in 1907 they were benched for the first time at a show in Claremont. The two first registered were owned by H. S. Wardner who was the first breeder of Otterhounds in the United States where they are still very popular.

The Otterhound's work in the field is remarkable, and he is noted for his fantastic nose and persistence. He is wary in the hunt, will rarely overrun a holt, and will stay on the trail through any sort of terrain and through deep fast-running water unwaveringly. Nothing will throw him off the trail, and when he gives tongue seriously, the location of his quarry is certain. He is a big strong noble looking hound in spite of his shaggy coat and somewhat unkempt appearance. He is described by George S. Lowe as requiring the courage of a Bulldog, the strength of a Newfoundland in water, the nose of a Pointer, the sagacity of a Retriever, the stamina of a Foxhound, the patience of a Beagle and the intelligence of a Collie. Praise indeed for a dog that has virtually disappeared in his home country. He is now rarely seen in his original form in Britain, and never on the show bench, whilst oddly enough, such is fashion, the Basset version of his probable ancestor is making rapid headway. The Otter Hound makes the most friendly and affectionate of companions and in addition to his prowess in the field, is a remarkably good guard and watch dog.

OFFICIAL STANDARD

General appearance
The Otter Hound is a large, rough-coated, squarely symmetrical hound. The length of a dog's body from withers to base of tail is approximately equal to its height at the withers. However, a bitch is not to be faulted if her length of body is slightly greater than her height. The Otter Hound is amiable and boisterous. It has an extremely sensitive nose, and is inquisitive and persevering in investigating scents. The Otter Hound should be shown on a loose lead. The Otter Hound hunts its quarry on land and water and requires a combination of characteristics unique among hounds—most notably a rough, double coat and webbed feet.

Head
The head is large, fairly narrow, and well covered with hair. The length from tip of nose to occiput is 11 to 12 inches in a hound 26 inches at the withers. This proportion should be maintained in larger and smaller hounds. The *skull* (cranium) is long, fairly narrow under the hair, and only slightly domed. The muzzle is long and square in cross-section with powerful jaws and deep flews. The *stop* is not pronounced. The *nose* is large, dark, and com-

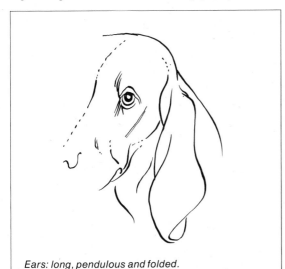

Ears: long, pendulous and folded.

pletely pigmented. The *ears* are long, pendulous, and folded. They are set low and hang close to the head. They are well covered and fringed with hair. The tips of the *ear* leather reach at least to the tip of the nose. The *eyes* are deeply set. The haw shows only slightly. The eyes are dark, but may vary with the color of the hound. The *jaws* are powerful and capable of a crushing grip. A scissors bite is preferred. *Faults:* bite grossly undershot or overshot.

Neck and body
The *neck* looks shorter than it really is because of the abundance of hair on it. The neck blends smoothly into the trunk. The *chest* is deep; the *ribs* extend well toward the rear of the trunk. The *topline* is level. The *tail* is fairly long, reaching at least to the hock. It is well feathered

(covered and fringed with hair). It is carried sickle-fashion (not over the back) when a dog is moving or alert, but may droop when the dog is at rest.

Forequarters
Shoulders clean, powerful, and well-sloped. *Legs* heavy-boned and straight.

Hindquarters
Thighs large and well-muscled. *Legs* moderately angulated. Legs parallel when viewed from the rear. *Feet* large, broad, compact, and well padded, with membranes connecting the toes (web-footed). *Dewclaws,* if any, on the hind legs are generally removed; dewclaws on the forelegs may be removed.

Coat
The rough outer coat is three to six inches long on the back, shorter on the extremities. It must be hard (coarse and crisp). A water-resistant inner coat of short woolly hair is an essential feature of the breed. A naturally stripped coat lacking length and fringes is correct for an Otter Hound that is being worked. A proper hunting coat will show the hard outer coat and woolly undercoat. *Faults:* a soft outer coat is a very serious fault as is a woolly-textured top coat. Lack of undercoat is a serious fault. An outer coat much longer than six inches becomes heavy when wet and is a fault.

Color
Any color or combination of colors is acceptable. The nose should be darkly pigmented, black or liver, depending on the color of the hound.

Gait
The Otter Hound moves freely with forward reach and drive. The gait is smooth and effortless and capable of being maintained for many miles. Otter Hounds single-track at slower speed than light-bodied hounds. Because they do not lift their feet high off the ground, Otter Hounds may shuffle when they walk or move at a slow trot.

Size
Dogs range from 24 to 27 inches at the withers, and weigh from 75 to 115 pounds, depending on the height and condition of the hound. Bitches are 22 to 26 inches at the withers and 65 to 100 pounds. A hound in hard working condition may weigh as much as 15 pounds less than one of the same height that is not being worked. Otter Hounds should not be penalized for being shown in working condition (lean, well-muscled, naturally stripped coat).

Approved by the AKC 12 October 1971

KC(GB) VARIATION TO STANDARD
This dog is not granted championship status by the KC(GB).

PHARAOH HOUND

NATIONAL GROUPING		
	Name	Number
AKC	—	—
KC(GB)	Hound	I
FCI	Coursing Dogs	10

The rise to popularity of the Pharaoh Hound has been one of the phenomena of the modern dog scene. In 1970 none were registered at the Kennel Club in England, and the breed was hardly known outside Malta. By 1975, the numbers had risen sufficiently for the breed to be granted championship status, and Mr. Hamilton-Renwick who had done so much to further the interests of the breed was judging them at Crufts. The more romantic among enthusiasts for the breed claim it as the most ancient form of dog in the world, and will date it back to some three thousand years BC. They will point to wall paintings in Egyptian tombs and claim that these depict early Pharaoh Hounds. In fact many of the prick-eared canine forms on early Egyptian works depicted the god Anubis, who was actually the Jackal God. The Pharaoh Hound was not the only prick-eared running hunting dog of the Mediterranean area. Italy, Spain and some of the islands can lay equal claim with similar dogs such as the Ibizan Hound. There is little doubt however, that the Pharaoh Hound is a very old breed. It was for a considerable length of time restricted to the island of Malta, and there it was bred true to type. It was at one time considered to be merely a colour variation of the Ibizan Hound, but has now been accepted as a separate breed.

It is probably this matter of colour which has affected the modern history of the dog. The dog now accepted as the Ibizan Hound, which was at one time known as the Podenco Ibicenco, was some years ago preferred as an all-red dog, the parti-coloured being less popular. Once the reds were separated and became a breed in their own right, their rapid rise was assured. The Pharaoh is a beautifully constructed Hound with most attractive body lines, long neck and straight bones, and his glowing reddish tan colour allied to a smooth glossy coat gain him many admirers. He was developed as a hunting dog from the even older dog known as the Egyptian Hound, which was noted for the ability to use his nose as well as his sight. He has retained this ability, and although he is what the Scandinavian countries would term a sight Hound he also has an excellent nose, something denied to the running Hounds proper such as the Greyhound.

As a show dog he has made a tremendous impression in many countries, being exhibited in large numbers in Britain and already being shown at major shows elsewhere. Although he is not yet recognised in the United States, there is little doubt that he will be one of the very popular show dogs of the future. He has the right temperament for the show ring, appearing to enjoy the admiration of the spectators and being in the company of others of his breed. He is steady in the ring, standing well and moving with great power and enjoyment when asked to do so. His coat repays attention as it is short and glossy and needs the minimum of brushing and polishing to look at its best. He is at his best at open-air shows, where when seen in numbers he creates a fine spectacle.

His temperament is most attractive as he is friendly, does not normally show signs of nervousness, is a happy dog and very good with children. He is clean and troublefree around the house, though in common with the other hunting dogs, he does need some exercise. Kept with others in sufficient space he will take exercise naturally, as his nature allows him to play with other dogs without quarrelling.

OFFICIAL STANDARD

Characteristics
An intelligent, friendly, affectionate, playful and alert breed. An alert keen hunter, the Pharaoh Hound hunts by scent and sight using its large ears to a marked degree when working close.

General appearance
The Pharaoh Hound is medium sized, of noble bearing with clean-cut lines. Graceful yet powerful. Very fast with free easy movement and alert expression.

Head and skull
Skull long, lean and well-chiselled. Foreface slightly longer than the skull. Only slight stop. Top of skull parallel with the foreface, the whole head representing a blunt wedge when viewed in profile and from above.

Eyes
Amber coloured, blending with the coat; oval, moderately deep set, with keen, intelligent expression.

Ears
Medium high set; carried erect when alert, but very mobile; broad at the base, fine and large.

Mouth
Powerful jaws with strong teeth. Scissor bite.

Nose
Flesh coloured only, blending with the coat.

Neck
Long, lean, muscular and slightly arched. Clean throat line.

Forequarters
Shoulders: strong, long and well laid back. *Forelegs:* straight and parallel. Elbows well tucked in. Pasterns strong.

Body
Lithe with almost straight topline. Slight slope down from croup to root of tail. Deep brisket extending down to point of elbow. Ribs well sprung. Moderate cut up. Length of body from breast to haunch bone slightly longer than height at withers.

Hindquarters
Strong and muscular. Moderate bend of stifle. Well developed second thigh. Limbs parallel when viewed from behind.

Feet
Strong, well knuckled and firm, turning neither in nor out. Paws well padded. Dew claws may be removed.

Gait
Free and flowing; the head should be held fairly high and the dog should cover the ground well without any apparent effort. The legs and feet should move in line with the body; any tendency to throw the feet sideways, or a high stepping 'hackney' action is a definite fault.

Tail
Medium set—fairly thick at the base and tapering (whip-like), reaching just below the point of hock in repose. Carried high and curved when the dog is in action. The tail should not be tucked between the legs. A screw tail is a fault.

Coat
Short and glossy, ranging from fine and close to slightly harsh; no feathering.

Colour
Tan or rich tan with white markings allowed as follows: White tip on tail strongly desired. White on chest (called 'The Star'). White on toes. Slim white blaze on centre line of face permissible. Flecking or white other than above undesirable.

Height
Dogs: ideally 56–63 cm (22 to 25 inches). *Bitches:* ideally 53–61 cm (21 to 24 inches). Overall balance must be maintained.

Faults
Any deviation from the foregoing is a fault, hunting blemishes excepted.

Note
Male animals should have two apparently normal testicles fully descended into the scrotum.

AKC VARIATION TO STANDARD
This dog is not granted championship status by the AKC. The above standards are those of the KC(GB).

149

RHODESIAN RIDGEBACK

On a farm called 'Valhalla' twenty miles north of Rusape, Rhodesia, there is a rock. The cow, the ox and the dogs depicted in the carving on the rock indicate that the scene is of the burial preparations for a chief, a Hottentot Chief. Hump-backed Zebu cattle and ridged hunting dogs were prize possessions of the Hottentot; the cattle were the forebears of the Afrikaner cattle, and the dogs the ancestors of the modern Rhodesian Ridgeback. These dogs were known in Rhodesia a long time before the coming of the white man, though probably the earliest published illustration showing the dog is in 'Livingstone's Missionary Travels in South Africa,' (1857), which clearly shows a dog with a ridge of hair on its back.

It is from this dog that the modern Rhodesian Ridgeback is descended. Undoubtedly there was some crossing with breeds brought in by the early settlers, but the resulting dog was a fine strong hunter that retained the ridge. There is record of dogs being brought to Matabeleland in 1875 and of their being crossed with a hunting pack by a big game hunter

NATIONAL GROUPING		
	Name	Number
AKC	Hounds	11
KC(GB)	Hound	1
FCI	Small Hounds	6

Cornelis van Rooyen and of dogs very like the modern hound being produced. In the 1920's there were a number of different ridged dogs in South Africa, and a meeting was held to compile a standard for the breed. That standard has stood the test of time, with certain minor changes. Since the 1920's the breed and the breed club have gone from strength to strength, and the Rhodesian Ridgeback has been constantly improved.

In the early days the dog was used by big game hunters for the hunting of lion, hence the additional name of 'lion dog', though it is certain that no dog exists that could succeed in a fight with a lion. What the dog did, and probably still does, is to torment the lion by feint attacks in much the same way as the Elkhound worries the Elk, until such time as the hunter can come up with it and shoot it. This means that the dog must have great agility as well as power, as the lion is one of the quickest beasts in spite of its size. He must also be able to run at speed to chase and cut off escaping game. The Rhodesian Ridgeback will, however, attack lesser game than the lion, and this is where the weight of the dog tells, the usual technique being for the dog to charge and knock over the game. He has a good nose and works quite well as a gundog.

As a showdog he is a fine animal, his size and muscularity in the ring giving a great impression of power. He handles well, and a ring full of the breed is usually quiet and well-behaved, though there is a certain amount of suspicion evident between them. When first introduced into Britain this dog was thought to be difficult to handle, but this may well have been due to one or two unfortunate importations,

as it has now settled down and has proved completely tractable.

The Ridgeback becomes very attached to his owner and family, proving an excellent guard, as he will stand no nonsense from strangers, and is very positive in his attention to intruders. Whilst the notice 'Beware of the Dog' rarely prevents anyone from entering property, the notice 'Beware of the Rhodesian Ridgeback' would ensure privacy. His warning is often a low growl rather than a bark, but it is very effective. Judges laying their hands on the dog in the ring will often feel this rumble even if they don't hear it, and whilst it does not mean that the dog is immediately about to attack, it does mean that the dog is wary of the attention being given it. He is still used a great deal as a guard in Southern Africa, being a multi-purpose animal, guarding the property day and night, available for a day's hunting at any time, and always prepared to make a fuss of the children.

OFFICIAL STANDARD

The peculiarity of this breed is the *ridge* on the back, which is formed by the hair growing in the opposite direction to the rest of the coat. The ridge must be regarded as the characteristic feature of the breed. The ridge should be clearly defined, tapering and symmetrical. It should start immediately behind the shoulders and continue to a point between the prominence of the hips, and should contain two identical crowns opposite each other. The lower edges of the crown should not extend further down the ridge than one third of the ridge.

General appearance
The Ridgeback should represent a strong muscular and active dog, symmetrical in outline, and capable of great endurance with a fair amount of speed.

Head
Should be of a fair length, the skull flat and rather broad

between the ears and should be free from wrinkles when in repose. The stop should be reasonably well defined. *Muzzle:* should be long, deep and powerful, jaws level and strong with well-developed teeth, especially the canines or holders. The lips clean, closely fitting the jaws. *Eyes:* should be moderately well apart, and should be round, bright and sparkling, with intelligent expression, their color harmonizing with the color of the dog. *Ears:* should be set rather high, of medium size, rather wide at base, and tapering to a rounded point. They should be

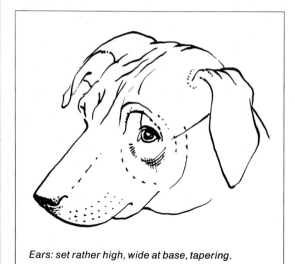

Ears: set rather high, wide at base, tapering.

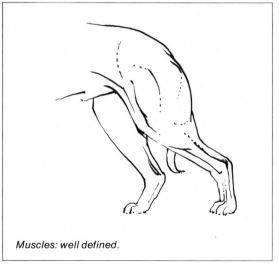

Muscles: well defined.

carried close to the head. *Nose:* should be black, or brown, in keeping with the color of the dog. No other colored nose is permissible. A black nose should be accompanied by dark eyes, a brown nose by amber eyes.

Neck and shoulders

The neck should be fairly strong and free from throatiness. The shoulders should be sloping, clean and muscular, denoting speed.

Body, back, chest and loins

The chest should not be too wide, but very deep and capacious; ribs moderately well sprung, never rounded like barrel hoops (which would indicate want of speed), the back powerful, the loins strong, muscular and slightly arched.

Legs and feet

The forelegs should be perfectly straight, strong and heavy in bone; elbows close to the body. The feet should be compact, with well-arched toes, round, tough, elastic pads, protected by hair between the toes and pads. In the hind legs the muscles should be clean, well defined, and hocks well down.

Tail

Should be strong at the insertion, and generally tapering towards the end, free from coarseness. It should not be inserted too high or too low, and should be carried with a slight curve upwards, never curled.

Coat

Should be short and dense, sleek and glossy in appearance, but neither woolly nor silky.

Color

Light wheaten to red wheaten. A little white on the chest and toes permissible but excessive white there and any white on the belly or above the toes is undesirable.

Size

A mature Ridgeback should be a handsome, upstanding dog; dogs should be of a height of 25 to 27 inches, and bitches 24 to 26 inches.

Weight

(Desirable) dogs 75 pounds, bitches 65 pounds.

Approved by the AKC November 1955

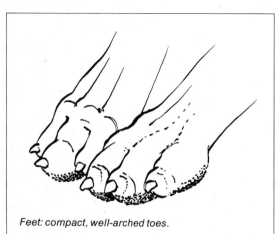

Feet: compact, well-arched toes.

KC(GB) VARIATION TO STANDARD

Head: not in one straight line from nose to occiput bone as required in a Bull Terrier. *Weight:* (desirable) dogs 80 pounds; bitches 70 pounds.

SALUKI

NATIONAL GROUPING		
	Name	Number
AKC	Hounds	II
KC(GB)	Hound	I
FCI	Coursing Dogs	10

When the ice age finally withdrew it moved gradually north. Some of the earliest evidence of man as he exists today was found in the areas that were the first to become fertile and warm, and it was there that the earliest traces of man's association with the canine race were found. Saluki breeders will claim that these early traces, found as cave paintings, show man with his dog, and that dog is a Saluki, or at least a Saluki type. Certainly the dog would have been a long-legged hunting dog, as this is the type that early man would have found useful. Whether it was anything like the Saluki as we know it today, is another matter, as many other breeds have also staked a claim.

The Saluki was, and probably still is, the dog of the Bedouin. Still a nomadic tribesman, the Bedouin needs to hunt to stay alive, as he still lives as his forefathers did, moving from place to place, living off the land and then moving on again when the resources of one area fail him. The dog has always been the prized possession of the tribesmen, being kept very close, even hidden away when strangers are around, and used for the hunt in the early hours of the morning before the heat of the sun. In the early days it was difficult to get a tribesman to part with his dog, as it was considered a member of the family as well as valuable.

As was the Afghan, the Saluki was used in conjunction with a hawk. The hawk was trained to swoop at the head of the game and slow it down until the dog could catch up with it and pull it down. This training was a long and complicated business, and tribes had their Hound attendants and huntsmen whose duty it was to train both bird and dog. Although the Saluki has been known for so long a time, it was not seen in Britain until 1840, and was not recognised by the American Kennel Club until 1927.

This dog is one of the most graceful dogs in the world. As yet another of the Greyhounds, it is the perfectly built running machine with long well angulated legs, great depth of ribs to give it heart and lung room, and a long neck to assist it to pick up game. It remains basically a hunter and a strong dog, capable of moving at high speeds over the roughest of going, picking its way over rocks and through gullies at a speed that would defy most animals. Like the Greyhound proper, its appearance has changed little over the centuries.

As a show dog the Saluki has reached the heights, winning consistently at all the major shows throughout the world, and a mature Saluki in full coat, moving round the ring with long flowing strides and great pride, is a fine sight.

He is a gentle, dignified dog with an attractive attitude towards human beings, being most friendly. He is somewhat aloof at first and does not take quickly to strangers, but once he attaches himself to a person, he does so for life.

OFFICIAL STANDARD

General appearance
The whole appearance of this breed should give an impression of grace and symmetry and of great speed and endurance coupled with strength and activity to enable it to kill gazelle or other quarry over deep sand or rocky mountains. The expression should be dignified and gentle with deep, faithful, far-seeing eyes. Dogs should average in height from 23 to 28 inches and bitches may be considerably smaller, this being very typical of the breed.

Head
Long and narrow, skull moderately wide between the ears, not domed, stop not pronounced, the whole showing great quality. Nose black or liver. *Ears:* long and covered with long silky hair hanging close to the skull and mobile. *Eyes:* dark to hazel and bright; large and oval, but not prominent. *Teeth:* strong and level.

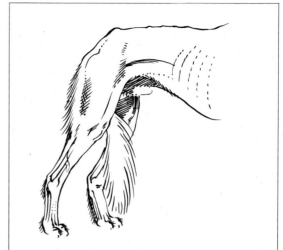
Hindquarter: stifle moderately bent, hocks low.

Head: long and narrow, great quality.

Loin and back
Back fairly broad, muscles slightly arched over loin.

Feet
Of moderate length, toes long and well arched, not splayed out, but at the same time not cat-footed; the whole being strong and supple and well feathered between the toes.

Tail
Long, set on low and carried naturally in a curve, well feathered on the underside with long silky hair, not bushy.

Coat
Smooth and of a soft silky texture, slight feather on the legs, feather at the back of the thighs and sometimes with slight woolly feather on the thigh and shoulder.

Colors
White, cream, fawn, golden, red, grizzle and tan, tricolor (white, black and tan) and black and tan.

The smooth variety: in this variety the points should be the same with the exception of the coat, which has no feathering.

Neck
Long, supple and well muscled.

Chest
Deep and moderately narrow.

Forequarters
Shoulders sloping and set well back, well muscled without being coarse.

Forelegs
Straight and long from the elbow to the knee.

Hindquarters
Strong, hipbones set well apart and stifle moderately bent, hocks low to the ground, showing galloping and jumping power.

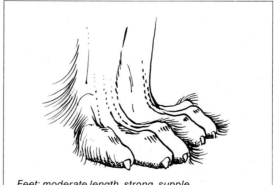
Feet: moderate length, strong, supple.

SCOTTISH DEERHOUND

NATIONAL GROUPING		
	Name	Number
AKC	Hounds	II
KC(GB)	Hound	I
FCI	Coursing Dogs	10

The Greyhound in some form has existed as long as records have been kept, and probably longer. Although the name has become synonymous with the English Greyhound, it was used at one time to describe all the long-legged coursing dogs. In Scotland it evolved in a very special form, now known as the Deerhound, as it was for the purpose of hunting the indigenous deer of Scotland that the breed was developed. Dr. Caius wrote of the family that 'some are smooth skinned and some are curled, the bigger therefore are appointed to hunt the bigger beastes'. Apart from the Elk, there are few members of the deer family larger than the Red Deer of Scotland, and it needed a large, fast and very agile dog to hunt them. It is closely related to the Irish Wolfhound, and there is every likelihood that the two have common ancestors somewhere among the early large running dogs described by Dr. Caius.

The Deerhound has always been associated with the castles of Scotland, and the vision brought to mind by most people when discussing them is of a large marble fireplace with a roaring log fire, a Deerhound or even a couple of Hounds curled up in front of the blaze whilst the laird sips his dram to the music of bagpipes. This is not far from the truth, as at one time only gentry were allowed to own these hounds for fear that the commoners might use them to poach his lordship's deer, as they undoubtedly would have done. Writers wrote of them and artists drew and painted them. The breed was a great favourite of Landseer's whose drawings and paintings of these dogs in the 19th century depict animals exactly like the ones that we have today.

Like so many of the game chasing dogs, the Deerhound has a dual personality, soft and even sentimental in his attachment to the family to which he belongs, yet an absolute killer when roused to the chase. He has the slightly mincing gait of the perfect running machine, with little of the striding out behind of the working dogs and with a somewhat delicate air. In full flight however he is a different creature, covering the ground with tremendous strides, almost leaps, and conveying his slender frame over rough territory at great speed.

The numbers of the breed are not high, as the Deerhound is a large dog needing a fair amount of food and is at his best on a large estate with acres of grass on which to exercise himself. The numbers have been growing steadily over recent years, however, largely because of the efforts of a few enthusiasts who have shown the breed fearlessly and kept it in front of the public. He is easily prepared for show, having the sort of coat that is natural and does not need a great deal of attention or trimming, and his behaviour in the ring is always gentlemanly.

Temperamentally the breed is most attractive, never boisterous, always obedient and what the running dog people call biddable. He is a lovely dog to own, attaching himself to one person and being extremely faithful. The Deerhound, like most of the running dogs is quiet and trustworthy, and centuries of domestication have developed a creature that enjoys human company and the comforts of the house.

OFFICIAL STANDARD

Head

Should be broadest at the ears, narrowing slightly to the eyes, with the muzzle tapering more decidedly to the nose. The muzzle should be pointed, but the teeth and lips level. The head should be long, the skull flat rather than round with a very slight rise over the eyes but nothing approaching a stop. The hair on the skull should be moderately

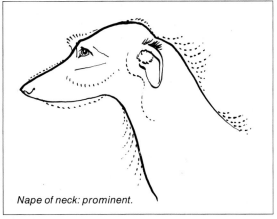

Nape of neck: prominent.

long and softer than the rest of the coat. The nose should be black (in some blue fawns—blue) and slightly aquiline. In lighter colored dogs the black muzzle is preferable. There should be a good mustache of rather silky hair and a fair beard.

Ears

Should be set on high; in repose, folded back like a Greyhound's, though raised above the head in excitement without losing the fold, and even in some cases semierect. A prick ear is bad. Big thick ears hanging flat to the head or heavily coated with long hair are bad faults. The ears should be soft, glossy, like a mouse's coat to the touch and the smaller the better. There should be no long coat or long fringe, but there is sometimes a silky, silvery coat on the body of the ear and the tip. On all Deerhounds,

irrespective of color of coat, the ears should be black or dark coloured.

Neck and shoulders

The neck should be long—of a length befitting the Greyhound character of the dog. Extreme length is neither necessary nor desirable. Deerhounds do not stoop to their work like the Greyhounds. The mane, which every good specimen should have, sometimes detracts from the apparent length of the neck. The neck, however, must be as strong as is necessary to hold a stag. The nape of the neck should be very prominent where the head is set on, and the throat clean cut at the angle and prominent. Shoulders should be well sloped; blades well back and not too much width between them. Loaded and straight shoulders are very bad faults.

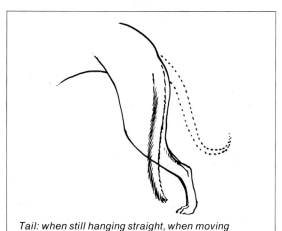

Tail: when still hanging straight, when moving curved, never over back.

Tail

Should be tolerably long, tapering and reaching to within $1\frac{1}{2}$ inches of the ground and about $1\frac{1}{2}$ inches below the hocks. Dropped perfectly down or curved when the Deerhound is still, when in motion or excited, curved, but in no instance lifted out of line of the back. It should be well covered with hair, on the inside, thick and wiry, underside longer and towards the end a slight fringe is not objectionable. A curl or ring tail is undesirable.

Ears: raised above head in excitement.

Eyes

Should be dark—generally dark brown, brown or hazel. A very light eye is not liked. The eye should be moderately full, with a soft look in repose, but a keen, far-away look when the Deerhound is roused. Rims of eyelids should be black.

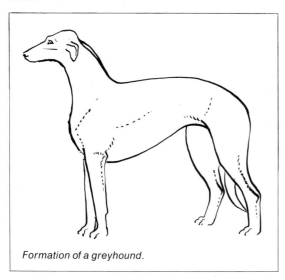

Formation of a greyhound.

Body

General conformation is that of a Greyhound of larger size and bone. Chest deep rather than broad but not too narrow or slab-sided. Good girth of chest is indicative of great lung power. The loin well arched and drooping to the tail. A straight back is not desirable, this formation being unsuited for uphill work, and very unsightly.

Legs and feet

Legs should be broad and flat, and good broad forearms and elbows are desirable. Forelegs must, of course, be as straight as possible. Feet close and compact, with well-arranged toes. The hindquarters drooping, and as broad and powerful as possible, the hips being set wide apart. A narrow rear denotes lack of power. The stifles should be well bent, with great length from hip to hock, which should be broad and flat. Cow hocks, weak pasterns, straight stifles and splay feet are very bad faults.

Coat

The hair on the body, neck and quarters should be harsh and wiry, about 3 or 4 inches long; that on the head, breast and belly much softer. There should be a slight fringe on the inside of the forelegs and hind legs but nothing approaching the 'feather' of a Collie. A woolly coat is bad. Some good strains have a mixture of silky coat with the hard which is preferable to a woolly coat. The climate of the United States tends to produce the mixed coat. The ideal coat is a thick, close-lying ragged coat, harsh or crisp to the touch.

Color

Is a matter of fancy, but the dark blue-gray is most preferred. Next come the darker and lighter grays or brindles, the darkest being generally preferred. Yellow and sandy red or red fawn, especially with black ears and muzzles, are equally high in estimation. This was the color of the oldest known strains—the McNeil and Chesthill Menzies. White is condemned by all authorities, but a white chest and white toes, occurring as they do in many of the darkest-colored dogs, are not objected to, although the less the better, for the Deerhound is a self-colored dog. A white blaze on the head, or a white collar, should entirely disqualify. The less white the better but a slight white tip to the stern occurs in some of the best strains.

Height

Height of dogs: from 30 to 32 inches, or even more if there be symmetry without coarseness, which is rare. *Height of bitches:* from 28 inches upwards. There is no objection to a bitch being large, unless too coarse, as even at her greatest height she does not approach that of the dog, and therefore could not be too big for work as overbig dogs are.

Weight

From 85 to 110 pounds in dogs, and from 75 to 95 pounds in bitches.

POINTS OF THE DEERHOUND
ARRANGED IN ORDER OF IMPORTANCE

1. *Typical:* a Deerhound should resemble a rough-coated Greyhound of larger size and bone. 2. *Movements:* easy, active and true. 3. As tall as possible consistent with quality. 4. *Head:* long, level, well balanced, carried high. 5. *Body:* long, very deep in brisket, well-sprung ribs and great breadth across hips. 6. *Forelegs:* strong and quite straight, with elbows neither in nor out. 7. *Thighs:* long and muscular, second thighs well muscled, stifles well bent. 8. *Loins:* well arched, and belly well drawn up. 9. *Coat:* rough and hard, with softer beard and brows. 10. *Feet:* close, compact, with well-knuckled toes. 11. *Ears:* small (dark) with Greyhoundlike carriage. 12. *Eyes:* dark, moderately full. 13. *Neck:* long, well arched, very strong with prominent nape. 14. *Shoulders:* clean, set sloping. 15. *Chest:* very deep but not too narrow. 16. *Tail:* long and curved slightly, carried low. 17. *Teeth:* strong and level. 18. *Nails:* strong and curved.

DISQUALIFICATION
White blaze on the head, or a white collar.

Approved by the AKC March 1935

KC(GB) VARIATION TO STANDARD

This dog is known simply as the Deerhound in GB. *Weight:* dogs 85 to 105 pounds; bitches 65 to 80 pounds. *Fault:* white markings.

WHIPPET

The history of many breeds of dog is shrouded in the obscurity that years of unrecorded progress brings. None more so than the Whippet. From its shape, use and character we can assume a great deal, but much of the early breeding went unrecorded, as it was carried out in areas where more attention was paid to breaking records than to keeping them, and only then to produce running and coursing dogs.

The origin of the name too is obscure. It has been suggested that it came from the word whip, to snap or crack like a whip, and that the sharp quick character of the dog led to the use of the name 'whippet' or little whip. There are however early mentions of a breed of dog that is not recorded pictorially called a Wappit, for example 'sporting dogs out of this question of which doubtless every farmer desires to possess some, the useful pack upon a farm consists of Sheepdogs, Rough Terriers, Vermin Curs and Wappits'. Around the latter part of the 19th century the racing of small dogs over a short straight course was extremely popular among the working classes of the North East of England. The area consisted largely of industrial towns and cities based upon the coalfields, and the miners needed a sport which was not too expensive, and in which they themselves could indulge as owners, whilst satisfying their native desire to keep animals and improve strains.

The Whippet fulfilled all the requirements. He is a small dog, easily housed and fed, and readily becomes a member of the household, living indoors, keeping the children company, and needing the type of exercise that can be given him on quiet walks round the streets and at the odd race or two at the weekend. Originally the dog used in the North East was a type of Terrier, often rough-coated, always long in the leg and very game, enthusiastic about chasing anything that moved,

NATIONAL GROUPING		
	Name	Number
AKC	Hounds	II
KC(GB)	Hound	I
FCI	Coursing Dogs	10

and prepared to kill at the end of the chase. This itself was important, as an occasional rabbit did not come amiss as a supplement to the often meagre family fare of the hard-working and underpaid underground worker and his family.

When dog shows became popular in England, and it is often suggested that this happened in the first instance in the Newcastle area, the breed rapidly changed to the dog that we now know so well. The smooth coats ousted the roughs, though the latter can still be seen racing in mining areas. The Whippet became a shapely dog, with all the beauty that the swiftest of animals possesses; indeed the Whippet is one of the fastest of all dogs over a short distance, capable of outdistancing even the Greyhound on its initial burst.

The breed has become popular as a show dog throughout the world, largely because of its temperament. The Whippet is among the easiest of dogs to prepare, transport and handle in the ring, even the youngest child being capable of achieving a rapport with one which would be impossible with most breeds. In addition there are few dogs that are as well-behaved in the house, clean in manner and as friendly.

OFFICIAL STANDARD

General appearance

A moderate size sight hound giving the appearance of elegance and fitness, denoting great speed, power, and balance without coarseness. A true sporting hound that covers a maximum of distance with a minumum of lost motion.

Head

Long and lean, fairly wide between the ears, scarcely perceptible stop, good length of muzzle which should be powerful without being coarse. Nose entirely black. *Ears:* small, fine in texture, thrown back and folded. Semi-pricked when at attention. Gay ears are incorrect and should be severely penalized. *Eyes:* large, dark, with keen intelligent alert expression. Lack of pigmentation around eyelids is undesirable. Yellow or dilute-colored eyes should be strictly penalized. Blue or china-colored eyes shall disqualify. Both eyes must be of the same color. *Muzzle:* muzzle should be long and powerful denoting great strength of 'bite' without coarseness. Teeth should be white and strong. Teeth of upper jaw should fit closely over teeth of lower jaw creating a strong scissors bite. Extremely short muzzle or lack of underjaw should be strictly penalized. An even bite is extremely undesirable. Undershot shall disqualify. Overshot one-quarter inch or more shall disqualify.

Neck

Long and muscular, well-arched and with no suggestion of throatiness, widening gradually into the shoulders. Must not have any tendency to a 'ewe' neck.

Shoulders

Long, well-laid back with long, flat muscles. Loaded shoulders are a *very* serious fault.

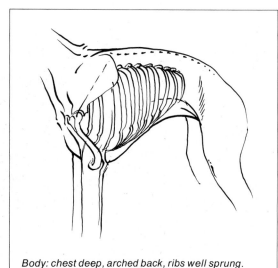

Body: chest deep, arched back, ribs well sprung.

Brisket

Very deep and strong, reaching as nearly as possible to the point of the elbow. Ribs well sprung but with no sugges-

tion of barrel shape. Should fill in the space between the forelegs so that there is no appearance of a hollow between them.

Forelegs

Straight and rather long, held in line with the shoulders and not set under the body so as to make a forechest. Elbows should turn neither in nor out and move freely with the point of the shoulder. Fair amount of bone, which should carry right down to the feet. Pasterns strong.

Feet

Must be well formed with strong, thick pads and well-knuckled-up paws. A thin, flat, open foot is a serious fault.

Hindquarters

Long and powerful, stifles well bent, hocks well let down and close to the ground. Thighs broad and muscular, the muscles should be long and flat. A steep croup is most undesirable.

Back

Strong and powerful, rather long with a good, natural arch over the loin creating a definite tuck-up of the underline but covering a lot of ground.

Tail

Long and tapering, should reach to a hipbone when drawn through between the hind legs. Must not be carried higher than the top of the back when moving.

Coat

Close, smooth, and firm in texture.

Color

Immaterial.

Size

Ideal height for dogs, 19 to 22 inches; for bitches, 18 to 21 inches, measured across the shoulders at the highest point. One-half inch above or below the above stated measurements will disqualify.

Gait

Low, free moving and smooth, as long as is commensurate with the size of the dog. A short, mincing gait with high knee action should be severely penalized.

DISQUALIFICATIONS
Blue or china-colored eyes. Undershot. Overshot one-quarter inch or more. A dog one-half inch above or below the measurements specified under 'Size'.

Approved by the AKC 12 October 1971

KC(GB) VARIATION TO STANDARD

Nose: in blues a bluish colour is permitted and in livers a nose of same colour and in whites or parti-colours a butterfly nose is permissible. *Tail:* no feathering. *Height:* (ideal) dogs $18\frac{1}{2}$ inches; bitches $17\frac{1}{2}$ inches.

GROUP III: WORKING DOGS

Akita

Alaskan Malamute

German Shepherd Dog

Belgian Malinois

Belgian Sheepdog

Belgian Tervuren

Bernese Mountain Dog

Bouvier des Flandres

Boxer

Briard

Bullmastiff

Bearded Collie

Collie

Giant Schnauzer

Doberman Pinscher

Great Dane

Puli

Komondor

Kuvasz

Standard Schnauzer

Norwegian Buhund

Mastiff

Newfoundland

Old English Sheepdog

Rottweiler

Great Pyrenees

Saint Bernard

Cardigan Welsh Corgi

Pembroke Welsh Corgi

Samoyed

Shetland Sheepdog

Siberian Husky

GROUP III: WORKING DOGS

Since early in the days of dog's association with man, he has been put to work, even if it was only as a guard dog. The group now known as the Working Group has dogs used for a multitude of purposes, from the tiny sheep-herding Shetland Sheepdog to the giant property-guarding Mastiff. Many of the tasks the dogs have learned to undertake are an extension of a natural instinct. The herding dogs for instance are trained to use their instinct to chase anything that runs, and the guard dogs merely exercising on someone else's behalf their natural desire to protect their own territory.

There are those which are essentially guards, those that work as draught animals, originally in sledges and small carts and more recently for sport. There are the herders, and this is probably the largest sub-group, as work with animals has been widespread throughout the world for centuries, and there are a few heelers and cattle dogs. All, however, have one thing in common, they are intelligent enough to be trained, often in very complicated tasks, and with a couple of exceptions, they are large, strong and muscular animals.

When the wild dog first came into contact with early man he would have done so almost certainly as a whelp from a litter of wolves or wild dogs, and partly tamed, his guarding of the area inhabited by the tribe would merely be an extension of his natural defence of his own territory as he exercised it in the wild state. In later years this defensive instinct was encouraged and breeds of dogs were evolved for the purpose, large strong and fierce dogs often used as war dogs and usually of the Mastiff type, though many of the herding dogs doubled as guard dogs, including the home in with the herd as part of their responsibility.

There is a mixed category of hauling dogs in the Group, those that were developed specifically for work in the snow and ice of the Arctic, such as the Huskies and the Samoyed, and others which were used to tow small carts in countries such as Switzerland and the Netherlands. These were used by tradesmen for delivery purposes as an inexpensive alternative to the horse. Though the use of dogs for draught purposes is now banned in most countries, they are still very much in demand as sledge dogs, and are used both seriously and for competitive purposes as racing teams.

By far the largest number of breeds in the Group are those which originally were herding dogs. As man ceased to be nomadic he collected around him herds of beasts that supplied almost everything that he needed, food, drink and clothing. These herds became very precious possessions, and needed to be protected from predatory wild animals as well as kept within the confines of the immediate area of the settlement. For this purpose a wide variety of breeds was evolved to suit both the work and the conditions under which it had to be carried out. In the mountainous country of the Pyrenees a large dog was needed, capable of herding but also of defending against the wolves that existed until recent years. In the less rigorous conditions of Britain the Collie or the Old English Sheepdog were more suitable, whilst in the severe climate of such places as Hungary dogs with protective coats were needed.

Other dogs were evolved for specific purposes. The heelers, the Corgis of Wales for driving cattle by nipping at their heels, and the Rottweilers of Southern Germany which were cattle drovers are typical examples. Subsequently the Collie was developed not just to work as a sheep herder, but to excel in competition, the Border Collie having a world-wide reputation in this field. In those countries where the rearing of sheep is an important industry such as Australia the sheepdog still plays a very important part even in these days of mechanisation, and a considerable degree of specialisation takes place.

The Group includes some of the most popular breeds of dogs in the world, underlining the fact that the process of breeding dogs for exhibition has in no way detracted from their usefulness as workers, as many countries insist on a dog being proved capable of carrying out the task for which it was evolved, before it can gain its full title as a show dog.

AKITA

NATIONAL GROUPING		
	Name	Number
AKC	Working Dogs	III
KC(GB)	—	–
FCI	Guard Dogs	2

The most important dog in Japan is without doubt the Akita. The breed is numerous, is a most trusted member of many families, and has become almost a legend for his combination of courage and kindness. To equate him with the Chow Chow is doing him a disservice even though there is a great deal of resemblance to that ancient breed. A breed exists on the waterfront of Hong Kong, which guards the godowns and timber yards which is nearer than the smooth Chow Chow is to the Akita, and those who only know the smooth Chow from the version seen in recent years in the Western World probably have a false impression of the original Chow. The Akita is a fairly long-legged version of the Chow type with curled tail and pricked ears, and it is more than likely that the two breeds descended from a common ancestor which looked rather like the present day harbour dogs of Hong Kong.

Records place the first development of the breed somewhere in the early part of the 17th century when an exiled nobleman with a keen interest in dogs took up residence in Akita Province. He encouraged the landowners of that province to breed a race of large hunting dogs from which, by selective breeding the Akita resulted. At one time the ownership of the breed was restricted to the aristocracy and the Imperial family, and they became as much a legend in their time as did the Pekingese of China, a special language being evolved for talking with and about them, and dog minders who looked after Akitas wore a special and elaborate costume. In 1927 the Akitainu Hozankai Society of Japan was established to preserve the breed as it had gone into serious decline. The Japanese Government supported the breed and the society to the extent of giving financial support to a dog which by this time had become accepted as something of a national symbol.

He is essentially a hunting dog, strong with a good nose and keen eyesight, and staunch enough to tackle bear and wild boar. He can be trained to retrieve, is a good water dog and is even said to have been used to drive fish into the fisherman's nets. The first to arrive in the United States of America were brought in by the celebrated Helen Keller who was presented with a puppy by the Ministry of Education in Akita in 1937. American servicemen returning from the Far East after the Second World War brought others back with them, and from that time onwards the breed's popularity has grown with remarkable speed in the West. The faithfulness of the breed is exemplified by a dog named Hachiko who continued to arrive at Shibuya station to meet his master for nine years after his owner had died, daily in fact until he himself died in 1934. A statue, erected by public subscription stands on the station to commemorate his devotion. The Akita Club of America was formed in 1956 and the breed is now admitted to register by the American Kennel Club though it remains unshown in Britain.

The whole tradition of the breed has been built around his faithfulness to the family and his loyalty to its members, and though reserved in general behaviour he is very affectionate and thrives on human companionship. He makes a very good house dog and pet, and is a first class guard, especially of children and stock.

OFFICIAL STANDARD

General appearance
Large, powerful, alert, with much substance and heavy bone. The broad head, forming a blunt triangle, with deep muzzle, small eyes and erect ears carried forward in line with back of neck, is characteristic of the breed. The large, curled tail, balancing the broad head, is also characteristic of the breed.

Head
Massive but in balance with body; free of wrinkle when at ease. Skull flat between ears and broad; jaws square and powerful with minimal dewlap. Head forms a blunt

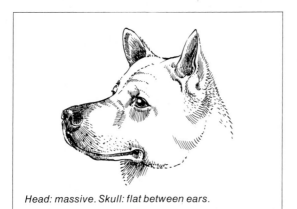

Head: massive. Skull: flat between ears.

triangle when viewed from above. *Fault:* narrow or snipy head. *Muzzle:* broad and full. Distance from nose to stop is to distance from stop to occiput as 2 is to 3. *Stop:* well defined, but not too abrupt. A shallow furrow extends well up forehead. *Nose:* broad and black. Liver permitted on white Akitas, but black always preferred. *Disqualification:* butterfly nose or total lack of pigmentation on nose. *Ears:* the ears of the Akita are characteristic of the breed. They are strongly erect and small in relation to rest of head. If ear is folded forward for measuring length, tip will touch upper eye rim. Ears are triangular, slightly rounded at tip, wide at base, set wide on head but not too low, and carried slightly forward over eyes in line with back of neck. *Disqualification:* drop or broken ears. *Eyes:* dark brown, small, deep-set and triangular in shape. Eye rims black and tight. *Lips and Tongue:* lips black and not pendulous; tongue pink. *Teeth:* strong with scissors bite preferred, but level bite acceptable. *Disqualification:* noticeably undershot or overshot.

Neck and body

Neck: thick and muscular; comparatively short, widening gradually toward shoulders. A pronounced crest blends in with base of skull. *Body:* longer than high, as 10 is to 9 in dogs; 11 to 9 in bitches. Chest wide and deep; depth of chest is one-half height of dog at shoulder. Ribs well sprung, brisket well developed. Level back with firmly-muscled loin and moderate tuck-up. Skin pliant but not loose. *Serious faults:* light bone, rangy body.

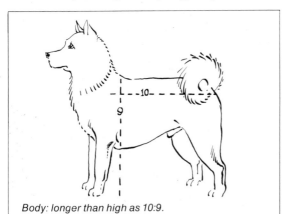

Body: longer than high as 10:9.

Tail

Large and full, set high and carried over back or against flank in a three-quarter, full, or double curl, always dipping to or below level of back. On a three-quarter curl, tip drops well down flank. Root large and strong. Tail bone reaches hock when let down. Hair coarse, straight and full, with no appearance of a plume. *Disqualification:* sickle or uncurled tail.

Forequarters and hindquarters

Forequarters: shoulders strong and powerful with moderate layback. Forelegs heavy-boned and straight as viewed from front. Angle of pastern 15 degrees forward from vertical. *Faults:* elbows in or out, loose shoulders. *Hindquarters:* width, muscular development and comparable to forequarters. Upper thighs well developed. Stifle moderately bent and hocks well let down, turning neither in nor out. *Dewclaws:* on front legs generally not removed; dewclaws on hind legs generally removed. *Feet:* cat feet, well knuckled up with thick pads. Feet straight ahead.

Coat

Double-coated. Undercoat thick, soft, dense and shorter than outer coat. Outer coat straight, harsh and standing somewhat off body. Hair on head, legs and ears short. Length of hair at withers and rump approximately two inches, which is slightly longer than on rest of body, except tail, where coat is longest and most profuse. *Fault:* Any indication of ruff or feathering.

Color

Any color including white; brindle; or pinto. Colors are brilliant and clear and markings are well balanced, with or without mask or blaze. White Akitas have no mask. Pinto has a white background with large, evenly placed patches covering head and more than one-third of body. Undercoat may be a different color from outer coat.

Gait

Brisk and powerful with strides of moderate length. Back remains strong, firm and level. Rear legs move in line with front legs.

Size

Dogs: 26 to 28 inches at the withers; bitches: 24 to 26 inches. *Disqualification:* dogs under 25 inches; bitches under 23 inches.

Temperament

Alert and responsive, dignified and courageous. Aggressive toward other dogs.

DISQUALIFICATIONS
Butterfly nose or total lack of pigmentation on nose. Drop or broken ears. Noticeably undershot or overshot. Sickle or uncurled tail. Dogs under 25 inches: bitches under 23 inches.

Approved by the AKC 12 December 1972

KC(GB) VARIATION TO STANDARD

This dog is not granted championship status by the KC(GB).

ALASKAN MALAMUTE

NATIONAL GROUPING		
	Name	Number
AKC	Working Dogs	III
KC(GB)	—	—
FCI	Guard Dogs	2

There are four recognised breeds of northern dogs which are used for hauling, the Siberian Husky, the Eskimo Dog, the Samoyed, and the Alaskan Malamute. Of the four, the Samoyed, though still used for exhibition hauling and competitions from time to time, has become so popular as a show breed that he is no longer thought of as belonging to the sledge hauling group. The others are still used, but are being seen more and more frequently in the show ring. The Alaskan Malamute is one of the oldest of the sledge hauling dogs, and was named after the Innuit tribe who were called Mahlemuts and who settled along the shores of Kotzebue Sound in Alaska.

When Alaska was opened up, and the richness of the territory was recognised, there was some intermingling of blood between the native dogs and those brought in by settlers. Sledge racing became popular and many crosses were tried to increase the strength and endurance of the hauling dogs, with the result that in the early part of this century there was considerable decline in the native Arctic sledge dog. The name Husky, often applied to all sledge dogs is unfortunate, as the only breed to which it should apply is the Siberian Husky. Jack London in his novels about the frozen North, for instance, wrote of Huskies when in fact he was almost certainly describing Malamutes. The Siberian Husky and the Eskimo Dog certainly existed, but the hauling dogs weighing eighty pounds, capable of towing heavily loaded sledges over considerable distances under very severe conditions, would certainly be Alaskan Malamutes.

Arctic exploration increased the interest in these powerful dogs that performed incredible feats of endurance under impossible conditions, living rough, subsisting on the absolute minimum of unappetising food, and making travel over frozen snow and ice possible before the days of the aeroplane and the powered sledge. Their prowess paralleled that of their human companions, and the stories about their power and abilities made them sound to be more than just dogs. Although the dogs are still used for serious work from time to time, they are now also used for the

fun of sledge racing. The Samoyed is used for showy teams, but the Alaskan Malamute for the serious competitive long-distance races. A team of six dogs will pull an eight hundred pound load at speeds of up to ten miles per hour for forty or fifty miles a day on a journey that may take days.

The Malamute has not achieved any degree of popularity in the show rings of Europe though specimens have been seen from time to time. Numbers are slowly growing, however, and one or two are now regularly entered in rare breed or unclassified classes. He is a large strong dog, rather positive in his reactions, and this may have had something to do with his lack of popularity as a show dog. He is friendly, becomes attached to people and especially to children, and makes an ideal companion for winter sports.

OFFICIAL STANDARD

General appearance and characteristics

The Alaskan Malamute is a powerful and substantially build dog with a deep chest and strong, compact body, not too short coupled, with a thick, coarse guard coat of sufficient length to protect a dense, woolly undercoat, from 1 to 2 inches in depth when dog is in full coat. Stands well over pads, and this stance gives the appearance of much activity, showing interest and curiosity. The head is broad, ears wedge-shaped and erect when alerted. The muzzle is bulky with only slight diminishing in width and depth from root to nose, not pointed or long, but not stubby. The Malamute moves with a proud carriage, head erect and eyes alert. Face markings are a distinguishing feature. These consist of either cap over head and rest of face solid color, usually grayish white, or face marked with the appearance of a mask. Combinations of cap and mask are not unusual. The tail is plumed and carried over the back, not like a fox brush, or tightly curled, more like a plume waving.

Malamutes are of various colors, but are usually wolfish gray or black and white. Their feet are of the 'snowshoe' type, tight and deep, with well-cushioned pads, giving a firm and compact appearance. Front legs are straight with big bone. Hind legs are broad and powerful, moderately bent at stifles, and without cowhocks. The back is straight, gently sloping from shoulders to hips. The loin should not be so short or tight as to interfere with easy, tireless movement. Endurance and intelligence are shown in body and expression. The eyes have a 'wolf-like' appearance by their position, but the expression is soft and indicates an affectionate disposition.

Temperament

The Alaskan Malamute is an affectionate, friendly dog, not a 'one-man' dog. He is a loyal, devoted companion, playful on invitation, but generally impressive by his dignity after maturity.

Head

The head should indicate a high degree of intelligence, and is broad and powerful as compared with other 'natural' breeds, but should be in proportion to the size of the dog so as not to make the dog appear clumsy or coarse. *Skull:* the skull should be broad between the ears, gradually narrowing to eyes, moderately rounded between ears, flattening on top as it approaches the eyes, rounding off to cheeks, which should be moderately flat. There should be a slight furrow between the eyes, the topline of skull and topline of the muzzle showing but little break downward

Head: showing typical markings.

from a straight line as they join. *Muzzle:* the muzzle should be large and bulky in proportion to size of skull, diminishing but little in width and depth from junction with skull to nose; lips close fitting; nose black; upper and lower jaws broad with large teeth, front teeth meeting with a scissors grip but never overshot or undershot.

Eyes

Brown, almond shaped, moderately large for this shape of eye, set obliquely in skull. Dark eyes preferred.

Ears

The ears should be of medium size, but small in proportion to head. The upper halves of the ears are triangular in shape, slightly rounded at tips, set wide apart on outside back edges of the skull with the lower part of the ear joining the skull on a line with the upper corner of the eye, giving the tips of the ears the appearance, when erect, of standing off from the skull. When erect, the ears point slightly forward, but when the dog is at work the ears are sometimes folded against the skull. High-set ears are a fault.

Neck

The neck should be strong and moderately arched.

Body

The chest should be strong and deep; body should be strong and compactly built but not short coupled. The back should be straight and gently sloping to the hips. The loins should be well muscled and not so short as to interfere with easy, rhythmic movement with powerful drive from the hindquarters. A long loin which weakens the back is also a fault. No excess weight.

Shoulders, legs and feet

Shoulders should be moderately sloping; forelegs heavily boned and muscled, straight to pasterns, which should be short and strong and almost vertical as viewed from the side. The feet should be large and compact, toes, tight-fitting and well arched, pads thick and tough, toenails short and strong. There should be a protective growth of hair between toes. Hind legs must be broad and powerfully muscled through thighs; stifles moderately bent, hock joints broad and strong, moderately bent and well let down. As viewed from behind, the hind legs should not appear bowed in bone, but stand and move true in line with movement of the front legs, and not too close or too wide. The legs of the Malamute must indicate unusual strength and tremendous propelling power. Any indication of unsoundness in legs or feet, standing or moving, is to be considered a serious fault. Dewclaws on the hind legs are undesirable and should be removed shortly after pups are whelped.

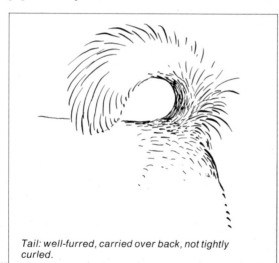

Tail: well-furred, carried over back, not tightly curled.

Tail

Moderately set and following the line of the spine at the start, well furred and carried over the back when not working—not tightly curled to rest on back—or short furred and carried like a fox brush, a waving plume appearance instead.

Coat

The Malamute should have a thick, coarse guard coat, not long and soft. The undercoat is dense, from 1 to 2 inches in depth, oily and woolly. The coarse guard coat stands out, and there is thick fur around the neck. The guard coat varies in length, as does the undercoat; however, in general, the coat is moderately short to medium along the sides of the body with the length of the coat increasing somewhat around the shoulders and neck, down the back

and over the rump, as well as in the breeching and plume. Malamutes usually have shorter and less dense coats when shed out during the summer months.

Color and markings

The usual colors range from light gray through the intermediate shadings to black, always with white on underbodies, parts of legs, feet, and part of mask markings. Markings should be either caplike and/or mask-like on face. A white blaze on forehead and/or collar or spot on nape is attractive and acceptable, but broken color extending over the body in spots or uneven splashings is undesirable. One should distinguish between mantled dogs and splash-coated dogs. The only solid color allowable is the all-white.

Size

There is a natural range in size in the breed. The desirable freighting sizes are:
Dogs: 25 inches at the shoulders—85 pounds.
Bitches: 23 inches at the shoulders—75 pounds.
However, size consideration should not outweigh that of type, proportion, and functional attributes, such as shoulders, chest, legs, feet, and movement. When dogs are judged equal in type, proportion, and functional attributes, the dog nearest the desirable freighting size is to be preferred.

IMPORTANT

In judging Alaskan Malamutes their function as a sledge dog for heavy freighting must be given consideration above all else. The judge must bear in mind that this breed is designed primarily as the working sledge dog of the North for hauling heavy freight, and therefore he should be a heavy-boned, powerfully built, compact dog with sound legs, good feet, deep chest, powerful shoulders, steady, balanced, tireless gait, and the other physical equipment necessary for the efficient performance of his job. He isn't intended as a racing sled dog designed to compete in speed trials with the smaller Northern breeds.
The Malamute as a sledge dog for heavy freighting is designed for strength and endurance and any characteristic of the individual specimen, including temperament, which interferes with the accomplishment of this purpose is to be considered the most serious of faults. Faults under this provision would be splayfootedness, any indication of unsoundness or weakness in legs, cowhocks, bad pasterns, straight shoulders, lack of angulation, stilted gait or any gait which isn't balanced, strong, and steady, ranginess, shallowness, ponderousness, lightness of bone, poor over-all proportion, and similar characteristics.

Approved by the AKC 12 April 1960

KC(GB) VARIATION TO STANDARD

This dog is not granted championship status by the KC(GB).

BELGIAN MALINOIS

Of the three types of Belgian Sheepdog recognised and registered by the American Kennel Club, the Malinois is the least well known. The other two are long-coated varieties and seem to have been more readily accepted by the public, possibly because they look rather more striking. It was towards the end of the 19th century that there was a revival of interest in the various sheep herding dogs of different countries, strangely enough at a time when the need for such dogs was declining with greater mechanisation, less droving and greatly increased areas of cultivation for food production purposes. The Belgian sheep herding dogs are very similar in structure, overall size and appearance to the

NATIONAL GROUPING		
	Name	Number
AKC	Working Dogs	III
KC(GB)	—	—
FCI	Guard Dogs	2

German Shepherd Dog, and there is little doubt that they shared a common ancestry.

The various dogs used for the herding of sheep in Europe were grouped together under the general term 'Chien de Berger' and the Malinois, to give it its full title should really be called the Chien de Berger Malinois, as it was first developed in the area around Malines. The dogs known as 'chiens de berger' during the last century were of just about every size and type, and so long as they could do the work, were given the title. The result has been a large number of breeds named after their country or place of origin, and many of them are now beginning to make their way on to the show scene. In 1891, Professor Reul made a study of the various types existing in Belgium, and began to sort them out into different breeds. He finally settled for six which could be distinguished one from the other and a group of three which were similar in size and conformation but different in coat and colour. It was these three that the Belgian Kennel Club finally recognised in 1897.

The Malinois first reached the United States of America in 1948, though they were registered and shown simply as Belgian Shepherd Dogs until 1959, when the three breeds were registered separately. In Britain the interest in the Malinois was delayed, and it is only in very recent years that specimens have been seen at shows and some litters bred.

He is a first class herding and working dog and a fine guard, and was at one time trained for police and army guard duties. Like many of the sheep herding dogs he has a certain reserve, and will not accept strangers without question, but he is at the same time friendly enough with those that he knows. He is a well-built powerful but flexible dog with a short coat of a distinctive fawn to mahogany colour with black tips to some of the hairs, and always a dark mask and ears. He is alert, intelligent and a little suspicious but his years of association with humans means that he quickly becomes one of the family. One of the characteristics of the breed is that the bitches always look smaller and feminine compared with the dogs.

OFFICIAL STANDARD

General appearance
The Belgian Malinois is a well-balanced, square dog, elegant in appearance, with an exceedingly proud carriage of the head and neck. The dog is strong, agile, well-muscled, alert and full of life. It stands squarely on all fours and viewed from the side, the topline, forelegs and hind legs closely approximate a square. The whole conformation gives the impression of depth and solidity without bulkiness. The expression indicates alertness, attention and readiness for activity, and the gaze is intelligent and questioning. The dog is usually somewhat more impressive and grand than its bitch counterpart, which has a distinctly feminine look.

Size and substance
Dogs, 24 to 26 inches in height; bitches, 22 to 24 inches, measured at the withers. The length, measured from point of breastbone to point of rump, should equal the height, but bitches may be slightly longer. Bone structure is moderately heavy in proportion to height so that the dog is well balanced throughout and neither spindly or leggy nor cumbersome and bulky.

Coat
Comparatively short, straight, with dense undercoat. Very short hair on the head, ears and lower legs. The hair is somewhat longer around the neck where it forms a collarette, and on the tail and the back of the thighs.

Color
Rich fawn to mahogany, with black overlay. Black mask and ears. The under parts of the body, tail, and breeches are lighter fawn, but washed-out fawn color on the body is a fault. The tips of the toes may be white and a small white spot on the chest is permitted.

Head
Clean-cut and strong, over-all size in proportion to the body. *Skull:* top flattened rather than rounded, the width approximately the same as the length but no wider. *Stop:* Moderate. *Muzzle, jaws, lips:* muzzle moderately pointed, avoiding any tendency to snipiness, and approximately equal in length to that of the topskull. The jaws are strong and powerful. The lips tight and black, with no pink showing on the outside. *Ears:* triangular in shape, stiff, erect and in proportion to the head in size. Base of the ear should not come below the center of the eye. *Eyes:* brown, preferably dark brown, medium size, slightly almond shaped, not protruding. *Nose:* black, without spots or discolored areas. *Teeth:* a full complement of strong, white teeth, evenly set and meeting in an even bite or a scissors bite, neither overshot nor undershot.

Torso
Neck: round and rather outstretched, tapered from head to body, well muscled with tight skin. *Topline:* the withers

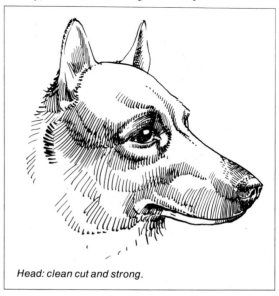

Head: clean cut and strong.

are slightly higher and slope into the back, which must be level, straight and firm from withers to hip joints. The loin section, viewed from above, is relatively short, broad and strong, but blending smoothly into the back. The croup is medium long, sloping gradually. *Tail:* strong at the base, bone to reach hock. At rest it is held low, the tip bent back level with the hock. In action it is raised with a curl, which is strongest toward the tip, without forming a hook. *Chest:* not broad, but deep. The lowest point reaches the elbow, forming a smooth ascendant curve to the abdomen, which is moderately developed, neither tucked up nor paunchy.

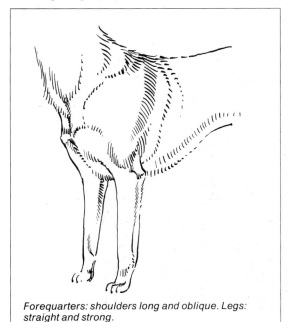

Forequarters: shoulders long and oblique. Legs: straight and strong.

Forequarters

Shoulders: long and oblique, laid flat against the body, forming a sharp angle (approximately 90°) with the upper arm. *Legs:* straight, strong and paralleled to each other. Bone oval rather than round. Length and substance well proportioned to the size of the dog. Pastern: Medium length, strong and very slightly sloped. Dewclaws may be removed. *Feet:* round (cat-footed), toes curved close together, well padded. Nails strong and black except that they may be white to match white toe tips.

Hindquarters

Thighs: broad and heavily muscled. The upper and lower thigh bones approximately parallel the shoulder blade and upper arm respectively, forming a relatively sharp angle at stifle joint. *Legs:* length and substance well proportioned to the size of the dog. Bone oval rather than round. Legs are parallel to each other. The angle at the hock is relatively sharp, although the Belgian Malinois does not have extreme angulation. Metatarsus medium length, strong and slightly sloped. Dewclaws, if any, should be removed. *Feet:* slightly elongated, toes curved close together, well padded. Nails strong and black except that they may be white to match white toe tips.

Gait

Smooth, free and easy, seemingly never tiring, exhibiting facility of movement rather than a hard driving action. The dog tends to single-track at a fast gait, the legs, both front and rear, converging toward the center line of gravity of the dog, while the backline remains firm and level, parallel to the line of motion with no crabbing. The Belgian Malinois shows a marked tendency to move in a circle rather than a straight line.

FAULTS

Any deviation from these specifications is a fault, the degree to which a dog is penalized depending on the extent to which the dog deviates from the standard and the extent to which the particular fault would actually affect the working ability of the dog.

DISQUALIFICATIONS

Ears hanging, as on a hound. Tail—cropped or stump. Dogs under 22½ or over 27½ inches in height. Bitches under 20½ or over 25½ inches in height.

Approved by the AKC 13 April 1965

KC(GB) VARIATION TO STANDARD

Classed by the KC(GB) as the Belgian Shepherd Dog (Malinois); and although it has been given an interim standard has not yet been granted championship status. *Nose:* nostrils well flared. *Mouth:* cheeks spare, quite flat but well muscled. *Eyes:* black ringed eyelids. Muzzle finely chiselled under eyes. *Neck:* nape very slightly arched. *Body:* length from point of shoulder to point of buttocks should be approximately equal to height at withers in case of dogs, in bitches it may be slightly greater. Ribs should be well sprung. *Skin:* springy but quite taut over whole body. All external mucous membranes highly pigmented.

BELGIAN SHEEPDOG

This variety is the black version of the Belgian Sheep-dog and is thus easily distinguished from the other two. For many years he has been shown in the United States of America as the Belgian Sheepdog and has only recently been awarded a separate identity in Britain. When Professor Reul did his study of the herding breeds of Belgium in 1891, he discovered that the long-haired black version was largely limited to one area and tended to breed true. M. Rose of the village of Groenendael had been breeding black long-hairs with considerable success. This had started with a bitch puppy named Petite, which was a long-haired black sport from parents of other colours. After a search he discovered a black male which he acquired, and these two when mated produced the beginnings of the black line which led to almost all of today's dogs.

The first came to the United States of America in 1907, at which time they were known of but unseen in Britain, where a contemporary book of the time de-scribes them amongst French, German and other Sheepdogs as being of ancient lineage, all having prick

NATIONAL GROUPING		
	Name	Number
AKC	Working Dogs	III
KC(GB)	Working	5
FCI	Herding Dogs	I

ears and bearing a suggestion of the wolf type. Those that were imported into the United States were used as police dogs. The breed soon became popular on both sides of the Atlantic and was appreciated as both a working and show dog some time before the other two Belgian Sheepdogs. In Belgium and indeed in France he has won a great reputation as a herding dog with tremendous versatility, and devotion to duty, and working trials are held regularly to encourage breeders to produce the type of dog that can work in the field and also look well on the show bench.

The disturbance caused by the Second World War did much to upset the progress of the breed, with none of the advantages that it enjoyed in the First World

War when it gained some recognition as a messenger and guard dog. He is a fairly big dog, but not a heavyweight, in fact he tends towards raciness, being rather slender in body and flexible in movement. He is elegant, proud and upstanding in posture and noted for his free, elegant and ground covering stride. As with the other varieties, the bitch is not nearly as prepossessing as the dog. The Groenendael is noted for his intelligence and his devoted companionship. His long association with humans makes him a very good dog to have in the house, where he settles into a remarkably small space for a large looking dog, is normally very quiet and self-effacing, but an excellent guard when roused who will defend his property to the last. As a show dog he is making many friends in most countries of the world, and is now seen both in the United States and Britain in fairly large numbers at most of the major shows. He makes an excellent show dog as he is amenable to command, takes very little preparation, and looks very imposing in the ring.

OFFICIAL STANDARD

Personality

The Belgian Sheepdog should reflect the qualities of intelligence, courage, alertness, and devotion to master. To his inherent aptitude as guardian of flocks should be added protectiveness of the person and property of his master. He should be watchful, attentive, and always in motion when not under command. In his relationship with humans he should be observant and vigilant with strangers but not apprehensive. He should not show fear or shyness. He should not show viciousness by unwarranted or unprovoked attack. With those he knows well, he is most affectionate and friendly, zealous of their attention, and very possessive.

General appearance

The first impression of the Belgian Sheepdog is that of a well-balanced, square dog, elegant in appearance, with an exceedingly proud carriage of the head and neck. He is a strong, agile, well-muscled animal, alert and full of life. His whole conformation gives the impression of depth and solidity without bulkiness. The male is usually somewhat more impressive and grand than his female counterpart. The bitch should have a distinctly feminine look.

Size and substance

Dogs should be 24 to 26 inches in height and bitches 22 to 24 inches, measured at the withers. The length, measured from point of breast-bone to point of rump, should equal the height. Bitches may be slightly longer. Bone structure should be moderately heavy in proportion to his height so that he is well balanced throughout and neither spindly or leggy nor cumbersome and bulky. *Stance:* the Belgian Sheepdog should stand squarely on all fours. Side view: the topline, front legs, and back legs should closely approximate a square.

Expression

Indicates alertness, attention, readiness for activity. Gaze should be intelligent and questioning.

Coat

The guard hairs of the coat must be long, well-fitting, straight, and abundant. They should not be silky or wiry. The texture should be a medium harshness. The undercoat should be extremely dense, commensurate, however, with climatic conditions. The Belgian Sheepdog is particularly adaptable to extremes of temperature or climate. The hair is shorter on the head, outside of the ears, and lower part of the legs. The opening of the ear is protected by tufts of hair. *Ornamentation:* especially long and abundant hair, like a collarette, around the neck; fringe of long hair down the back of the forearm; especially long and abundant hair trimming the hindquarters, the breeches; long, heavy, and abundant hair on the tail.

Color

Black. May be completely black or may be black with white, limited as follows: Small to moderate patch or strip on forechest. Between pads of feet. On *tips* of hind toes. On chin and muzzle (frost—may be white or gray). On *tips* of front toes—allowable but a fault.

Head

Clean-cut and strong, over-all size should be in proportion to the body. *Skull:* top flattened rather than rounded. The width approximately the same, but not wider, than the length. *Stop:* moderate. *Muzzle, jaws, lips:* muzzle moderately pointed, avoiding any tendency to snipiness, and approximately equal in length to that of the topskull. The jaws should be strong and powerful. The lips should be tight and black, with no pink showing on the outside. *Ears:* triangular in shape, stiff, erect, and in proportion to the head in size. Base of the ear should not come below the center of the eye. *Eyes:* brown, preferably dark brown. Medium size, slightly almond shaped, not protruding. *Nose:* black, without spots or discolored areas.

Head and skull: finely chiselled, fairly long, moderate stop.

Teeth: a full complement of strong, white teeth, evenly set. Should not be overshot or undershot. Should have either an even bite or a scissors bite.

Torso

Neck: round and rather outstretched, tapered from head to body, well muscled, with tight skin. *Topline:* the withers are slightly higher and slope into the back which must be level, straight, and firm from withers to hip joints. The loin section, viewed from above, is relatively short, broad and strong, but blending smoothly into the back. The croup is medium long, sloping gradually. *Tail:* strong at the base, bone to reach hock. At rest the dog holds it low, the tip bent back level with the hock. When in action he raises it and gives it a curl, which is strongest toward the tip, without forming a hook. *Chest:* not broad, but deep. The lowest point should reach the elbow, forming a smooth ascendant curve to the abdomen. *Abdomen:* moderate development. Neither tuck-up nor paunchy.

Forequarters

Shoulder: long and oblique, laid flat against the body, forming a sharp angle (approximately 90°) with the upper arm. *Legs:* straight, strong, and parallel to each other. Bone oval rather than round. Development (length and substance) should be well proportioned to the size of the dog. *Pastern:* Medium length, strong, and very slightly sloped. *Feet:* round (cat-footed), toes curved close together, well padded. Nails strong and black except that they may be white to match white toe tips.

Hindquarters: powerful but not bulky, good angulation, not excessive.

Hindquarters

Thighs: broad and heavily muscled. The upper and lower thigh bones approximately parallel the shoulder blade and upper arm respectively, forming a relatively sharp angle at stifle joint. *Legs:* length and substance well propor-

tioned to the size of the dog. Bone oval rather than round. Legs are parallel to each other. The angle at the hock is relatively sharp, although the Belgian Sheepdog does not have extreme angulation. Metatarsus medium length, strong, and slightly sloped. Dewclaws, if any, should be removed. *Feet:* slightly elongated. Toes curved close together, well padded. Nails strong and black except that they may be white to match white toe tips.

Gait

Motion should be smooth, free and easy, seemingly never tiring, exhibiting facility of movement rather than a hard driving action. He tends to single-track on a fast gait; the legs, both front and rear, converging toward the center line of gravity of the dog. The backline should remain firm and level, parallel to the line of motion with no crabbing. He shows a marked tendency to move in a circle rather than a straight line.

FAULTS

Any deviation from these specifications is a fault. In determining whether a fault is minor, serious, or major, these two factors should be used as a guide: 1. The extent to which it deviates from the Standard. 2. The extent to which such deviation would actually affect the working ability of the dog.

DISQUALIFICATIONS

Viciousness. Color—any color other than black, except for white in specified areas. Ears—hanging (as on a hound). Tail—cropped or stump. Dogs under 22½ or over 27½ inches in height. Bitches under 20½ or over 25½ inches in height.

Approved by the AKC 9 June 1959

KC(GB) VARIATION TO STANDARD

Classed by the KC(GB) as the Belgian Shepherd Dog (Groenendael). *Head:* nostrils well flared. *Eyes:* black ringed eyelids. Arches above eyes not prominent and muzzle finely chiselled under eyes. *Ears:* external ear well rounded at base. *Neck:* very supple; slightly arched. *Body:* length from point of shoulder to point of buttocks should be approximately equal to height at withers in case of dogs, in female it may be slightly greater. Ribs should be well sprung. *Forelegs:* bones joining feet and pastern joint should be strong and short. Pastern joint clearly defined. *Feet:* dewclaws not permitted. *Height:* (ideal) dogs 24½ inches; bitches 23 inches.

BELGIAN TERVUREN

NATIONAL GROUPING		
	Name	Number
AKC	Working Dogs	III
KC(GB)	Working	5
FCI	Herding Dogs	I

This is the third of the Chiens de Berger Belge to be recognised as a separate breed both in its country of origin and in the rest of the world. At one time they were very much interbred and were all shown as Belgian Shepherd Dogs, but in recent years most countries have only accepted registration of those dogs that have been bred true for a number of generations. As sheep herding declined, breeders of dogs that had been used, often for centuries for that purpose, looked elsewhere for an outlet for their enthusiasm, and dog showing offered a natural alternative. Prior to that time the only requirement for a herding dog was that it could do the work and do it well, and breeding programmes were devised not to produce the best-looking dog, but the best worker. A similar thing happened in Britain with the Border Collie, when breeding was established on the basis of ability and records kept of wins at trials rather than on the bench, with the result that although a magnificent race of working sheepdogs has been produced, few of them are good Border Collie types.

The evolution of the Tervuren was closely linked with that of the Groenendael, and they probably sprang from the same stock. A. M. Corbeel of Tervuren owned a pair of sheepdogs with long black-tipped hair that produced a litter of puppies, one of which came into the possession of M. Danhieux who mated her with a black long-haired dog. This mating in turn produced what has been described as the best Tervuren of the 19th century, a dog that became the first

Tervuren champion. In appearance the Tervuren is the same as the Groenendael apart from the colour, so it is natural that colour should become an important factor in the standards of the two breeds. The Groenendael must always be black with white allowed only as a small flash on the forechest, between the pads of the feet and the tips of the rear toes and a slight grizzling on the muzzle and chin. The Tervuren is always a warm mahogany colour with the black overlay typical of the breed; this black tipping being most pronounced on the shoulders, face and ears and the tip of the tail.

The first Tervurens went to the United States of America in the 1940s but were unregistered, the first

177

registered import being in 1954. In 1959 the breeds were granted separate registers but the progress of the Tervuren has been slow compared with the Groenendael. The same thing is true in Britain, where the breed is only slowly gaining ground. He is particularly suitable for obedience work, and it is probably in this field that he will gain most admirers, as in appearance he is so near to the German Shepherd Dog that many potential owners will prefer the well-established and more popular breed rather than risk having their dog mistaken for a poor specimen of that breed. Like the other Belgian Shepherd Dogs, he is very intelligent, and can be trained for guard duties as well as for normal work with sheep. He makes a very good show dog, as he is noble in outline, upstanding and elegant, and supremely biddable in the ring, willing to please and naturally obedient.

He is watchful and alert, constantly on the move when not relaxing, vigilant with strangers and suspicious without being vicious. With the members of his family he is kind and affectionate, and always desires attention.

OFFICIAL STANDARD

Personality
The Belgian Tervuren should reflect the qualities of intelligence, courage, alertness and devotion to master. To his inherent aptitude as guardian of flocks should be added protectiveness of the person and property of his master. He should be watchful, attentive and usually in motion when not under command. In his relationship with humans he should be observant and vigilant with strangers but not apprehensive. He should not show fear or shyness. He should not show viciousness by unwarranted or unprovoked attack. With those he knows well, he is most affectionate and friendly, zealous for their attention and very possessive.

General appearance
The first impression of the Belgian Tervuren is that of a well-balanced square dog, elegant in appearance, with proud carriage of the head and neck. He is a strong, agile, well-muscled animal, alert and full of life. His whole conformation gives the impression of depth and solidity without bulkiness. The male is usually somewhat more impressive and grand than the female. The female should have a distinctly feminine look. Because of frequent comparisons between the Belgian Tervuren and the German Shepherd Dog, it is to be noted that these two breeds differ considerably in size, substance and structure, the difference being especially noticeable in the formation of the topline and the hindquarters.

Size and substance
Dogs 24 to 26 inches in height, and bitches 22 to 24 inches, measured at the withers. The length, measured from point of breastbone to point of rump, should equal the height. Bone structure medium in proportion to height so that he is well balanced throughout and neither spindly or leggy nor cumbersome and bulky. *Stance:* the Belgian Tervuren should stand squarely on all fours. Viewed from the side, the topline, ground level, front legs, and back legs should closely approximate a perfect square.

Expression
Intelligent and questioning, indicating alertness, attention and readiness for action.

Coat
The guard hairs of the coat must be long, well-fitting, straight and abundant. They should not be silky or wiry. The texture should be a medium harshness. The undercoat should be very dense, commensurate, however, with climatic conditions. The Belgian Tervuren is particularly adapatable to extremes of temperature or climate. The hair is shorter on the head, outside the ears and on the lower part of the legs. The opening of the ear is protected by tufts of hair. *Ornamentation:* especially long and abundant hair, like a collarette, around the neck; fringe of long hair down the back of the forearm; especially long and abundant hair trimming the hindquarters—the breeches; long, heavy and abundant hair on the tail.

Color
Rich fawn to russet mahogany with black overlay. The coat is characteristically double pigmented, wherein the tip of each fawn hair is blackened. On mature males, this blackening is especially pronounced on the shoulders, back and rib section. The chest color is a mixture of black and gray. The face has a black mask, and the ears are mostly black. The tail typically has a darker or black tip. The underparts of the body, tail and breeches are light beige. A small white patch is permitted on the chest, not to extend to the neck or breast. The tips of the toes may be white. White or gray hair (frost) on chin or muzzle is normal. Although some allowance is to be made for dogs under 18 months of age, when the true color is attained, washed-out color or color too black resembling the Belgian Sheepdog is undesirable.

Head
Well chiseled, dry, long without exaggeration. *Skull and muzzle*, measuring from the stop, should be of equal length. Over-all size should be in proportion to the body. Top of skull flattened rather than rounded, the width approximately the same but not wider than the length. Stop moderate. Muzzle moderately pointed, avoiding any tendency to snipiness. *The jaws* should be strong and powerful. *The lips* should be tight and black, with no pink showing on the outside. *Ears* are equilateral triangles in shape, well cupped, stiff, erect, not too large. Set high, the base of the ear should not come below the center of the eye. *Eyes* brown, preferably dark brown, medium size, slightly almond shaped, not protruding. Light or yellow eyes are a fault. *Nose* black, without spots or discolored areas. Nostrils well defined. There should be a full complement of *strong white teeth* evenly set. Either a scissors or even bite is acceptable. Should not be overshot

Head: well-chiselled, long ears erect.

Hindquarters: thighs broad and heavily muscled.

or undershot. Teeth broken by accident should not be severely penalized, but worn teeth, especially incisors, are often indicative of the lack of proper bite, although some allowance should be made for age. Discolored (distemper) teeth are not to be penalized.

Torso

Neck round, muscular, rather outstretched, slightly arched and tapered from head to body. Skin well-fitting with no loose folds. Topline horizontal, straight and firm from withers to hip joints. The loin section, viewed from above, is relatively short, broad and strong, but blending smoothly into the back. The croup is medium long, sloping gradually. *Tail:* strong at the base, the last vertebra to reach the hock. At rest the dog holds it low, the tip bent back level with the hock. When in action he raises it and gives it a curl, which is strongest toward the tip, without forming a hook. Tail should not be carried too high nor turned to one side. *Chest:* not broad but deep, the lowest point should reach the elbow, forming a smooth ascendant curve to the abdomen. *Abdomen:* moderately developed, neither tucked-up nor paunchy.

Forequarters

Legs straight, parallel, perpendicular to the ground. Shoulders long and oblique, laid flat against the body, forming a sharp angle (approximately 90°) with the upper arm. Top of the shoulder blades should be roughly a thumb's width apart. Arms should move in a direction exactly parallel to the axis of the body. Forearms long and well muscled. Bone flat rather than round. Pasterns short and strong, slightly sloped. Feet round (cat-footed), toes curved close together, well padded, strong nails. Nail color can vary from black to transparent.

Hindquarters

Legs powerful without heaviness, moving in the same pattern as the limbs of the forequarters. Thighs broad and heavily muscled. Stifles clearly defined, with upper shank at right angles to the hip bones. Bone flat rather than round. Hocks moderately bent. Metatarsi short, perpendicular to the ground, parallel to each other when viewed from the rear. Dewclaws, if any, should be removed. Feet slightly elongated, toes curved close together, heavily padded, strong nails. Nail color may vary from black to transparent.

Gait

The gait is lively and graceful, covering the maximum of ground. Always in motion, seemingly never tiring, he shows facility of movement rather than a hard driving action. He tends to single-track at a fast gait, the legs both front and rear converging toward the center line of gravity of the dog. The back line should remain firm and level, parallel to the line of motion with no crabbing. His natural tendency is to move in a circle rather than a straight line.

DISQUALIFICATIONS
Ears—hanging, as on a hound. Tail—cropped or stump. Color—white markings anywhere except as specified. Teeth —pronounced undershot. Size—dogs under 22½ or over 27½ inches in height; bitches under 20½ or over 25½ inches in height.

Approved by the AKC 12 May 1959

KC(GB) VARIATION TO STANDARD

Classed by the KC(GB) as the Belgian Shepherd Dog (Tervueren); and although it has been given an interim standard it has not yet been granted championship status. *Eyes:* arches above eyes not prominent but muzzle finely chiselled under eyes. Blacked ringed eyelids. *Feet:* claws dark.

BERNESE MOUNTAIN DOG

NATIONAL GROUPING		
	Name	Number
AKC	Working Dogs	III
KC(GB)	Working	5
FCI	Guard Dogs	2

This breed is said to have been brought into Switzerland by the invading legions of Rome though this is difficult to prove. He is certainly a very ancient breed, and had been known for generations before he became the draught dog of the weavers of Berne. In this capacity he degenerated as the weavers were little interested in preserving the qualities of a particular breed so long as specimens were produced from time to time that were strong enough to tow a small cart. In 1892, one dog man in Switzerland determined to revive the breed and conducted a search to discover what he considered the correct type of dog with which to commence a breeding programme, and it was only after considerable difficulty that he managed to find sufficient dogs for his purpose. He was joined by other enthusiasts, and in 1907 a breed club was formed and the breed was saved from extinction.

The dog is one of the small group called Sennenhunde, including the Entlebuch which is quite small, and the large Swiss Mountain Dog proper, which form a very ancient group of Swiss national dogs. The only one that is well known outside his own country is the Bernese which also happens to be the only one with a long coat. If one had to place him in one of the old basic categories he would have to go into the Mastiff group, as he bears resemblance only to members of that group. With the basket weavers and cheese makers of Berne he lived very much as a working member of the family, and became the children's pet as well as a worker and guard dog.

In appearance he has been described, perhaps quite accurately as the child's vision of everything that a dog should be. He is large and rounded, warm and woolly. His colour is attractive, his markings distinct and typical, and his construction is in every way that of the average and normal dog. He is very strong and hardy being perfectly happy to live out of doors or in the house, and his coat, which tends towards softness and silkiness always has a fine sheen when he is groomed.

The Bernese Mountain Dog first entered the United States of America and was given recognition in the middle 1930s, and numbers both in that country and in Britain are steadily increasing. He makes a delightful show dog as he is much admired by the general public, who often see in him just the sort of dog that they would like to own. His shining coat and large heavyweight appearance make him a very impressive animal, and as a puppy he is particularly attractive. His temperament is good, and his long association with people gives him instinctive good manners. He is an affectionate and kindly dog, always willing to please and is easily trained to be obedient and trouble free. There is no doubt that he will become one of the important show dogs and companions of future years.

OFFICIAL STANDARD

General appearance
A well-balanced dog, active and alert; a combination of sagacity, fidelity and utility.

Height
Dogs, 23 to 27½ inches; bitches, 21 to 26 inches at shoulder.

Head
Skull flat, defined stop and strong muzzle. Dewlaps very slightly developed, flews not too pendulous, jaw strong with good, strong teeth. *Eyes:* dark, hazel-brown, full of fire. *Ears:* V-shaped, set on high, not too pointed at tips and rather short. When in repose, hanging close to head; when alert, brought slightly forward and raised at base.

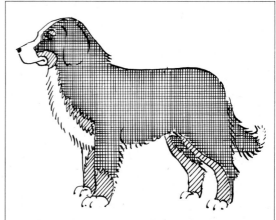

Colour: showing position of black, tan and white.

Color and markings
Jet-black with russet-brown or deep tan markings on all four legs, a spot just above forelegs, each side of white chest markings and spots over eyes, which may never be missing. The brown on the forelegs must always be between the black and white. *Preferable, but not a condition, are:* white feet, tip of tail, pure white blaze up foreface, a few white hairs on back of neck, and white star-shaped markings on chest. When the latter markings are missing, it is not a disqualification.

FAULTS

Too massive in head; light or staring eyes; too heavy or long ears; too narrow or snipy muzzle; undershot or overshot mouth; pendulous dewlaps; too long or Setter-like body; splay or hare feet; tail curled or carried over back; cowhocks; and white legs.

SCALE OF POINTS

General appearance (15). Size and height (5). Head (15). Body (15). Legs and feet (15). Tail (10). Coat (10). Color and markings (15). *Total (100).*

Approved by the AKC 13 April 1937

Head: defined stop, strong muzzle, slight dewlaps.

Body
Rather short than too long in back, compact and well ribbed up. Chest broad with good depth of brisket. Loins strong and muscular.

Legs and feet
Forelegs perfectly straight and muscular, thighs well developed and stifles well bent. Feet round and compact. Dewclaws should be removed.

Tail
Of fair thickness and well covered with long hair, but not to form a flag; moderate length. When in repose, should be carried low, upward swirl permissible; when alert, may be carried gaily, but may never curl or be carried over back.

Coat
Soft and silky with bright, natural sheen; long and slightly wavy but may never curl.

KC(GB) VARIATION TO STANDARD
Eyes: eyelids tight. *Mouth:* scissor bite. *Body:* back firm and straight. Rump smoothly rounded. *Forequarters:* shoulders strong, well laid back with upper forming an obtuse angle. *Hindquarters:* hocks, strong, well let down, turning neither in nor out. *Height:* at withers dogs 25 to 27½ inches (preferred 26 to 26¾ inches), bitches 23 to 26 inches (preferred 23½ to 25 inches).

BOUVIER DES FLANDRES

NATIONAL GROUPING		
	Name	Number
AKC	Working Dogs	III
KC(GB)	–	–
FCI	Herding Dogs	I

The word 'bouvier' translated from the French, means cowherd or oxherd which gives a good indication of this breed's original use. The word can also be translated figuratively as 'churl' which the dog certainly is not, as he is a handsome animal of noble bearing, and in recent years of impeccable breeding. The Bouvier des Flandres was first found in the South Western parts of Flanders and in Northern France, where he was being used as a cattle drover by the farmers and butchers. At that time, in the latter part of the 19th century, he was known by a number of rather uncomplimentary names, Koe Hond (cow dog), Toucheur de Boeuf (cattle driver) and Vuilbaard (dirty beard), and his appearance was as varied as his names. The breed appeared in almost every size, though all were fairly large, and in a variety of colours. He appeared on the show bench for the first time at the international show of 1910 when two were shown named Nelly and Even, but there was no standard for the breed until 1912 when a group of interested people encouraged by M. Fontaine, Vice-President of the Club St. Hubert

met and formed a society of Bouvier breeders.

From that time onwards the breed made rapid strides, only being halted by World War I, when the area in which the Bouvier des Flandres was mostly concentrated, was devastated. Some dogs however survived, and one, who was the property of the Veterinarian attached to the Belgian army was shown in Antwerp in 1920. Some time later a group of experts and enthusiasts gathered together with some examples of the breed and formulated a revised standard. By the 1930s the breed began to appear in the United States of America. Ch. Marios de Clos de Cerberus was imported after the Second World War and rapidly became an American champion and drew attention to the possibilities of the breed. Since that time, the breed has made steady progress in many countries outside Northern Europe, and is beginning to appear at major shows in Britain.

He is primarily a working dog, and though his shape and coat indicate that he will make a very successful show dog, modern breeders are not losing sight of the fact that he was originally designed for a certain task, and that he must remain capable of doing it. He is a strong dog of tremendous vitality, built along square and robust lines, but extremely fast. In South Africa, where for fun, races are sometimes staged between dogs towing miniature sulkies, jockeyed by children dressed in racing silks, one of the local Bouviers des Flandres is a regular winner. He is easily trained, being intelligent and naturally obedient, and he is one of those dogs which in his native country cannot gain the title of champion without succeeding at working trials.

He makes a very good show dog, being large, impressive, alert and smart. His native obedience makes him easily controlled in the ring despite his size and agility, and his coat is of the quality that repays just a little attention and shaping in the right places. He has a good steady but lively temperament, is an excellent guard and watchdog, being docile with those that he knows but distinctly suspicious of strangers.

OFFICIAL STANDARD

The Bouvier des Flandres is a rough-coated dog of notably rugged appearance as befitting an erstwhile cattle driver and farmers' helper of Flanders, and later an ambulance dog and messenger in World War I. He is a compact-bodied, powerfully built dog of upstanding carriage and alert, intelligent expression.

Head
The head is medium long, with the skull slightly longer than the muzzle. *Skull:* almost flat on top, moderately wide between the ears, and sloping slightly toward the muzzle. The brow is noticeably arched over the eyes. The stop is shallow, and the under-eye fill-in good. *Ears:* rough-coated, set high on the head and cropped to a triangular contour. They stand erect and are carried straight up. *Eyes:* neither protruding nor sunken, the eyes are set a trifle obliquely in the skull and not too far apart. They are of medium size and very nearly oval. Preferred color, a dark nut-brown. Black eyes, although not considered faulty, are less desirable as contributing to a somber expression. Light-colored eyes, and staring or wild expression are faulty. *Muzzle:* wide, deep and well filled out, the width narrowing gradually toward the tip of the nose. Cheeks are clean or flat-sided, the jaws powerful, and the lips dry and tight-fitting. A narrow muzzle, suggestive of weakness, is faulty. *Teeth:* strong and white, with the canines set well apart, the teeth meet in a scissors bite. *Nose:* black and well developed, the nostrils wide open. Across the top the contour is a trifle rounded as opposed to flat. Brown, pink and spotted noses are faulty.

Coat: topknot and beard.

Neck and shoulders
The neck is well rounded, slightly arched, and carried almost upright, its thickness gradually increasing as it fits gracefully into the shoulders. Clean and dry at the throat. The shoulders are long and sloping.

Body
The brisket is deep, extending down at least to the point of the elbows, and of moderate width. *Back:* short, strong and straight. *Loins:* short, taut, and slightly arched in topline, while the rump is broad and square rather than sloping. Ribs are deep and well sprung. As advantageous for breeding purposes, slightly greater length of loin is permissible in bitches.

Tail
Set high, carried up, and docked to about 4 inches.

Legs and feet
The leg bones, although only moderate in girth, are made to appear heavy because of their covering with thick, rough hair. *Forelegs:* straight as viewed from the front or side, with elbows turned neither in nor out. *Hind legs:* hindquarters are firm and well muscled, with large, powerful hams. Legs are strong and sturdy, with hocks well let down and wide apart. They are slightly angulated at stifle and hock joints. Viewed from the back, they are absolutely parallel. *Feet:* round, compact, with toes arched and close. The nails are black, the pads thick and tough.

Coat
Rough, touseled and unkempt in appearance, the coat is capable of withstanding the hardest work in the most inclement weather. *Topcoat:* harsh, rough and wiry, and so thick that when separated by the hand the skin is hardly visible. *Undercoat:* fine and soft in texture, and thicker in winter. On the skull the hair is shorter and almost smooth. On the brows it is longer, thus forming eyebrows. Longer growth on muzzle and underjaw form mustache and beard. On the legs it is thick and rough, on the feet rather short. Soft, silky or woolly topcoats are faulty.

Color
From fawn to black; pepper and salt, gray and brindle. A white star on the chest is allowed. Chocolate brown with white spots is faulty.

Height
Dogs from $23\frac{1}{2}$ to $27\frac{1}{2}$ inches; bitches, a minimum of $22\frac{3}{4}$ inches.

SCALE OF POINTS
Coat (20). Head, eyes, ears, skull, foreface (20). Shoulders and style (10). Hindquarters, hams and legs (10). Back, loin, brisket, belly (15). Feet and legs (10). Symmetry, size and character (15). *Total (100).*

Approved by the AKC 14 April 1959

KC(GB) VARIATION TO STANDARD
The dog is not granted championship status by the KC(GB).

BOXER

NATIONAL GROUPING		
	Name	Number
AKC	Working Dogs	III
KC(GB)	Working	5
FCI	Guard Dogs	2

Many of the breeds of dogs known today have changed very little from their ancestors of hundreds of years ago. The running dogs for instance are much the same now as they were in ancient Persia and medieval England. There are, however, a number of breeds which have been developed by man for specific purposes, which can be considered as manufactured dogs, and the Boxer is one of these. He is a member of the large family of Mastiff type dogs that were spread over most of Europe many centuries ago, but was changed in fairly recent years to an animal with an appearance distinct from any other breed of dog. The basic stock used was a dog called the Bullenbeisser, and around the 1830s German breeders commenced experimenting by crossing these dogs with other breeds including the Bulldog in an attempt to produce what was to be virtually a new breed. By 1895 the breed was well established, being shown at Munich, and from that time it has progressed until it is now not only one of the most popular dogs in Germany, but throughout the world.

The so-called sport of bull-baiting was carried on in Germany in the same way as it was in Britain until public opinion finally put an end to it, and there is no doubt that the German version of the Mastiff type of dog that was used as the basis for the Boxer, was used for this purpose. It is interesting therefore that when the German breeders wanted another dog to cross with their native bull-baiting type, they selected the Bulldog which had been used for the same purpose. There is not a great deal of similarity between the Bulldog and the Boxer, and it is not at all certain what other breeds were used. There is no doubt, however, that the final result had everything that the early breeders set out to achieve, as the animal that they eventually produced, the modern Boxer, is one of the smartest dogs in the world.

Types differ, and each country has worked on the breed to produce a dog that is fashionable in that country. It is a simple matter to differentiate between the Boxers of say Germany, Britain and the United States of America. Attempts are made from time to time to bring the forms of the dog closer together by importing from one country to another, but there remains a tendency for each country to go its own way. The dog generally is a very strong, boisterous and active dog with a very positive personality. It has the muscular development of the Mastiff, the agility of those breeds that needed to avoid the attentions of a furious bull, and the jaws and tenacity of the Bulldog.

There are few breeds that have made the progress of the Boxer as a show dog. Everything about him is expedient for the purpose. He is a big dog, statuesque in proportions with a magnificent presence, and with the sort of coat finish that shines in the sun and glows in artificial light. His behaviour in the ring is usually impeccable and he can be trained easily to stand remarkably still and move with great enthusiasm when the need arises. He allows himself to be handled by a complete stranger without objection knowing full well that he is in complete charge of the situation, and quite capable of handling any emergency.

He is a boisterous dog and yet not one with any vices, which he has proved by his proficiency as a guard and police dog, where fierceness needs to be allied to immediate control. He is a very good house dog, his appearance and positive behaviour deterring any intruder, and whilst it is unlikely that he would savage anyone, he always looks as though he might. He is wonderfully good with children, and though his sheer size and speed of reaction do from time to time cause some trouble, he would never intentionally injure anyone.

OFFICIAL STANDARD

General appearance

The Boxer is a medium-sized, sturdy dog, of square build, with short back, strong limbs, and short, tight-fitting coat. His musculation, well developed, should be clean, hard and appear smooth (not bulging) under taut skin. His movements should denote energy. The gait is firm yet elastic (springy), the stride free and ground-covering, the carriage proud and noble. Developed to serve the multiple purposes of guard, working and escort-dog, he must combine elegance with substance and ample power, not alone for beauty but to ensure the speed, dexterity and jumping ability essential to arduous hike, riding expedition, police or military duty. Only a body whose individual parts are built to withstand the most strenuous efforts, assembled as a complete and harmonious whole, can respond to these combined demands. Therefore, to be at his highest efficiency he must never be plump or heavy, and, while equipped for great speed, he must never be racy.

The head imparts to the Boxer a unique individual stamp, peculiar to him alone. It must be in perfect proportion to the body, never small in comparison to the over-all picture. The muzzle is his most distinctive feature, and great value is to be placed on its being of correct form and in absolute proper proportion to the skull.

In judging the Boxer, first consideration should be given to general appearance; next, over-all balance, including the desired proportions of the individual parts of the body to each other, as well as the relation of substance to elegance—to which an attractive color or arresting style may contribute. Special attention is to be devoted to the

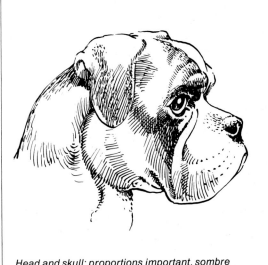

Head and skull: proportions important, sombre expression.

head, after which the dog's individual components are to be examined for their correct construction and function, and efficiency of gait evaluated. *General faults:* head not typical, plump, bulldoggy appearance, light bone, lack of balance, bad condition, lack of noble bearing.

Head

The beauty of the head depends upon the harmonious proportion of the muzzle to the skull. The muzzle should always appear powerful, never small in its relationship to the skull. The head should be clean, not showing deep wrinkles. Folds will normally appear upon the forehead when the ears are erect, and they are always indicated from the lower edge of the stop running downward on both sides of the muzzle. The dark mask is confined to the muzzle and is in distinct contrast to the color of the head. Any extension of the mask to the skull, other than dark shading around the eyes, creates a somber, undesirable expression. When white replaces any of the black mask, the path of any upward extension should be between the eyes. The muzzle is powerfully developed in length, width and depth. It is not pointed, narrow, short or shallow. Its shape is influenced first through the formation of both jawbones, second through the placement of the teeth, and third through the texture of the lips.

The Boxer is normally undershot. Therefore, the lower jaw protrudes beyond the upper and curves slightly upward. The upper jaw is broad where attached to the skull and maintains this breadth except for a very slight tapering to the front. The incisor teeth of the lower jaw are in a straight line, the canines preferably up front in the same line to give the jaw the greatest possible width. The line of incisors in the upper jaw is slightly convex toward the front. The upper corner incisors should fit snugly back of the lower canine teeth on each side, reflecting the symmetry essential to the creation of a sound, non-slip bite.

The lips, which complete the formation of the muzzle, should meet evenly. The upper lip is thick and padded,

filling out the frontal space created by the projection of the lower jaw. It rests on the edge of the lower lip and, laterally, is supported by the fangs (canines) of the lower jaw. Therefore, these fangs must stand far apart, and be of good length so that the front surface of the muzzle is broad and squarish and, when viewed from the side, forms an obtuse angle with the topline of the muzzle. Over-protrusion of the overlip or underlip is undesirable. The chin should be perceptible when viewed from the side as well as from the front without being over-repandous (rising above the bite line) as in the Bulldog. The Boxer must not show teeth or tongue when the mouth is closed. Excessive flews are not desirable.

The top of the skull is slightly arched, not rotund, flat, nor noticeably broad, and the occiput not too pronounced. The forehead forms a distinct stop with the topline of the muzzle, which must not be forced back into the forehead like that of a Bulldog. It should not slant down (down-faced), nor should it be dished, although the tip of the nose should lie somewhat higher than the root of the muzzle. The forehead shows just a slight furrow between the eyes. The cheeks, though covering powerful masseter muscles compatible with the strong set of teeth, should be relatively flat and not bulge, maintaining the clean lines of the skull. They taper into the muzzle in a slight,

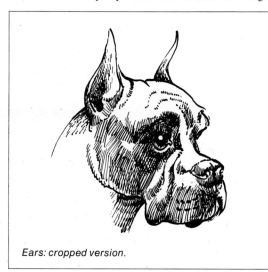

Ears: cropped version.

graceful curve. The ears are set at the highest points of the sides of the skull, cut rather long without too broad a shell, and are carried erect. The dark brown eyes, not too small, protruding or deep-set, are encircled by dark hair, and should impart an alert, intelligent expression. Their mood-mirroring quality combined with the mobile skin furrowing of the forehead gives the Boxer head its unique degree of expressiveness. The nose is broad and black, very slightly turned up; the nostrils broad, with the nasolabial line running between them down through the upper lip, which, however, must not be split. *Faults:* lack of nobility and expression, somber face, unserviceable bite. Pinscher or Bulldog head, sloping topline of muzzle, muzzle too light for skull, too pointed a bite (snipy). Teeth or tongue showing with mouth closed, driveling, split upper lip. Poor ear carriage, light ('Bird of Prey') eyes.

Neck

Round, of ample length, not too short; strong, muscular and clean throughout, without dewlap; distinctly marked nape with an elegant arch running down to the back. *Fault:* Dewlap.

Body

In profile, the build is of square proportions in that a horizontal line from the front of the forechest to the rear projection of the upper thigh should equal a vertical line dropped from the top of the withers to the ground.

Chest and forequarters

The brisket is deep, reaching down to the elbows; the depth of the body at the lowest point of the brisket equals half the height of the dog at the withers. The ribs, extending far to the rear, are well arched but not barrel-shaped. Chest of fair width and forechest well defined, being easily visible from the side. The loins are short and muscular; the lower stomach line, lightly tucked up, blends into a graceful curve to the rear. The shoulders are long and sloping, close-lying and not excessively covered with muscle. The upper arm is long, closely approaching a right angle to the shoulder blade. The forelegs, viewed from the front, are straight, stand parallel to each other, and have strong, firmly joined bones. The elbows should not press too closely to the chest wall or stand off visibly from it. The forearm is straight, long and firmly muscled. The pastern joint is clearly defined but not distended. The pastern is strong and distinct, slightly slanting, but standing almost perpendicular to the ground. The dewclaws may be removed as a safety precaution. Feet should be compact, turning neither in nor out, with tightly arched toes (cat feet) and tough pads. *Faults:* chest too broad, too shallow or too deep in front; loose or overmuscled shoulders; chest hanging between shoulders; tied-in or bowed-out elbows; turned feet; hare feet; hollow flanks; hanging stomach.

Back

The withers should be clearly defined as the highest point of the back; the whole back short, straight and muscular with a firm topline. *Faults:* roach back, sway back, thin lean back, long narrow loins, weak union with croup.

Hindquarters

Strongly muscled with angulation in balance with that of forequarters. The thighs broad and curved, the breech musculature hard and strongly developed. Croup slightly sloped, flat and broad. Tail attachment high rather than low. Tail clipped, carried upward. Pelvis long and, in bitches especially, broad. Upper and lower thigh long, leg well angulated with a clearly defined, well-let-down hock joint. In standing position, the leg below the hock joint (metatarsus) should be practically perpendicular to the ground, with a slight rearward slope permissible. Viewed from behind, the hind legs should be straight, with the hock joints leaning neither in nor out. The metatarsus should be short, clean and strong, supported by powerful rear pads. The rear toes just a little longer than the front toes, but similar in all other respects. Dewclaws, if any, may be removed. *Faults:* too rounded, too narrow, or falling off of croup; low-set tail; higher in back than in front; steep, stiff, or too slightly angulated hindquarters; light thighs; bowed or crooked legs; cowhocks; over-angulated hock joints (sickle hocks); long metatarsus (high hocks); hare feet; hindquarters too far under or too far behind.

Gait

Viewed from the side, proper front and rear angulation is manifested in a smoothly efficient, level-backed, ground-covering stride with powerful drive emanating from a freely operating rear. Although the front legs do not contribute impelling power, adequate 'reach' should be evident to prevent interference, overlap or 'side-winding' (crabbing). Viewed from the front, the shoulders should remain trim and the elbows not flare out. The legs are parallel until gaiting narrows the track in proportion to increasing speed, then the legs come in under the body but should never cross. The line from the shoulder down through the leg should remain straight, although not necessarily perpendicular to the ground. Viewed from the rear, a Boxer's breech should not roll. The hind feet should 'dig in' and track relatively true with the front. Again, as speed increases, the normally broad rear track will become narrower. *Faults:* stilted or inefficient gait, pounding, paddling or flailing out of front legs, rolling or waddling gait, tottering hock joints, crossing over or interference—front or rear, lack of smoothness.

Height

Adult dogs, $22\frac{1}{2}$ to 25 inches; bitches, 21 to $23\frac{1}{2}$ inches at the withers. Dogs should not go under the minimum nor

bitches over the maximum.

Coat

Short, shiny, lying smooth and tight to the body.

Color

The colors are fawn and brindle. Fawn in various shades from light tan to dark deer red or mahogany, the deeper colors preferred. The brindle variety should have clearly defined black stripes on fawn background. White markings on fawn or brindle dogs are not to be rejected and are often very attractive, but must be limited to one third of the ground color and are not desirable on the back of the torso proper. On the face, white may replace a part or all of the otherwise essential black mask. However, these white markings should be of such distribution as to enhance and not detract from true Boxer expression.

Character and temperament

These are of paramount importance in the Boxer. Instinctively a 'hearing' guard dog, his bearing is alert, dignified and self-assured, even at rest. In the show ring, his behaviour should exhibit constrained animation. With family and friends, his temperament is fundamentally playful, yet patient and stoical with children. Deliberate and wary with strangers, he will exhibit curiosity, but, most importantly, fearless courage and tenacity if threatened. However, he responds promptly to friendly overtures when honestly rendered. His intelligence, loyal affection and tractability to discipline make him a highly desirable companion. *Faults:* lack of dignity and alertness, shyness, cowardice, treachery and viciousness (belligerency toward other dogs should not be considered viciousness).

DISQUALIFICATIONS
Boxers with white or black ground color, or entirely white or black or any color other than fawn or brindle. (White markings, when present, must not exceed one third of the ground color.)

Approved by the AKC 12 December 1967

KC(GB) VARIATION TO STANDARD

Head: should never appear too small or too large. Length of muzzle to whole of head should be 3—1. *Ears:* cropping is illegal in the United Kingdom and dogs are shown with natural ears. *Weight and Size:* at withers: dogs 22 to 24 inches; bitches 21 to 23 inches. Heights above or below are not to be encouraged. A 23 inch dog should weigh about 66 pounds and bitches of about 22 inches weigh about 62 pounds.

BRIARD

NATIONAL GROUPING		
	Name	Number
AKC	Working Dogs	III
KC(GB)	Working	5
FCI	Herding Dogs	I

For as long as man has herded sheep and goats there have been long or rough coated sheepdogs. Their distant ancestors are unknown as they date back to the time when nomadic herdsmen moved as the climate changed and food for their animals changed with it. In more recent times, as nations became more stable, breeds developed which were best suited to local conditions. The result was such breeds as the Owtscharka in Russia, the Puli and the Komondor in Hungary and the Shepherd dogs of Germany. Among these different breeds that evolved in Northern Europe, the Briard, or Chien Berger de Brie, to give it its full name, is one of the oldest.

He is found in most parts of France but takes his name from the Province of Brie, and in records of the early part of the 19th century he is referred to as the dog of that area. At one time he was very much the guard dog as well as herder and he was expected to be capable of tackling wolves if need arose. In later years, however, after the French Revolution and the dividing up of the country into smaller parts, he became a herding dog entrusted with the task of keeping the flocks near to the homestead. He is now found doing this work in almost every part of France, as he is the most numerous of the herding dogs. In 1900 Les Amis du Briard was formed, a society dedicated to the welfare of the breed which wrote at that time a standard still in use today.

He was popular with the French troops during World War I, and it was at that time that the American troops became acquainted with him. By 1920 the breed was appearing in the United States and made steady progress. In Britain registrations began in 1971, and the breed's popularity increased at such a rate that by 1974 challenge certificates were on offer and by 1975, seventy-nine individual dogs were entered under the author at the Birmingham National Show. One of the most carefully guarded characteristics of the breed is the double dew claw on the hind legs, and breed club publications use this feature as their title.

He is square and strong, extremely muscular and active, and has a coat that will withstand relentless rain. He is seen in a wide range of colours, though principally black and slate grey, and the dogs of the other colours have a coat that can be either plain, or what is called *charbonnée* in which the longer hairs are tipped with black. As a show dog he is a tremendous success, being steady in the ring, easy-going in temperament, and responsive to command. He is easily prepared as apart from brushing the coat needs very little attention, and due to its quality, even looks good when the dog is thoroughly wet at an outdoor show. He is a well-mannered dog, easy to train, and a very good guard, being quiet until roused, when his voice is usually enough to deter intruders.

OFFICIAL STANDARD

General appearance
Vigorous and alert, powerful without coarseness, strong in bone and muscle, exhibiting the strength and agility required of the herding dog. Dogs lacking these qualities, however concealed by the coat, are to be penalized.

Character
A dog of handsome form. He is a dog at heart, with spirit and initiative, wise and fearless with no trace of timidity. Intelligent, easily trained, faithful, gentle and obedient, the Briard possesses an excellent memory and an ardent desire to please his master. He retains a high degree of his ancestral instinct to guard home and master. Although he is reserved with strangers, he is loving and loyal to those he knows. Some will display a certain independence.

Head and skull: strong. Fairly long moustache, beard and eyebrows.

Head
The head of a Briard always gives the impression of length, having sufficient width without being cumbersome. The correct length of a good head, measured from the occiput to the tip of the nose, is about forty per cent of the height of the dog at the withers. There is no objection to a slightly longer head, especially if the animal tends to a longer body line. The width of the head, as measured across the skull, is slightly less than the length of the skull from the occiput to the stop. Viewed from above, from the front or in profile, the fully-coated silhouette gives the impression of two rectangular forms, equal in length but differing in height and width, blending together rather abruptly. The larger rectangle is the skull and the other forms the muzzle. The topline of the muzzle is parallel to the topline of the skull, and the junction of the two forms a well-marked stop, which is midway between the occiput and the tip of the nose, and on a level with the eyes. The muzzle with mustache and beard is somewhat wide and terminates in a right angle. The muzzle must not be narrow or pointed. Although not clearly visible on the fully-coated head, the occiput is prominent and the forehead is very slightly rounded. The head joins the neck in a right angle and is held proudly alert. The head is sculptured in clean lines, without jowls or excess flesh on the sides, or under the eyes or temples.

The lips are of medium thickness, firm of line and fitted neatly, without folds or flews at the corners. The lips are black. The head is well covered with hair which lies down, forming a natural part in the center. The eyebrows do not lie flat but, instead, arch up and out in a curve that lightly veils the eyes. The hair is never so abundant that it masks the form of the head or completely covers the eyes.

Ears
The ears should be attached high, have thick leather and be firm at the base. Low-set ears cause the head to appear to be too arched. The length of the natural ear should be equal to or slightly less than one-half the length of the head, always straight and covered with long hair. The natural ear must not lie flat against the head and, when alert, the ears are lifted slightly, giving a square look to the top of the skull. The ears when cropped should be carried upright and parallel, emphasizing the parallel lines of the head; when alert, they should face forward, well open with long hair falling over the opening. The cropped ear should be long, broad at the base, tapering gradually to a rounded tip.

Neck
Strong and well constructed, the neck is in the shape of a truncated cone, clearing the shoulders well. It is strongly muscled and has good length.

Body
Chest: the chest is broad and deep with moderately curved ribs, egg-shaped in form, the ribs not too rounded. The breastbone is moderately advanced in front, descending smoothly to the level of the elbows and shaped to give good depth to the chest. The abdomen is moderately drawn up but still presents good volume. *Topline:* the Briard is constructed with a very slight incline, downward from the prominent withers to the back which is straight, to the broad loin and the croup which is slightly inclined. The topline is strong, never swayed nor roached. *Proportions:* the Briard is not cobby in build. In dogs the length of the body, measured from the point of the shoulder to the point of the buttock, is equal to or slightly more than his height at the withers. The bitch may be a little longer.

Tail
Uncut, well feathered, forming a crook at the extremity, carried low and not deviating to the right or to the left. In repose, the bone of the tail descends to the joint of the hock, terminating in the crook, similar in shape to the printed letter 'J' when viewed from the dog's right side. In action, the tail is raised in a harmonious curve, never going above the level of the back, except for the terminal crook. *Disqualification:* tail non-existent or cut.

Legs
The legs are powerfully muscled with strong bone. Viewed from the front or rear, the legs are straight and parallel to the median line of the body, never turned inward or outward. The distance between the front legs is equal to the distance between the rear legs. The construction of the legs is of utmost importance, determining the dog's ability

to work and his resistance to fatigue. The hindquarters are powerful, providing flexible, almost tireless movement.

Forequarters
Shoulder blades are long and sloping forming a 45-degree angle with the horizontal, firmly attached by strong muscles and blending smoothly with the withers. The forelegs are vertical when viewed from the side except the pasterns are very slightly inclined.

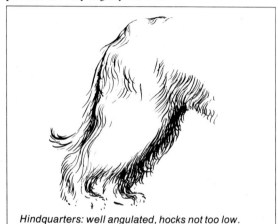

Hindquarters: well angulated, hocks not too low.

Hindquarters
The croup is well muscled and slightly sloped to a well-rounded finish. The pelvis slopes at a 30-degree angle from the horizontal and forms a right angle with the upper leg bone. Viewed from the side, the legs are well angled with the metatarsus slightly inclined, the hock making an angle of 135 degrees.

Feet
Strong and rounded, being slightly oval in shape. The feet travel straight forward in the line of movement. If the rear toes turn out very slightly when the hocks and metatarsus are parallel, then the position of the feet is correct. The nails are always black and hard. The pads are well developed, compact and elastic, covered with strong tissue. The toes are strong, well arched and compact.

Dewclaws
Two dewclaws are required on each rear leg, placed low on the leg, giving a wide base to the foot. Occasionally the nail may break off completely. The dog shall not be penalized for the missing nail so long as the digit itself is present. Ideally the dewclaws form additional functioning toes. Dewclaws on the forelegs may or may not be removed. *Disqualification:* anything less than two dewclaws on each rear leg.

Coat
The outer coat is coarse, hard and dry (making a dry rasping sound between the fingers). It lies down flat, falling naturally in long, slightly waving locks, having the sheen of good health. On the shoulders the length of hair is generally six inches or more. The undercoat is fine and tight on all the body.

Color
All uniform colors are permitted except white. The colors are black, various shades of gray and various shades of tawny. The deeper shades of each color are preferred. Combinations of two of these colors are permitted, provided there are no marked spots and the transition from one color to another takes place gradually and symmetrically. The only permissible white: white hairs scattered throughout the coat and/or a white spot on the chest not to exceed one inch in diameter at the root of the hair. *Disqualification:* white coat. Spotted coat. White spot on chest exceeding one inch in diameter.

Gait
The well-constructed Briard is a marvel of supple power. His movement has been described as 'quicksilver,' permitting him to make abrupt turns, springing starts and sudden stops required of the sheepherding dog. His gait is supple and light, almost like that of a large feline. The gait gives the impression that the dog glides along without touching the ground. Strong, flexible movement is essential to the sheep dog. He is above all a trotter, single-tracking, occasionally galloping and he frequently needs to change his speed to accomplish his work. His conformation is harmoniously balanced and strong to sustain him in the long day's work. Dogs with clumsy or inelegant gait must be penalized.

Nose
Square rather than round, always black with nostrils well opened. *Disqualification:* any color other than black.

Teeth
Strong, white and adapting perfectly in a scissors bite.

Eyes
Eyes set well apart with the inner corners and outer corners on the same level. Large, well opened and calm, they must never be narrow or slanted. The gaze is frank, questioning and confident. The color must be black or black-brown with very dark pigmentation of the rim of the eyelids, whatever the color of the coat. *Disqualification:* yellow eyes or spotted eyes.

Size
Dogs 23 to 27 inches at the withers; bitches 22 to $25\frac{1}{2}$ inches at the withers. *Disqualification:* all dogs and bitches under the minimum.

DISQUALIFICATIONS
Nose any color other than black. Yellow eyes or spotted eyes. Tail non-existent or cut. Less than two dewclaws on each rear leg. White coat. Spotted coat. White spot on chest exceeding one inch in diameter. All dogs or bitches under the minimum size limits.

Approved by the AKC 8 February 1975

KC(GB) VARIATION TO STANDARD
Feet: about mid-way between cat and hare-foot.

BULLMASTIFF

NATIONAL GROUPING		
	Name	Number
AKC	Working Dogs	III
KC(GB)	Working	5
FCI	Guard Dogs	2

The original Mastiff of Britain is one of the country's oldest breeds, but its descendant, the Bullmastiff is a comparatively recent development. It was bred by crossing the original Mastiff with other breeds, and probably the Bulldog, which was originally a much longer-legged breed than it is today. The Mastiff type is widespread over most of Europe, from the Neapolitan Mastiff of Italy to the Mountain Dogs of Switzerland. In Britain in the 13th century they were known as Bandogs, and were used principally for guarding property at night. In the middle of the 19th century attempts were made to improve the breed, as its use as a guard ended with increased urbanisation and better policing. Towards the end of the century classes were scheduled for Bullmastiffs belonging to gamekeepers, and clearly a dog of the size and reputed fierceness of the breed would be a useful companion to a gamekeeper at a time when poaching was a favourite country pastime.

There are early literary references to the breed, Buffon in 1791 stated that the cross between a Bulldog and a Mastiff produced a strong large Bulldog, much larger than a Bulldog but more like one of that breed than a Mastiff. In the *Field* of 1871 there appeared a report of a fight between two lions and Bullmastiffs, but the dogs of these early days were probably casual crosses between the two rather than a serious attempt to produce a new breed. From 1924, when the British Kennel Club first recognised the breed, there was a marked improvement, and from 1928, when challenge certificates were first offered, great strides were made and the breed settled down to something approaching the dog that we know today both in appearance and character. It was still much used as a guard dog, being a favourite among country people who needed a big strong dog to deter intruders from making raids on stock, and it was popular as an estate dog, some strains being traceable back to old family estates at the turn of the century.

He is a big strong active dog with a heavy body and very well made limbs which give him an appearance of squareness from every angle, and he should have no tendency towards elegance or legginess. His head, like that of one of his ancestors, the Bulldog, is his main feature, and much store is placed upon its squareness and character. He is supposed to look fierce but at the same time there should be a look of honesty about him so that he always looks trustworthy.

As a show dog he is readily trained, standing well without being set up too rigidly. He easily learns a few simple words of command, and rarely objects to being handled by strangers. He is a tough, likeable dog, has few vices, and whilst at first sight he does not look like the ideal animal to have as a house pet, those that own one rarely lose their love of the breed. He needs a considerable quantity of food to keep him in condition but he is not a fussy eater, subsisting well on any of the normal dog foods. Above all else he is a great guard, his appearance alone being enough to keep most intruders away, and whilst he is not prone to attacking anyone, his sheer weight is often enough to subdue anyone who persists in trespassing.

OFFICIAL STANDARD

General appearance

That of a symmetrical animal, showing great strength; powerfully built but active. The dog is fearless yet docile, has endurance and alertness. The foundation breeding was 60% Mastiff and 40% Bulldog.

Head and skull: skull large and square, muzzle short, underjaw broad.

Head

Skull large, with a fair amount of wrinkle when alert; broad, with cheeks well developed. Forehead flat. Muzzle broad and deep; its length, in comparison with that of the entire head, approximately as 1 is to 3. Lack of foreface with nostrils set on top of muzzle is a reversion to the Bulldog and is very undesirable. Nose black with nostrils large and broad. Flews not too pendulous, stop moderate, and the mouth (bite) preferably level or slightly undershot. Canine teeth large and set wide apart. A dark muzzle is preferable.

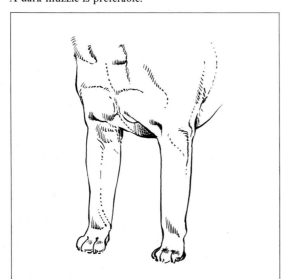

Forequarters: forelegs powerful and straight.

Eyes

Dark and of medium size.

Ears

V-shaped and carried close to the cheeks, set on wide and high, level with occiput and cheeks, giving a square appearance to the skull; darker in color than the body and medium in size.

Neck

Slightly arched, of moderate length, very muscular, and almost equal in circumference to the skull.

Body

Compact. Chest wide and deep, with ribs well sprung and well set down between the forelegs. *Forequarters:* shoulders muscular but not loaded, and slightly sloping. Forelegs straight, well boned and set well apart; elbows square. Pasterns straight, feet of medium size, with round toes well arched. Pads thick and tough, nails black. *Back:* short, giving the impression of a well balanced dog. *Loins:* wide, muscular and slightly arched, with fair depth of flank. *Hindquarters:* broad and muscular with well developed second thigh denoting power, but not cumbersome. Moderate angulation at hocks. Cowhocks and splay feet are bad faults. *Tail:* set on high, strong at the root and tapering to the hocks. It may be straight or curved, but never carried hound fashion.

Coat

Short and dense, giving good weather protection.

Color

Red, fawn or brindle. Except for a very small white spot on the chest, white marking is considered a fault.

Size

Dogs, 25 to 27 inches at the shoulder, and 110 to 130 pounds weight. Bitches, 24 to 26 inches at the shoulder, and 100 to 120 pounds weight. Other things being equal, the heavier dog is favored.

Approved by the AKC 6 February 1960

KC(GB) VARIATION TO STANDARD

Eyes: set apart the width of muzzle with furrow between. *Ears:* point level with eyes when alert. V-shaped or folded back. Small. *Fault:* light or yellow eyes. Rose ears.

BEARDED COLLIE

NATIONAL GROUPING		
	Name	Number
AKC	—	—
KC(GB)	Working	5
FCI	Herding Dogs	I

There was a time when much of the farming land of Europe was devoted to the raising of sheep and cattle, and particularly of sheep. The urban development that resulted from the industrial revolution changed the pattern and absorbed a great deal of the land. Enclosed farming restricted herding even further and in Britain nowadays, the free ranging of sheep is mostly confined to parts of Scotland and Wales. One of the results of this extensive herding was the development of breeds of dogs that would assist the shepherd in rounding up and controlling the sheep that roamed over the mountains as well as guarding the flocks. A special type of dog was developed for the purpose, known as the working sheepdog, a black and white Collie type, with variations in different areas, but basically a small mostly black and white working dog. In Scotland, and more specifically in Peeblesshire, the dog that was bred for sheep-herding was the Bearded Collie.

He looks something like an Old English Sheepdog though slender, less heavy in body, and much more freedom of choice is permitted in colour, some being similar to the Old English Sheepdog, but others being red, brown or sandy. He was known at one time as the Scottish Bearded or Highland Collie.

It was after World War II that the Bearded Collie began its rise to prominence in the British show ring. This was largely due to the efforts of Mrs. Willison whose successful search for a mate for her bitch started the Bothkennar line. She campaigned too for recognition for the breed which was finally granted in 1959 and she made up the first champion in the breed which was bred from a son of her original bitch.

The Bearded Collie is not so popular with flockmasters as some of the other breeds, as whilst he is hardy enough, he is temperamentally rather soft, and probably more suited to the gentle task of driving cattle than to using force on a difficult hill ewe with lambs. One of the other problems in the early days was that a Bearded Collie would hunt, and thus become easily diverted from the work that he was supposed to be doing. This was probably due to something deep-rooted in his ancestry dating back to the time when most dogs fulfilled a dual purpose.

As a showdog he is rapidly gaining popularity in Britain. The number of registrations have trebled in recent years, and he now vies with the once popular gundogs and Dachshunds. At the major shows the breed appears in large numbers, and has recently figured among the top awards for the first time. The Bearded Collie is one of those breeds that really repays attention to coat preparation. The modern Bearded Collie would probably meet with a certain amount of scorn from the working shepherd of a few years ago, who would consider such attention pampering, but there is no doubt that with its coat beautifully brushed out the modern Beardie makes a fine and very competitive spectacle in today's show ring.

Temperamentally he is a delightful dog, being affectionate, always willing to make friends, intelligent and faithful. He is a perfect dog with children, being very well-mannered and gentle, and it is one of the sights of today's shows to see a child handling a Bearded Collie in perfect harmony. The dogs that have won top awards have done so partly because of their demeanour in the ring as they can be trained to stand like a statue and move on command.

OFFICIAL STANDARD

Characteristics
The Bearded Collie should be alert, lively and self confident, good temperament essential.

General appearance
An active dog with long, lean body, and none of the stumpiness of the Bobtail and which though strongly made, shows plenty of daylight under the body and does not look too heavy. The face should have an enquiring expression. Movement should be free and active.

Head and skull
Broad, flat skull with ears set high, fairly long foreface with moderate stop. Nose black except with brown or fawn coats, when brown is permitted.

Eyes
To tone with coat in colour, the eyes to be set rather widely apart, big and bright. Eyebrows arched up and forward, but not long enough to obscure the eyes.

Forequarters: legs straight with good bone.

Ears: medium size, dropping, longish hair, slight lift at base.

Ears
Medium size, drooping with longish hair, slight lift at the base denoting alertness.

Mouth
Teeth large and white, never undershot or overshot.

Neck
Must be fair length, muscular and slightly arched.

Forequarters
Legs straight with good bone, pasterns flexible without weakness, covered with shaggy hair all round.

Body
Fairly long, back level, with flat ribs and strong loins, ribcage both deep and long, shoulders flat, straight front essential.

Hindquarters
Legs muscular at thighs, with well bent stifles and hocks, free from exaggeration.

Feet
Oval in shape, soles well padded, toes arched and close together, well covered with hair including between the pads.

Tail
Set low, should be moderately long with abundant hair or brush, carried low when the dog is quiet, with an upward swirl at the tip, carried gaily when the dog is excited, but not over the back.

Coat
Must be double, the under one soft, furry and close the outer one harsh strong and flat, free from woolliness or any tendency to curl. Sparse hair on the ridge of the nose, slightly longer on the sides just covering the lips. Behind this falls the long beard. A moderate amount of hair under the chin, increasing in length to the chest.

Colour
Slate grey or reddish fawn, black, all shades of grey, brown and sandy, with or without white Collie markings.

Size
Ideal height at the shoulder: dogs, 21 to 22 inches; bitches, 20 to 21 inches.

Note
Male animals should have two apparently normal testicles fully descended into the scrotum.

AKC VARIATION TO STANDARD
This dog is not granted championship status by the AKC. The above standards are those of the KC(GB).

COLLIE

Rough Collie

As is the case with a number of breeds there has been a fairly sharp division between the working and the show type of Collie. The working Collie of today is almost exactly like the one of a hundred years ago, whilst the show Collie is very different indeed, and it is unlikely that any show Collie would work sheep as his ancestors did. This divergence began something over a hundred years ago when a number of breeders recognised the potential in the rough-coated working Collie of Scotland, and by selective breeding, improved coat, stature and colouring to produce the magnificent dog that we know today. The breed was originally evolved for sheep herding as with the other Collie types, but today's version was produced almost entirely as a show dog. Queen Victoria took a great interest in the breed which increased its popularity, and around the turn of the century it commanded a very good export market, with prices that would seem high even by today's standards.

The popularity of the Rough Collie has continued, and the registration figures for the breed in Britain are second only to the German Shepherd Dog in the

NATIONAL GROUPING		
	Name	Number
AKC	Working Dogs	III
KC(GB)	Working	5
FCI	Herding Dogs	I

working group, whilst in the United States the figures have maintained a high level. At shows, the Rough Collie has always been a great draw, attracting a ring-side audience wherever he appears. This is hardly surprising as the Collie has been developed specifically as a show dog, the head becoming exaggerated by careful selection and the coat quality evolved in the same way. One of the problems has been to produce the perfect small semi-erect ears, and exhibitors go to great lengths to ensure that by care and attention to this feature at an early age, the mature dog has the desired ear.

The Rough Collie repays attention and a beautifully groomed dog in full coat is always much admired, whilst a ring full of them, in their subtle colour variations from light gold to silvery blue and black and tan, and in the United States even white, creates a spectacle that everyone admires. He is an easy dog to show, as he enjoys being admired, is attentive in the ring, and always willing to please his handler. Early critics of the direction in which the breed was developing complained that it was becoming too elegant and looking like a thoroughbred than the workhorse that it should resemble. These days this is no longer true, and the breeders have concentrated on producing a less attenuated animal, more compact and with better coupling.

As house pets Rough Collies have always had a following, as they are friendly, yet good guards, and whilst amenable to discipline, they are not easily cowed. They are by nature a dog for the fields and the open country and it is in this environment that they are perhaps at their happiest, but they fit in well to modern more confined living conditions, and are perfectly happy in a small house or apartment provided that they get sufficient exercise. Like all the working dogs they need exercise to prevent overweight, nothing looks worse than a fat Rough Collie.

Smooth Collie

The standard of the breed says that it is a replica of the Rough Collie in everything except coat. There are many breeds of dog that have a coat difference, the Wire and Smooth Fox Terrier, the variations in the Dachshund, and even in such well-established breeds as the German Shepherd Dog coat differences crop up from time to time. This is sometimes due to variations of climate in the country of origin of the breed, for example, the smooth Chow Chow tends to be found in the south of China whilst the rough-coated variety is found in the north where the weather is colder. This is, however, not true of the Collie, as the two types have developed alongside one another in the same area of Scotland. It has been suggested that the smooth coat resulted from a cross with the Greyhound, but this is improbable and it was more likely to have been just a natural variant.

It is interesting that the Australian Cattle Dog, which undoubtedly was produced from a Collie in the first instance, and indeed has still something of the collie colour variations, is in fact a smooth coated dog. The development of the Smooth Collie as a show dog was largely carried on south of the Border and in the early days both coats were shown in the same classes. It was only later that the two breeds were shown separately, and the smooth coated variety has never competed in numbers with the Rough Collie, less than two per-cent of the collies registered being smooth. It has always been said that though the Smooth Collie is an intelligent dog it is of little use as a worker with sheep, only the odd one being capable of rounding up a flock.

OFFICIAL STANDARD

ROUGH

General appearance

The Collie is a lithe, strong, responsive, active dog, carrying no useless timber, standing naturally straight and firm. The deep, moderately wide chest shows strength, the sloping shoulders and well-bent hocks indicate speed and grace, and the face shows high intelligence. The Collie presents an impressive, proud picture of true balance, each part being in harmonious proportion to every other part and to the whole. Except for the technical description that is essential to this Standard and without which no Standard for the guidance of breeders and judges is adequate, it could be stated simply that no part of the Collie ever seems to be out of proportion to any other part. Timidity, frailness, sullenness, viciousness, lack of animation, cumbersome appearance and lack of over-all balance impair the general character.

Head and skull: well-blunted, clean wedge, skull flat.

Head

The head properties are of great importance. When considered in proportion to the size of the dog the head is inclined to lightness and never appears massive. A heavy-headed dog lacks the necessary bright, alert, full-of-sense look that contributes so greatly to expression. Both in front and profile view the head bears a general resemblance to a well-blunted lean wedge, being smooth and clean in outline and nicely balanced in proportion. On the sides it tapers gradually and smoothly from the ears to the end of the black nose, without being flared out in backskull ('cheeky') or pinched in muzzle ('snipy'). In profile view the top of the backskull and the top of the muzzle lie in two approximately parallel, straight planes of equal length, divided by a very slight but perceptible stop or break. A mid-point between the inside corners of the eyes (which is the center of a correctly placed stop) is the center of balance in length of head.

The end of the smooth, well-rounded muzzle is blunt but not square. The underjaw is strong, clean-cut and the depth of skull from the brow to the under part of the jaw is not excessive. The teeth are of good size, meeting in a scissors bite. *Overshot or undershot jaws are undesirable, the latter being more severely penalized.* There is a very slight prominence of the eyebrows. The backskull is flat, without receding either laterally or backward and the occipital bone is not highly peaked. The proper width of backskull necessarily depends upon the combined length of skull and muzzle and the width of the backskull is less than its length. Thus the correct width varies with the individual and is dependent upon the extent to which it is supported by length of muzzle. Because of the importance of the head characteristics, *prominent head faults are very severely penalized.*

Eyes

Because of the combination of the flat skull, the arched eyebrows, the slight stop and the rounded muzzle, the foreface must be chiseled to form a receptacle for the eyes and they are necessarily placed obliquely to give them the required forward outlook. Except for the blue merles, they are required to be matched in color. They are almond-shaped, of medium size and never properly appear to be large or prominent. The color is dark and the eye does not show a yellow ring or a sufficiently prominent haw to affect the dog's expression. The eyes have a clear, bright appearance, expressing intelligent inquisitiveness, particularly when the ears are drawn up and the dog is on the alert. In blue merles, dark brown eyes are preferable, but either or both eyes may be merle or china in color without specific penalty. A large, round, full eye seriously detracts from the desired 'sweet' expression. *Eye faults are heavily penalized.*

Ears

The ears are in proportion to the size of the head and, if they are carried properly and unquestionably 'break' naturally, are seldom too small. Large ears usually cannot be lifted correctly off the head, and even if lifted, they will be out of proportion to the size of the head. When in repose the ears are folded lengthwise and thrown back into the frill. On the alert they are drawn well up on the backskull and are carried about three-quarters erect, with about one-fourth of the ear tipping or 'breaking' forward. *A dog with prick ears or low ears cannot show true expression and is penalized accordingly.*

Neck

The neck is firm, clean, muscular, sinewy and heavily frilled. It is fairly long, carried upright with a slight arch at the nape and imparts a proud, upstanding appearance showing off the frill.

Body

The body is firm, hard and muscular, a trifle long in proportion to the height. The ribs are well-rounded behind the well-sloped shoulders and the chest is deep, extending to the elbows. The back is strong and level, supported by powerful hips and thighs and the croup is sloped to give a well-rounded finish. The loin is powerful and slightly arched. *Noticeably fat dogs, or dogs in poor flesh, or with skin disease, or with no undercoat are out of condition and are moderately penalized accordingly.*

Legs

The forelegs are straight and muscular, with a fair amount of bone considering the size of the dog. A cumbersome appearance is undesirable. *Both narrow and wide placement are penalized.* The forearm is moderately fleshy and the pasterns are flexible but without weakness. The hind legs are less fleshy, muscular at the thighs, very sinewy and the hocks and stifles are well bent. *A cow-hocked dog or a dog with straight stifles is penalized.* The comparatively small feet are approximately oval in shape. The soles are well padded and tough, and the toes are well arched and close together. When the Collie is not in motion the legs and feet are judged by allowing the dog to come to a natural stop in a standing position so that both the forelegs and the hind legs are placed well apart, with the feet extending straight forward. Excessive 'posing' is undesirable.

Gait

The gait or movement is distinctly characteristic of the breed. A sound Collie is not out at the elbows but it does, nevertheless, move toward an observer with its front feet tracking comparatively close together at the ground. The front legs do not 'cross over,' nor does the Collie move with a pacing or rolling gait. Viewed from the front, one gains the impression that the dog is capable of changing its direction of travel almost instantaneously, as indeed it is. When viewed from the rear, the hind legs, from the hock to the ground, move in comparatively close-together, parallel, vertical planes. The hind legs are powerful and propelling. Viewed from the side, the gait is smooth not choppy. The reasonably long, 'reaching' stride is even, easy, light and seemingly effortless.

Tail

The tail is moderately long, the bone reaching to the hock joint or below. It is carried low when the dog is quiet, the end having an upward twist or 'swirl.' When gaited or when the dog is excited it is carried gaily but not over the back.

Coat

The well-fitting, proper-textured coat is the crowning glory of the rough variety of Collie. It is abundant except on the head and legs. The outer coat is straight and harsh to the touch. *A soft, open outer coat or a curly outer coat, regardless of quantity is penalized.* The undercoat, however, is soft, furry and so close together that it is difficult to see the skin when the hair is parted. The coat is very abundant on the mane and frill. The face or mask is smooth. The forelegs are smooth and well feathered to the back of the pasterns. The hind legs are smooth below the hock joints. Any feathering below the hocks is removed for the show ring. The hair on the tail is very profuse and on the hips it is long and bushy. The texture, quantity and the extent to which the coat 'fits the dog' are important points.

Color

The four recognized colors are sable and white, tri-color, blue merle and white. There is no preference among them. The sable and white is predominantly sable (a fawn sable color of varying shades from light gold to dark mahogany) with white markings usually on the chest, neck, legs, feet and the tip of the tail. A blaze may appear on the foreface or backskull or both. The tri-color is predominantly black, carrying white markings as in a sable and white

and has tan shadings on and about the head and legs. The blue merle is a mottled or 'marbled' color predominantly blue-gray and black with white markings as in the sable and white and usually has tan shadings as in the tri-color

White markings.

The white is predominantly white, preferably with sable or tri-color markings. Blue merle coloring is undesirable in whites.

Size
Dogs are from 24 to 26 inches at the shoulder and weigh from 60 to 75 pounds. Bitches are from 22 to 24 inches at the shoulder, weighing from 50 to 65 pounds. *An under-*

size or an oversize Collie is penalized according to the extent to which the dog appears to be undersize or oversize.

Expression
Expression is one of the most important points in considering the relative value of Collies. *Expression*, like the term 'character' is difficult to define in words. It is not a fixed point as in color, weight or height and it is something the uninitiated can properly understand only by optical illustration. In general, however, it may be said to be the combined product of the shape and balance of the skull and muzzle, the placement, size, shape and color of the eye and the position, size and carriage of the ears. An expression that shows sullenness or which is suggestive of any other breed is entirely foreign. The Collie cannot be judged properly until its expression has been carefully evaluated.

SMOOTH
The smooth variety of Collie is judged by the same standard as the rough variety, except that the references to the quantity and the distribution of the coat are not applicable to the smooth variety, which has a hard, dense, smooth coat.

Approved by the AKC 10 March 1959

KC(GB) VARIATION TO STANDARD
The rough-coated and smooth-coated varieties are classed as two separate breeds by the KC(GB). *Colour:* three only, sable, tri-colour, blue merle. *Weight:* dogs 45 to 65 pounds, bitches 40 to 55 pounds.

DOBERMAN PINSCHER

NATIONAL GROUPING		
	Name	Number
AKC	Working Dogs	III
KC(GB)	Working	5
FCI	Guard Dogs	2

It happens to few people that they have a breed of dog named after them to hand down to posterity, but when a man invents and produces a completely new breed as did Louis Dobermann in Germany about the year 1870, it would have been unjust had anything less happened. Herr Dobermann set out with a vision of the sort of dog that he wanted to breed, and beginning with the Rottweiler and the German Pinscher, he produced one of the finest and most popular breeds in the world. He is believed to have introduced into his cross the black and tan English Terrier and one of the shepherd dogs, probably the German Shepherd Dog. In the older books the dog is referred to as a distinctive German Terrier, but there is little of the Terrier look about him now. Originally he was a much coarser dog with a heavier body and a shorter and more rounded head, probably due to the Rottweiler blood. Others after Herr Dobermann, Otto Goeller and Daniel Elmer for instance, did a great deal towards the refinement of the breed and produced a more racy and elegant dog.

The first breed club was founded in 1912, and the breed began to be more widely accepted, finding its way rapidly to other European countries and to the United States and Britain. His qualities as a guard were quickly appreciated and he became a popular dog with the armed forces and police forces of the world. He has never quite achieved the popularity of the German Shepherd Dog for this work, as although he is somewhat lighter, he is tougher and harder to control. In the United States of America he soon became the third most popular dog and other countries followed suit, so that by the middle of the 20th century his fame as a guard, army dog and show dog has spread throughout the world, carrying the name of Herr Dobermann with him.

He is an elegant yet very strong dog, with a powerful body, great strength of limb and tremendous agility. He is fast, has great powers of endurance, and is an ardent worker, all of which make him very popular with the forces, as not only does he do the work that is required of him, but his smart appearance fits him well to the formality and precision of a trained body of men. As a show dog his progress has been amazing, and from small beginnings only a few years ago, he is now seen at shows throughout the world in large numbers. He is as popular in Malaysia as he is in Europe, and as numerous in Australia as he is in Scandinavia. His smart, elegant yet powerful appearance always guarantees him a good audience, and his smooth coat which can be polished until it shines makes him an outstanding dog in mixed company. He usually features among the big winners and the strength of the breed clubs, their enthusiasm and continued work on the breed ensure that this will continue.

At one time his temperament was suspect, and for this reason his use as a police dog declined in those parts of the world where undue force was frowned upon. In America it was recognised at an early stage that this would count against the breed, and his tendency to undue sharpness of reaction was carefully bred out, dogs which showed this trait suffering disqualification. Training programmes were instituted and owners and breeders were encouraged to train their dogs to obedience work, which at one and the same time reduced their aggression and gave them a better public image. In Britain this has not been done to the same extent, and from time to time the Doberman ring at one of the major shows will explode in fury. Properly trained they become obedient dogs, and within the family circle they are even affectionate, and there can hardly be a better guard dog in the world.

OFFICIAL STANDARD

General appearance

The appearance is that of a dog of medium size, with a body that is square; the height, measured vertically from the ground to the highest point of the withers, equalling the length measured horizontally from the forechest to the rear projection of the upper thigh. *Height:* at the withers —*Dogs:* 26 to 28 inches, ideal about $27\frac{1}{2}$ inches; *Bitches:* 24 to 26 inches, ideal about $25\frac{1}{2}$ inches. Length of head, neck and legs in proportion to length and depth of body. Compactly built, muscular and powerful, for great endurance and speed. Elegant in appearance, of proud carriage, reflecting great nobility and temperament. Energetic, watchful, determined, alert, fearless, loyal and obedient.

The judge shall dismiss from the ring any shy or vicious Doberman.
Shyness: a dog shall be judged fundamentally shy if, refusing to stand for examination, it shrinks away from the judge; if it fears an approach from the rear; if it shies at sudden and unusual noises to a marked degree. *Viciousness:* a dog that attacks or attempts to attack either the judge or its handler, is definitely vicious. An aggressive or belligerent attitude towards other dogs shall not be deemed viciousness.

Head

Long and dry, resembling a blunt wedge in both frontal and profile views. When seen from the front, the head widens gradually toward the base of the ears in a practically unbroken line. Top of skull flat, turning with slight stop to bridge of muzzle, with muzzle line extending parallel to top line of skull. Cheeks flat and muscular. Lips lying close to jaws. Jaws full and powerful, well filled under the eyes.

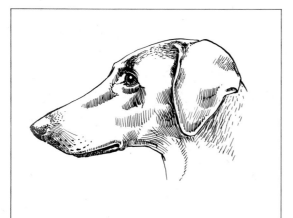

Head and skull: long, well-filled, clean out.

Eyes

Almond shaped, moderately deep set, with vigorous, energetic expression. Iris, of uniform color, ranging from medium to darkest brown in black dogs; in reds, blues, and fawns the color of the iris blends with that of the markings, the darkest shade being preferable in every case.

Teeth

Strongly developed and white. Lower incisors upright and touching inside of upper incisors—a true scissors bite. *42 correctly placed teeth,* 22 in the lower, 20 in the upper jaw. Distemper teeth shall not be penalized. *Disqualifying faults:* overshot more than $\frac{3}{16}$ of an inch. Undershot more than $\frac{1}{8}$ of an inch. Four or more missing teeth.

Ears

Normally cropped and carried erect. The upper attachment of the ear, when held erect, is on a level with the top of the skull.

Neck

Proudly carried, well muscled and dry. Well arched, with nape of neck widening gradually toward body. Length of neck proportioned to body and head.

Body

Back short, firm, of sufficient width, and muscular at the loins, extending in a straight line from withers to the *slightly* rounded croup. *Withers:* pronounced and forming the highest point of the body. *Brisket:* reaching deep to the elbow. *Chest:* broad with forechest well defined. *Ribs:* well sprung from the spine, but flattened in lower end to permit elbow clearance. *Belly:* well tucked up, extending in a curved line from the brisket. *Loins:* wide

and muscled. *Hips:* broad and in proportion to body, breadth of hips being approximately equal to breadth of body at rib cage and shoulders.

Tail
Docked at approximately second joint, appears to be a continuation of the spine, and is carried only slightly above the horizontal when the dog is alert.

Forequarters
Shoulder blade: sloping forward and downward at a 45-degree angle to the ground meets the upper arm at an angle of 90 degrees. Length of shoulder blade and upper arm are equal. Height from elbow to withers approximately equals height from ground to elbow. *Legs:* seen from front and side, perfectly straight and parallel to each other from elbow to pastern; muscled and sinewy, with heavy bone. In normal pose and when gaiting, the elbows lie close to the brisket. *Pasterns:* firm and almost perpendicular to the ground. *Feet:* well arched, compact, and catlike, turning neither in nor out. Dewclaws may be removed.

Hindquarters
The angulation of the hindquarters balances that of the forequarters. *Hip bone:* falls away from spinal column at an angle of about 30 degrees, producing a slightly rounded, well-filled-out croup. *Upper shanks:* at right angles to the hip bones, are long, wide, and well muscled on both sides of thigh, with clearly defined stifles. Upper and lower shanks are of equal length. While the dog is at rest, hock to heel is perpendicular to the ground. Viewed from the rear, the legs are straight, parallel to each other, and wide enough apart to fit in with a properly built body. *Cat feet:* as on front legs, turning neither in nor out. Dewclaws, if any, are generally removed.

Gait
Free, balanced, and vigorous, with good reach in the forequarters and good driving power in the hindquarters. When trotting, there is strong rear-action drive. Each rear leg moves in line with the foreleg on the same side. Rear and front legs are thrown neither in nor out. Back remains strong and firm. When moving at a fast trot, a properly built dog will single-track.

Coat, color, markings
Coat, smooth-haired, short, hard, thick and close lying. Invisible gray undercoat on neck permissible. *Allowed colors:* black, red, blue, and fawn (Isabella). *Markings:* rust, sharply defined, appearing above each eye and on muzzle, throat and forechest, on all legs and feet, and below tail. *Nose:* solid black on black dogs, dark brown on red ones, dark gray on blue ones, dark tan on fawns. White patch on chest, not exceeding ½ square inch, permisible.

FAULTS
The foregoing description is that of the ideal Doberman Pinscher. Any deviation from the above described dog must be penalized to the extent of the deviation.

DISQUALIFICATIONS
Overshot more than $\frac{3}{16}$ of an inch; undershot more than $\frac{1}{8}$ of an inch. Four or more missing teeth.

Approved by the AKC 14 October 1969

KC(GB) VARIATION TO STANDARD
Known simply as the Dobermann in GB.
Ears: erect or dropped. Erect preferred. *Body:* ribs well sprung, deep, reaching to elbow. *Feet:* all dewclaws to be removed. *Height:* (ideal) dogs 27 inches. *Faults:* hair forming ridge on back of neck and/or on spine.

GERMAN SHEPHERD DOG

There is no dog in what we now know as the Working Group that has achieved the German Shepherd Dog's popularity and ironically no dog has been more vilified. Its early name, the Alsatian Wolf-Dog would have been enough to guarantee this, but during the First World War, when everything that savoured of Germany was publicly denigrated there was a strong body of opinion against this quite remarkable dog. More recently, as urban attacks on people and especially upon children have increased, and as these attacks have often been carried out by German Shepherd Dogs or dogs very like them, the feeling against the breed has strengthened.

The ancestry of the German Shepherd Dog is fairly well defined. He was developed in Germany around a hundred years ago in an attempt to produce the ideal shepherd dog. It is very unlikely that the breed resulted from crossing wolves with local dogs as has been suggested, and any wolflike character which the dog is incorrectly said to have is most likely due to the vague similarity there is in physical type and colour. The modern dog almost certainly descends

NATIONAL GROUPING		
	Name	Number
AKC	Working Dogs	III
KC(GB)	Working	5
FCI	Herding Dogs	I

from three strains of working dogs in Württemburg, Thuringia and Krone.

The first appearance of a German Shepherd Dog at a show was in 1882 in Hanover and the first specialist club was formed in 1899. Since that time few breeds can have had such care in breeding and recording.

It is one of the most intelligent dogs, being capable of working independently of habit and training. There are many stories of dogs taking naturally to herding and guarding tasks with either no training at all or the absolute minimum. He is probably the best guard in the world, being very forceful and positive and as a result he is much in demand in police and military circles. He is fairly easily trained in apprehending criminals, and police forces throughout the world use the breed for that purpose, the training being carried to a high degree of proficiency, and there is much competition between forces and individual dogs. In addition the German Shepherd Dog is one of the most popular breeds in the world of obedience training.

The German Shepherd Dog's response to training results in a high degree of showmanship, and large numbers of these dogs standing like statues, or gaiting round the ring in their own particular manner is always tremendously popular as a spectacle. They are quiet in the ring, rarely interfering with one another, and their complete understanding of what is going on is shown by their joy and excitement at being released from the tension of the immediate competition.

Some doubt has been cast on the temperamental stability of this dog, largely due to the fact that used as guards in the early days they were discouraged very little from exercising their strength and courage. In recent years there have been many attacks upon people by dogs, sometimes by German Shepherd Dogs, but often by big strong dogs described by unreliable eye-witnesses and the media as such when they were probably mongrels or crossbreeds. In fact the temperament of the German Shepherd Dog is no more unreliable than that of any other dog. Correctly trained and housed he will prove every bit as amenable and friendly as a Toy breed or a Gundog. Incorrectly trained, and kept in conditions in which he sees strangers only as intruders to be driven off as in the guarding of dumps and other property, he exercises his strength and natural instincts as he has been encouraged to do.

OFFICIAL STANDARD

General appearance
The first impression of a good German Shepherd Dog is that of a strong, agile, well-muscled animal, alert and full of life. It is well balanced, with harmonious development of the forequarter and hindquarter. The dog is longer than tall, deep-bodied, and presents an outline of smooth curves rather than angles. It looks substantial and not spindly, giving the impression, both at rest and in motion, of muscular fitness and nimbleness without any look of clumsiness or soft living. The ideal dog is stamped with a look of quality and nobility—difficult to define, but unmistakable when present. Secondary sex characteristics are strongly marked, and every animal gives a definite impression of masculinity or femininity, according to its sex.

Character
The breed has a distinct personality marked by direct and fearless, but not hostile, expression, self-confidence and a certain aloofness that does not lend itself to immediate and indiscriminate friendships. The dog must be approachable, quietly standing its ground and showing confidence and willingness to meet overtures without itself making them. It is poised, but when the occasion demands, eager and alert; both fit and willing to serve in its capacity as companion, watchdog, blind leader, herding dog, or guardian, whichever the circumstances may demand. The dog must not be timid, shrinking behind its master or handler; it should not be nervous, looking about or upward with anxious expression or showing nervous reactions, such as tucking of tail, to strange sounds or sights. Lack of confidence under any surroundings is not typical of good character. Any of the above deficiencies in character which indicate shyness must be penalized as very serious faults. It must be possible for the judge to observe the teeth and to determine that both testicles are descended. Any dog that attempts to bite the judge must be disqualified. The ideal dog is a working animal with an incorruptible character combined with body and gait suitable for the arduous work that constitutes its primary purpose.

Head
The head is noble, cleanly chiseled, strong without coarseness, but above all not fine, and in proportion to the body. The head of the male is distinctly masculine, and that of the bitch distinctly feminine. The muzzle is long and strong with the lips firmly fitted, and its topline is parallel to the topline of the skull. Seen from the front, the forehead is only moderately arched, and the skull slopes into the long, wedge-shaped muzzle without abrupt stop. Jaws are strongly developed. *Ears:* ears are moderately pointed, in proportion to the skull, open toward the

front, and carried erect when at attention, the ideal carriage being one in which the center lines of the ears, viewed from the front, are parallel to each other and perpendicular to the ground. A dog with cropped or hanging ears must be disqualified. *Eyes:* of medium size, almond shaped, set a little obliquely and not protruding. The color is as dark as possible. The expression keen, intelligent and composed. *Teeth:* 42 in number—20 upper and 22 lower—are strongly developed and meet in a scissors bite in which part of the inner surface of the upper incisors meet and engage part of the outer surface of the lower incisors. An overshot jaw or a level bite is undesirable. An undershot jaw is a disqualifying fault. Complete dentition is to be preferred. Any missing teeth other than first premolars is a serious fault.

Neck

The neck is strong and muscular, clean-cut and relatively long, proportionate in size to the head and without loose folds of skin. When the dog is at attention or excited, the head is raised and the neck carried high; otherwise typical carriage of the head is forward rather than up and but little higher than the top of the shoulders, particularly in motion.

Forequarters

The shoulder blades are long and obliquely angled, laid on flat and not placed forward. The upper arm joins the shoulder blade at about a right angle. Both the upper arm and the shoulder blade are well muscled. The forelegs, viewed from all sides, are straight and the bone oval rather than round. The pasterns are strong and springy and angulated at approximately a 25-degree angle from the vertical.

Feet

The feet are short, compact, with toes well arched, pads thick and firm, nails short and dark. The dewclaws, if any, should be removed from the hind legs. Dewclaws on the forelegs may be removed, but are normally left on.

Proportion

The German Shepherd Dog is longer than tall, with the most desirable proportion as 10 to $8\frac{1}{2}$. The desired height for dogs at the top of the highest point of the shoulder blade is 24 to 26 inches; and for bitches, 22 to 24 inches. The length is measured from the point of the prosternum or breastbone to the rear of the pelvis, the ischial tuberosity.

Body

The whole structure of the body gives an impression of depth and solidity without bulkiness. *Chest:* commencing at the prosternum, it is well filled and carried well down between the legs. It is deep and capacious, never shallow, with ample room for lungs and heart, carried well forward, with the prosternum showing ahead of the shoulder in profile. *Ribs:* well sprung and long, neither barrel-shaped nor too flat, and carried down to a sternum which reaches to the elbows. Correct ribbing allows the elbows to move back freely when the dog is at a trot. Too round causes interference and throws the elbows out; too flat or short

causes pinched elbows. Ribbing is carried well back so that the loin is relatively short. *Abdomen:* firmly held and not paunchy. The bottom line is only moderately tucked up in the loin.

Topline

Withers: the withers are higher than and sloping into the level back. *Back:* the back is straight, very strongly developed without sag or roach, and relatively short. The desirable long proportion is not derived from a long back, but from over-all length with relation to height, which is achieved by length of forequarter and length of withers and hindquarter, viewed from the side. *Loin:* viewed from the top, broad and strong. Undue length between the last rib and the thigh, when viewed from the side, is undesirable. *Croup:* long and gradually sloping.

Tail

Bushy, with the last vertebra extended at least to the hock joint. It is set smoothly into the croup and low rather than high. At rest, the tail hangs in a slight curve like a saber. A slight hook—sometimes carried to one side—is faulty only to the extent that it mars general appearance. When the dog is excited or in motion, the curve is accentuated and the tail raised, but it should never be curled forward beyond a vertical line. Tails too short, or with clumpy ends due to ankylosis, are serious faults. A dog with a docked tail must be disqualified.

Hindquarters

The whole assembly of the thigh, viewed from the side, is broad, with both upper and lower thigh well muscled, forming as nearly as possible a right angle. The upper thigh bone parallels the shoulder blade while the lower thigh bone parallels the upper arm. The metatarsus (the unit between the hock joint and the foot) is short, strong and tightly articulated.

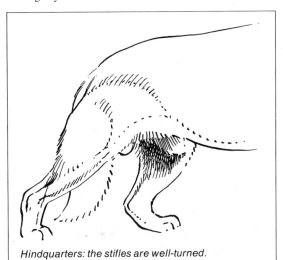

Hindquarters: the stifles are well-turned.

Gait

A German Shepherd Dog is a trotting dog, and its structure has been developed to meet the requirements of its work. *General impression:* the gait is outreaching, elastic, seemingly without effort, smooth and rhythmic, covering the maximum amount of ground with the minimum number of steps. At a walk it covers a great deal of ground, with long stride of both hind legs and forelegs. At a trot the dog covers still more ground with even longer stride, and moves powerfully but easily, with co-ordination and balance so that the gait appears to be the steady motion of a well-lubricated machine. The feet travel close to the ground on both forward reach and backward push. In order to achieve ideal movement of this kind, there must be good muscular development and ligamentation. The hindquarters deliver, through the back, a powerful forward thrust which slightly lifts the whole animal and drives the body forward. Reaching far under, and passing the imprint left by the front foot, the hind foot takes hold of the ground; then hock, stifle and upper thigh come into play and sweep back, the stroke of the hind leg finishing with the foot still close to the ground in a smooth follow-through. The over-reach of the hindquarter usually necessitates one hind foot passing outside and the other hind foot passing inside the track of the forefeet, and such action is not faulty unless the locomotion is crabwise with the dog's body sideways out of the normal straight line.

Transmission

The typical smooth, flowing gait is maintained with great strength and firmness of back. The whole effort of the hindquarters is transmitted to the forequarter through the loin, back and withers. At full trot, the back must

remain firm and level without sway, roll, whip or roach. Unlevel topline with withers lower than the hip is a fault. To compensate for the forward motion imparted by the hindquarters, the shoulder should open to its full extent. The forelegs should reach out close to the ground in a long stride in harmony with that of the hindquarters. The dog does not track on widely separated parallel lines, but brings the feet inward toward the middle line of the body when trotting in order to maintain balance. The feet track closely but do not strike or cross over. Viewed from the front, the front legs function from the shoulder joint to the pad in a straight line. Viewed from the rear, the hind legs function from the hip joint to the pad in a straight line. Faults of gait, whether from front, rear or side, are to be considered very serious faults.

Color

The German Shepherd Dog varies in color, and most colors are permissible. Strong rich colors are preferred. Nose black. Pale, washed-out colors and blues or livers are serious faults. A white dog or a dog with a nose that is not predominantly black, must be disqualified.

Coat

The ideal dog has a double coat of medium length. The outer coat should be as dense as possible, hair straight, harsh and lying close to the body. A slightly wavy outer coat, often of wiry texture, is permissible. The head, including the inner ear and foreface, and the legs and paws are covered with short hair, and the neck with longer and thicker hair. The rear of the forelegs and hind legs has somewhat longer hair extending to the pastern and hock, respectively. Faults in coat include soft, silky, too long outer coat, woolly, curly, and open coat.

DISQUALIFICATIONS
Cropped or hanging ears. Undershot jaw. Docked tail. White dogs. Dogs with noses not predominantly black. Any dog that attempts to bite the judge.

Approved by the AKC 9 April 1968

KC(GB) VARIATION TO STANDARD

Known as the Alsatian in GB. *Head:* well filled in under eyes. Should be plenty of substance in foreface. *Hindquarters:* stifles well turned, hocks strong and well let down. Ability to turn quickly is a necessary asset to Alsatians and this can only be if there is a good length of thigh-bone and leg, by bending hock. *Coat:* average length for hair on back is 1 to 2 inches. *Weight and size:* ideal height (to highest point of shoulder) is 22 to 24 inches for bitches and 24 to 26 inches for dogs. The proportion of length to height may vary between 10:9 and 10:8.5. *Faults:* a long narrow Collie or Borzoi head. Lack of heavy undercoat.

GIANT SCHNAUZER

The largest of the three Schnauzers, the Giant Schnauzer or Riesenschnauzer is the most recent of the three to arrive on the dog show scene outside Germany. Known for some time in European countries, it is only in recent years that it has appeared in the United States of America and Britain. The origin of the breed is somewhat obscure, but he is certainly a manufactured dog as were the Boxer and the Doberman. He was probably produced from some of the Belgian breeds such as the Bouvier Des Flandres and the Briard, both of which have his colours and something of his square look, though the strong wiry coat must have come from some other source.

He is a big, square, strong dog, built to combine strength and agility as he is in many ways the typical Terrier, having something of the look of a large strangely coloured Airedale. He can be trained to obedience work to a certain extent, which means that although he has a quickness of temper, he is normally very much under control, and he shows extremely well. His coat, like that of the two smaller Schnauzers, needs a great deal of preparation for the ring. The coat is hard and strong, and a good deal of trimming is needed which involves considerable work. In the rough he is still an attractive dog, but it is unlikely that he will ever become popular as a house pet. though his guarding instincts are well developed.

NATIONAL GROUPING		
	Name	Number
AKC	Working Dogs	III
KC(GB)	Utility	4
FCI	Guard Dogs	2

207

OFFICIAL STANDARD

General appearance

The Giant Schnauzer should resemble, as nearly as possible, in general appearance, a larger and more powerful version of the Standard Schnauzer, on the whole a bold and valiant figure of a dog. Robust, strongly built, nearly square in proportion of body length to height at withers, active, sturdy, and well muscled. Temperament which combines spirit and alertness with intelligence and reliability. Composed, watchful, courageous, easily trained, deeply loyal to family, playful, amiable in repose, and a commanding figure when aroused. The sound, reliable temperament, rugged build, and dense weather-resistant wiry coat make for one of the most useful, powerful, and enduring working breeds.

Head

Strong, rectangular in appearance, and elongated; narrowing slightly from the ears to the eyes, and again from the eyes to the tip of the nose. The total length of the head is about one-half the length of the back (withers to set-on of tail). The head matches the sex and substance of the dog. The top line of the muzzle is parallel to the top line of the skull; there is a slight stop which is accentuated by the eyebrows.

Skull (occiput to stop)

Moderately broad between the ears; occiput not too prominent. Top of skull flat; skin unwrinkled.

Cheeks

Flat, but with well-developed chewing muscles; there is no 'cheekiness' to disturb the rectangular head appearance (with beard).

Muzzle

Strong and well filled under the eyes; both parallel and

Head and skull: strong and elongated muzzle powerful.

equal in length to the topskull; ending in a moderately blunt wedge. The nose is large, black, and full. The lips are tight, and not overlapping, black in color.

Bite

A full complement of sound white teeth (6/6 incisors, 2/2 canines, 8/8 premolars, 4/6 molars) with a scissors bite. The upper and lower jaws are powerful and well formed. *Disqualifying faults:* overshot or undershot.

Ears

When cropped, identical in shape and length with pointed tips. They are in balance with the head and are not exaggerated in length. They are set high on the skull and carried perpendicularly at the inner edges with as little bell as possible along the other edges. When uncropped, the ears are V-shaped button ears of medium length and thickness, set high and carried rather high and close to the head.

Eyes

Medium size, dark brown, and deep-set. They are oval in appearance and keen in expression with lids fitting tightly. Vision is not impaired nor eyes hidden by too long eyebrows.

Neck

Strong and well arched, of moderate length, blending cleanly into the shoulders, and with the skin fitting tightly at the throat; in harmony with the dog's weight and build.

Body: compact, substantial, short-coupled, and strong, with great power and agility. The height at the highest point of the withers equals the body length from breastbone to point of rump. The loin section is well developed, as short as possible for compact build.

Forequarters

The forequarters have flat, somewhat sloping shoulders and high withers. Forelegs are straight and vertical when viewed from all sides with strong pasterns and good bone. They are separated by a fairly deep brisket which precludes a pinched front. The elbows are set close to the body and point directly backwards.

Chest

Medium in width, ribs well sprung but with no tendency toward a barrel chest; oval in cross section; deep through the brisket. The breastbone is plainly discernible, with strong forechest; the brisket descends at least to the elbows, and ascends gradually toward the rear with the belly moderately drawn up. The ribs spread gradually from the first rib so as to allow space for the elbows to move close to the body.

Shoulders

The sloping shoulder blades (scapulae) are strongly muscled, yet flat. They are well laid back so that from the side the rounded upper ends are in a nearly vertical line above the elbows. They slope well forward to the point where they join the upper arm (humerus), forming as nearly as possible a right angle. Such an angulation permits the maximum forward extension of the forelegs without binding or effort. Both shoulder blades and upper arm are long, permitting depth of chest at the brisket.

Back
Short, straight, strong, and firm.

Tail
The tail is set moderately high and carried high in excitement. It should be docked to the second or not more than the third joint (approximately one and one-half to about three inches long at maturity).

Hindquarters
The hindquarters are strongly muscled, in balance with the forequarters; upper thighs are slanting and well bent at the stifles, with the second thighs (tibiae) approximately parallel to an extension of the upper neckline. The legs from the hock joint to the feet are short, perpendicular to the ground while the dog is standing naturally, and from the rear parallel to each other. The hindquarters do not appear over-built or higher than the shoulders. Croup full and slightly rounded.

Feet
Well-arched, compact and catlike, turning neither in nor out, with thick tough pads and dark nails.

Dewclaws
Dewclaws, if any, on hind legs should be removed; on the forelegs, may be removed.

Gait
The trot is the gait at which movement is judged. Free, balanced and vigorous, with good reach in the forequarters and good driving power in the hindquarters. Rear and front legs are thrown neither in nor out. When moving at a fast trot, a properly built dog will single-track. Back

Hindquarters: vertical to stifle and in hock, flat and strongly muscled.

remains strong, firm, and flat.

Coat
Hard, wiry, very dense; composed of a soft undercoat and a harsh outer coat which, when seen against the grain, stands slightly up off the back, lying neither smooth nor flat. Coarse hair on top of head; harsh beard and eyebrows, the Schnauzer hallmark.

Color
Solid black or pepper and salt. *Black:* a truly pure black. A small white spot on the breast is permitted. *Pepper and salt:* outer coat of a combination of banded hairs (white with black and black with white) and some black and white hairs, appearing gray from a short distance. *Ideally:* an intensely pigmented medium gray shade with 'peppering' even distributed throughout the coat, and a gray undercoat. *Acceptable:* all shades of pepper and salt from dark iron-gray to silver-gray. Every shade of coat has a dark facial mask to emphasize the expression; the color of the mask harmonizes with the shade of the body coat. Eyebrows, whiskers, cheeks, throat, chest, legs, and under tail are lighter in color but include 'peppering.'

Height
The height of the withers of the dog is $25\frac{1}{2}$ to $27\frac{1}{2}$ inches, and of the bitch, $23\frac{1}{2}$ to $25\frac{1}{2}$ inches, with the mediums being desired. Size alone should never take precedence over type, balance, soundness, and temperament. It should be noted that too small dogs generally lack the power and too large dogs, the agility and maneuverability, desired in a working dog.

FAULTS

The foregoing description is that of the ideal Giant Schnauzer. Any deviation from the above described dog must be penalized to the extent of the deviation.

The judge shall dismiss from the ring any shy or vicious Giant Schnauzer. Shyness: a dog shall be judged fundamentally shy if, refusing to stand for examination, it repeatedly shrinks away from the judge; if it fears unduly any approach from the rear; if it shies to a marked degree at sudden and unusual noises. Viciousness: a dog that attacks or attempts to attack either the judge or its handler, is definitely vicious. An aggressive or belligerent attitude towards other dogs shall not be deemed visciousness.

DISQUALIFICATIONS
Overshot or undershot.

Approved by the AKC 13 February 1971

KC(GB) VARIATION TO STANDARD
This dog is granted championship status by the KC(GB) in the Utility Group of Non-sporting Breeds. *Ears:* not cropped. *Height:* any deviation of more than 1 inch either way should be penalised.

GREAT DANE

The Mastiff group is one of the oldest and most significant of all the groups of dogs. Amongst its breeds are guard dogs from almost every country in Europe and Asia, and examples of Mastiff type dogs exist in fact and myth in most parts of the world. Zeus is said to have had a golden dog created for him by a smith with miraculous powers and even that dog was a Mastiff. It is difficult to imagine how the large guard dog, often smooth-coated and invariably affectionate with those that it knows but fierce with intruders, developed from the common ancestor of the race *canis domesticus*, but it did, and at a very early stage. One of the finest examples, for sheer size and for the other qualities of the group is the Great Dane. He almost certainly goes back to the ancient Molossus, and to the Alaunt, antique breeds now disappeared, but the progenitors of many of the massive breeds in the world today.

Germany lays claim to having developed the breed in modern times. He was known as the 'Deutsche Dogge' at one time and is still known as the 'Dogo

NATIONAL GROUPING		
	Name	Number
AKC	Working Dogs	III
KC(GB)	Working	5
FCI	Guard Dogs	2

Alemanes' in Spain. In the early days of the breed in Britain he was also known as the German Boarhound, but the name Great Dane eventually became generally used, and it is by that name that he is now known almost everywhere. Denmark had in fact a large dog of the Mastiff type, but more stocky and shorter in the leg than the elegant dog that we know today, and it was certainly Germany that played the major part in developing the breed from the late part of the 19th century. A standard of points was agreed in about 1880, somewhat later in Britain, and adopted in the United States of America.

The first record of a Great Dane being shown in

Britain was in 1878 when one was entered in the stud book as an Ulmer Dogge. This name is a reference to one of the several breeds that were probably used in Germany to produce the breed, along with the Saufinder, Hatzreude and Grosse Dogge, but the history of the modern Great Dane in Britain really started in 1900 when Mrs. Violet Horsfall imported several.

There are few problems about the Great Dane apart from those of feeding and rearing. A dog that will grow from something of the size of a smallish cat to an animal standing over thirty inches high in around six months, needs vast quantities of the very best food at every stage of its growth. He has natural hunting instincts, and very well developed scenting powers. His strength and stamina is such that he will run for miles, swimming rivers and leaping walls on the way, yet he is remarkably tractable and responsive to commands and can be trained to be quite obedient.

There are few finer dogs in the show ring than the Great Dane. His very size, striking colour and manners in the ring which are usually impeccable, make him one of the favourites with the dog-show-going-public throughout the world. His temperament is excellent, as he is loving and kindly towards people and especially towards children. He is not aggressive, and although he is well able to take care of himself and will eventually lose patience if persistently annoyed, he will not seek trouble. At the same time he is a magnificent guard and watchdog, settles well in a house, and his short coat and clean habits make him easy to groom. He is very much a one-man dog, and will attach himself to one person sometimes even to the point of embarrassment, and for that one person he will do absolutely anything.

OFFICIAL STANDARD

General appearance
The Great Dane combines in its distinguished appearance dignity, strength and elegance with great size and a powerful, well-formed, smoothly muscled body. He is one of the giant breeds, but is unique in that his general conformation must be so well balanced that he never appears clumsy and is always a unit—the Apollo of dogs. He must be spirited and courageous—never timid. He is friendly and dependable. This physical and mental combination is the characteristic which gives the Great Dane the majesty possessed by no other breed. It is particularly true of this breed that there is an impression of great masculinity in dogs as compared to an impression of femininity in bitches. The male should appear more massive throughout than the bitch, with large frame and heavier bone. In the ratio between length and height, the Great Dane should appear as square as possible. In bitches, a somewhat longer body is permissible. *Faults:* lack of unity; timidity; bitchy dogs; poor musculature; poor bone development; out of condition; rickets; doggy bitches.

Color and markings
(i) Color—Brindle Danes: base color ranging from light golden yellow to deep golden yellow always brindled with strong black cross stripes. The more intensive the base color and the more intensive the brindling, the more attractive will be the color. Small white marks at the chest and toes are not desirable. *Faults:* brindle with too dark a base color; silver-blue and grayish-blue base color; dull (faded) brindling; white tail tip.
(ii) Fawn Danes: golden yellow up to deep golden yellow color with a deep black mask. The golden deep-yellow color must always be given the preference. Small white spots at the chest and toes are not desirable. *Faults:* yellowish-gray, bluish-yellow, grayish-blue, dirty yellow color (drab color), lack of black mask.
(iii) Blue Danes: the color must be a pure steel blue, as far as possible without any tinge of yellow, black or mouse gray. *Faults:* any deviation from a pure steel-blue coloration.
(iv) Black Danes: glossy black. *Faults:* yellow-black, brown-black or blue-black. White markings, such as stripes on the chest, speckled chest and markings on the paws are permitted but not desirable.
(v) Harlequin Danes: base color: pure white with black torn patches irregularly and well distributed over the entire body; pure white neck preferred. The black patches should never be large enough to give the appearance of a blanket nor so small as to give a stippled or dappled effect. (Eligible, but less desirable, are a few small gray spots; also pointings where instead of a pure white base with black spots, there is a white base with single black hairs showing through which tend to give a salt and pepper or dirty effect.) *Faults:* white base color with a few large spots; bluish-gray pointed background.

Size
The dog should not be less than 30 inches at the shoulders, but it is preferable that he be 32 inches or more, providing he is well proportioned to his height. The female should not be less than 28 inches at the shoulders, but it is preferable that she be 30 inches or more, providing she is well proportioned to her height.

Condition of coat
The coat should be very short and thick, smooth, and glossy. *Faults:* excessively long hair (stand-off coat); dull hair (indicating malnutrition, worms and negligent care).

Substance
Substance is that sufficiency of bone and muscle which rounds out a balance with the frame. *Faults:* Lightweight whippety Danes; coarse, ungainly proportioned Danes—always there should be balance.

Gait
Long, easy, springy stride with no tossing or rolling of body. The back line should move smoothly, parallel to

the ground. The gait of the Great Dane should denote strength and power. The rear legs should have drive. The forelegs should track smoothly and straight. The Dane should track in two parallel straight lines. *Faults:* short steps. The rear quarters should not pitch. The forelegs should not have a hackney gait (forced or choppy stride). When moving rapidly the Great Dane should not pace for the reason that it causes excessive side-to-side rolling of the body and thus reduces endurance.

Rear end *(croup, legs, paws)*
The croup must be full, slightly drooping and must continue imperceptibly to the tail root. *Faults:* a croup which is too straight; a croup which slopes downward too steeply; and too narrow a croup.

Hind legs, the first thighs (from hip joint to knee) are broad and muscular. The second thighs (from knee to hock joint) are strong and long. Seen from the side, the angulation of the first thigh with the body, of the second thigh with the first thigh, and the pastern root with the second thigh should be very moderate, neither too straight nor too exaggerated. Seen from the rear, the hock joints appear to be perfectly straight, turned neither towards the inside nor towards the outside. *Faults:* hind legs: soft flabby, poorly muscled thighs; cowhocks which are the result of the hock joint turning inward and the hock and rear paws turning outward; barrel legs, the result of the hock joints being too far apart; steep rear. As seen from the side, a steep rear is the result of the angles of the rear legs forming almost a straight line; overangulation is the result of exaggerated angles between the first and second thighs and the hocks and is very conducive to weakness. The rear legs should never be too long in proportion to the front legs.

Paws
Round and turned neither toward the inside nor toward the outside. Toes short, highly arched and well closed. Nails short, strong and as dark as possible. *Faults:* spreading toes (splay foot); bent, long toes (rabbit paws); toes turned toward the outside or toward the inside. Furthermore, the fifth toes on the hind legs appearing at a higher position and with wolf's claw or spur; excessively long nails; light-colored nails.

Front end *(shoulders, legs, paws)*
Shoulders: the shoulder blades must be strong and sloping and seen from the side, must form as nearly as possible a right angle in its articulation with the humerus (upper arm) to give a long stride. A line from the upper tip of the shoulder to the back of the elbow joint should be as nearly perpendicular as possible. Since all dogs lack a clavicle (collar bone) the ligaments and muscles holding the shoulder blade to the rib cage must be well developed, firm and secure to prevent loose shoulders. *Faults:* steep shoulders, which occur if the shoulder blade does not slope sufficiently; overangulation; loose shoulders which occur if the Dane is flabby muscled, or if the elbow is turned toward the outside; loaded shoulders.

Forelegs: the upper arm should be strong and muscular. Seen from the side or front, the strong lower arms run absolutely straight to the pastern joints. Seen from the

front, the forelegs and the pastern roots should form perpendicular lines to the ground. Seen from the side, the pastern root should slope only very slightly forward. *Faults:* elbows turned toward the inside or toward the outside, the former position caused mostly by too narrow or too shallow a chest, bringing the front legs too closely together and at the same time turning the entire lower part of the leg outward; the latter position causes the front legs to spread too far apart, with the pastern roots and paws usually turned inwards. Seen from the side, a considerable bend in the pastern toward the front indicates weakness and is in most cases connected with stretched and spread toes (splay foot); seen from the side, a forward bow in the forearm (chair leg); an excessively knotty bulge in the front of the pastern joint. *Paws:* round and turned neither toward the inside nor toward the outside. Toes short, highly arched and well closed. Nails short, strong and as dark as possible. *Faults:* spreading toes (splay foot), bent, long toes (rabbit paws); toes turned toward the outside or toward the inside; light-colored nails.

Head conformation
Long, narrow, distinguished, expressive, finely chiseled, especially the part below the eyes (which means that the skull plane under and to the inner point of the eye must slope without any bony protuberance in a pleasing line to the full square jaw), with strongly pronounced stop. The masculinity of the dog is very pronounced in the expression and structure of head (this subtle difference should be evident in the dog's head through massive skull and depth of muzzle); the bitch's head may be more delicately formed. Seen from the side, the forehead must be sharply set off from the bridge of the nose. The fore-

Eyes

Medium size, as dark as possible, with lively intelligent expression; almond-shaped eyelids, well-developed eyebrows. *Faults:* light-colored, piercing, amber-colored, light blue to a watery blue, red or bleary eyes; eyes of different colors; eyes too far apart; Mongolian eyes; eyes with pronounced haws; eyes with excessively drooping lower eyelids. In blue and black Danes, lighter eyes are permitted but are not desirable. In harlequins, the eyes should be dark. Light-colored eyes, two eyes of different color and walleyes are permitted but not desirable.

Nose

The nose must be large and in the case of brindled and 'single-colored' Danes, it must always be black. In harlequins, the nose should be black; a black spotted nose is permitted; a pink-colored nose is not desirable.

Ears

Ears should be high, set not too far apart, medium in size, of moderate thickness, drooping forward close to the cheek. Top line of folded ear should be about level with the skull. *Faults:* hanging on the side, as on a Foxhound.

Cropped ears

High set, not set too far apart, well pointed but always in proportion to the shape of the head and carried uniformly erect.

Neck

The neck should be firm and clean, high-set, well arched, long, muscular and sinewy. From the chest to the head, it should be slightly tapering, beautifully formed, with well-developed nape. *Faults:* short, heavy neck, pendulous throat folds (dewlaps).

Loin and back

The withers forms the highest part of the back which slopes downward slightly toward the loins which are imperceptibly arched and strong. The back should be short and tensely set. The belly should be well shaped and tightly muscled, and, with the rear part of the thorax, should swing in a pleasing curve (tuck-up). *Faults:* receding back; sway back; camel or roach back; a back line which is too high at the rear; an excessively long back; poor tuck-up.

Chest

Chest deals with that part of the thorax (rib cage) in front of the shoulders and front legs. The chest should be quite broad, deep and well muscled. *Faults:* a narrow and poorly muscled chest; strong protruding sternum (pigeon breast).

Tail

Should start high and fairly broad, terminating slender and thin at the hock joint. At rest, the tail should fall straight. When excited or running, slightly curved (saberlike). *Faults:* a too high, or too low set tail (the tail set is governed by the slope of the croup); too long or too short a tail; tail bent too far over the back (ring tail); a tail which is curled; a twisted tail (sideways); a tail

head and the bridge of the nose must be straight and parallel to one another. Seen from the front, the head should appear narrow, the bridge of the nose should be as broad as possible. The cheek muscles must show slightly, but under no circumstances should they be too pronounced (cheeky). The muzzle part must have full flews and must be as blunt vertically as possible in front; the angles of the lips must be quite pronounced. The front part of the head, from the tip of the nose up to the center of the stop should be as long as the rear part of the head from the center of the stop to the only slightly developed occiput. The head should be angular from all sides and should have definite flat planes and its dimensions should be absolutely in proportion to the general appearance of the Dane. *Faults:* any deviation from the parallel planes of skull and foreface; too small a stop; a poorly defined stop or none at all; too narrow a nose bridge; the rear of the head spreading laterally in a wedgelike manner (wedge head); an excessively round upper head (apple head); excessively pronounced cheek musculature; pointed muzzle; loose lips hanging over the lower jaw (fluttering lips) which create an illusion of a full deep muzzle. The head should be rather shorter and distinguished than long and expressionless.

Teeth

Strong, well developed and clean. The incisors of the lower jaw must touch very lightly the bottoms of the inner surface of the upper incisors (scissors bite). If the front teeth of both jaws bite on top of each other, they wear down too rapidly. *Faults:* even bite; undershot and overshot; incisors out of line; black or brown teeth; missing teeth.

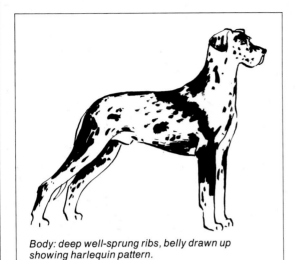

Body: deep well-sprung ribs, belly drawn up showing harlequin pattern.

carried too high over the back (gay tail); a brush tail (hair too long on lower side). Cropping tails to desired length is forbidden.

Ribs and brisket

Deals with that part of the thorax back of the shoulders and front legs. Should be broad, with the ribs sprung well out from the spine and flattened at the side to allow proper movement of the shoulders extending down to the elbow joint. *Faults:* narrow (slab-sided) rib cage; round (barrel) rib cage; shallow rib cage not reaching the elbow joint.

FAULTS

Disqualification faults

Danes under minimum height. White Danes without any black marks (albinos). Merles, a solid mouse-gray color or a mouse-gray base with black or white or both color spots or white base with mouse-gray spots. Harlequins and solid-colored Danes in which a large spot extends coatlike over the entire body so that only the legs, neck and point of the tail are white. Brindle, fawn, blue and black Danes with white forehead line, white collars, high white stockings and white bellies. Danes with predominantly blue, gray, yellow or also brindled spots. Docked tails. Split noses.

The faults below are important according to their groupings (very serious, serious, minor) and not according to their sequence as placed in each grouping:

Very serious: lack of unity. Poor bone development. Poor musculature. Lightweight whippety Danes. Rickets. Timidity. Bitchy dog. Swayback. Roach back. Cowhocks. Pitching gait. Short steps. Undershot teeth.

Serious: out of condition. Coarseness. Any deviation from the standard on all coloration. Deviation from parallel planes of skull and foreface. Wedge head. Poorly defined stop. Narrow nose bridge. Snipy muzzle. Any color but dark eyes in fawns and brindles. Mongolian eyes. Missing teeth. Overshot teeth. Heavy neck. Short neck. Dewlaps. Narrow chest. Narrow rib cage. Round rib cage. Shallow rib cage. Loose shoulders. Steep shoulders. Elbows turned inward. Chair legs (front). Knotty bulge in pastern joint (adult dog). Weak pastern roots.

Receding back. Too long a back. Back high in rear. In harlequins, a pink nose. Poor tuck-up (except in bitches that have been bred). Too straight croup. Too sloping croup. Too narrow croup. Overangulation. Steep rear. Too long rear legs. Poorly muscled thighs. Barrel legs. Paws turned outward. Rabbit paws. Wolf's claw. Hackney gait.

Minor: doggy bitches. Small white marks on chest and toes—blues, blacks, brindles and fawns. Few gray spots and pointings on harlequins. In harlequins, black-spotted nose. White-tipped tail except on harlequins. Excessively long hair. Excessively dull hair. Apple head. Small stop. Fluttering lips. Eyes too far apart. Drooping lower eyelids. Any color but dark eyes in blacks, blues and harlequins. Discolored teeth. Even bite. Pigeon breast. Loaded shoulders. Elbows turned outward. Paws turned inward. Splay foot. Excessively long toenails. Light nails (except in harlequins). Low-set tail. Too long a tail. Too short a tail. Gay tail. Curled tail. Twisted tail. Brush tail.

DISQUALIFICATIONS

Danes under minimum height. White Danes without any black marks (albinos). Merles, a solid mouse-gray color or a mouse-gray base with black or white or both color spots or white base with mouse-gray spots. Harlequins and solid-colored Danes in which a large spot extends coatlike over the entire body so that only the legs, neck and the point of the tail are white. Brindle, fawn, blue and black Danes with white forehead line, white collars, high white stockings and white bellies. Danes with predominantly blue, gray, yellow or also brindled spots. Docked tails. Split noses.

Approved by the AKC 14 November 1944

STANDARD OF POINTS

1. General Conformation (30): general appearance (10), color and markings (8), size (5), condition of coat (4), substance (3). *2. Movement (28):* gait (10), rear end (croup, legs, paws) (10), front end (shoulders, legs, paws) (8). *3. Head (20):* head conformation (12), teeth (4), eyes (nose and ears) (4). *4. Torso (20):* neck (6), loin and back (6), chest (4), ribs and brisket (4). *5. Tail (2). Total (100).*

KC(GB) VARIATION TO STANDARD

Head: entire length of head varies with height of dog. 13 inches from tip of nose to back of occiput is a good measurement for a dog of 32 inches at shoulder. There should be a decided rise or brow over eyes but no abrupt stop between. *Nose:* bridge of nose should be very wide, with slight ridge where cartilage joins bone. A butterfly or flesh-coloured nose is not objected to in Harlequins. *Mouth:* teeth should be level and not project one way or other. *Ears:* should be small, set high on skull, carried slightly erect with tips falling forward. *Feet:* light nails permissible in Harlequins. *Hindquarters:* stifle and hocks well bent, hocks set low. *Colour: brindle:* eyes and nails preferred dark. *Blues:* colour varies from light grey to deepest slate. *Height and size:* (minimum) dogs 30 inches and 120 pounds, bitches 28 inches and 100 pounds.

GREAT PYRENEES

Many of the large breeds used in Asia and Europe as guards and sheepdogs descended from the original Mastiff, and the Great Pyrenees Mountain Dog or Pyrenean is no exception. As the need for dogs to herd sheep decreased in Europe so those dogs used for the purpose declined in numbers. At the turn of the century it was estimated that no more than a dozen really typical Pyrenean Mountain Dogs remained in Europe. There is no doubt that the breed is of very ancient origin, based as it was on the Tibetan Mastiff. Used with sheep, its work was that of guard rather than herder, and like the Anatolian Karabash, which does similar work today in Turkey, its main purpose was to protect the flocks against wolves. This resulted in a very large tremendously strong and fierce dog not at all suited to being a family pet. The decline of the breed was halted by the efforts of a small number

NATIONAL GROUPING		
	Name	Number
AKC	Working Dogs	III
KC(GB)	Working	5
FCI	Herding Dogs	I

of enthusiasts such as M. Dretzen, who scoured the Pyrenees at the beginning of the century and finally found half a dozen specimens which he considered typical of the breed at its best. At the same time the breed appeared in Britain, and one very good specimen was shown in 1900 which was said to be thirty inches high at the shoulder.

As with so many of the larger breeds, conditions during wartime prevented the development of these heavy feeders, and no progress was made until the 1920s. Even after that very few were kept and the breed was not officially recognised by the Kennel Club in Britain until 1944. Since that time, in spite of their enormous size and very large appetites, progress has been remarkable, and the numbers throughout the world have risen until he is now among the more popular dogs, something like a thousand a year being registered with the Kennel Club in Britain and the same sort of progress is being made in the United States.

He is among the biggest, and is probably one of the strongest dogs around today, though some of the sledge hauling dogs could match his pulling power. His limbs are huge, and he can be ridden by children who use him as a pony, though the practice is not advised. He is a tremendous guard, his sheer size and very loud voice causing anyone who wanted to enter where he was not supposed to, to change his mind. He shares with some of the other herding dogs the double dewclaws on his hind legs. This gives a slight appearance of clumsiness, and although various reasons have been put forward for the practice of leaving them on, few are very convincing. It is probably just a tradition.

He is a noble looking animal in the show ring. Prepared as he invariably is to a state of snowy whiteness, he creates an impression that few other breeds can match. He carries his tail low when standing and curls it like a plume over his back when he moves, and this with his high head carriage and free ambling gait make him look even bigger than he really is. At one time there were temperament problems, and some of these dogs were far from trustworthy. Realising, however, that in a dog of this size this was a very dangerous trait, the breed club wrote into the standard that bad temperament should be considered a fault, and proceeded to breed from dogs selected for their steadiness as well as appearance, with the result that today's dogs are much more trustworthy and easy going than those of previous years. The fact that he is now a popular house pet in spite of his great size, his enormous appetite and that he tends to shed white hairs over the furniture, proves that he is now very acceptable in that capacity as well as being a fine show dog.

OFFICIAL STANDARD

General appearance

A dog of immense size, great majesty, keen intelligence, and kindly expression of unsurpassed beauty and a certain elegance, all white or principally white with markings of badger, gray, or varying shades of tan. In the rolling, ambling gait it shows unmistakably the purpose for which it has been bred, the strenuous work of guarding the flocks in all kinds of weather on the steep mountain slopes of the Pyrenees. Hence soundness is of the greatest importance and absolutely necessary for the proper fulfillment of his centuries' old task.

Size

The average height at the shoulder is 27 to 32 inches for dogs, and 25 to 29 inches for bitches. The average length from shoulder blades to root of tail should be the same as the height in any given specimen. The average girth is 36 to 42 inches for dogs and 32 to 36 inches for bitches. The weight for dogs run 100 to 125 pounds and 90 to 115 pounds for bitches. A dog heavily boned; with close cupped feet; double dewclaws behind and single dewclaws in front.

Head

Large and wedge-shaped, measuring 10 to 11 inches from dome to point of nose, with rounding crown, furrow only slightly developed and with no apparent stop. *Cheeks:* flat, *Ears:* V-shaped, but rounded at the tips, of medium size, set parallel with the eyes, carried low and close to the head except when raised in attention. *Eyes:* of medium size, set slightly obliquely, dark rich brown in color with close eyelids, well pigmented. *Lips:* close-fitting, edged with black. *Dewlaps:* developed but little. The head is in brief that of a brown bear, but with the ears falling down. *Neck:* short, stout and strongly muscular.

Head and skull: strong but not coarse, skull curved.

Body

Well-placed shoulders set obliquely, close to the body. *Back and loin:* well coupled, straight and broad. *Haunches:* fairly prominent. *Rump:* sloping slightly. *Ribs:* flat-sided. *Chest:* deep. *Tail:* of sufficient length to hang below the hocks, well-plumed, carried low in repose, and curled high over the back, 'making the wheel' when alert.

Coat

Created to withstand severe weather, with heavy fine white undercoat and long flat thick outer coat of coarser hair, straight or slightly undulating.

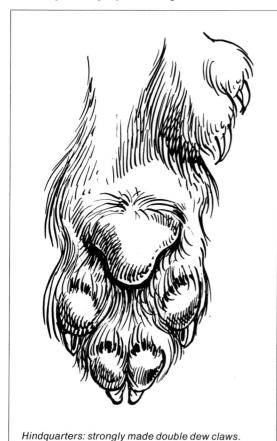

Hindquarters: strongly made double dew claws.

Qualities

In addition to his original age-old position in the scheme of pastoral life as protector of the shepherd and his flock, the Great Pyrenees has been used for centuries as a guard and watchdog on the large estates of his native France, and for this he has proven ideal. He is as serious in play as he is in work, adapting and molding himself to the moods, desires and even the very life of his human companions, through fair weather and foul, through leisure hours and hours fraught with danger, responsibility and extreme exertion; he is the exemplification of gentleness and docility with those he knows, of faithfulness and devotion for his master even to the point of self-sacrifice; and of courage in the protection of the flock placed in his care and of the ones he loves.

SCALE OF POINTS

Head (25): shape of skull (5), ears (5), eyes (5), muzzle (5), teeth (5). *General Conformation (25):* neck (5), chest (5), back (5), loins (5), feet (5). Coat (10). Size and Soundness (25). Expression and General Appearance (15). *Total (100).*

Approved by the AKC 13 February 1935

KC(GB) VARIATION TO STANDARD

Known as the Pyreneen Mountain Dog in GB. *Head:* well filled in below eyes. Nose black. *Mouth:* roof black. There should be a complete set of healthy strong even teeth. Meeting in either scissor or pincer bite. *Forequarters:* there should be medium angulation between shoulder-blade and upper arm. Forelegs should be straight, heavily boned and well muscled. Elbows should not be too close to chest nor should they stand off too far from it, so that a good width of stance and a free striding movement are obtained. Pasterns should show flexibility, but no weakness. *Body:* sides should be slightly rounded and rib-cage should extend well to rear. Back should be of good length, broad muscular, straight and level. *Hindquarters:* thighs should have great strength and be heavily muscled, tapering gradually down to strong hocks. Stifle and hock joints should both have medium angulation as seen from side. Hindlegs should each carry strongly-made double dewclaws and lack of this identifying characteristic is a very serious fault. Hind feet may turn out slightly, but legs themselves when viewed from behind should be straight. *Feet:* should be short and compact, toes being slightly arched and equipped with strong nails. *Coat:* should be longer around neck and shoulder, where it forms a mane, and towards tail. Forelegs should be fringed. Hair on rear of thighs should be long, very dense and more woolly in texture, giving a pantaloon effect. Bitches tend to be smoother-coated than dogs and usually have a less developed mane. *Weight and size:* minimum height at shoulder: dogs 28 inches; bitches 26 inches. Dogs 110 pounds; bitches 90 pounds.

KOMONDOR

NATIONAL GROUPING		
	Name	Number
AKC	Working Dogs	III
KC(GB)	Working	5
FCI	Herding Dogs	I

Three breeds of dog have traditionally had corded coats, that is, coats that have been encouraged to take on a natural twist and to mat in that position and continue to grow from the base until the whole dog is covered with a mass of long rope-like lengths of hair. The Komondor is one of these, and because of his size and colour, is quite the most spectacular. The earliest record of a dog known as a Komondor dates back to 1555, which leaves no doubt that it is an old established breed. It has been bred virtually without alteration from that time down as a herding and guard dog with the flocks of native sheep in Hungary. It is claimed that he wiped out the wolf in Hungary and that as a result he became a herding rather than a guarding dog, though he probably still fulfils both purposes.

During the 9th century the Magyar tribes entered Hungary bringing with them their dogs, and a breed of sheep known as Racka, which had a strange affinity of appearance with the dogs. They too had masses of curly rather than soft wool and they had the proud appearance of the dog rather than the 'sheepish' appearance normally associated with that animal. The Komondor was the perfect dog for the purpose of guarding these large and somewhat commanding animals, being a very positive dog with a strong personality. Later, in the 12th century smaller sheep were introduced, and the need for the particular qualities of the breed no longer existed. The Komondor stayed on as a guardian, and the smaller Puli served the purpose of herder to the more amenable smaller sheep.

The Komondor first reached the United States of America around 1933, and was recognised in that country in 1937, but it still remains a rare dog as it does in most countries outside Hungary. In recent years it has been introduced into Britain, where it still creates something of a sensation wherever it is shown. It is shown in Germany, Holland and Switzerland, and some fine examples have been seen in the Italian ring. Like many of the old working breeds, the Komondor is a very intelligent dog, readily trained and an obedient servant when kept under control. His coat is his most obvious point of identification, but that apart he is a big strong working dog with considerable powers of endurance under difficult conditions.

As a show dog he has certain problems, as it is not easy to keep the coat clean and yet at the same time maintain the much admired long cords. At about six months old the process of parting the cords commences, and if this were not continued, the animal would eventually be covered with one solid mat like a coat of armour. Each time that the Komondor is bathed, the coat has to be separated whilst drying, and the cords encouraged to remain as long narrow strips of hair rather than as bunches. The dog is never combed, even as a puppy, and needless to say, never brushed as this is impossible.

He is highly intelligent, and can be trained easily enough to obey simple commands. He needs firmness, and when correctly trained he makes an excellent guard and a pleasing companion. In the United States he is still used for his original purpose, to herd and guard flocks.

OFFICIAL STANDARD

General appearance

The Komondor is characterized by imposing strength, courageous demeanor and pleasing conformation. In general, it is a big muscular dog with plenty of bone and substance, covered with an unusual, heavy, white coat.

Nature and characteristics

An excellent houseguard. It is wary of strangers. As a guardian of herds, it is, when grown, an earnest, courageous, and very faithful dog. The young dog, however, is as playful as any other puppy. It is devoted to its master and will defend him against attack by any stranger. Because of this trait, it is not used for driving the herds, but only for guarding them. The Komondor's special task is to protect the animals. It lives during the greater part of the year in the open, without protection against strange dogs and beasts of prey.

Head

The head looks somewhat short in comparison to the seemingly wide forehead. The skull is somewhat arched when viewed from the side. Stop is moderate. The muzzle somewhat shorter than the length of the skull. The top of the muzzle is straight and about parallel with the line of the top of the skull. The muzzle is powerful, bite is scissors; level bite is acceptable. Any missing teeth is a serious fault. Distinctly undershot or overshot bite is a serious fault.

Ears

Medium set, hanging and V-shaped. Erect ears or ears that move toward an erect position are faults.

Eyes

Medium-sized and almond-shaped, not too deeply set. The edges of the eyelids are gray. The iris of the eyes is dark brown, light color is not desirable. Blue-white eyes are disqualifying.

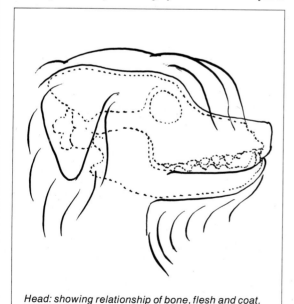

Head: showing relationship of bone, flesh and coat.

Muzzle

In comparison to the length given in the head description, the muzzle is wide, coarse and not pointed. Nostrils are wide. Color of the nose is black. A dark gray or dark brown nose is not desirable but is acceptable. Flesh-colored noses are disqualifying.

Neck

Muscular, of medium length, moderately arched. The head erect. Any dewlap is a fault.

Body

Characterized chiefly by the powerful, deep chest which is muscular and proportionately wide. Shoulders are moderately sloping. The back is level. Rump is wide, muscular, slightly sloping towards the root of the tail. The body is rectangular, only slightly longer than the height at the withers. The belly is somewhat drawn up at the rear.

Tail

A straight continuation of the rumpline, and reaches down to the hocks. Slightly curved upwards at its end. When the dog is excited, the tail is raised up to the level of the back. The tail is not to be docked. A short or curly tail is a fault. Bobtails are disqualifying.

Forelegs

Straight, well boned and muscular. Viewed from any side, the legs are like vertical columns. The upper arms join the body closely, without loose elbows.

Hindquarters and legs

The steely, strong bone structure is covered with highly developed muscles. The legs are straight as viewed from the rear. Stifles well bent. Dewclaws must be removed.

Feet

Strong, rather large and with close, well-arched toes. Nails are black or gray. Pads are hard, elastic and dark.

Movement

Light, leisurely and balanced. Takes long strides.

Coat

Characteristic of the breed is the dense, weather-resisting double coat. The puppy coat is relatively soft, but it shows a tendency to fall into cords. In the mature dog the coat consists of a dense, soft, woolly undercoat, much like the puppy coat, and a coarser outer coat that is wavy or curly. The coarser hairs of the outer coat trap the softer undercoat forming permanent strong cords that are felty to the touch. A grown dog is covered with a heavy coat of these tassel-like cords, which form themselves naturally, and once formed, require no care other than washing. Too curly a coat is not desired. Straight or silky coat is a serious fault. Short, smooth hair on the head and legs is a disqualification. Failure of the coat to cord by two years of age is a disqualification.

Coat: longest at rump and tail, medium length on back.

The coat is longest at the rump, loins and tail. It is of medium length on the back, shoulders and chest. Shorter on the cheeks, around the eyes, ears, neck, and on the extremities. It is shortest around the mouth and lower part of the legs up to the hocks.

Color

Color of the coat is white. Any color other than white is disqualifying.

In the ideal specimen the skin is gray. Pink skin is less desirable but is acceptable if no evidence of albinism. The nose, lips, outlines of eyelids and pads are dark or gray. It is good if the gums and palate are also dark.

Size

Dogs, $25\frac{1}{2}$ inches and upward at the withers; bitches, $23\frac{1}{2}$ inches and upward at withers. While size is important, type, character, symmetry, movement and ruggedness are of the greatest importance, and are on no account to be sacrificed for size alone.

Faults

Size below limit. Short or too curly coat. Straight or silky coat. Any missing teeth. Distinctly undershot or overshot bite. Looseness or slackness. Short or curly tail. Light-colored eyes. Erect ears or ears that move toward an erect position. Dewlaps on the neck.

DISQUALIFICATIONS
Blue-white eyes. Color other than white. Bobtails. Flesh-colored nose. Short, smooth hair on head and legs. Failure of the coat to cord by two years of age.

Approved by the AKC 13 February 1973

KC(GB) VARIATION TO STANDARD

Although this dog has been given an interim standard it has not yet been granted championship status by the KC(GB). *Feet:* toes slightly longer on hindfeet.

KUVASZ

NATIONAL GROUPING		
	Name	Number
AKC	Working Dogs	III
KC(GB)	—	—
FCI	Herding Dogs	I

When several breeds of dog are developed for roughly the same purpose, so that eventually they look very much alike, one might assume that they share a common ancestry. The Maremma Sheepdog, the Great Pyrenees and the Kuvasz are so generally similar in appearance, that if specimens of all three appear in the ring at the same time, and if the Pyrenean happens to be a reasonably small one, the average spectator will see them all as belonging to the same breed. They are all white, all have the same sort of gait, and all roughly the same sort of coat. Whilst the other two were both herding and guard dogs, the Kuvasz was evolved primarily for the latter duty. His ancestors came from Tibet, via Turkey, to Hungary, and as the court favourite only those who were in favour with the royal family were allowed to own one.

During the late 15th century he was kept by the big estates and had the treatment usually meted out to favourite animals, having a stud book, being carefully guarded and bred, and in turn guarding the person of the King and his family. He was trained for the chase and was capable of handling the large game which was plentiful in his country such as bear and wolf. King Matthias who reigned during the 15th century always had a Kuvasz with him wherever he went. He kept a large kennel at his palace, and with intrigue being a fashionable pursuit, placed more trust in his dogs than in his personal guards. The King developed a large pack for hunting, and it was mainly due to his efforts that the breed not only survived in those early years, but improved, becoming a bigger and stronger dog than he was originally.

In later centuries specimens of the breed came into the hands of commoners, and his value as a herding dog began to be appreciated. It was in the dual role of guard and herder that he made his reputation during the 19th century. Two World Wars, and the subsequent disturbances in Hungary brought about a serious decline in the breed, but fortunately by the 1930s, some had been imported into the United States of America and the future of the breed became assured. The American Kennel Club recognised the breed in 1935, and though the war years halted its progress in its own country, it has steadily gained ground elsewhere. It is seen regularly in most European countries, but not in Britain, where it has as yet failed to capture the public fancy.

He makes a really striking show dog, being large, stately and brilliant white in colour. He is a spirited dog, but very steady in the ring, where his strongly developed sense of curiosity gives him a great deal of interest in what is going on around him, and diverts his attention from possible high-spirited behaviour. Grooming is trouble-free as all that is needed is a constant brushing to remove dead hairs, the coat having a natural luxuriant sheen. His only problems are those that are shared by all large dogs, that he takes up a considerable amount of space and does not lend himself easily to travelling in a box in the back of the car. He is a very intelligent dog, sensitive and not to be dealt with harshly. He is devoted, gentle and patient without being too effusive, has a strongly developed inclination to guard children, and whilst friendly enough, has a natural aversion to making friends quickly with strangers.

OFFICIAL STANDARD

General characteristics
A spirited dog of keen intelligence, determination, courage and curiosity. Very sensitive to praise and blame. Primarily a one-family dog. Devoted, gentle and patient without being overly demonstrative. Always ready to protect loved ones even to the point of self-sacrifice. Extremely strong instinct to protect children. Polite to accepted strangers, but rather suspicious and very discriminating in making new friends. Unexcelled guard, possessing ability to act on his own initiative at just the right moment without instruction. Bold, courageous and fearless. Untiring ability to work and cover rough terrain for long periods of time. Has good scent and has been used to hunt game.

General appearance
A working dog of larger size, sturdily built, well balanced, neither lanky nor cobby. White in color with *no markings.* Medium boned, well muscled, without the slightest hint of bulkiness or lethargy. Impresses the eye with strength and activity combined with light-footedness, moves freely on strong legs. Trunk and limbs form a horizontal rectangle slightly deviated from the square. Slightly inclined croup. Hindquarters are particularly well developed. Any tendency to weakness or lack of substance is a decided fault.

Movement
Easy, free and elastic. Feet travel close to the ground. Hind legs reach far under, meeting or even passing the imprints of the front legs. Moving toward an observer, the front legs do not travel parallel to each other but rather close together at the ground. When viewed from the rear, the hind legs (from the hip joint down) also move close at the ground. As speed increases, the legs gradually angle more inward until the pads are almost single-tracking. Unless excited, the head is carried rather

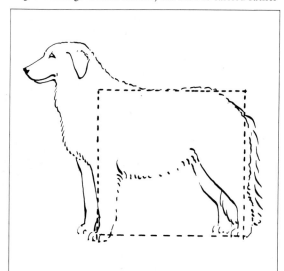

General: slightly longer proportions than high.

low at the level of the shoulders. Desired movement cannot be maintained without sufficient angulation and firm slimness of body.

Height
Measured at the withers: dogs, 28 to 30 inches; bitches, 26 to 28 inches.

Weight
Dogs, approximately 100 to 115 pounds; bitches, approximately 70 to 90 pounds.

Color
White.

Head
Proportions are of great importance as the head is considered to be the most beautiful part of the Kuvasz. Length of head measured from tip of nose to occiput is slightly less than half the height of the dog at the withers. Width is half the length of the head. The skull is elongated but not pointed. The stop is defined, never abrupt, raising the forehead gently above the plane of the muzzle. The longitudinal midline of the forehead is pronounced, widening as it slopes to the muzzle. Cheeks flat, bony arches above the eyes. The skin dry, no excess flews.

Muzzle
Length in proportion to the length of the head, top straight, not pointed, underjaw well developed. Inside of the mouth preferably black.

Nose
Large, black, nostrils well opened.

Lips
Black, closely covering the teeth. The upper lip covers tightly the upper jaw only. Lower lip tight and not pendulous.

Bite
Dentition full, scissors bite preferred. Level bite acceptable.

Eyes
Almond-shaped, set well apart, somewhat slanted. In profile, the eyes are set slightly below the plane of the muzzle. Lids tight, haws should not show. Dark brown, the darker the better.

Ears
V-shaped, tip is slightly rounded. Rather thick, they are well set back between the level of the eye and the top of the head. When pulled forward the tip of the ear should cover the eye. Looking at the dog face to face, the widest part of the ear is about level to the eye. The inner edge of the ear lies close to the cheek, the outer edge slightly away from the head forming a V. In the relaxed position, the ears should hold their set and are not cast backward. The ears should not protrude above the head.

Neck
Muscular, without dewlap, medium length, arched at the crest.

Forequarters
Shoulders muscular. The scapula and humerus form a right angle, are long and of equal length. Legs are medium boned, straight and well muscled. Elbows neither in nor out. When viewed from the side, the forechest protrudes slightly in front of the shoulders. The joints are dry, hard. Dewclaws on the forelegs should not be removed.

Body
Forechest is well developed, chest deep with long well-sprung ribs reaching almost to the elbows. Shoulders long with withers higher than back. Back is of medium length, straight, firm and quite broad. The loin is short, muscular and tight. The croup well muscled, slightly sloping. The brisket is deep, well developed and runs parallel to the ground. The stomach is well tucked up.

Bone
In proportion to size of body. Medium, hard. Never heavy or coarse.

Hindquarters
The portion behind the hip joint is moderately long producing wide, long and strong muscles of the upper thigh. The femur is long, creating well-bent stifles. Lower thigh is long, dry, well muscled. Metatarsus is short, broad and of great strength. Dewclaws, if any, are removed.

Tail
Carried low, natural length reaching at least to the hocks. In repose it hangs down resting on the body, the end but slightly lifted. In state of excitement, the tail may be elevated to the level of the loin, the tip slightly curved up. Ideally there should not be much difference in the carriage of the tail in state of excitement or in respose.

Feet
Well padded. Pads resilient, black. Feet are closed tight forming round 'cat feet'. The rear paws somewhat longer, some hair between the toes, the less the better. Dark nails are preferred.

Skin
The skin is heavily pigmented. The more slate gray or black pigmentation the better.

Coat
The Kuvasz has a double coat formed by a guard hair and fine undercoat. The texture of the coat is medium coarse. The coat ranges from quite wavy to straight. Distribution follows a definite pattern over the body regardless of coat type. The head, muzzle, ears and paws are covered with short, smooth hair. The neck has a mane that extends to and covers the chest. Coat on the front of the forelegs up to the elbows and the hind legs below the thighs is short and smooth. The backs of the forelegs are feathered to the pastern with hair 2 to 3 inches long. The body and sides of the thighs are covered with a medium length coat. The back of the thighs and the entire tail is covered with hair 4 to 6 inches long. It is natural for the Kuvasz to lose most of the long coat during hot weather. Full luxuriant coat comes in seasonably, depending on climate. Summer coat should not be penalized.

FAULTS
The foregoing description is that of the ideal Kuvasz. Any deviation from the above-described dog must be penalized to the extent of the deviation.

DISQUALIFICATIONS
Overshot bite. Undershot bite. Dogs smaller than 26 inches. Bitches smaller than 24 inches. Any color other than white.

Approved by the AKC 9 July 1974

KC(GB) VARIATION TO STANDARD
This dog is not granted championship status by the KC(GB).

MASTIFF

NATIONAL GROUPING		
	Name	Number
AKC	Working Dogs	III
KC(GB)	Working	5
FCI	Guard Dogs	2

Some breeds have emerged so recently from their countries of origin that information on them is hard to come by, others have been with us so long that books have been written about them as individual breeds. The Mastiff is one of these, the name not only indicating a specific breed of dog, but also a whole Group. Where the dog originated is obscure, but certainly the Mastiff that is now known by that name everywhere in the world was well known in England in Roman times. Records show that an officer was stationed at Winchester for the purpose of collecting and exporting these great dogs to Rome where they probably took part in battles in the Colosseum. Later Dame Juliana Berners, Prioress of Sopwell Nunnery in Hertfordshire wrote of them in the 15th century, and Doctor John Caius mentioned them in his book written in 1576.

In medieval times the Mastiff was a guard dog but was also used for hunting, and farmers living on the outskirts of forests were allowed to keep them only if they had been handicapped by the removal of toes to prevent them from chasing deer. During the Hundred Years War many were taken to France, and the devotion of one to Sir Piers Legh when he was wounded at Agincourt is a familiar story. She watched over him throughout the battle and guarded him against plunderers afterwards, but unfortunately her efforts were in vain as he died on the homeward journey.

In more recent times the story of the breed is equally romantic. During the Second World War owing to the difficulty of keeping dogs of any kind and large dogs as food was so scarce, the breed virtually disappeared from Britain. Fortunately a good many had been exported to the United States of America where the breed remained very much alive, and some were later reimported back into Britain to start up the breed again. Since that time the Mastiff has attained a degree of popularity and is now seen regularly at shows. He is still very much a dog with special rather than general appeal, and fortunately those who own the breed are interested in the preservation of a dog with a long history, so that it is in good hands.

It would be foolish to pretend that the Mastiff is the ideal show dog. He is very large to start with and does not fit easily into today's small cars. Few of them really enjoy showing, and would obviously be happier roaming round some large estate doing a little casual hunting and keeping a careful watch on the gates and fences. Being a fairly rare dog he is not appreciated by all judges and although he is admired for his sheer size by the general public, few of them would want to take him home to replace their own favourite cuddly pet. Even so he is a magnificent animal when he is standing in the ring, as he has great nobility and the slightly mournful expression of one who regrets past events.

His temperament, as with most of the large dogs, is that of the gentle giant. He has no vice, is absolutely friendly, even embarrassingly so to those to whom he becomes attached, and is one of the most faithful of all dogs. He is quiet and intelligent and rarely uses his immense power in an unfriendly act. As a guard he is supreme, as the instinct to look after his own territory and that of his owner is deeply imbedded in him, and his size and apparent ferocity when aroused are sufficient to deter the boldest of intruders.

OFFICIAL STANDARD

General character and symmetry
Large, massive, symmetrical and well-knit frame. A combination of grandeur and good nature, courage and docility.

Head and skull: nose broad, muzzle short broad under eyes, great depth.

General description of head
In general outline giving a massive appearance when viewed from any angle. Breadth greatly to be desired. *Skull:* broad and somewhat rounded between the ears, forehead slightly curved, showing marked wrinkles which are particularly distinctive when at attention. Brows (superciliary ridges) moderately raised. Muscles of the temples well developed, those of the cheeks extremely powerful. Arch across the skull a flattened curve with a furrow up the center of the forehead. This extends from between the eyes to halfway up the skull. *Ears:* small, V-shaped, rounded at the tips. Leather moderately thin, set widely apart at the highest points on the sides of the skull continuing the outline across the summit. They should lie close to the cheeks when in repose. Ears dark in color, the blacker the better, conforming to the color of the muzzle. *Eyes:* set wide apart, medium in size, never too prominent. Expression alert but kindly. The stop between the eyes well marked but not too abrupt. Color of eyes brown, the darker the better and showing no haw. *Face and muzzle:* short, broad under the eyes and running nearly equal in width to the end of the nose. Truncated, i.e. blunt and cut off square, thus forming a right angle with the upper line of the face. Of great depth from the point of the nose to underjaw. Underjaw broad to the end and slightly rounded. Canine teeth healthy, powerful and wide apart. Scissors bite preferred but a moderately undershot jaw permissible providing the teeth are not visible when the mouth is closed. Lips diverging at obtuse angles with the septum and sufficiently pendulous so as to show a modified square profile. Nose broad and always dark in color, the blacker the better, with spread flat nostrils (not pointed or turned up) in profile. Muzzle dark in color, the blacker the better. Muzzle should be half the length of the skull, thus dividing the head into three parts—one for the foreface and two for the skull. In other words, the distance from tip of nose to stop is equal to one-half the distance between the stop and the occiput. Circumference of muzzle (measured midway between the eyes and nose) to that of the head (measured before the ears) as 3 is to 5.

Neck
Powerful and very muscular, slightly arched, and of medium length. The neck gradually increases in circumference as it approaches the shoulder. Neck moderately 'dry' (not showing an excess of loose skin).

Chest and flanks
Wide, deep, rounded and well let down between the forelegs, extending at least to the elbow. Forechest should be deep and well defined. Ribs extremely well rounded. False ribs deep and well set back. There should be a reasonable, but not exaggerated, cut-up.

Shoulder and arm
Slightly sloping, heavy and muscular. No tendency to looseness of shoulders.

Forelegs and feet
Legs straight, strong and set wide apart, heavy-boned. Elbows parallel to body. Feet heavy, round and compact with well-arched toes. Pasterns strong and bent only slightly. Black nails preferred.

Hind legs
Hindquarters broad, wide and muscular. Second thighs

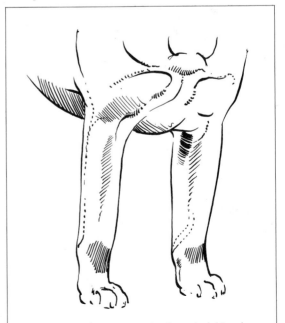

Forequarters: heavy muscular, legs straight and strong.

well developed, hocks set back, wide apart and parallel when viewed from the rear.

Back and loins

Back muscular, powerful and straight. Loins wide and muscular, slightly rounded over the rump.

Tail

Set on moderately high and reaching to the hocks or a little below. Wide at the root, tapering to the end, hanging straight in repose, forming a slight curve but never over the back when dog is in action.

Coat

Outer coat moderately coarse. Undercoat, dense, short and close lying.

Color

Apricot, silver fawn or dark fawn-brindle. Fawn-brindle should have fawn as a background color which should be completely covered with very dark stripes. In any case muzzle, ears and nose must be dark in color, the blacker the better, with similar color tone around the orbits, extending upwards between them.

Size

Dogs, minimum, 30 inches at the shoulder; bitches, minimum, $27\frac{1}{2}$ inches at the shoulder.

SCALE OF POINTS

General character and symmetry (10). Height and substance (10). Skull (10). Face and muzzle (12). Ears (5). Eyes (5). Chest and ribs (10). Forelegs and feet (10). Back, loins and flanks (10). Hind legs and feet (10). Tail (3). Coat and color (5). *Total (100)*.

Approved by the AKC 8 July 1941

KC(GB) VARIATION TO STANDARD

Head: forehead flat. *Eyes:* small. *Body:* girth should be one-third more than height at shoulder. Back and loins very wide in bitch, slightly arched in dog. Shoulder and arm slightly sloping, heavy and muscular. *Forelegs:* pasterns upright. *Coat:* short and close-lying, but not too fine over shoulders, neck and back.

NEWFOUNDLAND

NATIONAL GROUPING		
	Name	Number
AKC	Working Dogs	III
KC(GB)	Working	5
FCI	Guard Dogs	2

Some breeds of dogs attract attention by virtue of the romantic stories that have been woven about them (the Saint Bernard is a typical example), others because of particular abilities that they possess, such as the Bloodhound, and yet others because they have been portrayed by famous painters, but the Newfoundland has had attention for each of these reasons. Romantic rescue stories have been written about him, most of them true, his ability in water is legendary and the most famous of all animal painters, Sir Edwin Landseer painted him. Yet his origin is far from clear. One authority claims that the Beothuk Indians of Newfoundland had big black water-loving dogs as companions before the advent of the white man. Another reports that Lieut. John Cartwright in his exploration of the island in 1768 remarked that the native Indians did not even have the companionship of dogs to relieve their wretchedness.

There is, however, no doubt that a big black water-loving dog was evolved on the island, and that they were imported into Britain in numbers. There is no doubt too that he was of the Mastiff type, though whether he had evolved independently as such a type in Newfoundland or was originally taken over by early explorers and was a descendant of the Tibetan Mastiff is a moot point. By the 17th century a black and white version had evolved, since named the Landseer after the famous painting 'A distinguished Member of the Humane Society', giving some credence to the idea that the breed was a mixture of imported Mastiff type dogs which could carry coloured bloodlines and a native dog which might have been black. In some countries these black and white dogs are treated as a distinct variety.

By 1860 the breed was being shown. Six appeared at the Birmingham Show of that year and the breed made steady progress, classes at shows filling well, and the character and temperament of the breed gaining it some popularity. Two World Wars, and the difficulty encountered in feeding such large dogs decimated the breed in Britain, but fortunately it remained strong in the United States and Holland, and after the Second World War, when only some ten dogs were left in Britain, reimportations enabled the breed to survive. This was in some measure due to the generosity of the Newfoundland Club of America who presented the secretary of the British Club with a bitch in whelp which produced five puppies. As well as in Britain and the United States the breed is now firmly established in many countries. Australia has quite a number and the Scandinavians have taken a great interest.

The Newfoundland is a big dog, and very much the heavyweight, appearing somewhat lumbering and clumsy in action. It is when he takes to the water, however, that he really comes into his own, swimming with great power and apparently tirelessly, and usually doing it for sheer pleasure. The stories of rescues that he has carried out are endless, and he was a regular member of the crew of fishing boats off the coast of Newfoundland, joining in the work by carrying warps and from time to time affecting a spectacular rescue. As a show dog he is very spectacular too, his sheer size and bulk making him popular with the casual spectator, who enjoys showing a rescue dog to the children.

His temperament is near perfect, as he is one of the most kindly of dogs, very affectionate and becomes deeply attached to the members of a family. He is particularly noted for his care of children, keeping careful watch and placing himself in a position of guard between them and an approaching stranger. His ability in the water and his natural delight in towing things back to land allow those who own one to depend on his watchfulness and capabilities to ensure that the children of the family run no risk of drowning.

OFFICIAL STANDARD

General appearance

The Newfoundland is large, strong, and active, at home in water and on land, and has natural life-saving instincts. He is a multipurpose dog capable of heavy work as well as of being a devoted companion for child and man. To fulfill its purposes the Newfoundland is deep bodied, well muscled, and well coordinated. A good specimen of the breed has dignity and proud head carriage. The length of the dog's body, from withers to base of tail, is approximately equal to the height of the dog at the withers. However, a bitch is not to be faulted if the length of her body is slightly greater than her height. The dog's appearance is more massive throughout than the bitch's, with larger frame and heavier bone. The Newfoundland is free moving with a loosely slung body. When he moves, a slight roll is perceptible. Complete webbing between the toes is always present. Large size is desirable but never at the expense of gait, symmetry, balance, or conformation to the Standard herein described.

Head

The head is massive with a broad skull, slightly arched crown, and strongly developed occipital bone. The slope from the top of the skull to the tip of the muzzle has a definite but not steep stop. The forehead and face is smooth and free of wrinkles; the muzzle is clean cut and covered with short, fine hair. The muzzle is square, deep, and fairly short; its length from stop to tip of nose is less than from stop to occiput. The nostrils are well developed. The bitch's head follows the same general conformation as the dog's but is feminine and less massive. A narrow head and a snipy or long muzzle are to be faulted. The *eyes* are dark brown, relatively small, and deep-set; they are spaced wide apart and have no haw showing. Round, protruding, or yellow eyes are objectionable. The *ears* are relatively small and triangular with rounded tips. They are set well back on the skull and lie close to the head. When the ear is brought forward it reaches to the inner corner of the eye on the same side. The *teeth* meet in a scissors or level bite. The Newfoundland's

Hindquarters: strong, tail hanging to below the hocks.

expression is soft and reflects the character of the breed; benevolent, intelligent, dignified, and of sweet disposition. The dog never looks or acts either dull or ill-tempered.

Neck

The neck is strong and well set on the shoulders. It is long enough for proud head carriage.

Body

The Newfoundland's chest is full and deep with the brisket reaching at least down to the elbows. The back is broad, and the topline is level from the withers to the croup, never roached, slack, or swayed. He is broad at the croup, is well muscled, and has very strong loins. The croup slopes at an angle of about 30 degrees. Bone structure is massive throughout but does not give a heavy, sluggish appearance.

Forequarters

When the dog is not in motion, the forelegs are perfectly straight and parallel with the elbows close to the chest. The layback of the shoulders is about 45 degrees, and the upper arm meets the shoulder blade at an angle of about 90 degrees. The shoulders were well muscled. The pasterns are slightly sloping.

Hindquarters

Because driving power for swimming, pulling loads, or covering ground efficiently is dependent on the hindquarters, the rear assembly of the Newfoundland is of prime importance. It is well muscled, the thighs are fairly long, the stifles well bent, and the hocks wide and straight. Cowhocks, barrel legs, or pigeon toes are to be seriously faulted.

Feet

The feet are proportionate to the body in size, cat-foot in type, well-rounded and tight with firm, arched toes, and with webbing present. Dewclaws on the rear legs are to be removed.

Tail

The tail of the Newfoundland acts as a rudder when he is swimming. Therefore, it is broad and strong at the base.

Head and skull: broad and massive, no decided stop. Muzzle: short, clean cut and square.

The tail reaches down a little below the hocks. When the dog is standing the tail hangs straight down, possibly a little bent at the tip; when the dog is in motion or excited, the tail is carried straight out or slightly curved, but it never curls over the back. A tail with a kink is a serious fault.

Gait

The Newfoundland in motion gives the impression of effortless power, has good reach, and strong drive. A dog may appear symmetrical and well balanced when standing, but, if he is not structurally sound, he will lose that symmetry and balance when he moves. In motion, the legs move straight forward; they do not swing in an arc nor do the hocks move in or out in relation to the line of travel. A slight roll is present. As the dog's speed increases from a walk to a trot, the feet move in under the center line of the body to maintain balance. Mincing, shuffling, crabbing, too close moving, weaving, hackney action, and pacing are all faults.

Size

The average height for dogs is 28 inches, for bitches 26 inches. The average weight for dogs is 150 pounds, for bitches 120 pounds. Large size is desirable but is not to be favored over correct gait, symmetry, and structure.

Coat

The Newfoundland has a water-resistant double coat. The outer coat is moderately long and full but not shaggy. It is straight and flat with no curl, although it may have a slight wave. The coat, when rubbed the wrong way, tends to fall back into place. The undercoat, which is soft and dense, is often less dense during summer months or in tropical climates but is always found to some extent on the rump and chest. An open coat is to be seriously faulted. The hair on the head, muzzle, and ears is short and fine, and the legs are feathered all the way down. The tail is covered with long dense hair, but it does not form a flag.

Color

Black: a slight tinge of bronze or a splash of white on chest and toes is not objectionable. Black dogs that have only white toes and white chest and white tip to tail should be exhibited in the classes provided for 'black.' *Other than black:* should in all respects follow the black except in color, which may be almost any, so long as it disqualifies for the black class, but the colors most to be encouraged are bronze or white and black (Landseer) with black head marked with narrow blaze, even marked saddle and black rump extending on to tail. Beauty in markings to be taken greatly into consideration.

DISQUALIFICATIONS
Markings other than white on a solid-colored dog.

Approved by the AKC 9 June 1970

KC(GB) VARIATION TO STANDARD

Mouth: should be soft and well covered by lips. *Body:* well ribbed up.

NORWEGIAN BUHUND

NATIONAL GROUPING		
	Name	Number
AKC	—	—
KC(GB)	Working	5
FCI	Herding Dogs	I

There is a large group of dogs originating in the northern part of the globe which are classified as Spitz breeds. They occur in several Groups in many countries, from the Pomeranian in the Toy Group in Britain to the Chow Chow in the Utility Group, and the sledge dogs in the Working Group, and the number of such breeds is large enough for them to form a separate Group in Scandinavia. The various members of the Group perform many functions, from towing sledges in the Arctic to keeping madam's feet warm in bed, and even it is said at one time, to serve as food. The Norwegian Buhund, which is included in the Working Group in most countries is one of the typical breeds of the Spitz type. It has the short body, erect ears, curled tail and stand-off coat, all of which are common to the breeds in the Spitz Group in Scandinavia.

The history of the Buhund is rather obscure, though it is certainly Scandinavian in origin, and the name indicates that it was intended as a house guard and possibly a general farm dog. Whilst the most popular colour range seen in the showrings of the world today is between wheaten and red, colour is not important. Black or sable, with or without markings is permissible, which leads to the suggestion that such breeds as the Elkhound or the Jämthund played some part in its ancestry. In recent years the Buhund has been used as a guard and a herding dog, and its alert temperament and ability to move very, very quickly over rough ground seem to suit it to both purposes.

He is a sharp yet friendly dog with great strength for so small an animal. He is intelligent, as all the working dogs are, and he is capable of considerable endurance. His strong coat, excellent conformation and good balance without exaggeration fit him for the arduous work that he is expected to undertake.

The Buhund has never become really popular as a showdog, registrations in Britain rarely exceeding a hundred, and even less at one time. He does, however, make an excellent dog for the show ring, his coat quality, smart expression and sharp ears making him very attractive in the ring. Temperamentally he is very pleasant, being friendly and becoming most attached to one family or one member of the family. His kindly disposition towards children endears him to those who own the breed.

OFFICIAL STANDARD

Characteristics
The Norwegian Buhund should be fearless and brave.

General appearance
The Norwegian Buhund is a typical Spitz dog of under middle size, lightly built, with a short compact body, fairly smooth-lying coat, erect pointed ears, tail carried curled over the back, and with an energetic character.
It is of prime importance that the Buhund should be a well balanced dog, free from all exaggeration and should be capable of the arduous work for which it is bred.

Head and skull
Head lean, light, rather broad between the ears, wedge shaped, narrowing towards the point of the nose. Skull and back of head almost flat; marked but not sharp stop; muzzle of medium length, tapering evenly from above and side, with straight bridge; lips tightly closed.

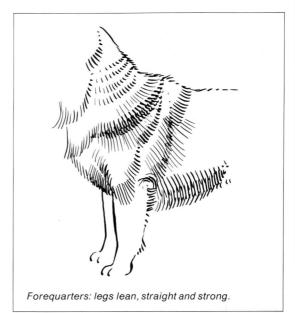

Forequarters: legs lean, straight and strong.

Head and skull: lean, light and wedge-shaped, ears erect.

Eyes
Not protruding, colour dark brown, lively with a fearless expression.

Ears
Placed high, erect, the height greater than the base; sharply pointed and very mobile.

Neck
Medium length, lean without loose skin, good carriage.

Forequarters
Legs lean, straight and strong, elbows tightly placed.

Body
Strong and short, but light; chest deep with good ribs; straight line of back, good loins, strong couplings, slightly drawn up.

Hindquarters
Only a little angulated, straight when seen from behind.

Feet
Rather small, oval in shape, with tightly closed toes.

Tail
Placed high on, short, thick and hairy, but without long hair tightly curled.

Coat
Close and harsh, but smooth; on head and front legs—short close and smooth; longer on chest, neck and shoulders and back of legs and inside of tail curl. The coat is made up of a harsh top hair, with soft wool undercoat.

Colour
Wheaten (biscuit), black, red (if the red is not too dark), wolf-sable. Preferably self-coloured but small symmetric markings such as white on chest and legs, blaize on head and narrow ring on neck, black masks and ears and black tips to the tail are permissible.

Size
Dogs not more than $17\frac{3}{4}$ inches (45 centimetres); bitches somewhat less.

Faults
White dogs. Light eyes. Light nose. Undershot or overshot mouth. Drop ear.

Note
Male animals should have two apparently normal testicles fully descended into the scrotum.

AKC VARIATION TO STANDARD
The dog is not granted championship status by the AKC. The above standards are those of the KC(GB).

OLD ENGLISH SHEEPDOG

NATIONAL GROUPING		
	Name	Number
AKC	Working Dogs	III
KC(GB)	Working	5
FCI	Herding Dogs	I

There are a number of different reasons why certain breeds of dog attain popularity. At its best this is because of the qualities of the animal itself, but there are other and less admirable reasons. Connections with courts and noble families, or more recently with the stars of stage and screen, their inclusion in literature as characters in a story, their stardom in films such as Lassie and Rin Tin Tin, all have helped to popularise different breeds. More recently it has been the media, and particularly the advertising media that has had its effect. Two breeds of dog owe their enormous rise in popularity to worldwide use in connection with advertising, and one of these is the Old English Sheepdog. Early records show that a dog very much like the present Old English Sheepdog existed in 1771 when Gainsborough painted a portrait of the Third Duke of Buccleuch with what is palpably a specimen of the breed, and the engraving of Reinagle's painting of a Shepherd Dog in the Sportsman's Cabinet of 1803 is certainly of an unbobbed bobtail.

It is suggested that the Bearded Collie and the Old English Sheepdog share a common ancestry, and this may well be true, as there are certainly points of similarity, though overall they now differ fairly widely. The Old English Sheepdog as we now know it was developed from the older herder's dog into its present form in England rather than in Scotland, and throughout the 19th century the breed was fairly well established in Suffolk, Hampshire and Dorset as well as in Wales. By the beginning of this century the numbers had grown until at the Clerkenwell Show of 1905 there were over a hundred on exhibition. Since then growth was fairly steady until the early 1970s, when the numbers suddenly quadrupled almost certainly because of the considerable exposure of the breed.

As a show dog the Old English Sheepdog has always had an enthusiastic following, and as long ago as the turn of the century ringside applause for the breed was recorded. Today, his appearance is so striking that his entrance into the big ring at many shows is again greeted with applause. His striking coat, which varies in colour from grey, through grizzle to blue, (with duck-egg blue being considered by many to be the most desirable), the volume of coat that modern breeders and exhibitors have managed to encourage on the dog, and his peculiar ambling gait which is so different from that of any other breed, make him a great favourite with spectators. Although his preparation and presentation present some problems, as the heavy coat needs constant and expert attention, he is still a grand dog to show, being big, friendly and very tractable. A ring full of these large beautifully groomed dogs is always guaranteed a large audience.

Temperamentally the Old English Sheepdog is a lovely animal. He is playful and somewhat boisterous when young (even sometimes when quite mature) and he is very intelligent and friendly. He is reputed to be extremely good with children, making a good guard as well as a decorative addition to any household.

OFFICIAL STANDARD

General appearance and characteristics

A strong, compact-looking dog of great symmetry, practically the same in measurement from shoulder to stern as in height, absolutely free from legginess or weaselness, very elastic in his gallop, but in walking or trotting he has a characteristic ambling or pacing movement, and his bark should be loud, with a peculiar 'pot-casse' ring in it. Taking him all round, he is a profusely, but not *excessively* coated, thick-set, muscular, able-bodied dog with a most intelligent expression, free from all Poodle or Deerhound character. *Soundness should be considered of greatest importance.*

Coat: profuse and hard, showing fashionable grooming pattern.

Head and skull: nose large, black and capacious, head covered with hair.

Skull

Capacious and rather squarely formed, giving plenty of room for brain power. The parts over the eyes should be well arched and the whole well covered with hair. *Jaw:* fairly long, strong, square and truncated. The stop should be well defined to avoid a Deerhound face. (The attention of judges is particularly called to the above properties, as a long, narrow head is a deformity.) *Eyes:* vary according to the color of the dog. Very dark preferred, but in the glaucous or blue dogs a pearl, walleye or china eye is considered typical. (A light eye is most objectionable.) *Nose:* always black, large and capacious. *Teeth:* strong and large, evenly placed and level in opposition. *Ears:* medium-sized, and carried flat to side of head, coated moderately.

Legs

The forelegs should be dead straight, with plenty of bone, removing the body a medium height from the ground, without approaching legginess, and well coated all around. *Feet:* small, round; toes well arched, and pads thick and hard.

Tail

It is preferable that there should be none. Should never, however, exceed 1½ to 2 inches in grown dogs. When not natural-born bobtails however, puppies should be docked at the first joint from the body and the operation performed when they are from three to four days old.

Neck and shoulders

The neck should be fairly long, arched gracefully and well coated with hair. The shoulders sloping and narrow at the points, the dog standing lower at the shoulder than at the loin.

Body

Rather short and very compact, ribs well sprung and brisket deep and capacious. *Slabsidedness highly undesirable.* The loins should be very stout and gently arched, while the hindquarters should be round and muscular and with well-let-down hocks, and the hams densely coated with a thick, long jacket in excess of any other part.

Coat

Profuse, but not so excessive as to give the impression of the dog being overfat, and of a good hard texture; not straight, but shaggy and free from curl. *Quality and texture of coat to be considered above mere profuseness.* Softness or flatness of coat to be considered a fault. The undercoat should be a waterproof pile, when not removed by grooming or season.

Color

Any shade of gray, grizzle, blue or blue-merled with or without white markings or in reverse. *Any shade of brown or fawn to be considered distinctly objectionable and not to be encouraged.*

Size

Twenty-two inches and upwards for dogs and slightly less for bitches. Type, character and symmetry are of the greatest importance and are on no account to be sacrificed to size alone.

SCALE OF POINTS

Skull (5). Eyes (5). Ears (5). Teeth (5). Nose (5). Jaw (5). Foreface (5). Neck and shoulders (5). Body and loins (10). Hindquarters (10). Legs (10). Coat, texture, quality and condition (15). General appearance and movement (15). *Total (100).*

Approved by the AKC 13 October 1953

PULI

NATIONAL GROUPING		
	Name	Number
AKC	Working Dogs	III
KC(GB)	—	—
FCI	Herding Dogs	I

Fairly wild claims are made for different breeds of dogs concerning their early history, and if all the breeds that laid claim to being depicted on ancient Egyptian carvings and paintings were gathered together, it would be possible to hold a very successful dog show. The Puli is a typical example, attempts having been made to trace him back eight thousand years, to a time when dogs were just dogs, and no particular breeds had established themselves. There is no denying that the Puli is an ancient breed, but it would probably be unwise to go back more than a thousand years to the time when the Magyars migrated into the area now known as Hungary. He was the sheepherding dog of the Magyars, and the smallest of the breeds that they used for this purpose. The others, the Komondor and the Kuvasz almost certainly also existed alongside the Puli, and whilst the larger dogs were used as guards as well as herders, the Puli was probably the daytime herding dog, his darker colour helping in the control of flocks as the sheep would see him more easily. He was probably connected ancestrally with the Tibetan Terrier, a somewhat similar type of dog used for the same purpose, and even today, though the Puli is a much more heavily built dog, there is a good deal of similarity.

The modern history of the Puli dates back to 1751 when Heppe wrote of 'The Hungarian Water Dog' which resembled the Puli. This raises an interesting point, as the Water Dog, described in the Sportsman's Repository of 1820 describes this dog in some detail, and though it speaks of it as a hunting dog, it was almost certainly the ancestor of the Poodle, and has the type of coat, which if allowed to grow would certainly cord as does that of the Puli, and as did that of the Poodle in the early days. Under the Austrian occupation of Hungary the habits of the country were forcibly changed including the breeds of cattle and sheep that were kept. However, the Hungarian shepherds did their best to preserve the Puli, and persisted with a breeding programme which ensured that the breed remained pure, selecting stock with great care and often travelling great distances to arrange matings.

During the first half of this century there has been considerable concentration on the show qualities of the Puli rather than upon his working ability, though even dogs bred from generations of show stock will work sheep naturally. From 1900 the breeding of the Puli was undertaken as a serious study, scientists and veterinarians joining in the efforts of breeders to retain the purity of the breed. The director of the Zoo in Budapest co-operated and arranged for a part of the Zoo to be devoted to a breeding programme, and the stock produced from this experiment formed the foundation of many of the modern kennels.

The Second World War reduced dog breeding to the minimum in Hungary and the Puli sadly declined, but by one of those odd quirks of fate, the fleeing of the people of Hungary to many other parts of Europe taking with them their dogs, did more to make the Puli generally known than anything else could have done. By the mid-fifties the breed was back to something like its pre-war strength and by the sixties was being regularly shown in its native country and was fairly well-known in other parts of the world. The first had arrived in The United States of America in the 1930s when they were imported primarily as herding dogs, and by 1936 he was recognised as one of the Working Group. He was much slower invading Britain, and has only just begun to gain a foothold. Now, however, he is seen regularly at shows in Britain and in most of the European countries.

He is a sound, solid dog that suffers from very little sickness, is virtually waterproof and very hardy. He is intelligent, alert and very active, takes to obedience work very easily, and makes an excellent property guard.

OFFICIAL STANDARD

General appearance

A dog of medium size, vigorous, alert, and extremely active. By nature affectionate, he is a devoted and home-loving companion, sensibly suspicious of strangers and therefore an excellent guard. Striking and highly characteristic is the shaggy coat which centuries ago fitted him for the strenuous work of herding the flocks on the plains of Hungary.

Head

Of medium size, in proportion to the body. The *skull* is slightly domed and not too broad. *Stop:* clearly defined but not abrupt, neither dished nor downfaced, with a strong muzzle of medium length ending in a nose of good size. *Teeth:* are strong and comparatively large, and the bite may be either level or scissors. Flews tight. *Ears:* hanging and set fairly high, medium size, and V-shaped. *Eyes:* Deep-set and rather large, should be dark brown, but lighter color is not a serious fault.

Neck and shoulders

Neck strong and muscular, of medium length, and free of throatiness. Shoulders clean-cut and sloping, with elbows close.

Body

The chest is deep and fairly broad with ribs well sprung. Back of medium length, straight and level, the rump sloping moderately. Fairly broad across the loins and well tucked up.

Tail

Occasionally born bobtail, which is acceptable, but never cut. The tail is carried curled over the back when alert, carried low with the end curled up when at rest.

Legs and feet

Forelegs straight, strong, and well-boned. Feet round and compact with thick-cushioned pads and strong nails. Hindquarters well developed, moderately broad through the stifle which is well bent and muscular. Dewclaws, if any, may be removed from both forelegs and hind legs.

Body: relationship of body and coat.

Coat

Characteristic of the breed is the dense, weather-resisting double coat. The outer coat, long and of medium texture, is never silky. It may be straight, wavy, or slightly curly, the more curly coat appearing to be somewhat shorter. The undercoat is soft, woolly, and dense. The coat mats easily, the hair tending to cling together in bunches, giving a somewhat corded appearance even when groomed. The hair is profuse on the head, ears, face, stifles and tail, and the feet are well haired between the toes. Usually shown combed, but may also be shown uncombed with the coat hanging in tight, even cords.

Color

Solid colors, black, rusty-black, various shades of gray, and white. The black usually appears weathered and rusty or slightly gray. The inter-mixture of hair of different colors is acceptable and is usually present in the grays, but must be uniform throughout the coat so that the over-all appearance of a solid color is maintained. Nose, flews, and eyelids are black.

Height

Dogs about 17 inches, and should not exceed 19 inches. Bitches about 16 inches, and should not exceed 18 inches.

Serious faults

Overshot or undershot. Lack of undercoat, short or sparse coat. White markings such as white paws or spot on chest. Flesh color on nose, flews, or eyelids. Coat with areas of two or more colors at the skin.

Approved by the AKC 12 April 1960

KC(GB) VARIATION TO STANDARD

Although this dog has been given an interim standard it has not yet been granted championship status by the KC(GB). *Head:* muzzle is one-third length of head. *Eyes:* medium size. Arches of eye socket well defined. *Ears:* length of ears should be about half length of head. Ears must not appear noticeable even when alert. *Mouth:* roof of mouth should be dark. *Neck:* held at 45 degrees to horizontal. *Hindquarters:* hocks set fairly low, toes slightly longer than on forefeet. *Body:* withers slightly higher than level of back. *Coat:* combed coat is as undesirable as a neglected one. *Colour:* white spot of not more than 2 inches in diameter permissible on chest, also few white hairs on feet. Skin well pigmented slate grey in colour. *Weight and size:* (ideal) dogs 16 to 18 inches and 29 to 33 pounds; bitches 14 to 16 inches and 22 to 29 pounds.

ROTTWEILER

NATIONAL GROUPING		
	Name	Number
AKC	Working Dogs	III
KC(GB)	Working	5
FCI	Guard Dogs	2

One of the favourite sports in Germany over the centuries has been boar hunting. Though today it is not carried out in quite the same way as it once was, the advent of gunpowder making life easier for the hunter and more conclusive for the game, the race of dogs used then, or at least something very like it, exists still. At one time it was a question of chasing the boar, cornering him and then despatching him with a spear. The dogs used were the ancestors of the modern Great Dane, the Saufinder and the Hatzrüden, tough fierce dogs, strong and short in the leg and with powerful jaws. The Hatzrüden has disappeared, but the dog that most closely resembles the sort of dog that he probably was, is the Rottweiler. He originated in Rottweil in Southern Germany, and was used by butchers as a droving dog, being known as the Rottweiler Metzgerhund, helping to drive the cattle from the countryside to the market and acting as guards to the drovers when the cattle had been converted into cash.

In 1900 it was reported that the breed had declined to such an extent that it was likely to disappear, which undoubtedly it would have done had not a breed club been established to look after its interests. This proved to be the turning point in the history of the breed as from then on not only did it take its rightful place in the show rings of the world, but increasing interest in the breed was taken by those who wished to use it as a working and guard dog. Since the Second World War the breed has thrived, and is today one of the more popular dogs in Germany. The first Rottweilers came to Britain in 1936 and were exhibited at Crufts in the following year, though they were known in the United States of America some years earlier and the breed was recognised in 1935 by the American Kennel Club. A good deal of work has been done on the breed in Scandinavia, and a very flourishing club exists in Sweden where extensive trials are held to improve the working qualities and temperament of the breed.

For his size the Rottweiler must be one of the strongest dogs in the world, being very heavy for his height and standing four square on very powerful legs. He is powerful and compact and capable of great endurance, and when fit, is very muscular, carrying no excess weight and being remarkably agile for a large dog. His massive head and well-armed powerful jaws are those of the one time boar hunter, and there is no doubt that when roused he would be a formidable opponent.

Although he appears regularly in the show rings of many countries, he has never made quite the impression that perhaps he deserves, but the numbers are steadily increasing and the enthusiasm of the breed clubs will ensure that his popularity will certainly not decline. He is usually in competition in a group that includes breeds that more regularly win top honours, and they have perhaps stolen the limelight. He is not a difficult dog to show, as his descent from a long line of hunting dogs has given him a natural ability to learn obedience to commands, and though the occasional dog will object to the close attentions of another one in the ring, it is by no means rare to see one handled by a child.

He is a very intelligent dog, and can be taught simple tricks as well as the more usual exercises of the obedience ring. At one time he was not so settled temperamentally as he is now, but careful elimination of the bloodlines that carried too much temper has produced a dog that is friendly and a very good companion. As a guard he is first class, having a very strong sense of duty and well developed sense of territory. At night, when as a dark coloured dog he is difficult to see, his deep roar and obvious powerful presence is usually sufficient.

OFFICIAL STANDARD

General appearance and character

The Rottweiler, is a good-sized, strongly built, active dog. He is affectionate, intelligent, easily trained to work, naturally obedient and extremely faithful. While not quarrelsome, he possesses great courage and makes a splendid guard. His demeanor is dignified and he is not excitable.

Head

Is of medium length, the skull broad between the ears. Stop well pronounced as is also the occiput. Muzzle is not very long. It should not be longer than the distance from the stop to the occiput. Nose is well developed, with relatively large nostrils and is always black. Flews which should not be too pronounced are also black. Jaws should be strong and muscular; teeth strong—incisors of lower jaw must touch the inner surface of the upper incisors. Eyes are of medium size, dark brown in color and should express faithfulness, good humor and confidence. The ears are comparatively small, set high and wide and hang over about on a level with top of head. The skin on head should not be loose. The neck should be of fair length, strong, round and very muscular, slightly arched and free from throatiness.

Forequarters

Shoulders should be well placed, long and sloping, elbows well let down, but not loose. Legs muscular and with plenty of bone and substance, pasterns straight and strong. Feet strong, round and close, with toes well arched. Soles very hard, toe nails dark, short and strong.

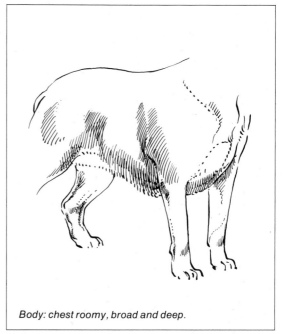

Body: chest roomy, broad and deep.

Body

The chest is roomy, broad and deep. Ribs well sprung. Back straight, strong and rather short. Loins strong and deep, the flanks should not be tucked up. Croup short, broad, but not sloping.

Hindquarters

Upper thigh is short, broad and very muscular. Lower thigh very muscular at top and strong and sinewy at the bottom. Stifles fairly well bent, hocks strong. The hind feet are somewhat longer than the front ones, but should be close and strong with toes well arched. There should be no dewclaws.

Tail

Should be short, placed high (on level with back) and carried horizontally. Dogs are frequently born with a short stump tail and when tail is too long it must be docked close to body.

Coat

Hair should be short, coarse and flat. The undercoat which is absolutely required on neck and thighs should not show through outer coat. The hair should be a little longer on the back of front and hind legs and on tail.

Color

Black, with clearly defined markings on cheeks, muzzle, chest and legs, as well as over both eyes. Color of markings: tan to mahogany brown. A small spot of white on chest and belly is permissible but not desirable.

Height

Shoulder height for dogs is $23\frac{3}{4}$ to 27 inches, for bitches, $21\frac{3}{4}$ to $25\frac{3}{4}$ inches, but height should always be considered in relation to the general appearance and conformation of the dog.

FAULTS

Too lightly built or too heavily built. Swayback. Roach back. Too long body. Lack of spring of ribs. Head too long and narrow, or too short and plump. Lack of occuput, snipy muzzle, cheekiness, top line of muzzle not straight. Light or flesh-colored nose. Hanging flews. Overshot or undershot. Loose skin on head. Ears set too low, or ears too heavy. Long or narrow or rose ear, or ears uneven in size. Light, small or slanting eyes, or lack of expression. Neck too long, thin or weak, or very noticeable throatiness. Lack of bone and muscle. Short or straight shoulders. Front legs too close together, or not straight. Weak pasterns. Splay feet, light nails, weak toes. Flat ribs. Sloping croup. Too heavy or plump body. Flanks drawn up. Flat thighs. Cowhocks or weak hocks. Dewclaws. Tail set too high or too low, or that is too long or too thin. Soft, too short, too long or too open coat. Wavy coat or lack of undercoat. White markings on toes, legs or other parts of the body. Markings not too well defined or smudgy. The one-color tan Rottweiler with either black or light mask, or with black streak on back as well as other colors such as brown or blue, are not recognized and are believed to be crossbred, as is also a longhaired Rottweiler. Timid or stupid-appearing animals are to be positively rejected.

Approved by the AKC 9 April 1935

KC(GB) VARIATION TO STANDARD

Head: cheeks well muscled but not prominent. *Eyes:* almond shaped. Eyelids close lying. *Ears:* lying flat and close to cheek. *Forelegs:* pasterns should be bent slightly forward and not be completely vertical. Front legs seen from all sides must be straight and not placed too closely to one another. *Feet:* pads should be very hard and toenails short dark and strong. *Height:* at shoulder: dogs 25 to 27 inches; bitches 23 to 25 inches.

SAINT BERNARD

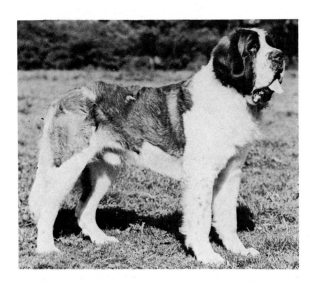

NATIONAL GROUPING		
	Name	Number
AKC	Working Dogs	III
KC(GB)	Working	5
FCI	Guard Dogs	2

Legend has it that this great dog spent a good deal of its time ploughing through the deep snow surrounding the Hospice of St. Bernard with a small keg of brandy fastened to his collar, rescuing snowbound travellers. How much credence should be placed on this story it is difficult to estimate. The only thing that is known is that the Hospice sticks to the story and the dog is certainly large enough and powerful enough to perform the deeds that it is reputed to have done. They would be able to scent out travellers lost in the snow and act as guides in extreme weather, and the monks still keep these striking animals even though the pass is now completely negotiable and more modern methods of rescue are employed. There is some evidence that there were dogs at the Hospice in the 17th century, and these would probably have been the Alpine Mastiff or some similar dog used largely as a guard. It is known that the dogs at the Hospice virtually died out and that the monks had to recourse to using other breeds as an outcross, the Newfoundland and the Great Pyrenees are suggested as possibilities.

1866 saw the first Saint Bernards being shown in Britain. They had been imported from the Hospice of St. Bernard where reputedly only the worst specimens were allowed to leave by the monks. They in fact created an immediate sensation, and a club was formed shortly afterwards to look after the interests of the breed. The dogs at the Hospice are said to have been half-coated, neither rough nor smooth, but the out-cross with other breeds resulted in two coats, and dogs that were brought into Britain produced stock that was both smooth or rough indiscriminately, something that still happens. The original Alpine Mastiff was a fairly smooth-coated dog and it is probable that the smooth coats of today are a reversion to this type. After considerable popularity around the turn of the century, when a great deal of breeding took place and dogs changed hands for very large sums of money (Sir Bedivere being sold to the United States of America for instance for £1,300 which was a fortune in those days) the breed went into a decline. The St. Bernard Club is one of the old established clubs in Britain, but even they could not prevent the fall in numbers that took place. But fashion is fickle, and now that one of the breed has won the Supreme Award at Crufts, there could easily be an upsurge in its fortunes.

He is still one of the heaviest dogs in the world, weights of two hundred pounds not being unknown, and his strength is enormous. It would be foolish to pretend that he is an easy dog to keep. To begin with he takes up a great deal of space, and needs a large amount of high quality food to maintain his immense bulk in condition. In the search for size, soundness was for a long time sacrificed, and even now in order to rear a Saint Bernard, a great deal of correct exercising is needed to prevent weakness of the hindquarters. He has moreover the habit of drooling, and it is not unusual to see one of these dogs sitting in a car with a bib tied round his neck to prevent him soiling the upholstery.

Given those slight drawbacks, he makes a magnificent show dog. The rich mixture of colours and well-defined markings distinguishes him from all the other large breeds, and his sheer size makes his presence felt especially when a number of these dogs are grouped together. He has a very steady temperament as most of the large dogs have, and though he objects to the close attention of another dog, he is perfectly friendly with people and especially with those that he knows.

OFFICIAL STANDARD

SHORTHAIRED
General appearance
Powerful, proportionately tall figure, strong and muscular in every part, with powerful head and most intelligent expression. In dogs with a dark mask the expression appears more stern, but never ill-natured.

Head and skull: massive, dignified expression.

Head
Like the whole body, very powerful and imposing. The massive skull is wide, slightly arched and the sides slope in a gentle curve into the very strongly developed high cheek bones. Occiput only moderately developed. The supra-orbital ridge is very strongly developed and forms nearly a right angle with the horizontal axis of the head. Deeply imbedded between the eyes and starting at the root of the muzzle, a furrow runs over the whole skull. It is strongly marked in the first half, gradually disappearing toward the base of the occiput. The lines at the sides of the head diverge considerably from the outer corner of the eyes toward the back of the head. The skin of the forehead, above the eyes, forms rather noticeable wrinkles, more or less pronounced, which converge toward the furrow. Especially when the dog is in action, the wrinkles are more visible without in the least giving the impression of morosity. Too strongly developed wrinkles are not desired. The slope from the skull to the muzzle is sudden and rather steep.
The muzzle is short, does not taper, and the vertical depth at the root of the muzzle must be greater than the length of the muzzle. The bridge of the muzzle is not arched, but straight; in some dogs, occasionally, slightly broken. A rather wide, well-marked, shallow furrow runs from the root of the muzzle over the entire bridge of the muzzle to the nose. The flews of the upper jaw are strongly developed, not sharply cut, but turning in a beautiful curve into the lower edge, and slightly overhanging. The flews of the lower jaw must not be deeply pendant. The teeth should be sound and strong and should meet in either a scissors or an even bite; the scissors bite being preferable. The undershot bite, although sometimes found with good specimens, is not desirable. The overshot bite is a fault. A black roof to the mouth is desirable. *Nose* (Schwamm): very substantial, broad, with wide open nostrils, and, like the lips, always black. *Ears:* of medium size, rather high set, with very strongly developed burr (Muschel) at the base. They stand slightly away from the head at the base, then drop with a sharp bend to the side and cling to the head without a turn. The flap is tender and forms a rounded triangle, slightly elongated toward the point, the front edge lying firmly to the head, whereas the back edge may stand somewhat away from the head, especially when the dog is at attention. Lightly set ears, which at the base immediately cling to the head, give it an oval and too little marked exterior, whereas a strongly developed base gives the skull a squarer, broader and much more expressive appearance. *Eyes:* set more to the front than the sides, are of medium size, dark brown, with intelligent, friendly expression, set moderately deep. The lower eyelids, as a rule, do not close completely and, if that is the case, form an angular wrinkle toward the inner corner of the eye. Eyelids which are too deeply pendant and show conspicuously the lachrymal glands, or a very red, thick haw, and eyes that are too light, are objectionable.

Neck
Set high, very strong and in action is carried erect. Otherwise horizontally or slightly downward. The junction of head and neck is distinctly marked by an indentation. The nape of the neck is very muscular and rounded at the sides which makes the neck appear rather short. The dewlap of throat and neck is well pronounced: too strong development, however, is not desirable.

Shoulders
Sloping and broad, very muscular and powerful. The withers are strongly pronounced.

Chest
Very well arched, moderately deep, not reaching below the elbows.

Back
Very broad, perfectly straight as far as the haunches, from there gently sloping to the rump, and merging imperceptibly into the root of the tail.

Hindquarters
Well-developed. Legs very muscular.

Belly
Distinctly set off from the very powerful loin section, only little drawn up.

Tail
Starting broad and powerful directly from the rump is long, very heavy, ending in a powerful tip. In repose it hangs straight down, turning gently upward in the lower third only, which is not considered a fault. In a great many specimens the tail is carried with the end slightly bent and

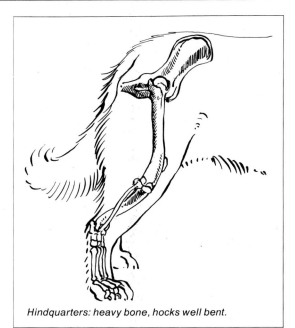
Hindquarters: heavy bone, hocks well bent.

therefore hangs down in the shape of an 'f'. In action all dogs carry the tail more or less turned upward. However it may not be carried too erect or by any means rolled over the back. A slight curling of the tip is sooner admissible.

Forearms
Very powerful and extraordinarily muscular.

Forelegs
Straight, strong.

Hind legs
Hocks of moderate angulation. Dewclaws are not desired; if present, they must not obstruct gait.

Feet
Broad, with strong toes, moderately closed, and with rather high knuckles. The so-called dewclaws which sometimes occur on the inside of the hind legs are imperfectly developed toes. They are of no use to the dog and are not taken into consideration in judging. They may be removed by surgery.

Coat
Very dense, short-haired (stockhaarig), lying smooth, tough, without however feeling rough to the touch. The thighs are slightly bushy. The tail at the root has longer and denser hair which gradually becomes shorter toward the tip. The tail appears bushy, not forming a flag.

Color
White with red or red with white, the red in its various shades; brindle patches with white markings. The colors red and brown-yellow are of entirely equal value. Necessary markings are: white chest, feet and tip of tail, noseband, collar or spot on the nape; the latter and blaze are very desirable. Never of one color or without white. Faulty are all other colors, except the favorite dark

shadings on the head (mask) and ears. One distinguishes between mantle dogs and splash-coated dogs.

Height at shoulder
Of the dog should be $27\frac{1}{2}$ inches minimum, of the bitch $25\frac{1}{2}$ inches. Bitch animals are of finer and more delicate build.

Considered as faults: are all deviations from the Standard, as for instance a swayback and a disproportionately long back, hocks too much bent, straight hindquarters, upward growing hair in spaces between the toes, out at elbows, cowhocks and weak pasterns.

LONGHAIRED
The longhaired type completely resembles the shorthaired type except for the coat which is not shorthaired (stockhaarig) but of medium length plain to slightly wavy, never rolled or curly and not shaggy either. Usually, on the back especially from the region of the haunches to the rump, the hair is more wavy, a condition, by the way, that is slightly indicated in the shorthaired dogs. The tail is bushy with dense hair of moderate length. Rolled or curly hair on the tail is not desirable. A tail with parted hair, or a flag tail, is faulty. Face and ears are covered with short and soft hair; longer hair at the base of the ear is permissible. Forelegs only slightly feathered; thighs very bushy.

Approved by the AKC 12 May 1959

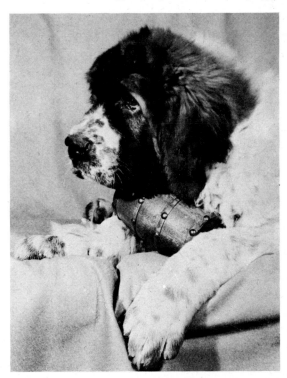

KC(GB) VARIATION TO STANDARD
Head: cheeks flat. Great depth from eye to lower jaw.
Hindlegs: hocks well bent, thighs very muscular.

SAMOYED

Many dogs in their early association with man, were put to work by him: they herded stock, guarded property or hunted game for food. Some, where conditions were suitable, were used as haulers and the Samoyed is a typical example of this. He is one of the sledge hauling dogs used under arctic conditions, where teams of dogs could be harnessed together to tow loads through snow. He is typical of the Spitz group of dogs with erect ears, curled tail and stand-off coat, and is one of a small group used for work in snow. Unlike the others, however, his somewhat more glamorous appearance attracted popular attention and he was soon drawn into the world of the show dog, becoming very popular all over the world whilst the others remained in comparative obscurity.

He is said to have originated in the north west of Siberia among the Samoyed tribe who were originally a nomadic people who herded reindeer and used their dogs for this purpose as well as for pulling their sledges. The tribe is now settled, but their dogs have spread their influence over the whole world, to such an extent that most people would know what a Samoyed was. Originally he was a multi-coloured dog, and in the early days of importation into Britain there were many that were black, black and tan, or black and white, but the white specimens eventually predominated. In the United States racing with teams of Samoyeds is still popular, which means that the working propensities of the breed are preserved, but little is done in this direction in other countries and he is now primarily a show dog, and a very popular one. Having first arrived in Britain only at the turn of the century, registration figures are now running at nearly a thousand each year.

The Samoyed is a strong, well built dog, and sturdy though not as short and cobbily built as some of the Spitz breeds. His coat is one of his most striking features, the white being the glistening white of snow, and the fullness and density of the coat being reminiscent of the most expensive of furs. He is intelligent, alert and friendly, being almost affectionate towards his owners and never unfriendly even to strangers. He is tremendously hardy, and though it is not now the general practice, he will sleep out of doors in the coldest weather, burying himself in the snow and making a sort of igloo in which his body heat, retained by his heavy coat allows him to remain reasonably comfortable as it did his ancestors of long ago.

As a show dog he is a most attractive breed. Exhibitors vie with presentation, bathing their dogs until the white coat is pure glistening white, with the result that a ring full of these dogs is a brilliant sight at any large modern show. He is an easy dog to show, as he appears to enjoy the atmosphere of the ring as so many of the Spitz breeds do, and he is rarely overawed by the surroundings of the dog show. He enjoys a game, loves plenty of exercise, and even though he does from time to time tend to shed white hairs on the furniture, he makes a wonderful house pet.

OFFICIAL STANDARD

GENERAL CONFORMATION
General appearance

The Samoyed, being essentially a working dog, should present a picture of beauty, alertness and strength, with agility, dignity and grace. As his work lies in cold climates, his coat should be heavy and weather-resistant, well groomed, and of good quality rather than quantity. The dog carries more of a 'ruff' than the bitch. He should not be long in the back as a weak back would make him practically useless for his legitimate work, but at the same time, a close-coupled body would also place him at a great disadvantage as a draft dog. Breeders should aim for the happy medium, a body not long but muscular, allowing liberty, with a deep chest and well-sprung ribs, strong neck, straight front and especially strong loins. Dogs should be masculine in appearance and deportment without unwarranted aggressiveness; bitches feminine without weakness of structure or apparent softness of temperament. Bitches may be slightly longer in back than dogs. They should both give the appearance of being capable of great endurance but be free from coarseness. Because of the depth of chest required, the legs should be moderately long. A very short-legged dog is to be deprecated. Hindquarters should be particularly well developed, stifles well bent and any suggestion of unsound stifles or cowhocks severely penalized. General appearance should include movement and general conformation, indicating balance and good substance.

Substance

Substance is that sufficiency of bone and muscle which rounds out a balance with the frame. The bone is heavier than would be expected in a dog of this size but not so massive as to prevent the speed and agility most desirable in a Samoyed. In all builds, bone should be in proportion to body size. The Samoyed should never be so heavy as to appear clumsy nor so light as to appear racy. The weight should be in proportion to the height.

Height

Dogs, 21 to 23½ inches; bitches, 19 to 21 inches at the withers. An oversized or undersized Samoyed is to be penalized according to the extent of the deviation.

Coat (texture and condition)

The Samoyed is a double-coated dog. The body should be well covered with an undercoat of soft, short, thick, close wool with longer and harsh hair growing through it to form the outer coat, which stands straight out from the body and should be free from curl. The coat should form a ruff around the neck and shoulders, framing the head (more on dogs than on bitches). Quality of coat should be weather resistant and considered more than quantity. A droopy coat is undesirable. The coat should glisten with a silver sheen. The female does not usually carry as long a coat as most males and it is softer in texture.

Color

Samoyeds should be pure white, white and biscuit, cream, or all biscuit. Any other colors disqualify.

MOVEMENT
Gait

The Samoyed should trot, not pace. He should move with a quick agile stride that is well timed. The gait should be free, balanced and vigorous, with good reach in the forequarters and good driving power in the hindquarters. When trotting, there should be a strong rear action drive. Moving at a slow walk or trot, they will not single-track, but as speed increases the legs gradually angle inward until the pads are finally falling on a line directly under the longitudinal center of the body. As the pad marks converge the forelegs and hind legs are carried straight forward in traveling, the stifles not turned in nor out. The back should remain strong, firm and level. A choppy or stilted gait should be penalized.

Rear end

Upper thighs should be well developed. Stifles well bent—approximately 45 degrees to the ground. Hocks should be well developed, sharply defined and set at approximately 30 per cent of hip height. The hind legs should be parallel when viewed from the rear in a natural stance, strong, well developed, turning neither in nor out. Straight stifles are objectionable. Double-jointedness or cowhocks are a fault. Cowhocks should only be determined if the dog has had an opportunity to move properly.

Front end

Legs should be parallel and straight to the pasterns. The pasterns should be strong, sturdy and straight, but flexible with some spring for proper let-down of feet. Because of depth of chest, legs should be moderately long. Length of leg from the ground to the elbow should be approximately 55 per cent of the total height at the withers—a very short-legged dog is to be deprecated. Shoulders should be long and sloping, with a layback of 45 degrees and be firmly set. Out at the shoulders or out at the elbows should be penalized. The withers separation should be approximately 1 to 1½ inches.

Feet

Large, long, flattish—a hare-foot, slightly spread but not splayed; toes arched; pads thick and tough, with protective growth of hair between the toes. Feet should turn neither in nor out in a natural stance but may turn in slightly in the act of pulling. Turning out, pigeon-toed, round or cat-footed or splayed are faults. Feathers on feet are not too essential but are more profuse on bitches than on dogs.

HEAD
Conformation

Skull is wedge-shaped, broad, slightly crowned, not round or apple-headed, and should form an equilateral triangle on lines between the inner base of the ears and the center point of the stop. *Muzzle:* muzzle of medium length and medium width, neither coarse nor snipy; should taper toward the nose and be in proportion to the size of the dog and the width of skull. The muzzle must have depth. *Stop:* not too abrupt, nevertheless well defined. *Lips:* should be black for preference and slightly curved up at the corners of the mouth, giving the 'Sam-

Head and skull: powerful and wedge-shaped.

Expression

The expression, referred to as 'Samoyed expression,' is very important and is indicated by sparkle of the eyes, animation and lighting up of the face when alert or intent on anything. Expression is made up of a combination of eyes, ears and mouth. The ears should be erect when alert; the mouth should be slightly curved up at the corners to form the 'Samoyed smile.'

TORSO
Neck

Strong, well muscled, carried proudly erect, set on sloping shoulders to carry head with dignity when at attention. Neck should blend into shoulders with a graceful arch.

Chest

Should be deep, with ribs well sprung out from the spine and flattened at the sides to allow proper movement of the shoulders and freedom for the front legs. Should not be barrel-chested. Perfect depth of chest approximates the point of elbows, and the deepest part of the chest should be back of the forelegs—near the ninth rib. Heart and lung room are secured more by body depth than width.

Loin and back

The withers forms the highest part of the back. Loins strong and slightly arched. The back should be straight to the loin, medium in length, very muscular and neither long nor short-coupled. The dog should be 'just off square'—the length being approximately 5 per cent more than the height. Bitches allowed to be slightly longer than dogs. The belly should be well shaped and tightly muscled and, with the rear of the thorax, should swing up in a pleasing curve (tuck-up). Croup must be full, slightly sloping, and must continue imperceptibly to the tail root.

Tail

The tail should be moderately long with the tail bone terminating approximately at the hock when down. It should be profusely covered with long hair and carried forward over the back or side when alert, but sometimes dropped when at rest. It should not be high or low set and should be mobile and loose—not tight over the back. A double hook is a fault. A judge should see the tail over the back once when judging.

Disposition

Intelligent, gentle, loyal, adaptable, alert, full of action, eager to serve, friendly but conservative, not distrustful or shy, not overly aggressive. Unprovoked aggressiveness to be severely penalized.

oyed smile.' Lip lines should not have the appearance of being coarse nor should the flews drop predominately at corners of the mouth. *Ears:* strong and thick, erect, triangular and slightly rounded at the tips; should not be large or pointed, nor should they be small and 'bear-eared.' Ears should conform to head size and the size of the dog; they should be set well apart but be within the border of the outer edge of the head; they should be mobile and well covered inside with hair; hair full and stand-off before the ears. Length of ear should be the same measurement as the distance from inner base of ear

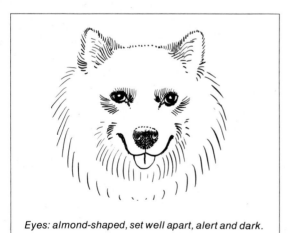
Eyes: almond-shaped, set well apart, alert and dark.

to outer corner of eye. *Eyes:* should be dark for preference; should be placed well apart and deep-set; almond shaped with lower lid slanting toward an imaginary point approximating the base of ears. Dark eye rims for preference. Round or protruding eyes penalized. Blue eyes disqualifying. *Nose:* black for preference but brown, liver, or Dudley nose not penalized. Color of nose sometimes changes with age and weather. *Jaws and teeth:* strong, well-set teeth, snugly overlapping with scissors bite. Undershot or overshot should be penalized.

DISQUALIFICATIONS
Any color other than pure white, cream, biscuit, or white and biscuit. Blue eyes.

Approved by the AKC 9 April 1963

KC(GB) VARIATION TO STANDARD
Colour: not biscuit. *Faults:* bull neck. Long body. Black or black spots.

SHETLAND SHEEPDOG

NATIONAL GROUPING		
	Name	Number
AKC	Working Dogs	III
KC(GB)	Working	5
FCI	Herding Dogs	I

It is notable that the islands off the north coast of Scotland have over the years produced much reduced versions of a number of domestic animals. They have a small hardy breed of sheep, the Shetland Ponies, and a small breed of sheepdog. It is probably not true that the severe climatic conditions have stunted the growth of these animals, but simply that with the lack of space the smaller animals have been more suitable. It was the habit, and indeed still is in some remote parts, to move the farm animals under cover in the same building as the family during the winter, with a separate space but a common roof, and clearly large animals would create some difficulties. The breed was at one time known as the Miniature Collie or the Shetland Collie, and the islanders were said to have used these little dogs as sheepherders, a task which they performed with considerable skill, being active, intelligent and as one writer put it, 'as hardy as Terriers'.

It was not until after 1908 that the first breed club was formed, and since that time the breed has never looked back, the original clubs settling their differences, deciding on a standard for the breed and encouraging shows to put on separate classes for them rather than scheduling them as Miniature Collies. The breed is now third in popularity in the Working Group after the German Shepherd Dog and the Rough-coated Collie, and boasts in Britain some six thousand registrations each year.

The Shetland Sheepdog still retains many of the characteristics of its working ancestors, being a sturdy and hardy little dog capable of withstanding a great deal of bad weather being well-protected by its soft undercoat and long harsh outer coat in spite of its somewhat delicate appearance. He is active and gay, enjoys exercise as most of the working breeds do, being virtually tireless.

It would be a mistake these days to look upon the Shetland Sheepdog as just a miniature of the Rough Collie, as there are distinct differences, especially about the head, where the proportions are quite distinctive to the breed. It must be remembered too that they are essentially a working breed, and a Shetland Sheepdog that looks weedy, or begins to look like a toy dog is not a typical Sheltie.

As a show dog he is very popular, and the numbers appearing at the major shows throughout the world are very high. His size helps, as where an exhibitor would take two Rough Collies, the same exhibitor could easily take half a dozen Shetland Sheepdogs to a show because of less time needed for preparation and less space occupied in transport. The colours are attractive too, and whilst sables in the range from gold to mahogany predominate, there is always a sprinkling of tricolours and blue merles which add colour to the ring. They repay attention to coat, as do most breeds, but the Shetland Sheepdog more than most, and when he has his coat really well sorted out, with his pronounced mane and abundant feathering prepared to full advantage, he is a very handsome little dog.

He is a happy dog, alert and friendly, not always prepared to accept strangers immediately, and a very good guard and housedog. He makes a very good companion, rapidly becoming part of the family and loving to join the children in their games. He is not difficult to train, and he is from time to time seen in the obedience ring where he acquits himself well in competition with the more usual breeds.

OFFICIAL STANDARD

The Shetland Sheepdog, like the Collie, traces to the Border Collie of Scotland, which, transported to the Shetland Islands and crossed with small, intelligent, longhaired breeds, was reduced to miniature proportions. Subsequently crosses were made from time to time with Collies. This breed now bears the same relationship in size and general appearance to the Rough Collie as the Shetland Pony does to some of the larger breeds of horses. Although the resemblance between the Shetland Sheepdog and the Rough Collie is marked, there are differences which may be noted.

General description
The Shetland Sheepdog is a small, alert, rough-coated, longhaired working dog. He must be sound, agile and sturdy. The outline should be so symmetrical that no part appears out of proportion to the whole. Dogs should appear masculine; bitches feminine.

Size
The Shetland Sheepdog should stand between 13 and 16 inches at the shoulder. Note: Height is determined by a line perpendicular to the ground from the top of the shoulder blades, the dog standing naturally, with forelegs parallel to line of measurement. *Disqualification:* heights below or above the desired size range are to be disqualified from the show ring.

Coat
The coat should be double, the outer coat consisting of long, straight, harsh hair; the undercoat short, furry, and so dense as to give the entire coat its 'stand-off' quality. The hair on face, tips of ears and feet should be smooth. Mane and frill should be abundant, and particularly impressive in dogs. The forelegs well feathered, the hind legs heavily so, but smooth below the hock joint. Hair on tail profuse. Note: Excess hair on ears, feet, and on hocks may be trimmed for the show ring. *Faults:* coat short or flat, in whole or in part; wavy, curly, soft or silky. Lack of undercoat. Smooth-coated specimens.

Head and skull: refined, wedge-shaped.

Color
Black, blue merle, and sable (ranging from golden through mahogany); marked with varying amounts of white and/or tan. *Faults:* rustiness in a black or a blue coat. Washed out or degenerate colors, such as pale sable and faded blue. Self-color in the case of blue merle, that is, without any merling or mottling and generally appearing as a faded or dilute tri-color. Conspicuous white body spots. Specimens with more than 50 per cent white shall be so severely penalized as to effectively eliminate them from competition. *Disqualification:* brindle.

Temperament
The Shetland Sheepdog is intensely loyal, affectionate, and responsive to his owner. However, he may be reserved towards strangers but not to the point of showing fear or cringing in the ring. *Faults:* shyness, timidity, or nervousness. Stubbornness, snappiness, or ill temper.

Head
The head should be refined and its shape, when viewed from top or side, be a long, blunt wedge tapering slightly from ears to nose, which must be black. *Skull and muzzle:* top of skull should be flat, showing no prominence at nuchal crest (the top of the occiput). Cheeks should be flat and should merge smoothly into a well-rounded muzzle. Skull and muzzle should be of equal length, balance point being inner corner of eye. In profile the top line of skull should parallel the top line of muzzle, but on a higher plane due to the presence of a slight but definite stop. Jaws clean and powerful. The deep, well-developed under-jaw, rounded at chin, should extend to base of nostril. Lips tight. Upper and lower lips must meet and fit smoothly together all the way around. Teeth level and evenly spaced. Scissors bite. *Fault:* two-angled head. Too prominent stop, or no stop. Overfill below, between, or above eyes. Prominent nuchal crest. Domed skull. Prominent cheekbones. Snipy muzzle. Short, receding, or shallow under-jaw, lacking breadth and depth. Overshot or undershot, missing or crooked teeth. Teeth visible when mouth is closed. *Eyes:* medium size with dark, almond-shaped rims, set somewhat obliquely in skull. Color must be dark, with blue or merle eyes permissible in blue merles only. *Faults:* light, round, large or too small. Prominent haws. *Ears:* small and flexible, placed high, carried three-fourths erect, with tips breaking forward. When in repose the ears fold lengthwise and are thrown back into the frill. *Faults:* set too low. Hound, prick, bat, twisted ears. Leather too thick or too thin.

Expression
Contours and chiseling of the head, the shape, set and use of ears, the placement, shape and color of the eyes, combine to produce expression. Normally the expression

should be alert, gentle, intelligent and questioning. Toward strangers the eyes should show watchfulness and reserve, but no fear.

Neck

Neck should be muscular, arched, and of sufficient length to carry the head proudly. *Faults:* too short and thick.

Body

In over-all appearance the body should appear moderately long as measured from shoulder joint to ischium (rearmost extremity of the pelvic bone), but much of this length is actually due to the proper angulation and breadth of the shoulder and hindquarter, as the back itself should be comparatively short. Back should be level and strongly muscled. Chest should be deep, the brisket reaching to point of elbow. The ribs should be well sprung, but flattened at their lower half to allow free play of the foreleg and shoulder. Abdomen moderately tucked up. *Faults:* back too long, too short, swayed or roached. Barrel ribs. Slab-side. Chest narrow and/or too shallow.

Forequarters

From the withers the shoulder blades should slope at a 45-degree angle forward and downward to the shoulder joints. At the withers they are separated only by the vertebra, but they must slope outward sufficiently to accommodate the desired spring of rib. The upper arm should join the shoulder blade at as nearly as possible a right angle. Elbow joint should be equidistant from the ground or from the withers. Forelegs straight viewed from all angles, muscular and clean, and of strong bone. Pasterns very strong, sinewy and flexible. Dewclaws may be removed. *Faults:* Insufficient angulation between shoulder and upper arm. Upper arm too short. Lack of outward slope of shoulders. Loose shoulders. Turning in or out of elbows. Crooked legs. Light bone.

Feet (front and hind)

Feet should be oval and compact with the toes well arched and fitting tightly together. Pads deep and tough, nails hard and strong. *Faults:* feet turning in or out. Splay-feet. Hare-feet. Cat-feet.

Hindquarters

There should be a slight arch at the loins, and the croup should slope gradually to the rear. The hipbone (pelvis) should be set at a 30-degree angle to the spine. The thigh should be broad and muscular. The thighbone should be set into the pelvis at a right angle corresponding to the angle of the shoulder blade and upper arm. Stifle bones join the thighbone and should be distinctly angled at the stifle joint. The over-all length of the stifle should at least equal the length of the thighbone, and preferably should slightly exceed it. Hock joint should be clean-cut, angular, sinewy, with good bone and strong ligamentation. The hock (metatarsus) should be short and straight viewed from all angles. Dewclaws should be removed. Feet (*see* Forequarters). *Faults:* croup higher than withers. Croup too straight or too steep. Narrow thighs. Cowhocks. Hocks turning out. Poorly defined hock joint. Feet (*see* Forequarters).

Tail

The tail should be sufficiently long so that when it is laid along the back edge of the hind legs the last vertebra will reach the hock joint. Carriage of tail at rest is straight down or in a slight upward curve. When the dog is alert the tail is normally lifted, but it should not be curved forward over the back. *Faults:* too short. Twisted at end.

Gait

The trotting gait of the Shetland Sheepdog should denote effortless speed and smoothness. There should be no jerkiness, nor stiff, stilted, up-and-down movement. The drive should be from the rear, true and straight, dependent upon correct angulation, musculation, and ligamentation of the entire hindquarter, thus allowing the dog to reach well under his body with his hind foot and propel himself forward. Reach of stride of the foreleg is dependent upon correct angulation, musculation and ligamentation of the forequarters, together with correct width of chest and construction of rib cage. The foot should be lifted only enough to clear the ground as the leg swings forward. Viewed from the front, both forelegs and hind legs should move forward almost perpendicular to ground at the walk, slanting a little inward at a slow trot, until at a swift trot the feet are brought so far inward toward center line of body that the tracks left show two parallel lines of footprints actually touching a center line at their inner edges. *There should be no crossing of the feet nor throwing of the weight from side to side. Faults:* stiff, short steps, with a choppy, jerky movement. Mincing steps, with a hopping up and down, or a balancing of weight from side to side (often erroneously admired as a 'dancing gait' but permissible in young puppies). Lifting of front feet in hackney-like action, resulting in loss of speed and energy. Pacing gait.

SCALE OF POINTS

General Appearance (25): symmetry (10), temperament (10), coat (5). *Head (20):* skull and stop (5), muzzle (5), eyes, ears and expression (10). Body (20): neck and back (5), chest, ribs and brisket (10), loin, croup and tail (5). Forequarters (15): shoulder (10), forelegs and feet (5). Hindquarters (15): hip, thigh and stifle (10), hocks and feet (5). Gait (5): gait—smoothness and lack of waste motion when trotting (5). *Total (100).*

DISQUALIFICATIONS

Heights below or above the desired range, i.e. 13–16 inches. Brindle color.

Approved by the AKC 12 May 1959

KC(GB) VARIATION TO STANDARD

Ears: moderately wide at base, fairly close together. *Size:* ideal height measured at withers: dogs $14\frac{1}{2}$ inches, bitches 14 inches. Anything more than 1 inch above these heights to be considered a serious fault.

SIBERIAN HUSKY

NATIONAL GROUPING		
	Name	Number
AKC	Working Dogs	III
KC(GB)	—	—
FCI	Guard Dogs	2

There are several breeds that were originally used for sledge towing that have some similarities, the Siberian Husky, the Alaskan Malamute and the Eskimo Dog are the three most obvious ones. Their points of similarity lead some people to believe that they date back to the time when there was a land ridge between Alaska and Siberia. Even if this is not a fact, there is every possibility that arctic fishermen moved with their dogs from one continent to the other. The Siberian Husky was originally the sledge dog of the Chukchis of the far north-eastern part of Asia. The Chukchis are said to have maintained the breed in the 19th century as a pure breed, treasuring them for their speed and endurance, and this is the race of dogs that were the ancestors of today's Siberian Husky.

During the 19th century sledge dogs were in constant use in Alaska, as they were virtually the only way of carrying loads over snow and ice between stations. The people of Alaska had their own dog, the Malamute, but he was heavier, and proved slower, and the men who wished to travel further and faster turned their attention to the Siberian Husky whose reputation had spread from its native country. Early Russian explorers had made extensive journeys and charted the coastline of Siberia using these Huskies, realising the value of having a large number of lighter and faster dogs, and later both Peary and Nansen followed suit, using a mixed force of both East and West Siberian dogs. The first team of Siberian Huskies appeared in a race on the North American Continent in the All Alaska Sweepstakes Race in 1909, and in the following year a number were imported, Fox Maule Ramsay won with a team which covered four hundred miles in the race.

One of the most dramatic stories of the Siberian Husky's prowess was when Nome in Alaska suffered an epidemic of diphtheria, and the serum was relayed to the stricken town by teams of Huskies. This event focussed attention on the breed, and it was taken up in a big way both for work and for competition. The breed became established in the United States and was granted recognition in 1930. The Siberian Husky is now seen in many countries, and is growing in popularity in Britain where at the moment it competes only in rare breed and variety classes. It is, however, making its mark, and wins such classes frequently. He makes a good show dog, being striking in appearance with his colour and marking, and unusual coat, which is more dense than anything seen in other dogs. He is quick on his feet, and very graceful when moving, his gait appearing completely effortless. He stands well in the ring, enjoying the experience, watching the other dogs, and from time to time breaking off to look into the distance as if he was expecting snow. He is a strong well-made dog with good bone, and the bitches manage to look feminine without losing anything in power and nobility.

He is a friendly dog, affectionate almost with those that he becomes attached to, makes a very good guard, and is adaptable to any conditions, living equally happily indoors or out of doors in any weather. He is hardy, suffers from few illnesses, and is a perfectly amiable dog despite the stories of team dogs fighting to the death.

OFFICIAL STANDARD

General appearance

The Siberian Husky is a medium-sized working dog, quick and light on his feet and free and graceful in action. His moderately compact and well-furred body, erect ears and brush tail suggest his Northern heritage. His characteristic gait is smooth and seemingly effortless. He performs his original function in harness most capably, carrying a light load at moderate speed over great distances. His body proportions and form reflect this basic balance of power, speed and endurance. The dogs of the Siberian Husky breed are masculine but never coarse; the bitches are feminine but without weakness of structure. In proper condition, with muscle firm and well-developed, the Siberian Husky does not carry excess weight.

Head: eyes almond-shaped, ears triangular, erect, well-furred.

Head

Skull: of medium size and in proportion to the body; slightly rounded on top and tapering gradually from the widest point to the eyes. *Faults:* head clumsy or heavy; head too finely chiseled. *Muzzle:* of medium length; that is, the distance from the tip of the nose to the stop is equal to the distance from the stop to the occiput. The stop is well-defined and the bridge of the nose is straight from the stop to the tip. The muzzle is of medium width, tapering gradually to the nose, with the tip neither pointed nor square. The lips are well-pigmented and close fitting; teeth closing in a scissors bite. *Faults:* muzzle either too snipy or too coarse; muzzle too short or too long; insufficient stop; any bite other than scissors. *Ears:* of medium size, triangular in shape, close fitting and set high on the head. They are thick, well-furred, slightly arched at the back, and strongly erect, with slightly rounded tips

pointing straight up. *Faults:* ears too large in proportion to the head; too wide-set; not strongly erect. *Eyes:* almond shaped, moderately spaced and set a trifle obliquely. The expression is keen, but friendly; interested and even mischievous. Eyes may be brown or blue in color; one of each or parti-coloured are acceptable. *Faults:* eyes set too obliquely; set too close together. *Nose:* black in gray, tan or black dogs; liver in copper dogs; may be flesh-colored in pure white dogs. The pink-streaked 'snow nose' is acceptable.

Body

Neck: medium in length, arched and carried proudly erect when dog is standing. When moving at a trot, the neck is extended so that the head is carried slightly forward. *Faults:* neck too short and thick; neck too long. *Shoulders:* the shoulder blade is well laid back at an approximate angle of 45 degrees to the ground. The upper arm angles slightly backward from point of shoulder to elbow, and is never perpendicular to the ground. The muscles and ligaments holding the shoulder to the rib cage are firm and well-developed. *Faults:* straight shoulders; loose shoulders. *Chest:* deep and strong, but not too broad, with the deepest point just behind and level with the elbows. The ribs are well-sprung from the spine but flattened on the sides to allow for freedom of action. *Faults:* chest too broad; 'barrel ribs'; ribs too flat or weak. *Back:* The back is straight and strong, with a level topline from withers to croup. It is of medium length, neither cobby nor slack from excessive length. The loin is taut and lean, narrower than the rib cage, and with a slight tuck-up. The croup slopes away from the spine at an angle, but never so steeply as to restrict the rearward thrust of the hind legs. In profile, the length of the body from the point of the shoulder to the rear point of the croup is slightly longer than the height of the body from the ground to the top of the withers. *Faults:* weak or slack back; roached back; sloping topline.

Legs and feet

Forelegs: when standing and viewed from the front, the legs are moderately spaced, parallel and straight, with elbows close to the body and turned neither in nor out. Viewed from the side, pasterns are slightly slanted, with pastern joint strong, but flexible. Bone is substantial but never heavy. Length of the leg from elbow to ground is slightly more than the distance from the elbow to the top of withers. Dewclaws or forelegs may be removed. *Faults:* weak pasterns, too heavy bone; too narrow or too wide in the front; out at the elbows. *Hindquarters:* when standing and viewed from the rear, the hind legs are moderately spaced and parallel. The upper thighs are well-muscled and powerful, the stifles well-bent, the hock joint well-defined and set low to the ground. Dewclaws, if any, are to be removed. *Faults:* straight stifles, cowhocks, too narrow or too wide in the rear. *Feet:* oval in shape, but not long. The paws are medium size, compact and well-furred between the toes and pads. The pads are tough and thickly cushioned. The paws neither turn in nor out when dog is in natural stance. *Faults:* soft or splayed toes; paws too large and clumsy; paws too small and delicate; toeing in or out.

Tail

The well-furred tail of fox-brush shape is set on just below the level of the topline, and is usually carried over the back in a graceful sickle curve when the dog is at attention. When carried up, the tail does not curl to either side of the body, nor does it snap flat against the back. A trailing tail is normal for the dog when working or in repose. Hair on the tail is of medium length and approximately the same length on top, sides and bottom, giving the appearance of a round brush. *Faults:* a snapped or tightly curled tail; highly plumed tail; tail set too low or too high.

Gait

The Siberian Husky's characteristic gait is smooth and seemingly effortless. He is quick and light on his feet, and when in the show ring should be gaited on a loose lead at a moderately fast trot, exhibiting good reach in the forequarters and good drive in the hindquarters. When viewed from the front to rear, while moving at a walk the Siberian Husky does not single-track, but as the speed increases the legs gradually angle inward until the pads are falling on a line directly under the longitudinal center of the body. As the pad marks converge, the forelegs and hind legs are carried straight forward, with neither elbows nor stifles turned in or out. Each hind leg moves in the path of the foreleg on the same side. While the dog is gaiting, the topline remains firm and level. *Faults:* short, prancing or choppy gait, lumbering or rolling gait; crossing; crabbing.

Coat

The coat of the Siberian Husky is double and medium in length, giving a well-furred appearance, but is never so long as to obscure the clean-cut outline of the dog. The undercoat is soft and dense and of sufficient length to support the outer coat. The guard hairs of the outer coat are straight and somewhat smooth-lying, never harsh nor standing straight off from the body. It should be noted that the absence of the undercoat during the shedding season is normal. Trimming of the whiskers and fur between the toes and around the feet to present a neater appearance is permissible. Trimming of the fur on any other part of the dog is not to be condoned and should be severely penalized. *Faults:* long, rough or shaggy coat; texture too harsh or too silky; trimming of the coat, except as permitted above.

Color

All colors from black to pure white are allowed. A variety of markings on the head is common, including many striking patterns not found in other breeds.

Temperament

The characteristic temperament of the Siberian Husky is friendly and gentle, but also alert and outgoing. He does not display the possessive qualities of the guard dog, nor is he overly suspicious of strangers or aggressive with other dogs. Some measure of reserve and dignity may be expected in the mature dog. His intelligence, tractability, and eager disposition make him an agreeable companion and willing worker.

Size

Height: dogs: 21 to 23½ inches at the withers. Bitches: 20 to 22 inches at the withers. *Weight:* dogs: 45 to 60 pounds. Bitches: 35 to 50 pounds. Weight is in proportion to height. The measurements mentioned above represent the extreme height and weight limits, with no preference given to either extreme. *Disqualification:* dogs over 23½ inches and bitches over 22 inches.

Summary

The most important breed characteristics of the Siberian Husky are medium size, moderate bone, well-balanced proportions, ease and freedom of movement, proper coat, pleasing head and ears, correct tail, and good disposition. Any appearance of excessive bone or weight, constricted or clumsy gait, or long, rough coat should be penalized. The Siberian Husky never appears so heavy or coarse as to suggest a freighting animal; nor is he so light and fragile as to suggest a sprint-racing animal. In both sexes the Siberian Husky gives the appearance of being capable of great endurance. In addition to the faults already noted, obvious structural faults common to all breeds are as undesirable in the Siberian Husky as in any other breed, even though they are not specifically mentioned herein.

DISQUALIFICATION
Dogs over 23½ inches and bitches over 22 inches.

Approved by the AKC 9 November 1971

KC(GB) VARIATION TO STANDARD
This dog is not granted championship status by the KC(GB).

STANDARD SCHNAUZER

Britain is the home of the Terriers, by far the majority of the breeds in the Group originating in that country, but there are Terriers in other countries, and particularly in Germany, Terriers which have existed in one form or another for centuries. The best known of these is the Schnauzer. He exists in three forms, the Schnauzer proper, known in some countries as the Standard Schnauzer or Medium Schnauzer, the Miniature Schnauzer or Zwergschnauzer and the Giant or Riesenschnauzer, all of which stem from a common stock dating back to around 1500. Central Europe has always had its Terriers, and it was from a mixture of several of these, probably the Schafer Pudel and the Wire-haired German Pinscher that this now very distinctive breed of dog was produced. The result of using one breed that was essentially a working dog and crossing it with another which was a Terrier, was a dog that combined most of the admirable characteristics of both, a strong, staunch positive sort of dog that was capable of doing most things likely to be required of it.

The breed first appeared in the show ring in the late part of the 19th century and gained such immediate popularity that a club was formed, a standard drawn up, and speciality shows soon held. Soon after the turn of the century the first was imported into the United States and was considered to be a Terrier and shown as such. There had been a certain amount of confusion concerning the naming of the breed, and both Schnauzers and Dobermans were being called Pinschers which for all practical purposes means Terrier. Later the breed was moved in the AKC from the Terrier Group to the Working Group whilst in Britain it was classified as one of the Utility dogs. The Schnauzer was introduced much later into Britain and it was not until 1928 that the first one appeared in the foreign dog class at Crufts.

He has never achieved the popularity that the Miniature Schnauzer has, and registration numbers are running at only about one tenth of the more popular little version. In Germany, with the change from agriculture to industry, the Schnauzer found a new role as a guard dog rather than the herder that he had undoubtedly been formerly, and in this he has proved very successful. He is a strong dog, very stout in limb, and a particularly active and ferocious guard. He is not vicious and will not normally persist in an attack, but his aspect is sufficient usually to deter intruders.

He has in recent years become reasonably popular as a show dog, especially in the Scandinavian countries, and a few very enthusiastic breeders have kept him in front of the public eye and he is regularly seen at most of the major shows. He is not a particularly easy dog to show as he has a good deal of the Terrier temperament and his coat needs considerable attention. Left in the rough he is a fairly ragged sort of individual, and it is only when an expert has spent some hours on his coat, trimming and shaping him, and brushing up on the legs and muzzle that he begins to look the picture of the smart Terrier type dog. He makes a very good guard indeed, and those who own a Schnauzer will say that there is not a better house dog and watchdog in the world.

OFFICIAL STANDARD

General appearance
The Standard Schnauzer is a robust, heavy-set dog, sturdily built with good muscle and plenty of bone; square-built in proportion of body-length to height. His nature combines high-spirited temperament with extreme reliability. His rugged build and dense harsh coat are accentuated by the hallmark of the breed, the arched eyebrows, bristly mustache, and luxuriant whiskers.

Head
Strong, rectangular, and elongated; narrowing slightly from the ears to the eyes and again to the tip of the nose. The total length of the head is about one half the length of the back measured from the withers to the set-on of the tail. The head matches the sex and substance of the dog. The top line of the muzzle is parallel with the top line of the skull. There is a slight stop which is accentuated by the wiry brows. *Skull (occiput to stop):* moderately broad between the ears with the width of the skull not exceeding two thirds the length of the skull. The skull must be flat; neither domed nor bumpy; skin unwrinkled. *Cheeks:* well-developed chewing muscles, but not so much that 'cheekiness' disturbs the rectangular head form. *Muzzle:* strong, and both parallel and equal in length to the top-skull; it ends in a moderately blunt wedge with wiry whiskers accenting the rectangular shape of the head.

Head and skull: strong and elongated skull, moderately broad, medium stop, crop-eared version.

Nose is large, black and full. The lips should be black, tight and not overlapping. *Eyes:* medium size; dark brown; oval in shape and turned forward; neither round nor protruding. The brow is arched and wiry, but vision is not impaired nor eyes hidden by too long an eyebrow. *Bite:* a full complement of white teeth, with a strong, sound scissors bite. The canine teeth are strong and well developed with the upper incisors slightly overlapping and engaging the lower. The upper and lower jaws are powerful and neither overshot nor undershot. *Faults:* a level bite is considered undesirable but a lesser fault than an overshot or undershot mouth. *Ears:* evenly shaped, set high and carried erect when cropped. If uncropped, they are small, V-shaped button ears of moderate thickness and carried rather high and close to the head.

Neck
Strong, of moderate thickness and length, elegantly arched and blending cleanly into the shoulders. The skin is tight, fitting closely to the dry throat with no wrinkles or dewlaps.

Shoulders
The sloping shoulder blades are strongly muscled, yet flat and well laid back so that the rounded upper ends are in a nearly vertical line above the elbows. They slope well forward to the point where they join the upper arm, forming as nearly as possible a right angle when seen from the side. Such an angulation permits the maximum forward extension of the forelegs without binding or effort.

Chest
Of medium width with well-sprung ribs, and if it could be seen in cross-section would be oval. The breastbone is plainly discernible. The brisket must descend at least to the elbows and ascend gradually to the rear with the belly moderately drawn up.

Body
Compact, strong, short-coupled and substantial so as to permit great flexibility and agility. The height at the highest point of the withers equals the length from breastbone to point or rump. *Faults:* too slender or shelly; too bulky or coarse; excessive tuck-up.

Back
Strong, stiff, straight and short, with a well-developed loin section; the distance from the last rib to the hips as short as possible. The top line of the back should not be absolutely horizontal, but should have a slightly descending slope from the first vertebra of the withers to the faintly curved croup and set-on of the tail.

Forelegs
Straight, vertical, and without any curvature when seen from all sides; set moderately far apart; with heavy bone; elbows set close to the body and pointing directly to the rear.

Hindquarters
Strongly muscled, in balance with the forequarters, never appearing higher than the shoulders. Croup full and slightly rounded. Thighs broad with well-bent stifles. The second thigh, from knee to hock, is approximately parallel with an extension of the upper-neck line. The legs, from the clearly defined hock joint to the feet, are short and perpendicular to the ground and when viewed from the rear are parallel to each other.

Feet
Small and compact, round with thick pads and strong black nails. The toes are well closed and arched (cat's paws) and pointing straight ahead. *Dewclaws:* dewclaws, if any, on the hind legs are generally removed. Dewclaws on the forelegs may be removed.

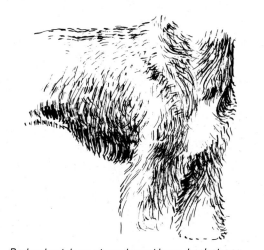
Body: chest deep, strong breast bone, back strong and straight.

Tail
Set moderately high and carried erect. It is docked to not less than 1 inch nor more than 2 inches. *Faults:* squirrel tail.

Height
Ideal height at the highest point of the shoulder blades, 18½ to 19½ inches for dogs and 17½ to 18½ inches for bitches. Dogs measuring over or under these limits must be faulted in proportion to the extent of the deviation. Dogs measuring more than one half inch over or under these limits must be disqualified.

Coat
Tight, hard, wiry and as thick as possible, composed of a soft, close undercoat and a harsh outer coat which, when seen against the grain, stands up off the back, lying neither smooth nor flat. The outer coat (body coat) is trimmed (by plucking) only to accent the body outline. When in show condition, the outer coat's proper length is approximately 1½ inches, except on the ears, head, neck, chest, belly and under the tail where it may be closely trimmed to give the desired typical appearance of the breed.
On the muzzle and over the eyes the coat lengthens to form luxuriant beard and eyebrows; the hair on the legs is longer than that on the body. These 'furnishings' should be of harsh texture and should not be so profuse so as to detract from the neat appearance or working capabilities of the dog. *Faults:* soft, smooth, curly, wavy or shaggy; too long or too short; too sparse or lacking undercoat; excessive furnishings; lack of furnishings.

Color
Pepper and salt or pure black. *Pepper and salt:* the typical pepper and salt color of the topcoat results from the combination of black and white hairs, and white hairs banded with black. Acceptable are all shades of pepper and salt from dark iron-gray to silver gray. Ideally, pepper and salt Standard Schnauzers have a gray undercoat, but a tan or fawn undercoat is not to be penalized. It is desirable to have a darker facial mask that harmonizes with the particular shade of coat color. Also, in pepper and salt dogs, the pepper and salt mixture may fade out to light gray or silver white in the eyebrows, whiskers, cheeks, under throat, across chest, under tail, leg furnishings, under body, and inside legs. *Black:* ideally the black Standard Schnauzer should be a true rich color, free from any fading or discoloration or any admixture of gray or tan hairs. The undercoat should also be solid black. However, increased age or continued exposure to the sun may cause a certain amount of fading and burning. A small white smudge on the chest is not a fault. Loss of color as a result of scars from cuts and bites is not a fault. *Faults:* any colors other than specified, and any shadings or mixtures thereof in the topcoat such as rust, brown, red, yellow or tan; absence of peppering; spotting or striping; a black streak down the back; or a black saddle without typical salt and pepper coloring—and gray hairs in the coat of a black; in blacks, any undercoat color other than black.

Gait
Sound, strong, quick, free, true and level gait with powerful, well-angulated hindquarters that reach out and cover ground. The forelegs reach out in a stride balancing that of the hindquarters. At a trot, the back remains firm and level, without swaying, rolling or roaching. When viewed from the rear, the feet, though they may appear to travel close when trotting, must not cross or strike. Increased speed causes feet to converge toward the center line of gravity. *Faults:* crabbing or weaving; paddling, rolling, swaying; short, choppy, stiff, stilted rear action; front legs that throw out or in (East and West movers); hackney gait, crossing over, or striking in front or rear.

FAULTS

Any deviation from the specifications in the Standard is to be considered a fault and should be penalized in proportion to the extent of the deviation. In weighing the seriousness of a fault, greatest consideration should be given to deviation from the desired alert, highly intelligent, spirited, reliable character of the Standard Schnauzer's desired general appearance of a robust, active, square-built, wire-coated dog. Dogs that are shy or appear to be highly nervous should be seriously faulted and dismissed from the ring. Vicious dogs shall be disqualified.

DISQUALIFICATIONS

Vicious dogs. Dogs under 18 inches or over 20 inches in height. Bitches under 17 inches or over 19 inches in height.

Approved by the AKC 14 May 1968

KC(GB) VARIATION TO STANDARD
This dog is granted championship status by the KC(GB) in the Utility Group of Non-Sporting Breeds. *Ears:* not cropped. *Tail:* cut down to 3 joints. *Height:* (ideal) dogs 19 inches, bitches 18 inches.

CARDIGAN WELSH CORGI

As long as Welshmen exist, the debate over the origin of the Corgi, and which variety came first, will continue. The protagonists of the Pembroke will insist that theirs was earlier, whilst those who favour the Cardigan will insist that their favourite breed not only existed before the Pembroke, but was probably responsible for all the other heelers and the Swedish Vallhund as well. Most opinion tends towards the Cardigan as being the more ancient of the two corgis, and there is little doubt that dogs used for rounding up and driving cattle were used in Wales centuries ago. These dogs were almost certainly short-legged, to enable them to move in quickly behind the cattle, give a sharp nip and escape before the resultant kick could reach them. It is odd, however, that many of the old books completely ignore the breed, and that it was not until the formation of the Welsh Corgi Club in 1926

NATIONAL GROUPING		
	Name	Number
AKC	Working Dogs	III
KC(GB)	Working	5
FCI	Herding Dogs	I

that attention was drawn to these attractive little dogs.

At first the two varieties were mixed, and were shown together, competing against one another for the challenge certificates offered by the Kennel Club, and it was only in 1934 that certificates were offered to both varieties. Fashion is unpredictable, and it is difficult to reason why it should be that the Pembroke variety should become one of the most popular dogs in the world, whilst the Cardigans remained very much in the background, with only a small number of enthusiasts keeping the breed alive. In recent years the Cardigan Corgi has had something of a revival and numbers crept slowly up, particularly in Australia.

The Cardigan is a sturdy little dog, heavy for its height, and with strong short legs that carry it over the ground at a remarkable speed and allow it to whip round quickly in its own length. He is a real all-weather dog, being just as happy in the pouring rain as basking in sunshine, and staunch enough to face up to exercise all day without undue tiring. His coat is hard and water-resistant and his very sharp hearing allows him to wander considerable distances and still retain contact with his owner.

As a show dog he is much admired for his steady character. He rarely shows nerves in the ring, and whilst suspicious of strangers, he allows himself to be handled rather than encouraging it.

Temperamentally he is somewhat stolid compared with many other breeds, tending to enjoy a romp with others of his kind rather than with people. With those to whom he becomes attached, however, he is remarkably companionable, affectionate without being over-fussy, and attentive without fawning. He is an even tempered dog, both with people and with other dogs, and will rarely enter a fight unless forced into it, preferring to retain his somewhat aloof exterior whilst other and lesser canines join battle. He does retain the working instinct, and can easily be trained to be quite obedient, obeying commands at quite long distances as he once needed to when working with cattle.

OFFICIAL STANDARD

General appearance
Low-set, sturdily built, with heavy bone and deep chest. Over-all silhouette long in proportion to height, culminating in low tail-set and foxlike brush. Expression alert and foxy, watchful yet friendly.

General impression
A handsome, powerful, small dog, capable of both speed and endurance, intelligent, sturdy, but not coarse.

Head and skull
Skull moderately wide and flat between the ears, with definite though moderate stop. *Muzzle:* to measure about 3 inches in length, or in proportion to the skull as 3 to 5. Muzzle medium, *i.e.* neither too pointed nor too blunt but somewhat less fine than the Pembroke. *Nose:* black.

Nostrils of moderate size. Under-jaw clean-cut and strong. *Eyes:* medium to large, and rather widely set, with distinct corners. Color dark to dark amber but clear. Blue eyes, or one dark and one blue eye, permissible in blue merles. *Mouth:* teeth strong and regular, neither overshot nor undershot. Pincer (level) bite permissible but scissors bite preferred, *e.g.*, the inner side of the front teeth resting closely over the front of the lower front teeth. *Ears:* large and prominent in proportion to size of dog. Slightly rounded at the tips, moderately wide at the base, and carried erect, set well apart and well back, sloping slightly forward when erect. Flop ears a serious fault.

Neck
Muscular, well developed, especially in dogs, and in proportion to dog's build; fitting into strong, well-shaped shoulders.

Forequarters
Chest broad, deep, and well let down between forelegs. Forelegs short, and slightly bowed around chest, and with distinct but not exaggerated crook below the carpus. Elbows close to side. A straight, terrier-like front is a fault.

Body
Long and strong, with deep brisket, well-sprung ribs with moderate tuck-up of loin. Topline level except for slight slope of spine above tail.

Hindquarters
Strong, with muscular thighs. Legs short and well boned.

Feet
Round and well padded. Hind dewclaws, if any, should be removed. Front dewclaws may be removed.

Tail
Long to moderately long, resembling a fox brush. Should be set fairly low on body line, carried low when standing or moving slowly, streaming out when at a dead run, lifted when tracking or excited, but never curled over the back. A rat tail or a whip tail are faults.

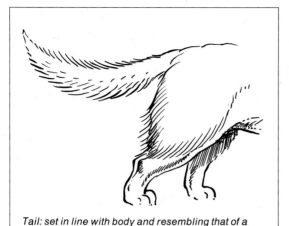

Tail: set in line with body and resembling that of a fox.

Size

Height approximately 12 inches at the highest point of the shoulder blades. Length usually between 36 and 44 inches from nose to tip of tail. In considering the height, weight, and length of a dog, over-all balance is a prime factor.

Colors

Red, sable, red-brindle, black-brindle, black, tri-color, blue merle. Usually with white flashings on chest, neck, feet, face or tip of tail. No preferences among these colors. A dog predominantly white in color should be seriously faulted. Pure white is a disqualification.

DISQUALIFICATIONS
A distinctly long coat. Pure white.

Approved by the AKC 11 February 1967

Coat

Medium length but dense. Slightly harsh texture, but neither wiry nor silky. Weather-resistant. An overly short coat or a long and silky and/or curly coat are faults. Normal grooming and trimming of whiskers is permitted. Any trimming that alters the natural length of the coat is not permitted and is a serious fault. A distinctly long coat is a disqualification.

KC(GB) VARIATION TO STANDARD

Skull: slightly domed above eyes, nose black except in blue merles. *Eyes:* silver eyes permissible in blue merles. *Ears:* set about 3½ inches apart. *Feet:* rather large. *Weight:* dogs 22 to 26 pounds; bitches 20 to 24 pounds.

PEMBROKE WELSH CORGI

NATIONAL GROUPING		
	Name	Number
AKC	Working Dogs	III
KC(GB)	Working	5
FCI	Herding Dogs	I

It is difficult to understand why when two breeds of dog are so close together in appearance, temperament and origin as the two varieties of Corgi, one should remain fairly rare whilst the other is to be seen on every street corner. The Cardigan is still a comparatively rare breed, whilst the Pembroke is one of the most popular breeds in the world. The origins of the two varieties are so closely interwoven that there can be no doubt that at one time they were one and the same breed, used for centuries in the Welsh hills for the herding of cattle. They were probably used for sheep too, and almost certainly for the herds of small Welsh Ponies that run wild on the hills of some parts of Wales. It is interesting that although almost every book that deals with the breed mentions its antiquity, no book prior to the turn of the century mentions them at all.

It was in 1926 that the Welsh Corgi Club was formed, but its interests covered both varieties, the Pembroke and the Cardigan, and though challenge certificates were granted in 1928, they were for competition between both types. The division did not come about until 1934, and from that time the Pembroke Welsh Corgi has never looked back, increasing in popularity at a tremendous rate, and becoming one of the most popular pet dogs in the world. The enormous growth in recent years has undoubtedly been partly due to the fact that the breed became the favourite of the British Royal Family. The Queen owns a number, and is frequently seen, either being greeted by them on her return from overseas, or bidding them farewell before leaving the country. The registration figures of the breed reached a peak in the late sixties in Britain, since when they have shown some decline, but their popularity in other countries, particularly in Australia and South Africa does not appear to be on the wane.

The Pembroke Corgi is a slightly smaller dog than the Cardigan, the head is generally sharper and the ears smaller. He is a thoroughly sturdy little dog, and although his popularity as a pet may have generally softened him, a fit Pembroke is still very much the tough little working dog, very muscular, and still capable of considerable exercise without distress in spite of his short legs. He is a particularly clean, neat little dog and fits well into modern living conditions, being easily trained, intelligent and obedient, and not subject to some of the ailments to which other dogs are prone.

As a show dog he is a near perfect subject especially if he is shown as a hobby. He is easily fed and housed, small enough to transport in numbers, grooming is no problem, and he is so easily trained to behave well and comport himself with dignity in the ring, that even very young puppies can be trained to show like veterans. He is a dog that is anxious to please, and his reactions to people bred into him from generations of being a working dog housed under small-family conditions, are friendly and willing.

Temperamentally he is completely suited to the life of a pet dog. If he has a vice at all, and it is by no means certain that he has, it could be gluttony, and his appealing expression has such an effect on people, and especially children, that many that are kept as pets become overweight. He is one of the most friendly of dogs, being particularly attached to children with whom he loves to play, prefers a game to a fight at any time, and is great fun to have either in the house or on country walks. As a working dog he is not easily tired, and his enthusiasm for investigation and native inquisitiveness make him the ideal companion for the country life as he entertains himself. He has the additional advantage of being an excellent guard, being naturally suspicious of strangers and with a strongly developed sense of territory.

OFFICIAL STANDARD

General appearance
Low-set, strong, sturdily built and active, giving an impression of substance and stamina in a small space. Should not be so low and heavy-boned as to appear coarse or overdone, nor so light-boned as to appear racy. Outlook bold, but kindly. Expression intelligent and interested. Never shy nor vicious.

Size and proportions
Moderately long and low. The distance from the withers to base of tail should be approximately 40 per cent greater than the distance from the withers to the ground. *Height:* (from ground to highest point on withers) should be 10 to 12 inches. *Weight:* is in proportion to size, not exceeding 30 pounds for dogs and 28 pounds for bitches. In show condition, the preferred medium-size dog of correct bone and substance will weigh approximately 27 pounds, with bitches approximately 25 pounds. Obvious oversized specimens and diminutive toylike individuals must be very seriously penalized.

Head and skull
Head to be foxy in shape and appearance, but not sly in expression. Skull to be fairly wide and flat between the ears. Moderate amount of stop. Very slight rounding of cheek, and not filled in below the eyes, as foreface should be nicely chiseled to give a somewhat tapered muzzle. Distance from the occiput to center of stop to be greater than the distance from stop to nose tip, the proportion being five parts of total distance for the skull and three parts for the foreface. Muzzle should be neither dish-faced nor Roman-nosed. *Nose:* black and fully pigmented.

Eyes
Oval, medium in size, not round nor protruding, nor deep-set and piglike. Set somewhat obliquely. Variations of brown in harmony with coat color. Eye rims dark, preferably black. While dark eyes enhance the expression, true black eyes are most undesirable, as are yellow or bluish eyes.

Ears
Erect, firm, and of medium size, tapering slightly to a rounded point. Ears are mobile, and react sensitively to sounds. A line drawn from the nose tip through the eyes to the ear tips, and across, should form an approximate equilateral triangle. Bat ears, small catlike ears, large weak ears, hooded ears, ears carried too high or too low, are undesirable. Button, rose or drop ears are very serious faults.

Mouth
Scissors bite, the inner side of the upper incisors touching the outer side of the lower incisors. Level bite is acceptable. Lips should be tight, with little or no fullness, and black. Overshot or undershot bite is a very serious fault.

Neck
Fairly long, of sufficient length to provide over-all balance of the dog. Slightly arched, clean and blending well into

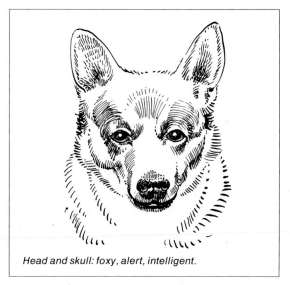
Head and skull: foxy, alert, intelligent.

the shoulders. A very short neck giving a stuffy appearance, and a long, thin or ewe neck, are faulty.

Body
Rib cage should be well sprung, slightly egg-shaped, and moderately long. Deep chest, well let down between forelegs. Exaggerated lowness interferes with the desired freedom of movement and should be penalized. Viewed from above, the body should taper slightly to end of the loin. Loin short. Firm level topline, neither riding up to nor falling away at the croup. A slight depression behind the shoulders caused by heavier neck coat meeting the shorter body coat is permissible. Round or flat rib cage, lack of brisket, extreme length or cobbiness, are undesirable.

Forequarters
Legs short; forearms turned slightly inward, with the distance between the wrists less than between the shoulder joints, so that the front does not appear absolutely straight. Ample bone carried right down into the feet. Pasterns firm and nearly straight when viewed from the side. Weak pasterns and knuckling over are serious faults. Shoulder blades long and well laid back along the rib cage. Upper arms nearly equal in length to shoulder blades. Elbows parallel to the body, not prominent, and well set back to allow a line perpendicular to the ground to be drawn from the tip of the shoulder blade through to elbow.

Hindquarters
Ample bone, strong and flexible, moderately angulated at stifle and hock. Exaggerated angulation is as faulty as too little. Thighs should be well muscled. Hocks short, parallel, and when viewed from the side are perpendicular to the ground. Barrel hocks or cowhocks are most objectionable. Slipped or double-jointed hocks are very faulty.

Tail
Docked as short as possible without being indented.

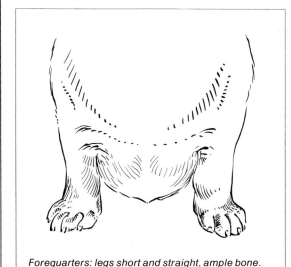

Forequarters: legs short and straight, ample bone.

Occasionally a puppy is born with a natural dock, which if sufficiently short, is acceptable. A tail up to two inches in length is allowed, but if carried high tends to spoil the contour of the topline.

Feet
Oval, with the two center toes slightly in advance of the two outer ones. Turning neither in nor out. Pads strong and feet arched. Nails short. Dewclaws on both forelegs and hind legs usually removed. Too round, long and narrow, or splayed feet are faulty.

Movement
Free and smooth. Forelegs should reach well forward, without too much lift, in unison with the driving action of hind legs. The correct shoulder assembly and well-fitted elbows allow the long, free stride in front. Viewed from the front, legs do not move in exact parallel planes, but incline slightly inward to compensate for shortness of leg and width of chest. Hind legs should drive well under the body and move on a line with the forelegs, with hocks turning neither in nor out. Feet must travel parallel to the line of motion with no tendency to swing out, cross over, or interfere with each other. Short, choppy movement, rolling or high-stepping gait, close or overly wide coming or going, are incorrect. This is a herding dog which must have the agility, freedom of movement, and endurance to do the work for which he was developed.

Color
The outer coat is to be of self colors in red, sable, fawn, black and tan, with or without white markings. White is acceptable on legs, chest, neck (either in part or as a collar), muzzle, underparts, and as a narrow blaze on head.

VERY SERIOUS FAULTS
Whitelies: body color white with red or dark markings. *Mismarks:* self colors with any area of white on back between withers and tail, on sides between elbows and back of hindquarters, or on ears. Black with white markings and no tan present. *Bluies:* colored portions of the coat have a distinct bluish or smoky cast. This coloring is associated with extremely light or blue eyes and liver or gray rims, nose and lip pigment.

Coat
Medium length; short, thick, weather-resistant undercoat with a coarser, longer outer coat. Over-all length varies, with slightly thicker and longer ruff around neck, chest and on the shoulders. The body coat lies flat. Hair is slightly longer on back of forelegs and underparts, and somewhat fuller and longer on rear of hindquarters. The coat is preferably straight, but some waviness is permitted. This breed has a shedding coat, and seasonal lack of undercoat should not be too severely penalized, providing the hair is glossy, healthy, and well groomed. A wiry, tightly marcelled coat is very faulty, as is an overly short, smooth and thin coat.

VERY SERIOUS FAULT
Fluffies: a coat of extreme length with exaggerated feathering on ears, chest, legs and feet, underparts and hindquarters. Trimming such a coat does not make it any more acceptable.

The Corgi should be shown in its natural condition, with no trimming permitted except to tidy the feet, and, if desired, remove the whiskers.

OVER-ALL PICTURE
Correct type, including general balance and outline, attractiveness of head-piece, intelligent outlook and correct temperament, is of primary importance. Movement is especially important, particularly as viewed from the side. A dog with smooth and free gait has to be reasonably sound and must be highly regarded. A minor fault must never take precedence over the above desired qualities.

A dog must be very seriously penalized for the following faults, regardless of whatever desirable qualities the dog may present: Whitelies, Mismarks or Bluies; Fluffies; Button, Rose or Drop Ears; Overshot or Undershot Bite; Oversize or Undersize.

The judge shall dismiss from the ring any Pembroke Welsh Corgi that is vicious or excessively shy.

Approved by the AKC 13 June 1972

KC(GB) VARIATION TO STANDARD
Tail: short, preferably natural. *Weight:* dogs 20 to 24 pounds, bitches 18 to 22 pounds.

GROUP IV: TERRIERS

Airedale Terrier

American Staffordshire Terrier

Australian Terrier

Border Terrier

Bull Terrier

Bedlington Terrier

Bull Terrier
(Miniature)

Cairn Terrier

Irish Terrier

Dandie Dinmont Terrier

Fox Terrier (Wire)

Kerry Blue Terrier

Lakeland Terrier

Manchester Terrier

Miniature Schnauzer

Norwich Terrier

Scottish Terrier

Sealyham Terrier

Skye Terrier

Soft-coated Wheaten Terrier

Staffordshire Bull Terrier

Welsh Terrier

West Highland White Terrier

GROUP IV: TERRIERS

This Group is fairly recent in its development. The very name 'Terrier', which refers to the native inclination to dig into the ground, infers that most of the breeds included in the Group grew up with domestication and industry. They are largely vermin hunters, have little to do with the more ancient sports, and have never needed to take upon themselves the mantle of the sheep-herding dogs or the game hunters. For some reason which is difficult to explain, the majority of the Terriers originated in Britain. It is not logical to suppose, as some of the older writers did, that this resulted from their use by hunts, as the basic stock from which they descended must have existed long before fox-hunting became fashionable. They were certainly known in the 15th century as Dame Juliana Berners included them in her list of types.

They all have one thing in common, and that is that given the opportunity they will dig and attempt to go to ground after vermin. This has become difficult for some breeds as they have been evolved and perfected to be too long in the leg for the purpose, for example one cannot imagine an Airedale having much success attempting to dig out a rabbit. Nicholas Cox in 1677 divided the Terriers of his time into two groups, the short-haired and the crook-legged type which in his words 'will take earth well, and will lie very long at fox or badger' and the long-legged shaggy sort which will not only hunt above ground but will also enter the earth with much fury. At the time that Cox was writing this would probably have been the only general division, but since then things have changed considerably.

In the first instance a great deal of selective breeding has taken place to produce dogs of very differing types. This process was speeded up with the advent of the dog show, and whole new breeds have appeared. In addition, there were a number of Terriers which by accidents of geography were being bred along fairly rigid lines in Ireland and the islands off the coast of Scotland. These developments not only produced different breeds of dogs for different forms of fox-hunting with packs of hounds, but as fashions changed, even produced entirely different types for other purposes. The country sport of badger digging demanded a much stronger dog than the ordinary Terriers used for the fox, and crosses with Bulldogs were resorted to which produced formidable terriers with fighting instincts. These were encouraged and resulted in yet another sport, that of dog fighting.

Generally speaking the smaller Terriers were used by working men for a little weekend sport hunting rats around the industrial buildings that mushroomed as the result of the country's greatly increased dependence on coal and steel. The middle-sized Terriers with rather longer legs such as the Fox Terriers and the Border Terriers remained the favourites of the hunts and were used in conjunction with packs of hounds to drive the fox from his earth or hold him there until the huntsmen could dig him out. The more heavily built low-to-ground Terriers such as the Sealyham and the Dandie Dinmont proved to be the best badger dogs, their greater strength and stronger jaws dealing effectively with their much stronger and fiercer quarry, whilst the more recent developments from the Bulldog and Terrier crosses became the fighting dogs of the 18th century.

Dog fighting became illegal, the badger became a subject for preservation, and the number of hunts declined over the past hundred years. Fortunately, however, the Terriers prospered as show dogs and from the very early days of dog shows the Terriers held a very important position. In Britain dog shows first started as one of the pastimes of the working man, taking place in public houses, and being an increasingly important recreation towards the latter part of the 18th century. Many areas had produced their own breeds of Terrier in which the locals took a great deal of pride so that there was always considerable rivalry for instance between the men of Bedlington and those of Manchester. They tended to look down on such things as Spaniels as foreign dogs, and Terriers became very popular. Unfortunately the golden age did not last, and at shows today the Terrier breeds are on the whole the worst supported.

AIREDALE TERRIER

NATIONAL GROUPING		
	Name	Number
AKC	Terriers	IV
KC(GB)	Terrier	3
FCI	Terriers	3

The word 'terrier' when applied to a dog, implies the ability to go to ground, and to call a dog as large as an Airedale a Terrier seems to many people to be a complete misuse of the word. Yet in fact he is the absolute essence of Terrier, and is known as the King of the Terriers, not just because of his size, but because he combines all the Terrier characteristics. He is a fairly recent dog, having been produced in the area of the valley of the river Aire in South Yorkshire around the middle of the 19th century, probably as the result of crossing the old fashioned black and tan hard-coated northern tyke with the Otterhound. The natives of Yorkshire have always been sportsmen, and have for centuries been interested in animals, dogs in particular, and the production of new varieties. They will redesign the canary, grow new varieties of chrysanthemums or produce a new strain of dog at the drop of a hat. Otter hunting was a favourite sport in the valleys of the Aire and the Wharfe where several packs were kept, and there were always at one time a number of hounds in private ownership. Ratting, and the casual sport of hunting vermin has been going on in the county for as long as people can remember, and when the sportsmen of the Otley district decided that they wanted a large game terrier-type dog, it was natural for them to take the two available types and cross them. The dog that resulted, having been perfected, is not only the largest of the true Terriers, but is a noble animal worthy of the county of the White Rose.

In the early years he was known as the Waterside Terrier or the Bingley Terrier, and he was not the smart dog that he is today, being bad in colour, shaggy in appearance and with rather large ears. But after about twenty years the breed had settled down and in 1883 three classes were scheduled at the Birmingham Show and by 1886 the breed was recognised and admitted to the stud book. From this time onwards the breed progressed both in numbers and in quality, the coat and colour improving and the hound type gradually disappearing in favour of a true Terrier. Just before the turn of the century the Airedale Terrier Club was formed and the success of the breed was assured.

He is one of the finest guards and protectors of property in the canine world, and many a successful show dog has first been discovered as a yard dog in South Yorkshire. He has proved his value in this respect in many countries, and especially in those places where protection against wild animals is needed, as he is completely fearless and willing to tackle anything. During the First World War he was trained as a messenger dog and sentry, and has even been trained for police work. In recent years, however, it has been as a show dog that he has proved supreme, winning major awards at the larger shows throughout the world.

As with most of the hard-coated Terriers, a considerable amount of work is involved in his preparation for show, as the coat has to be shaped and trimmed to make the most of his smart outline. This can be tedious work that goes on for a fairly lengthy period before a show, and it is for this reason that many of these dogs are in the hands of professional handlers who are experts at presentation and who know the short cuts to success. He is still, however, very much in demand as a guard and house dog, as his qualities of faithfulness and affection to the members of the family are well known.

OFFICIAL STANDARD

Head

Should be well balanced with little apparent difference between the length of skull and foreface. *Skull:* should be long and flat, not too broad between the ears and narrow-

Head: stop hardly visible, cheeks level, foreface well filled.

ing very slightly to the eyes. Scalp should be free from wrinkles, stop hardly visible and cheeks level and free from fullness. *Ears:* should be V-shaped with carriage rather to the side of the head, not pointing to the eyes, small but not out of proportion to the size of the dog. The topline of the folded ear should be above the level of the skull. *Foreface:* should be deep, powerful, strong and muscular. Should be well filled up before the eyes. *Eyes:* should be dark, small, not prominent, full of terrier expression, keenness and intelligence. *Lips:* should be tight. *Nose:* should be black and not too small. *Teeth:* should be strong and white, free from discoloration or defect. Bite either level or vise-like. A slightly overlapping or scissors bite is permissible without preference.

Neck

Should be of moderate length and thickness gradually widening towards the shoulders. Skin tight, not loose.

Shoulders and chest

Shoulders long and sloping well into the back. Shoulder blades flat. From the front, chest deep but not broad. The depth of the chest should be approximately on a level with the elbows.

Body

Back should be short, strong and level. Ribs well sprung. Loins muscular and of good width. There should be but little space between the last rib and the hip joint.

Hindquarters

Should be strong and muscular with no droop.

Tail

The root of the tail should be set well up on the back. It should be carried gaily but not curled over the back. It

should be of good strength and substance and of fair length.

Legs

Forelegs: should be perfectly straight, with plenty of muscle and bone. *Elbows:* should be perpendicular to the body, working free of sides. *Thighs:* should be long and powerful with muscular second thigh, stifles well bent, not turned either in or out, hocks well let down parallel with each other when viewed from behind. *Feet:* should be small, round and compact with a good depth of pad, well cushioned; the toes moderately arched, not turned either in or out.

Coat

Should be hard, dense and wiry, lying straight and close, covering the dog well over the body and legs. Some of the hardest are crinkling or just slightly waved. At the base of the hard very stiff hair should be a shorter growth of softer hair termed the undercoat.

Color

The head and ears should be tan, the ears being of a darker shade than the rest. Dark markings on either side of the skull are permissible. The legs up to the thighs and elbows and the under-part of the body and chest are also tan and the tan frequently runs into the shoulder. The sides and upper parts of the body should be black or dark grizzle. A red mixture is often found in the black and is not to be considered objectionable. A small white blaze on the chest is a characteristic of certain strains of the breed.

Size

Dogs should measure approximately 23 inches in height at the shoulder; bitches, slightly less. Both sexes should be sturdy, well muscled and boned

Movement

Movement or action is the crucial test of conformation. Movement should be free. As seen from the front the forelegs should swing perpendicular from the body free from the sides, the feet the same distance apart as the elbows. As seen from the rear the hind legs should be parallel with each other, neither too close nor too far apart, but so placed as to give a strong well-balanced stance and movement. The toes should not be turned either in or out.

FAULTS

Yellow eyes, hound ears, white feet, soft coat, being much over or under the size limit, being undershot or overshot, having poor movement, are faults which should be severely penalized.

SCALE OF POINTS

Head (10). Neck, shoulders and chest (10). Body (10). Hindquarters and tail (10). Legs and feet (10). Coat (10). Color (5). Size (10). Movement (10). General characteristics and expression (15). *Total (100).*

Approved by the AKC 14 July 1959

AMERICAN STAFFORDSHIRE TERRIER

NATIONAL GROUPING		
	Name	Number
AKC	Terriers	IV
KC(GB)	—	–
FCI	Terriers	3

This breed is a typical example of a split in a breed resulting eventually in two distinct breeds. The division by ears of the Norwich and Norfolk Terriers is another. The American Staffordshire Terrier and the Staffordshire Bull Terrier were originally one and the same animal, resulting from a cross between the Bulldog and the old English Smooth Terrier. In Britain the result remained the Staffordshire Bull Terrier, and was recognised as such in 1935. He was not, however, recognised in the United States of America at that time, but the Staffordshire Terrier was, and the name was changed to the American Staffordshire Terrier in 1972. In the meantime the Staffordshire Bull Terrier had been growing in status and numbers in Britain, and in 1974 he too was recognised as a different breed by the American Kennel Club. This means that two breeds with a common ancestry and many similarities of appearance now exist in the United States.

In Britain the size of the breed was kept down, the height at the shoulder being fourteen to sixteen inches, and it was here that the major change took place. In America it was decided that a bigger dog was desirable, and the standard requires a male to be between eighteen and nineteen inches high with weight in proportion. A glance at other breeds shows that a fully grown dog could weigh around forty-five pounds.

It was in the late 19th century that the Staffordshire dog first arrived in America. He was known at that time as the Pit Dog because of his association with the rat pit and the dog fighting pit, as it was in this particular sphere that his considerable abilities as a fighting dog were usually employed. There is little doubt that this now illegal, so-called sport, was as much enjoyed in the early days in his new country as it was in the old.

It has really only been in this century that the qualities of the dog have been fully appreciated. His admission to register was held up in Britain by the fact that he was always associated with what were considered to be the rougher and less gentlemanly elements of society. In fact the 'gentry' as they were known, were frequenters of dog fights albeit often in disguise, and were certainly the heaviest betters. It was comparable with cock fighting, in that although it was frowned upon, a blind eye was turned upon it by the authorities for fear that the squire, the local doctor or even the mayor might be present!

Like his British cousin, the American Staffordshire Terrier is a remarkably strong dog for his size, built with tremendous power in both his sholders and his hindquarters, but with a gracefulness that reminds one of the well-trained boxer, always ready for anything, and always on his toes.

He will never turn tail on anything however large, looking around himself constantly in the ring or out of it, facing up to other and often considerably larger dogs with a positive though not threatening attitude. He will not pick a fight, but he will never run away from one, and his very attitude frequently deters potential opposition which usually discovers that it has a pressing engagement elsewhere. With people he is the essence of kindness and affection, and makes a wonderful companion for either children or the elderly, being very possessive and a good guard.

OFFICIAL STANDARD

General impression
The American Staffordshire Terrier should give the impression of great strength for his size, a well put-together dog, muscular, but agile and graceful, keenly alive to his surroundings. He should be stocky, not long-legged or racy in outline. His courage is proverbial.

Head
Medium length, deep through, broad skull, very pronounced cheek muscles, distinct stop; and ears are set high. *Ears:* cropped or uncropped, the latter preferred. Uncropped ears should be short and held half rose or prick. Full drop to be penalized. *Eyes:* dark and round, low down in skull and set far apart. No pink eyelids. *Muzzle:* medium length, rounded on upper side to fall away abruptly below eyes. Jaws well defined. Underjaw

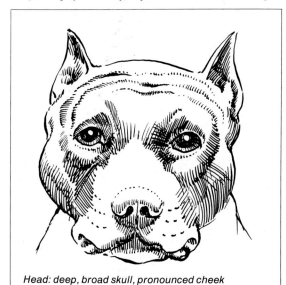

Head: deep, broad skull, pronounced cheek muscles, distinct stop, cropped-eared version.

to be strong and have biting power. Lips close and even, no looseness. Upper teeth to meet tightly outside lower teeth in front. Nose definitely black.

Neck
Heavy, slightly arched, tapering from shoulders to back of skull. No looseness of skin. Medium length.

Shoulders
Strong and muscular with blades wide and sloping.

Back
Fairly short. Slight sloping from withers to rump with gentle short slope at rump to base of tail. Loins slightly tucked.

Body
Well-sprung ribs, deep in rear. All ribs close together. Forelegs set rather wide apart to permit of chest development. Chest deep and broad.

Tail
Short in comparison to size, low set, tapering to a fine point; not curled or held over back. Not docked.

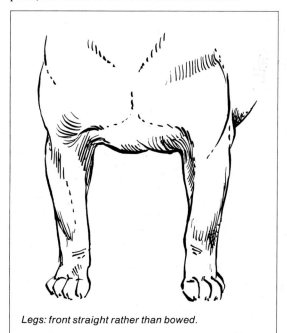

Legs: front straight rather than bowed.

Legs
The front legs should be straight, large or round bones, pastern upright. No resemblance of bend in front. Hindquarters well-muscled, let down at hocks, turning neither in nor out. Feet of moderate size, well-arched and compact. Gait must be springy but without roll or pace.

Coat
Short, close, stiff to the touch, and glossy.

Color
Any color, solid, parti, or patched is permissible, but all white, more than 80 per cent white, black and tan, and liver not to be encouraged.

Size
Height and weight should be in proportion. A height of about 18 to 19 inches at shoulders for the dog and 17 to 18 inches for the bitch is to be considered preferable.

Faults
Faults to be penalized are: Dudley nose, light or pink eyes, tail too long or badly carried, undershot or overshot mouths.

Approved by the AKC 10 June 1936

KC(GB) VARIATION TO STANDARD
This dog is not granted championship status by the KC(GB).

AUSTRALIAN TERRIER

NATIONAL GROUPING		
	Name	Number
AKC	Terriers	IV
KC(GB)	Terrier	3
FCI	Terriers	3

The history of the Australian Terrier is comparatively recent, as it was not exhibited until 1872, when it was shown in Melbourne as a Broken-coated Terrier of blackish blue sheen. By 1880 it had become the Blue and Tan, by 1884 the Toy, in 1888 it was the Blue Terrier and finally in 1900 it was shown as the Rough-coated Terrier, Blue and Tan. It has been reported that early in the 19th century settlers in Tasmania were breeding broken-coated terriers that were blue and tan and were excellent guards and weighed around ten pounds. By 1906 this little dog was being shown in Britain, though he did not achieve breed status until 1933, and was even later in the United States of America where he arrived during the first quarter of the century and was finally recognised in 1960.

It is almost certain that the Australian Terrier and the Australian Silky Terrier shared a common ancestry, both descending from the old broken-coated terriers of Tasmania, New South Wales and Victoria. That dog in its turn probably resulted from crossing the Skye, the Dandie Dinmont and the Scottish Terrier, traces of all of these appearing in the present breed. From the Skye came the coat, from the Scottie the head and conformation and from the Dandie the tendency towards a soft topknot. From time to time Yorkshire Terrier blood was introduced to improve colour and even later the Manchester, to give the breed a better tan. At some stage the Australian Terrier and the Silky Terrier parted company, and whilst the Silky was bred down to a size to conform with the requirements of the Toy dog Group, the other became the hard-bitten tough little Terrier that we see today.

There is no question that he is tough, for his size he is a bundle of terrier characteristics, being sharp in his reactions, tough with other dogs, and a splendid little hunting dog. For some time he was essentially a blue and tan dog, but Mr. McPharlane of Adelaide introduced the red colour, probably by using a Cairn Terrier cross, so that now, whilst the blue and tans predominate, some reds are regularly seen. He is one of the smallest of the working Terriers, standing only ten inches at the withers and weighing a mere twelve to fourteen pounds, but his air of importance makes him appear a much larger dog. He was used as a guard in Australia for farms and mines, and even looked after flocks of sheep, where his keen eyesight and hearing permitted him to give early warning of danger and his native fierceness was sufficient to deter anything but the boldest predator.

He makes a smart little show dog, very little preparation being needed to keep him in show trim as he is not heavily coated, and his love of exercise and will to work, keeps him in fine muscular condition. He is an affectionate and generally quiet little dog for a Terrier, and makes a very pleasing housedog and pet, being well mannered and very good with children.

OFFICIAL STANDARD

General appearance
Small, sturdy, rough-coated terrier of spirited action and self-assured manner.

Head
Long, flat-skulled, and full between the eyes, with the stop moderate. The muzzle is no longer than the distance from the eyes to the occiput. Jaws long and powerful,

Head and skull: long, skull flat, long powerful jaw.

teeth of good size meeting in a scissors bite, although a level bite is acceptable. *Nose:* black. *Ears:* set high on the skull and well apart. They are small and pricked, the leather either pointed or slightly rounded and free from long hairs. *Eyes:* small, dark, and keen in expression; not prominent. Light-colored and protruding eyes are faulty.

Neck
Inclined to be long, and tapering into sloping shoulders; well furnished with hair which forms a protective ruff.

Body
Low-set and slightly longer from the withers to the root of the tail than from the withers to the ground. *Chest:* medium wide, and deep, with ribs well sprung but not round. Topline level.

Tail
Set on high and carried erect but not too gay; docked leaving two fifths.

Legs and feet
Forelegs straight and slightly feathered to the carpus or so-called knee; they are set well under the body with elbows close and pasterns strong. Hindquarters strong and well muscled but not heavy; legs moderately angulated at stifles and hocks, with hocks well let down. Bone medium in size. Feet are small, clean, and catlike, the toes arched and compact, nicely padded and free from long hair. Nails strong and black.

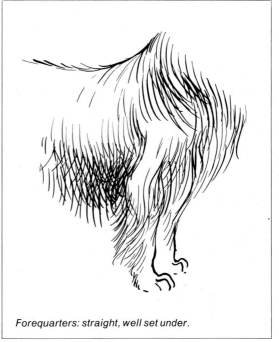
Forequarters: straight, well set under.

Coat
Outer coat harsh and straight, and about two and one half inches all over the body. Undercoat short and soft. The topknot, which covers only the top of the skull, is of finer texture and lighter color than the body coat.

Color
May be blue-black or silver-black, with rich tan markings on head and legs, sandy color or clear red. The blue-black is bluish at the roots and dark at the tips. In the silver-blacks each hair carries black and silver alternating with black at the tips. The tan is rich and deep, the richer the better. In the sandies, any suggestion of smuttiness is undesirable.

Gait
Straight and true; sprightly, indicating spirit and assurance.

Temperament
That of a hard-bitten terrier, with the aggressiveness of the natural ratter and hedge hunter, but as a companion, friendly, affectionate, and biddable.

Size
Shoulder height, about 10 inches. Average weight 12 to 14 pounds.

Approved by the AKC 13 October 1970

KC(GB) VARIATION TO STANDARD
Ears: pricked or dropped towards the front. *Weight and size:* average weight 10 to 11 pounds. *Faults:* flesh coloured toe nails or nose; white on feet; white breast; curly or woolly coat; all black coat (puppies excepted). Overshot or undershot mouths.

BEDLINGTON TERRIER

A mason named Joseph Aynsley can claim the credit for naming this delicate yet gamest of Terriers. It was previously known as the Rothbury Terrier or the Northern Counties Fox Terrier, but in 1825 Aynsley christened it the Bedlington Terrier and the name had a certain ring about it and it stuck. His bitch, called Phoebe came from a friend of his at Alnwick and was mated to a Rothbury dog and they produced the dogs that became the first of the Bedlington Terriers. The North country working man has always been involved in developing new varieties of almost everything and in the Newcastle area he set about producing a dog that

NATIONAL GROUPING		
	Name	Number
AKC	Terriers	IV
KC(GB)	Terrier	3
FCI	Terriers	3

was distinctive, particular to the area, and capable of helping him enjoy himself, and from time to time to assist in feeding the family. He took Aynsley's dog, and by the introduction of other blood, probably the Whippet to give some speed and the Dandie Dinmont to give the coat and the Terrier toughness that that breed has in abundance, he produced the sort of dog he wanted.

He was capable of joining the steelworker on a mornings ratting around the warehouse and factories of his native Northumberland and Durham, and, if the gamekeeper happened not to be on the lookout, would sneak off into the nearby fields and catch a rabbit which would help out the meagre rations of the family. In 1877 the National Bedlington Club was formed in England to further the interest of the breed and put him before the public. In this the club at first failed, and at the Crystal Palace show of 1895, only six dogs were shown which was certainly less than the number exhibited at the first show for the breed held in Bedlington in 1870. Since that time there has been a steady increase as the breed was taken up by fanciers outside its own area who realised the potential of this delightful little dog, that paid so well for care in presentation. It was this preparation, the trimming of the coat particularly, which prevented the breed from becoming very popular, as there is considerable art in shaping the coat to make the most of the dog. It is more like the work of the sculptor than the dog handler, and the finished product often bears little relationship to the dog underneath. The result is that over the years the less expert have been completely overshadowed by those who could do the job well, and have ceased to exhibit even when they had a good dog. He is a delicate looking, mincing little dog whose appearance completely belies his actual nature, as he is tough, very willing to take part in a scrap at a moments notice, and whilst rarely seeking a fight, is quite capable of looking after himself.

He is hardy, not difficult to raise or feed, takes up very little space, and is quiet and unobtrusive in the house. Like most of the terriers he is very friendly, attaches himself to one particular place and family, and even to one individual. Provided he has enough exercise, hunting around anywhere where there is the smell of small game, he remains a very fit and happy dog.

OFFICIAL STANDARD

General appearance
A graceful, lithe, well-balanced dog with no sign of coarseness, weakness or shelliness. In repose the expression is mild and gentle, not shy or nervous. Aroused, the dog is particularly alert and full of immense energy and courage. Noteworthy for endurance, Bedlingtons also gallop at great speed, as their body outline clearly shows.

Head
Narrow, but deep and rounded. Shorter in skull and longer in jaw. Covered with a profuse topknot which is lighter than the color of the body, highest at the crown, and tapering gradually to just back of the nose. There must be no stop and the unbroken line from crown to nose end reveals a slender head without cheekiness or snipiness. Lips are black in the blue and tans and brown in all other solid and bi-colors. *Eyes:* almond-shaped, small, bright and well sunk with no tendency to tear or water. Set is oblique and fairly high on the head. Blues have dark eyes; blues and tans, less dark with amber lights; sandies, sandies and tans, light hazel; liver, livers and tans, slightly darker. Eye rims are black in the blue and blue and tans, and brown in all other solid and bi-colors. *Ears:* triangular with rounded tips. Set on low and hanging flat to the cheek in front with a slight projection at the base. Point of greatest width approximately 3 inches. Ear tips reach the corners of the mouth. Thin and velvety in texture, covered with fine hair forming a small silky tassel at the tip. *Nose:* nostrils large and well defined. Blue and blues and tans have black noses. Livers, livers and tans, sandies, sandies and tans have brown noses. *Jaws:* long and tapering. Strong muzzle well filled up with bone beneath the eye. Close-fitting lips, no flews. *Teeth:* large, strong and white. Level or scissors bite. Lower canines clasp the outer surface of the upper gum just in front of the upper canines. Upper premolars and molars lie outside those of the lower jaw.

Neck and shoulders
Long, tapering neck with no throatiness, deep at the base and rising well up from the shoulders which are flat and sloping with no excessive musculature. The head is carried high.

Body
Muscular and markedly flexible. Chest deep. Flat-ribbed and deep through the brisket, which reaches to the elbows. Back has a good natural arch over the loin, creating a definite tuck-up of the underline. Body slightly greater in length than height. Well-muscled quarters are also fine and graceful.

Head and skull: narrow, deep and rounded.

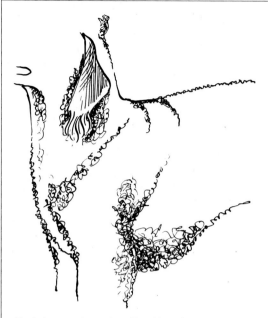

Neck: long and tapering. Shoulders: flat and sloping.

Legs and feet

Lithe and muscular. The hind legs are longer than the forelegs, which are straight and wider apart at the chest than at the feet. Slight bend to pasterns which are long and sloping without weakness. Stifles well angulated. Hocks strong and well let down, turning neither in nor out. Long hare feet with thick, well-closed-up, smooth pads. Dewclaws should be removed.

Coat

A very distinctive mixture of hard and soft hair standing well out from the skin. Crisp to the touch but not wiry, having a tendency to curl, especially on the head and face. When in show trim must not exceed 1 inch on body; hair on legs is slightly longer.

Tail

Set low, scimitar-shaped, thick at the root and tapering to a point which reaches the hock. Not carried over the back or tight to the underbody.

Color

Blue, sandy, liver, blue and tan, sandy and tan, liver and tan. In bicolors the tan markings are found on the legs, chest, under the tail, inside the hindquarters and over each eye. The topknots of all adults should be lighter than the body color. Patches of darker hair from an injury are not objectionable, as these are only temporary. Darker body pigmentation of all colors is to be encouraged.

Height

The preferred Bedlington Terrier dog measures $16\frac{1}{2}$ inches at the withers, the bitch $15\frac{1}{2}$ inches. Under 16 inches or over $17\frac{1}{2}$ inches for dogs and under 15 inches or over $16\frac{1}{2}$ inches for bitches are serious faults. Only where comparative superiority of a specimen outside these ranges clearly justifies it, should greater latitude be taken.

Weight

To be proportionate to height within the range of 17 to 23 pounds.

Gait

Unique lightness of movement. Springy in the slower paces, not stilted or hackneyed. Must not cross, weave or paddle.

Approved by the AKC 12 September 1967

KC(GB) VARIATION TO STANDARD

Head: lips are black in blue and tans, and brown in all other colours. *Eyes:* ideal eye has the appearance of being triangular. *Ears:* filbert shaped. *Forequarters:* forelegs should be straight, but wider apart at chest than at feet. Pasterns long and slightly sloping without weakness. *Weight:* 18 to 23 pounds.

BORDER TERRIER

NATIONAL GROUPING		
	Name	Number
AKC	Terriers	IV
KC(GB)	Terrier	3
FCI	Terriers	3

Some of the smaller Terriers were one of the trappings of fox-hunting. The Wire and Smooth Fox Terriers show this association in their name, but the Terrier that has by tradition been connected with the hunt, is the Border. There is evidence of tough hard-bitten small Terriers in the Border country between England and Scotland back in the 18th century, and it is probable that the Dandie Dinmont and the Bedlington came from these originally. He is said to have acquired his name from the Border Hunt whose master Mr. Jacob Robson did much to make the qualities of these little dogs more widely known. The work that he was required to do, dictated what sort of dog he should be. He had to be long in the leg to follow a horse, though in more sophisticated later years he was supplied with a saddle bag in which he rode when distances became too long for a small dog. He had to be small enough to go to ground after a fox, and hardy enough to look after himself when he got down an earth and found himself face to face with his quarry. For this purpose he needed an even more powerful jaw than the normal Terrier as he could quite easily find himself facing the much rougher badger. He had to be active, strong and tireless, have endless patience, and the sort of waterproof coat that would enable him to face up to a long day in the pouring rain without wilting, in fact he had to be a very remarkable dog.

It says much for the early breeders that they did in fact produce such a dog. Starting with the old rough Terrier they introduced other blood to develop the qualities that they needed, and by the turn of the century the breed was perfected and fixed. Soon after the First World War their fame began to spread, and enthusiasts in the south of England began to hear of the Terrier shows that were being held in the Border country. These events became so important a part of the northern dog scene that by 1921 a Border Terrier Club was formed and shortly afterwards the breed was recognised by the Kennel Club in England. From that time onwards they were not only taken up by exhibitors, but appeared as working terriers with hunts further south, and their future was assured.

The breed has become quite popular in Britain, and is one of the most generally adopted family pets among the terriers in recent years, many litters being bred purely for the pet market, and show quality puppies becoming very difficult to obtain. He has just begun to appear in the United States of America, and in a few other countries, though there are many places in the world that have not yet begun to appreciate his qualities. On the bench one or two very good specimens have begun to take Groups at major shows, with the result that there is increasing interest in him as a show dog, and registrations are rising.

He makes a very good housedog, being remarkably good with children and somewhat quieter than many of the Terriers. He is a fine guard and very possessive about property. He enjoys being in the company of people, and is never happier than when out for a country walk with the children or enjoying the warmth of the fireside in the evenings.

OFFICIAL STANDARD

Since the Border Terrier is a working terrier of a size to go to ground and able, within reason, to follow a horse, his conformation should be such that he be ideally built to do his job. No deviations from this ideal conformation should be permitted, which would impair his usefulness in running his quarry to earth and in bolting it therefrom. For this work he must be alert, active and agile, and capable of squeezing through narrow apertures and rapidly traversing any kind of terrain. His head, 'like that of an otter,' is distinctive, and his temperament ideally exemplifies that of a terrier. By nature he is good-tempered, affectionate, obedient, and easily trained. In the field he is hard as nails, 'game as they come' and driving in attack. It should be the aim of Border Terrier breeders to avoid such over-emphasis of any point in the Standard as might lead to unbalanced exaggeration.

Head: moderately broad with strong short muzzle.

General appearance

He is an active terrier of medium bone, strongly put together, suggesting endurance and agility, but rather narrow in shoulder, body and quarter. The body is covered with a somewhat broken though close-fitting and intensely wiry jacket. The characteristic 'otter' head with its keen eye, combined with a body poise which is 'at the alert,' gives a look of fearless and implacable determination characteristic of the breed. The propor- tions should be that the height at the withers is slightly greater than the distance from the withers to the tail, *i.e.* by possibly $1-1\frac{1}{2}$ inches in a 14-pound dog.

Weight

Dogs, $13-15\frac{1}{2}$ pounds, bitches, $11\frac{1}{2}-14$ pounds, are

appropriate weights for Border Terriers in hard-working condition.

Head

Similar to that of an otter. Moderately broad and flat in skull with plenty of width between the eyes and between the ears. A slight, moderately broad curve at the stop rather than a pronounced indentation. Cheeks slightly full. *Ears:* small, V-shaped and of moderate thickness, dark preferred. Not set high on the head but somewhat on the side, and dropping forward close to the cheeks. They should not break above the level of the skull. *Eyes:* dark hazel and full of fire and intelligence. Moderate in size, neither prominent nor small and beady. *Muzzle:*

Ears: small v-shaped dropping to cheek.

Short and 'well filled.' A dark muzzle is characteristic and desirable. A few short whiskers are natural to the breed. *Teeth:* strong, with a scissors bite, large in proportion to size of dog. *Nose:* black, and of a good size.

Neck

Clean, muscular and only long enough to give a well-balanced appearance. It should gradually widen into the shoulder. *Shoulders:* well laid back and of good length, the blades converging to the withers gradually from a brisket not excessively deep or narrow.

Forelegs

Straight and not too heavy in bone and placed slightly wider than in a Fox Terrier. *Feet:* small and compact. Toes should point forward and be moderately arched with thick pads.

Body

Deep, fairly narrow and of sufficient length to avoid any suggestions of lack of range and agility. Deep ribs carried well back and not oversprung in view of the desired depth and narrowness of the body. The body should be capable of being spanned by a man's hands behind the shoulders. Back strong but laterally supple, with no suspicion of a dip behind the shoulder. Loin strong and the underline fairly straight.

Tail

Moderately short, thick at the base, then tapering. Not

set on too high. Carried gaily when at the alert, but not over the back. When at ease, a Border may drop his stern.

Hindquarters

Muscular and racy, with thighs long and nicely molded. Stifles well bent and hocks well let down.

Coat

A short and dense undercoat covered with a very wiry and somewhat broken top coat which should lie closely, but it must not show any tendency to curl or wave. With such a coat a Border should be able to be exhibited almost in his natural state, nothing more in the way of trimming being needed than a tidying-up of the head, neck and feet. *Hide:* very thick and loose fitting.

Movement

Straight and rhythmical before and behind, with good length of stride and flexing of stifle and hock. The dog should respond to his handler with a gait which is free, agile and quick.

Color

Red, grizzle and tan, blue and tan, or wheaten. A small amount of white may be allowed on the chest but white on the feet should be penalized.

SCALE OF POINTS
Head, ears, neck and teeth (20). Legs and feet (15). Coat and skin (10). Shoulders and chest (10). Eyes and expression (10). Back and loin (10). Hindquarters (10). Tail (5). General appearance (10). *Total (100).*

Approved by the AKC 14 March 1950

KC(GB) VARIATION TO STANDARD
Faults: over or undershot mouth.

BULL TERRIER

NATIONAL GROUPING		
	Name	Number
AKC	Terriers	IV
KC(GB)	Terrier	3
FCI	Terriers	3

The Bull Terrier is by no means an ancient breed, though he is descended from the earliest Terriers in Britain and the now extinct Old English White Terrier. By a process of evolution, selective breeding and crossing with other breeds, notably the Bulldog, the Staffordshire Bull Terrier was produced, and around the middle of the 19th century, James Hinks, a well known dog dealer of Birmingham perfected a strain of pure white Bull Terriers based on these early dogs. He was originally nothing of the aristocrat that he is today, being essentially connected with ratting and fighting, and considered to be the associate of low fellows. He was bred and trained to fight, and contests took place on which considerable sums of money were wagered.

Mr. Hinks's strain of pure whites lifted the Bull Terrier out of his somewhat murky surroundings, and placed him alongside all the other pedigree dogs on the show bench. He became a popular dog with fashionable young men, and the all-white strain swept the board at shows in the 1860s. One of Mr. Hinks's better known bitches, Puss, was challenged by some of the adherents of the old type who maintained that in breeding for the show bench he had lost the fighting qualities of the breed. Mr. Hinks accepted the challenge, and backed his bitch against one of the old bull-faced types for a five pound note and a case of champagne. The fight took place at Tuppers in Long Acre, and Puss had killed her opponent in half an hour, and was so little injured herself that she took an award on the following morning at a dog show.

After this time the long-faced type became popular, and the more graceful dog with less of a pugilistic look about him, longer and straighter legs and the longer muzzle, completely ousted the older type. In recent years a good deal of attention has been paid to head qualities, the eyes have become smaller, the stop non-existent, and the whole head now has a filled in oval appearance from any aspect, being compared to an egg or a rugby football. Not only have his associates become more gentlemanly, but he himself has ceased to look a rough sort of dog. He is now refined, both in appearance and nature, though he is still capable of looking after himself.

He has become one of the top show dogs of the world, winning major awards at all the large shows, on both sides of the Atlantic, in South Africa and Australia. He is noted in the ring for his gladiatorial attitude to competition, standing four square, scorning the opposition, and demanding that he should be not only looked at but considered seriously as the potential winner, which, should he escape from his lead he would undoubtedly be. He is, however, the kindest of dogs with people, even soft and affectionate, especially with children with whom he seems to have a particular rapport. Naturally enough he makes a magnificent guard, as he is completely fearless, and will tackle anything or anyone that he feels is threatening the property which he believes is his responsibility.

OFFICIAL STANDARD

WHITE

The Bull Terrier must be strongly built, muscular, symmetrical and active, with a keen determined and intelligent expression, full of fire but of sweet disposition and amenable to discipline.

Head should be long, strong and deep right to the end of the muzzle, but not coarse. Full face it should be oval in outline and be filled completely up giving the impression of fullness with a surface devoid of hollows or indentations, *i.e.*, egg shaped. In profile it should curve gently downwards from the top of the skull to the tip of the nose. The forehead should be flat across from ear to ear. The distance from the tip of the nose to the eyes should be perceptibly greater than that from the eyes to the top of the skull. The underjaw should be deep and well defined. *Lips* should be clean and tight. *Teeth* should meet in either a level or in a scissors bite. In the scissors bite the

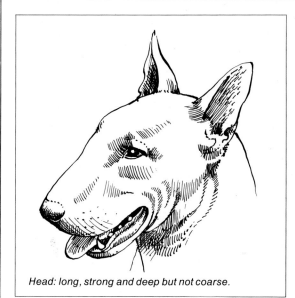

Head: long, strong and deep but not coarse.

upper teeth should fit in front of and closely against the lower teeth, and they should be sound, strong and perfectly regular. *Ears* should be small, thin and placed close together. They should be capable of being held stiffly erect, when they should point upwards. *Eyes* should be well sunken and as dark as possible, with a piercing glint and they should be small, triangular and obliquely placed; set near together and high up on the dog's head. Blue eyes are a disqualification. *Nose* should be black, with well-developed nostrils bent downwards at the tip. *Neck* should be very muscular, long, arched and clean, tapering from the shoulders to the head and it should be free from loose skin. *Chest* should be broad when viewed from in front, and there should be great depth from withers to brisket, so that the latter is nearer the ground than the belly.

Body should be well rounded with marked spring of rib, the back should be short and strong. The back ribs deep.

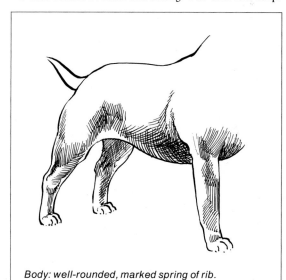

Body: well-rounded, marked spring of rib.

Slightly arched over the loin. The shoulders should be strong and muscular but without heaviness. The shoulder blades should be wide and flat and there should be a very pronounced backward slope from the bottom edge of the blade to the top edge. Behind the shoulders there should be no slackness or dip at the withers. The underline from the brisket to the belly should form a graceful upward curve.

Legs should be big boned but not to the point of coarseness; the forelegs should be of moderate length, perfectly straight, and the dog must stand firmly upon them. The elbows must turn neither in nor out, and the pasterns should be strong and upright. The hind legs should be parallel viewed from behind. The thighs very muscular with hocks well let down. Hind pasterns short and upright. The stifle joint should be well bent with a well-developed second thigh. *Feet* round and compact with well-arched toes like a cat.

Tail should be short, set on low, fine, and ideally should be carried horizontally. It should be thick where it joins the body, and should taper to a fine point.

Coat should be short, flat, harsh to the touch and with a fine gloss. The dog's skin should fit tightly. *Color* is white though markings on the head are permissible. Any markings elsewhere on the coat are to be severely faulted. Skin pigmentation is not to be penalized.

Movement

The dog shall move smoothly, covering the ground with free, easy strides, fore and hind legs should move parallel each to each when viewed from in front or behind. The forelegs reaching out well and the hind legs moving smoothly at the hip and flexing well at the stifle and hock. The dog should move compactly and in one piece but with a typical jaunty air that suggests agility and power.

FAULTS

Any departure from the foregoing points shall be considered a fault, and the seriousness of the fault shall be in exact proportion to its degree, *i.e.* a very crooked front is a very bad fault; a rather crooked front is a rather bad fault; and a slightly crooked front is a slight fault.

DISQUALIFICATION

Blue eyes.

COLORED

The Standard for the colored variety is the same as for the white except for the sub-head 'Color' which reads: *Color.* Any color other than white, or any color with white markings. Other things being equal, the preferred color is brindle. A dog which is predominantly white shall be disqualified.

DISQUALIFICATIONS

Blue eyes. Any dog which is predominantly white.

Approved by the AKC 9 July 1974

KC(GB) VARIATION TO STANDARD

Faults: under Kennel Club Show Regulations deafness is a disqualification.

BULL TERRIER (MINIATURE)

Everything that one can say about the Bull Terrier holds good for the Miniature Bull Terrier, as he is virtually the same breed. He has escaped the problems that are usually associated with miniaturisation, as there have always been many smaller Bull Terriers occurring in litters of the larger dog. This appears to be one of the peculiarities of the Bull breeds; the same thing happens in Bulldogs, where the weight differential has from time to time been as much as forty pounds. To produce the Miniature Bull Terrier all that has been necessary is to select the smaller Bull Terriers and to breed from them. This is not to say that the breed is a recent development, as many exhibitors, taking advantage of the standard which allowed weights between fifteen and fifty pounds at the beginning of this century, bred and continued to show

NATIONAL GROUPING		
	Name	Number
AKC	—	—
KC(GB)	Terrier	3
FCI	Terriers	3

the smallest specimens. They were often scheduled by size, and divided into the smaller and the larger dogs at shows and at the Islington Show of 1863 there were even classes for dogs under ten pounds.

They are now recognised as a separate variety, and although until recently interbreeding was permitted, that will shortly cease. These small but quite typical Bull Terriers will then exist as a breed in their own right throughout the world as they do in Britain.

OFFICIAL STANDARD

General appearance

The Bull Terrier is the Gladiator of the canine race and must be strongly built, muscular, symmetrical and active, with a keen, determined and intelligent expression, full of fire and courageous but of even temperament and amenable to discipline. Irrespective of size, dogs should look masculine, and bitches feminine. Male animals should have two apparently normal testicles fully descended into the scrotum. The moving dog shall appear well-knit, smoothly covering the ground with free easy strides and with a typical jaunty air. Fore and hind legs should move parallel each to each when viewed from in front or behind, the forelegs reaching out well and the hindlegs moving smoothly at the hip and flexing well at the stifle and hock with great thrust.

Head

The head should be long, strong and deep, right to the end of the muzzle, but not coarse. Viewed from the front it should be egg-shaped and completely filled, its surface being free from hollows or indentations. The top of the skull should be almost flat from ear to ear. The profile should curve gently downwards from the top of the skull to the tip of the nose, which should be black and bent downwards at the tip. The nostrils should be well developed. The underjaw should be strong.

Eyes

The eyes should appear narrow, obliquely placed, and triangular, well sunken, black, or as dark brown as possible, so as to appear almost black, and with a piercing glint. The distance from the tip of the nose to the eyes should be perceptibly greater than that from the eyes to the top of the skull.

Ears

The ears should be small, thin and placed close together. The dog should be able to hold them stiffly erect, when they should point straight upwards.

Mouth

The teeth should be sound, clean, strong, of good size and perfectly regular. The upper front teeth should fit in front of and closely against the lower front teeth. The lips should be clean and tight.

Neck

The neck should be very muscular, long, arched, tapering from the shoulders to the head, and free from loose skin.

Forequarters

The shoulders should be strong and muscular but without loading. The shoulder blades should be wide, flat and attached closely to the chest wall, and should have a very pronounced backward slope of the front edge from bottom to top. The forelegs should have the strongest type of round quality bone and the dog should stand solidly upon them; they should be moderately long and perfectly parallel. The elbows should be held straight and the strong pasterns upright.

Body

The body should be well rounded with marked spring of rib, and great depth from withers to brisket, so that the latter is nearer the ground than the belly. The back should be short and strong with the top line level behind the withers and arching or roaching slightly over the loin. The underline from brisket to belly should form a graceful upward curve. The chest should be broad viewed from in front.

Hindquarters

The hind legs should be in parallel viewed from behind. The thighs must be muscular and the second thigh well developed. The stifle joint should be well bent and the hock well angulated, with the bone to the foot short and strong.

Feet

The feet should be round and compact with well arched toes.

Tail

The tail should be short, set on low, it should be carried horizontally. Thick at the root it should taper to a fine point.

Coat

The coat should be short, flat, even and harsh to the touch, with a fine gloss. The skin should fit the dog tightly.

Colour

For white, pure white coat. Skin pigmentation and markings on the head should not be penalised. For coloured, the colour should predominate; all other things equal, brindle to be preferred.

Weight and size

Height should be not more than 14 inches. Weight should be not more than 20 pounds.

Faults

Any departure from the foregoing points should be considered a fault and the seriousness of the fault should be in exact proportion to its degree.

Note

Under Kennel Club Show Regulations deafness is a disqualification.

AKC VARIATION TO STANDARD

This dog is not granted championship status by the AKC. The above standards are those of the KC(GB). *The standard of the Miniature is the same as that of the Bull Terrier with the exception of the following: Weight and size: height should be not more than 14 inches. Weight should be not more than 20 pounds.*

CAIRN TERRIER

NATIONAL GROUPING		
	Name	Number
AKC	Terriers	IV
KC(GB)	Terrier	3
FCI	Terriers	3

Although the Cairn Terrier has only existed as a show dog since the beginning of this century, and before that no book concerned with the exhibition of dogs even gives them a mention, there is no doubt at all that they existed as a separate breed many years before that time. The breed was developed on the Island of Skye, and this led to confusion with the Skye Terrier which became the show dog associated with that island and somewhat overshadowed his less glamorous cousin.

The Cairn was essentially a working dog, used to bolt foxes and otters from among the rocks, and it is from this skill that he draws his name. He was probably at that time not the standardised dog that he is today, but existed in different forms in different parts of Scotland as each breeder exercised his own choice of type and colour. He would, however, even in those days be a sturdy, hard-coated active dog with the temperament that was needed for him to face up to some fairly strong adversaries.

On its formation the Cairn Terrier Club of England had as its object the maintenance of the old working type of dog, an ambition that it shared with the Cairn Terrier Club of the United States of America. They have adopted the same standard and the same size of dog as the ideal, and in that the modern Cairn is still

a hardy tough active dog, they have succeeded in their object.

He was first exhibited in Britain at the Inverness Show in 1909 by Mrs. Alastair Campbell and was described as a short-haired Skye Terrier. The colours varied from those that we know today, to black, but they were similar to the modern Terrier. They were unrecognised by the British Kennel Club and the established Skye Terrier exhibitors raised considerable objection both to the dogs and to their name but by 1912 challenge certificates were on offer and the breed became recognised. Since that time the dog has become one of the most popular of the Terriers, second in registration numbers only to the West Highland White, and the Cairn Terrier Club is still looking after his interests, holding shows and very jealously maintaining the original type.

He differs physically from the other Terriers in a number of ways. His head is shorter and broader than most and his great activity demands that whilst he remains a short-legged Terrier to enable him to go to ground, he must be longer in the leg than say the modern Scottish Terrier. He is shown in the rough, in that he looks natural, though this is deceptive, as a great deal of skilful work goes into reducing what would otherwise be a very ragged dog indeed into something looking fairly smart in a very natural sort of way. His coat is one of his characteristics, as it is hard, double and weather-resistant with the typical somewhat softer hair on the skull.

He is popular with the public as a show dog who see in him their idea of a natural Terrier very much more appealing than some of the other Terrier breeds which some people look on as being overdressed. He is a great little sport, loves hunting, and is happy to spend the whole day out in the country just ferreting around. He does, however, make an excellent house dog as he is friendly, has no vices, and is a very good guard.

OFFICIAL STANDARD

General appearance

That of an active, game, hardy, small working terrier of the short-legged class; very free in its movements, strongly but not heavily built, standing well forward on its forelegs, deep in the ribs, well coupled with strong hindquarters and presenting a well-proportioned build with a medium length of back, having a hard, weather-resisting coat; head shorter and wider than any other terrier and well furnished with hair giving a general foxy expression.

Head

Skull: broad in proportion to length with a decided stop and well furnished with hair on the top of the head, which may be somewhat softer than the body coat. *Muzzle:* strong but not too long or heavy. *Teeth:* large, mouth neither overshot nor undershot. *Nose:* black. *Eyes:* set wide apart, rather sunken, with shaggy eyebrows, medium in size, hazel or dark hazel in color, depending on body color, with a keen terrier expression. *Ears:* small, pointed, well carried erectly, set wide apart on the side of the head. Free from long hairs.

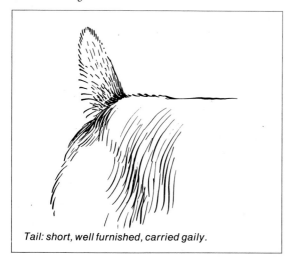

Tail: short, well furnished, carried gaily.

Tail

In proportion to head, well furnished with hair but not feathery. Carried gaily but must not curl over back. Set on at back level.

Body

Well muscled, strong, active body with well-sprung, deep ribs, coupled to strong hindquarters, with a level back of medium length, giving an impression of strength and activity without heaviness.

Shoulders, legs and feet

A sloping shoulder, medium length of leg, good but not too heavy bone; forelegs should not be out at elbows, and be perfectly straight, but forefeet may be slightly turned out. Forefeet larger than hind feet. Legs must be covered with hard hair. Pads should be thick and strong and dog should stand well up on its feet.

Coat

Hard and weather-resistant. Must be double-coated with profuse harsh outer coat and short, soft, close furry undercoat.

Color

May be of any color except white. Dark ears, muzzle and tail tip are desirable.

Ideal size

Involves the weight, the height at the withers and the length of body. Weight for bitches, 13 pounds; for dogs, 14 pounds. Height at the withers—bitches, 9½ inches; dogs, 10 inches. Length of body from 14¼ to 15 inches from the front of the chest to back of hindquarters. The dog must be of balanced proportions and appear neither leggy nor too low to ground; and neither too short nor too long in body. Weight and measurements are for matured dogs at two years of age. Older dogs may weigh slightly in excess and growing dogs may be under these weights and measurements.

Condition

Dogs should be shown in good hard flesh, well muscled and neither too fat or thin. Should be in full good coat with plenty of head furnishings, be clean, combed, brushed and tidied up on ears, tail, feet and general outline. Should move freely and easily on a loose lead, should not cringe on being handled, should stand up on their toes and show with marked terrier characteristics.

FAULTS

1. *Skull:* too narrow in skull.
2. *Muzzle:* too long and heavy a foreface; mouth overshot or undershot.
3. *Eyes:* too large, prominent, yellow, and ringed are all objectionable.
4. *Ears:* too large, round at points, set too close together, set too high on the head; heavily covered with hair.
5. *Legs and feet:* too light or too heavy bone. Crooked forelegs or out at elbow. Thin, ferrety feet; feet let down on the heel or too open and spread. Too high or too low on the leg.
6. *Body:* too short back and compact a body, hampering quickness of movement and turning ability. Too long, weedy and snaky a body, giving an impression of weakness. Tail set on too low. Back not level.
7. *Coat:* open coats, blousy coats, too short or dead coats, lack of sufficient undercoat, lack of head furnishings, lack of hard hair on the legs. Silkiness or curliness. A slight wave permissible.
8. *Nose:* flesh or light-colored nose.
9. *Color:* white on chest, feet or other parts of body.

Approved by the AKC 10 May 1938

KC(GB) VARIATION TO STANDARD

Mouth: jaw strong. *Neck:* well set on, but not short. *Hindquarters:* very strong. *Colour:* red, sandy, grey, brindled or nearly black.

DANDIE DINMONT TERRIER

NATIONAL GROUPING		
	Name	Number
AKC	Terriers	IV
KC(GB)	Terrier	3
FCI	Terriers	3

This very distinctive little dog, with his individual outline, somewhat strange coat and soulful eyes, is one of the older breeds of Terrier. He first appeared in about 1700 and was probably bred from the rough native Terriers of the Border country by selective breeding. He was used for the hunting of the badger and the otter as well as the fox, and no-one should be misled by his large soulful eyes, as he is one of the fiercest of all the Terriers when he is roused. He was popularised, and indeed named by Sir Walter Scott, who, in his travels is said to have encountered Mr. James Davidson of Hawick with his dogs, and immediately made him the hero of his story called Guy Mannering published in 1814. The name of Scott's character in the novel, 'Dandie Dinmont' was seized upon as the name for the dog.

It is recorded that a letter existed at one time in the handwriting of James Davidson concerning his dogs in which he said 'Tarr, reddish and wire-haired, a bitch; Pepper, shaggy and light, from Dr. Brown, of Borjenwood. The race of Dandies are all bred from the two last.' If authentic, and there is no reason to suppose that it is not, we know from this letter the actual names of the two dogs from which the whole race of Dandie Dinmont Terriers descended. Since those early days of popularity the breed has never quite captured the public fancy which has meant that he has never become too numerous. This suits the enthusiasts who feel that by keeping it in the hands of a smaller number of people who are dedicated to retaining the original qualities and characteristics, the breed will not degenerate. His numbers in Britain remain fairly steady, though they are on the increase in Europe where quite large numbers of them are seen at the major shows.

He is no longer used for working, but has retained the working characteristics and temperament. He is not easily roused, but when he is he is completely fearless and will tackle anything, which makes him an excellent guard of property. He is stronger than his somewhat attenuated figure would suggest, extremely hardy and virtually impervious to adverse weather conditions. He has a rough double coat which looks a little sparse at times, and he boasts two colours only, called pepper and mustard, which describes the main part of the coat, but which in each instance is highlighted by lighter points and topknot. His coat needs regular care and frequent plucking to improve the colour as otherwise it grows long and has a faded appearance.

He is intelligent, fond of children and makes an excellent guard and housedog. He is not the most obedient of dogs, having a will of his own and at times will go about his own business in a rather superior manner. As a show dog he is excellent, though he does not always appreciate the close attention of another dog and will react somewhat violently. He is on the whole, however, quiet and obedient in the ring, and whilst he rarely manages to gain major awards, is always popular with the spectators, largely because of his rather quaint appearance.

OFFICIAL STANDARD

Head
Strongly made and large, not out of proportion to the dog's size, the muscles showing extraordinary development, more especially the maxillary. *Skull* broad between

Head and skull: large, skull broad, forehead domed.

the ears, getting gradually less towards the eyes, and measuring about the same from the inner corner of the eye to back of skull as it does from ear to ear. The forehead well domed. The head is *covered* with very soft silky hair, which should not be confined to a mere topknot, and the lighter in color and silkier it is the better. *Cheeks*, starting from the ears proportionately with the skull have a gradual taper towards the muzzle, which is deep and strongly made, and measures about three inches in length, or in proportion to skull as 3 is to 5. *Muzzle* is covered with hair of a little darker shade than the topknot, and of the same texture as the feather of the forelegs. The top of the muzzle is generally bare for about an inch from the back part of the nose, the bareness coming to a point towards the eye, and being about one inch broad at the nose. The nose and inside of *Mouth* black or dark-colored. *Teeth* very strong, especially the canines, which are of extraordinary size for a small dog. The canines mesh well with each other, so as to give the greatest available holding and punishing power. The incisors in each jaw are evenly spaced and six in number, with the upper incisors overlapping the lower incisors in a tight, scissors bite. *Eyes:* set wide apart, large, full, round, bright, expressive of great determination, intelligence and dignity; set low and prominent in front of the head; color, a rich dark hazel. *Ears:* pendulous, set well back, wide apart, and low on the skull, hanging close to the cheek, with a very slight projection at the base, broad at the junction of the head and tapering almost to a point, the forepart of the ear tapering very little—the tapering being mostly on the back part, the forepart of the ear coming almost straight down from its junction with the head to the tip. They should harmonize in color with the

body color. In the case of a Pepper dog they are covered with a soft straight brownish hair (in some cases almost black). In the case of a Mustard dog the hair should be mustard in color, a shade darker than the body, but not black. All should have a thin feather of light hair starting about 2 inches from the tip, and of nearly the same color and texture as the topknot, which gives the ear the appearance of a *distinct point*. The animal is often 1 or 2 years old before the feather is shown. The cartilage and skin of the ear should not be thick, but rather thin. Length of ear from 3 to 4 inches.

Neck
Very muscular, well-developed and strong, showing great power of resistance, being well set into the shoulders.

Body
Long, strong and flexible; ribs well sprung and round, chest well developed and let well down between the forelegs; the back rather low at the shoulder, having a slight

Body: long, low at shoulders, arch over loin.

downward curve and a corresponding arch over the loins, with a very slight gradual drop from top of loins to root of tail; both sides of backbone well supplied with muscle.

Tail
Rather short, say from 8 to 10 inches, and covered on the upper side with wiry hair of darker color than that of the body, the hair on the under side being lighter in color and not so wiry, with nice feather about 2 inches long, getting shorter as it nears the tip; rather thick at the root, getting thicker for about 4 inches, then tapering off to a point. It should not be twisted or curled in any way, but should come up with a curve like a scimitar, the tip, when excited, being in a perpendicular line with the root of the tail. It should neither be set on too high nor too low. When not excited it is carried gaily, and a little above the level of the body.

Legs
The forelegs short, with immense muscular development and bone, set wide apart, the chest coming well down between them. The feet well formed *and not flat*, with

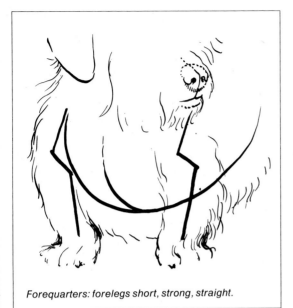

Forequarters: forelegs short, strong, straight.

very strong brown or dark-colored claws. Bandy legs and flat feet are objectionable. The hair on the forelegs and feet of a Pepper dog should be tan, varying according to the body color from a rich tan to a pale fawn; of a Mustard dog they are of a darker shade than its head, which is a creamy white. In both colors there is a nice feather, about 2 inches long, rather lighter in color than the hair on the forepart of the leg. The hind legs are a little longer than the forelegs, and are set rather wide apart but not spread out in an unnatural manner, while the feet are much smaller; the thighs are well developed, and the hair of the same color and texture as the forelegs, but having no feather or dewclaws; the whole claws should be dark; but the claws of all vary in shade according to the color of the dog's body.

Coat

This is a very important point; the hair should be about 2 inches long; that from skull to root of tail, a mixture of hardish and soft hair, which gives a sort of crisp feel to the hand. The hard should not be wiry; the coat is what is termed piley or penciled. The hair on the under part of the body is lighter in color and softer than on the top. The skin on the belly accords with the color of dog.

Color

The color is pepper or mustard. The pepper ranges from a dark bluish black to a light silvery gray, the intermediate shades being preferred, the body color coming well down the shoulder and hips, gradually merging into the leg color. The mustards vary from a reddish brown to a pale fawn, the head being a creamy white, the legs and feet of a shade darker than the head. The claws are dark as in other colors. (Nearly all Dandie Dinmont Terriers have some white on the chest; some have also white claws.)

Size and weight

The height should be from 8 to 11 inches at the top of shoulder. Length from top of shoulder to root of tail should not be more than twice the dog's height, but preferably 1 or 2 inches less. The preferred weight from 18 to 24 pounds. These weights are for dogs in good working condition.

SCALE OF POINTS

Head (10). Eyes (10). Ears (10). Neck (5). Body (20). Tail (5). Legs and feet (10). Coat (15). Color (5). Size and weight (5). General appearance (5). *Total (100).*

Approved by the AKC 10 June 1969

KC(GB) VARIATION TO STANDARD

Feet: white feet are objectionable. *Weight:* as near 18 pounds as possible.

FOX TERRIER

Smooth Fox Terrier

Few breeds of dog have retained their popularity as the Smooth Fox Terrier has. He was known at the beginning of the 19th century, and was popular before dog shows started. Arthur Wardle depicted the famous 'Totteridge Eleven' at the start of this century, and they are still being shown in fairly large numbers to this day. He has become one of the most widely known of all British dogs, and invariably when thinking about Terriers, and British Terriers in particular, most people think of one or other of the two Fox Terriers. He started life as the old English Terrier, the sort of dog mentioned by Dame Juliana Berners in 1486, and a century later by Dr. Caius when he speaks of 'Another sorte there is which hunteth the Fox and the Badger or Greye onely, whom we call Terrars'. This is the same sort of basic Terrier depicted in a Reinagle engraving in The Sportsman's Repository of 1820, though in that instance they are a slightly rougher type.

The modern Smooth Fox Terrier starts from about 1860 from which time pedigrees can be traced, and with the advent of the Fox Terrier Club in 1876 and the care that was taken in the compiling of the stud books, the history of the breed since that time is clear. One of the first dogs of note was Old Jock who was first shown in 1862 at Birmingham and for the last time at Crystal Palace in 1870. He was said to have been a smart, well-balanced Terrier, with perhaps too much daylight under him and wanting something in jaw power, but at least he was away from the Bull

NATIONAL GROUPING		
	Name	Number
AKC	Terriers	IV
KC(GB)	Terrier	3
FCI	Terriers	3

Terrier type. Some idea of the value placed on these early dogs is shown by the fact that when Mr. Burbidge's kennel was sold in 1892, the dogs fetched up to £135 each, which was a vast sum of money in those days. That the breed has changed very little is shown by the fact that the standard devised by the Fox Terrier Club in the very early days, holds good today except for the question of size which has been reduced from twenty to eighteen pounds.

It would be a very bold enthusiast for the modern Smooth Fox Terrier who would claim that today's show dog would go to ground and work as his ancestors did, even though he retains all the old fire and hunting instinct. He has come a long way in appearance since

the days of the Rev. John Russell and his stocky shorter-legged dogs. He is now a beautifully balanced little dog with a symmetrical outline, great refinement of head and a dignified movement, all qualities that make him a very popular show dog. His neat ears, straight bone and mostly all-white colour with interesting markings make him most attractive to look at in the ring, and the manner in which he sets off his fellow Terriers and appears to sparkle underlines the fact that he is still very much the Terrier. Although he was historically first in the ring, he has never quite attained the popularity numerically of his wire-coated brother, which is probably due to the fact that so many people have always associated the word 'terrier' with a dog that has a rough coat.

He is a dog of great charm, friendly, as most of the Terriers are, a pleasant companion with a love of exercise, never lazy, always ready for a game whether it is just a romp on the lawn or a more serious go at the local rabbits. He is clean and mannerly in the house, quiet except when he feels that intrusion of some sort is imminent, when he becomes one of the best guards.

Wire Fox Terrier

The original basic stock from which both the Smooth Fox Terrier and the Wire Fox Terrier descended was probably what one might call half-coated. He was neither rough nor smooth, and old paintings and engravings endorse this opinion. The Terriers in the Sportsman's Repository of 1820 are neither rough nor smooth, and a contemporary model of one of the dogs belonging to the Rev. John Russell, at present in the possession of the Kennel Club in London, shows a Terrier with a somewhat mixed coat, fairly short in places but with a certain amount of feathering and roughness around the neck and shoulders. It is generally accepted that the old black and tan, Wire-

haired Terrier which was among the earliest terriers in Britain was used to produce the coat of the Wire Fox Terrier. At the same time, there existed the old English White Terrier which was smooth coated and which probably helped in the evolution of the Smooth Fox Terrier. It was probably by the judicious crossing of the two types that the white colour of the one and the hard coat of the other were retained.

In the early days of the breed there was considerable crossing between the smooth and wire-haired variety. This was probably with the intention of improving both, but certainly as far as the Wire is concerned, it was with the intention of retaining the large proportion of white as this was fashionable. It was also felt that the Smooth had the neater and smarter head, smaller ears and a better outline. There was also a determined effort at one time to reduce the size of both Terriers, and whilst one succeeded to a certain degree in that a miniature Fox Terrier with a smooth coat was evolved and enjoyed a vogue for a time as a Toy Fox Terrier, the eighteen pound dog is still the accepted version of the breed.

One of the problems with the Wire Fox Terrier is that in order to keep him looking neat and smart, his coat needs constant attention, having to be plucked and trimmed regularly, and from time to time taken right down so that the new coat will grow strong and hard. This has led to the breed being very much the province of the professional handler as far as showing is concerned, and the number of dogs shown by their owners is now very much in the minority. Even many of those that are handled in the ring by their proud proprietors are prepared professionally. The result is a very high degree of presentation in the breed, and any dog that enters the ring in a state of unpreparedness, has little chance of success. This has caused the criticism that the breed is artificial and wooden, and that it has lost its terrier character, but nothing could be further from the truth. The Wire Fox Terrier is still every bit as much a devil as he always was, full of fun and fire, always ready to have a go at anything, however large, and still one of the real sports of the race. It has also been claimed that the breeding for a long narrow head has resulted in a dog that has no brains, but this is equally untrue. Accepted into the family and treated as a normal dog, he is as intelligent and responsive as he has always been, even if untrimmed he looks like a floor mop!

There are few breeds that have more consistently reached the top at dog shows all over the world. From America to Britain, from Australia to Scandinavia, he is constantly winning Groups and Best in Show, and these wins are always greeted with thunderous applause as he looks the part of the perfect show dog. His temperament is all Terrier, affectionate with those that he knows, suspicious of those that he does not, sharp, even fierce towards anything or anyone who offends him, but an excellent companion in the house, and a bright cheerful animal to have around.

OFFICIAL STANDARD

SMOOTH

The following shall be the Standard of the Fox Terrier, amplified in part in order that a more complete description of the Fox Terrier may be presented. The Standard itself is set forth in ordinary type, the amplification in italics.

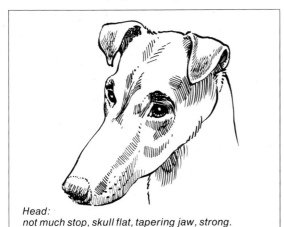

Head:
not much stop, skull flat, tapering jaw, strong.

Head

The skull should be flat and moderately narrow, gradually decreasing in width to the eyes. Not much stop should be apparent, but there should be more dip in the profile between the forehead and the top jaw than is seen in the case of a Greyhound. The cheeks must not be full. The ears should be V-shaped and small, of moderate thickness, and drooping forward close to the cheek, not hanging by the side of the head like a Foxhound. *The top line of the folded ear should be well above the level of the skull.* The jaws, upper and lower, should be strong and muscular and of fair punishing strength, but not so as in any way to resemble the Greyhound or modern English Terrier. There should not be much falling away below the eyes. This part of the head should, however, be moderately chiseled out, so as not to go down in a straight slope like a wedge. The nose, toward which the muzzle must gradually taper, should be black. *It should be noticed that although the foreface should gradually taper from eye to muzzle and should tip slightly at its juncture with the forehead, it should not 'dish' or fall away quickly below the eyes, where it should be full and well made up, but relieved from 'wedginess' by a little delicate chiseling.* The eyes and the rims should be dark in color, *moderately* small and rather deep-set, full of fire, life and intelligence and as nearly as possible circular in shape. *Anything approaching a yellow eye is most objectionable.* The teeth should be as nearly as possible together, *i.e. the points* of the upper (*incisors*) teeth on the outside of or *slightly overlapping* the lower teeth. *There should be apparent little difference in length between the skull and foreface of a well-balanced head.*

Neck

Should be clean and muscular, without throatiness, of fair length, and gradually widening to the shoulders.

Shoulders

Should be long and sloping, well laid back, fine at the points, and clearly cut at the withers.

Chest

Deep and not broad.

Back

Should be short, straight, (*i.e. level*), and strong, with no appearance of slackness. *Brisket should be deep, yet not exaggerated.*

Loin

Should be very powerful, *muscular* and very slightly arched. The foreribs should be moderately arched, the back ribs deep *and well sprung*, and the dog should be well ribbed up.

Hindquarters

Should be strong and muscular, quite free from droop or crouch; the thighs long and powerful; *stifles well curved and turned neither in nor out*; hocks *well bent* and near the ground *should be perfectly upright and parallel each with the other when viewed from behind*, the dog standing well up on them like a Foxhound, and not straight in the stifle. *The worst possible form of hindquarters consists of a short second thigh and a straight stifle.*

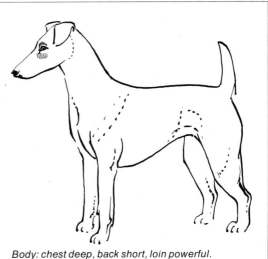

Body: chest deep, back short, loin powerful.

Stern

Should be set on rather high and carried gaily, but not over the back or curled. It should be of good strength, anything approaching a 'pipe-stopper' tail being especially objectionable.

Legs

The forelegs viewed from any direction must be straight with bone strong right down to the feet, showing little or no appearance of ankle in front, and being short and straight in pasterns. Both forelegs and hind legs should be carried straight forward in traveling, the stifles not turning outward. The elbows should hang perpendicu-

larly to the body, working free of the sides. *Feet:* should be round, compact and not large; the soles hard and tough; the toes moderately arched and turned neither in nor out.

Coat
Should be smooth, flat, but hard, dense and abundant. The belly and under side of the thighs should not be bare.

Color
White should predominate; brindle, red, or liver markings are objectionable. Otherwise this point is of little or no importance.

Symmetry, size and character
The dog must present a generally gay, lively and active appearance; bone and strength in a small compass are essentials, but this must not be taken to mean that a Fox Terrier should be cloddy, or in any way coarse—speed and endurance must be looked to as well as power, and the symmetry of the Foxhound taken as a model. The terrier, like the hound, must on no account be leggy, nor must he be too short in the leg. He should stand like a cleverly made hunter, covering a lot of ground, yet with a short back, as before stated. He will then attain the highest degree of propelling power, together with the greatest length of stride that is compatible with the length of his body. Weight is not a certain criterion of a terrier's fitness for his work—general shape, size and contour are the main points; and if a dog can gallop and stay, and follow his fox up a drain, it matters little what his weight is to a pound or so. *According to present-day requirements, a full-sized, well-balanced dog should not exceed 15½ inches at the withers, the bitch being proportionately lower—nor should the length of back from withers to root of tail exceed 12 inches, while, to maintain the relative proportions, the head should not exceed 7¼ inches or be less than 7 inches. A dog with these measurements should scale 18 pounds in show condition—a bitch weighing some 2 pounds less—with a margin of 1 pound either way.*

Balance
This may be defined as the correct proportions of a certain point, or points, when considered in relation to a certain other point or points. It is the keystone of the terrier's

anatomy. The chief points for consideration are the relative proportions of skull and foreface; head and back; height at withers and length of body from shoulder-point to buttock—the ideal of proportion being reached when the last two measurements are the same. It should be added that, although the head measurements can be taken with absolute accuracy, the height at withers and length of back and coat are approximate, and are inserted for the information of breeders and exhibitors rather than as a hard and fast rule.

Movement

Movement, or action, is the crucial test of conformation. The terrier's legs should be carried straight forward while traveling, the forelegs hanging perpendicular and swinging parallel with the sides, like the pendulum of a clock. The principal propulsive power is furnished by the hind legs, perfection of action being found in the terrier possessing long thighs and muscular second thighs well bent at the stifles, which admit of a strong forward thrust or 'snatch' of the hocks. When approaching, the forelegs should form a continuation of the straight line of the front, the feet being the same distance apart at the elbows. When stationary, it is often difficult to determine whether a dog is slightly out at shoulder, but, directly he moves, the defect—if it exists—becomes more apparent, the forefeet having a tendency to cross, 'weave' or 'dish'. When, on the contrary, the dog is tied at the shoulder, the tendency of the feet is to move wider apart, with a sort of paddling action. When the hocks are turned in—cowhock—the stifles and feet are turned outwards, resulting in a serious loss of propulsive power. When the hocks are turned outwards the tendency of the hind feet is to cross, resulting in an ungainly waddle.

N.B.: old scars or injuries, the result of work or accident, should not be allowed to prejudice a terrier's chance in the show ring, unless they interfere with its movement or with its utility for work or stud.

WIRE

This variety of the breed should resemble the smooth sort in every respect except the coat, which should be broken. The harder and more wiry the texture of the coat

General appearance: relative proportions important, height and length the same.

Head and skull: balanced, skull flat, well-developed jaw.

is, the better. On no account should the dog look or feel woolly; and there should be no silky hair about the poll or elsewhere. The coat should not be too long, so as to give the dog a shaggy appearance, but, at the same time, it should show a marked and distinct difference all over from the smooth species.

SCALE OF POINTS

Head and ears (15). Neck (5). Shoulders and chest (10). Back and loin (10). Hindquarters (15). Stern (5). Legs and feet (15). Coat (15). Symmetry, size and character (10). *Total (100).*

DISQUALIFICATIONS

Nose: white, cherry or spotted to a considerable extent with either of these colors. Ears: prick, tulip or rose. Mouth: much undershot or much overshot.

KC(GB) VARIATION TO STANDARD

This dog is granted championship status by the KC(GB) separately for the Smooth and Wire varieties. The AKC standard for the Fox Terrier corresponds most directly to the KC(GB) standard for the Wire-haired. *Coat:* principal difference between that of Smooth and Wire varieties is that, whereas former is straight and flat, that of latter appears to be broken—hairs having a tendency to twist. Best coats are of a dense, wiry texture—like cocoanut matting—hairs growing so close and strongly together that when parted with fingers skin cannot be seen. At base of these stiff hairs is a shorter growth of finer and softer hair—termed undercoat. Coat on sides is never quite so hard as that on back and quarters. Some of hardest coats are 'crinkly' or slightly waved, but a curly coat is very objectionable. Hair on upper and lower jaws should be crisp and only sufficiently long to impart an appearance of strength to the fore-face, thus effectually differentiating them from Smooth variety. Hair on forelegs should also be dense and crisp. Coat should average in length from $\frac{3}{4}$ to 1 inch on shoulders and neck, lengthening to $1\frac{1}{2}$ inches on withers, backs, ribs and quarters. *Weight:* dogs 18 pounds; bitches 16 pounds. Margin of 1 pound either way.

IRISH TERRIER

Ireland has produced three or four native Terriers, and they are all very different from anything else that we know in the Group. Whether for size, colour, or even shape, they cannot easily be traced back to either a combination of any of the old established breeds or to any of the basic Terrier types. This is probably due to the relative isolation of the island which resulted in breeds being kept fairly free from dilution from other quarters in the days before transport improved and freedom of movement between Ireland and the mainland became as quick and easy as it is now. Certainly the Irish Terrier developed as a very individual dog, with a colour of its own, from wheaten to bright red, a size between the Lakeland and the Airedale, and a temperament which has earned him the reputation for fearlessness and devilishness second to none in the Terrier group. Though classes for the breed were staged in Lisburn in 1875 and in Dublin during the previous year, he was virtually unknown in England and it was not until some time later that he became generally known outside his native country.

Prior to the end of the 19th century the colour of

NATIONAL GROUPING		
	Name	Number
AKC	Terriers	IV
KC(GB)	Terrier	3
FCI	Terriers	3

the Irish Terrier was by no means fixed, black and tan, grey, and brindle being quite common colours, and it was from a bitch called Poppy who was a rich red colour and who threw puppies of the same hue, that the breed probably owes its present distinctive colouration. The black and grey, as well as the brindle was rigidly bred out of the breed, until by this century all the members of the breed were self-coloured and of the colours accepted today. The conformation of the modern Irish Terrier is very different from most of the other members of the group. His body is longer for one thing and his lines much more racy. He is leggier than many of the other Terriers, showing a good deal more daylight under his body than say the

292

Airedale or his own fellow Irishman, the Kerry Blue Terrier.

He has never become very popular, and registration figures have fallen steadily in recent years so that he is now in something of a decline. This may in part be due to his reputation, as he is definitely included among the dogs that are not easy to handle in the show ring. It has been the habit in the Irish Terrier ring to set off one dog against another to smarten him up and make him show. The skirmishes that resulted never meant a great deal, as they were more in the nature of skirmishes than serious warfare, but unfortunately in the eyes of the public who witnessed them the breed was seen as a fierce and intractable dog. In fact he is nothing of the sort, and whilst full of spirit and always prepared to look after himself, he can be very obedient and trains easily. This was proved during the First World War, when he was used successfully as a messenger dog.

He is tremendously staunch and loyal, a wonderful protector of property and persons, and is most adaptable, living happily enough out in the country where he can roam at will, or in a town house or flat where he settles down in complete harmony with his surroundings. He remains however very much a sporting dog, and as the dog man will say, he is all Terrier.

OFFICIAL STANDARD

General appearance

The over-all appearance of the Irish Terrier is important. In conformation he must be more than a sum of his parts. He must be all-of-a-piece, a balanced vital picture of symmetry, proportion and harmony. Furthermore, he must convey character. This terrier must be active, lithe and wiry in movement, with great animation; sturdy and strong in substance and bone structure, but at the same time free from clumsiness, for speed, power and endurance are most essential. The Irish Terrier must be neither 'cobby' nor 'cloddy', but should be built on lines of speed with a graceful, racing outline.

Head

Long, but in nice proportion to the rest of the body; the skull flat, rather narrow between the ears, and narrowing slightly toward the eyes; free from wrinkle, with the stop hardly noticeable except in profile. The jaws must be strong and muscular, but not too full in the cheek, and of good punishing length. The foreface must not fall away appreciably between or below the eyes; instead, the modeling should be delicate. An exaggerated foreface, or a noticeably short foreface, disturbs the proper balance of the head and is not desirable. The foreface and the skull from occiput to stop should be approximately equal in length. Excessive muscular development of the cheeks, or bony development of the temples, conditions which are described by the fancier as 'cheeky', or 'strong in head', or 'thick in skull' are objectionable. The 'bumpy' head, in which the skull presents two lumps of bony structure above the eyes, is to be faulted. The hair on the upper and lower jaws should be similar in quality and texture to that on the body, and of sufficient length to present an appearance of additional strength and finish to the foreface. Either the profuse, goat-like beard, or the absence of beard, is unsightly and undesirable.

Teeth

Should be strong and even, white and sound; and neither overshot nor undershot.

Lips

Should be close and well-fitting, almost black in color.

Nose

Must be black.

Eyes

Dark brown in color; small, not prominent; full of life, fire and intelligence, showing an intense expression. The light or yellow eye is most objectionable, and is a bad fault.

Ears

Small and V-shaped; of moderate thickness; set well on the head, and dropping forward closely toward the outside corner of the eye. The top of the folded ear should be well above the level of the skull. A 'dead' ear, houndlike in appearance, must be severely penalized. It is not characteristic of the Irish Terrier. The hair should be much shorter and somewhat darker in color than that on the body.

Neck

Should be of fair length and gradually widening toward the shoulders; well and proudly carried, and free from throatiness. Generally there is a slight frill in the hair at each side of the neck, extending almost to the corner of the ear.

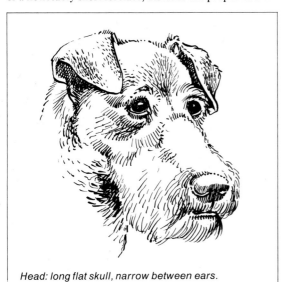
Head: long flat skull, narrow between ears.

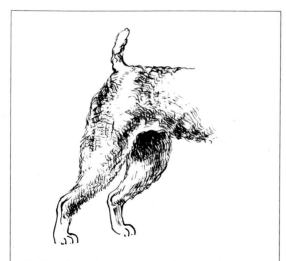

Hindquarters: strong and muscular, powerful, hocks low.

Shoulders and chest
Shoulders must be fine, long, and sloping well into the back. The chest should be deep and muscular, but neither full nor wide.

Body
The body should be moderately long. The short back is not characteristic of the Irish Terrier, and is extremely objectionable. The back must be strong and straight, and free from an appearance of slackness or 'dip' behind the shoulders. The loin should be strong and muscular, and slightly arched, the ribs fairly sprung, deep rather than round, reaching to the level of the elbow. The bitch may be slightly longer than the dog.

Hindquarters
Should be strong and muscular; thighs powerful; hocks near the ground; stifles moderately bent.

Stern
Should be docked, taking off about one quarter. It should be set on rather high, but not curled. It should be of good strength and substance; of fair length and well covered with harsh, rough hair.

Feet and legs
The feet should be strong, tolerably round, and moderately small; toes arched and turned neither out nor in, with dark toenails. The pads should be deep, and must be perfectly sound and free from corns. Cracks alone do not necessarily indicate unsound feet. In fact, all breeds have cracked pads occasionally, from various causes.
Legs moderately long, well set from the shoulders, perfectly straight, with plenty of bone and muscle; the elbows working clear of the sides; pasterns short, straight, and hardly noticeable. Both fore and hind legs should move straight forward when traveling; the stifles should not turn outwards. 'Cow-hocks'—that is, the hocks turned in and the feet turned out—are intolerable. The legs should be free from feather and covered with hair of similar texture to that on the body to give proper finish to the dog.

Coat
Should be dense and wiry in texture, rich in quality, having a broken appearance, but still lying fairly close to the body, the hairs growing so closely and strongly together that when parted with the fingers the skin is hardly visible; free of softness or silkiness, and not so long as to alter the outline of the body, particularly in the hindquarters. On the sides of the body the coat is never as harsh as on the back and quarters, but it should be plentiful and of good texture. At the base of the stiff outer coat there should be a growth of finer and softer hair, lighter in color, termed the undercoat. Single coats, which are without any undercoat, and wavy coats are undesirable; the curly and the kinky coats are most objectionable.

Color
Should be whole-colored: bright red, golden red, red wheaten, or wheaten. A small patch of white on the chest, frequently encountered in all whole-colored breeds, is permissible but not desirable. White on any other part of the body is most objectionable. Puppies sometimes have black hair at birth, which should disappear before they are full grown.

Size
The most desirable weight in show condition is 27 pounds for the dog and 25 pounds for the bitch. The height at the shoulder should be approximately 18 inches. These figures serve as a guide to both breeder and judge. In the show ring, however, the informed judge readily identifies the oversized or undersized Irish Terrier by its conformation and general appearance. Weight is not the last word in judgment. It is of the greatest importance to select, insofar as possible, terriers of moderate and generally accepted size, possessing the other various characteristics.

Temperament
The temperament of the Irish Terrier reflects his early background: he was family pet, guard dog, and hunter. He is good tempered, spirited and game. It is of the utmost importance that the Irish Terrier show fire and animation. There is a heedless, reckless pluck about the Irish Terrier which is characteristic, and which, coupled with the headlong dash, blind to all consequences, with which he rushes at his adversary, has earned for the breed the proud epithet of 'Daredevil'. He is of good temper, most affectionate, and absolutely loyal to mankind. Tender and forebearing with those he loves, this rugged, stout-hearted terrier will guard his master, his mistress and children with utter contempt for danger or hurt. His life is one continuous and eager offering of loyal and faithful companionship and devotion. He is ever on guard, and stands between his home and all that threatens.

Approved by the AKC 10 December 1968

KC(GB) VARIATION TO STANDARD
Mouth: top teeth slightly overlapping lower.

KERRY BLUE TERRIER

This is another of the purely Irish dogs. He was first found in the fabulous piece of country known as the Ring of Kerry; an area, which, until tourism became one of the major industries of Ireland, remained very much a backwater of hills and valleys, small subsistence farms and tiny fishing ports. He had been known in Kerry for at least a century, and was another breed that had benefitted by the comparative isolation of his native country, until he was discovered by the English around the turn of the century. It is in fact quite remarkable that a breed of such distinction should remain unknown in a neighbouring dog-conscious country such as England for so long, but he gets no mention in any dog book prior to this century and it was not until 1922 in England and 1926 in the United States of America that breed clubs were formed.

Since that time he has become increasingly popular as a show dog, winning major awards in a great many countries, especially on the continent and in Austral-

NATIONAL GROUPING		
	Name	Number
AKC	Terriers	IV
KC(GB)	Terrier	3
FCI	Terriers	3

asia. He remains very much a sporting dog and the Irish Blue Terrier Club of Ireland has established the preservation of that side of the dog's character as one of its aims. For some time the Irish club discouraged the trimming of the dog's coat though some cleaning up has not been declared undesirable in other countries. In the rough he carries too much coat, and the quality of it, which is soft and wavy, makes it difficult to deal with when it grows too long, which meant that a good deal of surreptitious trimming has always gone on. All puppies are born black, which creates yet another slight difficulty, as the colour change takes place at any time between nine months and two years, generally the ones that change too early eventually become too pale in colour and those that change late grow the desired and fashionable deeper blue. At any stage the coat may go through stages of showing patches of black and even a brownish tinge, all of which makes the selection of puppies a gamble. Many breeders run on a litter until the colour change has started which is an expensive and time-consuming business in which there is very little profit.

He is a real all-round Terrier, making an excellent guard, being easily trained to the gun and will retrieve like a gundog. He loves the water and with his farming background it is not surprising that he has even proved successful as a herder. He has a good many advantages as a house dog, not the least of which being that his coat, although it needs attention to keep it tidy, does not shed like some breeds.

As a show dog he often reigns in the Group, and from time to time takes Best in Show All-breeds at some of the large shows. Being somewhat larger than others in the group, and having his distinctive colour, he is always spectacular in the ring. Being a positive dog, something of an extrovert and a flashy mover, he usually looks like a potential winner. His temperament is excellent, although like the other Irish Terriers, and indeed like many in the Group he does not take kindly to what he considers interference by other dogs, when a scrap usually results. He is very kind with people, is not snappy or nasty tempered, and fits in well with the average household.

OFFICIAL STANDARD

Head
Long, but not exaggerated and in good proportion to the rest of the body. Well-balanced, with little apparent difference between the legth of the skull and foreface. *Skull:* flat, with very slight stop, of but moderate breadth between the ears, and narrowing very slightly to the eyes. *Cheeks:* clean and level, free from bumpiness. *Ears:* V-shaped, small but not out of proportion to the size of the dog, of moderate thickness, carried forward close to the cheeks with the top of the folded ear slightly above the level of the skull. A 'dead' ear houndlike in appearance is very undesirable. *Foreface:* jaws deep, strong and muscular. Foreface full and well made up, not falling away appreciably below the eyes but moderately chiseled out to relieve the foreface from wedginess. *Nose:* black, nostrils large and wide. *Teeth:* strong, white and either level or with the upper (incisors) teeth slightly overlapping the lower teeth. An undershot mouth should be strictly penalized. *Eyes:* dark, small, not prominent, well placed and with a keen terrier expression. Anything approaching a yellow eye is very undesirable.

Neck
Clean and moderately long, gradually widening to the shoulders upon which it should be well set and carried proudly.

Shoulders and chest
Shoulders fine, long and sloping, well laid back and well knit. Chest deep and of but moderate breadth.

Legs and feet
Legs moderately long with plenty of bone and muscle. The forelegs should be straight from both front and side view, with the elbows hanging perpendicularly to the body and working clear of the sides in movement, the pasterns short, straight and hardly noticeable. Both forelegs and hind legs should move straight forward when traveling, the stifles turning neither in nor out. Feet should be strong, compact, fairly round and moderately small, with good depth of pad free from cracks, the toes arched, turned neither in nor out, with black toenails.

Body
Back short, strong and straight (*i.e.* level), with no appearance of slackness. Loin short and powerful with a slight tuck-up, the ribs fairly well sprung, deep rather than round.

Head and skull: long, lean, flat skull. Ears: small v-shaped.

Body: short-coupled, good depth of brisket, well-sprung ribs.

well knit and in good balance, showing a well developed and muscular body with definite terrier style and character throughout. A low-slung Kerry is not typical.

Height
The ideal Kerry should be 18½ inches at the withers for a dog, slightly less for a bitch. In judging Kerries, a height of 18–19½ inches for a dog, and 17½–19 inches for a bitch should be given primary preference. Only where the comparative superiority of a specimen outside of the ranges noted clearly justifies it, should greater latitude be taken. In no case should it extend to a dog over 20 inches or under 17½ inches, or to a bitch over 19½ inches or under 17 inches. The minimum limits do not apply to puppies.

Weight
The most desirable weight for a fully developed dog is from 33–40 pounds, bitches weighing proportionately less.

DISQUALIFICATIONS
Solid black. Dewclaws on hind legs.

Approved by the AKC 15 September 1959

Hindquarters and stern
Hindquarters strong and muscular with full freedom of action, free from droop or crouch, the thighs long and powerful, stifles well bent and turned neither in nor out, hocks near the ground and, when viewed from behind, upright and parallel with each other, the dog standing well up on them. Tail should be set on high, of moderate length and carried gaily erect, the straighter the tail the better.

Color
The correct mature color is any shade of blue gray or gray blue from deep slate to light blue gray, of a fairly uniform color throughout except that distinctly darker to black parts may appear on the muzzle, head, ears, tail and feet. Kerry color, in its process of 'clearing' from an apparent black at birth to the mature gray blue or blue gray, passes through one or more transitions—involving a very dark blue (darker than deep slate), shades or tinges of brown, and mixtures of these, together with a progressive infiltration of the correct mature color. Up to 18 months such deviations from the correct mature color are permissible without preference and without regard for uniformity. Thereafter, deviation from it to any significant extent must be severely penalized. Solid black is never permissible in the show ring. Up to 18 months any doubt as to whether a dog is black or a very dark blue should be resolved in favor of the dog, particularly in the case of a puppy. Black on the muzzle, head, ears, tail and feet is permissible at any age.

Coat
Soft, dense and wavy. A harsh, wire or bristle coat should be severely penalized. In show trim the body should be well covered but tidy, with the head (except for the whiskers) and the ears and cheeks clear.

General conformation and character
The typical Kerry Blue Terrier should be upstanding,

KC(GB) VARIATION TO STANDARD
Head: nostril of due proportion. *Mouth:* dark gums and roof. *Forequarters:* shoulders flat as possible with elbows carried close to body. *Weight and size:* dogs 18 to 19 inches at shoulder; bitches slightly less. Desirable weight dogs 33 to 37 pounds; bitches 35 pounds. *Faults:* rose ears, snipy foreface.

LAKELAND TERRIER

It was only during the 19th century that the Terriers of Britain began to sort themselves out. The breeds peculiar to Scotland kept themselves very much to themselves as did those in Ireland, but with the growth of fox hunting with packs of hounds, each area of the rest of Britain seemed to develop a strain of its own that suited the terrain over which the pack worked, that is the conditions under which the fox went to ground. At one time it was even the fashion of the day for visiting sportsmen to bring their own personal Terriers to the hunt. The English Lake District was a

NATIONAL GROUPING		
	Name	Number
AKC	Terriers	IV
KC(GB)	Terrier	3
FCI	Terriers	3

very strong hunting area, and in addition to the regular packs, there were always a considerable number of irregular hunts organised to keep down the number of foxes, something that was always important in a sheep-

298

rearing area. The origins of the Lakeland Terrier are linked, as are those of many other Terriers with the Old English Black and Tan rough-coated Terrier, but as time went by the different strains became known by names which denoted the area of their origin, so we had the Patterdale Terrier, the Elterwater Terrier and the Fell Terrier.

They were all in fact Lakeland Terriers in that they belonged to that district, but they were not known as such until a club was formed in 1912. The advent of the First World War put a stop to further progress and it was 1921 before the breed was formally recognised and a standard drawn up. Cumberland was the county of origin of the breed and is still one of its strongholds, the large agricultural shows of the county usually having a good display of the breed, often alongside classes of hunt Terriers, shown under different rules and mostly composed of his nearest rival, the Border Terrier. By 1931 the breed was well established and was granted challenge certificates in Britain though there was still considerable discussion about which was the correct type. The colour range that is acceptable in the United States of America and in Britain gives some indication of the broad Terrier basis on which the breed was built, and whilst at one time the mixed colours were the most popular in

Britain, there is a growing tendency for more self-coloureds to be shown.

In a very few years he has made his mark on the show scene all over the world, having taken many group wins and Best in Shows and his handy size, attractive personality and pleasing colour range has made him one of the popular Terriers. In recent years the number of registrations has steadied down around the same figure as for Bedlingtons and Welsh Terriers and there is little doubt that after a shaky and rather late start, he is very much here to stay. He is one of those Terriers that pays for trimming and attention to coat, though his critics will claim that perhaps at times there is too much attention, and that there is a wide gap between the appearance of a Lakeland in the ring and a pet one at home. He is however very smart, bright and sparkling in the ring, and a great little showman.

Temperamentally he is ideal as a house dog, being an excellent guard, small and easily accommodated, yet very happy and sporting, enjoying a game as all the Terriers seem to, and being very much on his toes when exploring the countryside. He is not a quarrelsome dog, but is well able to look after himself if attacked, being agile, very muscular with powerful jaws for his size.

OFFICIAL STANDARD

General appearance
The Lakeland Terrier is a small, workman-like dog of square, sturdy build and gay, friendly, self-confident demeanor. He stands on his toes as if ready to go, and he moves, lithe and graceful, with a straight-ahead, free stride of good length. His head is rectangular in contour, ears V-shaped, and wiry coat finished off with fairly long furnishings on muzzle and legs.

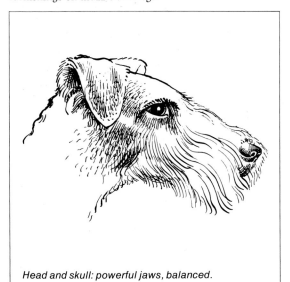

Head and skull: powerful jaws, balanced.

Head
Well balanced, rectangular, the length of skull equaling the length of the muzzle when measured from occiput to stop, and from stop to nosetip. The *skull* is flat on top and moderately broad, the cheeks almost straightsided, and the stop barely perceptible. The *muzzle* is broad with straight nose bridge and good fill-in beneath the eyes. The *nose* is black, except that liver-colored noses shall be permissible on liver-coated dogs. *Jaws* are powerful. The *teeth*, which are comparatively large, may meet in either a level, edge-to-edge bite, or a slightly overlapping scissors bite. Specimens with teeth overshot or undershot are to be disqualified. The *ears* are small, V-shaped, their fold just above the top of the skull, the inner edge close to the cheeks, and the flap pointed down. The *eyes*, moderately small and somewhat oval in outline, are set squarely in the skull, fairly wide apart. Their normally dark color may be a warm brown or black. The *expression* depends upon the dog's mood of the moment; although typically alert, it may be intense and determined, or gay and even impish.

Neck
Reachy and of good length; refined but strong; clean at the throat, slightly arched, and widening gradually into the shoulders. The withers, that point at the back of the neck where neck and body meet, are noticeably higher than the level of the back.

Body
In over-all length-to-height proportion, the dog is approximately square. The moderately narrow *chest* is

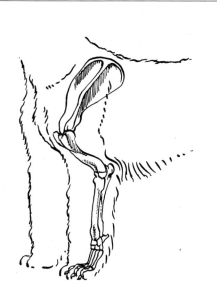

Forequarters: shoulders well laid back, forelegs straight.

deep; it extends to elbows which are held close to the body. Shoulder blades are sloping, that is, well laid back, their musculature lean and almost flat in outline. The *ribs* are well sprung and moderately rounded. The *back* is short and level in topline. *Loins* are taut and short, although they may be a trifle longer in bitches than in dogs. *Quarters* are strong, broad, and muscular.

Legs and feet
Forelegs are strongly boned, clean, and absolutely straight as viewed from the front or side, and devoid of appreciable bend at the pasterns. *Hind legs* too are strong and sturdy, the second thighs long and nicely angulated at the stifles and the hocks. *Hocks* are well let down, with the bone from hock to toes straight and parallel to each other. The small *feet* are round, the toes compact and well padded, the nails strong. Dewclaws, if any, are to be removed.

Tail
Set high on the body, the tail is customarily docked so that when the dog is set up in show position, the tip of the docked tail is on an approximate level with the skull. In carriage it is gay or upright, although a slight curve in the direction of the head is considered desirable. The tail curled over the back is faulty.

Coat and color
Two-ply or double, the outer coat is hard and wiry in texture, the undercoat soft. Furnishings on muzzle and legs are plentiful as opposed to profuse. The *color* may be blue, black, liver, black and tan, blue and tan, red, red grizzle, grizzle and tan, or wheaten. Tan is desirable in the Lakeland Terrier, is a light wheaten or straw color, with rich red or mahogany tan to be penalized. Otherwise, colors, as specified, are equally acceptable. Dark-saddled specimens (whether black grizzle or blue) are nearly solid

black at birth, with tan points on muzzle and feet. The black recedes and usually turns grayish or grizzle at maturity, while the tan also lightens.

Size
The ideal *height* of the mature dog is 14½ inches from the withers to the ground, with up to a ½-inch deviation either way permissible. Bitches may measure as much as one inch less than dogs. The *weight* of the well-balanced, mature specimen in hard, show condition, averages approximately 17 pounds, those of other heights proportionately more or less.

Size is to be considered of lesser importance than other qualities, that is, when judging dogs of equal merit, the one nearest the ideal size is to be preferred. Symmetry and proportion, however, are paramount in the appraisal, since all qualities together must be considered in visualizing the ideal.

Movement
Straight and free, with good length of stride. Paddling, moving close, and toeing-in are faulty.

Temperament
The typical Lakeland Terrier is bold, gay, and friendly, with a self-confident, cock-of-the-walk attitude. Shyness, especially shy-sharpness, in the mature specimen is to be heavily penalized.

SCALE OF POINTS
Head (15). Eyes, ears, expression (15). Neck (5), Body (10). Coat (15). Legs and feet (10). Size and symmetry (10). Movement (10). Temperament (10). *Total (100)*.

DISQUALIFICATION
The front teeth overshot or undershot.

Approved by the AKC 14 May 1963

KC(GB) VARIATION TO STANDARD
Ears: carried alertly. *Weight and size:* should not exceed 14½ inches at shoulder. Dogs 17 pounds; bitches 15 pounds.

MANCHESTER TERRIER

Tough, somewhat cloddy smooth-coated black-and-tan Terriers have existed in Britain for centuries. They were often more tan than black, and did not follow the fashion for the carefully placed areas of this colour that is so much a feature of the breed today. The black-and-tan colour is remarkable in that the general pattern of the patches of the two colours is very much the same in a number of breeds all over the world, the Rottweiler, the Doberman and the Afghan Hound for example all display the same basic pattern. The old Black-and-Tan Terrier in Britain was marked in roughly the same way. He was, however, a bull-headed dog often with cropped ears, and was used as a fighter and vermin killer. In the mining areas of Britain the rat pit was an accepted sport, and matches were regularly held to find which dog could kill the most rats in a given time. The dog most generally used for the purpose was the Black-and-Tan Terrier and a very famous dog named Billy is said to have dispatched one hundred rats in eight and a half minutes, and to have then capped this performance by destroying the same number in six minutes and thirteen seconds. Needless to say, apart from the thrill of the fight, a great deal of wagering on the result took place.

One of the early dogs, famed for his prowess in the rat pit was also a very good rabbiting dog and as the coursing of the rabbit was also very popular, the experiment of crossing this dog with a Whippet was made. The result was a strain of dogs in the Man-chester area which were faster and more refined than the old Black-and-Tan, and were known as Manchester Terriers. In those early days there were few dog shows, and those that were held were casual affairs usually held in a public house. In the Manchester area these meetings became a regular feature of the weekend life of the working man, and soon his favourite dog, the Manchester, was playing an important part in the proceedings with classes of his own. By the end of the 19th century the breed was widespread. It had lost some of its original association with Manchester and was called the Black-and-Tan Terrier. It had reached the United States of America, and in 1923 when the Manchester Terrier Club of America was formed, the name reverted to the original.

Since those early days he has had his ups and downs, as many breeds have, and the Terriers in particular. It seems that once the original purpose of a breed has disappeared either through fashion or because of legislation against it, the breed tends to go into a decline, and though no-one would wish to see the rat pit back again, it would be a fillip for many of the Terrier breeds if their usefulness could be proved in some way. As a show dog he has always had his adherents in many countries, but particularly in the United States and in his country of origin. He has not been an easy dog to maintain in his original form, as with the emphasis on colour and markings, some of the structural requirements were lost sight of and he went through a bad patch. Now, however, he is being shown as a very sound and showy dog with a lean attractive head, neat ears and a close-fitting glossy coat.

He makes a very good pet and house dog, as although his background is in some respects not a salubrious one, he has always been associated with people and families, living as one of the household and being kept in small numbers rather than in large kennels. The result is that he is very domesticated, friendly with people and especially with children, and clean and mannerly around the house.

OFFICIAL STANDARD

Head

Long, narrow, tight-skinned, almost flat, with a slight indentation up the forehead; slightly wedge-shaped, tapering to the nose, with no visible cheek muscles, and well filled up under the eyes; tight-lipped jaws, level in mouth, and functionally level teeth, or the incisors of the upper jaw may make a close, slightly overlapping contact with the incisors of the lower jaw. *Eyes:* small, bright, sparkling and as near black as possible; set moderately close together; oblong in shape, slanting upwards on the outside; they should neither protrude nor sink in the skull. *Nose:* black. *Ears (toy variety):* of moderate size; set well up on the skull and rather close together; thin, moderately narrow at base; with pointed tips; naturally erect carriage. Wide, flaring, blunt-tipped or 'bell' ears are a serious fault; cropped or cut ears shall disqualify. *Ears (standard variety):* erect, or button, small and thin; smaller at the root and set at close together as possible at the top of the head. If cropped, to a point, long and carried erect.

Neck and shoulders

The neck should be a moderate length, slim and graceful; gradually becoming larger as it approaches, and blend smoothly with the sloping shoulders; free from throatiness; slightly arched from the occiput.

Chest

Narrow between the legs; deep in the brisket.

Body

Moderately short, with robust loins; ribs well sprung out behind the shoulders; back slightly arched at the loin, and falling again to the tail to the same height as the shoulder.

Legs

Forelegs straight, of proportionate length, and well under body. Hind legs should not turn in or out as viewed from the rear; carried back; hocks well let down. *Feet:* compact, well arched, with jet black nails; the two middle toes in the front feet rather longer than the others; the hind feet shaped like those of a cat.

Tail

Moderately short, and set on where the arch of the back ends; thick where it joins the body, tapering to a point, not carried higher than the back.

Coat

Smooth, short, thick, dense, close and glossy; not soft.

Color

Jet black and rich mahogany tan, which should not run or blend into each other but abruptly forming clear, well-defined lines of color division. A small tan spot over each eye; a very small tan spot on each cheek; the lips of the upper and lower jaws should be tanned, extending under the throat, ending in the shape of the letter V; the inside of the ears partly tanned. Tan spots, called 'rosettes',

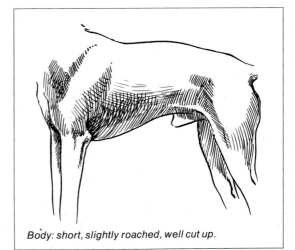
Body: short, slightly roached, well cut up.

on each side of the chest above the front legs, more pronounced in puppies than in adults. There should be a black 'thumb mark' patch on the front of each foreleg between the pastern and the knee. There should be a distinct black 'pencil mark' line running lengthwise on the top of each toe on all four feet. The remainder of the forelegs to be tan to the knee. Tan on the hind legs should continue from the penciling on the feet up the inside of the legs to a little below the stifle joint; the outside of the hind legs to be black. There should be tan under the tail, and on the vent, but only of such size as to be covered by the tail. White in any part of the coat is a serious fault, and shall disqualify whenever the white shall form a patch or stripe measuring as much as ½-inch in its longest dimension.

Weight *(Toy variety)*

Not exceeding 12 pounds. It is suggested that clubs consider dividing the American-bred and open classes by weight as follows: 7 pounds and under, over 7 pounds and not exceeding 12 pounds.

Weight *(Standard variety)*

Over 12 pounds and not exceeding 22 pounds. Dogs weighing over 22 pounds shall be disqualified. It is suggested that clubs consider dividing the American-bred and open classes by weight as follows: over 12 pounds and not exceeding 16 pounds, over 16 pounds and not exceeding 22 pounds.

DISQUALIFICATIONS
Color: white in any part of the coat, forming a patch or stripe measuring as much as ½ inch in its longest dimension. Weight (Standard variety): over 22 pounds. Ears (Toy variety): cropped or cut ears.

Approved by the AKC 12 June 1962

KC(GB) VARIATION TO STANDARD

Ears: v-shaped, carried well above top line of head and hanging close to head above eyes. *Feet:* small, semi-harefooted. *Height:* (desired) dogs 16 inches; bitches 15 inches.

MINIATURE SCHNAUZER

By breeding from the smaller dogs in a litter and probably by introducing new blood from other breeds, a steady process of miniaturisation produced the smallest of the three Schnauzers, the Miniature. Compared with the other two he is quite a tiny dog in his modern form, and whilst the standard suggests that an ideal height of thirteen to fourteen inches should be aimed at, there are many fine specimens that are smaller even than this. He came from the same root stock as the Schnauzer, but it is suggested

NATIONAL GROUPING		
	Name	Number
AKC	Terriers	IV
KC(GB)	Utility	4
FCI	Companion Dogs	9

that the Affenpinscher was used to help reduce the size whilst at the same time retaining the Terrier characteristics. He became a very popular dog in the

United States of America, and has been bred in that country successfully for the past half century or so, though they decided at an early date that he was a Terrier, something with which many countries disagree, not the least Britain where he is firmly established in the Utility group.

The breed has steadily increased throughout the world, and there is no sign that numbers are decreasing. His handy size, pleasant temperament and delightful showmanship constantly gaining new admirers for him. He is a square dog, and this is exaggerated by his presentation, the head having very pronounced hair on the eyebrows, the body coat being kept very short with the leg hair encouraged as much as possible. The total appearance is that of a very sharp, smart little dog. He is still a great vermin hunter, and likes nothing better than a good rat hunt, but his small size and cleanliness suit him admirably to life in a small apartment with a nearby park for exercise.

As a show dog he is ideal, few dogs repaying care and attention to presentation as he does. He can be shaped and trimmed to make the most of his characteristics, and whilst he always looks the epitome of smartness in show trim there is never anything artificial about him. When released from the tension of being shown his exuberance is infectious. He can be trained to stand absolutely still in the ring with just a little temptation by his handler, and in competition with other breeds usually scores on sheer ring performance. As a pet he is completely reliable, with no vice, great good spirits, and very friendly with everyone including children.

OFFICIAL STANDARD

General appearance
The Miniature Schnauzer is a robust, active dog of terrier type, resembling his larger cousin, the Standard Schnauzer, in general appearance, and of an alert, active disposition. He is sturdily built, nearly square in proportion of body length to height, with plenty of bone, and without any suggestion of toyishness.

Head
Strong and rectangular, its width diminishing slightly from ears to eyes, and again to the tip of the nose. The

Neck: moderately long, nape strong, slightly arched, skin close.

forehead is unwrinkled. The topskull is flat and fairly long. The foreface is parallel to the topskull, with a slight stop, and is at least as long as the topskull. The muzzle is strong in proportion to the skull; it ends in a moderately blunt manner, with thick whiskers which accentuate the rectangular shape of the head. *Teeth:* the teeth meet in a scissors bite. That is, the upper front teeth overlap front teeth in such a manner that the inner surface of the upper incisors barely touches the outer surface of the lower incisors when the mouth is closed. *Eyes:* small, dark brown and deep-set. They are oval in appearance and keen in expression. *Ears:* when cropped the ears are identical in shape and length, with pointed tips. They are in balance with the head and not exaggerated in length. They are set high on the skull and carried perpendicularly at the inner edges, with as little bell as possible along the outer edges. When uncropped, the ears are small and V-shaped, folding close to the skull.

Neck
Strong and well arched, blending into the shoulders, and with the skin fitting tightly at the throat.

Body
Short and deep, with the brisket extending at least to the elbows. Ribs are well sprung and deep, extending well back to a short loin. The underbody does not present a tucked-up appearance at the flank. The topline is straight; it declines slightly from the withers to the base of the tail. The over-all length from chest to stern bone equals the height at the withers.

Forequarters
The forequarters have flat, somewhat sloping shoulders and high withers. Forelegs are straight and parallel when viewed from all sides. They have strong pasterns and good bone. They are separated by a fairly deep brisket which precludes a pinched front. The elbows are close, and the ribs spread gradually from the first rib so as to allow space for the elbows to move close to the body.

Hindquarters
The hindquarters have strong-muscled, slanting thighs: they are well bent at the stifles and straight from hock to so-called heel. There is sufficient angulation so that, in stance, the hocks extend beyond the tail. The hindquarters never appear overbuilt or higher than the shoulders.

Feet
Short and round (cat-feet) with thick, black pads. The toes are arched and compact.

Action
The trot is the gait at which movement is judged. The dog must gait in a straight line. Coming on, the forelegs are parallel, with the elbows close to the body. The feet turn neither inward nor outward. Going away, the hind legs are parallel from the hocks down, and travel wide. Viewed from the side, the forelegs have a good reach, while the hind legs have a strong drive with good pick-up of hocks.

Tail
Set high and carried erect. It is docked only long enough to be clearly visible over the topline of the body when the dog is in proper length of coat.

Coat
Double, with a hard, wiry outer coat and a close undercoat. The body coat should be plucked. When in show condition, the proper length is not less than three-quarters of an inch except on neck, ears and skull. Furnishings are fairly thick but not silky.

Size
From 12 to 14 inches. Ideal size $13\frac{1}{2}$ inches. (*See disqualifications.*)

Color
The recognized colors are salt and pepper, black and silver, and solid black. The typical color is salt and pepper in shades of gray; tan shading is permissible. The salt and pepper mixture fades out to light gray or silver white in the eyebrows, whiskers, cheeks, under throat, across chest, under tail, leg furnishings, under body, and inside legs. The light under-body hair is not to rise higher on the sides of the body than the front elbows.

The black and silvers follow the same pattern as the salt and peppers. The entire salt-and-pepper section must be black.

Black is the only solid color allowed. It must be a true black with no gray hairs and no brown tinge except where the whiskers may have become discolored. A small white spot on the chest is permitted.

FAULTS

Type: toyishness, raciness, or coarseness. *Structure:* head coarse and cheeky. Chest too broad or shallow in brisket. Tail set low. Sway or roach back. Bowed or cowhocked hindquarters. Loose elbows. *Action:* sidegaiting. Paddling in front, or high hackney knee action. Weak hind action. *Coat:* too soft or too smooth and slick in appearance. *Temperament:* shyness or viciousness. *Bite:* undershot or overshot jaw. Level bite. *Eyes:* light and/or large and prominent in appearance.

DISQUALIFICATIONS

Dogs or bitches under 12 inches or over 14 inches. Color solid white or white patches on the body.

Approved by the AKC 13 May 1958

KC(GB) VARIATION TO STANDARD
This dog is granted championship status by the KC(GB) in the Utility Group of Non-Sporting Breeds. *Eyes:* medium size. *Ears:* not cropped. *Feet:* dark nails. *Height:* (ideal) dogs 14 inches; bitches 13 inches. *Faults:* spotty, tigered or red colours.

NORWICH TERRIER

This attractive little short-legged Terrier was first accepted to the KC(GB) register as a recognised breed in 1932. He had however been recognised as a well-established breed for many years prior to that time. He is in fact one of the old native Terrier types of Norfolk, a county of wide areas under cultivation, large tracts of grassland and countless woods, lakes and rivers, an area rich in game and in the history of hunting. Dr. Caius, writing in 1576, said 'Another sort there is that hunteth the fox and the badger only, whom we call Terrars, they creep into the ground, and by that means make afraid, nip and bite the fox and badger in such sort that either they tear them in pieces with their teeth being in the earth, or else hail and pull them out perforce out of their lurking angles, dark dungeons, and close caves.'

This paints a very graphic picture of what a Terrier

NATIONAL GROUPING		
	Name	Number
AKC	Terriers	IV
KC(GB)	Terrier	3
FCI	Terriers	3

is supposed to do, and making allowances for the somewhat picturesque language, gives a very good idea of the conditions under which he is supposed to work. The protagonists of the short-legged Terriers will say that the long-legged ones are incapable of doing this sort of work and will point to other breeds and even to other Groups for examples of the build of the dogs that go to ground. The ideal dog for the purpose is obviously a strong one, low to the ground with powerful legs and hindquarters to push and probe, with the sort of jaw power that will allow it to deal with a fairly fierce trapped adversary whilst taking care of itself. Those who produced this Terrier from East Anglia will say that they solved the problem.

Although an old breed, he first came to public attention in the middle of the 19th century. He was at that time, and the date 1880 is often quoted as the time when his popularity began to climb, already being used as a hunting Terrier, but he became something of a cult with the university fraternity of Cambridge. The young bloods, seeking sport outside the walls of the university, and many of them being unable to afford the keeping of a horse and riding to hounds, indulged in more casual hunting trips with their own dogs. The Cantab Terrier, as it became known at that time, was the obvious solution, being small enough to live in lodgings but sporting enough to satisfy the tastes of the times.

After the First World War, a number of specimens were imported into the United States of America, being known as Jones Terriers after the man who bred them in Britain. They joined various packs of Fox-hounds as hunt Terriers, and for some time the Cheshire Hunt in Philadelphia kept a small kennel. In 1932 the breed was recognised by the KC(GB) and in 1936 the American Kennel Club also granted recognition. In the United States of America the breed has remained one, both the drop-eared and the prick-eared varieties being recognised as the Norwich Terrier. However, after considerable pressure from breeders and breed clubs, the breed was divided in Britain, the prick-eared variety being known as the Norwich Terrier, and the drop-eared as the Norfolk Terrier. Those breeders who did not favour the change accused those who did of wishing to divide the breed merely because they could not consistently breed prick-eared dogs, but this was probably fallacious. For a time, as is customary, interbreeding between the two varieties was permitted, the progeny being registered according to the ear placement. This has now ceased, and the Norwich and the Norfolk are now two quite distinct varieties in Britain.

He has made steady progress towards popularity over the years since 1935, and now matches the Scottish and Dandie Dinmont Terriers in numbers of registrations in Britain. His attractive appearance, small size and engaging personality are rapidly spreading his popularity throughout the world, and he now appears at shows regularly in most countries. A few very good specimens are making their mark in the show world in his country of origin owing to the efforts of a small number of enthusiastic and dedicated breeders and exhibitors. He is in fact a very good show dog, being easy to keep in trim, as though his coat needs the same sort of care and attention to keep it looking neat as does that of other hard-coated terriers, he is much smaller and merely needs tidying up rather than sculpting. He is small, easily transported, and his appetite is moderate, which makes him an ideal house

pet. His temperament is attractive, as he has the spirit of a Terrier, but is more stolid and easy-going than many of them. He is loyal, quite affectionate, and is an extremely good house guard, having sharp hearing and a strong sense of territory.

Britain is the country of Terriers; of the dogs listed throughout the world as belonging to this group, a mere handful originated in other countries. Yet the Norwich Terrier is distinct from any of the others and it is difficult to claim that he descended from other breeds. Of the short-legged Terriers, only the Cairn resembles him in general physical characteristics, and there are many fundamental differences. He has a head rather like a Border Terrier, the smartness of the Scottish Terrier, the hard coat of the Wire Fox Terrier and the tail carriage of the Sealyham, yet in total he is unlike any of these. Over the years there have been crossbred Terriers in many parts of Britain that have looked very like the Norwich that we know today, and one is forced to the conclusion that he is probably a thoroughly basic Terrier type. There have been claims that he was produced from the Irish Terrier, with possibly Scottish Terrier and Cairn blood, but this

can be discounted, and he is almost certainly a very ancient East Anglian form that has been developed over the years into the form that we know today.

He is a very active little dog, his short legs in no way handicapping him. He enjoys long runs in the country following a horse and hunting the undergrowth in the typical Terrier fashion. Weather in no way deters him from this, and he stands up to extremes of climate, is virtually waterproof, and being a dog with no abnormalities, he stands the heat as well as the cold, which makes him a suitable dog for almost any country. He is easily fed, remains remarkably fit with very little organised exercise as most of the Terriers do, and has no inherent weaknesses. As a show dog he is most successful, as he is rarely nervous, stands up well to the rigours of travelling, and is not disturbed by conditions or by other dogs.

OFFICIAL STANDARD

General appearance
A small, low rugged terrier, tremendously active. A perfect demon, yet not quarrelsome, and of a lovable

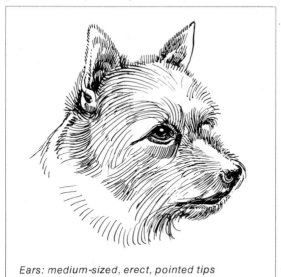

Ears: medium-sized, erect, pointed tips

disposition, and a very hardy constitution. Honorable scars from fair wear and tear shall not count against.

Head
Skull wide, slightly rounded with good width between the ears. Muzzle strong but not long or heavy, with slightly 'foxy' appearance. Length about one-third less than the measurement from the occiput to the bottom of the stop, which should be well defined. *Faults:* a long narrow head; over square muzzle; highly rounded dome.

Ears: medium-sized, drooping to cheek.

Ears
Prick or drop. If pricked, small, pointed, erect and set well apart. If dropped, neat, small, with break just above the skull line, front edge close to cheek, and not falling lower than the outer corner of the eye. *Faults:* oversize; poor carriage.

Eyes
Very bright, dark and keen. Full of expression. *Faults:* light or protruding eyes.

Jaw
Clean, strong, tight lipped, with strong, large, closely-fitting teeth; scissors bite. *Faults:* a bite over- or undershot.

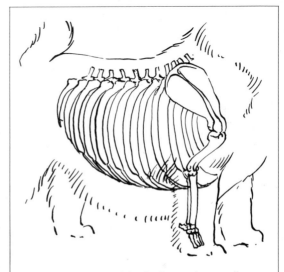

Body: compact, good depth, rib cage long, well sprung.

Neck
Short and strong, well set on clean shoulders.

Body
Moderately short, compact and deep with level topline, ribs well sprung. *Faults:* long weak back, loaded shoulders.

Legs
Short and powerful and as straight as is consistent with the short legs for which we aim. Sound bone, round feet, thick pads. *Faults:* out at elbow, badly bowed, knuckled over. Too light in bone.

Quarters
Strong, rounded, with great powers of propulsion. *Faults:* Cowhocks.

Tail
Medium docked, carriage not excessively gay.

Forequarters: short, powerful, straight legs.

full coat longer and rougher forming almost a mane on shoulders and neck. Hair on head, ears and muzzle, except for slight eyebrows and slight whiskers, is absolutely short and smooth. These dogs should be shown with as nearly a natural coat as possible. A minimum amount of tidying is permissible but excessive trimming, shaping and clipping shall be heavily penalized by the judge. *Faults:* silky or curly coat.

Weight
Ideal, 11 to 12 pounds.

Height
Ideal, 10 inches at the withers.

General appearance
A small, low rugged terrier, tremendously active. A perfect demon, yet not quarrelsome, and of a lovable disposition, and a very hardy constitution. Honorable scars from fair wear and tear shall not count against.

DISQUALIFICATION
Cropped ears shall disqualify.

Approved by the AKC 10 June 1969

Color
All shades of red, wheaten, black and tan and grizzle. White markings on the chest, though allowable, are not desirable. *Faults:* white markings elsewhere or to any great extent on the chest.

Coat
As hard and wiry as possible, lying close to the body, with a definite undercoat. Top coat absolutely straight; in

KC(GB) VARIATION TO STANDARD
The drop ear variety is shown under the name Norfolk Terrier in the UK. *Ears:* medium size; v-shaped but slightly rounded at tip. *Eyes:* oval shaped and deep set. *Neck:* medium length. *Hindquarters:* good turn of stifle; hocks well let down.

SCOTTISH TERRIER

NATIONAL GROUPING		
	Name	Number
AKC	Terriers	IV
KC(GB)	Terrier	3
FCI	Terriers	3

There are few dogs about which as much controversy has raged as about the origin of the Scottish Terrier. In the early days a number of different breeds existed in Scotland, almost all of which, being Terriers from Scotland, were known or wished to be known as Scottish Terriers—which indeed but for the capital letters they were, as they were all 'terriers' from Scotland. Add to that the confusion that was caused when early Terriers of the type that we now know as the Scottish Terrier were bred on the Isle of Skye, and were first exhibited as Skye Terriers though they were nothing like the dog that we now know by that name. There have always been Terriers of different sorts in Scotland, and on the islands particularly, isolation led to fairly close inter-breeding and the early establishment of fixed types. Although he had been in existence for a long time, he was superseded into the ring by some of the other Scottish Terrier breeds such as the Dandie and the Skye, which were known and recognised, with the result that a number of somewhat odd looking dogs were exhibited as Scottish Terriers in the second half of the 19th century.

In 1877 so mixed up had the situation become, that the editor of the *Live Stock Journal* having endured a lengthy and sometimes scurrilous correspondence on what in fact constituted a Scottish Terrier, finally put a stop to the flood of letters with the comment, 'We see no use in prolonging this discussion except each correspondent describes the dog he is talking about and holds to be the true type'. Capt. Gordon Murray eventually in 1879 described what he felt the Scottish Terrier should look like, deplored the exhibiting of what he called mongrels with hair ten and a half inches long, and thus started a movement towards the breed as we know it today. S. E. Shirley supported him, and arranged for two classes of the type of dog that he described to be staged at the Kennel Club show at Alexandra Palace, and the breed was on its way to present day popularity. The Scottish Terrier often went by the name of Aberdeen Terrier, and still does to this day in some parts of Britain.

The Scottish Terrier Club was formed in 1882 and in that year a joint committee of representatives from Scotland and South of the Border drew up a standard for the breed which has varied very little from that time. The American standard was adopted in 1925 by a small committee, the only real difference between that and the British standard being in the matter of weight, the American standard allowing a slightly lighter dog.

To many people, the Scottish Terrier is a black dog, largely because many of them were at one time black and this colour featured in a well-known publicity campaign for a famous Scottish product. He may, however, be any one of several colours, and some of the lighter dogs are very striking. He is a strong heavily built little dog, short on the leg and with strong bone and very good muscle. His head has for many years been one of his important features, with its square well-furnished muzzle and long skull. His ears are neat and carried high, his neck long and his body strong, and in total he presents a picture of one of the smartest show dogs possible. His temperament is keen, as might be expected of a dog that is very much the Terrier, but he is kindly with those he knows, and he makes an excellent pet and house dog.

OFFICIAL STANDARD

General appearance

The face should wear a keen, sharp and active expression. Both head and tail should be carried well up. The dog should look very compact, well muscled and powerful, giving the impression of immense power in a small size.

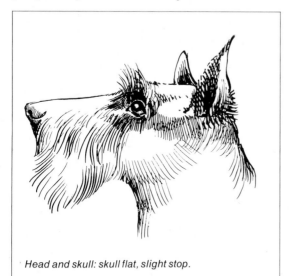

Head and skull: skull flat, slight stop.

Skull

Long, of medium width, slightly domed and covered with short, hard hair. It should not be quite flat, as there should be a slight stop or drop between the eyes.

Muzzle

In proportion to the length of skull, with not too much taper toward the nose. Nose should be black and of good size. The jaws should be level and square. The nose projects somewhat over the mouth, giving the impression that the upper jaw is longer than the lower. The teeth should be evenly placed, having a scissors or level bite, with the former being preferable.

Eyes

Set wide apart, small and of almond shape, not round. Color to be dark brown or nearly black. To be bright, piercing and set well under the brow.

Ears

Small, prick, set well up on the skull, rather pointed but not cut. The hair on them should be short and velvety.

Neck

Moderately short, thick and muscular, strongly set on sloping shoulders, but not so short as to appear clumsy.

Chest

Broad and very deep, well let down between the forelegs.

Body

Moderately short and well ribbed up with strong loin, deep flanks and very muscular hindquarters.

Legs and feet

Both forelegs and hind legs should be short and very heavy in bone in proportion to the size of the dog. Forelegs straight or slightly bent with elbows close to the body. Scottish Terriers should not be out at the elbows. Stifles should be well bent and legs straight from hock to heel. Thighs very muscular. Feet round and thick with strong nails, forefeet larger than the hind feet. *Note:* the gait of the Scottish Terrier is peculiarly its own and is very characteristic of the breed. It is not the square trot or walk that is desirable in the long-legged breeds. The forelegs do not move in exact parallel planes—rather in reaching out incline slightly inward. This is due to the shortness of leg and width of chest. The action of the rear legs should be square and true and at the trot both the hocks and stifles should be flexed with a vigorous motion.

Tail

Never cut and about 7 inches long, carried with a slight curve but not over the back.

Coat

Rather short, about 2 inches, dense undercoat with outer coat intensely hard and wiry.

Size and weight

Equal consideration must be given to height, length of back and weight. Height at shoulder for either sex should be about 10 inches. Generally, a well-balanced Scottish Terrier dog of correct size should weigh from 19 to 22 pounds and a bitch, from 18 to 21 pounds. The principal objective must be symmetry and balance.

Color

Steel or iron gray, brindled or grizzled, black, sandy or wheaten. White markings are objectionable and can be allowed only on the chest and that to a slight extent only.

Penalties

Soft coat, round, or very light eye, overshot or undershot jaw, obviously oversize or undersize, shyness, timidity to show with head and tail up are faults to be penalized. No judge should put to Winners or Best of Breed any Scottish Terrier not showing real terrier character in the ring.

SCALE OF POINTS
Skull (5). Muzzle (5). Eyes (5). Ears (10). Neck (5). Chest (5). Body (15). Legs and feet (10). Tail (2½). Coat (15). Size (10). Color (2½). General appearance (10). *Total (100)*.

Approved by the AKC 10 June 1947

KC(GB) VARIATION TO STANDARD

Head: the skull is nearly flat and cheek bones do not protrude. *Feet:* well padded toes, well arched. *Weight:* from 19 to 23 pounds.

SEALYHAM TERRIER

NATIONAL GROUPING		
	Name	Number
AKC	Terriers	IV
KC(GB)	Terrier	3
FCI	Terriers	3

The evolution of the Sealyham Terrier began in the second half of the 19th century when Capt. John Edwardes of Sealyham, Haverfordwest in Pembrokeshire developed from some obscure Terrier strains a dog to use on badger and fox, one small enough to go to ground and game enough to tackle such large and fierce quarry. It is suggested that he imported Dandie Dinmont blood into his kennels to shorten the legs whilst maintaining the pluck of his Terriers, as there are few Terriers as persistent in attack on vermin as the Dandie. It is possible, too, that Bull Terriers were used to increase jaw power, but whatever went into the make-up of the Sealyham, one thing remains clear and that is that the end result was a very game and very smart Terrier. The breed was first shown in 1903 in Haverfordwest, and in 1908 the Sealyham Terrier Club of Haverfordwest was founded. The Great Joint Terrier Show was the first show in Britain to have challenge certificates on offer in 1911, and in March of that year the breed attained recognition for the first time. By that year too the breed had been recognised in the United States of America and made its debut at the San Mateo Show in California.

The breed went ahead very quickly after those early days, even though for a while many of the dogs shown were indifferent in type and little like the classy dog of today. After the First World War the breed really came into its own and a great deal of careful selective breeding for type took place so that by the 1920s he was a breed that not only looked really smart, but was still capable of doing the work for which he was first intended. He is one of the few Terriers that happily hunts in a pack, and one very well-known English gentleman, Sir Jocelyn Lucas, was to be seen at one time with a large number of these dogs that ran together. By the mid-twenties the demand was very great, many being exported to the United States and becoming a very popular show dog in that country, taking Group and Best in Show awards at major All-breed shows.

The sporting side of the breed had not been ignored, and the Sealyham Terrier Badger Digging Association was formed to preserve the dogs' working qualities. Winnie Barber writing in 1948 said that contrary to gloomy predictions that the breeders of show Sealyhams were ruining the breed, in spite of the interruption of the Second World War, the Sealyham has not only retained his beauty and brains, but his pluck and sporting proclivities as well. It will be interesting to see what happens in future years with the badger becoming a protected animal.

The Sealyham has been a tremendously successful show dog in many parts of the world and though the registration figures in Britain show a steady decline he is in no danger of becoming rare. He is one of those dogs that pays for most careful preparation work, and whilst he retains his basic shape when put down in the ring rather more than some breeds do, he does look so much better for a certain amount of clever shaping. He is bold and carefree in the ring, outward looking, almost invariably interested in what is going on around him, and moves with the commanding presence of one who knows that he looks well and has an admiring public.

Those who have owned one say that they never wish to own any other breed, as temperamentally he is quite captivating. He has an entertaining sense of humour, thoroughly enjoys a game or a romp, and tends to invent tricks and games of his own. He makes a grand companion and house pet, is a very good guard and child minder, and his voice sounds like that of a much larger dog to any intending intruder.

OFFICIAL STANDARD

The Sealyham should be the embodiment of power and determination, ever keen and alert, of extraordinary substance, yet free from clumsiness.

Head

Long, broad and powerful without coarseness. It should, however, be in perfect balance with the body, joining neck smoothly. Length of head roughly, three-quarters height at withers, or about an inch longer than neck. Breadth between ears a little less than one-half length of head. *Skull:* very slightly domed, with a shallow indentation running down between the brows, and joining the muzzle with a moderate stop. *Cheeks:* smoothly formed and flat, without heavy jowls. *Jaws:* powerful and square. Bite level or scissors. Overshot or undershot bad faults. *Teeth:* sound, strong and white, with canines fitting closely together. *Nose:* black, with large nostrils. White, cherry or butterfly bad faults. *Eyes:* very dark, deeply set and fairly wide apart, of medium size, oval in shape with keen terrier expression. Light, large or protruding eye bad faults. Lack of eye rim pigmentation not a fault. *Ears:* folded level with top of head, with forward edge close to cheek. Well rounded at tip, and of length to reach outer corner of eye. Thin, not leathery, and of sufficient thickness to avoid creases. Prick, tulip, rose or hound ears bad faults.

Neck

Length slightly less than two-thirds of height of dog at withers. Muscular without coarseness, with good reach, refinement at throat, and set firmly on shoulders.

Shoulders

Well laid back and powerful, but not over-muscled. Sufficiently wide to permit freedom of action. Upright or straight shoulder placement highly undesirable.

Legs

Forelegs strong, with good bone; and as straight as is consistent with chest being well let down between them.

Forequarters: forelegs short, strong and straight.

Down on pasterns, knuckled over, bowed, and out at elbow, bad faults. Hind legs longer than forelegs and not so heavily boned. *Feet:* large but compact, round with thick pads, strong nails. Toes well arched and pointing straight ahead. Forefeet larger, though not quite so long as hind feet. Thin, spread or flat feet bad faults.

Body

Strong, short-coupled and substantial, so as to permit great flexibility. Brisket deep and well let down between forelegs. Ribs well sprung.

Back

Length from withers to set-on of tail should approximate height at withers, or $10\frac{1}{2}$ inches. Topline level, neither roached nor swayed. Any deviations from these measurements undesirable. *Hindquarters:* very powerful, and protruding well behind the set-on of tail. Strong second thighs, stifles well bent, and hocks well let down. Cow-hocks bad fault.

Tail

Docked and carried upright. Set on far enough forward so that spine does not slope down to it.

Coat

Weather-resisting, comprised of soft, dense undercoat and hard, wiry top coat. Silky or curly coat bad fault.

Color

All white, or with lemon, tan or badger markings on head and ears. Heavy body markings and excessive ticking should be discouraged.

Height

At withers about $10\frac{1}{2}$ inches.

Weight

23 to 24 pounds for dogs; bitches slightly less. It should be borne in mind that size is more important than weight.

Action

Sound, strong, quick, free, true and level.

SCALE OF POINTS
General character, balance and size (15). Head (5). Eyes (5). Mouth (5). Ears (5). Neck (5). Shoulders and brisket (10). Body, ribs and loin (10). Hindquarters (10). Legs and feet (10) Coat (10). Tail (5). Color (body marking and ticking) (5). *Total (100).*

Approved by the AKC 9 February 1974

KC(GB) VARIATION TO STANDARD

Eyes: round. *Weight and size:* should not exceed 12 inches at shoulder. Dogs not to exceed 20 pounds. Bitches not to exceed 18 pounds.

SKYE TERRIER

The appearance of the Skye Terrier completely belies his character. He looks like what one might call the 'fancy pants' of the Terriers, but in the words of one Scot, he is a 'terrible fetcher'. If two get to grips their steel-trap jaws are extremely difficult to prise apart, and they will attempt to fight to the death. He is one of the oldest of all the Terrier breeds, and Dr. Caius, writing at the time of Queen Elizabeth I, describes a dog from the north which he said came from Iceland, which almost completely fits the description of the breed as we know it today. He came, as his name suggests from the Island of Skye, which is so far north that to Dr. Caius it could well have appeared to be Iceland, and is one of two of today's breeds that emanated from that island. There is a tradition sometimes referred to, that he was evolved from dogs that swam from the ships of the Armada wrecked off the Isle of Skye, but Dr. Caius's description predates the Armada by some twenty years.

He was very much a working dog, and his low-to-the-

NATIONAL GROUPING		
	Name	Number
AKC	Terriers	IV
KC(GB)	Terrier	3
FCI	Terriers	3

ground build enabled him to go to ground to fox or badger, whilst his long hard outer coat and short close undercoat protected him from the undergrowth and from the teeth of the animals with which he often found himself engaged. He has always been a great hunter, and his apparently soft appearance completely disappears when he joins some of his fellows in a cross-country hunt. That is not to say that he becomes a ravening beast, but that his strength and fitness prove him to be the able hunter that he always has been. He has been used to produce several other breeds as exhibitors envied his lovely coat, and there is little doubt that he was ancestor to the Yorkshire Terrier in Britain and the Australian Silky. He had become one of the pre-eminent show breeds in the United States of America before the turn of the century, and though since that time his popularity has declined he is still regularly seen in top competition.

In Britain too his popularity is on the wane, though he has been readily accepted in many other countries who see in him one of the glamour dogs of the Terrier Group and a potential Group and Best in Show winner. He is not a difficult dog to prepare for show as his coat repays for regular brushing and combing, and does not soften with the occasional bath as does that of some of the hard-coated Terriers. There is no trimming, and all that is needed is to keep him in a fit condition and to encourage his coat to grow. His coat is clearly one of his most striking features, and not only are the colours themselves striking but there is also some very subtle shading, and the black fringes on his ears complete a very pleasing picture.

He is game, staunch and courageous with great stamina and agility and is generally good tempered. With those whom he knows he is friendly, gay and loyal, but with strangers he is somewhat cautious and wary. His coat is not the sort that sheds easily which means that he can be kept as a house dog, a situation which he makes quite clear that he prefers. His appearance certainly gives any owner a feeling of one-upmanship when the dog is compared with the more prosaic animals usually kept by the neighbours.

OFFICIAL STANDARD

General appearance
The Skye Terrier is a dog of style, elegance, and dignity; agile and strong with sturdy bone and hard muscle. Long, low, and lank—he is twice as long as he is high—he is covered with a profuse coat that falls straight down either side of the body over oval-shaped ribs. The hair well feathered on the head veils forehead and eyes to serve as protection from brush and briar as well as amid serious encounters with other animals. He stands with head high and long tail hanging, and moves with a seemingly effortless gait. Of suitable size for his hunting work, strong in body, quarters, and jaw.

Temperament
That of the typical working terrier capable of overtaking game and going to ground, displaying stamina, courage, strength, and agility. Fearless, good-tempered, loyal and canny, he is friendly and gay with those he knows and reserved and cautious with strangers.

Head
Long and powerful, strength being deemed more important than extreme length. Moderate width at the back of the skull tapers gradually to a strong muzzle. The stop is slight. The dark muzzle is just moderately full as opposed to snipy, and the nose is always black. A Dudley, flesh-colored, or brown nose shall disqualify. Powerful and absolutely true jaws and mouth with the incisor teeth closing level, or with the upper teeth slightly overlapping the lower. *Eyes:* brown, preferably dark brown, medium in size, close-set, and alight with life and intelligence. *Ears:* symmetrical and gracefully feathered. They may be carried prick or drop. When prick, they are medium in size, placed high on the skull, erect at their outer edges, and slightly wider apart at the peak than at the skull. Drop ears, somewhat larger in size and set lower, hang flat against the skull.

Neck
Long and gracefully arched, carried high and proudly.

Body
Pre-eminently long and low. The backline is level, the chest deep, with oval-shaped ribs. The sides appear flattish due to the straight falling and profuse coat.

Legs and feet
Forequarters: legs short, muscular, and straight as possible. 'Straight as possible' means straight as soundness and chest will permit; it does not mean 'terrier straight.' Shoulders well laid back, with tight placement of shoulder blades at the withers, and elbows should fit closely to the sides and be neither loose nor tied. Forearm should curve slightly around the chest. *Hindquarters:* strong, full, well developed, and well angulated. Legs short, muscular, and straight when viewed from behind. *Feet:* large harefeet preferably pointing forward, the pads thick and nails strong and preferably black.

Movement
The legs proceed straight forward when traveling. When

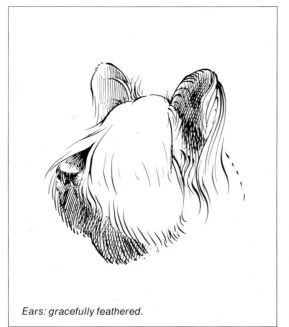

Ears: gracefully feathered.

approaching the forelegs form a continuation of the straight line of the front, the feet being the same distance apart as the elbows. The principal propelling power is furnished by the hind legs, which travel straight forward. Forelegs should move well forward, without too much lift. The whole movement may be termed free, active, and effortless and give a more or less fluid picture.

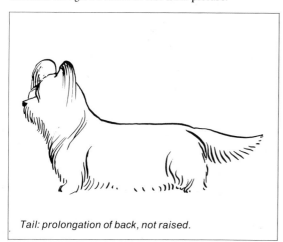

Tail: prolongation of back, not raised.

Tail

Long and well feathered. When hanging, its upper section is pendulous, following the line of the rump, its lower section thrown back in a moderate arc without twist or curl. When raised, its height makes it appear a prolongation of the backline. Though not to be preferred, the tail is sometimes carried high when the dog is excited or angry. When such carriage arises from emotion only, it is permissible. But the tail should not be constantly carried above the level of the back nor hang limp.

Coat

Double. Undercoat short, close, soft, and woolly. Outer coat hard, straight and flat, $5\frac{1}{2}$ inches long without extra credit granted for greater length. The body coat hangs straight down each side, parting from head to tail. The head hair, which may be shorter and softer, veils forehead and eyes and forms a moderate beard and apron. The long feathering on the ears falls straight down from the tips and outer edges, surrounding the ears like a fringe and outlining their shape. The ends of the hair should mingle with the coat at the sides of the neck.

Color

The coat must be of one over-all color at the skin but may be of varying shades of the same color in the full coat, which may be black, blue, dark or light gray, silver platinum, fawn, or cream. The dog must have no distinctive markings except for the desirable black points of ears, muzzle, and tip of tail, all of which points are preferably dark even to black. The shade of head and legs should approximate that of the body. There must be no trace of pattern, design, or clear-cut color variations, with the exception of the breed's only permissible white which occasionally exists on the chest not exceeding 2 inches in diameter.

The puppy coat may be very different in color from the adult coat. As it is growing and clearing, wide variations of color may occur; consequently this is permissible in dogs under 18 months of age. However, even in puppies there must be no trace of pattern, design, or clear-cut variations with the exception of the black band of varying width frequently seen encircling the body coat of the cream-colored dog, and the only permissible white which, as in the adult dog, occasionally exists on the chest not exceeding 2 inches in diameter.

Size

Dogs: Shoulder height, 10 inches. Length, chest bone over tail at rump, 20 inches. Head, $8\frac{1}{2}$ inches. Tail, 9 inches. Bitches: Shoulder height, $9\frac{1}{2}$ inches. Length, chest bone over tail at rump, 19 inches. Head, 8 inches. Tail, $8\frac{1}{2}$ inches. A slightly higher or lower dog of either sex is acceptable, providing body, head, and tail dimensions are proportionately longer or shorter. The ideal ratio of body length to shoulder height is 2 to 1, which is considered the correct proportion.

Measurements are taken with the Skye standing in natural position with feet well under. A box caliper is used vertically and horizontally. For the height, the top bar should rest on the withers. The head is measured from the tip of the nose to the back of the occipital bone, and the tail from the root to tip. Dogs 8 inches or less at the withers and bitches $7\frac{1}{2}$ inches or less at the withers are to be penalized.

DISQUALIFICATIONS
A Dudley, flesh-colored or brown nose.

Approved by the AKC 8 May 1973

KC(GB) VARIATION TO STANDARD

Weight and size: dogs: height 10 inches; total length $41\frac{1}{2}$ inches; weight 25 pounds. Bitches slightly smaller in same proportions. *Faults:* yellow eyes, tail curled over back or any deformity.

SOFT-COATED WHEATEN TERRIER

NATIONAL GROUPING		
	Name	Number
AKC	Terriers	IV
KC(GB)	Terrier	3
FCI	Terriers	3

This is one of the three large Terriers native to Ireland, and in most countries the least known of the three though its origins are ancient and it has a very active breed club looking after its interests. In spite of a long tradition the people of Ireland have not been great record keepers, and although it is suspected that this breed goes back hundreds of years, there is nothing written down which has yet been discovered to confirm the fact. Agriculturally Ireland is a fascinating country in that there are a few fairly large estates but very few large farms. In fact most are what is called subsistence farms where the work is carried out by members of the family over a small acreage surrounding an enclosed farm consisting of dwellings and buildings for the stock and its winter feed, and peat for the family fire. In these surroundings a good all-round dog was an essential, the sort that would deal with vermin, of which there would usually be an ample supply around the buildings, would help to round up the stock, and could even at a pinch be trained as a gundog. He needed too to be a good guard, as although there are no longer any dangerous wild beasts in Ireland, many farms are very isolated and it was not the habit to lock, bolt and bar doors as constantly as it is in some other countries.

He is believed to have played a part in the evolution of the Kerry Blue Terrier, and apart from the colour,

everything else about him would confirm that belief. Originally a good deal of cross-breeding took place, and there is little doubt that prior to some form of control, the Irish farmer would breed from those dogs around him irrespective of their blood lines in order to produce the sort of working dog that he wanted. In 1934 a breed club was formed and although application was made for the breed to be recognised, it was not until 1937 that the Irish Kennel Club granted this. In that year, fittingly enough on St. Patrick's Day, the breed made its debut at the IKC Championship Show in Dublin. Dr. G. J. Pierse was a great campaigner for the breed in those early days of its acceptance into the show world, and it is largely due to his efforts that early difficulties were overcome. For many years the breed was required to prove itself in the field, and even now the working qualities are considered to be important.

Considerable controversy has centred around the question of whether he should be left in the rough, or trimmed as is the Kerry Blue Terrier. There are two quite definite schools of thought on this, but a compromise seems now to have been reached and in the future a certain amount of tidying up will probably be the policy, leaving it largely to the judges to decide how far this should be allowed.

The first dogs of the breed arrived in the United States of America in 1946 and were shown at Westminster in 1947, though recognition was not granted at that time. On St. Patrick's Day in 1962 the Soft-Coated Wheaten Terrier Club of America was formed, and since then the breed has made steady progress. In Britain the first were registered in 1971 and numbers have since increased sufficiently for the breed to be awarded championship status.

He is a straightforward Terrier to show, having spirit, but being quite obedient, and apart from the tidying up process his preparation is a simple matter. He is affectionate, and devoted to his owner, can easily be trained to be obedient, and is fond of children. He is game, full of fun, extremely hardy, and makes an excellent house dog.

OFFICIAL STANDARD

General appearance

The Soft-Coated Wheaten Terrier is a medium-sized, hardy, well-balanced sporting terrier covered abundantly with a soft, naturally wavy coat of a good clear wheaten color. The breed requires moderation in all points and any exaggerated features are to be shunned. The head is only moderately long, is well balanced and should be free of any coarseness; the back is level with tail set on high and carried gaily; legs straight in front and muscular behind with well-laid-back shoulders and well-bent stifles to provide a long graceful stride. The dog should present an overall appearance of a hardy, active and happy animal, strong and well-coordinated.

Head

Well balanced and moderately long, profusely covered with coat which may fall forward to shade the eyes. *Skull:* flat and not too wide with no suggestion of coarseness. Skull and foreface about equal length. *Cheeks:* clean and stop well defined. *Muzzle:* square, powerful and strong, with no suggestion of snipiness. Lips are tight and black. *Nose:* is black and large for size of the dog.

Eyes

Dark hazel or brown, medium in size and well protected under a strong brow; eye rims black.

Head: well-balanced, moderately long, profusely covered with coat.

Ears

Break level with the skull and drop slightly forward close to the cheeks rather than pointing to the eyes; small to medium in size.

Teeth

Large, clean and white with either level or scissors bite.

Neck

Medium in length, strong and muscular, well covered with protective coat.

Shoulders
Well laid back, clean and smooth.

Body
Body is compact; back strong and level. Ribs are well sprung but without roundness to provide a deep chest with relatively short coupling.

Length of back from point of withers to base of tail should measure about the same as from point of withers to ground. Tail is docked and well set on, carried gaily but never over the back.

Legs and feet
Forelegs, straight and well boned; hind legs well developed with well bent stifles; hocks well let down, turned neither in nor out.

Feet are round and compact with good depth of pad. Nails dark.

Dewclaws on forelegs may be removed; dewclaws on hind legs should be removed.

Coat
Abundant, soft and wavy, of a good clear wheaten color; may be shaded on the ears and muzzle.

The Soft-Coated Wheaten Terrier is a natural dog and should so appear. Dogs that appear to be overly trimmed should be penalized.

Coat on ears may be left natural or relieved of the fringe to accent smallness.

Coat color and texture do not stabilize until about 18–24 months and should be given some latitude in young dogs. For show purposes the coat may be tidied up merely to present a neat outline but may not be clipped, plucked or stylized.

Size
Dogs should measure 18 to 19 inches at the withers and should weigh between 35–45 pounds, bitches somewhat less.

Movement
Free; gait graceful and lively having reach in front and good drive behind; straight action fore and aft.

Temperament
Good tempered, spirited and game; exhibits less aggressiveness than is sometimes encouraged in terriers in the show ring; alert and intelligent.

Major faults
Overshot. Undershot. Coat texture deviation. Any color save wheaten.

Approved by the AKC 12 June 1973

Body: compact, back strong and level, deep chest.

KC(GB) VARIATION TO STANDARD
Head: distance from eyes to nose not longer, and preferably shorter, than distance from eye to occiput. Topline of muzzle absolutely straight and parallel with skull. *Neck:* slightly arched without throatiness gradually widening toward and running clearly into shoulders. *Body:* powerful short loins. Thighs strong and muscular. *Forelegs:* pasterns strong and springy. *Feet:* turned neither in nor out. *Tail:* about 4 to 5 inches long. Not curled and not too thick.

STAFFORDSHIRE BULL TERRIER

NATIONAL GROUPING		
	Name	Number
AKC	Terriers	IV
KC(GB)	Terrier	3
FCI	Terriers	3

The origins of the Staffordshire Bull Terrier are far from attractive. In the first quarter of the 19th century, attempts were being made to improve the types of Terrier existing in Britain, and fanciers were seeking new breeds. At that time rat killing was a favourite pastime among the working classes and the young bloods with time on their hands, and the dogs used were tough and agile. Stories of the prowess of these dogs are probably on the whole apocryphal, but it is recorded that Jimmy Shaw's Jacko could finish off a thousand rats in one and a half hours. The young sportsmen who frequented these rat-pit meetings wanted something more exciting and thought up the idea of organised dog fights as an alternative. They wanted a dog with all the gameness of the Terrier and the courage and fighting instinct of the Bulldog so they proceeded to mate the two. The result was an agile dog with tremendous strength of jaw and an insatiable desire to fight.

These early dogs were indisputably ugly, and one that Lord Camelford presented to Belcher the pugilist is described as a short-legged, thick set fawn coloured individual with closely amputated ears, a broad blunt muzzle and considerable lay-back. For some reason this type of dog became popular among undergraduates and was considered a very manly possession for a young man to have. The dog fight of those early days was quite ritualistic, and no hit-or-miss affair. Meets were arranged, often in public house yards, some of which sported these pits as objects of curiosity long after the so-called sport was declared illegal. Naturally enough a great deal of money often depended on the result of a match, which led to a considerable amount of unsportsmanlike behaviour.

The rules were simple enough, and it was not so much an attempt to kill the other dog, as to be game enough to try. The arena was a boarded-in rectangle over which the spectators watched. There were such tricks as rubbing a contestant with pepper or other distasteful substance, and dogs were frequently washed to remove this. Each owner was permitted to lick or 'taste' the opposing dog as an additional precaution. Each dog was released in turn to cross a 'scratch' line drawn across the centre of the ring, being encouraged to do so by his 'setter'. The battle was lost by the first dog that failed 'to come up to scratch'. The result of all this was a race of remarkably fit and game dogs that would tackle anything that looked like a dog, and would fight to the death.

Attempts to show a dog of this type were doomed, as by 1863 Mr. Hinks had perfected his long-faced all-white smart Bull Terrier proper, and the Bull and Terrier, which is virtually what the fighting dog was, was being completely outshone.

An official campaign to have the sport of dog fighting banned was eventually successful and the breed that had been evolved for this purpose found itself with no future as a fighter. Fortunately he had developed other qualities, descending as he had done partly from the Bulldog, which in spite of appearance is one of the kindest dogs in the world, and there was a future for him as a pet and a show dog. He was finally recognised as such by the Kennel Club in England in 1935 and in the United States of America in 1974, and has made his mark in both these countries as well as throughout the world.

He is one of the kindest and most friendly dogs around, though he still has the inherent tendency to dispute with other dogs, and particularly with other Bull Terriers. With humans, however, he is faithful, affectionate and tremendously loyal, and his love of children is well known.

OFFICIAL STANDARD

From the past history of the Staffordshire Bull Terrier, the modern dog draws its character of indomitable courage, high intelligence, and tenacity. This, coupled with its affection for its friends, and children in particular, its off-duty quietness and trustworthy stability, makes it a foremost all-purpose dog.

General appearance
The Staffordshire Bull Terrier is a smooth-coated dog. It should be of great strength for its size and, although muscular, should be active and agile.

Head and skull: short, deep, broad, pronounced cheek muscles.

Head and skull
Short, deep through, broad skull, very pronounced cheek muscles, distinct stop, short foreface, black nose. Pink (Dudley) nose to be considered a serious fault.

Eyes
Dark preferable, but may bear some relation to coat color. Round, of medium size, and set to look straight ahead. Light eyes or pink eye rims to be considered a fault, except that where the coat surrounding the eye is white the eye rim may be pink.

Ears
Rose or half-pricked and not large. Full drop or full prick to be considered a serious fault.

Mouth
A bite in which the outer side of the lower incisors touches the inner side of the upper incisors. The lips should be tight and clean. The badly undershot or overshot bite is a serious fault.

Neck
Muscular, rather short, clean in outline and gradually widening toward the shoulders.

Forequarters
Legs straight and well boned, set rather far apart, without

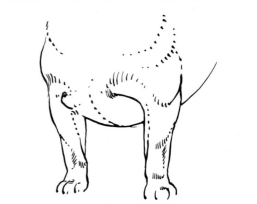

Forequarters: legs straight, feet turn out a little.

looseness at the shoulders and showing no weakness at the pasterns, from which point the feet turn out a little.

Body
The body is close coupled, with a level topline, wide front, deep brisket and well sprung ribs being rather light in the loins.

Hindquarters
The hindquarters should be well muscled, hocks let down with stifles well bent. Legs should be parallel when viewed from behind.

Feet
The feet should be well padded, strong and of medium size. Dewclaws, if any, on the hind legs are generally removed. Dewclaws on the forelegs may be removed.

Tail
The tail is undocked, of medium length, low set, tapering to a point and carried rather low. It should not curl much and may be likened to an old-fashioned pump handle. A tail that is too long or badly curled is a fault.

Coat
Smooth, short and close to the skin, not to be trimmed or dewhiskered.

Color
Red, fawn, white, black or blue, or any of these colors with white. Any shade of brindle or any shade of brindle with white. Black-and-tan or liver color to be disqualified.

Size
Weight: dogs, 28 to 38 pounds; bitches, 24 to 34 pounds. Height at shoulder: 14 to 16 inches, these heights being related to weights. Non-conformity with these limits is a fault.

DISQUALIFICATIONS
Black-and-tan or liver color.

Approved by the AKC 5 March 1975

WELSH TERRIER

This long-legged Terrier is one of the two that are claimed as native to Wales, and there is little doubt that they have been known in the Principality for a considerable time. Like so many of the medium-sized Terriers, he almost certainly descended from the old rough Black-and-Tan Terrier that was fairly common in Britain in the 18th and 19th centuries. Old prints and paintings depict a Terrier of that time which was not far removed from the Welsh Terrier of today. It was, however, towards the end of the 18th century that he was first seen as a distinct breed in North Wales, and they were running with a pack of hounds at that time under the name Ynysfor. They were definitely working dogs as all Terriers were, and it was not until towards the end of the 19th century that anyone thought of them as a show breed.

In 1885 the Welsh Terrier Club was formed, and in the following year the breed was recognised by the Kennel Club in England. It was not until 1901 that classes were staged at the Westminster Show, but since that time their popularity has grown. The club did a great deal to improve and refine the breed, as the Old English Black-and-Tan was a roughish little dog with a head that lacked the square-cut character

NATIONAL GROUPING		
	Name	Number
AKC	Terriers	IV
KC(GB)	Terrier	3
FCI	Terriers	3

that has become desirable in most Terriers, and the coat, though strong and wiry, did not have the desired quality. Many of the old working Terriers were bowed in front too, but selective breeding from good specimens has produced a straight-fronted dog with an attractive head and a pleasing coat.

He has often been confused with the Lakeland Terrier, but the differences are quite marked, especially around the head. He has been described too as a miniature Airedale, but he differs in proportion as well as in detail from the king of the Terriers. He is in fact an individual dog with a great many admirers, particularly in his own country still, where he is looked upon as something of a mascot. There are few shows, however small, where one or two specimens of the breed do not appear. In Britain registration figures remain remarkably steady around the three hundred per year mark, and he is beginning to spread to other countries where he has been seen as a possible addition to the Terrier list.

As a show dog he has been remarkably successful without hitting the high spots. He is no more difficult to prepare than any other Terrier, and indeed because of his darker colour is easier than some. He is somewhat steadier than some of the others in the Group and is very easy to handle. His long tradition of obedience to command which comes from his working background results in a willingness to please, and although he retains all the gameness of the other Terriers, he lacks some of their independent spirit. He is a gay yet not over-exuberant companion, very good with children, and compact enough in size to fit in with modern living conditions. Although many are kept as kennel dogs, a way of life that they fit into naturally enough, they are excellent house dogs.

323

OFFICIAL STANDARD

Head

The skull should be flat, and rather wider between the ears than the Wirehaired Fox Terrier. The jaw should be powerful, clean-cut, rather deeper, and more punishing— giving the head a more masculine appearance than that usually seen on a Fox Terrier. Stop not too defined, fair length from stop to end of nose, the latter being of a black color. *Ears:* the ear should be V-shaped, small, not too thin, set on fairly high, carried forward and close to the cheek. *Eyes:* the eye should be small, not being too deeply set in or protruding out of skull, of a dark hazel color, expressive and indicating abundant pluck.

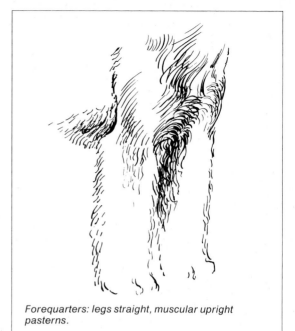

Forequarters: legs straight, muscular upright pasterns.

Head and skull: flat and wider than wire-haired fox terrier.

Neck

The neck should be of moderate length and thickness, slightly arched and sloping gracefully into the shoulders.

Body

The back should be short, and well-ribbed up, the loin strong, good depth, and moderate width of chest. The shoulders should be long, sloping, and well set back. The hindquarters should be strong, thighs muscular and of good length, with the hocks moderately straight, well let down, and fair amount of bone. The stern should be set on moderately high, but not too gaily carried.

Legs and feet

The legs should be straight and muscular, possessing fair amount of bone, with upright and powerful pasterns. The feet should be small, round and catlike.

Coat

The coat should be wiry, hard, very close and abundant.

Color

The color should be black and tan, or black grizzle and tan, free from black penciling on toes.

Size

The height at shoulder should be 15 inches for dogs, bitches proportionately less. Twenty pounds shall be considered a fair average weight in working condition, but this may vary a pound or so either way.

DISQUALIFICATIONS

(1) Nose: white, cherry or spotted to a considerable extent with either of these colors. (2) Ears: prick, tulip or rose. (3) Undershot jaw or pig-jawed mouth. (4) Black below hocks or white to an appreciable extent.

SCALE OF POINTS

Head and jaws (10). Ears (5). Eyes (5). Neck and shoulders (10). Body (10). Loins and hindquarters (10). Legs and feet (10). Coat (15). Color (5). Stern (5). General appearance (15). *Total (100).*

KC(GB) VARIATION TO STANDARD

Hindquarters: hocks well bent. *Tail:* well set on but not carried too gaily. *Coat:* a single coat undesirable. *Height:* at shoulder should not exceed 15½ inches. *Faults:* a white, cherry, or spotted nose. Prick, tulip or rose ears. An appreciable amount of black below hocks.

WEST HIGHLAND WHITE TERRIER

NATIONAL GROUPING

	Name	Number
AKC	Terriers	IV
KC(GB)	Terrier	3
FCI	Terriers	3

It is very likely that all the Terriers of Scotland came originally from the same root stock, and that it was only by selective breeding from those that displayed difference of size, type and colour, that we now have such diverse breeds as the Dandie Dinmont Terrier and the Scottish Terrier, or the Skye and the Cairn. The relative isolation of various parts of the country and of its islands made the maintenance of pure lines a simple matter once a type had been established, as even the most ardent of dogs would find some trouble in trying to swim some of the lochs and seaways. Col. E. D. Malcolm of Poltalloch first drew attention to these little short-legged white Terriers, which in 1907 he had been breeding for sixty years, and which were first shown as Poltalloch Terriers. Though he confessed to being no dog man, he got together with one or two other interested gentlemen and formed the first club to further the interest of the breed. Early photographs show his dogs as being rather longer in the leg than is now fashionable but all-white, and with the same keen expression and smartly pricked ears that have become such a feature of the breed.

The original Poltalloch Terriers were built along foxy lines, tremendously hard and flexible, and fitted to the work of hunting the fox in a rocky terrain. In that sort of country a fox's earth is not a hole dug in soft ground, but a passageway scraped between huge immovable rocks, often very narrow and always impossible to dig through. The Terrier had to be prepared to force his way through narrow openings, often against stiff opposition, and frequently with no opportunity of turning round to get out again. He had to be prepared to fight his way through, and struggle out backwards if he was able, which meant that he had to be an extremely fit, agile and active little animal. Fortunately the early fears of enthusiasts that the West Highland White would develop into merely a white Scottish Terrier have not been realised, and the modern respresentatives of the breed have all the sporting characteristics of their ancestors.

It is true that they have been taken in hand for show purposes, often by professional handlers, and have been given an external appearance which is very different from that of the old Poltalloch dogs, but underneath this they are still sporting, flexible and agile. He is now recognised as one of the top winning Terriers in the Group, with many Best in Shows to his credit including Crufts, and his reputation is high in most countries. He has the sort of character that makes him an ideal show dog, cocky, full of fun, and enjoying the admiration that comes to those that win. His coat is such that expert attention brings out the best in him, and he can be shaped to give a delightfully smart outline, extending his neck, giving his legs the desirable sturdy appearance, and accentuating the whiskers of his head until his face looks like three little black spots in a white circle.

He is an affectionate character, hardy, loving to romp and play under any conditions, rolling in the sunshine or digging in the snow, it all comes alike to him. He is a fine house dog, being very alert and protective about his family, and having the acute hearing of all the prick-eared Terriers. He is a wonderful companion and pet, and a tremendous dog to have around the house.

OFFICIAL STANDARD

General appearance

The West Highland White Terrier is a small, game, well-balanced, hardy-looking terrier, exhibiting good showmanship, possessed with no small amount of self-esteem, strongly built, deep in chest and back ribs, straight back and powerful hindquarters on muscular legs, and exhibiting in marked degree a great combination of strength and activity. The coat should be about 2 inches long, white in color, hard, with plenty of soft undercoat.

Head and skull: slightly domed, thickly coated with hair.

The dog should be neatly presented. Considerable hair should be left around the head to act as a frame for the face to yield a typical Westie expression.

Color and pigmentation

Coat should be white, as defined by the breed's name. Nose should be black. Black pigmentation is most desirable on lips, eye-rims, pads of feet, nails and skin. *Faults:* any coat color other than white and nose color other than black are serious faults.

Coat

Very important and seldom seen to perfection; must be double-coated. The outer coat consists of straight hard hair, about 2 inches long, with shorter coat on neck and shoulders, properly blended. *Faults:* any silkiness or tendency to curl is a serious fault, as is an open or single coat.

Size

Dogs should measure about 11 inches at the withers, bitches about one inch less. *Faults:* any specimens much over or under height limits are objectionable.

Skull

Should be fairly broad, being in proportion to his powerful jaw, not too long, slightly domed, and gradually tapering to the eyes. There should be a defined stop, eyebrows heavy. *Faults:* a too long or too narrow skull.

Muzzle

Should be slightly shorter than the skull, powerful and gradually tapering to the nose, which should be large. The jaws should be level and powerful, the teeth well set and large for the size of the dog. There shall be six incisor teeth between the canines of both lower and upper jaws. A tight scissors bite with upper incisors slightly overlapping the lower incisors or level mouth are equally acceptable. *Faults:* muzzle longer than skull. Teeth much undershot or overshot are a serious fault, as are teeth defective or missing.

Ears

Small, carried tightly erect, set wide apart and terminating in a sharp point. They must never be cropped. The hair on the ears should be short, smooth and velvety, and trimmed free of fringe at the tips. *Faults:* round-pointed, drop, broad and large ears are very objectionable, as are mule-ears, ears set too closely together or not held tightly erect.

Eyes

Widely set apart, medium in size, dark in color, slightly sunk in the head, sharp and intelligent. Looking from under heavy eyebrows, they give a piercing look. *Faults:* too small, too full or light-colored eyes are very objectionable.

Neck

Muscular and nicely set on sloping shoulders. *Faults:* short neck or too long neck.

Chest

Very deep and extending at least to the elbows with breadth in proportion to size of the dog. *Faults:* shallow chest.

Body: compact, back level, distance from last rib short.

Body

Compact and of good substance, level back, ribs deep and well arched in the upper half of rib, presenting a flattish side appearance, loins broad and strong, hindquarters strong, muscular, and wide across the top. *Faults:* long or weak back; barrel ribs; high rump.

Legs and feet

Both forelegs and hind legs should be muscular and relatively short, but with sufficient length to set the dog up so as not to be too close to the ground. The shoulder blades should be well laid back and well knit at the backbone. The chest should be relatively broad and the front legs spaced apart accordingly. The front legs should be set in under the shoulder blades with definite body overhang before them. The front legs should be reasonably straight and thickly covered with short hard hair. The hind legs should be short and sinewy; the thighs very muscular and not set wide apart, with hocks well bent. The forefeet are larger than the hind ones, are round, proportionate in size, strong, thickly padded, and covered with short hard hair; they may properly be turned out a slight amount. The hind feet are smaller and thickly padded. *Faults:* steep shoulders, loaded shoulders, or out at the elbows. Too light bone. Cowhocks, weak hocks and lack of angulation. A 'fiddle-front' is a serious fault.

Tail

Relatively short, when standing erect it should never extend above the top of the skull. It should be covered with hard hairs, no feather, as straight as possible, carried gaily but not curled over the back. The tail should be set on high enough so that the spine does not slope down to it. The tail must never be docked. *Faults:* tail set too low; tail too long or carried at half mast or over back.

Movement

Should be free, straight and easy all around. In front, the leg should be freely extended forward by the shoulder. The hind movement should be free, strong and fairly close. The hocks should be freely flexed and drawn close under the body; so that when moving off the foot the body is thrown or pushed forward with some force. *Faults:* stiff, stilty or too wide movement behind. Lack of reach in front, and/or drive behind.

Temperament

Must be alert, gay, courageous and self-reliant, but friendly. *Faults:* excess timidity or excess pugnacity.

Approved by the AKC 10 December 1968

KC(GB) VARIATION TO STANDARD

Head: the distance from occiput to eyes should be slightly greater than length of foreface. Head should be thickly coated with hair, and carried at a right-angle or less, to axis of neck. On no account should head be carried in extended position. Nose black.

GROUP V: TOYS

Affenpinscher

Cavalier King Charles Spaniel

Brussels Griffon

Chihuahua

Italian Greyhound

Japanese Chin

English Toy Spaniel

Lowchen

Maltese

Manchester Terrier (Toy)

Papillon

Miniature Pinscher

Pug

Pekingese

Poodle (Toy)

Pomeranian

Yorkshire Terrier

Shih Tzu

Silky Terrier

GROUP V: TOYS

This Group contains some of the dogs claiming the greatest antiquity as specific breeds. Whilst the working dogs certainly were part of the early life of mankind, they were not so clearly developed into breeds, and were bred for performance as were the early Hounds, rather than for appearance. The toy dogs, however, carefully bred for appearance for centuries (some claim even for thousands of years), and as small lap dogs and companion dogs, have been favourites of the courts and noble families for as long as records have been kept. They are recognised by their size, though some of the recent additions to the group do not entirely conform in this aspect. They have without exception been produced by a process of selective miniaturisation, as none of the wild stock from which all dogs descended is as small as they are, and in most cases their ancestry can be traced back to other and larger breeds.

The members of the Group can be split up roughly into dogs related to the other Groups. There is a Spaniel sub-group, consisting of such breeds as the Toy Spaniels and the Japanese. The running group is represented by the Italian Greyhound, the Spitz group by the Pomeranian and the Terrier Group by the Yorkshire Terrier and the English Toy Terrier. In addition to these, the foreign Terriers are represented by the Miniature Pinscher and the Griffon, whilst in the United States the Toy Poodle is included by reason of its lack of size, as is the Shih Tzu, though both appear elsewhere in other countries.

We are fortunate in that we have better visual records of the breeds in the Toy Group than in almost any of the others. Down through the centuries it has been the habit of ladies of the courts, and gentlemen too for that matter, to include their favourite dog, usually a lap dog, when having their portrait painted. As a result of this we have a very clear picture of what the early Toy Spaniels looked like in the time of Charles II; we know with some certainty that the Italian Greyhound has changed very little since the time of Anne of Denmark; and that Hogarth's pet Pug painted in 1745 was a fair representative of the breed even by today's standards.

The early civilisations of the Far East have preserved for us some of the best ancient records of many of the toy breeds, as several of them originated in that part of the world, the Pekingese for example occupying a very important place in the history of Imperial China. In Tibet too the smaller dogs were revered and the pure breeding of some of the older types of toy dogs was practised by the monasteries of that country where they were used in religious ceremonies. Some of the smaller dogs in other parts of the world have been said to have an association with religion, the Chihuahua from South America for example, and myth and legend play a formidable part in the history of the members of the Group.

Some of the early writers were extremely scornful about the toy breeds, steeped as they were in the world of the coursing and shooting dog. Dr. Caius for instance describes them as 'These dogges are little, pretty, and proper, and fyne, and sought for to satisfie the delicatenesse of daintie dames and wanton women's wiles, instruments of folly for them to play and dally withall, to tryfle away the treasure of time, to withdraw their mindes from their commendable exercises'. In fact, many of the toy dogs are very sporting indeed, and it has been placed on record that at the beginning of this century one gentleman regularly shot over his team of Toy Spaniels.

In more recent times Europe has been the centre of the breeding of the toy dogs, and breeds that have their origin in the Far East, found their way into Europe as world trade grew during the last two hundred years. The Papillon for instance, looked upon as a French breed and even carrying a French name, almost certainly came from the Orient. Similarly, the Pug, known at one time as the Dutch Pug, is an ancient Chinese breed that was developed in Europe. Some of the newcomers to the Group, the Chihuahua, the Bichon and the Lowchen are making tremendous strides in popularity, evidence of the fact that there always was and always will be an interest in the toy dogs.

AFFENPINSCHER

NATIONAL GROUPING		
	Name	Number
AKC	Toys	V
KC(GB)	—	—
FCI	Companion Dogs	9

sed by the American Kennel Club in 1936, but the Second World War slowed down his progress. After the cessation of hostilities, however, his numbers began to grow steadily and the toy dog people became interested in him. He is still hardly known outside the United States of America and in his home country, and has made no impression in Britain at all.

He is a small—under ten inches—dog with a sturdy build, strong straight-backed terrier-like body and straight legs. He is covered with a short dense coat that develops on the legs and around the eyes, nose and chin into a shaggy, hard wiry and much longer coat which gives the square appearance and the monkey expression. He is game, alert and intelligent, and though he can be quite aggressive for his size, and makes a good guard, he is an affectionate little dog that makes a fine pet and house dog. Although overshadowed by the Brussels Griffon as a show dog in numbers, he is rapidly gaining ground.

This quaint little dog is one of the oldest toy dogs of Europe, having been known for at least the past three centuries and in his early days, with the delightful title of Monkey Pinscher. The word 'pinscher' means simply 'terrier' in the German language and the prefix 'Affe' can be freely translated as 'monkey'. He is believed to have been one of the ancestors of two other well-known breeds, the Brussels Griffon and Miniature Schnauzer, in both of which similarities about the head and expression can be seen. His origin is obscure. All that is known for certain is that there were originally two sizes and that it is the smaller version that has survived and which is now accepted worldwide.

At the turn of the century there existed a dog known as the Wire-haired Pinscher 'Deuthscher Rauhhaariger Pinscher' that could have been the larger type. He was described as being from twelve to eighteen inches high and having a short beard and whiskers. He was known familiarly as the Rattler, and appeared mostly as a black dog, though other colours were seen. As the Schnauzer gets no mention at that time, this dog could well have been that breed and it is likely that in fact the breeds were so intermingled that a considerable amount of confusion existed. He was recogni-

OFFICIAL STANDARD

General appearance
Small, but rather sturdy in build and not delicate in any way. He carries himself with comical seriousness and he is generally quiet and a very devoted pal. He can get vehemently excited, however, when attacked and is fearless toward any aggressor.

Coat
A very important factor. It is short and dense in certain parts and shaggy and longer in others, but should be hard and wiry. It is longer and more loose and shaggy on the legs and around the eyes, nose and chin, giving the typical monkey-like appearance from whence comes his name. The best color is black, matching his eyes and fiery temperament. However, black with tan markings, red, gray and other mixtures are permissible. Very light colors and white markings are a fault.

Body: proportions square, chest deep.

Legs
Front legs should be straight as possible. Hind legs without much bend at the hocks and set well under the body. *Feet:* should be round, small and compact. Turned neither in nor out, with preferably black pads and nails.

Head: showing arrangement of facial hair.

Hindquarters: little bend.

Head
Should be round and not too heavy, with well-domed forehead. *Eyes:* should be round, of good size, black and very brilliant. *Ears:* rather small, set high, pointed and erect, usually clipped to a point. *Muzzle:* must be short and rather pointed with a black nose. The upper jaw is a trifle shorter than the lower jaw, while the teeth should close together; a slight undershot condition is not material. The teeth, however, should not show.

Neck
Short and straight.

Body
The back should be straight with its length about equal to the height at the shoulder. Chest should be reasonably deep and the body should show only a slight tuck-up at the loin.

Tail
Cut short, set and carried high.

Size
The smaller dog, if of characteristic type, is more valuable, and the shoulder height should not exceed $10\frac{1}{4}$ inches in any case.

Approved by the AKC 15 September 1936

KC(GB) VARIATION TO STANDARD
This dog is not granted championship status by the KC(GB).

BRUSSELS GRIFFON

NATIONAL GROUPING		
	Name	Number
AKC	Toys	v
KC(GB)	Toy	6
FCI	Companion Dogs	9

This little dog started life as a guard on the front seats of cabs in Brussels, where his wonderful spirit in spite of lack of size, endeared him to a great number of people. Something of a street urchin still, the 'gamin' of the dog world, his quaint appearance and cockiness make him one of the personality dogs if not one of the beauties of the Toy Group. His ancestry is a little confused, but he probably descended from the German Affenpinscher and a mixture of street curs that frequented the less fashionable areas of Brussels during the last century and earlier. There were a number of breeds in Belgium and Northern France at one time that had the rough coat and moustachioed appearance of the Brussels Griffon, but most of them were considerably larger and were hunting dogs. It is not difficult, however, to picture a situation in which smaller specimens unsuitable for chasing game would find their way into the hands of pet owners who used them as a basis for a particular breed of their own.

Later this little rough-coated dog was crossed with the Pug and produced a smooth-coated variety. By 1880 the breed was established and was being shown, and some authorities suggest that at around that time Schnauzer and Yorkshire Terrier blood was introduced to improve the coat and reduce the size of the breed. It has also been suggested that the English Toy Spaniel was used to give the breed the characteristic very short nose. The Brussels Griffon first began to appear at shows in Europe in the late 19th century, and was soon adopted in other countries, his quaint assurance endearing him to exhibitors in Britain and the United States.

Those who own a Griffon become addicted to the breed, finding them extremely intelligent and very good guards and companions. Compared with others in the Toy Group he lacks any hint of aristocratic background, but in any case he lays no claim to this, and is prepared to be accepted at face value. He is certainly no beauty, but his facial expression and the peculiar whiskered foreface give him a charm all of his own. He is very much the man-in-the-street's toy dog as far as appearance goes, but he has now outlived his lowly background and has become accepted as something of a society pet among the few who own the breed. He is still something of the Terrier, will hunt if he is given the opportunity, and he is among the strongest and sturdiest built of any in the Toy Group.

The Griffon has never made a great impact as a show dog, one or two kennels only showing the breed at the highest level. Registrations have hardly varied over the years from their fairly low figure which compares with the Maltese or the Lakeland Terrier in Britain, and is considerably lower in some countries. He has the sort of coat that does not need a great deal of attention, having something of the quality of the Irish Terrier's and not requiring the excessive trimming that many of the Terriers do. Some tend to be rather nervous in the ring, the smooth-coated version perhaps more so than the rough-coated but the ones that have confidence show remarkably well.

In the home he is a fearless little dog, having a strongly developed territorial sense, and being very possessive about the family to which he belongs. To them he is most affectionate, and having no vices, he makes a splendid pet and companion. He needs to be appreciated as the intelligent dog that he is, and when trained he becomes very obedient and easily managed.

OFFICIAL STANDARD

General appearance

A toy dog, intelligent, alert, sturdy, with a thick-set short body, a smart carriage and set-up, attracting attention by an almost human expression.

Head

Skull: large and round, with a domed forehead. *Ears:* small and set rather high on the head. May be shown cropped or natural. If natural they are carried semi-erect. *Eyes:* should be set well apart, very large, black, prominent, and well open. The eyelashes long and black. Eyelids edged with black. *Nose:* very black, extremely short, its tip being set back deeply between the eyes so as to form a lay-back. The nostrils large, the stop deep. *Lips:* edged with black, not pendulous but well brought together, giving a clean finish to the mouth. *Jaws:* chin must be undershot, prominent, and large with an upward sweep. The incisors of the lower jaw should protrude over the upper incisors, and the lower jaw should be rather broad. Neither teeth nor tongue should show when the mouth is closed. A wry mouth is a serious fault.

Head and skull: large, rounded, furnished with beard.

Body and legs

Brisket should be broad and deep, ribs well sprung, back level and short. *Neck:* medium length, gracefully arched. *Tail:* set and held high, docked to about one third. *Forelegs:* of medium length, straight in bone, well muscled, set moderately wide apart and straight from the point of the shoulders as viewed from the front. Pasterns short and strong. *Hind legs:* set true, thighs strong and well muscled, stifles bent, hocks well let down, turning neither in nor out. *Feet:* round, small, and compact, turned neither in nor out. Toes well arched. Black pads and toenails preferred.

Coat

There are two distinct types of coat—rough and smooth. The rough coat should be wiry and dense, the harder and more wiry the better. On no account should the dog look or feel woolly, and there should be no silky hair anywhere. The coat should not be so long as to give a shaggy appearance, but should still be distinctly different all over from the smooth coat. The head should be covered with wiry hair slightly longer around the eyes, nose, cheeks, and chin, thus forming a fringe. The smooth coat is similar to that of the Boston Terrier or Bulldog, with no trace of wire hair.

Color

In the rough-coated type, coat is either 1. reddish brown, with a little black at the whiskers and chin allowable, or 2. black and reddish brown mixed, usually with black mask and whiskers, or 3. black with uniform reddish brown markings, usually appearing under the chin, on the legs, over the eyebrows, around the edges of the ears and around the vent, or 4. solid black. The colors of the smooth-coated type are the same as those of the rough-coated type except that solid black is not allowable. Any white hairs in either the rough or smooth coat are a serious fault, except for 'frost' on the black muzzle of a mature dog, which is natural.

Weight

Usually 8 to 10 pounds, and should not exceed 12 pounds. Type and quality are of greater importance than weight, and a smaller dog that is sturdy and well proportioned should not be penalized.

SCALE OF POINTS
Head (35): skull (5), nose and stop (10), eyes (5), chin and jaws (10), ears (5). Coat (25): color (12), texture (13). *Body and General Conformation (40):* body (brisket and rib) (15), legs (10), feet (5), general appearance (neck, topline, and tail carriage) 10. *Total (100).*

DISQUALIFICATIONS
Dudley or butterfly nose, white spot or blaze anywhere on coat. Hanging tongue. Jaw overshot. Solid black coat in the smooth type.

Approved by the AKC 6 February 1960

KC(GB) VARIATION TO STANDARD

Rough-coated variety called 'Griffon Bruxellois', and the smooth-coated variety called 'Petit Brabançon' by the KC(GB). *Head:* forehead not domed. *Ears:* better small —not cropped. *Feet:* black toenails. *Weight:* 3 to 10 pounds; most desirable 6 to 9 pounds. *Faults:* showing teeth. Light eyes, brown nose, eyerims or toenails, curly coat. Roaching or dipping of back should be penalised.

CAVALIER KING CHARLES SPANIEL

NATIONAL GROUPING		
	Name	Number
AKC	—	—
KC(GB)	Toy	6
FCI	Companion Dogs	9

A good deal of confusion existed in the various breeds of toy Spaniels up to the early part of this century, old paintings depicting dogs that were either Cavaliers or English Toy Spaniels or something produced from oriental Spaniels arriving by way of France. The Cavalier King Charles Spaniel really owes its existence to an enthusiast in the United States of America who was so impressed with the differences shown in old paintings that he decided to resurrect the longer tailed and longer nosed variety as a separate breed. The main distinctive features of the Cavalier that the others did not have were the longer face, flat skull, less stop and the much-prized spot in the middle of the skull of the Blenheims. The English Toy Spaniel was known at one time as the 'Comforter' and according to chroniclers of the time, Charles II enjoyed the company of his dogs more than he did that of the members of his court. He kept a number of these little dogs around him, and according to Pepys 'he often suffered the bitches to puppy and give suck, which rendered it very offensive and indeed made the whole court nasty and stinking'. The dog that was the favourite of Charles II was almost certainly the black and tan version of the English Toy, or King Charles as it is known in England. The others were the Prince Charles, which was a tricolour, the Blenheim, which was red and white and first bred by the Duke of Marlborough at Blenheim, and the Ruby, which was a solid rich red.

The colours have remained, but the division took place in the early 1920s, when Mr. Eldridge of Long Island, New York, gave special prizes for those Toy Spaniels which most nearly fitted the description that he preferred from among those that he had studied on old paintings. A club was formed in 1928 to promote the Cavalier King Charles Spaniel, and since that time the breed has gone from strength to strength. Whilst it is not numerically the strongest breed in the Toy Group, that distinction going to the Yorkshire Terrier, it is easily the most popular at shows.

Apart from the detailed differences between the Cavalier and the King Charles Spaniel, the Cavalier is much the larger of the two, the standard allowing from twelve to eighteen pounds as against the eight to fourteen of the King Charles. In fact fashion has decreed that the King Charles and Cavaliers should be at opposite ends of the popularity scale so that the difference in size is even more acute than the standard would suggest. In recent years in Britain, and probably in other countries too, the breed has suffered as many breeds do when their popularity takes a sharp upward turn. The award of Best in Show All-breeds at Crufts to a Cavalier King Charles Spaniel in 1973 led to a great deal of indiscriminate breeding and the standard of the breed has suffered as a result. He is one of the heavy-weights of the Toy dog Group, and when one of the larger specimens manages to win Best of Breed and appears in the Group, it can look somewhat out of place alongside some of the much smaller breeds.

The Cavalier King Charles is sturdy for a toy dog, having a short strong body and straight bone, and retains something of the characteristic Spaniel quality of his ancestors. He will enjoy a good deal of exercise, being very active and not tiring easily, and is a good companion on a country walk. As a show dog he presents few problems. Some are a little shy or reserved, but few are really nervous, and the coat needs no special preparation, the only problem being keeping coat rather than trimming off excess. He is an enjoyable dog to own, as he is kindly and affectionate, with no vices at all, and with centuries of domestication behind him, he takes naturally to living indoors.

OFFICIAL STANDARD

General appearance
An active, graceful and well-balanced dog. Absolutely fearless and sporting in character and very gay and free in action.

Head and skull
Head almost flat between the ears, without dome. Stop shallow. Length from base of stop to tip about 1½ inches. Nostrils should be well developed and the pigment black. Muzzle well tapered. Lips well-covering but not hound like. Face should be well filled out underneath the eyes. Any tendency to appear 'snipy' is undesirable.

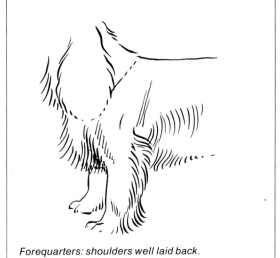

Forequarters: shoulders well laid back.

Ears
Long and set high with plenty of feather.

Mouth
Level; scissor-bite preferred.

Neck
Moderate length—slightly arched.

Eyes
Large, dark and round but not prominent. The eyes should be spaced well apart.

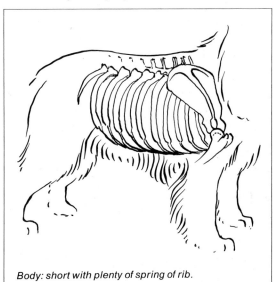

Body: short with plenty of spring of rib.

Forequarters
Shoulders well laid back; legs moderate bone and straight.

Body
Short-coupled with plenty of spring of rib. Back level. Chest moderate leaving ample heart room.

Hindquarters
Legs with moderate bone; well-turned stifle—no tend-

Ears: long, set high, plenty of feather.

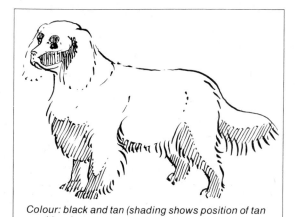

Colour: black and tan (shading shows position of tan markings).

ency to cow or sickle hocks.

Feet
Compact, cushioned and well-feathered.

Tail
The docking of tails is optional. No more than one-third to be removed. The length of the tail should be in balance with the body.

Coat
Long, silky and free from curl. A slight wave is permissible. There should be plenty of feather.

Colour
The only recognised colours are: Black and tan: Raven black with tan markings above the eyes, on cheeks, inside ears, on chest and legs and underside of tail. The tan should be bright. Ruby: Whole coloured rich red. Blenheim: Rich chestnut marking well broken up on a pearly white ground. The markings should be evenly divided on the head, leaving room between the ears for the much valued lozenge mark or spot (a unique characteristic of the breed). Tricolour: Black and white well spaced and broken up, with tan markings over the eyes, on cheeks, inside ears, inside legs, and on underside of tail. Any other colour or combination of colours is most undesirable.

Weight and size
Weight: 12 to 18 pounds. A small well-balanced dog well within these weights is desirable.

Faults
Light eyes. Undershot and crooked mouths and pig jaws. White marks on whole-coloured specimens. Coarseness of type. Putty noses. Flesh marks. Nervousness.

Note
Male animals should have two apparently normal testicles fully descended into the scrotum.

AKC VARIATION TO STANDARD
This dog is admitted to the Miscellaneous Class by the AKC. The above standards are those of the KC(GB).

CHIHUAHUA (LONG AND SMOOTH COAT)

One of the real tinies of the Toy Group is the Chihuahua. It takes its name from the Mexican city of the same name, and the stories of its origin are almost as numerous as the dog itself. It is said to have been the sacred dog of the Aztecs, to be descended from an early mute dog of South America, to have started life with the Incas, and even to have been reared for food. Whatever the real truth is, there is no doubt at all that it is a real South American product. The first record of the breed is of the purchase of a litter of three in 1888, all black and white and with mixed coats. It has been established that he existed as a separate breed as early as the 9th century called the Techichi and kept by the Toltecs. Carvings in the monastery of Huejotzingo depict a dog very like the present day Chihuahua, and this building dates in part to the pyramids of the Toltecs. It is, however, by no means certain that this original Mexican dog was the sole ancestor of the Chihuahua of today, and it is suspected that a small hairless dog such as the Chinese Crested came across from Asia and was used to produce the modern dog.

Columbus in writing to the King of Spain reported that he found small barkless domesticated dogs. Archaeologists have found remains of these little dogs in Mexico and the United States of America. He is said to have played a part in the religious ceremonies of the Aztecs, perhaps even being sacrificed. According to Aztec mythology the souls of the dead had to be

NATIONAL GROUPING		
	Name	Number
AKC	Toys	V
KC(GB)	Toy	6
FCI	Companion Dogs	9

guarded over the rivers on their way to the other world, and payment had to be made by means of slips of paper to the dogs that performed this duty. This possibility led to the practice of sacrificing dogs and burning the corpses as part of the funeral rite. Whatever the truth of the ancestry of the Chihuahua there is no doubt at all that the modern dog that has resulted from selective breeding from the original imports from Mexico has become not only the smallest, but one of the most popular dogs in the world. From the two dozen or so dogs imported into the United States between 1850 and the end of the century almost all the Chihuahuas of today are descended. The breeders worked hard on their dogs and in 1904 the American Kennel Club recognised the breed, and accepted the registration of the Chihuahua Club of America in 1923.

He was certainly known in Britain in the early part of this century, and probably before, but it was not until considerably later, in 1934 that a breeding pair was imported into the country, and not until after the Second World War that the breed became in any way popular. Since that time its rise has been phenomenal and something over four thousand registrations in both coats are now recorded annually at the Kennel Club. For some time the two coats were exhibited together, but in recent years, in 1952 in the United States and 1965 in Britain, the varieties were separated.

The Chihuahua is a wonderful show dog as he completely forgets his lack of size, and refuses to be intimated by any other dog in the ring, however large it may happen to be. He is of course remarkably portable, and it is not unusual for one exhibitor to take as many as twenty to one show at a time. In the ring he is completely fearless, accepting being handled by a stranger, not disturbed by extraneous noises, and in the Group is always very competitive. As a pet he is delightful, being a real toy, a mere handful of a dog but at the same time an excellent guard, being most alert and noisy at the approach of strangers. Oddly enough he prefers the company of his own kind, and whilst he will suffer the company of any number of other Chihuahuas, he objects strongly to any other breed of dog.

OFFICIAL STANDARD

General appearance
A graceful, alert, swift-moving little dog with saucy expression. Compact, and with terrier like qualities.

Head
A well-rounded 'apple dome' skull, with or without molera. Cheeks and jaws lean. Nose moderately short, slightly pointed (self-colored, in blond types, or black). In moles, blues, and chocolates, they are self-colored. In blond types, pink nose permissible.

Ears
Large, held erect when alert, but flaring at the sides at about an angle of 45 degrees when in repose. This gives breadth between the ears. In *Long Coats*, ears fringed. (Heavily fringed ears may be tipped slightly, never down.)

Eyes
Full, not protruding, balanced, set well apart—dark ruby, or luminous. (Light eyes in blond types permissible.)

Teeth
Level or scissors bite. Overshot or undershot bite or any

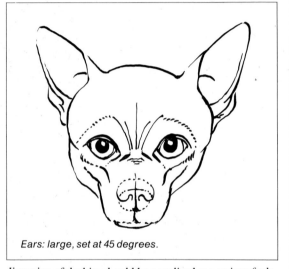

Ears: large, set at 45 degrees.

distortion of the bite should be penalized as a serious fault.

Neck and shoulders
Slightly arched, gracefully sloping into lean shoulders, may be smooth in the very short types, or with ruff about

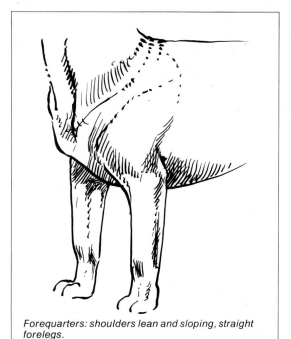

Forequarters: shoulders lean and sloping, straight forelegs.

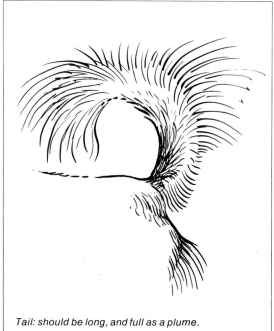

Tail: should be long, and full as a plume.

neck preferred. In *Long Coats*, large ruff on neck desired and preferred. Shoulders lean, sloping into a slightly broadening support above straight forelegs that are set well under, giving a free play at the elbows. Shoulders should be well up, giving balance and soundness, sloping into a level back. (Never down or low.) This gives a chestiness, and strength of forequarters, yet not of the 'Bulldog' chest; plenty of brisket.

Back and body
Level back, slightly longer than height. Shorter backs desired in males. Ribs rounded (but not too much 'barrel-shaped').

Hindquarters
Muscular, with hocks well apart, neither out nor in, well let down, with firm sturdy action.

Tail
Moderately long, carried sickle either up or out, or in a loop over the back, with tip just touching the back. (Never tucked under.) Hair on tail in harmony with the coat of the body, preferred furry in *Smooth Coats*. In *Long Coats*, tail full and long (as a plume).

Feet
Small, with toes well split up but not spread, pads

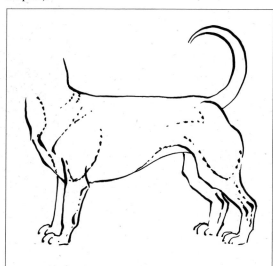

Body: level back, slightly longer than height at shoulder.

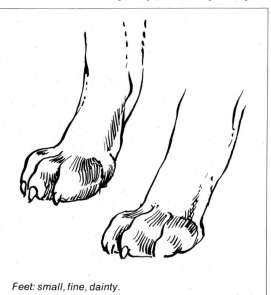

Feet: small, fine, dainty.

Coat: a large ruff on the neck is desired.

on head and ears. In *Long Coats*, the coat should be of a soft texture, either flat or slightly curly, with undercoat preferred. Ears fringed (heavily fringed ears may be tipped slightly, never down), feathering on feet and legs, and pants on hind legs. Large ruff on neck desired and preferred. Tail full and long (as a plume).

Color
Any color—solid, marked or splashed.

Weight
A well-balanced little dog not to exceed 6 pounds.

SCALE OF POINTS
Head, incl. ears (20). Body, incl. tail (20). Coat (20). Legs (20). General appearance and action (20). *Total (100)*.

DISQUALIFICATIONS
Cropped tail, bobtail. Broken down or cropped ears. Any dog over 6 pounds in weight. In Long Coats, too thin coat that resembles bareness.

Approved by the AKC 14 November 1972

cushioned, with fine pasterns. (Neither the hare nor the cat-foot.) A dainty, small foot with nails moderately long.

Coat
In the *Smooth*, the coat should be soft texture, close and glossy. (Heavier coats with undercoats permissible.) Coat placed well over body with ruff on neck, and more scanty

KC(GB) VARIATION TO STANDARD
Long and smooth coats shown as separate classes. *Head:* nose has definite stop. *Neck:* medium length. *Weight:* given two equally good dogs, more diminutive preferred.

ENGLISH TOY SPANIEL

NATIONAL GROUPING		
	Name	Number
AKC	Toys	V
KC(GB)	Toy	6
FCI	Companion Dogs	9

Many of the toy dogs have their origin in breeds that still exist in other Groups, for example the Italian Greyhound is descended from the gazelle hounds and probably from the Greyhound proper. The English Toy Spaniel, or the King Charles Spaniel as he is known in Britain, is another example. The word 'spaniel' itself suggests Spain as the origin of the race, and there is little doubt that although variations on the spaniel theme have occurred in many countries the whole family originated on the Iberian peninsula. At one time the present differences were not so clearly defined and it is unlikely that the King Charles Spaniel and the Cavalier King Charles existed as different breeds; they were all toy Spaniels. This particular little dog descended from a breed that was a great favourite of King Charles II, and Macaulay writes of the King that he could be seen before the dew was off the grass in St. James's Park, striding among the trees and playing with his Spaniels.

It is claimed by some sources that the Spaniel originated in the Far East, and that it was in Spain that larger specimens were developed as gundogs and sporting dogs, the smaller ones remaining as toy dogs. The fact, however, that Dr. Caius, physician to Queen Elizabeth described Spaniels, and toy Spaniels at that, indicates that the breed has been around for many centuries. Ellis's letters recording the execution of Mary Queen of Scots describes how her toy Spaniel refused to leave her body after her beheading. The dogs so beloved by King Charles II were of the black and tan variety and were later called King Charles in Britain, but the division into the two breeds did not take place until fairly recent times. A good deal of confusion over the name exists even now in the minds of those who do not have the two breeds clearly defined. This has probably led to the situation in which the Cavalier, having completely outstripped the numbers of English Toy Spaniels in Britain, still remains in the Miscellaneous Class in the United States.

The breed still varies a good deal in size and length of leg, and one of the problems is to produce a dog of the desirable weight that retains the soundness of its Spaniel ancestors. The standard describes a compact strong little dog with a wide and deep chest and short straight legs, but in fact the attempts to breed down to a fashionable size have produced a dog that rarely measures up to this. It is probably this as much as anything which has kept him very much a minority breed in recent years and the numbers appearing at major shows in Britain are now comparatively small. He does in fact make a delightful little show dog, having a very appealing look, with his very large dark eyes and low hanging ears, and he needs very little preparation to get him ready for the ring. The dog tends to grow a little rough or woolly coat in patches which needs tidying up, but otherwise it is largely a matter of washing and grooming and maintaining the long silky coat. He makes a most attractive pet, being very affectionate and friendly, somewhat reserved towards strangers, but once he has made friends, is very welcoming. His small size, clean habits and quietness endear him to those who own the breed, and those who become attached to him, rarely look for another breed of dog.

OFFICIAL STANDARD

KING CHARLES, PRINCE CHARLES, RUBY AND BLENHEIM
Head
Should be well domed, and in good specimens is absolutely semi-globular, sometimes even extending beyond the half-circle, and absolutely projecting over the eyes, so as nearly to meet the upturned nose. *Eyes:* the eyes are set wide apart, with the eyelids square to the line of the face—not oblique or foxlike. The eyes themselves are large and dark as possible, so as to be generally considered black, their enormous pupils, which are absolutely of that color, increasing the description. *Stop:* the stop, or hollow between the eyes, is well marked, as in

Head and skull: domed and full over the eyes, muzzle square, wide, deep and well turned up.

the Bulldog, or even more so; some good specimens exhibit a hollow deep enough to bury a small marble in it. *Nose:* the nose must be short and well turned up between the eyes, and without any indication of artificial displacement afforded by a deviation to either side. The color of the end should be black, and it should be both deep and wide with open nostrils. A light-colored nose is objectionable, but shall not disqualify. *Jaw:* the muzzle must be square and deep, and the lower jaw wide between the branches, leaving plenty of space for the tongue, and for the attachment of the lower lips, which should completely conceal the teeth. It should also be turned up or 'finished,' so as to allow of its meeting the end of the upper jaw, turned up in a similar way as above described. A protruding tongue is objectionable, but does not disqualify. *Ears:* the ears must be long, so as to approach the ground. In an average-sized dog they measure 20 inches from tip to tip, and some reach 22 inches or even a trifle more. They should be set low down on the head and hang flat to the sides of the cheeks, and be heavy-feathered.

Size

The most desirable size is from 9 pounds to 12 pounds. *Shape:* in compactness of shape these Spaniels almost rival the Pug, but the length of coat adds greatly to the apparent bulk, as the body, when the coat is wetted, looks small in comparison with that dog. Still, it ought to be decidedly 'cobby,' with strong, stout legs, short broad back and wide chest.

Coat

The coat should be long, silky, soft and wavy, but not curly. There should be a profuse mane, extending well down in the front of the chest. The feather should be well displayed on the ears and feet, and in the latter case so thickly as to give the appearance of being webbed. It is also carried well up the backs of the legs. In the Black and Tan the feather on the ears is very long and profuse, exceeding that of the Blenheim by an inch or more. The feather on the tail (which is cut to the length of about 1½

inches) should be silky, and from 3 to 4 inches in length, constituting a marked 'flag' of a square shape, and not carried above the level of the back.

COLORS OF THE TWO VARIETIES
King Charles and Ruby: the King Charles and Ruby types which comprise one show variety are solid-colored dogs. The King Charles are black and tan (considered a solid color), the black rich and glossy with deep mahogany tan markings over the eyes and on the muzzle, chest and legs. The presence of a few white hairs intermixed with the black on the chest is to be faulted, but a white patch on the chest or white appearing elsewhere disqualifies. The Ruby is a rich chestnut red and is whole-colored. The presence of a few white hairs intermixed with the red on the chest is to be faulted, but a white patch on the chest or white appearing elsewhere disqualifies.

Blenheim and Prince Charles: the Blenheim and Prince Charles types which comprise the other show variety are broken-colored dogs. The Blenheim is red and white. The ground color is a pearly white which has bright red chestnut or ruby red markings evenly distributed in large patches. The ears and cheeks should be red, with a blaze of white extending from the nose up the forehead and ending between the ears in a crescentic curve. In the center of the blaze at the top of the forehead, there should be a clear 'spot' of red, the size of a dime. The Prince Charles, a tri-colored dog, is white, black and tan. The ground color is a pearly white. The black consists of markings which should be evenly distributed in large patches. The tan appears as spots over the eyes, on the muzzle, chest and legs; the ears and vent should also be lined with tan. The Prince Charles has no 'spot,' that being a particular feature of the Blenheim.

SCALE OF POINTS
King Charles (black and tan).
Prince Charles (white, with black and tan markings).
Ruby (red).
Symmetry, condition, size and soundness of limb (20).
Head (15). Stop (5). Muzzle (10). Eyes (10). Ears (15).
Coat and feathering (15). Color (10). *Total (100)*.

Blenheim (white with red markings).
Symmetry, condition, size and soundness of limb (15).
Head (15). Stop (5). Muzzle (10). Eyes (10). Ears (10).
Coat and feathering (15). Color and markings (15).
Spot (5). *Total (100)*.

DISQUALIFICATIONS
King Charles and Ruby: A white patch on the chest, or white on any other part.

Approved by the AKC 14 July 1959

KC(GB) VARIATION TO STANDARD
This dog is known as the King Charles Spaniel in Great Britain. *Weight:* most desirable 6 to 12 pounds.

ITALIAN GREYHOUND

There can be few dogs with the ancient history of the Italian Greyhound, and even if there are those which compete, few have been recorded as well as he has. He has been a favourite of royalty and the noble families as we know from portraits, and there is even evidence that he existed in that capacity as far back as the glorious days of Pompeii. He is one of the few breeds that has not changed in appearance over the centuries, and the little dogs portrayed in paintings of court favourites by the Spanish and Italian painters of three or four hundred years ago vary hardly at all from those seen in the showrings of today. His actual origin is obvious from his appearance, as he is simply a Greyhound in miniature, and there is little doubt that he was the product of miniaturisation by careful selective breeding. This process, which must have taken many years was itself quite a remarkable achievement as the Greyhound proper can weigh as much as eighty

NATIONAL GROUPING		
	Name	Number
AKC	Toys	V
KC(GB)	Toy	6
FCI	Coursing Dogs	10

pounds whilst the toy has been bred down to as little as five pounds.

The first specimens were brought over to Britain in the 17th century during the reign of Charles I, and they quickly became the court favourites they had been in their own country. In later years, the Sportsman's Repository published in 1820, mentions the Italian Greyhound, one of only two toy breeds included in the book, which indicates that he predates most of the Group. He was the favourite of the Court in Britain for many years, and reached the peak of his popularity during the reign of Queen Victoria. Since that time enthusiasm for the breed has declined and in the years immediately following World War II it had almost disappeared from Britain. There is now an upward trend once more, and though it is still one of the minority breeds, numbers are slowly increasing.

One of the problems with the breed was the result of the very miniaturisation that produced it. In the first instance, its sturdiness decreased in proportion to the reduction in size, and some difficulty was experienced in producing really sound specimens of the tiny size that was fashionable. In the early days, when the breed was purely decorative, and when it was expected to do little more than grace a silken cushion, this was not important, but in more recent years, when everyone, and not the least of all, judges, preferred a sound dog even in the tiniest of breeds, this lack of good conformation was a distinct handicap. Fortunately in some countries, and particularly in Scandinavia, the ability to course has been encouraged, and as a result, whilst some of the Scandinavian dogs are a little larger than was at one time fashionable, they can at least perform as a running dog.

In fact the Italian Greyhound is not nearly so tender a dog as has been made out. There are old stories that his bones were not strong enough to stand any sort of rough and tumble, and one writer even gave instructions on how to pick up an Italian Greyhound without breaking it. The same writer would have been surprised to see one belonging to the author jump from a bedroom window at a height of fifteen feet, shake on landing and run off across the lawn. He will still chase small game, and he has a leaping ability that even permits him to capture small and unsuspecting birds in flight. He does, however, need rather more shelter and warmth than many breeds as his coat is fine and silky, and he does not enjoy either cold or strong winds.

As a show dog he has suffered from the fault, already mentioned, of lack of good conformation, but he is still a delightful dog to exhibit. He has the natural good manners of his ancestral cousin the Greyhound, and the ability of the Whippet to stand still. He is not an easy dog to condition as his appetite is small and unless he is given a great deal of exercise to build up muscle and encourage eating, he tends to look rather frail. Temperamentally he is quite delightful, and those who have owned one can readily understand why he became a Court favourite. He is a little reserved, becomes very attached to one person only, and occupies so little space that he can accompany his owner everywhere.

OFFICIAL STANDARD

The Italian Greyhound is very similar to the Greyhound, but much smaller and more slender in all proportions and of ideal elegance and grace.

Head
Narrow and long, tapering to nose, with a slight suggestion of stop.

Skull
Rather long, almost flat.

Muzzle
Long and fine.

Nose
Dark. It may be black or brown or in keeping with the color of the dog. A light or partly pigmented nose is a fault.

Teeth
Scissors bite. A badly undershot or overshot mouth is a fault.

Eyes
Dark, bright, intelligent, medium in size. Very light eyes are a fault.

Ears
Small, fine in texture; thrown back and folded except when alerted, then carried folded at right angles to the head. Erect or button ears severely penalized.

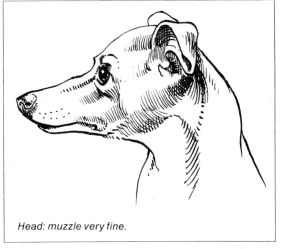

Head: muzzle very fine.

Neck
Long, slender and gracefully arched.

Body
Of medium length, short coupled; high at withers, back curved and drooping at hindquarters, the highest point of curve at start of loin, creating a definite tuck-up at flanks.

Shoulders
Long and sloping.

Chest
Deep and narrow.

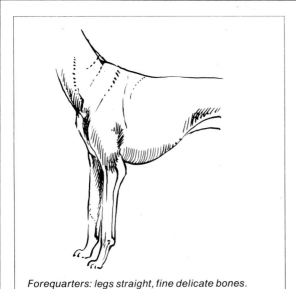

Forequarters: legs straight, fine delicate bones.

Forelegs
Long, straight, set well under shoulder; strong pasterns, fine bone.

Hindquarters
Long, well-muscled thigh; hind legs parallel when viewed from behind, hocks well let down, well-bent stifle.

Feet
Harefoot with well-arched toes. Removal of dewclaws optional.

Tail
Slender and tapering to a curved end, long enough to reach the hock; set low, carried low. Ring tail a serious fault, gay tail a fault.

Coat
Skin fine and supple, hair short, glossy like satin and soft to the touch.

Color
Any color and markings are acceptable except that a dog with the tan markings normally found on black and tan dogs of other breeds must be disqualified.

Action
High stepping and free, front and hind legs to move forward in a straight line.

Size
Height at withers, ideally 13 inches to 15 inches.

DISQUALIFICATION
Dogs with the tan markings normally found on black and tan dogs of other breeds.

Approved by the AKC 13 April 1971

KC(GB) VARIATION TO STANDARD
Eyes: rather large. *Teeth:* level. *Feet:* long. *Weight:* 6 to 8 pounds, not exceeding 10 pounds.

JAPANESE CHIN

NATIONAL GROUPING		
	Name	Number
AKC	Toys	V
KC(GB)	Toy	6
FCI	Companion dogs	9

Several of the small dogs that have become part of the everyday dog show scene in the modern Western World, started off as breeds that were favoured by the courts of the Orient. The Japanese Spaniel, or Chin is one of them. Although its name implies that it owes its origins to Japan, it almost certainly in fact originated in China and it has been reported that a pair was presented by the emperor of China to the emperor of Japan some thousand years ago. The similarity between this little dog and the Pekingese is no accident, and there is little doubt that the one is the result of changes brought about by the selective breeding from the other, though which came first it is impossible to say.

In 1853 Commodore Perry was presented with a pair of these dogs which he brought back to Britain and presented to Queen Victoria whose interest in dogs is well known. Later others were brought out of the Orient by sailors who realised the potential profit in taking these tiny dogs back to Europe and the United States. In 1894 the breed was recognised by the Kennel Club in Britain and soon afterwards its influence on the toy dog world was felt in many other countries. The early specimens brought into the Western World were larger than the dogs seen today, and some miniaturisation was resorted to. This was probably done by selection, but possibly by the introduction of the English Toy Spaniel blood already available, and

individuals were eventually bred which weighed as little as two and a half pounds as adults. The efforts of the Japanese Chin Club in Britain did much to settle the standard of the breed and it is largely due to them that we now have a very sound little dog of around seven pounds in weight.

Numbers in recent years have remained very steady and the breed is firmly established as a show dog. At one time he was said to be a dog that was constitutionally delicate and needed special care in feeding. Opinion has changed, however, and there is now no reason why because his origin was oriental that he should be considered incapable of standing up to western climate or that his diet should largely consist of rice. Most of the breed are black and white, but other colours such as red, or lemon or even brindle markings are acceptable. He has one breed characteristic which differentiates him from many other breeds in that his eyes are placed wide apart on his skull which, in his effort to look straight ahead give him a perpetual astonished and even apparently cross-eyed look.

He makes a delightful little show dog, as he is something of an extrovert and enjoys being in the public eye, but it is probably as a puppy that he is at his most attractive, being just a tiny ball of black and white fluff which children find adorable. He has never been among the top winners at major shows in Britain, but is always much admired for his aristocratic and stylish appearance. Many carry profuse coats of great quality and his sparkling colours in contrast with his white coat make him an attraction whenever he appears in the ring. His manners are impeccable and he is a bright, intelligent and alert companion. He is sensitive and responsive to human companionship becoming very much part of the family that adopts him, and his diminutive size makes him an ideal pet for the small house or apartment.

OFFICIAL STANDARD

General appearance
That of a lively, high-bred little dog with dainty appearance, smart, compact carriage and profuse coat. These dogs should be essentially stylish in movement, lifting the feet high when in action, carrying the tail (which is heavily feathered, proudly curved or plumed) over the back. In size they vary considerably, but the smaller they are the better, provided type and quality are not sacrificed. When divided by weight, classes should be under and over 7 pounds.

Head
Should be large for the size of the dog, with broad skull, rounded in front.

Head and skull: broad skull rounded in front. Muzzle short and wide. Eyes large, dark, set wide apart.

Eyes
Large, dark, lustrous, rather prominent and set wide apart.

Ears
Small and V-shaped, nicely feathered, set wide apart and high on the head and carried slightly forward.

Nose
Very short in the muzzle part. The end or nose proper should be wide, with open nostrils, and must be the color of the dog's markings, i.e. black in black-marked dogs, and red or deep flesh color in red or lemon-marked dogs. It shall be a disqualification for a black and white Japanese Spaniel to have a nose any other color than black.

Neck
Should be short and moderately thick.

Body
Should be squarely and compactly built, wide in chest, 'cobby' in shape. The length of the dog's body should be about its height.

Tail
Must be well twisted to either right or left from root and carried up over back and flow on opposite side; it should be profusely covered with long hair (ring tails not desirable).

Legs
The bones of the legs should be small, giving them a slender appearance, and they should be well feathered.

Feet
Small and shaped somewhat long; the dog stands up on its toes somewhat. If feathered, the tufts should never increase in width of the foot, but only its length a trifle.

Coat
Profuse, long, straight, rather silky. It should be absolutely free from wave or curl, and not lie too flat, but have a tendency to stand out, especially at the neck, so as to give a thick mane or ruff, which with profuse feathering on thighs and tail gives a very showy appearance.

Color
The dogs should be either black and white or red and white, i.e. parti-colored. The term red includes all shades of sable, brindle, lemon and orange, but the brighter and clearer the red the better. The white should be clear white, and the color, whether black or red, should be evenly distributed patches over the body, cheek and ears.

SCALE OF POINTS
Head and neck (10). Eyes (10). Ears (5). Muzzle (10). Nose (5). Body (15). Tail (10). Feet and legs (5). Coat and markings (15). Action (5). Size (10). *Total (100)*.

DISQUALIFICATION
In black and whites, a nose any other color than black.

KC(GB) VARIATION TO STANDARD
Head: nostrils should be large and black except in case of red and white dogs, in which brown-coloured noses are as common as black. *Eyes:* it is desirable that white shows in inner corners, giving dog characteristic look of astonishment that should on no account be lost. *Feet:* hare shaped. *Tail:* carried proudly over back. *Faults:* flying ears, wry mouth, tongue showing, tri-colour.

LOWCHEN

NATIONAL GROUPING		
	Name	Number
AKC	—	—
KC(GB)	Toy	6
FCI	Companion Dogs	9

Although this is one of the latest breeds to be admitted to championship level in Britain it is a very ancient type of dog that has been known and exhibited in Europe for a considerable time. It is said variously to have originated in Russia, the Mediterranean and France, and in addition to its two more usual names is also known as the Petit Chien Lion. It was known in Britain at the beginning of this century, but was not imported, and was often said to be found in Germany and Holland. Like many of the small European companion dogs, its origins are fairly obscure. It is clearly related to the Bichon and Barbet, which were themselves connected with the Miniature and Toy Poodles, and there is a certain resemblance though a superficial one, with those breeds.

It would be a mistake to connect the breed with the Lion Dogs of the Far East, which gained their name from the myths connected with their courage rather than with their appearance. The name of the Lowchen, the Little Lion Dog came from the manner in which it was trimmed, giving it the look of a well-maned male lion in miniature. Vero Shaw in 1881 wrote of the Poodle being trimmed to imitate the Lion Dog (*Canis Leoninus*), of which a degenerate scion still exists in Malta; whilst Richard Cope even earlier in 1840 described an animal very like today's Lowchen which he too attributed to Malta but said that it was extremely timid, feeble and inactive, which is completely unlike the dog that we now know. One or two breeders in Europe kept the breed alive during its depressed period in the early part of the present century, Madame M. de Conninck of Dieghem showing them prior to the First World War with some success. It was not, however, until after the Second World War that there was a real revival of interest, principally in Germany.

None were registered in Britain until 1971, but since that time their growth in popularity has been one of the phenomena of the British dog scene, and by 1976 their numbers had risen to such an extent that they were granted championship status, the first challenge certificates being on offer at Crufts of that year. The popularity of the breed continues to grow and they are now being exported to many countries.

He is a sturdy little dog, with a remarkably strong body and stouter construction than the average Poodle of a similar size. His general appearance on casual acquaintance is reminiscent of the Poodle but he differs in many respects, principally in the head, where he is broader and stronger in muzzle, and in proportionately greater strength of body and hindquarters. His coat too is softer and more silky in texture, with a slight wave. He makes a very good show dog, being quite striking in appearance, with considerable variation in colour, and remarkably steady in the ring.

His temperament is quite delightful. He is not the timid, feeble dog that was described a century or so ago, but is bold and very active. He is friendly with everyone, becomes very attached to his owner, and though gay and boisterous, is kind and playful with no vices. He makes an admirable house pet and friend of the family and is very good with children.

OFFICIAL STANDARD

General appearance
Small intelligent dog, affectionate and lively disposition combining all the good qualities of a companion dog. The body is clipped in the traditional lion clip and the tail, also clipped, is topped with a pom pom, thus giving the dog the appearance of a little lion.

Head
Short. Skull wide in proportion.

Nose
Black.

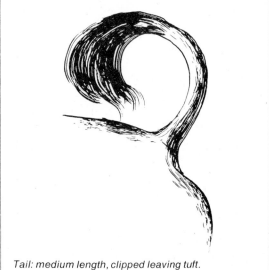

Tail: medium length, clipped leaving tuft.

Head: short, broad, well furnished.

Eyes
Round, large and intelligent, dark in colour.

Ears
Pendant, long and well fringed.

Forequarters
Forelegs straight and fine boned.

Body
Short and well proportioned.

Hindquarters
Hindlegs straight when viewed from the rear, with good turn of stifle.

Feet
Small and round.

Tail
Of medium length, clipped with a tuft of hair left to form a pom pom.

Coat
Fairly long and wavy but not curly.

Colour
Any colour permissible, be it self colour or parti-colour. The most sought after colours are white, black and lemon.

Weight and size
Height 8 to 14 inches (20 to 35 centimetres) at the withers. Weight 4 to 9 pounds.

Faults
Any departure from the foregoing points should be considered a fault and the seriousness of the fault should be in exact proportion to its degree.

Note
Male animals should have two apparently normal testicles fully descended into the scrotum.

AKC VARIATION TO STANDARD
This dog is not granted championship status by the AKC. The above standards are those of the KC(GB).

MALTESE

Malta as an island has a very ancient and noble history. Its geographical position has always made it an important place in the Mediterranean since it was settled by the Phoenicians some four thousand years ago. It developed a culture and a race of people with distinctive characteristics, and a race of dogs in the little Maltese which differs from almost every other breed. Malta's situation gave it an ecology which remained undiluted by outside influences much as in a very large way did that of Australia, and the Maltese was bred as a pure breed for centuries as a result. Dr. Caius referred to the breed in 1576 when he wrote 'the dogges of this kind doth Callimachus call Melitaers of the Iseland Melita in the sea of Sicily'. They were favourites in the time of Phidias and of the Imperial Court of Rome and Theophrastus wrote 'When his favourite dog dies he deposits the remains in a tomb and erects a monument over the grave with the inscription "Offspring of the stock of Malta"'. Early Italian painters often depicted the breed, or something very like it in court paintings, and though there may

NATIONAL GROUPING		
	Name	Number
AKC	Toys	V
KC(GB)	Toy	6
FCI	Companion Dogs	9

be some confusion with the Shock Dog and the Bichon, many of the early works depict these little dogs so clearly that there is no doubt at all that they are indeed Maltese.

Maltese were first imported into Britain during the reign of Henry VIII and were certainly favourites in the time of Queen Elizabeth I to whose physician we owe our early reference. By the middle of the 19th century the breed was well established as a pet dog in Britain, and when dog shows began, the Maltese featured among the early exhibits. In the period 1860 to 1870 Mr. Mandeville had a brace of dogs that were winning at all the big shows and later other breeders took the Maltese up seriously, giving the breed greater prominence. Later still, by the turn of the century there was some decline and the Maltese was being overtaken by some of the newer Toy breeds being imported into the country. At that time specimens were being exported from Britain into the United States of America, where the splendid coat and sheer showmanship of these beautiful dogs made a rapid impression.

The fact that the Maltese has for centuries been the pampered pet of house and court must to a certain extent account for his refinement and fastidiousness, though it would be a mistake to consider him as just a soft little dog needing special care and attention. He was at one time known as the Maltese Terrier, and there is a good deal of the Terrier in his makeup. He is strong, very active and muscular, and thoroughly enjoys a good deal of exercise. His long silky coat does need, however, a great deal of attention if it is to retain its length and tidiness. He needs considerable bathing to keep the coat white and clean, and only a dog in perfect health will carry the coat of the desired length and quality.

As a show dog he is supreme, having all those qualities which serve a dog so well. He is easily trained to stand still and to move with spirit, he is amenable to discipline and is not easily scared by strangers which means that he will allow himself to be handled in the ring without shrinking away from the judge. His snowy whiteness makes him very attractive in the ring, and he is one of those dogs that looks at his best at an indoor show under powerful artificial light. He makes a very good pet dog and companion, being friendly and attentive to his owner, and enjoying the warmth and comfort of a house, being very much a furniture and fireside dog.

OFFICIAL STANDARD

General appearance
The Maltese is a toy dog covered from head to foot with a mantle of long, silky, white hair. He is gentle-mannered and affectionate, eager and sprightly in action, and, despite his size, possessed of the vigor needed for the satisfactory companion.

Head
Of medium length and in proportion to the size of the dog. The *skull* is slightly rounded on top, the stop moderate. The *drop ears* are rather low set and heavily feathered with long hair that hangs close to the head. *Eyes* are set not too far apart; they are very dark and round, their black rims enhancing the gentle yet alert expression. The *muzzle* is

Body: balanced, short, cobby.

of medium length, fine and tapered but not snipy. The *nose* is black. The *teeth* meet in an even, edge-to-edge bite, or in a scissors bite.

Neck
Sufficient length of neck is desirable as promoting a high carriage of the head.

Body
Compact, the height from the withers to the ground equaling the length from the withers to the root of the tail. Shoulder blades are sloping, the elbows well knit and held close to the body. The back is level in topline, the ribs well sprung. The chest is fairly deep, the loins, taut, strong, and just slightly tucked up underneath.

Tail
A long-haired plume carried gracefully over the back, its tip lying to the side over the quarter.

Legs and feet
Legs are fine-boned and nicely feathered. Forelegs are

Head and skull: equally balanced, stop defined.

ion of kinkiness, curliness, or woolly texture is objectionable. Color, pure white. Light tan or lemon on the ears is permissible, but not desirable.

Size
Weight under 7 pounds, with from 4 to 6 pounds preferred. Over-all quality is to be favored over size.

Gait
The Maltese moves with a jaunty, smooth, flowing gait. Viewed from the side, he gives an impression of rapid movement, size considered. In the stride, the forelegs reach straight and free from the shoulders, with elbows close. Hind legs to move in a straight line. Cowhocks or any suggestion of hind leg toeing in or out are faults.

Temperament
For all his diminutive size, the Maltese seems to be without fear. His trust and affectionate responsiveness are very appealing. He is among the gentlest mannered of all little dogs, yet he is lively and playful as well as vigorous.

Approved by the AKC 10 March 1964

straight, their pastern joints well knit and devoid of appreciable bend. Hind legs are strong and moderately angulated at stifles and hocks. The feet are small and round, with toe pads black. Scraggly hairs on the feet may be trimmed to give a neater appearance.

Coat and color
The coat is single, that is, without undercoat. It hangs long, flat, and silky over the sides of the body almost, if not quite, to the ground. The long head-hair may be tied up in a topknot or it may be left hanging. Any suggest-

KC(GB) VARIATION TO STANDARD
Eyes: should be dark brown. *Tail:* well arched over back. *Size:* not over 10 inches from ground to top of shoulder. *Faults:* bad mouth, over or undershot; gay tail; curly or woolly coat; brown nose; pink eye rims; unsound in any way.

MANCHESTER TERRIER (TOY)

Most of the toy dogs have an ancestry that is based on one or more of the dogs that form the other Groups, so that we have toy Spaniels, toy Greyhounds and of course toy Terriers. Towards the end of the 19th century one of the most popular of Terriers in England was the Black and Tan Terrier, known as the Manchester Terrier, a breed which exists to this day, and in the United States the English Toy Terrier is known as the Manchester Terrier (Toy). They were vermin killers and one of the favourite dogs for use in the rat pits, a popular form of sport among the working classes, and indeed among the gentry too at that time. The common practice of miniaturisation produced the Manchester, and this was done either by selecting smaller specimens to breed from, or as has been

NATIONAL GROUPING		
	Name	Number
AKC	Toys	V
KC(GB)	Toy	6
FCI	Companion Dogs	9

suggested by crossing with the Italian Greyhound. The second method is likely as the Manchester Toy is a much more delicate animal than the Manchester proper or the old-fashioned Black and Tan Terrier from which he is supposed to have descended, which looked rather like a Staffordshire Bull Terrier. An early standard of the Black and Tan of 1881 reveals that miniatures existed at a very early stage, as the

357

weight permitted is from seven to twenty pounds indicating that small and normal Terrier sized specimens were exhibited together.

The pattern of the colouring of the breed has been considered so important that the breed club and the Kennel Club have laid down strict standards that must be adhered to. The black parts of the coat must be jet black, the tan a rich mahogany and this must appear on the muzzle, the underjaw and the throat with a small spot on each cheek. The tan on the forelegs must reach up to the knee in front and the elbow behind with a thin black line called the 'pencilling' up each toe and with a black thumb mark on each pastern. The colour requirements are just as strict on other parts of the body and this very carefully devised pattern is an attempt to retain the original black and tan markings of the parent stock, which dates back centuries.

In recent years, the breed, along with its larger cousin the Manchester Terrier, has gone into something of a decline. It seems that fewer and fewer people are interested in the traditional and tend to become involved in things that are more modern and exotic. Whilst the registration figures in the country of origin of this attractive little dog have dropped to below fifty each year and the Manchester likewise, breeds that only a comparative short time ago were being exhibited among the foreign dogs at our major shows boast ten times as many. One reason for this is probably that breeders in recent years have failed to produce a sound dog, sacrificing construction to the more specialist features such as the colour and markings, and many of the dogs entered at shows nowadays are rather weak and weedy specimens with none of the staunch terrier character of their forebears.

He has never made much of a mark in the show ring, being overshadowed by the more picturesque 'comforter' breeds in the Toy Group, and many people

prefer a breed of dog that has been associated with man—or more particularly in some cases with woman —down through the centuries. He suffers from the disadvantage of being considered by some to have a rather plebeian background rather than to have descended from the pets of kings and princes. A good one is, however, very attractive in the ring, and judges who have studied the dog's past history and who understand him, will sometimes look with favour on a good specimen in strong competition.

OFFICIAL STANDARD

The Standard for the Manchester Terrier (Toy Variety) is the same as for the Manchester Terrier except as regards weight and ears. (See page 303.)

KC(GB) VARIATION TO STANDARD
This dog is known as the English Toy Terrier (Black and Tan) in GB.

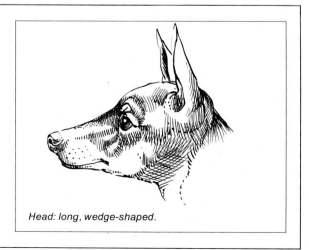

Head: long, wedge-shaped.

MINIATURE PINSCHER

The Miniature Pinscher is an ancient breed, though probably not in the style that we know it today. He is a German dog descended from Terrier types indigenous in Germany for centuries, the word 'pinscher' meaning 'terrier' in the German language. The fact that the Doberman is known as the Doberman Pinscher was a miniaturisation of this breed, a belief heightened by the fact that there is a superficial resemblance. In fact the two are not related and the Miniature Pinscher is probably the older breed. There was at one time a large Pinscher in Germany that existed in two coats, wire and smooth, and it was probably from the latter that the Miniature Pinscher was developed. He was a strong active dog about the size of an Irish Terrier and seems to have had a fondness for stables where he was employed keeping down the rat population. He probably still exists in Germany in his original form, but since the late 19th century, when there was a medley of types, things

NATIONAL GROUPING		
	Name	Number
AKC	Toys	V
KC(GB)	Toy	6
FCI	Companion Dogs	9

have been sorted out and the rough-coated version has been developed into the Schnauzer.

The German *Pinscher Klub* was formed in 1895 and it was this club which gave the breed its standard and improved it prior to the First World War, but it was after the war that the breed really began to make progress. Before 1928 and until the breed club was formed in the United States there were few Miniature Pinschers to be seen in the show rings there. Since that time the breed has developed steadily on both sides of the Atlantic, and whilst the numbers in Britain remain fairly steady at around the same figure

359

as the Japanese, specimens are now finding their way into a great many countries.

The Miniature Pinscher is a tremendously sturdy and active little dog, hard as nails, so muscular that he can outjump many dogs far larger than he is, and is built in a square and stylish fashion. He is sporting, will hunt all day given the opportunity, and likes nothing better than a scramble through the woods in search of small game, and for that matter not-so-small game too, as he is fearless and will tackle anything several times his size. He is one of the most soundly constructed dogs in the Toy Group, having straight limbs, an excellent conformation, and many of the physical attributes of the working and hunting dogs.

As a show dog there is hardly anything in the Toy Group that can approach him for smartness, style and spirit. He stands like a rock in the ring, and yet is always fully prepared to whip round at the too-near approach of another dog, being continually on guard against intrusion into what he feels is his territory. His outline has the smart clean-cut look of the trotting pony, an illusion which is increased by his straight legs and close, hard and lustrous coat. He is a dog that always has the appearance of supreme fitness, and it is this look, combined with his snappy appearance in the ring which always makes him a very keen competitor at the major shows.

He is very much the house dog these days, as the need for vermin hunters in modern society has declined, but he makes a very good one, being an extremely keen guard, with an alert sense of hearing and well-developed quick reactions to anything unusual. He is friendly though somewhat reserved at first approach, and until he has ascertained that a visitor is welcome, he is somewhat guarded in his approach. Once he has made friends, however, he is pleasant and sociable, and towards his own household he is free from vice and amenable to discipline.

OFFICIAL STANDARD

General appearance

The Miniature Pinscher was originated in Germany and named the 'Reh Pinscher' due to his resemblance in structure and animation to a very small species of deer found in the forests. This breed is structurally a well-balanced, sturdy, compact, short-coupled, smooth-coated toy dog. He is naturally well groomed, proud, vigorous and alert. The natural characteristic traits which identify him from other toy dogs are his precise Hackney gait, his fearless animation, complete self-possession, and his spirited presence. *Faults:* structurally lacking in balance, too long- or short-coupled, too coarse or too refined (lacking in bone development causing poor feet and legs), too large or too small, lethargic, timid or dull, shy or vicious, low in tail placement and poor in action (action not typical of the breed requirements). Knotty over-developed muscles.

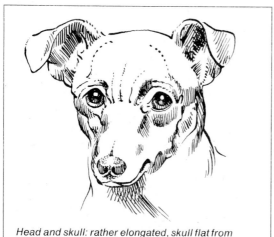

Head and skull: rather elongated, skull flat from front, drop-ear version.

Head

In correct proportion with the body. *From top:* tapering, narrow with well-fitted but not too prominent foreface which should balance with the skull. No indication of coarseness. *From front:* skull appears flat, tapering forward toward the muzzle. Muzzle itself strong rather than fine and delicate, and in proportion to the head as a whole; cheeks and lips small, taut and closely adherent to each other. Teeth in perfect alignment and apposition. *From side:* Well-balanced with only a slight drop to the muzzle, which should be parallel to the top of the skull. *Eyes:* full, slightly oval, almost round, clear, bright and dark even to a true black; set wide apart and fitted well into the sockets. *Ears:* well-set and firmly placed, upstanding (when cropped, pointed and carried erect in balance with the head). *Nose:* black only (with the exception of chocolates, which may have a self-colored nose). *Faults:* too large or too small for the body, too coarse or too refined, pinched and weak in foreface, domed in skull, too flat and lacking in chiseling, giving a vapid expression. *Jaws and teeth* overshot or undershot. *Eyes* too round and full, too large, bulging, too deep-set or set too far apart; or too small, set too close (pig eyes). Light-colored eyes not desirable. *Ears* poorly placed, low-set hanging ears (lacking in cartilage) which detracts from head conformation. (Poorly cropped ears if set on the head properly and having sufficient cartilage should not detract from head points, as this would be a man-made fault and automatically would detract from general appearance.) *Nose* any color other than black (with the exception of chocolates which may have a self-colored nose).

Neck

Proportioned to head and body. Slightly arched, gracefully curved, clean and firm, blending into shoulders, length well-balanced, muscular and free from a suggestion of dewlap or throatiness. *Faults:* too straight or too curved; too thick or too thin; too long or short; knotty muscles; loose, flabby or wrinkled skin.

Body

From top: compact, slightly wedge-shaped, muscular with well-sprung ribs. *From side:* depth of brisket, the base line of which is level with the points of the elbows; short and strong in loin with belly moderately tucked up to denote grace in structural form. Back level or slightly sloping toward the rear. Length of males equals height at withers. Females may be slightly longer. *From rear:* high tail-set; strong, sturdy upper shanks, with croup slope at about 30 degrees; vent opening not barreled. *Forequarters:* forechest well-developed and full, moderately broad, shoulders clean, sloping with moderate angulation, co-ordinated to permit the true action of the Hackney pony. *Hindquarters:* well-knit muscular quarters set wide enough apart to fit into a properly balanced body. *Faults: from top:* too long, too short, too barreled, lacking in body development. *From side:* too long, too short, too thin or too fat, hips higher or considerably lower than the withers, lacking depth of chest, too full in loin, sway back, roach back or wry back. *From rear:* quarters too wide or too close to each other, overdeveloped, barreled vent, underdeveloped vent, too sloping croup, tail set low. *Forequarters:* forechest and spring of rib too narrow (or too shallow and underdeveloped), shoulders too straight, too loose, or too short and overloaded with muscles. *Hindquarters:* too narrow, undermuscled or overmuscled, too steep in croup.

Legs and feet

Strong bone development and small clean joints; feet catlike, toes strong, well-arched and closely knit with deep pads and thick blunt nails. *Forelegs and feet:* as viewed from the front straight and upstanding, elbows close to body, well-knit, flexible yet strong with perpendicular pasterns. *Hind legs:* all adjacent bones should appear well-angulated with well-muscled thighs or upper shanks, with clearly well-defined stifles, hocks short, set well apart turning neither in nor out, while at rest should stand perpendicular to the ground and upper shanks, lower shanks and hocks parallel to each other. *Faults:* too thick or thin bone development, large joints, spreading flat feet.

Forelegs and feet

Bowed or crooked, weak pasterns, feet turning in or out, loose elbows. *Hind legs:* thin undeveloped stifles, large or crooked hocks, loose stifle joints.

Tail

Set high, held erect, docked to $\frac{1}{2}$ to 1 inch. *Faults:* set too low, too thin, drooping, hanging or poorly docked.

Coat

Smooth, hard and short, straight and lustrous, closely adhering to and uniformly covering the body. *Faults:* thin, too long, dull; upstanding; curly; dry; area of various thickness or bald spots.

Color

1. Solid red or stag red. 2. Lustrous black with sharply defined tan, rust-red markings on cheeks, lips, lower jaw, throat, twin spots above eyes and chest, lower half of forelegs, inside of hind legs and vent region, lower portion of hocks and feet. Black pencil stripes on toes. 3. Solid brown or chocolate with rust or yellow markings. *Faults:* any color other than listed; very dark or sooty spots. *Disqualifications:* thumb marks or any area of white on feet or forechest exceeding one-half inch in its longest dimension.

Size

Desired height 11 inches to $11\frac{1}{2}$ inches at the withers. A dog of either sex measuring under 10 inches or over $12\frac{1}{2}$ inches shall be disqualified. *Faults:* oversize; undersize; too fat; too lean.

SCALE OF POINTS

General appearance and movement*(very important)* (30). (30). Skull (5). Muzzle (5). Mouth (5). Eyes (5). Ears (5). Neck (5). Body (15). Feet (5). Legs (5). Color (5). Coat (5). Tail (5). *Total (100).*

DISQUALIFICATIONS

Color: thumb marks or any area of white on feet or forechest exceeding one-half ($\frac{1}{2}$) inch in its longest dimension.
Size: a dog of either sex measuring under 10 or over $12\frac{1}{2}$ inches.

Approved by the AKC 13 May 1958

KC(GB) VARIATION TO STANDARD

Nose: black only with exception of livers and blues which may have self coloured nose. *Mouth:* scissors bite. *Feet:* nails dark.

PAPILLON

This little dog is another of the dwarf Spaniels evolved in Europe from the root stock which was either Oriental or Spanish in origin, and opinions differ on that point. He was known centuries ago, as there is a record of one having been sold as early as 1545, and certainly Madame de Pompadour and Marie Antoinette were both owners and admirers of the breed. The dog first became popular in Spain, where it was the pet of the courts, and it soon spread as fashion decreed that it should, through Italy where it became very popular and to France where it gained its name. The overall appearance of the head, with its large upstanding fringed ears and clearly defined blaze down the face was said to resemble the butterfly, hence the name

NATIONAL GROUPING		
	Name	Number
AKC	Toys	V
KC(GB)	Toy	6
FCI	Companion Dogs	9

Papillon. They were at one time known as Squirrel Spaniels because they carried their heavily plumed tail over their back as does the squirrel, and the version with the folded down ears, accepted as a separate breed in some continental countries, was called the Phalene as the head was then said to resemble a moth.

By the turn of the century the breed was being shown

at dog shows in France, and soon afterwards it found its way across the Channel and appeared in the show rings in Britain and the United States. When he first came into Britain he was a much larger dog than is fashionable at the present time, and only careful selective breeding produced the sound very small dog that can be seen today, though even now from time to time larger specimens are produced which are unsuitable for the show ring but which make very attractive pets. In the early days too, they were often self-coloured, red-mahogany, ruby, reddish chestnut or dark yellow, lending weight to the argument that they were closely related to some of the other small Spaniels. It became fashionable, however, to breed the white dogs with patches of these colours, and this is the type that has survived and the standard now states that he should always be a parti-coloured dog.

The Papillon is a hardy little dog, not nearly so delicate as his appearance might suggest, and certainly not needing as much coddling as some people give him. He has a fairly long fine coat which is weather resistant and neither winter cold nor summer heat appears to worry him. He is a refined and not a cobby dog, but his bone though slender is straight and this, together with his well-developed hindquarters make him one of the more active members of the Group. He is still something of a hunter, enjoys pursuing vermin, and will kill a rat if given the opportunity.

He makes a fine show dog, being smart, active in the ring and very amenable to discipline. The variation in the colours, and the snowy whiteness of the white parts of his coat make an attractive picture when a number of them are gathered in the ring together. He is steady, and when trained to the ring, carries his head with great pride and his tail curled over giving a picture of a very alert little dog doing his best to please. Preparation is no problem, as keeping the coat in condition is largely a matter of physical fitness and of washing and brushing to get the best out of the fine long silky coat. The fringes on the ears are a desirable feature, and exhibitors spend considerable time and ingenuity in growing and keeping these as long as possible. As a pet he is delightful, being merry and sociable and liking nothing better than being in the company of those to whom he becomes firmly attached.

OFFICIAL STANDARD

General appearance
The Papillon is a small, friendly, elegant toy dog of fine-boned structure, light, dainty and of lively action; distinguished from other breeds by its beautiful butterfly-like ears.

Head
Small. The skull of medium width, and slightly rounded between the ears. A well-defined stop is formed where the muzzle joins the skull. The muzzle is fine, abruptly thinner than the head, tapering to the nose. The length of the muzzle from the tip of nose to stop is approximately one third the length of the head from tip of nose to occiput.

Nose
Black, small, rounded and slightly flat on top.

Eyes
Dark, round, not bulging, of medium size and alert in expression. The inner corner of the eyes is on a line with the stop. Eye rims black.

Mouth
Lips are tight, thin and black. Teeth meet in a scissors bite. Tongue must not be visible when jaws are closed. *Fault:* overshot or undershot.

Ears
The ears of either the erect or drop type should be large with rounded tips and set on the sides and toward the back of head.
(1) Ears of the erect type are carried obliquely and move like the spread wings of a butterfly. When alert, each ear forms an angle of approximately 45 degrees to the head. The leather should be of sufficient strength to maintain the erect position.
(2) Ears of the drop type, known as Phalene, are similar to the erect type, but are carried drooping and must be completely down.
Faults: ears small, pointed, set too high, one ear up or ears partly down.

Ears: large, rounded tips, heavily fringed.

Ears: dropped ear version or Phalene.

Neck
Of medium length.

Body
Must be slightly longer than the height at withers. It is not a cobby dog. Topline straight and level. The chest is of medium depth with well-sprung ribs. The belly is tucked up.

Forequarters
Shoulders well developed and laid back to allow freedom of movement. Forelegs slender, fine-boned and must be straight. Removal of dewclaws on forelegs optional.

Hindquarters
Well developed and well angulated. Hocks inclined neither in nor out. The hind legs are slender, fine-boned, and parallel when viewed from behind. Dewclaws, if any, must be removed from hind legs.

Feet
Thin and elongated (harelike), pointing neither in nor out.

Tail
Long, set high and carried well arched over the body. The plume may hang to either side of the body. *Fault:* Low-set tail, one not arched over back or too short.

Coat
Abundant, long, fine, silky, flowing, straight with resilient quality, flat on back and sides of body. A profuse frill on chest. There is no undercoat. Hair short and close on skull, muzzle, front of forelegs and from hind feet to hocks. Ears well fringed with the inside covered with silken hair of medium length. Backs of the forelegs are covered with feathers diminishing to the pasterns. Hind legs are covered to the hocks with abundant breeches (culottes). Tail is covered with a long flowing plume. Hair on feet is short but fine tufts may appear over toes and grow beyond them forming a point.

Size
Height at highest point of shoulder blades, 8 to 11 inches.

Weight is in proportion to height. *Fault:* over 11 inches.

Gait
Free, quick, easy, graceful, not paddle-footed, or stiff in hip movements.

Color
Always parti-color, white with patches of any color. On the head color other than white must cover both ears, back and front, and extend without interruption from the ears over both eyes. A clearly defined white blaze and noseband are preferred to a solidly marked head. Symmetry of facial markings is desirable. The size, shape, placement or absence of patches on the body are without importance. Papillons may be any parti-color, provided nose, eye rims and lips are well-pigmented black. Among the colors there is no preference.

The following faults shall be severely penalized:
(1) Nose not black.
(2) Color other than white not covering both ears, back and front, or not extending from the ears over both eyes. A slight extension of the white collar onto the base of the ears or a few white hairs interspersed among the color, shall not be penalized provided the butterfly appearance is not sacrificed.

DISQUALIFICATIONS
Height: over 12 inches. An all white dog or a dog with no white.

Approved by the AKC 8 February 1975

KC(GB) VARIATION TO STANDARD
Faults: muzzle over long or coarse. Skull flat or apple shaped. Eyes light in colour, too small or too large or protruding. Wry mouth. Shoulders straight; out at elbow. Topline roached dipped or cobby. Legs malformed and crooked; cow hocked; too long or too short. Stifles straight; coupled with weak hindquarters. Harsh curly or stand-off coat.

PEKINGESE

NATIONAL GROUPING		
	Name	Number
AKC	Toys	V
KC(GB)	Toy	6
FCI	Companion Dogs	9

The ancient oriental background of this dog makes him one of the most fascinating as well as one of the most popular of all the Toy dogs. His origins are well documented as the country that produced him was one with a long history of keeping written and illustrated records of everything including its animal life. We know therefore more about what the Pekingese looked like centuries ago than we do about almost any other breed. They were the Royal Dogs of China and their history goes back to at least the Tang dynasty. They were held as sacred, and the theft of a dog from the Imperial Palace was punishable by death. The bloodlines were kept pure by breeding them only within the walls of the palace, and staff were kept whose sole duty it was to look after the imperial dogs. Emperors had dog portraits painted in books kept for the purpose, and which formed a pictorial standard of the breed. The staff of eunuchs who looked after the dogs vied with one another as to who should produce the best dogs to present to the Emperor, and remarkable lengths were gone to to encourage desirable features of stunted growth, short nose and exaggerated width of front.

The Emperor's favourites were given rank and were treated as people rather than as dogs, visitors even being expected to pay homage to them. Legend has it that the Pekingese was produced by crossing a marmoset with a lion and that he has had the heart of a lion ever since. Certainly he was a good little fighter, and the eunuchs often staged fights for entertainment. He came into the Western World as the result of the looting of the Imperial Palace at Peking in 1860, when a number of these little dogs were found by the British troops, in spite of the fact that many of them had been killed to prevent them falling into the hands of the enemy. Admiral Lord John who was present at the overrunning of the palace brought five back to Britain on his return, one being presented to Queen Victoria and the other two pairs being kept by the officers concerned. Two of these, that spent the rest of their days at Goodwood were the ancestors of the modern Pekingese.

The Pekingese was first exhibited in Britain in 1893 when the breed appeared at Chester and from that time on, their appearance and their remarkable history captured the public imagination so thoroughly that they quickly became very popular. By 1909 the Pekingese Club of America was in being and since that time this appealing little dog has spread all over the world. His sporting character as well as his somewhat quaint appearance has endeared him to a great number of people. Despite the fact that for centuries he was a pampered pet, he is nothing of the 'softie' being quite fierce when aroused, and by no means averse to having a scrap, something that often leads to trouble as his eyes are particularly vulnerable. He is a strong dog for his size, and when picking one up the impression should be that he is surprisingly heavy for so small a dog.

He makes a wonderful show dog, being very picturesque with his enormous coat, strong colouring and distinctive shape. His head, which is one of his major features, is full of character and to see as one often does, a line of these little dogs being held up for the judge to examine their heads, or being lined up on a table for the same purpose is one of the sights of the show rings of the world. Temperamentally he is very positive and opinionated, wilful even and with fixed ideas about what constitutes his own affairs. He is at the same time extremely friendly. He can be pompous as indeed he has every right to be with his history, and he almost always remains calm and good-tempered. Although rarely aggressive, he remembers that he is supposed to have the heart of a lion and will never turn tail if attacked; and he remains one of the greatest of all the pet dogs.

OFFICIAL STANDARD

Expression
Must suggest the Chinese origin of the Pekingese in its quaintness and individuality, resemblance to the lion in directions and independence and should imply courage, boldness, self-esteem and combativeness rather than prettiness, daintiness or delicacy.

Skull
Massive, broad, wide and flat between the ears (not dome-shaped), wide between the eyes. *Nose:* black, broad, very short and flat. *Eyes:* large, dark, prominent, round, lustrous. *Stop:* deep. *Ears:* heart-shaped, not set too high, leather never long enough to come below the muzzle, nor carried erect, but rather drooping, long feather. *Muzzle:* wrinkled, very short and broad, not overshot nor pointed. Strong, broad underjaw, teeth not to show.

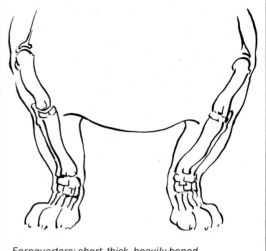
Forequarters: short, thick, heavily boned.

Head: skull broad, wide, flat.

Color
All colors are allowable. Red, fawn, black, black and tan, sable, brindle, white and parti-color well defined: black masks and spectacles around the eyes, with lines to ears are desirable. *Definition of parti-color Pekingese:* the coloring of a parti-colored dog must be broken on the body. No large portion of any one color should exist. White should be shown on the saddle. A dog of any solid color with white feet and chest is not a parti-color.

Tail
Set high; lying well over back to either side; long, profuse, straight feather.

Size
Being a toy dog, medium size preferred, providing type and points are not sacrificed; extreme limit 14 pounds.

SCALE OF POINTS
Expression (5). Skull (10). Nose (5). Eyes (5). Stop (5). Ears (5). Muzzle (5). Shape of body (15). Legs and feet (15). Coat, feather and condition (15). Tail (5). Action (10). *Total (100).*

FAULTS
Protruding tongue, badly blemished eye, overshot, wry mouth.

DISQUALIFICATIONS
Weight: over 14 pounds. Dudley nose.

Approved by the AKC 10 April 1956

Shape of body
Heavy in front, well-sprung ribs, broad chest, falling away lighter behind, lionlike. Back level. Not too long in body; allowance made for longer body in bitch. *Legs:* short forelegs, bones of forearm bowed, firm at shoulder; hind legs lighter but firm and well shaped. *Feet:* flat, toes turned out, not round, should stand well up on feet, not on ankles.

Action
Fearless, free and strong, with slight roll.

Coat, feather and condition
Long, with thick undercoat, straight and flat, not curly nor wavy, rather coarse, but soft; feather on thighs, legs, tail and toes long and profuse. *Mane:* profuse, extending beyond the shoulder blades, forming ruff or frill round the neck.

KC(GB) VARIATION TO STANDARD
Colour: all colours except albino or liver. *Weight:* not to exceed 11 pounds for dogs or 12 pounds for bitches. *Gait:* a slow dignified rolling gait in front, with a close gait behind, this typical movement not to be confused with a roll caused by slackness of shoulders.

POMERANIAN

The smallest of the Spitz group of dogs, the Pomeranian is a descendent of the much larger sledge hauling dogs of the Arctic countries. He came to the modern show ring via Germany and more particularly Pomerania, where he was bred down in size from the Deutscher Spitz to the Deutscher Kleinspitz, and from where he took his name once he left his country of origin. In the early stages he was a fairly large dog with herding capabilities, and was often white. This version still survives in some countries where it is known as the Japanese Spitz, but is almost certainly a descendant of the original Pomeranian. In the early years of the breed in the United States of America and Britain white was the fashionable colour and it is only recently that this

NATIONAL GROUPING		
	Name	Number
AKC	Toys	v
KC(GB)	Toy	6
FCI	Companion Dogs	9

has been superseded by the now more popular sables and oranges. Some books on the breed prefer to consider that the origin of the breed goes back to much earlier days, and quote Greek and Roman sources for their theories, but the evidence is vague and the sledgedog theory is much more realistic.

The Pomeranian was hardly known in Britain until 1870 when the Kennel Club in Britain recognised the Spitz dog, but the interest shown in the breed by Queen Victoria in 1890 when a number entered her kennels soon popularised the breed, though her large greyish specimens were very different from the much smaller and more colourful ones that soon became fashionable. The formation of the Pomeranian Club in 1891 and the establishment of a standard for the breed was to ensure the future popularity of the smaller dogs. In the United States the first classes for the breed were staged at Westminster in 1900 and it is interesting to note that at that time blues and chocolates were being shown. In the same year the American Pomeranian Club was formed, and the admission of that club to the American Kennel Club brought about an immediate increased interest in the breed and began its rise to present popularity.

In the early days white was a very popular colour, but there is no doubt that the bloodline for this colour was too near the origins of the breed, and dogs that were white were almost always far too big, some of them weighing upwards of thirty pounds. In their efforts to produce smaller and smaller dogs, breeders concentrated on the other colours, and the browns and sables together with the blacks formed the bulk of the show stock. The first clear orange dog, Mrs. Parker's Ch. Mars, created a sensation when he first appeared and there were many theories as to where the colour came from. In fact it probably confirmed the origins of the breed among the northern Spitz dogs, as bright red regularly appears in both the Finnish Spitz and the Chow Chow, members of the northern Spitz group.

The Pomeranian is one of the great little show dogs of the world. In recent years more and more emphasis has been placed on coat length and quality until now the top specimens are just tiny balls of beautifully prepared stand-off coat in glowing colour. Careful control of the shape of the coat has been developed to a fine art and the Spitz outline with tail well over the back and head carried well back has been encouraged until he stands in the ring like a beautifully sculptured little statue. The ideal show size is now around four or five pounds, and to see these tiny dogs battling for Best in Show awards against enormous dogs, and defying them, is one of the exciting sights of the modern dog show world. This tremendous spirit and vivacity is one of the characteristics of the breed, and that, with his normally docile temper and great affection makes him an ideal family pet.

OFFICIAL STANDARD

Appearance
The Pomeranian in build and appearance is a cobby, balanced, short-coupled dog. He exhibits great intelligence in his expression, and is alert in character and deportment.

Head
Well-proportioned to the body, wedge-shaped but not domed in outline, with a foxlike expression. There is a pronounced stop with a rather fine but not snipy muzzle, with no lippiness. The pigmentation around the eyes, lips, and on the nose must be black, except self-colored in brown and blue. *Teeth:* the teeth meet in a scissors bite, in which part of the inner surface of the upper teeth meets and engages part of the outer surface of the lower teeth. One tooth out of line does not mean an undershot or overshot mouth. *Eyes:* bright, dark in color, and medium in size, almond-shaped and not set too wide apart nor too close together. *Ears:* small, carried erect and mounted high on the head, and placed not too far apart.

Neck and shoulders
The neck is rather short, its base set well back on the shoulders. The Pom is not straight-in-shoulder, but has sufficient layback of shoulders to carry the neck proudly and high.

Body
The back must be short and the topline level. The body is cobby, being well ribbed and rounded. The brisket is fairly deep and not too wide.

Legs
The forelegs are straight and parallel, of medium length in proportion to a well balanced frame. The hocks are perpendicular to the ground, parallel to each other from hock to heel, and turning neither in nor out. The Pomeranian stands well-up on toes.

Tail
The tail is characteristic of the breed. It turns over the

Ears: small, erect.

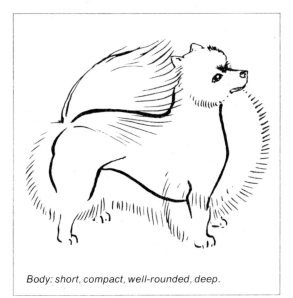

Body: short, compact, well-rounded, deep.

back and is carried flat, set high. It is profusely covered with hair.

Coat

Double-coated; a short, soft, thick undercoat, with longer, coarse, glistening outer coat consisting of guard hairs which must be harsh to the touch in order to give the proper texture for the coat to form a frill of profuse, standing-off straight hair. The front legs are well feathered and the hindquarters are clad with long hair or feathering from the top of the rump to the hocks.

Color

Acceptable colors to be judged on an equal basis; any solid color, any solid color with lighter or darker shadings of the same color, any solid color with sable or black shadings, parti-color, sable and black and tan. Black and tan is black with tan or rust, sharply defined, appearing above each eye and on muzzle, throat, and forechest, on all legs and feet and below the tail. Parti-color is white with any other color distributed in even patches on the body and a white blaze on head.

Movement

The Pomeranian moves with a smooth, free, but not loose action. He does not elbow out in front nor move excessively wide nor cow-hocked behind. He is sound in action.

Size

The weight of a Pomeranian for exhibition is 3 to 7 pounds. The ideal size for show specimens is from 4 to 5 pounds.

Trimming and dewclaws

Trimming for neatness is permissible around the feet and up the back of the legs to the first joint; trimming of unruly hairs on the edges of the ears and around the anus is also permitted. Dewclaws, if any, on the hind legs are generally removed. Dewclaws on the forelegs may be removed.

Classifications

The Open Classes at Specialty shows may be divided by color as follows: Open Red, Orange, Cream and Sable; Open Black, Brown and Blue; Open Any Other Allowed Color.

Approved by the AKC 9 March 1971

KC(GB) VARIATION TO STANDARD

Colour: all whole colours are admissible, but they should be free from black or white shadings. At present *whole-coloured dogs* are: white, black, brown, light or dark, blue as pale as possible. Orange, which should be as self-coloured and bright as possible. Beaver. Cream dogs should have black noses and black rims around eyes. Whites must be quite free from lemon or any other colour. A few white hairs, in any of self-coloured dogs, shall not heavily penalise. Dogs (other than white) with white or tan markings, are decidedly objectionable and should be discouraged. They cannot compete as whole coloured specimens. In *parti-coloured* dogs, the colours should be evenly distributed on body in patches; a dog with white or tan feet or chest would not be a parti-coloured dog. Shaded-sables should be shaded throughout with three or more colours, hair to be as uniformly shaded as possible, with no patches of self-colour. In mixed classes, where whole-coloured and parti-coloured dogs compete together, preference should, if in other points they are equal, be given to whole-coloured specimens. *Faults:* Undershot or overshot mouths; double jointed; light eyes; off-coloured nose; a tail carried to side; hare feet.

POODLE (TOY)

One of the results of more and more people living closer together and in smaller houses has been the increased popularity of the smaller dogs. Miniaturisation was either an accident seized upon and developed by someone who wanted something different, or it was done for a purpose, as in the case of the smaller Dachshunds. More recently small breeds have been evolved to suit modern conditions, and the Toy Poodle is one of these. He was virtually unknown as a breed until this century. It is true that small long-coated dogs existed in France, such as the Bichon, and in Germany the Lowchen, though they were not the typical, but tiny Poodle that we know today. Perhaps the Barbet was nearest, though even this was often much larger than the modern Toy Poodle.

NATIONAL GROUPING		
	Name	Number
AKC	Toys	v
KC(GB)	Utility	4
FCI	Companion Dogs	9

In the early days of the attempt to produce a very small version of the Poodle, small, and often rather weak Miniature Poodle offspring were selected, and by continually breeding from these, animals were produced which were certainly small enough, but in many cases were rather grotesque as well. Bent fore-legs would bring the shoulders under the ten inch or eleven inch measure, and short legs on long bodies would do the same thing, so that when the variety first began to appear in the show rings they were somewhat ludicrous compared with the miniatures and the standards. They were very much objects of scorn among those who owned what they called real dogs. Fortunately some of the more serious breeders continued with a careful programme and eventually succeeded in evolving a tiny dog that was a replica of his larger cousins, and with all their smartness and temperament. This success was finally crowned when one of these tiny dogs was Best in Show All-breeds at Crufts in 1966.

Progress continues in the breed, and where at one time only the blacks had pleasing heads, now all the other colours have caught up, and equally attractive whites and apricots as well as silvers are regularly seen. The rigid standard for height laid down in the early days of the breed has now been relaxed in Britain, and whereas at one time those that would not go under the measure were disqualified and required to leave the ring, now they may in fact remain and may win provided that in the opinion of the judge the degree of their oversize is a lesser fault than those of other exhibits and that the oversize dog is of better quality.

Now that the breeding of the Toy Poodle has settled down, there is no longer the fear of a litter of puppies all growing to be oversize. He is a sturdy little dog, solid and well-made, and remarkably hardy. Although by size he is included in the Toy Group in some countries, he remains in the Utility Group in Britain alongside the other two varieties. It is believed that he earns that place by virtue of his ancestry, which is not comparable with the small companion dogs that form most of the Toy Group, and because of his sturdy independence. In the ring he is certainly not overshadowed by either of the other two, or for that matter any breed for spirit and game performance, as he will continue to stride out in the ring at the end of a long hard day, full of confidence and independence. For his size he sparkles, moving with very rapid long strides, and covering the

ground at a speed which many people find remarkable until they recall that he is in fact just a small version of what was once a hunting dog.

His temperament is quite delightful, and like his larger relatives he has no vice, being easy going and cheerful at all times, welcoming family and visitors alike with effusion, standing on his hind legs and bouncing up and down in his excitement. It is this gay spirit that endears him to everyone, and though he is not a toy, children love him for his small size and playfulness.

OFFICIAL STANDARD

The Standard for the Poodle (Toy variety) is the same as for the Standard and the Miniature varieties except as regards height. (See pages 405—7.)

KC(GB) VARIATION TO STANDARD

This dog is granted championship status by the KC(GB) in the Utility Group of Non-Sporting Breeds. *Height:* must be under 11 inches at shoulder.

Coat: traditional lion clip.

PUG

NATIONAL GROUPING		
	Name	Number
AKC	Toys	v
KC(GB)	Toy	6
FCI	Companion Dogs	9

This member of the Toy dog Group, originating in the Orient, is something of an oddity in the Group, as whilst most of the others descend from the Spaniels or the Terriers, this one is undoubtedly a very tiny Mastiff type. He has the large head, the wrinkled face and the heavy-weight body of that group, which numbers among its members some of the largest dogs in the world. He was known at one time as the Dutch Pug and it was rather taken for granted that he was of Dutch origin, but the trade carried on between Holland and the Far East during the time of the Dutch East India Company gave every opportunity for him to have been brought into Holland from China. The name is said by some to have originated from the latin word 'pugnus'—a fist, as the head was said to have borne some resemblance to the human clenched fist. Others maintain that the name means 'monkey-faced'. In China the wrinkles on the head of the Pug were considered extremely important and the so-called 'prince mark' the vertical wrinkle on the forehead which was similar to the Chinese character for 'prince', was a very much sought after feature.

The pug was first brought to Britain during Victorian times, and like so many other breeds, particularly toys, found favour with the Monarch who quickly added some to her kennels. At that time his ears were cropped very short to give a smart appearance and to emphasize the wrinkles, and it is in this form that so many of them were depicted in early ceramic sculpture at such factories as Meissen where they were called Mopser, a name still used for the breed in some parts of Europe. The breed became a great favourite with sculptors and painters and one of the most famous of all, a dog named Trump which was owned by Hogarth, was not only painted by the artist, but used as a model by sculptors of the time. Lady Willoughby de Eresby of Lincoln and Mr. Morrison of Waltham Green established early kennels in Britain and during their time fawn Pugs were known as Willoughby or Morrison Pugs. The two types were later interbred and the early colour differences vanished.

The black Pug came some time later, in about 1886 when some were exhibited at the Maidstone show, and there was considerable difference of opinion as to how he originated. It was suggested that he resulted from an infusion of blood from Japan, or that some non-descript small black dog was used to start off the strain. The most likely answer is that an occasional black dog cropped up as happens sometimes in the self-coloured darker dogs and by using these more and more blacks eventually resulted. The modern Pug varies very little from his ancestors, and photographs of Pugs taken seventy years ago show dogs that have all the characteristics of today's breed and which would conform to the modern standard. Though numbers have declined a little in recent years, in Britain for example from the near one-and-a-half thousand per year to something like half that number, he still remains one of the more popular of the toy dogs. The esteem with which he was held in Victorian Britain can be seen from the fact that there are still in existence stuffed remains of family pets set up in glass cases, dating back to the time when the family could not bear to be parted from their companion and kept him on the sideboard.

As a show dog he is simple to transport and prepare. He travels happily enough in a box and his short coat needs the minimum of grooming, a quick rub down with a hound glove or chamois leather is all that is required. He normally stands very quietly in the ring and moves off with his characteristic rolling gait. His temperament is near perfect, and he is extremely friendly, attaches himself to a household and the family with complete acceptance of the fact that he is an essential part of their lifestyle, and in his old age becomes very much the rather wheezy old relation sitting in the most comfortable chair in front of the fire.

OFFICIAL STANDARD

Symmetry
Symmetry and general appearance, decidedly square and cobby. A lean, leggy Pug and a dog with short legs and a long body are equally objectionable.

Size and condition j
The Pug should be *multum in parvo*, but this condensation (if the word may be used) should be shown by compactness of form, well-knit proportions, and hardness of developed muscle. Weight from 14 to 18 pounds (dog or bitch) desirable.

Body
Short and cobby, wide in chest and well ribbed up.

Legs
Very strong, straight, of moderate length and well under.

Feet
Neither so long as the foot of the hare, nor so round as that of the cat; well-split-up toes, and the nails black.

Muzzle
Short, blunt, square, but not up-faced.

Head
Large, massive, round—not apple-headed, with no indentation of the skull.

Head and skull: large, massive, round.

Eyes
Dark in color, very large, bold and prominent, globular in shape, soft and solicitous in expression, very lustrous, and, when excited, full of fire.

Ears
Thin, small, soft, like black velvet. There are two kinds—the 'rose' and 'button.' Preference is given to the latter.

Markings
Clearly defined. The muzzle or mask, ears, moles on cheeks, thumb mark or diamond on forehead, back-trace should be as black as possible.

Mask
The mask should be black. The more intense and well defined it is the better.

Trace
A black line extending from the occiput to the tail.

Wrinkles
Large and deep.

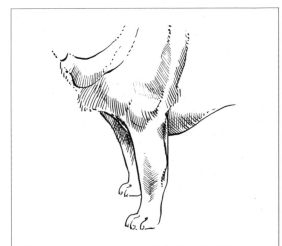
Forequarters: legs strong, straight, well under.

Tail
Curled tightly as possible over the hip. The double curl is perfection.

Coat
Fine, smooth, soft, short and glossy, neither hard nor woolly.

Color
Silver or apricot-fawn. Each should be decided, to make the contrast complete between the color and the trace and the mask. Black.

SCALE OF POINTS
FAWN: symmetry (10), size (5), condition (5), body (10), legs and feet (5), head (5), muzzle (10), ears (5), eyes (10), mask (5), wrinkles (5), tail (10), trace (5), coat (5), color (5). *Total (100)*.

BLACK: symmetry (10), size (10), condition (5), body (10), legs and feet (5), head (5), muzzle (10), ears (5), eyes (10), wrinkles (5), tail (10), coat (5), color (10). *Total (100)*.

SHIH TZU

NATIONAL GROUPING		
	Name	Number
AKC	Toys	V
KC(GB)	Utility	4
FCI	Companion Dogs	9

Several dogs have their origin in the Far East, and one or two in China. The Shih Tzu is undoubtedly one of these though a good deal of confusion exists because of the resemblance between a number of the small dogs that began life in that country. The Tibetan Spaniel, the Lhasa Apso and the Pekingese all bear a superficial resemblance to the Shih Tzu. The ancient myths and legends woven around the Lion Dog of China, half lion and half dog, playing with his ball, could refer to any one of these tiny dogs. In Tibet the small Lion Dogs were kept as house pets and for indeterminate duties round the temples. They were treated with considerable reverence, and their supposed relationship to the lion which is an animal that is much respected in the Buddhist religion, added to the esteem in which they were held. It is possible that these dogs were bred in the temples of Tibet and taken to China as tributes, as gifts of dogs were considered a great honour, largely because there were always dogs at the Imperial Courts of China. Much of the early history of these small companion dogs in China depends on the written word which tells of small short-nosed dogs which could have been anything from a Pug to a Pekingese, which makes the distinguishing of the Shih Tzu as a separate breed extremely difficult.

It was not until the 1930s that the breed really began to be recognised as a separate one outside China. At a dog show held in Peking in 1936 a European with an interest in these little dogs, recognised them as something other than a Pekingese or an Apso. The first recorded importation into Britain was of a bitch which entered the country in 1931, and when first shown in 1933 the dogs were classified with the Apsos,

and it was not until the Tibetan Breed Association sorted things out in 1934 that they were recognised as a separate breed. They arrived in the United States of America in 1938 and were reregistered as Apsos. In 1940 the breed was granted a separate register in Britain, and from that time it has never looked back. Something like two thousand are registered in Britain every year, and the breed now draws very large classes at all the major championship shows. It is rapidly gaining in popularity in most countries of the world, and has outstripped all the other Tibetan breeds.

The Shih Tzu is a very sturdy little dog with few of the toy dog characteristics being heavy for his size, and with strong limbs and great stamina. He is bold and sporty without being belligerent, and happy to hunt with other dogs, thoroughly enjoying being one of the pack. As a show dog he has achieved real prominence in the short time since he first arrived on the scene in the Western World, and he now features regularly as a Group or Best in Show winner at many of the major shows. He is a pleasant dog to show, being very amenable to the discipline of the ring, and almost always the complete extrovert, enjoying putting on a performance in front of admirers, and never disturbed by other dogs or the big occasion. His preparation is not a hardship as his coat is strong and fairly straight, and if kept constantly groomed, show preparation is reduced to a simple matter of a bath and brushing and combing.

Temperamentally he is one of the most delightful dogs in the world, being almost human in his response to the companionship of the human race, settling into living in a house as if it were his natural right, which it probably is as he has lived thus for centuries. He is gay, forthcoming and resilient, bouncing back from a reprimand with an entertaining charm that is irresistible, and joins in the games of the children with an enthusiasm that is infectious. There is no doubt that he appreciates that as a dog he is something special, and he probably dreams of the times when he was the revered inmate of a Tibetan temple.

OFFICIAL STANDARD

General appearance
Very active, lively and alert, with a distinctly arrogant carriage. The Shih Tzu is proud of bearing as befits his noble ancestry, and walks with head well up and tail carried gaily over the back.

Head
Broad and round, wide between the eyes. Muzzle square and short, but not wrinkled, about one inch from tip of nose to stop. *Definite Stop. Eyes:* large, dark and round but not prominent, placed well apart. Eyes should show warm expression. *Ears:* large, with long leathers, and carried drooping; set slightly below the crown of the skull; so heavily coated that they appear to blend with the hair of the neck. *Teeth:* level or slightly undershot bite.

Body: longer than height, well coupled, sturdy.

Head and skull: head broad and round, good beard and whiskers.

Forequarters
Legs short, straight, well boned, muscular, and heavily coated. Legs and feet look massive on account of the wealth of hair.

Body
Body between the withers and the root of the tail is somewhat longer than the height at the withers; well coupled and sturdy. Chest broad and deep, shoulders firm, back level.

Hindquarters
Legs short, well boned and muscular, are straight when viewed from the rear. Thighs well rounded and muscular. Legs look massive on account of wealth of hair.

Feet
Of good size, firm, well padded, with hair between the pads. Dewclaws, if any, on the hind legs are generally removed. Dewclaws on the forelegs may be removed.

Tail
Heavily plumed and curved well over the back; carried gaily, set on high.

Coat
A luxurious, long, dense coat. May be slightly wavy but *not* curly. Good woolly undercoat. The hair on top of the head may be tied up.

Color
All colors permissible. Nose and eye rims black, except that dogs with liver markings may have liver noses and slightly lighter eyes.

Gait
Slightly rolling, smooth and flowing, with strong rear action.

Size
Height at withers—9 to 10½ inches—should be no more than 11 inches nor less than 8 inches. Weight of mature dogs—12 to 15 pounds—should be no more than 18 pounds nor less than 9 pounds. However, type and breed characteristics are of the greatest importance.

FAULTS
Narrow head; overshot bite; snipiness; pink on nose or eye rims; small or light eyes; legginess; sparse coat; lack of definite stop.

Approved by the AKC 13 May 1969

KC(GB) VARIATION TO STANDARD
This dog is granted championship status by the KC(GB) in the Utility Group of Non-Sporting Breeds. *Colour:* white blaze on forehead and white tip to tail are highly prized.

SILKY TERRIER

This interesting little dog has been established as a breed in fairly recent years. Prior to the Second World War it was virtually unknown outside Australia, but afterwards became quite popular in the United States of America though there are still none in Britain. The two main ancestors of the breed were the Yorkshire Terrier and the Australian Terrier. The first was developed from crossing the Skye, the Black and Tan and the Maltese, and the second from the Skye, the Dandie Dinmont and the indigenous broken-coated Terrier of Australia. The result is a well set up dog, somewhat larger than the Yorkshire Terrier but with a silky coat. At first in Australia the two breeds were closely involved, the Yorkshire Terrier and the Australian Silky, the two breeds sharing a breed club in 1900. The first record of a small dog resembling the Australian Silky Terrier is of Broken-coated Terriers being shown at the second Royal Melbourne Show in Victoria in 1872. Later in 1884 they were shown as Broken-coated Toy Terriers and later still in 1900 the Victorian Silky and Yorkshire Terrier Club drew up standards for the two breeds as obviously there was danger of confusion, and indeed perhaps even fusion

NATIONAL GROUPING		
	Name	Number
AKC	Toys	v
KC(GB)	–	–
FCI	Terriers	3

of the two breeds.

Soon after the turn of the century breeders in Sydney commenced the Sydney Silky Club and the breed became widely known as the Sydney Silky. It was not until 1959 that the Australian National Kennel Council adopted a standard for the breed and changed its name to the Australian Silky Terrier. Breeders in Australia are still anxious lest there should be any confusion between the Yorkshire Terrier and the Australian Silky. They prefer a dog that is around nine inches high and that weighs about eight to ten pounds, and they are quite firm that the coat should be only some five or six inches long and should not trail on the ground as does that of the Yorkshire Terrier. They prefer too that the coat should be a real blue colour rather than the steely colour of the Yorkie.

The Silky Terrier is a compact low set dog with enough substance to look as though he can hunt, which indeed he can, being very much the vermin killer. He is much more the Terrier than the Toy, being very alert, and extremely active. He now appears in quite large numbers at the Australian dog shows, and having had challenge certificates awarded since 1924, is well-established in his home country. His popularity extends to New Zealand and he is still quite familiar to showgoers in the United States where it is called simply the Silky Terrier. He looks at his best at the outdoor championship shows of Australia, where the brilliant sunshine shows off his silky coat to the fullest advantage. He is a very attractive pet dog, and whilst he is included among the Toys, has more fire and sparkle than some, being just as much at home sniffing at a rat hole as he is lying around on the furniture. He is a very picturesque dog, decorative and handsome, and looks well in a modern apartment. He is a good guard, making a noise out of all proportion to his size, and being very possessive about his family and their property.

OFFICIAL STANDARD

The Silky Terrier is a lightly built, moderately low-set toy dog of pronounced terrier character and spirited action.

Head
The head is strong, wedge-shaped, and moderately long. The skull is a trifle longer than the muzzle, in proportion about three-fifths for the skull, two-fifths for the muzzle. *Skull:* flat, and not too wide between the ears. *Stop:* shallow. *Ears:* small, V-shaped and pricked. They are set high and carried erect without any tendency to flare obliquely off the skull. *Eyes:* small, dark in color, and piercingly keen in expression. Light eyes are a fault. *Teeth:* strong and well aligned, scissors bite. A bite markedly undershot or overshot is a serious fault. *Nose:* the nose is black.

Neck and shoulders
The neck fits gracefully into sloping shoulders. It is medium long, fine and to some degree crested along its topline.

Body
Low-set, about one fifth longer than the dog's height at the withers. A too short body is a fault. The back line is straight, with a just perceptible rounding over the loins. Brisket medium wide, and deep enough to extend down to the elbows.

Tail
The tail is set high and carried erect or semi-erect but not over-gay. It is docked and well coated but devoid of plume.

Forequarters
Well laid back shoulders, together with good angulation at the upper arm, set the forelegs nicely under the body. Forelegs are strong, straight and rather fine-boned.

Hindquarters
Thighs well muscled and strong, but not so developed as to appear heavy. Legs moderately angulated at stifles and hocks, with the hocks low and equidistant from the hock joints to the ground.

Feet
Small, cat-like, round, compact. Pads are thick and springy while the nails are strong and dark colored. White or flesh-colored nails are a fault. The feet point straight ahead, with no turning in or out. Dewclaws, if any, are removed.

Coat
Flat, in texture fine, glossy, silky; on matured specimens the desired length of coat from behind the ears to the set-on of the tail is from five to six inches. On the top of the head the hair is so profuse as to form a topknot, but long hair on face and ears is objectionable. Legs from knee and hock joints to feet should be free from long hair. The hair is parted on the head and down over the back to the root of the tail.

Color
Blue and tan. The blue may be silver blue, pigeon blue or slate blue, the tan deep and rich. The blue extends from the base of the skull to the tip of the tail, down the forelegs to the pasterns, and down the thighs to the hocks. On the tail the blue should be very dark. Tan appears on muzzle and cheeks, around the base of the ears, below the pasterns and hocks, and around the vent. There is a tan spot over each eye. The topknot should be silver or fawn.

Temperament
The keenly alert air of the terrier is characteristic, with shyness or excessive nervousness to be faulted. The manner is quick, friendly, responsive.

Movement
Should be free, light-footed, lively, and straightforward. Hindquarters should have strong propelling power. Toeing in or out is to be faulted.

Size
Weight ranges from eight to ten pounds. Shoulder height from nine to ten inches. Pronounced diminutiveness (such as height of less than 8 inches) is not desired; it accentuates the quality of toyishness as opposed to the breed's definite terrier character.

Approved by the AKC 14 April 1959

KC(GB) VARIATION TO STANDARD
This dog is known as the Australian Silky Terrier in GB but has not yet been granted championship status.

YORKSHIRE TERRIER

This little dog has no claim at all to being an ancient breed. It is well known that he has been produced in comparatively recent years, and it is not difficult to conjecture which of the other breeds went to his make-up. As Robert Leighton said, Bradford and not Babylon was his ancestral home. Yorkshire, however, is not only England's largest county, it is also the county that is steeped in the breeding and development of livestock of all kinds from cats to canaries, and certainly of dogs. One needs only to remember that not only has it given its name to a breed of dog, but even one of its very small areas, Airedale, produced and gave its name to Britain's largest Terrier. It is obvious from the result that no haphazard mixture produced this little dog, but that wise livestock breeders knew exactly what they wanted and set out to get it. There have apparently always been Terriers in York-

NATIONAL GROUPING		
	Name	Number
AKC	Toys	V
KC(GB)	Toy	6
FCI	Companion Dogs	9

shire. Since the time of the industrial revolution they have been the companions of the working man who spent his days in the pits or mills of the county and found in vermin hunting his relaxation at weekends. Before that time when the county was purely agricultural and arboreal it was rich in wildlife such as rabbits and foxes and the Terriers were used in hunting these.

The designers of the breed, and they could hardly be called anything else, probably took the Clydesdale

Terrier as the starting point. He himself was the progenitor of the Skye Terrier, was described as rare in 1900 and has now disappeared. He had many of the characteristics of the Skye but was a smaller dog, his weight rarely exceeding eighteen pounds which is the minimum weight for a Skye, which meant that he was a good start towards miniaturisation.

At first the Yorkshire Terrier was exhibited as a Scotch Terrier and was broken-coated. The introduction of the old English Black and Tan Terrier would give the desired colour and markings, especially as at that time there was a blue and tan version of this dog. Skye blood and probably the Maltese would give the length and silkiness of coat, and possibly even the Dandie Dinmont Terrier was used. At first the Yorkshire Terrier was not a particularly small dog and show classes divided them into over and under five pounds. Fashion decreed, however, that the smaller ones were preferable, and at the same time also decided that the longer the coat the better, and in 1900 a dog that was five and a half pounds in weight had a coat of a uniform length of twenty-four inches. Continued attempts to produce smaller dogs have resulted in a strange state of affairs now, when the larger bitches are often retained by breeders for breeding purposes and mated to considerably smaller dogs. Whelps from the resulting litters can grow into dogs with considerable variation in size. This has meant that there have always been large numbers of dogs unwanted for show and available to the pet market. More Yorkshire Terriers are now being bred and exported from Britain than any other breed, yet the entries at shows in no way reflect this fact.

As a show dog he is a wonderful proposition, as his tiny size makes transportation a simple matter (the writer having seen two being taken to a show in a shopping bag on one occasion) and their coat repaying the tremendous amount of care and attention that is paid to it. In between shows the coat of the dog is tied up in small ribbons or papers to prevent it becoming damaged and in this way a great length of fine silky coat is encouraged. When brushed out, and standing in the ring shining in the sun or artificial lights, there is hardly a breed that is more striking. He appears to enjoy being shown and will stand still for considerable periods of time with his ears erect and having a jaunty appearance. Although very much a pampered pet, he is at the same time still a Terrier, enjoying games and walks, and reverting to his ancestral hunting background at every opportunity.

OFFICIAL STANDARD

General appearance
That of a long-haired toy terrier whose blue and tan coat is parted on the face and from the base of the skull to the end of the tail and hangs evenly and quite straight down each side of body. The body is neat, compact and well proportioned. The dog's high head carriage and confident manner should give the appearance of vigor and self-importance.

Ears: small, 'v'-shaped, erect.

Head
Small and rather flat on top, the *skull* not too prominent or round, the *muzzle* not too long, with the *bite* neither undershot nor overshot and teeth sound. Either scissors bite or level bite is acceptable. The *nose* is black. *Eyes* are medium in size and not too prominent; dark in color and sprakling with a sharp, intelligent expression. Eye rims are dark. *Ears* are small, V-shaped, carried erect and set not too far apart.

Body
Well proportioned and very compact. The back is rather short, the back line level, with height at shoulder the same as at the rump.

Colors
Puppies are born black and tan and are normally darker in body color, showing an intermingling of black hair in the tan until they are matured. Color of hair on body and richness of tan on head and legs are of prime importance in *adult dogs*, to which the following color requirements apply:
BLUE: is a dark steel-blue, not a silver-blue and not mingled with fawn, bronzy or black hairs.
TAN: all tan hair is darker at the roots than in the middle, shading to still lighter tan at the tips. There should be no sooty or black hair intermingled with any of the tan.

Legs and feet
Forelegs should be straight, elbows neither in nor out. *Hind legs* straight when viewed from behind, but stifles are moderately bent when viewed from the sides. *Feet* are round with black toenails. Dewclaws, if any, are

Body: compact, level back.

generally removed from the hind legs. Dewclaws on the forelegs may be removed.

Tail
Docked to a medium length and carried slightly higher than the level of the back.

Coat
Quality, texture and quantity of coat are of prime importance. Hair is glossy, fine and silky in texture. Coat on the body is moderately long and perfectly straight (not wavy). It may be trimmed to floor length to give ease of movement and a neater appearance, if desired. The fall on the head is long, tied with one bow in center of head or parted in the middle and tied with two bows. Hair on muzzle is very long. Hair should be trimmed short on tips of ears and may be trimmed on feet to give them a neat appearance.

Color on body
The blue extends over the body from back of neck to

root of tail. Hair on tail is a darker blue, especially at end of tail.

Headfall
A rich golden tan, deeper in color at sides of head, at ear roots and on the muzzle, with ears a deep rich tan. Tan color should not extend down on back of neck.

Chest and legs
A bright, rich tan, not extending above the elbow on the forelegs nor above the stifle on the hind legs.

Weight
Must not exceed seven pounds.

Approved by the AKC 12 April 1966

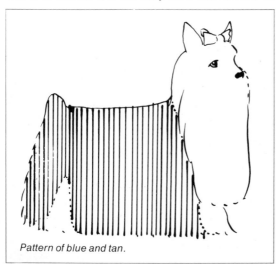

Pattern of blue and tan.

KC(GB) VARIATION TO STANDARD
Mouth: perfectly even.

GROUP VI: NON-SPORTING DOGS

Bichon Frise

Boston Terrier

Chow Chow

Bulldog

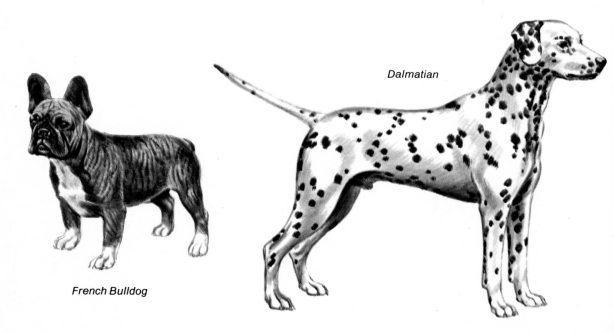

Dalmatian

French Bulldog

Lhasa Apso

Keeshond

Poodle

Schipperke

Tibetan Terrier

Tibetan Spaniel

GROUP VI: NON-SPORTING DOGS

When dog shows first started in Britain in the middle of the 19th century, all the dogs were lumped together, so that the Boston Terriers, the Maltese, the Bulldogs and the Spaniels all appeared in the local public house at the same time. The first division into Sporting and Non-Sporting was fairly straightforward, as breeds identified themselves by purpose. The next division within the Non-Sporting Group by extracting the Toy Dogs and giving them a Group of their own was a simple matter, but it was in recent years in Britain when the remainder of the Non-Sporting Group became so large as to be unwieldy that problems were encountered. There was a great deal of discussion concerning which breeds should go into the Working Group and which should go into the new Group and what it should be called. There are still those who find it difficult to understand why the Doberman for instance which is a guard dog should be in the Working Group, whilst the Schnauzer, which is also a guard dog and is in the Working Group in the United States of America is placed in the Utility Group in Britain.

A more or less parallel Group now exists, however, on each side of the Atlantic, and unless some system such as the Scandinavian one of dividing into yet more Groups is adopted, there will always be anomalies. The Group consists of those dogs which were not developed for any specific purpose, or those whose purpose if it once existed, has now disappeared. They are the larger dogs bred for appearance rather than for performance, such as the Dalmatian and the Poodle which are decorative rather than useful. This does not mean in fact that they were not originally bred as working dogs. The Poodles for instance are descended from the Old Water Dog which was very much a sporting dog, and a case could even be made out for the Bulldog, which for no fault of its own is now out of work, whilst the Boxer, which is also descended from a race of bull-baiting dogs is included everywhere as a working dog.

The breeds within this Group are a very mixed bag indeed, originating as they did in a number of countries as wide apart as America and Tibet, and it is interesting that they include a number of breeds which are recognised as national dogs. The Boston Terrier is as American as any dog could be, whilst the Bulldog typifies everything that is British. The Poodle is immediately associated with France even though it was not originally a French dog. The Chow Chow is Chinese to everyone, the Keeshond even takes its name from national upheavals in Holland and is the national dog of that country, whilst nothing could be more redolent of Tibet than the Tibetan Terrier.

The one thing that is noticeable about the Group when it is seen in the ring with all the breeds represented, is that it is full of interest. The dogs are of no particular size, as they are in the Toy Group, nor are they roughly of the same shape, as they are in the Working Group, which gives them great spectator appeal. The breeds within the Group are very much talking points. The Bulldog with his squat formidable conformation, the decorative quality of the Dalmatian with all its association with tradition, elegance and the silver screen, and the quaint appearance of the dogs from the roof of the world in Tibet, give additional flavour to what might otherwise be just a collection of dogs. It so happens, too, that just about every type and colour of coat is also seen in the Group.

It is possible that at some future date world agreement will be reached concerning the placing of breeds within groups, and possibly the international acceptance of names for those groups. It could then well be that those breeds which have ceased for one reason or another to practice the purpose for which they were evolved, will be placed in a group known by a name which best describes their reason for existing in a modern world. The title 'Large Companion Dogs' is already in use in some countries and might be adopted.

BICHON FRISE

NATIONAL GROUPING		
	Name	Number
AKC	Non-Sporting Dogs	VI
KC(GB)	Toy	6
FCI	Companion Dogs	9

This little dog is recorded back into history more faithfully than most, as having been a favourite with court families he appears in portraits and genre paintings of many centuries ago. The portrait dog is not immediately recognisable as the Bichon Frise we know today, but he is so similar that there is little doubt that small curly-coated dogs existed that must have been his ancestors. He is said to have originated in the Mediterranean area around the 18th century, discovered by Italian sailors who brought him back to the mainland from the Canary Islands. He was certainly known in France in the 16th century and in the courts of Spain, figuring frequently in the paintings by Murillo. His 'The Holy Family and the Little Bird' is a typical example, in which a small white dog which can hardly have been anything else but a Bichon is a central figure. In later paintings by Goya similar dogs appear.

Like the Poodle and many of the other curly-coated dogs of Europe, the Bichon descended from the Water Spaniel or Barbet, a much larger sporting dog, by a process of selective breeding and miniaturisation. He existed at first in four forms, the Maltais which probably became the Maltese or dogs of Melita, the Bolognaise, which seems to have disappeared (but which is depicted somewhat wildly in a porcelain by Kirchner in the Metropolitan Museum of Art in New York), the Havanais and the Tenerife. Another porcelain of 1750, said to represent a dog belonging to the Marquise de Pompadour depicts a typical Bichon Frise. During the late 19th century the breed lost its aristocratic connections and became the plaything of stage and circus, running the streets, acting as a catchpenny for beggars and generally going into something of a decline as a pedigree dog as the bloodlines became diluted.

At the end of the First World War the breed had virtually disappeared, and it was only the interest of a small number of enthusiasts that kept it alive. In 1933 an official standard was adopted and the breed became established under two names, the 'Bichon' and the 'Tenerife', and it was Madame de Leemans who proposed the name Bichon Frise as describing both the antiquity of the breed and its appearance. The breed is now recognised and is becoming popular in most countries. The first entered the United States of America in 1956 and further imports took place during the following years. Recognition was granted by the American Kennel Club in 1972 and the breed then enjoyed a rapid climb to popularity. Britain was much later in the field, when a few specimens came into the country in the mid-seventies. Their climb to popularity has been one of the phenomena of the modern show scene in Britain and there is no doubt that the Bichon Frise will be one of the popular dogs of the next decade.

The Bichon is a most attractive little dog, full of charm, and very appealing. He is sturdy, very stylish and full of confidence, attracting great attention wherever he appears. His coat, which consists of a mass of loose silky curls is trimmed to show the eyes and to give a full rounded appearance to the head and the body, with the result that he looks like a well-made, snow-white fluffy child's toy when he appears in the show ring. He is intelligent and attentive, shows really well, with great mobility for so small a dog. His generations of dependence on human beings gives him a sense of belonging to the family which comes out in his enjoyment of comfort and company, and his love of people.

OFFICIAL STANDARD

General appearance
A sturdy, lively dog of stable temperament, with a stylish gait and an air of dignity and intelligence.

Color
Solid white, or white with cream, apricot, or gray on the ears and/or body.

Body: slightly longer than tall, covered in profuse, silky, loosely-curled coat.

Head: skull broad and round, covered with hair.

Head
Proportionate to the size of the dog. Skull broad and somewhat round, but not coarse; covered with a topknot of hair.

Muzzle
Of medium length, not heavy or snipy. Slightly accentuated stop.

Ears
Dropped, covered with long flowing hair. The leather should reach approximately halfway the length of the muzzle.

Eyes
Black or dark brown, with black rims. Large, round, expressive, and alert.

Lips
Black, fine, never drooping.

Nose
Black, round, pronounced.

Bite
Scissors.

Neck
Rather long, and gracefully and proudly carried behind an erect head.

Shoulders
Well laid back. Elbows held close to the body.

Body
Slightly longer than tall. Well developed with good spring of ribs. The back inclines gradually from the withers

to a slight rise over the loin. The loin is large and muscular. The brisket, well let down.

Tail
Covered with long flowing hair, carried gaily and curved to lie on the back.

Size
The height at the withers should not exceed 12 inches nor be under 8 inches.

Legs and feet
Strong boned; forelegs appearing straight, with well-knit pasterns. Hindquarters well angulated. Feet, resembling cat's paws, are tight and round.

Coat
Profuse, silky and loosely curled. There is an undercoat.

Grooming
Scissored to show the eyes and give a full rounded appearance to the head and body. Feet should have hair trimmed to give a rounded appearance. When properly brushed, there is an overall 'powder puff' appearance. Puppies may be shown in short coat, but the minimum show coat for an adult is two inches.

Faults
Cowhocks, snipy muzzle, poor pigmentation, protruding eyes, yellow eyes, undershot or overshot bite.

Serious faults
Corkscrew tail, black hair in the coat.

Approved by the AKC 14 November 1972

KC(GB) VARIATION TO STANDARD
Ears: narrow and delicate. Hanging close to head and well covered with tightly curled, long hair. Carried forward when dog is alert but in such manner that forward edge touches skull and not carried obliquely away from head. *Mouth:* lower lip should be neither heavy, protruding nor flabby and should never show mucous membrane when mouth is closed. *Neck:* about one-third length of body. *Shoulders:* not prominent and equal in length to upper arm. *Feet:* well knuckled up. *Coat:* $2\frac{1}{2}$ to 4 inches long.

BOSTON TERRIER

There are many breeds in the world that have a history stretching so far back that their origins are obscure, but there are others whose development has been well recorded and whose origins are so recent that they can easily be traced. Such a breed is the Boston Terrier. He is very much an American dog, and is recognised in many countries as the national dog of America, though in fact his ancestors came from Britain. The very first was a dog called Hooper's Judge, a cross between a Bulldog and an English Terrier, and he was purchased by a Mr. Robert C. Hooper of Boston, and was a dark brindle with a white blaze and throat, cropped ears and a screw tail. From this original dog the Boston Terrier as it is known today descended and by careful breeding for colour, markings and type, the breed was fixed. It is suggested that the careful introduction of French Bulldog blood helped in perfecting the breed.

Several were exhibited at the Boston Show in 1878, and in 1891 the American Bull Terrier Club of Boston applied for registration and was refused until the name Bull Terrier was removed, and the club became

NATIONAL GROUPING		
	Name	Number
AKC	Non-Sporting Dogs	VI
KC(GB)	Utility	4
FCI	Companion Dogs	9

the Boston Terrier Club, being given full recognition in 1893. The Bostonians persevered with their efforts to produce a strain of dogs removed from the old Bull Terrier image and their dogs gradually became recognised outside Massachusetts until they were one of the most popular breeds in the United States. Soon after the First World War the breed appeared in Europe, and a number came to Britain in the mid-twenties. Whilst they have not achieved the popularity that they have in the United States, they have steady registration figures of some hundreds per year, and are shown fairly extensively in Britain.

The first Bostons were tough, as would be expected from a cross between a Bulldog and a Terrier proper, both of which are noted for their pugnacious qualities, and there is some suggestion that the early ones were encouraged to fight. There was some diversity of opinion as to the correct size, and for a time they were exhibited in weight classes. Eventually, however, the weight was standardised at something more generally acceptable to a dog with a fighting background.

He is a dapper little dog these days with a settled temperament, a certain ruggedness and the ability to take care of himself. He still has something of the jaw power of the Bulldog, the agility and sharpness of a Terrier and the quickness of reaction of the Bull Terrier that was his ancestor.

As a show dog the Boston Terrier is supreme, being smart to look at, gay and classy in ring behaviour, and easily trained to stand imperturbably among a collection of much larger dogs. He is easily cared for, having a short shiny coat that needs very little more than a brisk rub down to bring out its natural shine. He is easily transported, being small, and will allow himself to be boxed with little protest. His temperament is first class, and he is claimed by those who own one to be the most affectionate dog on earth. Certainly as a house dog there are few breeds with his qualities. He rapidly becomes one of the family, will occupy his favourite—and usually the most comfortable—chair, and will not be offended if a human expresses a desire to join him on it. He loves company, has remarkable understanding, and whilst remaining soft and sweet-tempered, is a very good guard, being very possessive about his own territory.

OFFICIAL STANDARD

General appearance

The general appearance of the Boston Terrier should be that of a lively, highly intelligent, smooth-coated, short-headed, compactly built, short-tailed, well-balanced dog of medium station, of brindle color and evenly marked with white. The head should indicate a high degree of intelligence, and should be in proportion to the size of the dog; the body rather short and well knit, the limbs strong and neatly turned; tail short; and no feature to be so prominent that the dog appears badly proportioned. The dog should convey an impression of determination, strength and activity, with style of a high order; carriage easy and graceful. A proportionate combination of 'color' and 'ideal markings' is a particularly distinctive feature of a representative specimen, and a dog with a preponderance of white on body, or without the proper proportion of brindle and white on head, should possess sufficient merit otherwise to counteract its deficiencies in these respects. The ideal 'Boston Terrier expression' as indicating 'a high degree of intelligence,' is also an important characteristic of the breed. 'Color and markings' and 'expression' should be given particular consideration in determining the relative value of 'general appearance' to other points.

Skull

Square, flat on top, free from wrinkles; cheeks flat; brow abrupt, stop well defined. *Eyes:* wide apart, large and round, dark in color, expression alert, but kind and intelligent. The eyes should set square in the skull, and the outside corners should be on a line with the cheeks as viewed from the front. *Muzzle:* short, square, wide and deep, and in proportion to skull; free from wrinkles; shorter in length than in width and depth, not exceeding in length approximately one third of length of skull; width and depth carried out well to end; the muzzle from stop to end of nose on a line parallel to the top of the skull; nose black and wide, with well defined line between nostrils. The jaws broad and square, with short regular teeth. Bite even or sufficiently undershot to square muzzle. The chops of good depth but not pendulous, completely covering the teeth when mouth is closed. *Ears:* carried

Head and skull: square, free from wrinkles, muzzle short, square, wide, and deep.

erect, either cropped to conform to the shape of head, or natural bat, situated as near the corners of skull as possible. *Head faults:* skull 'domed' or inclined; furrowed by a medial line; skull too long for breadth, or *vice versa*; stop too shallow; brow and skull too slanting. Eyes small or sunken; too prominent; light color or walleye; showing too much white or haw. Muzzle wedge-shaped or lacking depth; down-faced; too much cut out below the eyes; pinched or wide nostrils; butterfly nose; protruding teeth; weak lower jaw; showing turn-up, layback, or wrinkled. Ears poorly carried or in size out of proportion to head.

Neck

Of fair length, slightly arched and carrying the head gracefully; setting neatly into shoulders. *Neck faults:* ewe-necked; throatiness; short and thick.

Body

Deep with good width of chest; shoulders sloping; back

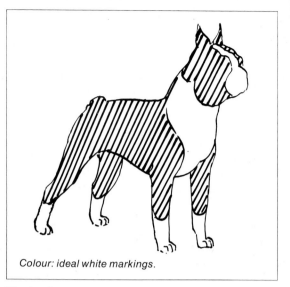

Colour: ideal white markings.

short; ribs deep and well sprung, carried well back to loins; loins short and muscular; rump curving slightly to set-on of tail; flank very slightly cut up. The body should appear short but not chunky. *Body faults:* flat sides; narrow chest; long or slack loins; roach back; swayback; too much cut up in flank.

Elbows

Standing neither in nor out. *Forelegs:* set moderately wide apart and on a line with the point of the shoulders; straight in bone and well muscled; pasterns short and strong. *Hind legs:* set true; bent at stifles; short from hocks to feet; hocks turning neither in nor out; thighs strong and well muscled. *Feet:* round, small and compact and turned neither in nor out; toes well arched. *Leg and feet faults:* loose shoulders or elbows; hind legs too straight at stifles; hocks too prominent; long or weak pasterns; splay feet.

Gait

The gait of the Boston Terrier is that of a sure-footed, straight-gaited dog, forelegs and hind legs moving straight ahead in line with perfect rhythm, each step indicating grace with power. *Gait faults:* there shall be no rolling, paddling or weaving when gaited and any crossing movement, either front or rear, is a serious fault.

Tail

Set-on low; short, fine and tapering; straight; or screw; devoid of fringe or coarse hair, and not carried above horizontal. *Tail faults:* a long or gaily carried tail; extremely gnarled or curled against body. (Note: the preferred tail should not exceed in length approximately half the distance from set-on to hock.)

Ideal color

Brindle with white markings. The brindle to be evenly distributed and distinct. Black with white markings permissible but brindle with white markings preferred. *Ideal markings:* white muzzle, even white blaze over head, collar, breast, part or whole of forelegs, and hind legs below hocks. *Color and markings faults:* all white; absence of white marking; preponderance of white on body; without the proper proportion of brindle and white on head; or any variations detracting from the general appearance.

Coat

Short, smooth, bright and fine in texture. *Coat faults:* long or coarse; lacking luster.

Weight

Not exceeding 25 pounds, divided by classes as follows: lightweight, under 15 pounds; middleweight, 15 and under 20 pounds; heavyweight, 20 and not exceeding 25 pounds.

DISQUALIFICATIONS
Solid black; black and tan; liver or mouse colors. Dudley nose. Docked tail or any artificial means used to deceive the judge.

Approved by the AKC 9 April 1957

SCALE OF POINTS
General appearance (10). Skull (10). Eyes (5). Muzzle (10). Ears (2). Neck (3). Body (15). Elbows (4). Forelegs (5). Hind legs (5). Gait (10). Feet (5). Tail (5). Color (4). Ideal markings (5). Coat (2). *Total (100).*

FAULTS
Ring or low-set tail. Undersize or oversize.

KC(GB) VARIATION TO STANDARD
Ears: small and thin.

BULLDOG

NATIONAL GROUPING		
	Name	Number
AKC	Non-Sporting Dogs	VI
KC(GB)	Utility	4
FCI	Guard Dogs	2

It sometimes happens that countries adopt as their national symbol an animal which is native to their country, but which has no special significance apart from that, the kangaroo of Australia for instance or the bear of Russia. There is one animal, however, which has been accepted as a symbol of something more, of the character of a nation, and that is the Bulldog of Britain. Whether it is a true reflection or a hopeful one is a matter for some argument, but the fact remains that throughout the world the Bulldog is recognised as something peculiarly British. The origins of the breed lie certainly in the Mastiff which is one of the oldest of British breeds, and there is no doubt that by continuous selective breeding for shorter and shorter legs the Bulldog was produced. The so-called sport of bull-baiting was a regular scene in Britain prior to 1835, when it became illegal, and the Bulldog was produced for this sport alone. The practice was for the bull to be tied to a stake usually on a village green or similar space in an urban area, and the dogs were encouraged by handlers to attack and lay hold on the bulls by what was called pinning him by nose. The bull defended himself by keeping his nose close to the ground, and even sometimes digging a hole for the purpose, tossing the indiscreet dogs, which the handlers attempted to catch to break their fall. Considerable betting took place and large sums of money changed hands on the performance of an individual dog or bull.

After the banning of bull-baiting the Bulldog was still bred as a fighting dog but the Bull Terrier proved a much better breed for this purpose, and it needed the formation of the Bulldog Club Incorporated in 1864 to ensure the continuance of the breed. Since that time a certain amount of exaggeration of characteristics has taken place, and the opponents of the pedigree dog usually use the Bulldog as a typical example of how selective breeding can ruin the appearance and health of a breed of dog. In fact a fit modern Bulldog has all the power and agility of its forebears, is capable of running at considerable speed and has still the quick reaction that would be the envy of many of its ancestors. The modern dog has become something of a cult, and there are now probably more Bulldog clubs than those of any other breed, each with its specialist shows.

At his best the Bulldog is a powerful superbly muscled fighting machine of a dog with tremendous weight for his height, with enormous chest and shoulders and the look of an animal planted firmly on the ground and difficult to upset. His head is his great feature, and much store is placed on the head details, the standard for which occupies a large part of the standard for the whole dog. His head is massive, and out of proportion by the standards of a more normal dog, and the jaw is enormously powerful. At his worst, overweight and underexercised he loses attraction more quickly than most breeds, which gives rise to some of the criticism levelled at him.

He is something of a specialist's problem as a show dog, being by no means the easiest of dogs to show to best advantage, as he rarely adopts his best stance in the ring, and needs a considerable amount of attention. This is not for any reason of temperament, as he is an easy dog to handle, but fashion has dictated that he should stand in a certain way. In fact, temperamentally he is quite delightful, being most affectionate and friendly towards people, and not overprone towards being aggressive to other dogs. The puppies in the breed are most attractive, and so irresistible that many people who do not understand the later problems of the breed enter into owning one and sometimes regret it later. Those who become addicted to the breed never want any other sort of dog.

OFFICIAL STANDARD

General appearance, attitude, expression, etc.

The perfect Bulldog must be of medium size and smooth coat; with heavy, thick-set, low-swung body, massive, short-faced head, wide shoulders and sturdy limbs. The general appearance and attitude should suggest great stability, vigor and strength. The disposition should be equable and kind, resolute and courageous (not vicious or aggressive), and demeanor should be pacific and dignified. These attributes should be countenanced by the expression and behavior.

Gait

The style and carriage are peculiar, his gait being a loose-jointed, shuffling, sidewise motion, giving the characteristic 'roll.' The action must, however, be unrestrained, free and vigorous.

Proportion and symmetry

The 'points' should be well distributed and bear good relation one to the other, no feature being in such prominence from either excess or lack of quality that the animal appears deformed or ill-proportioned. *Influence of sex:* in comparison of specimens of different sex, due allowance should be made in favor of the bitches, which do not bear the characteristics of the breed to the same degree of perfection and grandeur as do the dogs.

Size

The size for mature dogs is about 50 pounds; for mature bitches about 40 pounds.

Coat

The coat should be straight, short, flat, close, of fine texture, smooth and glossy. (No fringe, feather or curl.)

Color of coat

The color of coat should be uniform, pure of its kind and brilliant. The various colors found in the breed are to be preferred in the following order: (1) red brindle, (2) all other brindles, (3) solid white, (4) solid red, fawn or fallow, (5) piebald, (6) inferior qualities of all the foregoing. *Note:* a perfect piebald is preferable to a muddy brindle or defective solid color. Solid black is very undesirable, but not so objectionable if occurring to a moderate degree in piebald patches. The brindles to be perfect should have a fine, even and equal distribution of the composite colors. In brindles and solid colors a small white patch on the chest is not considered detrimental. In piebalds the color patches should be well defined, of pure color and symmetrically distributed.

Skin

The skin should be soft and loose, especially at the head, neck and shoulders. *Wrinkles and dewlap:* the head and face should be covered with heavy wrinkles, and at the throat, from jaw to chest, there should be two loose pendulous folds, forming the dewlap.

Skull

The skull should be very large, and in circumference, in

Head and skull: large, broad, square, skin loose and well-wrinkled.

front of the ears, should measure at least the height of the dog at the shoulders. Viewed from the front, it should appear very high from the corner of the lower jaw to the apex of the skull, and also very broad and square. Viewed at the side, the head should appear very high, and very short from the point of the nose to occiput. The forehead should be flat (not rounded or domed), neither too prominent nor overhanging the face. *Cheeks:* the cheeks should be well rounded, protruding sideways and outward beyond the eyes. *Stop:* the temples or frontal bones should be very well defined, broad, square and high, causing a hollow or groove between the eyes. This indentation, or stop, should be both broad and deep and extend up the middle of the forehead, dividing the head vertically, being traceable to the top of the skull. *Eyes and eyelids:* the eyes, seen from the front, should be situated low down in the skull, as far from the ears as possible, and their corners should be in a straight line at right angles with the stop. They should be quite in front of the head, as wide apart as possible, provided their outer corners are within the outline of the cheeks when viewed from the front. They should be quite round in form, of moderate size, neither sunken nor bulging, and in color should be very dark. The lids should cover the white of the eyeball, when the dog is looking directly forward, and the lid should show no 'haw.' *Ears:* the ears should be set high in the head, the front inner edge of each ear joining the outline of the skull at the top back corner of the skull, so as to place them as wide apart, and as high, and as far from the eyes as possible. In size they should be small and thin. The shape termed 'rose ear' is the most desirable. The rose ear folds inward at its back lower edge, the upper front edge curling over, outward and backward, showing part of the inside of the burr. (The ears should not be carried erect or prick-eared or buttoned and should never be cropped.)

Face

The face, measured from the front of the cheekbone to the tip of the nose, should be extremely short, the muzzle being very short, broad, turned upward and very deep from the corner of the eye to the corner of the mouth. *Nose:* the nose should be large, broad and black, its tip being set back deeply between the eyes. The distance from bottom of stop, between the eyes, to the tip of nose should be as short as possible and not exceed the length from the tip of nose to the edge of under lip. The nostrils should be wide, large and black, with a well-defined line between them. Any nose other than black is objectionable, and a brown or liver-colored nose shall disqualify. *Chops:* the chops or 'flews' should be thick, broad, pendant and very deep, completely overhanging the lower jaw at each side. They join the under lip in front and almost or quite cover the teeth, which should be scarcely noticeable when the mouth is closed. *Jaws:* the jaws should be massive, very broad, square and 'undershot,' the lower jaw projecting considerably in front of the upper jaw and turning up. *Teeth:* the teeth should be large and strong, with the canine teeth or tusks wide apart, and the six small teeth in front, between the canines, in an even, level row.

Neck

The neck should be short, very thick, deep and strong and well arched at the back.

Shoulders

The shoulders should be muscular, very heavy, widespread and slanting outward, giving stability and great power.

Chest

The chest should be very broad, deep and full.

Brisket and body

The brisket and body should be very capacious, with full sides, well-rounded ribs and very deep from the shoulders down to its lowest part, where it joins the chest. It should be well let down between the shoulders and forelegs, giving the dog a broad, low, short-legged appearance. The body should be well ribbed up behind with the belly tucked up and not rotund.

Back

The back should be short and strong, very broad at the shoulders and comparatively narrow at the loins. There should be a slight fall in the back, close behind the shoulders (its lowest part), whence the spine should rise to the loins (the top of which should be higher than the top of the shoulders), thence curving again more suddenly to the tail, forming an arch (a very distinctive feature of the breed), termed 'roach back' or, more correctly, 'wheelback.'

Legs and feet

Forelegs: the forelegs should be short, very stout, straight and muscular, set wide apart, with well developed calves, presenting a bowed outline, but the bones of the legs should not be curved or bandy, nor the feet brought too close together. *Elbows:* the elbows should be low and stand well out and loose from the body. *Hind legs:* the hind legs should be strong and muscular and longer than the forelegs, so as to elevate the loins above the shoulders. Hocks should be slightly bent and well let down, so as to give length and strength from loins to hock. The lower leg should be short, straight and strong, with the stifles turned slightly outward and away from the body. The hocks are thereby made to approach each other, and the hind feet to turn outward. *Feet:* the feet should be moderate in size, compact and firmly set. Toes compact, well split up, with high knuckles and with short stubby nails. The front feet may be straight or slightly out-turned, but the hind feet should be pointed well outward.

Tail

The tail may be either straight or 'screwed' (but never curved or curly), and in any case must be short, hung low, with decided downward carriage, thick root and fine tip. If straight, the tail should be cylindrical and of uniform taper. If 'screwed' the bends or kinks should be well defined, and they may be abrupt and even knotty, but no portion of the member should be elevated above the base or root.

SCALE OF POINTS

General Properties (22): proportion and symmetry 5, attitude 3, expression 2, gait 3, size 3, coat 2, color of coat 4. *Head (39):* skull 5, cheeks 2, stop 4, eyes and eyelids 3, ears 5, wrinkle 5, nose 6, chops 2, jaws 5, teeth 2. *Body, Legs, etc. (39):* neck 3, dewlap 2, shoulders 5, chest 3, ribs 3, brisket 2, belly 2, back 5, forelegs and elbows 4, hind legs 3, feet 3, tail 4. *Total (100)*.

DISQUALIFICATION

Dudley or flesh-colored nose.

Approved by the AKC 20 July 1976

KC(GB) VARIATION TO STANDARD

Mouth: when viewed from front under jaw should be central under upper jaw with which it should be parallel. *Tail:* round and smooth, devoid of fringe and coarse hair. *Size:* most desirable weight is dogs 55 pounds, bitches 50 pounds. *Colour:* colour should be whole or smut, that is a whole colour with black mask or muzzle. *General appearance:* from its formation dog has a peculiar heavy and constrained gait, appearing to walk with short, quick steps on tips of its toes, its hind-feet not being lifted high, but appearing to skim ground, and running with right shoulder rather advanced, similar to manner of a horse cantering.

CHOW CHOW

NATIONAL GROUPING		
	Name	Number
AKC	Non-Sporting Dogs	VI
KC(GB)	Utility	4
FCI	Companion Dogs	9

When man first took the dog as his companion, he almost certainly saw him as a guard, as an assistant on a hunt, and later as a herder. It is most unlikely, however, that he saw him as a potential source of food. Wild game was so plentiful that in most parts of the world there was no need to look upon dogs as part of the diet, but in China things were rather different. The Chow Chow has existed in China for at least the past two thousand years, in the north the rough-coated variety and in the south the smooth, indeed the smooth-coated Chow Chow, or at least a dog very like it still exists in fair numbers in southern China and Hong Kong. It is longer in the leg and looks something like an Akita, but it is basically a Chow. The coat of the northern rough-coated Chow Chow was so rich and warm, that in that very cold country the skins were looked upon as a useful article of clothing, and dog skins were sold in the markets of Manchuria and Mongolia. Not only was the skin used, but in a thickly populated country such as China, nothing that was edible could be wasted, and the flesh of the Chow Chow was an acceptable adjunct to the normal diet. Dog ranches were by no means unusual, and the breeding of these dogs on a commercial basis was quite common.

He is one of the Spitz types, allied to the other rough-coated prick-eared curled-tailed breeds, and his history in China goes back to very early days even in that country where time is measured in tens of centuries. The first report of the breed in Britain is in the letters of Gilbert White the naturalist, who in the 18th century wrote that he had seen a pair belonging to a neighbour who had brought them from Canton, the description of which is clearly that of a Chow Chow. He was certainly in Britain by the 19th century, and began to appear at shows, and by the turn of the century he was well-established. There was some interest before the First World War, but it was not until the 1920s that they began to hit the headlines, a number being shown at Crufts in 1925, and one particularly outstanding dog being exported to Mrs. Earl Hoover of Chicago.

Since that time the breed has made steady progress and registrations increase each year. He is a massive short-backed heavily boned dog with one peculiarity of hind movement, having little or no angulation of stifle. His coat is a very important feature, and whilst the short-coat crops up from time to time, some breeders even deliberately breeding for that characteristic, it is the rough-coated variety which has captured the public interest. He has another peculiarity in that the inside of his mouth should always be black.

The Chow Chow has always been a great performer and very popular at shows, his colourful character, his very showy coat, and his strange gait endearing him to spectators. Chows have been among the biggest winners in the show rings of the world since the First World War, and one alive at present in Britain holds the all-time record for winning challenge certificates over every other breed. As puppies Chow Chows are quite delightful, looking more like woolly toys than dogs, and children find them irresistible. His temperament is very different from many dogs. He is somewhat aloof and distant at times, gazing away from those who speak to him and appearing very haughty, but with people that he likes he is most affectionate. He has no vice, though he is not easily trained in the normal way, and is seldom if ever seen in say the obedience ring, as he has a will of his own. He is fairly obedient without being servile, and well-behaved without being selfconscious about it.

OFFICIAL STANDARD

General appearance
A massive, cobby, powerful dog, active and alert, with strong, muscular development, and perfect balance. Body squares with height of leg at shoulder; head, broad and flat, with short, broad, and deep muzzle, accentuated by a ruff; the whole supported by straight, strong legs. Clothed in a shining, offstanding coat, the Chow is a masterpiece of beauty, dignity, and untouched naturalness.

Head
Large and massive in proportion to size of dog, with broad, flat skull; well filled under the eyes; moderate stop; and proudly carried. *Expression:* essentially dignified, lordly, scowling, discerning, sober, and snobbish—one of independence. *Muzzle:* short in comparison to length of skull; broad from eyes to end of nose, and of equal depth. The lips somewhat full and overhanging. *Teeth:* strong and level, with a scissors bite; should neither be overshot, nor undershot. *Nose:* large, broad, and black in color. (Disqualification—Nose spotted or distinctly other than black, except in blue Chows, which may have solid blue or slate noses.) *Tongue:* a blue-black. The tissues of the mouth should approximate black. (Disqualification—Tongue red, pink, or obviously spotted with red or pink.) *Eyes:* dark, deep-set, of moderate size, and almond-shaped. *Ears:* small, slightly rounded at tip, stiffly carried. They should be placed wide apart, on top of the skull, and set with a slight, forward tilt. (Disqualification—Drop ear or ears. A drop ear is one which is not stiffly carried or stiffly erect, but which breaks over at any point from its base to its tip.)

Head and skull: flat, broad well filled out.

Body
Short, compact, with well-sprung ribs, and let down in the flank.

Neck
Strong, full, set well on the shoulders.

Shoulders
Muscular, slightly sloping.

Chest
Broad, deep, and muscular. A narrow chest is a serious fault.

Back
Short, straight, and strong.

Loins
Broad, deep, and powerful.

Tail
Set well up and carried closely to the back, following line of spine at start.

Forelegs
Perfectly straight, with heavy bone and upright pasterns.

Hindquarters: hocks well let down and straight.

Hind legs
Straight-hocked, muscular, and heavy boned. *Feet:* compact, round, catlike, with thick pads.

Gait
Completely individual. Short and stilted because of straight hocks.

Coat
Abundant, dense, straight, and off-standing; rather coarse in texture with a soft, woolly undercoat. It may be any clear color, solid throughout, with lighter shadings on ruff, tail, and breechings.

DISQUALIFICATIONS
Nose spotted or distinctly other color than black, except in blue Chows, which may have solid blue or slate noses. Tongue red, pink or obviously spotted with red or pink. Drop ear or ears.

Approved by the AKC 11 March 1941

KC(GB) VARIATION TO STANDARD
Nose: with cream and whites a light coloured nose is permissible and in blues or fawns a self-coloured nose. *Neck:* slightly arched. *Height:* minimum 18 inches.

DALMATIAN

NATIONAL GROUPING		
	Name	Number
AKC	Non-Sporting Dogs	VI
KC(GB)	Utility	4
FCI	Companion Dogs	9

The decorative value of a dog has been recognised by the ladies, and for that matter the gentlemen, of court circles at least since the Imperial Court of Rome. The pampered pet of the gentlewomen of the Italian and the Spanish courts was depicted as a foil to the lady's beauty, almost as part of her personality. The Dalmatian is a typical example of a dog that has been evolved for just that purpose. He is not a working dog, nor does he hunt or course. He was developed simply as an adjunct to the fashionable person's equipage. The breed is quite an ancient one, and it has been suggested that it was originally a guard dog, and even a war dog in Dalmatia or Croatia, though there is a possibility that here it was being confused with the spotted German Mastiff known at one time as the Tiger Dog, which was a hunting and fighting dog. In the middle of the 19th century it was considered to be fashionable to have one of these spotted dogs trotting along with one's carriage. In Dalmatia where these dogs are said to have originated they were probably a small version of the spotted or harlequin Great Dane, and probably these were later crossed with Pointers to reduce the size and improve the markings.

In Victorian England the Dalmatian was certainly a carriage dog, often living in the stables, not normally entering the house, and appearing only when the horses were being prepared, when they would join the carriage, and either trot alongside, even in front, or what was considered the height of fashion, beneath the rear axle. For a while, with the advent of the motorcar, the Dalmatian went into something of a decline, but a dog with all the qualities that he has could not be kept down for long, and he has climbed up once more into a very strong position in the popularity poll. As happened with some other breeds, it needed a book and Walt Disney to give him the boost that he needed.

He is a very intelligent dog, as his ancestry would suggest, as both the Great Dane and the Pointer which are supposed to have been used to produce the breed are very intelligent dogs. In order to accomplish the feats of running that he did during his carriage dog days, he had to be a very muscular well-built dog with great powers of endurance and persistence, and these qualities he has to this day, never appearing to tire, and being one of the most symmetrically built dogs in the world. As a showdog he has proved remarkably successful, and there is little at any of today's shows that attracts more attention than a ring full of these beautifully spotted animals. Being always willing to please, and attentive to his handler, he is easily trained to stand perfectly still in the ring, and his excellent conformation makes him a pleasure to see as he moves freely up and down the ring. He has no vices, and a ring full of Dalmatians is one of the quietest and the best behaved rings at any show.

Temperamentally he is the perfect companion dog. Years of association with man have given him a natural sense of what is correct behaviour, and whilst he enjoys life as much as any dog, he is amenable to discipline and makes a wonderful pet and housedog. He still enjoys a hunt as his forebears undoubtedly did, and he is at his happiest on a walk through the country, but enjoys the fireside in the winter too, and he is remarkably well-behaved and troublefree in the house. His intelligence and good manners have endeared him to circus and stage folk and in the United States he has been associated with the Fire Service, for which he has been used as a badge for many years.

OFFICIAL STANDARD

The Dalmatian should represent a strong, muscular, and active dog; poised and alert; free of shyness; intelligent in expression; symmetrical in outline; and free from coarseness and lumber. He should be capable of great endurance, combined with a fair amount of speed.

Head
Should be of a fair length, the skull flat, proportionately broad between the ears, and moderately well defined at the temples, and not in one straight line from the nose to the occiput bone as required in a Bull Terrier. It should be entirely free from wrinkle. *Muzzle:* should be long and powerful—the lips clean. The mouth should have a scissors bite. Never undershot or overshot. It is permissible to trim whiskers. *Eyes:* should be set moderately well apart, and of medium size, round, bright, and sparkling, with an intelligent expression; their color greatly depending on the markings of the dog. In the black-spotted variety the eyes should be dark (black or brown or blue). In the liver-spotted variety they should be lighter than in the black-spotted variety (golden or light brown or blue). The rim around the eyes in the black-spotted variety should be black; in the liver-spotted variety, brown. Never flesh-colored in either. Lack of pigment a major fault. *Ears:* should be set rather high, of moderate size, rather wide at the base, and gradually tapering to a rounded point. They should be carried close to the head, be thin and fine in texture, and preferably spotted. *Nose:* in the black-spotted variety should always be black; in the liver-spotted variety, always brown. A butterfly or flesh-colored nose is a major fault.

Neck and shoulders
The neck should be fairly long, nicely arched, light and tapering, and entirely free from throatiness. The shoulders should be oblique, clean, and muscular, denoting speed.

Body, back, chest and loins
The chest should not be too wide, but very deep and capacious, ribs well sprung but never rounded like barrel hoops (which would indicate want of speed). Back powerful; loin strong, muscular and slightly arched.

Legs and feet
Of great importance. The forelegs should be straight, strong, and heavy in bone; elbows close to the body; feet compact, well-arched toes, and tough, elastic pads. In the hind legs the muscles should be clean, though well defined; the hocks well let down. Dewclaws may be removed from legs. *Nails:* in the black-spotted variety, black or white; or a nail may be both black and white. In the liver-spotted variety, brown or white; or a nail may be both brown and white.

Gait
Length of stride should be in proportion to the size of the dog, steady in rhythm of 1, 2, 3, 4 as in the cadence count in military drill. Front legs should not paddle, nor should there be a straddling appearance. Hind legs should neither cross nor weave; judges should be able to see each leg move with no interference of another leg. Drive and reach are most desirable. Cowhocks are a major fault.

Tail
Should ideally reach the hock joint, strong at the insertion, and tapering toward the end, free from coarseness. It should not be inserted too low down, but carried with a slight curve upwards, and never curled.

Coat
Should be short, hard, dense, and fine, sleek and glossy in appearance, but neither woolly nor silky.

Color and markings
Are most important points. The ground color in both varieties should be pure white, very decided, and not intermixed. The color of the spots in the black-spotted variety should be dense black; in the liver-spotted variety they should be liver brown. The spots should not intermingle, but be as round and well defined as possible, the more distinct the better. In size they should be from that of a dime to a half-dollar. The spots on the face, head, ears, legs, and tail to be smaller than those on the body. Patches, tricolors, and any color markings other than black or liver constitute a disqualification. A true patch is a solid, sharply defined mass of black or liver that is appreciably larger than any of the markings on the dog. Several spots that are so adjacent that they actually touch one another at their edges do not constitute a patch.

Size
The desirable height of dogs and bitches is between 19 and 23 inches at the withers, and any dog or bitch over 24 inches at the withers is to be disqualified.

MAJOR FAULTS
Butterfly or flesh-colored nose. Cowhocks. Flat feet. Lack of pigment in eye rims. Shyness. Trichiasis (abnormal position or direction of the eyelashes).

SCALE OF POINTS
Body, back, chest and loins (10). Coat (5), Color and markings (25). Ears (5). Gait (10). Head and eyes (10). Legs and feet (10). Neck and shoulders (10). Size, symmetry, etc. (10). Tail (5). *Total (100).*

DISQUALIFICATIONS
Any color markings other than black or liver. Any size over 24 inches at the withers. Patches. Tri-colors. Undershot or overshot bite.

Approved by the AKC 11 December 1962

KC(GB) VARIATION TO STANDARD
Size: ideal height: dogs 23 to 24 inches; bitches 22 to 23 inches. *Fault:* blue eyes.

FRENCH BULLDOG

NATIONAL GROUPING		
	Name	Number
AKC	Non-Sporting Dogs	VI
KC(GB)	Utility	4
FCI	Companion Dogs	9

From time to time there have cropped up in some lines of British Bulldogs, specimens much smaller than average. Indeed, whilst there have been Bulldogs that weighed nearer to eighty than the fifty pounds which is the average, there have been many which have weighed as little as twenty pounds. Around the middle of the 19th century, a Toy Bulldog existed, and was shown as such until the British Kennel Club at the turn of the century decided that this was a contradiction in terms and insisted on the use of the name 'Miniature Bulldog'. There is little doubt that the French Bulldog is descended from some of these very small Bulldogs. The French authorities claim that the breed was in fact native to their country. Some claim that the breed originated with the Dogue de Bordeaux which still exists as a very large Mastiff type of up to twenty-six inches at the shoulder, but which was miniaturised to produce both the Bulldog and the French Bulldog. All will agree, however, that the miniature version of the Bulldog had something to do with the ancestry of the French Bulldog.

The breed in some form has been known since the 17th century, and in its early days in Paris was bred by the Lutetian bootmakers and other artisans, and became popular as a fighting dog. One stalwart breeder, Mr. George Krehl brought dogs over from France to exhibit them in Britain around the turn of the century, and at that time an attempt was made to reintroduce the miniature or toy Bulldog. This failed, however, and in 1902 the French Bulldog Club of England was formed against considerable opposition from the established Bulldog clubs and the Toy Bull-

dog Club which was still in existence. The first show was held shortly afterwards in Britain, and the breed was recognised by the Kennel Club. In the United States of America the adoption of the breed took place somewhat earlier, and by 1898 the first breed show had already been held, the breed soon becoming very popular.

The attempt to revive the toy Bulldog in Britain persisted until the First World War, and for a while the very small Bulldog of under fifteen pounds was recognised, and whilst some breeders still prefer the smaller type, the fifty pound average is now accepted generally as the norm. The real parting of the ways between the two breeds came with the acceptance of the bat-ears, which are a feature of the French Bulldog, but abhorrent to those who breed the Bulldog proper.

He is a heavy little dog with a large chest and a wide front, and apart from the head is just like a smaller version of the Bulldog with a roach, a dip towards the withers and an impression of great strength in a small compass. He is tremendously active, keeping remarkably fit by virtue of the great deal of exercise that he takes normally in play and adventure. He makes a wonderful show dog, as he reacts so well to human companionship. He can be trained to stand perfectly still without losing his natural alertness and looking cowed, and he enjoys himself so obviously in the ring that his spirit is infectious. When he moves, providing he is a fit and healthy dog, he moves with freedom and with the sort of assurance that the earlier Bulldogs had.

His temperament is delightful, and it is in this respect that it is so easy to visualise that he had the Bulldog as an ancestor. He has the same sort of personality, being very charming and quaint on the one hand and extremely positive on the other. There are few half-measures about a French Bulldog, when he plays he does so wholeheartedly, but if he sulks it takes a great deal to console him. He is intelligent enough to make the most of the comfortable surroundings with which most people indulge him, and he soon becomes very much a part of the family.

OFFICIAL STANDARD

General appearance

The French Bulldog should have the appearance of an active, intelligent, muscular dog, of heavy bone, smooth coat, compactly built, and of medium or small structure. *Proportion and symmetry:* the points should be well distributed and bear good relation one to the other, no feature being in such prominence from either excess or lack of quality that the animal appears deformed or poorly proportioned. *Influence of sex:* In comparison of specimens of different sex, due allowance should be made in favor of the bitches, which do not bear the characteristics of the breed to the same marked degree as do the dogs.

Weight

A lightweight class under 22 pounds; heavyweight class, 22 pounds, and not over 28 pounds.

Head and skull: massive, square, broad, domed forehead with loose skin.

Head

The head should be large and square. The top of the skull should be flat between the ears; the forehead should not be flat but slightly rounded. The stop should be well defined, causing a hollow or groove between the eyes. The muzzle should be broad, deep and well laid back; the muscles of the cheeks well developed. The nose should be extremely short; nostrils broad with well defined line between them. The nose and flews should be black, except in the case of the lighter-colored dogs, where a lighter color nose is acceptable. The flews should be thick and broad, hanging over the lower jaw at the sides, meeting the underlip in front and covering the teeth which should not be seen when the mouth is closed. The underjaw should be deep, square, broad, undershot and well turned up. *Eyes:* the eyes should be wide apart, set low down in the skull, as far from the ears as possible, round in form, of moderate size, neither sunken nor bulging, and in color dark. No haw and no white of the eye showing when looking forward.

Ears

The ears shall hereafter be known as the bat ear, broad at the base, elongated, with round top, set high on the head, but not too close together, and carried erect with the orifice to the front. The leather of the ear, fine and soft.

Neck

The neck should be thick and well arched, with loose skin at throat.

Body

The body should be short and well rounded. The chest, broad, deep and full, well ribbed with the belly tucked up. The back should be a roach back, with a slight fall close behind the shoulders. It should be strong and short, broad at the shoulders and narrowing at the loins.

Legs

The forelegs should be short, stout, straight and muscular, set wide apart. The hind leg should be strong and muscular, longer than the forelegs, so as to elevate the loins above the shoulders. Hocks well let down. *Feet:* the feet should be moderate in size, compact and firmly set. Toes compact, well split up, with high knuckles and short, stubby nails; hind feet slightly longer than forefeet.

Tail

The tail should be either straight or screwed (but not curly), short, hung low, thick root and fine tip; carried low in repose.

Color, skin and coat

Acceptable colors are: All brindle, fawn, white, brindle and white, and any color except those which constitute disqualification. The skin should be soft and loose, especially at head and shoulders, forming wrinkles. Coat moderately fine, brilliant, short and smooth.

DISQUALIFICATIONS

Other than bat ears. Black and white, black and tan, liver, mouse or solid black (black means black without any trace of brindle). Eyes of different color. Nose other than black, except in the case of the lighter-colored dogs, where a lighter color nose is acceptable. Hare lip. Any mutilation. Over 28 pounds in weight.

General Properties (20): proportion and symmetry 5, expression 5, gait 4, color 4, coat 2. *Head (40):* skull 6, cheeks and chops 2, stop 5, ears 8, eyes 4, wrinkles 4, nose 3, jaws 6, teeth 2. *Body, Legs, etc. (40):* shoulders 5, back 5, neck 4, chest 3, ribs 4, brisket 3, belly 2, forelegs 4, hind legs 3, feet 3, tail 4. *Total (100).*

Approved by the AKC 11 February 1947

KC(GB) VARIATION TO STANDARD

Mouth: tongue must not protrude. *Feet:* small, with absolutely sound pasterns. *Weight:* (ideal) dogs 28 pounds; bitches 24 pounds, but soundness must not be sacrificed to smallness.

KEESHOND

NATIONAL GROUPING		
	Name	Number
AKC	Non-Sporting Dogs	VI
KC(GB)	Utility	4
FCI	Companion Dogs	9

One of the most typical of the Spitz group of dogs after the Finnish Spitz, is the Keeshond. He is rather like a very large Pomeranian of a different colour. He is really the product of the Netherlands, and when first imported into Britain was known as the Dutch Barge Dog. He is by no means a recently developed dog, and probably descended from the Wolf Spitz of Germany and has been known in Europe in one form or another for the past two hundred years or more. The dog probably takes his name from the two patriots Kees de Witt and Kees de Gyselaer, and he became the mascot of Keezen, an 18th century peoples' party which opposed the House of Orange. He was best known, however, as a dog used as a companion and guard by the barge people of Holland.

The modern Keeshond has been known in Britain from the turn of the century since when it has made steady progress both there and in the United States. More recently it has achieved a degree of worldwide popularity and is seen more frequently almost everywhere than it is in its country of origin. The first one shown outside its native country was probably a dog called simply Kees which was exhibited around 1900 and was described as a Wolf Spitz though undoubtedly from its description it was in fact a Keeshond. It was shown in the foreign dog class, and was immediately objected to by another exhibitor who claimed that it should have been shown in the class for Pomeranians, which is not so odd as it may sound, as many Pomeranians at that time were as large as the modern Keeshond.

He is a strong and active dog with a very distinctive and clear bark, and the typical stand-off coat, prick ears and curled tail of the Spitz dogs. He has one particular mark of difference which distinguishes him from other breeds in the pencilling of dark marks around and behind the eyes known as the spectacles, which are a feature of the breed and very desirable.

As a show dog he has the one attribute of all the Spitz group, the ability to adopt a completely statuesque attitude in the ring and to hold it for a considerable time. This takes some training, and is usually done by food attraction, but it is not unusual to see a whole line of these dogs standing almost head to tail in the ring and completely motionless, watching every move of the handler's free hand which is usually somewhere near his mouth. He has no vice in the ring, or for that matter out of it, and will rarely interfere with any of the other dogs. His coat, when well-prepared is quite spectacular, with its distinctive wolf-grey colour, profuse feathering and well-developed ruff. An occasional dog will get into the habit of barking in the ring, when his loud bell-like tones will tell anyone in the vicinity which breed is being judged.

Long years of association with man have produced a dog ideally suited to life in a house. Although he is a fairly large dog, he curls himself up into a corner much as his close cousins in the group, the arctic dogs, curl themselves up in the snow, and he occupies the minimum of space. He is friendly, even affectionate, becomes very attached to those that he knows well, but still remains very much the guard dog, in which role his acute hearing and strong voice prove extremely valuable.

OFFICIAL STANDARD

General appearance and conformation

The Keeshond is a handsome dog, of well-balanced, short-coupled body, attracting attention not only by his alert carriage and intelligent expression, but also by his luxurious coat, his richly plumed tail, well curled over his back, and by his foxlike face and head with small pointed ears. His coat is very thick round the neck, fore part of the shoulders and chest, forming a lionlike mane. His rump and hind legs, down to the hocks, are also thickly coated forming the characteristic 'trousers.' His head, ears and lower legs are covered with thick short hair.

The ideal height of fully matured dogs (over 2 years old),

measured from top of withers to the ground, is: for dogs, 18 inches; bitches, 17 inches. However, size consideration should not outweigh that of type. When dogs are judged equal in type, the dog nearest the ideal height is to be preferred. Length of back from withers to rump should equal height as measured above.

Head

Expression: expression is largely dependent on the distinctive characteristic called 'spectacles'—a delicately penciled line slanting slightly upward from the outer corner of each eye to the lower corner of the ear, coupled with distinct markings and shadings forming short but expressive eyebrows. Markings (or shadings) on face and head must present a pleasing appearance, imparting to the dog an alert and intelligent expression. *Fault:* absence of 'spectacles.' *Skull:* the head should be well proportioned to the body, wedge-shaped when viewed from above. Not only in muzzle, but the whole head should give this impression when the ears are drawn back by covering the nape of the neck and the ears with one hand. Head in profile should exhibit a definite stop. *Fault:* apple head, or absence of stop. *Muzzle:* the muzzle should be dark in color and of medium length, neither coarse nor snipy, and well proportioned to the skull. *Mouth:* the mouth should be neither overshot nor undershot. Lips should be black and closely meeting, not thick, coarse or sagging; and with no wrinkle at the corner of the mouth. *Faults:* overshot or undershot. *Teeth:* the teeth should be white, sound and strong (but discoloration from distemper not to penalize severely); upper teeth should just overlap the lower teeth. *Eyes:* eyes should be dark brown in color, of medium size, rather oblique in shape and not set too wide apart. *Fault:* protruding round eyes or eyes light of color. *Ears:* ears should be small, triangular in shape, mounted high on head and carried erect; dark in color and covered with thick, velvety short hair. Size should be proportionate to the head—length approximating the distance from outer corner of the eye to the nearest edge of the ear. *Fault:* ears not carried erect when at attention.

Body

Neck and shoulders: the neck should be moderately long, well shaped and well set on shoulders; covered with a profuse mane, sweeping from under the jaw and covering the whole of the front part of the shoulders and chest, as well as the top part of the shoulders. *Chest, back and loin:* the body should be compact with a short straight back sloping slightly downward toward the hindquarters; well ribbed, barrel well rounded, belly moderately tucked up, deep and strong of chest. *Legs:* forelegs should be straight seen from any angle and well feathered. Hind legs should be profusely feathered down to the hocks—not below, with hocks only slightly bent. Legs must be of good bone and cream in color. *Fault:* black markings below the knee, penciling excepted. *Feet:* the feet should be compact, well rounded, catlike, and cream in color. Toes are nicely arched, with black nails. *Fault:* white foot or feet.

Tail

The tail should be set on high, moderately long, and well feathered, tightly curled over back. It should lie flat and close to the body with a very light gray plume on top where curled, but the tip of the tail should be black. The tail should form a part of the 'silhouette' of the dog's body, rather than give the appearance of an appendage. *Fault:* tail not lying close to the back.

Action

Dogs should show boldly and keep tails curled over the back. They should move cleanly and briskly; and the movement should be straight and sharp (not lope like a German Shepherd). *Fault:* tail not carried over back when moving.

Coat

The body should be abundantly covered with long, straight, harsh hair; standing well out from a thick, downy undercoat. The hair on the legs should be smooth and short, except for a feathering on the front legs and 'trousers,' as previously described, on the hind legs. The hair on the tail should be profuse, forming a rich plume. Head, including muzzle, skull and ears, should be covered with smooth, soft, short hair—velvety in texture on the ears. Coat must not part down the back. *Fault:* silky, wavy or curly coats. Part in coat down the back.

Color and markings

A mixture of gray and black. The undercoat should be very pale gray or cream (not tawny). The hair of the outer coat is black tipped, the length of the black tips producing the characteristic shading of color. The color may vary from light to dark, but any pronounced deviation from the gray color is not permissible. The plume of the tail should be very light gray when curled on back, and the tip of the tail should be black. Legs and feet should be cream. Ears should be very dark—almost black. Shoulder line markings (light gray) should be well defined. The color of the ruff and 'trousers' is generally lighter than that of the body. 'Spectacles' and shadings, as previously described, are characteristic of the breed and must be present to some degree. There should be no pronounced white markings. *Very serious faults:* entirely black or white or any other solid color; any pronounced deviation from the gray color.

SCALE OF POINTS
General conformation and appearance (20). Head (20): shape 6, eyes 5, ears 5, teeth 4. *Body (35):* chest, back and loin 10, tail 10, neck and shoulders 8, legs 4, feet 3. *Coat (15). Color and markings (10). Total (100).*

Approved by the AKC 12 July 1949

KC(GB) VARIATION TO STANDARD

Ears: not widely set, yet not meeting.

LHASA APSO

NATIONAL GROUPING		
	Name	Number
AKC	Non-Sporting Dogs	VI
KC(GB)	Utility	4
FCI	Companion Dogs	9

The history of the dogs of Tibet is closely connected with the history of the monasteries of that country. Many of the dogs were kept in monasteries and were considered to be holy animals, and some, particularly the Tibetan Spaniels are said to have turned prayer wheels as part of their duty. Of these sacred dogs, the Apso is the most recent one to have become popular in the Western World. His name is believed to have evolved from a corruption of the Tibetan word for goat, 'rapso', as his coat resembles that of this animal. It was said that the souls of lamas entered the bodies of Apsos on death, and the dogs were therefore treated with considerable respect. The ancient Chinese myth of the Lion Dog complements the beliefs concerning the dog in Tibet, and although the story is more generally applied to the history of the Pekingese, the lamas of Tibet had a very similar story. This supposed transfer of the soul leaving a body and entering a dog was accepted at one time so completely that it became a rite, and dogs were used to identify the presence of evil in a corpse.

Tibetan dogs were known to the rest of the world more than fifty years ago, the first to become well-known being the Tibetan Spaniel, and it was some time after that that the Lhasa Apso first made its mark. The first came into the possession of Colonel Kennedy, a medical officer who was given a couple in 1921. They were brought to England and were exhibited at a show in London in 1929. A breed club was formed in 1933 and from that time the breed has never looked back, the number of registrations rapidly overtaking those of the other Tibetan breeds.

He is a very sturdy little dog, strongly made and with a coat that protects him from the most rigorous weather conditions. In spite of his lack of size he is a forceful character and very much a guard dog and it would be unfortunate if because of his lack of size he became considered as a toy dog. In recent films emanating from Tibet this little dog can still be seen running around the monasteries, apparently little changed over the centuries by the influx of foreign blood, the comparative inaccessability of the country probably accounting for this. Seen thus they are fairly rough, with a comparatively short, hard and somewhat neglected coat. As we see them today in the rest of the world they are very different.

The Lhasa Apso is one of those dogs that really repays attention to his coat. The hair is long, and easily separated, with the result that today's exhibitors spend considerable time preparing their dogs for exhibition. His coat now normally reaches the ground, giving him a very glamorous appearance which makes him attractive to spectators and constantly encourages more people to own one. In the ring he is well-behaved, being steady, ignoring in an amusingly pompous manner the presence of other dogs, however large, and when asked to move, strides out with all the drive and presence of a very much larger dog.

He is an amusing little character, giving the impression all the time that inside his small frame there is a much larger dog trying to express himself. He is always full of confidence, even cheeky, and behaves in a playful, gay and attractive manner. He is very active, needs a great deal of exercise, which he fortunately gets with the endless games that he will play with anything or anyone, and he makes one of the most entertaining companions. He looks at his best when kept in the company of his fellows, and there are few more attractive sights in the canine world than a number of these little dogs enjoying the games that they invent for themselves on a sunny day in the garden.

OFFICIAL STANDARD

Character
Gay and assertive, but chary of strangers.

Size
Variable, but about 10 inches or 11 inches at shoulder for dogs, bitches slightly smaller.

Color
Golden, sandy, honey, dark grizzle, slate, smoke, parti-color, black, white or brown. This being the true Tibetan Lion-dog, golden or lionlike colors are preferred. Other colors in order as above. Dark tips to ears and beard are an asset.

Body shape
The length from point of shoulders to point of buttocks longer than height at withers, well ribbed up, strong loin, well-developed quarters and thighs.

Coat
Heavy, straight, hard, not woolly nor silky, of good length, and very dense.

Body: length greater than height.

Mouth and muzzle
Mouth level, otherwise slightly undershot preferable. Muzzle of medium length; a square muzzle is objectionable.

Head
Heavy head furnishings with good fall over eyes, good whiskers and beard; skull narrow, falling away behind the eyes in a marked degree, not quite flat, but not domed or apple-shaped; straight foreface of fair length. Nose black, about $1\frac{1}{2}$ inches long, or the length from tip of nose to eye to be roughly about one-third of the total length from nose to back of skull.

Eyes
Dark brown, neither very large and full, nor very small and sunk.

Ears
Pendant, heavily feathered.

Legs
Forelegs straight; both forelegs and hind legs heavily furnished with hair.

Feet
Well feathered, should be round and catlike, with good pads.

Tail and carriage
Well feathered, should be carried well over back in a screw; there may be a kink at the end. A low carriage of stern is a serious fault.

Approved by the AKC 9 April 1935

KC(GB) VARIATION TO STANDARD
Head: medium stop. *Eyes:* medium sized frontally placed. *Neck:* strong, well covered with a dense mane which is more pronounced in dogs. *Body:* level top line. *Forequarters:* shoulders well laid back. *Hindquarters:* well developed with good muscle. Good angulation. Hocks when viewed from behind should be parallel and not too close together. *Coat:* dense undercoat.

POODLE

NATIONAL GROUPING		
	Name	Number
AKC	Non-Sporting Dogs	VI
KC(GB)	Utility	4
FCI	Companion Dogs	9

The Poodle family is divided into three varieties by size in most countries, but the history of the breed is the same for all of them. The Poodle is the most entertaining of dogs and has a long association with the stage as a performer. He is a wonderful companion as one is never quite certain what he will do next, and he is full of fun and inventiveness. He will constantly surprise by his actions, and although he can be trained to repeat actions easily enough, he will indulge in activities which are the result of spur-of-the-moment decisions. His history is complicated somewhat by the fact that for many years France laid claim to him as the country of origin of the breed, whereas in fact it was almost certainly Germany that can claim the honour. He started off life as the Water Dog or Pudel of Germany, and old engravings of this dog look almost exactly like a somewhat neglected poodle.

The Standard Poodle was almost certainly origin-ally a large gundog, though the uses to which he was subsequently put changed his appearance to some extent. In Russia the same dog became almost in-variably large and black, in Germany the dogs were used as load pullers and became heavier and stronger, being used for pulling milk carts, whilst in France they became smaller and were almost exclusively companions. Many other breeds were probably used

to produce the dog as we know him today, and it would not be simply a case of selective breeding. There were a number of long-coated breeds of sheepdog in Hungary and Germany whose coats corded as the Poodle's will, and the very ancient Little Lion Dog has something of the look of a Poodle.

For a great number of years the Poodle was a regular part of the French circus, as he can be trained to perform apparently most difficult tricks with ease, and at the same time can be trimmed and clipped into patterns which themselves are entertaining. In more modern times his history has been less lowly, as he has become one of the finest of show dogs. Many of the early Poodles shown had what is called a corded coat which means that the coat was oiled and persuaded to mat into long separate cords which in a good speci-men reached to the ground. This went out of fashion largely because of the difficulty encountered in keeping the coat in that condition, but the Puli exhibitors do the same thing successfully with the coat of their dogs today and it would be interesting to see what the modern Standard Poodle would look like with cords down to the ground.

He is a big fine dog, very elegant yet at the same time having great strength. His height has not caused him to sacrifice anything in the way of robustness, and his love of exercise and play means that he can be kept in excellent muscular condition with little difficulty. His coat needs constant attention to keep it in mat-free condition, but as it is quite acceptable that a dog not intended for exhibition may be clipped all over and still look very presentable, this is what most owners do.

He is one of the most striking and noble of all show dogs. His sheer height, and he can now be as much as twenty-five or more inches at the shoulder makes him very spectacular. Add to that the fact that at least four colours are often seen in the ring together, and that each in its way is a lovely clear colour and the whole picture becomes a very attractive one. To keep him in show trim means a considerable amount of work, and he will need a daily brushing as well as hours of trimming and clipping to put him into the ring looking his best. That it is worth while is proved by the fact that Standard Poodles have won major awards at every

OFFICIAL STANDARD

General appearance, carriage and condition

That of a very active, intelligent and elegant-appearing dog, squarely built, well proportioned, moving soundly and carrying himself proudly. Properly clipped in the traditional fashion and carefully groomed, the Poodle has about him an air of distinction and dignity peculiar to himself.

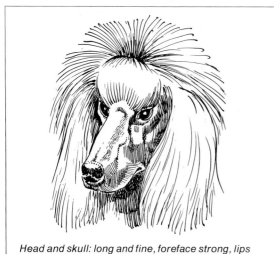

Head and skull: long and fine, foreface strong, lips tight-fitting.

Head and expression

Skull: moderately rounded, with a slight but definite stop. Cheekbones and muscles flat. *Muzzle:* long, straight and fine, with slight chiseling under the eyes. Strong without lippiness. The chin definite enough to preclude snipiness. Teeth white, strong and with a scissors bite. *Eyes:* set far apart, very dark, oval in appearance and showing alert intelligence. *Ears:* hanging close to the

Ears: leather long and wide, low set on.

head, set at or slightly below eye level. The ear leather is long, wide, and thickly feathered, but the ear fringe should not be of excessive length.

Neck and shoulders

Neck well proportioned, strong and long enough to permit the head to be carried high and with dignity. Skin snug at throat. The neck rises from strong, smoothly muscled shoulders. The shoulder blade is well laid back and approximately the same length as the upper foreleg.

Body

The chest deep and moderately wide with well sprung ribs. The back short, strong and slightly hollowed; the loins short, broad and muscular. Length of body and height at shoulder are in such proportion as to insure the desirable squarely built appearance.

Tail

Straight, set on high and carried up, docked, but sufficient in length to insure a balanced outline.

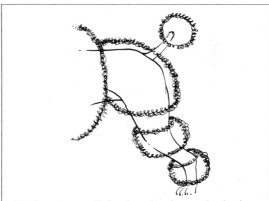

Hindquarters: well-developed and muscular, hocks well let down.

Legs

The forelegs are straight and parallel when viewed from the front. When viewed from the side with a leg vertical, the elbow is directly below the highest point of the shoulder blade. The hind legs are muscular with width in the region of the stifles. The pasterns are strong and the stifles well bent. The length of the leg from the stifle joint to the hock joint is considerably greater than the length from the hock joint to the foot.

Feet

The feet are rather small, oval in shape with toes well arched and cushioned on thick firm pads. Nails short but not excessively shortened. The feet turn neither in nor out. Dewclaws may be removed.

Coat

Quality: of naturally harsh texture, profuse and dense throughout. *Clip:* a Poodle may be shown in the 'Puppy' clip or the 'English Saddle' clip or the traditional 'Continental' clip. A Poodle shown in any other type of clip shall be disqualified. A Poodle under a year old may be shown

big show in the world including Westminster and Crufts.

He is a joyous animal to own, being very playful and full of high spirits, friendly and completely without vice. One never hears of a Poodle attacking anyone or biting at a show, or indeed anywhere else, but he is a natural guard with a very strong sense of territory.

Miniature and Toy Poodles

It is almost certain that the Miniature Poodle as we now know it, was developed from the normal sized Pudel of Germany. The Standard Poodle of today is much taller than his ancestors would have been, and the Toy Poodle much smaller. It is the Miniature Poodle which is probably nearer in height to the original, though these days he is much more slender and refined and does not have the strength that the Pudel had. Some authorities state that the original was the Standard Poodle, but the dog shown in Europe today, where the sizes are not so clearly defined as they are in the United States and Britain, is not nearly as tall as the modern Standard Poodle. This would lead one to believe that the original Pudel was not a particularly tall dog, and an engraving of German Poodles dated around 1880 shows them as a medium sized dog,

incidentally, with long tails.

In 1907 the Miniature Poodle was described as the Toy Poodle, and had to be less than fifteen inches at the shoulder, and it was not until later, when in the United States they required a Toy Poodle to be under ten inches and Britain under eleven, that the position was finally cleared up. Descended from the larger dog, which was often used as a gundog, the Miniature Poodle still retains the instinct to work. Though many of today's dogs are far from steady enough to work satisfactorily, the fact that they can easily be trained to take part in obedience tests proves that they still retain the ability. The rise of the Miniature Poodle was meteoric in the years after World War II, and by the 1960s he was one of the most popular dogs in the world. As a result of this puppies fetched very high prices and a great deal of indiscriminate breeding took place, puppies being produced with little regard for quality, and the standard of the breed declined. Fortunately, the position improved as the numbers decreased, and most of today's stock is most carefully bred.

It is impossible to lose sight of the fact that the Poodle was once a performing dog, and indeed still is in many parts of the world, particularly in France, where he is used extensively on the stage. He can be taught to perform a multitude of tricks, many of them apparently completely outside the natural habits of a dog. The result is that he is a very popular pet, having the sort of personality that endears him to elderly people particularly, as he has certain childlike qualities. He is still, however, a sporty little dog, needing a good deal of exercise, and in spite of his somewhat quaint appearance when clipped he is more of the sportsman than the dandy.

Few breeds of dog have had the success in the show ring of the Poodle, and particularly the Miniature Poodle. In Britain where variety classes are a feature at shows, the scene is frequently stolen by the beautifully presented Miniature Poodle. He appears to enjoy showing off, seems to appreciate the fact that he is being admired, and usually storms round the ring behaving like a dog twice his size. Coat preparation is vital, and nothing looks worse than a badly prepared Miniature Poodle. This preparation starts weeks before the show and continues right up until the dog enters the ring, and often beyond.

He is a lovely dog to own, or, as some suggest, to be owned by. He has to be accepted as part of the household, does not take kindly to being shut in kennels, and probably only reveals his true and complete personality when he is kept as a member of the family. Under these conditions he becomes a complete extrovert, and gains such confidence that he is clearly of the opinion that he is quite indispensable. He makes a good guard, as all the Poodles do, being very noisy at the approach of any intruder on to what he believes is his property, and putting up a show of fierceness remarkable in so small a dog.

in the 'Puppy' clip with the coat long. The face, throat, feet and base of the tail are shaved. The entire shaven foot is visible. There is a pompon on the end of the tail. In order to give a neat appearance, a slight shaping of the coat is permissible; however, a Poodle in 'Puppy' clip that is excessively scissored shall be dismissed. Dogs one year old or older must be shown in either the 'English Saddle' clip or the 'Continental' clip. In the 'English Saddle' clip the face, throat, feet, forelegs and base of the tail are shaved, leaving puffs on the forelegs and a pompon on the end of the tail. The hindquarters are covered with a short blanket of hair except for a curved shaved area on each flank and two shaved bands on each hind leg. The entire shaven foot and a portion of the shaven leg above the puff are visible. The rest of the body is left in full coat but may be shaped in order to insure over-all balance. In the 'Continental' clip the face, throat, feet and base of the tail are shaved. The hindquarters are shaved with pompons (optional) on the hips. The legs are shaved, leaving bracelets on the hind legs and puffs on the forelegs. There is a pompon on the end of the tail. The entire shaven foot and portion of the shaven foreleg above the puff are visible. The rest of the body is left in full coat but may be shaped in order to insure over-all balance. In all clips the hair of the topknot may be held in place by an elastic band or barrette. The hair is only of sufficient length to present a smooth outline.

Color

The coat is an even and solid color at the skin. In blues, grays, silvers, browns, cafe-au-laits, apricots, and creams the coat may show varying shades of the same color. This is frequently present in the somewhat darker feathering of the ears and in the tipping of the ruff. While clear colors are definitely preferred, such natural variation in the shading of the coat is not to be considered a fault. Brown and cafe-au-lait Poodles have liver-colored noses, eye rims and lips, dark toenails and dark amber eyes. Black, blue, gray, silver, cream and white Poodles have black noses, eye rims and lips, black or self-colored toenails and very dark eyes. In the apricots while the foregoing coloring is preferred, liver-colored noses, eye rims and lips, and amber eyes are permitted but are not desirable.

Parti-colored dogs shall be disqualified. The coat of a parti-colored dog is not an even solid color at the skin but is of two or more colors.

Gait

A straightforward trot with light springy action and strong hindquarter drive. Head and tail carried high. Forelegs and hind legs move parallel turning neither in nor out. Sound movement is essential.

SIZE

Standard: the Standard Poodle is over 15 inches at the highest point of the shoulders. Any Poodle which is 15 inches or less in height shall be disqualified from competition as a Standard Poodle.

Miniature: the Miniature Poodle is 15 inches or under at the highest point of the shoulders, with a minimum

Intelligent, elegant looking.

height in excess of 10 inches. Any Poodle which is over 15 inches or 10 inches or less at the highest point of the shoulders shall be disqualified from competition as a Miniature Poodle.

Toy: the Toy Poodle is 10 inches or under at the highest point of the shoulders. Any Poodle which is more than 10 inches at the highest point of the shoulders shall be disqualified from competition as a Toy Poodle.

MAJOR FAULTS

Eyes: round in appearance, protruding, large or very light. *Jaws:* undershot, overshot or wry mouth. *Feet:* flat or spread. *Tail:* set low, curled or carried over the back. *Hindquarters:* cowhocks. *Temperament:* shyness or sharpness.

DISQUALIFICATIONS

Clip: a dog in any type of clip other than those listed under 'Coat' shall be disqualified.
Parti-colors: the coat of a parti-colored dog is not an even solid color at the skin but is of two or more colors. Parti-colored dogs shall be disqualified.
Size: a dog over or under the height limits specified under 'Size' shall be disqualified.

VALUE OF POINTS

General appearance, temperament, carriage and condition (30). Head, expression, ears, eyes, and teeth (20). Body, neck, legs, feet and tail (20). Gait (20). Coat, color and texture (10).

Approved by the AKC 10 November 1970

KC(GB) VARIATION TO STANDARD

Head: long and fine with a slight peak at back. Skull not broad and with a moderate stop. *Coat:* it is strongly recommended that traditional lion clip be adhered to. (Known as the English Saddle Clip in the US). All three varieties are given separate championship status by the KC(GB). *Standard*—15 inches and over. *Miniature*—11 to 15 inches. *Toy*—under 11 inches.

SCHIPPERKE

NATIONAL GROUPING		
	Name	Number
AKC	Non-Sporting Dogs	VI
KC(GB)	Utility	4
FCI	Companion Dogs	9

It is virtually impossible to write an extended history of the Schipperke, as the background to the breed is so simple. With some of the characteristics of the Spitz group, insofar as the body shape is typical and the ears are erect, he is so much smaller than the remainder of the Group that he does not seem to belong. This diminutive size does not appear to have been a matter of miniaturisation, as he has always been small. He was in use for many years as a barge dog in Belgium and Holland, living on board, guarding property and probably from time to time encouraging the lazier towing horses to move a little faster. His name comes from a corruption of the word for little skipper, and his somewhat pompous attitude as he made his way around the canals, probably led to the description.

He first appeared in Britain and the United States at about the same time, probably because the Queen of the Belgians purchased a specimen in 1888 and three came into Britain in about the same year. They immediately became popular, and it was this popularity which may have persuaded the dog people of Belgium that their little dog had a future, and led to the formation of a breed club there which devised the standard of the breed. The first burst of enthusiasm soon lost its impetus, and after a time during the 1920s when he was seen at almost every show, numbers declined and the Schipperke is now one of the minority breeds in Britain, though in some countries, and particularly in South Africa he is still very popular.

Although described in the early days as a tailless dog, this was not entirely correct, as some were born with them. An early meeting of representatives of the Schipperke Club with a sub-committee of the Kennel Club in Britain agreed that the tail if present, could be docked, and modern examples always appear in the ring without a tail. The question of colour was a much-vexed one too, as by tradition the Schipperke had always been looked upon as a black dog though from time to time specimens were born which were of other colours. By the early 1900s it had been agreed that other colours could be permitted so long as they were whole colours, and some very attractive dogs have now been bred in cream and fawn.

He is an extremely active little dog, always on the alert, very much the guard dog, and very suspicious of strangers. One of the characteristics of the breed is his extreme inquisitiveness, and encouraged, he makes a very effective vermin dog, though there is little of the Terrier in his make-up. He is a sturdy, strong-bodied little dog, wiry and very strong for his size. His coat is virtually waterproof, and the distinctive mane is a feature of the breed. He is not a heavy-boned dog, his tendency being towards activity and agility rather than towards the miniature cart-horse type.

As a show dog he has always had adherents, as he is something of the natural showman that all the Spitz types are. He stands rock-steady in the ring, ignores other dogs and pays attention only to his handler. His size makes transport a simple matter as he can be boxed in comfort and will travel long distances in the back of a car without being a nuisance to passengers. Preparation is no problem, simply a matter of the glow of good health, the removal of a few white hairs which are almost always present in whole coloured dogs, and some nail trimming.

The Schipperke does not make friends easily with strangers and is something of a one-man dog, defending his territory and his family with a fearlessness that belies his lack of size. At the same time he is affectionate with children and has few vices, and his generations of association with families make him one of the best of house dogs.

OFFICIAL STANDARD

Appearance and general characteristics
Excellent and faithful little watchdog, suspicious of strangers. Active, agile, indefatigable, continually occupied with what is going on around him, careful of things that are given him to guard, very kind with children, knows the ways of the household; always curious to know what is going on behind closed doors or about any object that has been moved, betraying his impressions by his sharp bark and upstanding ruff, seeking the company of horses, a hunter of moles and other vermin; can be used to hunt, a good rabbit dog.

Color
Solid black.

Head
Foxlike, fairly wide, narrowing at the eyes, seen in profile slightly rounded, tapering muzzle not too elongated nor too blunt, not too much stop. *Nose:* small and black. *Eyes:* dark brown, small, oval rather than round, neither sunken nor prominent. *Expression:* should have a questioning expression: sharp and lively, not mean or wild. *Ears:* very erect, small, triangular, placed high, strong enough not to be capable of being lowered except in line with the body. *Teeth:* meeting evenly. A tight scissors bite is acceptable.

Head and skull: foxy, skull fairly broad.

Neck
Strong and full, slightly arched, rather short.

Shoulders
Muscular and sloping.

Chest
Broad and deep in brisket.

Body
Short, thick-set and cobby. Broad behind the shoulders, seeming higher in front because of ruff. Back strong, short, straight and level or slightly sloping down toward rump. Ribs well sprung. *Loins:* muscular and well drawn

Body: chest deep, back short, loins powerful.

up from the brisket but not to such an extent as to cause a weak and leggy appearance of the hindquarters. *Forelegs:* straight under body, with bone in proportion, but not coarse. *Hindquarters:* somewhat lighter than the foreparts, but muscular, powerful, with rump well rounded, tail docked to no more than 1 inch in length. *Feet:* small, round and tight (not splayed), nails straight, strong and short.

Coat
Abundant and slightly harsh to the touch, short on the ears and on the front of legs and on the hocks, fairly short on the body, but longer around neck beginning back of the ears, and forming a ruff and a cape; a jabot extending down between the front legs, also longer on rear where it forms a culotte, the points turning inward. Undercoat dense and short on body, very dense around neck making ruff stand out. Culotte should be as long as the ruff.

Weight
Up to 18 pounds.

FAULTS
Light eyes; large round prominent eyes; ears too long or too rounded; narrow head and elongated muzzle; too blunt muzzle; domed skull; smooth short coat with short ruff and culotte; lack of undercoat; curly or silky coat; body coat more than three inches long; slightly overshot or undershot; swayback; Bull Terrier shaped head; straight hocks. Straight stifles and shoulders; cowhocks; feet turning in or out; legs not straight when viewed from front. Lack of distinction between length of coat, ruff and culotte.

DISQUALIFICATIONS
Any color other than solid black. Drop or semi-erect ears. Badly overshot or undershot.

Approved by the AKC 12 May 1959

KC(GB) VARIATION TO STANDARD
Weight: 12 to 16 pounds. *Faults:* drop or semi-erect ears. Dudley noses in coloured variety.

TIBETAN SPANIEL

NATIONAL GROUPING		
	Name	Number
AKC	—	–
KC(GB)	Utility	4
FCI	Companion Dogs	9

This delightful little dog was one of the first of the Tibetan breeds to arrive in the West. It had been used for centuries by the monks of Tibet as a Prayer Dog being trained to turn the prayer wheels by means of a small treadmill. Each turn of the wheel which contained rolled up parchment scrolls is believed to give the prayers the necessary push to bring them nearer to heaven. He was highly prized and was often given as a special gift to the Emperors of China, where it is claimed that he could easily have been one of the ancestors of the Pekingese. Certainly when the breed first arrived in Britain in around 1900 they were considered to resemble the Pekingese very closely and it was only the efforts of early breeders to eliminate the short-nosed specimens that resulted in the present clear distinction. Even so to this day they are often mistaken for Pekingese by the general public.

As with the other small dogs from the Far East, the origins are obscured by time and lack of information, and it is probable that in the very early days of its development, when trade between China and Tibet was a feature of the daily life of those countries, the breeds were very interbred. It is only in recent years—recent that is in the context of development of a breed of dog—that the distinct separation has taken place. Even since the introduction of the Tibetan Spaniel to the Western World it has been hinted that some outcrossing took place to improve certain characteristics of the breed, and from time to time even now certain specimens have too much of the Pekingese look about them. Early Chinese drawings depict dogs that look

different yet have a good deal in common, and allowing for a certain amount of artistic licence, could be any one of three or four different breeds in their early stages of development.

He is a very positive little dog, outgoing temperamentally and strong physically, and though his size—or rather lack of it—persuades some people that he is really a Toy dog, his manner and his conviction that he is as big as a Great Dane places him, at least in his own opinion, very firmly outside that Group. Since his early days as a show dog he has made tremendous strides, very enthusiastic and efficient clubs have watched carefully over the progress of the breed, and the Tibetan Breeds Association included the breed among its interests from 1934 onwards. He is still invading new countries and the first specimens have just arrived in South Africa. The number of registrations have climbed steadily and although one writer stated as recently as 1948 that in his opinion it was the Tibetan Terrier that was most likely to succeed as a fancy, the Tibetan Spaniel has completely outstripped its rival and now numbers something like three times that of the Terrier.

He is an enjoyable little dog to show, as when part of a team he travels happily boxed up with the rest, waits his turn patiently, watching his kennelmates and all that is going on around him with keen interest, and then when it is his turn, enjoys the experience to the full. There are few problems with preparation, some removal of excess soft woolly coat being all that is needed.

The temperament of this little dog is delightful. He is full of fun, enjoys life to the full, and is every bit as happy racing through the woods after a rabbit, real or imaginary, as he is sitting on a silk cushion on the most comfortable chair in the house. It is perhaps in the latter environment that his sense of superiority shows most clearly. There is little doubt that he is subconsciously aware that his ancestors were part of the ritual of the monasteries.

OFFICIAL STANDARD

Characteristics
Gay and assertive, highly intelligent, aloof with strangers.

General appearance
Should be small, active and alert. The outline should give a well balanced appearance, slightly longer in body than height at withers.

Head and skull
Small in proportion to body and proudly carried giving an impression of quality. Masculine in dogs but free from coarseness. Skull slightly domed, moderate width and length. Stop slight, but defined. Medium length of muzzle, blunt with cushioning, free from wrinkle. The chin should show some depth and width. Nose black preferred.

Head and skull: skull slightly domed, stop slight but defined.

Eyes
Dark brown in colour, oval in shape, bright and expressive, of medium size set fairly well apart but forward looking giving an ape-like expression. Eye rims black.

Ears
Medium size, pendant, well feathered in the adult and set fairly high. They may have a slight lift from the skull, but should not fly. Large heavy low set ears are not typical.

Mouth
Ideally slightly undershot, the upper incisors fitting neatly inside and touching the lower incisors. Teeth should be evenly placed and the lower jaw wide between the canine tusks. Full dentition desired. A level mouth is permissible providing there is sufficient width and depth of chin to preserve the blunt appearance of muzzle. Teeth must not show when mouth is closed.

Neck
Moderately short, strong and well set on. Covered with a mane or 'shawl' of longer hair which is more pronounced in dogs than bitches.

Forequarters
The bones of the forelegs slightly bowed but firm at shoulder. Moderate bone. Shoulder well placed.

Body
Slightly longer from point of shoulder to root of tail than the height at withers, well ribbed with good depth, level back.

Hindquarters
Well made and strong, hocks well let down and straight when viewed from behind. Stifle well developed, showing moderate angulation.

Feet
Harefooted, small and neat with feathering between toes often extending beyond the feet. White markings allowed.

Gait
Quick moving, straight, free, positive.

Tail
Set high, richly plumed and carried in a gay curl over the back when moving. Should not be penalised for dropping tail when standing.

Coat
Double coat, silky in texture, smooth on face and front of legs, of moderate length on body, but lying rather flat. Ears and back of forelegs nicely feathered, tail and buttocks well furnished with longer hair. Should not be overcoated and bitches tend to carry less coat and mane than dogs.

Colour
All colours and mixture of colours allowed.

Weight and size
Weight 9 to 15 pounds being ideal. Height about 10 inches.

Faults
Large full eyes, broad flat muzzle, very domed or flat wide skull, accentuated stop, pointed weak or wrinkled muzzle, overshot mouth, long plain down face without stop, very bowed or loose front, straight stifle, cow hocks, nervousness, cat feet, coarseness of type, mean expression, liver or putty coloured pigmentation, light eyes, protruding tongue.

Note
Male animals should have two apparently normal testicles fully descended into the scrotum.

AKC VARIATION TO STANDARD
This dog is not granted championship status by the AKC. The above standards are those of the KC(GB).

TIBETAN TERRIER

NATIONAL GROUPING		
	Name	Number
AKC	Non-Sporting Dogs	VI
KC(GB)	Utility	4
FCI	Companion Dogs	9

Whilst the other Tibetan breeds were largely the urban dogs of their native country, the Tibetan Terrier was the rural one. Whilst the others spent most of their time being cossetted to a certain extent in and around the villages and monasteries, this dog was working for his living as a herding dog and as a guard. He is supposed to have been the original 'holy dog' of Tibet, and when that country was subjected to paying tribute in the form of goods and treasures to China, this little dog was the one that guarded the caravans. It was in fact the awe in which the dog was held rather than his size or ferocity that prevented the caravans from being raided, as he is a small and fairly quiet animal.

The confusion that affected all the small Tibetan breeds in the early days of their introduction to the Western World, was seen in the Tibetan Terrier as much as in the others. An early photograph of what is described as the best Lhasa Terrier imported into Britain around 1900, shows a dog that is very little like the Tibetan Terrier that we know today, and was clearly more of an Apso or a Shih Tzu than the breed that it purported to be. Fortunately for the breed Mrs. Greig and her daughter, Dr. A. R. H. Greig took the breed to their hearts, and almost all the dogs being shown today have, way back in their pedigrees the names 'Ladkok' or 'Lamleh'. Dr. Greig showed her dogs fearlessly all over Britain, and survived to see the breed well-established as a show dog, and would have been very happy to see the great wins of recent speci-

mens. The first Best in Show All-breeds was recorded at an Open show in Britain in August 1963 when the author was the judge.

Registrations have quadrupled since that time, and the rings at most important shows are well-filled when the breed is scheduled. He is a strong dog of considerable activity, and at first sight conveys the impression of a miniature Old English Sheepdog as he is square, has considerable hair over his eyes, and his tail curved well over his back gives the same appearance as the upward lift over the hindquarters of the Bobtail. He is the only dog with a standard that states that he should stand well down on his pads. This was a point that Dr. Greig always felt was very important, maintaining that the large flat feet gave the breed the ability to perform well over very rough mountainous country which by tradition it had to do, and over which small terrier type feet would prove a handicap.

The breed now appears in the show rings in a great variety of colours, which makes a parade of them a very attractive spectacle. The only colour that is barred in the standard is chocolate. In recent years a great deal of attention has been paid to grooming and presentation as was necessary to compete an equal terms with such glamorous animals as Afghan Hounds and Poodles, and a Tibetan Terrier shown now in the rough, as once was the practice, would look very out of place. The coat still retains its strong weatherproof qualities, however, and though the breed has been glamorised, it has lost none of its original character.

He is as delightful temperamentally as all the other Tibetan breeds, and though somewhat sharper than the others as would be expected of a dog that needs to live up to the title of Terrier, he has no vice, and is an amenable and affectionate companion. He makes a good house dog, is small enough to fit into a modern home and modern transport, and makes a very good guard.

OFFICIAL STANDARD

Skull and head
Skull of medium length, not broad or coarse, narrowing slightly from ear to eye, not domed but not absolutely flat between the ears. The malar bones are curved, but should not be overdeveloped so as to bulge. There should be a marked stop in front of the eyes, but this must not be exaggerated. The head should be well furnished with long hair, falling forward over the eyes. The lower jaw should carry a small but not over-exaggerated amount of beard. Jaws between the canines should form a distinct curve. The length from the eye to tip of nose should be equal to that from eye to base of skull, not broad or massive.

Nose
Black. Any color other than black shall disqualify.

Eyes
Large, dark, neither prominent nor sunken; should be set fairly wide apart. Eyelids dark.

Ears
Pendant, not too close to the head, 'V' shaped, not too large; heavily feathered.

Mouth
Level by preference but a slight undershot should not be penalized.

Forequarters
Legs straight, heavily furnished.

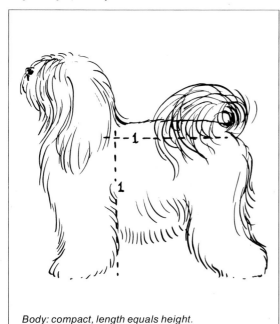

Body: compact, length equals height.

Body
Compact and powerful. Length from point of shoulder to root of tail equal to height at withers. Well ribbed up. Loin slightly arched.

Hindquarters
Heavily furnished, hocks well let down.

Feet
The feet should be large, round, and heavily furnished with hair between the toes and pads. The dog should stand well down on its pads.

Tail
Medium length, set on fairly high and carried in a gay curl over the back. Very well feathered. There is often a kink near the tip.

Coat
Double-coated. The undercoat fine wool, the top coat profuse, fine, but not silky or woolly; long; either straight or waved.

Color
Any color or colors including white.

Weight and size
Average weight 22 to 23 pounds, but may be 18 to 30 pounds. Height from 14 to 16 inches.

Faults: poor coat; mouth very undershot or overshot; a weak snipy foreface.

DISQUALIFICATION
Nose any color other than black.

Approved by the AKC 12 June 1973

PART TWO:
Breeds recognised by the Fédération Cynologique Internationale (FCI)

In every country in the world in which the breeding of pedigree dogs, their preservation, exhibition, and their welfare, are considered important, there is an organisation to govern canine affairs. In some countries where the world of the pedigree dog is under the control of separate states there is more than one organisation. There is, however, one international body whose sphere of influence is wider than any one country. It began in Europe and has spread to many other countries including South America, and is known to everyone connected with dogs, as the *FCI*.

Most countries, and the United States of America and Britain are typical examples, have their show dogs organised on a two-tier basis. The upper tier is composed of those breeds which are considered important enough and which are numerically strong enough within that country to warrant the award of champion status, and a second tier which is made up of those breeds which are recognised, but because they are at the moment few in number, are shown but not granted champion status.

The *Féderation Cynologique Internationale*, with its headquarters in Belgium, recognises a great many more breeds than any individual country and awards champion status to them even though they are often very few in number, or indeed have not been shown outside their own country. Thirty-one countries are federated within the *FCI*, and all the breeds recognised by those countries are accepted by the *FCI*, and are eligible for the award of the title International Champion. A further fifteen countries are associated with the *FCI* though not federated, and in those countries the title of International Champion is not available. The *FCI* recognises nearly three hundred breeds of dogs, which is something like twice as many as any other individual country.

The standards of the breeds from each member country are submitted to the *FCI* council for approval, and only when this has been given is the breed then admitted to the *FCI* list. The standards are then kept on register by the *FCI* and may only be altered by the country of origin in consultation with the council. The *FCI* then publishes the standard in several languages. In addition to this rather detailed involvement in the canine affairs of many of the countries of the world, the *FCI* holds an annual international congress in a different centre each year at which many important topics are discussed concerning canine affairs internationally. There has been a move in recent years towards the acceptance of standardised forms of breed standards throughout the world, and the *FCI* has been one of the principal advocates of this. At present standards, even of the same breed, vary from country to country though in the main these variations are minor ones only, and in many cases countries adopt the standards of the country of origin.

In the subsequent chapters of this book the breeds which are recognised by the FCI (other than those granted championship status by the United States of America and Britain) are described, and are arranged in *FCI* groups which are ten in number.

FCI GROUP 1:

Herding dogs, guard dogs, sheepdogs and dogs that are useful

Australian Cattle Dog

In the early days the Australian settlers were faced with the problem of controlling vast herds of cattle and flocks of sheep grazing over huge tracts of land, and the answer lay in using dogs. They started with a dog known as the Smithfield the origin of which is itself obscure, but it was a large and somewhat cumbersome beast that was too noisy and disturbed the herds. A man named Timmins of New South Wales, and a drover by trade, crossed the Smithfield with the native Dingo around 1830 and produced a litter of red, bob-tailed pups which were known as Timmins Biters. In 1840 a landowner named Hall imported a couple of smooth blue merle Collies from Scotland and these, in turn crossed with the Dingo and the Timmins dogs, produced what were known as Hall Heelers.

From that time onwards there were continued efforts to improve the breed, and the present-day blue and red mottled Cattle Dogs are the result. A standard was drawn up in 1897 for what was then

known as the Australian Heeler and the name has since been changed to Australian Cattle Dog, the standard being updated and adopted in 1963. He is a fantastic working dog with tremendous powers of endurance and courage. He will work in the exhausting conditions of the Australian climate all day, and rarely flags. As a show dog he has proved an immediate success, as he is most impressive for his appearance of sheer strength and absolute doggedness. He still works, however, and that side of his character has not been neglected.

Australian Kelpie

In 1870 a grazier named Allen imported into Australia a pair of so-called Fox Collies from Scotland, they

were black and tan with prick ears. They mated on board ship and whelped a litter, one red, and the others black and tan. They proved to be good workers, fast and quiet and capable of working over wide areas. At about the same time a smooth black and tan bitch named 'Kelpie' appeared in New South Wales and was mated to one of the original litter and produced a famous winning dog also named 'Kelpie'. She was the foundation of the breed as all her progeny turned out to be good workers with sheep, and more or less in her honour they were all called Kelpies.

The breed was first exhibited at Melbourne in 1908. From the same line there descended a black strain which for a while were known as Barbs, a name which has now died out, but which still sometimes crops up when sheep men are talking about a black Kelpie, which they will refer to as a 'Barb'. They were shown for a time as a separate breed, but now appear together. The Kelpie is one of the cleverest and certainly one of the hardest working sheep dogs in the world, being famed for the use of what is called 'eye', which is the almost mesmeric manner in which they control the sheep by just gazing at them. They are fine show dogs, being easily prepared, almost always in good muscular condition, and obedient in the ring. Their guarding qualities have become a legend.

Beauceron (Berger de Beauce)

There are a number of French sheep-herding dogs probably developed from common stock, somewhat similar in size and type, but varying in some details from one area to another, and having been bred true to type in those areas. The Beauceron, comes oddly enough from the region of Brie rather than from Beauce, and was probably given the name to differentiate him from the Briard which originated in more or less the same area. He looks something like a short-coated German Shepherd Dog though with rather more elegance. He was bred originally to herd the large flocks of sheep which at one time were common in France, and he is still a farmer's dog as well as one recognised as a specific breed by the FCI.

Like many of the other breeds which were used for guarding the flocks as well as working them, he has a certain aggressiveness allied to his tractability, which,

when controlled gives him a positive quality. He is highly intelligent, easily trained and very obedient. He is not seen a great deal outside his own country, and has not achieved the popularity of his countryman the Briard.

Belgian Shepherd Dog (Laekenois)

This is the one variety of Belgian Shepherd Dog which so far has not become known outside his own country as have the Groenendael, the Malinois and the Tervuren. His origins are in a small area of Belgium near Antwerp where one of his duties was to guard the fields in which linen was put out to bleach in the rain and sun, known in Britain as 'bleachcrofts'. Like the

others of the family he is every bit as much a guard dog as a herder, and it is in this capacity that in recent years he has found a place in society. The breed appears in small numbers at the larger dog shows in Belgium and other European countries.

He is very like the Groenendael in some ways, but is fawn in colour with some black on the muzzle, and his coat is quite different. In the main it is rough and shaggy with a certain hardness of texture, long on the body and shorter on the head. He is an intelligent dog, easily trained and a very good guard and companion. He stands about twenty-five inches high at the shoulder with long neck and the general outline of an active working dog.

Berger Polonais de Vallée (Owczarek Nizinny)

This is an old breed of herding dog native to Poland, to which country it was probably taken by the Huns. In order to work on the terrain of its native country, a smaller and more active dog than some of the large Mastiff type guard and herding mountain dogs of other countries was needed, and yet because of the climate a dog with a protective coat was essential. For this reason the Nizinny was developed. He is a medium-sized dog up to twenty inches at the shoulder and is well-proportioned and strongly built. He is resistant to bad weather conditions, is lively and intelligent and capable of feats of memory.

He is somewhat like a small Old English Sheepdog with his long shaggy coat which covers his eyes, and his lack of tail, which is either rudimentary or docked soon after birth. His coat is long, very thick and shaggy, and though with a tendency to wave, does not cord as does that of some of the other European sheepdogs. All colours and markings are acceptable, but he is usually self-coloured or marked with very large patches of colour on white. He is very intelligent, alert and friendly, an excellent guard and has an inbuilt tendency to herd.

Cane da Pastore Bergamasco

This breed is one of the herding dogs traditionally used in the mountains of Northern Italy. His appearance suggests some connection with the Briard, but at the same time he also has something of the look of the herding dogs of Eastern Europe. He is a large dog, up to twenty-five inches at the shoulder with a short back, and is flexible and agile rather than heavy and slow. He is descended from the herding dogs described at least two thousand years ago, and until such time as modern transport methods opened up the mountainous districts he was probably bred fairly true to type.

He has a long, somewhat wavy coat, which when brushed out has something of the quality of that of the Briard, but with a thick undercoat which allows a certain amount of cording on the sides of the body

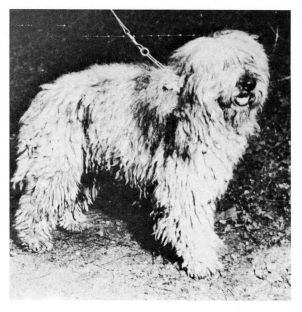

similar to that of the Puli. He is a trustworthy and courageous dog that makes a very good guard.

Catalan Sheepdog (Gos d'Atura)

Though dogs of definite types have existed in Spain for centuries, and the use of dogs for sport, particularly hunting, has been popular in that country for a considerable length of time, the organisation of dog shows and the recognition of the importance of native breeds has been a comparatively recent development.

This little herding dog with his great character and individual appearance originated in Catalonia, and probably descended from some of the original mastiff types indigenous to the Iberian peninsula. He has now spread throughout Spain and has to a certain extent lost his original name being known as the Catalan Sheepdog. He was one of the dogs brought into military service during the Spanish Civil War, and there earned

himself a reputation as a guard and messenger.

He exists in two forms, the short-haired, which has gained favour as a companion and show dog, and the long-haired which is the one more commonly used as a sheep dog. He has great courage and tenacity and will drive the most stubborn and obstinate cattle single-handed, appearing to understand what is required with the minimum of instruction. He seems to have developed the same sort of 'eye' as the Australian herding dogs and can hold a herd merely by imposing his will upon them. He is a small dog, somewhat smaller than a Springer Spaniel and very strong and flexible. His size and temperament suit him perfectly to life as a companion or house dog.

Croatian Sheepdog (Kraski and Hrvatski Ovčar)

This is one of the oldest established and individual working dogs of Yugoslavia originating in Croatia, where it was used as a herder in mountainous country, but has now become much more widespread. He exists in two sizes, listed by the FCI as the Kraski Ovčar and the Hrvatski Ovčar, the Kraski standing up to twenty-four inches at the shoulder whilst the Hrvatski stands only up to twenty. The breed was one of the old indigenous breeds peculiar to a limited part of Yugoslavia and was used as a herding dog and watch dog.

He is a long-coated dog with erect, or sometimes pendant ears, and is reminiscent of the working sheepdog seen in many other parts of the world. He is strongly built with a wide chest and a strong loin with some curve towards the hindquarters and a bushy tail which he carries low but curls up when he becomes excited. His coat is quite long, three or four inches, soft and strong with a slight wave or curl on the body and shorter on the head and legs. He has considerable feathering and the long hair over the shoulders gives the effect of a soft mane. He is normally black in colour with some grey hairs, and white on the legs, feet and chest is not objected to. He is extremely hardy, virtually weatherproof, and is a fast and active worker.

Dutch Sheepdog

This very old sheep-herding dog from the Netherlands exists in three coat forms. The smooth and the rough, which look something like the Belgian sheep-dogs, and the long-coated which has something of the appearance of the long-coated shepherd dogs of the southern European countries. The breed had been in existence for a good many years before the breeders got together in the late 19th century to form a club to look after the interests of the breed and ensure its survival.

Most of these dogs come from the area of North Brabant but are very much working dogs and until recently were not seen very frequently at shows. This is, however, changing and the breed is being exhibited.

The wire-haired variety is particularly attractive looking rather like a small Bouvier des Flandres, and has a very pleasing temperament. He is extremely hardy, very faithful and attached to places and people and can be trained very easily not only as a herder, but in what is called 'man work', as a police dog, for example. He is in fact capable of doing most of the work that a German Shepherd Dog does, but unfortunately the rapid growth of popularity of that breed has ousted the Dutch from public favour.

Iceland Dog

This small dog, only some twelve to sixteen inches at the shoulder has existed for centuries in Iceland, though he is rarely seen outside his own country. He is rather like a small Elkhound, though with less coat, and of mixed as well as plain colours. In the early years of this century he was known in Britain, several specimens being imported and recognised by the Kennel

Club, but he did not gain favour. Unlike so many of the other Spitz types he does not have a very highly developed hunting instinct, but he is an excellent herder and guard dog, being used for driving both sheep and horses. A standard for the breed was accepted by the Danish authorities in 1898.

Lapinporokoira (Lapponian Vallhund)

This breed was produced in southern Finland by crossing the existing Lapphund, which is better known and seen more frequently in other countries, with such breeds as the German Shepherd Dog and the Collie. A dog was needed that had the highly developed herding instincts of the Collie and the German Shepherd Dog allied to the hardiness and guarding instincts of the indigenous Lappland Spitz.

He is a medium-sized dog with many of the Spitz characteristics, but somewhat longer in the back than most of the family. He has an alert-looking head with

tapering muzzle and erect ears, though tipped ears are permitted. He is strongly made with muscular hindquarters and loin and tail curled over his back, though this may droop at times. He has a double coat, the outer coat long, hard and glossy, and fitting fairly close to the body, and a soft woolly undercoat as protection against the weather which in his country can be fairly rigorous. His colour varies from white with darker shading, through brown to black, with some white markings. He is an extremely hardy dog and will work in all weathers, with tremendous stamina and willingness. His hunting instincts have virtually disappeared which has improved his performance as a herder. He was approved as a separate breed by the FCI in 1946 but is not seen outside Scandinavia.

Lapphund (Lapinkoira, Swedish Lapp Spitz)

This is one of the oldest Spitz breeds in Scandinavia, having been used originally as a herding dog for reindeer in Lappland. It was more or less adopted by

Sweden and a standard was written for the breed by the Svenska Kennelklubben. The breed has been taken up by the Swedish army who are breeding these dogs with the intention of using them as guard dogs, a task which they undoubtedly have often doubled with their herding activities from very early days. The breed is very much the Spitz type with the pricked ears, the dense coat and the curled tail of all the members of the group, though in the case of this breed the coat is rather longer and more glossy than some of the others.

He is a fairly small dog standing around eighteen inches which is about the size of a Whippet, but he is a strong square dog with roomy body and very stout, not too long legs. He is not a hunter, which makes him

more valuable as a guard and herder than some of the other Scandinavian Spitz breeds which would sooner chase game than stay at home. He is, however, courageous in protecting his home, intelligent and faithful, and makes a very affectionate companion. He is as yet not recognised by the American or British Kennel Clubs, but enjoys a reasonable vogue in Scandinavian countries where he is regularly seen among the native breeds at the important shows.

Maremma Sheepdog (Cane da Pastore Maremano-Abruzzese)

This very ancient breed of herding dog probably descended from the old white working dogs of the Magyars. Large white dogs of this type have been described in manuscripts and paintings for several hundreds of years. The area of Maremma from which the breed takes its name is the stretch of open rolling country down the coast as far as Rome and has been a grazing as well as a hunting area for centuries. The flocks were moved from plains to mountains as the weather dictated, and whilst some of the dogs stayed behind to guard the farms, others went with the flocks to act both as herders and guards. The result was that

for a time two forms of the breed were recognised by the farmers, and it was not until well into the present century that it was finally agreed that they were one and the same dog.

He is a large dog with a certain independence of spirit, and being naturally very intelligent he almost scorns training. He becomes attached to people, but only in the capacity of a guard and not as a house-pet, retaining his freedom of spirit and not allowing himself to fawn on anyone. He is a wonderful guard of anything, flocks, property and children, and can be very fierce when these responsibilities are challenged by animal or human. He first appeared in the show ring in Britain before the end of the 19th century, but disappeared again, to be seen once more from the early 1930s, when a number were introduced and have steadily increased. Upwards of a hundred are now registered with the Kennel Club in Britain and they are seen regularly at some of the major shows, where classes for the breed are staged.

Mudi

This breed originated in Hungary as a natural development of the ancient sheep-herding dogs of that country. It was unknown at the end of the 19th century, the

role of the herder and guard being filled by the Komondor and the Puli which are much older breeds. There was, however, a need for an active dog with the build that would allow it to work over difficult territory, and without the coat problems of the corded breeds. He is a taller and heavier animal than the Puli, and is very much a guard as well as a herder, being capable of tackling large predators and is even used for the hunting of wild boar. He is a very useful animal around the farm or household, being a keen and watchful guard and an enthusiastic rodent hunter.

His coat, like Jacob's, is of many colours. Although black predominates, white or parti-colours are permitted and one colour, the so called 'pepita' which is an evenly distributed mixture of colours, is a peculiarity of the breed. He has a wavy and shiny coat which is shorter and smoother on the muzzle and legs, and which needs considerably less attention than that of the corded Hungarian dogs. He is docile and affectionate and very easily trained, but is brave in the face of danger. He is virtually unknown outside his own country.

Berger Picard

The Picard is one of the oldest of the French sheepdogs, originating in the North of France and believed

to have been brought to that country in the time of the Celts, in the 9th century. He is not only one of the most ancient breeds, but one of the biggest, standing as high as twenty-six inches at the shoulder, which makes him the size of a German Shepherd Dog. He is a medium-coated dog with a strong rough outer coat and a thick weatherproof undercoat.

He is very intelligent, easily trained, and affectionate, particularly with children. He is not known outside his own country, and not frequently seen inside France, as he remains very much a working dog and has not

been taken up by the show fraternity. He is a somewhat pugnacious guard and makes a very good housedog.

Polish Tatra Herddog (Owczarek Podhalanski)

This large white herding dog is one of the ancient breeds of Poland, where it has been used by the mountain people as a sheepdog and guard against the attacks of wolves and bears. The interest in these fine dogs began during the middle of the 19th century

when mountain exploration became popular, and between the two World Wars a standard for the breed was approved. During the Second World War the breed almost ceased to exist and breeders needed to make a fresh start. The FCI recognised the breed in 1967 and its future is now secure. Dog shows incorporating trials for sheep herding dogs are regularly staged.

He is a large dog, standing up to twenty-six inches at the shoulder, and is very strong and muscular with it, with a massive body and well-boned legs. One of the characteristics of the breed is that the dogs are shorter in the body than the bitches. His general appearance is that of the Kuvasz, or the Maremma. His coat is close and fairly short on the head, and longer and dense on the body with a distinct feather on the tail and some feathering on the hindquarters. He is almost always white, though at times this is a creamy white rather than pure white. He is a fine worker, intelligent and alert and an excellent guard. His temperament is steady and friendly though reserved with strangers.

Portuguese Sheepdog (Cão da Serra de Aires)

This is one of the old-established breeds of Portuguese Sheepdogs, descending from the early indigenous types. He is unrelated to the other sheepdog, the

Laboreiro, and is different in appearance, being considerably smaller, up to nineteen inches at the shoulder only, and having a long coat. He looks rather like a smallish Bearded Collie though with less coat and minus the beard, and it could be that the origins were the same, as small hairy herding dogs have been native to the whole of Europe, and as far east as Hungary, for centuries.

He is a deep-chested dog with strong limbs and a long, smooth or rather wavy coat which is waterproof but without the tendency to cord as in some of the Hungarian dogs. His colours vary between fawn and black through the greys and chestnut and though a few white marks are permitted, parti-coloured or white dogs are not. He is tough and reliable, quick and a very good worker with sheep. He is not normally seen outside his own country.

Pyrenean Sheepdog (Berger des Pyrénées)

The rapid rise to popularity throughout the world of the other herding dog from the Pyrenees, the Pyrenean Mountain Dog, has overshadowed this very attractive working dog, due partly to the fact that there is some variation in type from one district to another. There are in fact at least five recognisable varieties, different from one another mostly in colour, though most of them look like small Collies or Bearded Collies, and a short-coated version also exists. His general description is of a handy-sized, up to twenty inches high, fairly heavily coated dog of the working type, strong and flexible, very active and intelligent.

He is very much the working dog, tough, hardy and lively. He is rather reserved and shy of strangers, but easily trained and an eager worker. He is rarely seen outside his own country, and is unlikely to become a popular show dog.

Pumi

This little terrier type dog evolved in Hungary during the 17th and 18th centuries, by the crossing of the ancient Puli with the drovers' dogs from France and Germany that entered the country. From the Puli came its tendency to a long and somewhat unruly coat and from the visiting droving dogs came the semi-erect ears and volatile temperament. The crossing with different breeds to produce a keen droving dog went on for a considerable number of years, and it was not until the beginning of this century that he finally became accepted as a fixed breed of dog with a recognised pedigree. It is remarkable in the light of this that a dog evolved so like the Tibetan Terrier in many ways.

He is an extremely lively dog, quite incapable of remaining quiet except when at rest. He has developed into a very forceful and audacious drover of cattle, and in spite of his lack of size, as he is only about the same size as a Fox Terrier, he is quite capable of driving the most obstinate of cattle. He has good scenting powers too, and is a very good exterminator of pests and even of predators. He is a strongly built square little dog with strong jaws. The favourite colours are silver, dove grey or slate, though other colours frequently occur. Mixed colours and marking are not allowed. He makes a good house pet, though he is a noisy and volatile guard.

Schapendoes

This is the smaller very ancient breed of sheep-herding dog from the Netherlands. His origins are obscure, but his appearance is very like that of many of the other European working dogs, being shaggy-coated like the Bearded Collie and with the proportions of the Puli. He was at his peak as a breed in Holland when there were large flocks of sheep in that country, but with the changes that have taken place in the agricultural economy of the country, he has declined in numbers. Fortunately there is now a club which preserves an interest in the breed, and he is seen from time to time at shows.

He is a very lively, gay and active dog, courageous and yet friendly, has a very good intellect, is easily trained to perform most of the duties of a herder and guard. He makes a good housedog, and there is little doubt that with his coat, which repays attention, he could easily become a fairly popular show dog.

Swedish Vallhund (Väsgötaspets)

This is the most recent dog to invade the British show scene from Sweden, recent importations already making their mark and winning regularly, largely owing to the efforts of one British judge who brought in the first ones. The breed is an ancient one, though their close resemblance to the Corgi results in a constant discussion as to which is ancestor and which descendant. It has been suggested that the Vikings either took Corgis back with them, or brought the Väsgötaspets over with them, and this discussion will probably never end. In Sweden he has been known for a great number of years as a cattle-herding dog as well as a vermin catcher and a watch dog, but although he had been bred true for a considerable length of time, he was so much a part of the agricultural scene that few people paid him much attention.

It was only in the beginning of the present century that one or two breeders began to make serious attempts to popularise the breed as a show dog, and in 1943 it

was recognised by the Svenska Kennelklubben. Throughout the world, those accustomed to the bright colours of the Pembroke Corgis will find it strange at first that there is another breed of the same type but of considerably duller colours, as this little dog is often grey, brownish yellow or brindle. He has, however, a most attractive temperament, being very intelligent, friendly and affectionate with those whom he knows, but is a sharp and active guard when needed.

Yugoslavian Herder (Jugoslovenski Ovčarski Pas Sarplaninas)

This large grey herding dog has been in existence in Yugoslavia for centuries in the mountainous areas of the South East, and has recently become fairly widespread throughout the whole of the country. The breed was registered with the FCI in 1939 as the Ilirski Ovčar, but approaches from the Yugoslavian Kennel Authority in 1957 resulted in the name being changed to Chein De Berger Yougoslave de Charplanina. The origins of the breed are obscure, but there is little doubt that it shared ancestry with the other large Mastiff type breeds common in Southern Europe. Though the breed is essentially a herding dog, it doubles up as a flock guard, protecting domesticated animals against the attacks of wolves and other predators.

He is a big dog, at least twenty-five inches at the shoulder, and this is considered so important that smaller specimens are not allowed to be used for breeding. His head, ears and front of his legs are covered with short dense hair whilst the rest of the body carries a long fairly hard coat which is longer still on the neck and shoulders and on the feathering. He is uniformly coloured in various shades of grey with some white on the chest and legs. He has a good steady temperament, is easily trained, and whilst a staunch guard, is well-mannered towards people.

FCI GROUP 2:
Guard dogs, dogs that are useful and hauling dogs

Aidi (Chien de l'Atlas)

The flocks of Morocco are not comparable in size or behaviour with those of Europe, with the result that sheep-herding as it is practised elsewhere is unknown in that country. The herds consist of goats and native sheep which are more domesticated than those of other countries, and more accustomed to being moved about quietly by young shepherds. Sheepdogs as such are not needed, but at the same time there is a need for flock-guarding dogs, and it is for this purpose that the Aidi has been developed. He is a big strong dog standing up to twenty-five inches at the shoulder and very solidly built, but quick and active.

He is a mountain dog with a protective coat which is very thick and rough, and he is quite capable of protecting his charges against the possible attack of wild beasts. He can be almost any colour from fawn, through red to black and white. In some parts of the country it is the habit to crop the ears and dock the tail of the working dogs though the practice is not a desirable one. He is not known outside his own country.

Ainu (Hokkaido-Ken)

This is one of the older Japanese native breeds, having been bred by the Ainu on the island of Hokkaido for centuries as a hunting and watch dog. He is essentially one of the Spitz type, but nearer to the Scandinavian Spitz dogs than the other Japanese breeds such as the Akita, being rather more stockily built. He is a small dog, around sixteen inches at the shoulder, and has the prick ears and curled tail of the family. His coat is fairly short and dense with a thick undercoat. In colour he is red, white or black, and can be grizzle or black and tan. He is an excellent guard, having plenty of courage for a small dog, is intelligent and easily trained, and is lively and active.

Appenzell Mountain Dog (Appenzeller Sennenhund)

This is one of the four breeds known as the Swiss mountain dogs, the most generally popular of which is the Bernese. This is one of the smaller members of the family and in its native country one of the more popular. Starting off as a farmer's dog and a worker, it is now gaining popularity among townspeople. He is one of a number of ancient working dogs used as a herder and drover of cattle in and around the canton of Appenzell, and is still used for those purposes. Like many of the working dogs of the world, he suffered the effects of mechanisation on farming, and became reduced in numbers during the second half of the 19th century. Fortunately, around the turn of the century a breed club was formed to protect his interests, and since that time preservation has been assured.

The first example of the breed was imported into Britain in the 1930s, but he has never gained the popularity of his larger cousin the Bernese. He is fairly well known in Germany and some other European countries where he is seen from time to time at shows. He is a kindly and friendly dog, very attached to his owners, and an excellent guard. He is intelligent and easily trained, and small enough to be suitable as a house dog.

Austrian Pinscher (Oesterreichische Kurzhaarige Pinscher)

This is one of the old indigenous breeds of Austria which has existed as a working terrier-type for a considerable length of time without becoming known elsewhere. He is a smallish dog, only up to about twenty inches at the shoulder and often much smaller. He is short-haired, with small neat ears which may be pendant, but are preferred when tight and 'button'. In build he is very much like the other Pinschers, having a short deep body with good spring of rib and standing on shortish, strong straight legs and neat terrier feet.

His coat is short and strong rather like that of the Smooth Fox Terrier, and he is usually fawn, red, black or brown with white markings on cheeks, neck and legs. His tail, which is high-set is either docked, or left on, when it is short and curled. He is a lively little dog, a typical terrier and is seen at shows only in his own country.

Canaan Dog

This breed is accepted as almost the national breed of Israel though its origins are obscure. It has been suggested that it was developed by selective breeding from the Pariah dogs of the Middle East, though these vary considerably in type, and it is generally accepted that they themselves are descended from various domesticated types which have become feral. The Pariah dog varies according to the area in which it lives, and indiscriminate breeding eventually results in a similarity of character which is sometimes mistaken for type. The Canaan Dog is a fixed type, looking

rather like a heavy-weight Smooth Collie, but with a curled tail.

He is a medium-sized dog standing up to twenty-four inches at the shoulder, has a short deep strong body and prick ears. He is sturdy and well-boned and has neat round feet. His coat is medium length straight and hard, and though longer coat is permissible it is not considered desirable. He is parti-coloured in white, tan or black. He is a good watch-dog, being alert and courageous, is intelligent and easily trained and becomes attached to one family. Only recently is he being seen outside Israel, when shown in small numbers in other countries.

Dogue de Bordeaux

This French breed like many other ancient breeds is said to have descended from the Molossus of Rome, and he certainly appears the very essence of the ancient Mastiff type, being very heavily built and with a massive head. The influence of the forces of England on the

Bordeaux area centuries ago probably resulted in the mixing of Mastiff blood from the other side of the Channel, as these dogs frequently travelled with the armies and courts of England. It is possible too that there was an influx of blood from Spain in the form of the ancient Alaunt. They were at one time used for fighting bears and wolves in Southern France and later became the butchers' dogs of the Bordeaux area.

He is rarely seen outside European countries as he is not recognised by either the American or the British Kennel Clubs, and is unlikely to become popular in either of these countries where in his particular field the Mastiff is already established. He is a real heavy-weight, being massively built and standing up to twenty-six inches at the shoulder. He was used both to fight and guard, and these elements seem to have remained to some extent in his character, as he is very independent and can be somewhat short-tempered. One of the popular colours is a very distinctive pale

golden yellow which certainly gives him the appeal of looking very different from the ordinary run of dogs.

Entlebuch Mountain Dog (Entlebucher Sennenhund)

This dog is one of the closely related group which originated in Switzerland as drovers and general purpose dogs. Centuries ago there was a good deal of

trading carried on through the mountain passes of Switzerland, and travellers took with them not only goods, but their cattle and flocks. They also needed largely to live off the land, so that a dog which could drive cattle, guard them at night, and do a little hunting when needed, was invaluable. This dog is the medium-sized member of the family and is shorter in the leg and lower to the ground than the others.

The various breeds were established mainly by the efforts of a Mr Heim who, working with the Swiss Kennel Club established the differences and the standards for each variety during the early years of the present century. The Entlebuch was the latest of the family to gain any popularity, but is now well established and in no danger of becoming extinct. He is rarely seen outside his native country and has not yet appeared in British and American show rings as has his larger cousin the Bernese Mountain Dog. He is a very quiet dog, completely trustworthy and easily trained, and makes an excellent watchdog and guard.

Eskimo Dog

The Eskimo Dog is one of the most famous working dogs in the world, but unfortunately has suffered from confusion as the result of other, smaller and less popular sledge dogs being credited with his name. The Eskimo Dog proper originated in Greenland and is the most generally useful of the hauling dogs of all the Arctic countries. He is very much part of the heritage of northern Canada, and known to the Inuit people as the 'Kingmik', he was the only breed of domestic animal known to the early Arctic peoples. He hauled sledges, carried packs and was used for hunting. He guarded the camps and property, was the plaything of the children when he was young, and whilst working hard he lived frugally and made little inroad into the limited resources of the people with whom he lived.

These dogs were first encountered by explorers who immediately found them the only answer to their

transport problems. He was first written about one hundred and fifty years ago and was accepted as a separate breed by the Canadian Kennel Club before the turn of the century. Although mechanisation has restricted the absolute need for these magnificent dogs, they are still used competitively. There was at one time danger that the breed would disappear, but recent efforts to ensure its continuance are proving entirely successful. He is a large strong dog of rugged build with a weatherproof coat, and the more attractively marked ones that are appearing in the show rings of the world are gaining the breed new friends all the time. He is a very intelligent and good-natured dog.

Estrela Mountain Dog (Cão Serra da Estrela)

When the first specimens of this breed entered Britain they were called Portuguese Mountain Dogs, but it was decided that to avoid possible confusion later they should be named after the location from which they originated and the name Estrela Mountain Dog was adopted. The breed is certainly an ancient one, though the conditions under which it evolved were not conducive to the keeping of accurate records, and it is impossible to be certain about which breeds were its ancestors. He is large enough and heavy enough to be considered one of the Mastiff family and is more of a watchdog and guard than he is a herder of stock, so it is more than likely that he has a close relationship with the Spanish Mastiffs and even the similar dogs of France and Italy.

He is very much a farmer's dog, and in a country and

at a time when predators were common, he acted as a day and night guard for property and stock and was strong enough and staunch enough to tackle anything. During this century he has grown in stature as a show dog and is seen regularly at major shows both in his own and in neighbouring countries. His coat varies from the short and rather harsh to the long and wavy. He is an extremely strong dog that can be difficult to handle unless he is trained to obey from an early age.

Eurasier

This is one of the newest breeds of dog to be evolved as the result of the whims and efforts of virtually one man, within the past two or three decades. In the 1950s a gentleman named Wipfel, living in Bergstrasse in the German town of Weinheim decided to create, or perhaps recreate would be more accurate, a dog which resembled the ancient German Wolfspitz. He used the Chow Chow and the Samoyed type of sledge dog of Asia which he originally called the Wolf-Chow. The development of the breed reached its peak in the 1960s, and it was recognised by the German Kennel Club and the FCI and the name Eurasier was adopted in deference to its origins in Europe and Asia.

The Eurasier Club was formed, to look after the interests of the breed, and the development has been carefully controlled by a small number of enthusiasts centred on Weinheim, the town of its origin. He is a medium-sized Spitz type of dog with a stand-off coat short enough to allow the body contours to remain visible, and varies in colour from red in various shades, wolf-grey to black or black with well-defined markings.

Fila Brasileiro (Cão de Fila)

During the conquest of Central America in the 16th century the Portuguese and the Spaniards took with them some of the native Mastiff type dogs indigenous to the Iberian peninsula at that time. A good example of the type of dog is seen in Velasquez's painting of the 'Family of Philip IV' in the middle of the following century. These mastiffs, crossed with the indigenous dogs of the natives produced the Filo Brasileiro. They are still used as guards and drovers on the large estates, and are also used as hunters.

He is a big dog, standing twenty-seven inches at the shoulder and has many of the characteristics of his Spanish and Portuguese ancestors, a large and heavy head, pendant ears, heavy bone and a short dense coat. He varies in colour, being any solid colour except white, and is often brindle. He is extremely strong with long stout bone and great musculation. He is a forceful dog with a strong personality, tremendous courage, (as he has to have in a country where there are still large wild cats) and very active. He is friendly with those whom he knows, but is suspicious of strangers which makes him a valuable watch-dog. He is unknown outside his own country.

Great Swiss Mountain Dog (Grosser Schweizer Sennenhund)

This is the larger, smooth-coated version of the much better known Bernese Mountain Dog, standing a couple of inches higher at the shoulder, but in many ways similar. He was almost certainly descended from the Alpine Mastiff and was known at least two hundred years ago.

He was once popular throughout Switzerland, where he was used for hauling small carts, and after almost disappearing at the beginning of this century, has since that time made a steady comeback. At one time he was lumped together, under the one general name of Sennenhunden, with the other similar dogs, but it was realised that there were in fact at least four different types, and these have now been sorted out and established.

In colour he is really what we now call a tricolour, being mainly black, with red markings on cheeks, over the eyes and on the legs, with white flashes on chest, tail and feet. He is a large strongly made dog with a very short dense and shiny coat which is virtually weatherproof. He is easily trained and most obedient, being used from time to time as a rescue dog. He is a natural watchdog, very faithful to the family that he serves, and is well known for his attachment to children. He was recognised in 1908 by the Swiss Kennel Club, but is not seen outside his own country to any extent, and remains unrecognised by either the American or the British Kennel Clubs.

Greenland Dog (Grønlandshund)

Considerable difference of opinion still exists concerning the names of the arctic sledge-hauling dogs. The Alaskan Malamute and the Siberian Husky have been successfully separated in name, classification and recognition by the major canine authorities, but there is still some confusion concerning the Grønlandshund and the Eskimo Dog, some authorities still dividing the two. The FCI however recognises the Grønlandshund, whilst the Canadian Kennel Club recognise the Eskimo Dog. He is big, up to twenty-five inches at the shoulder and strong and well-built with it, his stand-off coat making him look even more massive.

As a sledge-hauling dog he played his part in the exploration of the Arctic regions, and is still used competitively in sledge races. The Eskimoes used dogs for work for centuries before mechanisation took over, and in addition to the actual hauling that he did, the Greenland dog proved to be an excellent guard, and watchdog. His coat is long and hard, and he has a thick soft undercoat which affords him protection from the weather. He is extremely hardy, capable of existing on the minimum of sustenance and out of doors in the worst weather. His colour is not considered to be an important feature, but white, grey, black and a little

tan in almost any proportions are acceptable. He is reserved with strangers but becomes attached to those with whom he lives.

Hovawart

This is a very old breed of guard dog, known as long ago as the 15th century as the Hofewart, or 'warden of the estate and farmyard'. He went out of fashion, and apparently disappeared during the 19th century, but was revived by a group of German breeders in the early part of this century. They took several breeds of local guard dogs, from the Harz and Black Forest regions, and by careful selective breeding reproduced a dog which closely resembled the original. Their work and patience was rewarded when the German Kennel Club recognised the breed in 1936 with the name Hovawart.

He is a big dog of roughly the same size and with

427

something of the general appearance of the Flat-Coated Retriever. He is usually black, black and gold, or deep gold in colour, and whilst used principally as a guard dog as his ancestors were, he has a good nose and can be used for hunting. He is very intelligent, and is easily trained. He makes a particularly good dog to have as a companion either in or around the house as he becomes attached to the members of a family and can be quite affectionate.

Japanese Middle Size Dog (Sanshu)

This is another of the Spitz type dogs from Japan, and is a smaller version of the Akita, only up to twenty-one inches at the shoulder. He has the same reputation for complete faithfulness as his larger relative, and stories of his attachment to families are legion. It is interesting that a dog which looks very like him is seen

frequently on the waterfront at Hong Kong, being bred there and being used as a guard dog among the boats and wharves. There he tends to be called a smooth Chow Chow, but he is far too tall to qualify as a member of that breed.

He has the typical prick ears and curled over tail of the Spitz race and is a beautifully constructed dog with a strong body and stout straight limbs. He has an intelligent-looking head with a calm and even kindly expression, a medium-to-short coat with dense soft warm undercoat. His colour varies considerably from almost white to black through brown, grey and tan. He could well be the same dog that was imported into Europe at the turn of this century and was known as the Phu Quoc Dog having been brought from Cambodia.

Landseer

In most countries the Newfoundland is accepted in all its normal colours including black-and-white, which is known as the Landseer variety because the artist of that name in 1838 painted a work entitled 'A distinguished member of the Humane Society'. As his subject he took a black-and-white Newfoundland, a colour which was particularly popular at the end of the 18th century, and became even more so as a result of the painting. History of the breed shows that in the 18th century Newfoundlands were varicoloured, some being liver and white.

European countries, and those others which have associated themselves with the FCI, have decided, however, that the black-and-white variety is a separate breed, and it is this which is known as the Landseer. At present those specimens which are exhibited appear to differ from the Newfoundland as he is known in other countries by being rather less heavily built and without the same strength of bone as the majority of the breed. Beauty of marking is very important, and the head should be black with a white muzzle and blaze and the body and legs should be white with large patches of black on the saddle and quarters with some other smaller spots on both body and legs permitted but not desirable. He is an affectionate and very intelligent guard, kindly with those whom he knows, and supreme in water, where he is almost certainly the strongest swimmer of all the canine race.

Leonberger

It is amusing that in 1907 the Leonberger was dismissed as a cross between a Newfoundland and a St Bernard when it was first introduced into Britain. One writer of the time stating that its merits were only recognised by the enterprising gentleman who had presented it as a 'new breed'. In fact it was such a cross, but that is how many of today's recognised breeds made their start. Herr Essig of Leonberg returned a couple of St Bernards to the hospice of St Bernard to help replace the stock lost when an avalanche and an outbreak of distemper decimated the kennels there. Before returning the bitch she was mated to a Newfoundland and the resultant litter were the first Leonbergers.

By 1907 a few were being shown in the Chiens de Montagne classes in Paris, and since that time the breed has made rapid progress. He is now shown regularly at most European championship shows, and at the 1976 Winners Show in Amsterdam there were fifty-six on exhibition. He is one of those breeds developed for no particular purpose except to look attractive, and Herr Essig in taking as his model the heraldic lions on the coat of arms of Leonberg was ambitious, but successful, as he produced a very handsome dog that is rapidly becoming admired in many countries outside his own. Leonberg is still inordinately proud of the dog that carries the name of the city. At one time he is said to have been used for herding flocks of sheep and cattle, but that side of his character, even if it ever existed has not been developed. He is an intelligent strong dog that makes an excellent watch-

dog, and could well be one of the popular large show-dogs of the future.

Neapolitan Mastiff (Mastino Napoletano)

This very ancient breed of dog, peculiar to Southern Italy, is, like many ancient breeds, a descendant of the Roman Mollossus. He has been bred with considerable care and in small numbers in his home country and the type frequently seen today varies very little from the dogs seen in ancient paintings and manuscripts. He is a somewhat terrifying dog as he is very large and heavy with a particularly forbidding head, an appearance which is increased by the fact that in Italy the ears are frequently so closely cropped as almost to disappear. In fact his appearance is deceptive, as, with one or two exceptions, in which the hereditary fierceness of the original fighting dog comes uppermost, the dog is a comparatively gentle and kindly creature.

He is a guard dog almost without peer, as not only is his appearance alone usually sufficient to deter intruders, he is also immensely strong and will attack,

usually only on command. There is a small number of breeders in Italy who keep the breed alive, but outside his home country he is rarely seen. One or two specimens have recently been imported into Britain but have not yet appeared in the show rings there. In Italy he is regularly exhibited, and has a staunch following.

Norbottenspets

This small Spitz dog from the North of Sweden is typical of the family, having prick ears, curly tail and the thick stand-off coat of the race. His origins are obscure, though there is a family resemblance to the even smaller Lundehund from the same area. It is

probable that he descended from the German Spitz and the Arctic Spitz types, but that can only be conjecture. He almost became extinct in the early part of the present century before the value of native breeds was fully appreciated, and the breed has increased since its recognition in 1960.

He is a medium sized dog, not more than fifteen inches at the shoulder with a short strong body and pointed muzzle. His coat is hard and stand-off with a soft dense undercoat, and he is white with black, red or cream patches. Like most of the Spitz breeds he was undoubtedly bred formerly as a hunting dog, but has now become more of a housedog and watchdog. He is cheerful, active and lively, and becomes attached to a family. He is rarely seen outside his own country.

Pinscher

This is a very old established German breed of terrier-type dog developed centuries ago and probably descending from a medieval hunting dog. As a basic type he has been produced along very specific lines and is now a medium-sized short-coated dog shown only in the one size in his home country, but he was used to produce other breeds including the Doberman and the Miniature Pinscher both of which are popular throughout the world. He was officially recognised in 1879, and during the present century his interests have been looked after by the parent Pinscher-Schnauzer Club.

He is a sporting dog, a great vermin killer and a first-class watchdog. His coat is smooth and glossy and although he appears in a variety of colours, black and tan or brown seem to be the most popular. He makes a very good show dog as he is responsive and obedient, and is seen regularly at the larger shows in Europe. So far he has made no headway in other countries though a few have been imported into Britain from time to time. He makes a friendly and lively companion, and is an adventurous hunter.

Perro de Presa Mallorquin

This is a very ancient breed of Mastiff type dog from the Azores. He is a hunting dog capable of dealing with big game, and is descended from the Spanish Mastiffs and the Portuguese dogs carried by early explorers. In appearance he is rather like the Alano, but his leonine look is increased by the fact that at one time his ears were trimmed short and round like those of the big cats. The Perro de Presa is a big, heavy dog, some twenty-three inches at the shoulder; weighing up to one hundred and fifty pounds, and has a massive head and strong bone. His coat is very short and smooth and he is almost invariably a shade of yellow in colour with some white or darker patches. Little has been heard of him lately and numbers could well be on the decline. He is unknown outside his own country.

Portuguese Cattle Dog (Cão de Castro Laboreiro)

This very old breed of Portuguese dog was used exclusively for the herding of cattle. Principally found in the north of the country, in those parts where sheep were less plentiful, a smaller more active but even harder type of dog was needed. The area being fairly isolated for many years, the breed was fixed by using local dogs with the right temperament and physical properties rather than importing other breeds. Although as a breed he was always fairly popular, he was not seen at shows until comparatively recently. A standard has now been drawn up, however, and the breed has been considerably encouraged by the efforts of the Portuguese canine authorities.

He is a particularly tough and well-built dog as his height to weight ratio of twenty-three inches and sixty-five pounds would suggest. (Oddly enough this suggests a dog of the build of the Australian Cattle Dog.) He is a well-muscled dog but very flexible and quick-moving despite this. He has a short coat with a certain harshness on the body which renders it waterproof, and he is usually grey to dark grey with a darker mask. He is not a particularly friendly dog, is suspicious of strangers and makes a very good guard and watch dog.

Portuguese Shepherd Dog (Cão Rafeiro do Alentejo)

This very ancient Portuguese herding dog is one of the largest and most imposing of the country. He comes originally from the Alentejo province south of Lisbon and is descended from the early Mastiff types. Years of responsibility for guarding flocks and herds at night have given him the habit of being particularly alert at that time, when he becomes a keen guard and even aggressive. He is a strong dog that can weigh over one hundred pounds when adult and has a short and dense coat with weather-resisting properties. His appearance is striking as he is strongly marked with large white patches on a dark coloured or black ground.

He is not normally a show dog, and is rarely seen outside Portugal.

Portuguese Water Dog (Cão de Agua)

This is an ancient breed that has always been associated with the fishermen of the coasts of Portugal. His ancestry is obviously closely linked with the old

Water Dog of other European countries, the dog that produced the modern poodle and even the Irish Water Spaniel. Over the centuries he has accompanied the fishermen on their boats and has been used to retrieve equipment washed overboard and even to recover lost fish. On shore they were used to guard boards and nets. Numbers shrank around the beginning of this century and the breed was virtually restricted to the Algarve coast, but efforts in the period between the two World Wars encouraged a revival of interest in the breed, and examples were seen at the major Portuguese shows.

He is a very fit and hardy dog that will spend a considerable time in the water under trying conditions. His coat is usually clipped, but not in the extreme fashion of some other breeds, and he retains his essential working dog appearance. He is strongly built, very active, and an excellent guard. In temperament he is somewhat forceful, and though he has over the centuries been the companion of fishermen, it is unlikely that he will ever become very popular as a house pet. The earliest known animal portrait in English art, that of Sir John Harington's dog Bungy, painted nearly four hundred years ago, is undoubtedly a portrait of a Portuguese Water Dog.

Pyrenean Mastiff (Mastin de los Pirineos)

This breed, along with the Pyrenean Mountain Dog, descended from the ancient Tibetan Mastiff, and thus probably originally from the even more ancient Molossus. The Mountain Dog and the Mastiff were almost certainly originally one breed. Selective breeding for two types, however, produced some differences which were due to some extent to the the dog evolved in Spain and France. A large guard dog which would tackle the fierce predators of the mountain regions was needed, and yet at the same time a general purpose animal that could do some herding and act as a companion was preferred. The Pyrenean Mastiff filled all these roles, and though there is some divergence of type, he exists as a separate breed.

He is a large dog, up to thirty-two inches at the shoulder, massive, though not quite as large as the Pyrenean Mountain Dog, and is white with grey, dark grey or yellow patches on the head, and some are allowed on the body. He is intelligent, obedient and friendly with people he knows.

Spanish Mastiff (Mastin Español)

This is another descendant of the ancient Mastiffs of Europe which probably themselves descended from the Roman Molossus. Unlike the Italian version which has a very short coat, this breed has a dense medium length coat and greater refinement of head. He was used originally as a guard dog, but has a well-developed hunting instinct and will tackle large game. He is also

strong enough to be used as a military guard and all-purpose dog. He was at one time known as the Spanish Bulldog though he is much longer in the leg than the British Bulldog.

Several examples of the breed were imported into Britain in the late 18th century and were exhibited. Like the Italian Mastiff he had his ears cropped and was used for fighting, but was certainly one of the heavyweights of the arena, as a good specimen even in hard fighting condition could weigh as much as a hundred pounds. He is now not seen outside his own country and it is likely that he has degenerated from the original type by crossing with other breeds, particularly the British Bulldog. He is courageous, obedient and responsive to training, and is a great protector of both stock and property.

Tibetan Mastiff

This large guard dog, originating in the foothills of the Himalayas and Central Asia is considered by many not to be a true Mastiff. He is fairly large and has a head which resembles some of the other so-called Mastiffs, but there the likeness ends, as he is not particularly heavy for his size, nor does he have the typical heavy jowl and furrowed brows of the other members of the family. In their native country they were used as guards, to herd sheep and cattle, and as hunting dogs from time to time, but they have little of the native ferocity of the other Mastiffs. He is, however, a big handsome dog with a well-developed sense of belonging to the tribe or family, and whilst he will not normally persist in an attack, he puts on a brave show that deters any intruder.

He was well-known in Britain in the latter part of the 19th century, two good examples of the breed having been imported by King George IV. At the end of the century a dozen were imported into Britain by a

Mr Jamrach but were said to be not typical of the breed. Though they were shown, and one specimen, said to be an exceedingly good one of which photographs exist was shown at the Crystal Palace in 1906, they never became popular, and are now unknown in Britain. He is said to be a docile dog, and though attached to his owner, very suspicious of strangers.

Tosa Fighting Dog

This large Mastiff type dog was bred from the middle of the 19th century onwards when dog-fighting was popular in Japan. The biggest and toughest breeds were used to produce him, including the Mastiff, the Bull Terrier and the Bulldog, which were crossed with the original fighting dogs bred in the area of Kochi. It is interesting that the smaller tougher type of Mastiff was spread over so large an area, appearing in countries as far apart as South America and Tibet,

and it is probably from the ancient Molossus that the Tibetan and thus the Japanese Mastiff type was evolved.

The Tosa is described as deep, broad and massive with a short, hard and dense coat. His ears are small and his eyes hard and tiny as befits a fighting dog. He has some loose protective skin around the neck and throat, and is said to be gentle but full of courage. In the light of this it is noteworthy that some specimens recently exhibited were shown on double leads and with two handlers.

FCI GROUP 3:
The working Terriers

Cesky Terrier

This short-legged terrier from the Bohemia district of what is now Czechoslovakia is a fairly modern creation. The sportsmen of the country, looking for a dog that would go to ground and yet would be strong enough and sufficiently courageous to tackle fox and badger underground, crossed the Scottish and Sealyham Terriers. The German Jagdterriers which were available to them were longer in the leg, and though they are great hunting Terriers they were not quite suitable for the purpose.

He is a dog that is slightly larger than either of his fashionable ancestors, being up to fourteen inches at the shoulder and with a build that is commensurate with that height. He has a long punishing head, strong body and short well-boned legs. His coat is not so hard as that of many of the Terriers, and is wavy with some sheen. He is an excellent working terrier, and is becoming increasingly popular as a show dog, appearing at many of the large shows in Europe. He has most of the Terrier qualities and characteristics and makes an excellent companion and house dog.

German Hunting Terrier (Deutscher Jagdterrier)

This breed did not exist at the beginning of this century, and is another product of man looking for certain qualities in existing breeds, failing to find what he wanted and setting out to produce it by selective breeding and crossing. The sportsmen of Bavaria

wanted a tough working terrier that combined the keen qualities of the Fox Terriers with the strength of some of the old original Terriers which they thought had largely disappeared as the result of breeding for show purposes. Starting with a Welsh Terrier bitch, and a dog who descended from the old-fashioned Broken Coated Terrier of Britain, they crossed with both wire and smooth Fox Terriers and produced a very tough fierce hunting dog.

He is capable of going to ground to most game, with a very good nose and tremendous terrier pluck, and yet a dog that can double-up as a Retriever if need be.

He is a small dog, very slightly larger than a Wire Fox Terrier but considerably more robust with a strong body, well-muscled legs and larger feet than would be acceptable in a Fox Terrier. He has moreover a wide head, very strong jaws and a dense smooth close-lying coat. In colour he is a dark dog, black, brown or dark grey with tan markings, and is reminiscent of a stout rather tough-looking Welsh Terrier. He is somewhat fierce, and distrustful of strangers.

Japanese Terrier (Nihon Terrier)

This is a small Terrier, bred in Japan by crossing the indigenous dogs of Japan with Short-haired Terriers from other countries, probably the Smooth Fox Terrier from Britain or the small Toy Terrier, the Amertoy of America. He is a small dog, up to fifteen inches at the shoulder though often smaller, has a smooth coat and prick ears and is white with black or tan markings. He is not known outside Japan.

FCI GROUP 4:

Dachshunds. See Hound Group pages 93-160

FCI GROUP 5:

Hounds for hunting large game

Billy

The larger pack Hounds of France were used for hunting the stag which was restricted to the forests of the north and the west as well as to some areas of Burgundy. A good many packs existed, and the hunt was carried out with a considerable amount of ritual with a method and a language of its own. The Billy was bred by M. G. Hublot du Rivault and takes its name from his home in Poitou. It is a descendant of some of the ancient pack Hounds of the time of Louis XII, which were themselves probably evolved from the old Southern Hound and the St Hubert Hound.

In later years many of the Hounds of France were crossed with Foxhounds from Britain to produce

what were known as Batards, and combined the best qualities of the French forest Hounds and those more accustomed to working open country. The Billy is distinguished as many of the French Hounds are by his colour. He is large, up to twenty-six inches at the shoulder and is white with markings of lemon or orange. He is used for hunting deer and wild boar and is a scent hunting dog that hunts in packs.

Black Elkhound

This variety of Elkhound was once much more widespread than it now is, being fairly well-known in Norway and seen from time to time in other parts of Scandinavia. It is now less popular, however, and has been superseded by the more common grey Elkhound which has been accepted by all other countries as the more typical variety. The Black Elkhound is a smaller and lighter dog and carries considerably less coat than the more generally accepted form, and completes the trio of Elkhound types known to Scandinavia which includes the much larger Jämthund. He is a Spitz dog with all the characteristics of that

group, the pricked ears, curled tail and dense coat, and has the independence of temperament common to most of them.

He is now rarely seen at shows in his own country, and never outside it, and can really be numbered among those breeds in danger of extinction. He is a hunting dog used for big game in the difficult terrain and intense cold of his native country. He is tough, active and hardy, somewhat quarrelsome with other dogs but friendly enough with people. He makes an excellent guard as he has the distinctive bell-like voice of his near relatives and has considerable territorial conscientiousness. His colour is a jet black, but white marks on feet and chest are permitted.

Chambray

This is another of the very large family of French hunting dogs. When one remembers that in France at the turn of the century, hunting was so popular a pastime that there were three hundred packs of Hounds, and remembering too that the average hunt has a very partisan attitude towards its own Hounds, it is hardly surprising that so many different breeds of Hounds have survived in that country. He is a large dog, and somewhat less elegant than many of the other French breeds. He stands up to twenty-eight inches high at the shoulder and is wide, muscular and deep-chested.

He has a short fine close coat, and a white and yellow parti-coloured pattern which tends to disappear with age until he is almost white. Occasionally he has ticking of yellow and even grey, and has the yellow spot on the skull which is seen in many other breeds of dogs. He is not fast, but has great stamina and is a steady but enthusiastic hunter.

Chien de Trait (Matin Belge)

As the name implies, this was a Mastiff type dog, used as a leash dog or *limier*, which suggests that it was in fact comparable with the St Hubert Hound or Bloodhound. He is reputed in fact to be the darker coloured form of the French large Hound which can still be seen as an influence on the British Bloodhound. It is probable that the French and the Belgian versions of this dog were indistinguishable, but in any case the Société Royale Saint Hubert of Belgium state that the breed is now extinct.

Chien Français Blanc et Noir

The number of packs of Hounds in France was severely reduced when the great estates and courts ceased to occupy the important position that they once did in the social life of the country. For centuries the descendants of the old Celtic Hound had flourished, and it is unlikely that any other country could have competed at one time with France in the number and

variety of dogs for the chase which were once kept. Many of the varieties have disappeared, but the Blanc et Noir has survived.

He is one of the bigger Hounds standing up to nearly thirty inches at the shoulder and is a survivor of the Hounds that hunted deer, wild boar and other big game when these existed in large numbers in the country. When the authorities held a survey in 1957 of the hounds still extant in France, sufficient numbers of the Blanc et Noir remained for them to be listed as a separate breed. He is a big handsome well-balanced hound with long neck and straight bone. His coat is short and hard and his colour is important. His ground colour is white, and he has large black patches including a mantle and some ticking. Some red is permitted on the legs, and pale russet marks on head, under the ears and root of tail are allowed. He is friendly, and a forceful hunter. He is not known outside France.

Chien Français Tricolore

This is yet another of the large hunting dogs of France, a breed that survived the disturbances of the end of the

18th century. He is another of the tall Hounds used for the hunting of big game and especially deer. Prior to the reign of Louis XV these Hounds were bred true to type, but after that time the English Foxhound cross was used to improve speed with the result that many of the older breeds disappeared. When the French authorities carried out a survey of the remaining Hounds however in 1957, there were enough of these Hounds for acceptance as a separate breed.

He is a tall Hound, up to twenty-eight inches at the shoulder, and has the soft, long slightly folded ears that denote his ancient lineage. He has a long neck and very elegant body and limbs, and soft expression denoting intelligence and friendliness. His coat is short, fine and smooth, and he is always tricolour, black, white and tan. He is an excellent hunter with great stamina, is intelligent and friendly and though he has many friends in his own country, is hardly known outside it.

Grahund

A number of the stockily built Spitz type dogs were developed in Scandinavia as hunting dogs to cope with the extreme conditions of snow and ice in Norway and Sweden. The more commonly known of these are of course the Elkhound and in Sweden the Jämthund, but these are both larger dogs. The Grahund, which translates simply enough into grey dog, is one of the varieties that has evolved from the original Scandinavian dogs as a separate breed. He first appeared and was recognised by the Svenska Kennelklubben under the name 'Nørsk Elghund' in 1891, which makes the present use of the name Norwegian when added to the Elkhound, somewhat confusing.

He is a medium sized dog, up to twenty inches, powerfully built and with the typical stand-off coat, pricked ears and curled tail of the Spitz group. He is rather less bulky in appearance than the Elkhound, but is similar in colour, with various shades of grey, black tips to the ends of the outer coat and a soft paler undercoat. The pale colour shows on the chest, hindquarters and throat. He is a hunting dog and is lively and enthusiastic, but remains friendly with those that he knows. He is seen frequently in Sweden, but is not known elsewhere.

Grand Bleu de Gasgogne

This is one of the old breeds of French Hounds descending from the Grands Chiens Courants of the early days of hunting in France. He has something of the St Hubert Hound in his ancestry as can be seen from his head qualities and his long folded ears. He is distinguished from the Hounds by his colour, and is more lightly built than some of the Hounds, weighing up to around sixty pounds, but is very strong and has great stamina. Henry IV of France owned a famous pack of these Hounds.

He is always white with black patches, and so ticked with the same colour that the overall effect is that of a blue dog. He has very distinctive head markings, with a black patch on either side of the head and a small patch on the skull. The head, legs and rump are marked with red or tan. Like so many of the pack-hunting Hounds, he is friendly and calm in temperament. A smaller version exists known as the Petit Bleu de Gascogne which must not exceed twenty-two inches at the shoulder.

Grand Gascon-Saintongeois

This French Hound is very unlike any Hound that is commonly seen in other countries, being larger, up to twenty-eight inches at the shoulder, and leggy, and having a considerable amount of loose skin around the head and neck. He was produced by crossing the Saintongeois with the Gascon, and is used for hunting

the roe deer. He is white, with black mantle or patches and a considerable amount of ticking, and has the distinctive feature of a small fawn spot on the hind legs above the hock known as the 'marque de chevreuil.'

He is not seen outside France, but remains well known in his own country as a pack dog. He is said to be gentle, quiet and affectionate. A smaller version known as the Gascon Saintongeois Petit which is identical in all other respects to the 'Grand' version has been produced exclusively for hare hunting.

Grand Griffon Vendéen

This is one of the more famous of the French hunting breeds, being well-known by name if not in fact in

many countries among dog people. He is shorter and higher on the leg than some of the other Griffons, and is constructed in such a way that he exemplifies the tough hunting dog accustomed to working under arduous conditions and even in water. Many packs of these Hounds, often mixed with the Nivernais, were at one time in existence in France.

His prevailing colour is white or wheaten, with vari-coloured markings, and his coat is rough and hard with a thick undercoat. He is a remarkably friendly dog, even jolly and appears to enjoy a joke, an appearance which is added to by his somewhat large and quizzical head with its long furry ears and heavy furnishing of hair. He is rarely seen outside France in the long-legged form though the Basset variety is rapidly gaining favour in some countries. There is a smaller version known as the Briquet Griffon Vendéen.

It is his quaint appearance, resulting from his heavily whiskered face, that is endearing him to so many people who are acquainted with the rather more popular smooth-coated dogs, and who are seeking something a little out of the ordinary.

Hanoverian Schweisshund

This old breed of tracking Hounds from Hanover was produced by crossing the heavier type of Bracke, a dog rather like the St. Hubert Hound, with the lighter breed from the Harz mountains. The connection with the St Hubert type is shown by his larger head and loose folds of skin, whilst the colour recalls the old Haidbracke from the lighter form of Hound. He was originally used by huntsmen on a long lead to track the game in the first instance before laying on lighter Hounds. Other breeds were similarly used in France and Britain, where the Bloodhound performed the same duties.

He dates back to around 1800 and has remained fairly true to type since that time. He is a patient and persistent tracker and is still used by huntsmen. He is, like the Bloodhound, a quiet and dignified Hound, and completely trustworthy. Being smaller and handier than his larger relatives, he might well have a future

in the show world, but at present he is unknown outside his own country.

Hungarian Hound (Erdélyi Kopo)

This very ancient breed of Hungarian Foxhound, originated in the heavily wooded districts of Eastern Hungary, a district rich in game. Early writings report that there were at one time two forms of Hound, a larger black variety used for hunting big game, and a smaller red version which hunted the hare and the fox. The smaller type can now be considered extinct, but the larger one has been carefully preserved. During the process of conservation some cross-breeding with other Hounds has taken place, but this was eventually abandoned in favour of trying to retain the original characteristics of the breed.

In appearance he is something akin to the Swedish Hounds, but with the longer ears of some of the French dogs, though he lacks the skin folds of those breeds which descended from the St Hubert Hound. He is usually black in colour with tan legs and head markings and some white marks on chest and paws. He has a smooth but hard coat, and is rather longer in the body than some Hounds. He is not a pack hunter, but something of a loner, becoming very attached to one master who usually finds that he can be trained as a retriever as well as a hunter.

Karelian Bear Dog (Karelsk Björnhund)

Around the area between Russia and Finland there have been tough bear-hunting dogs for centuries. They have served two purposes, as guard dogs they were fierce enough to drive off dangerous predators, and the step from that task to actually going out and hunting these animals was a natural and simple one. They have always been of the Spitz type, hardy, dense-coated with pricked ears and stubborn temperament. In Russia they were accepted as a variety of Laika

but in recent years the Russians have decreed otherwise and now claim all the varieties of that breed as their own.

The Bear Dog was at one time used exclusively for bear hunting, but more recently it has been used for other game and particularly for elk. He is noted for his courage and persistence, but it is those very qualities that have led him into some trouble, as he is notoriously quarrelsome and fierce, and over the years every attempt has been made to moderate those qualities without losing any of his tenacity as a hunting dog. Since 1935 he has been pure bred in Finland where he is frequently seen in shows, and is now growing in popularity in other Scandinavian countries. He is an interesting dog, and there is little doubt that he will soon be taken up by other countries where his striking black and white appearance will soon gain him adherents.

Levesque

Lord Ribblesdale who had had experience with the French packs of Hounds, once said 'There can be little doubt that a good Batard is a better hound for forest hunting than a draft hound from the Holdernesse or the Tedworth'. The Batard to which he referred was in fact a cross between the traditional French Hound and the English Foxhound. One of the most popular of these for some time was the Levesque which was a mixture of the Gascon, the Saintongeois and the English Foxhound.

He is a big fine dog with a smooth coat, and is invariably black and white, the black, which at times appears almost blue-black is in the form of a saddle and patches and some irregular ticking of black in other parts of the body, and there may be some small tan markings especially on the hocks. He is, like so many of the pack hounds, very friendly.

Podengo

Many of the native dogs of Portugal remain little known outside their own country, and the Podengo is no exception. The breed is an old one, though a fair amount of crossing with other breeds has taken place at various times in order to improve the hunting qualities. There are three sizes, the largest being around twenty-five inches and being used mainly for the hunting of hare, the medium of about eighteen inches and the small which is fourteen inches, the two latter being used mostly for hunting rabbits. For the most part the larger dogs are hunted in pairs or singly and course in the manner of a Greyhound, whilst the smaller dogs are hunted in packs.

Many of the countrymen and farmers of Portugal have one or even a small pack of these dogs, and they have never lost their popularity outside the towns and cities. They are regularly shown at the Portuguese shows and it is surprising that their size and sporting

inclinations have not found them a wider public in other countries. He is a strong little dog with great flexibility, and a short hard coat which appears in many colours, though fawn or tan predominate. He is intelligent, has something of the alertness of the Terriers, and is affectionate and faithful. He makes an excellent house pet and companion and is a good guard.

Poitevin

This is one of the older varieties of French Hound, dating back at least to the 18th century, when packs were well-established in the Haut-Poitou region. These were decimated by rabies in 1842, leaving just a few

specimens from which all the present dogs are descended. English Foxhound blood was introduced to help preserve the breed, with the result that of all the French hounds, this one resembles more closely the common conception of a Foxhound.

He is a fairly big hound, up to twenty-eight inches at the shoulder, is more symmetrical than many of the traditional French hounds, and has less loose skin. His colour too is reminiscent of many of the English packs, being what is usually referred to as hound-marked, in other words, tricolor, with a black mantle on a red and white background. He is a lively and intelligent hound and very friendly, but is rarely seen outside his own country.

Polish Hound (Ogar Polski)

This is a traditional breed, known for centuries as both a hunting dog and a guard. During the troubled times of the early part of the present century and during the two World Wars the breed, in common with many of the other native dogs went into a decline. It was only after the Second World War that attempts were made to regenerate the breed and to evolve it

along uniform lines. The standard was eventually accepted by the FCI and the breed is now no longer in danger of becoming extinct. He is a dog with a remarkable inborn ability for orientation, a great hunter and tracker with well-developed tendencies to quarter ground thoroughly.

He is used extensively for the hunting of the wild boar, and the natural toughness that assists him in this work has to be controlled at an early age, when he needs fairly rigorous training. He is a medium-sized dog up to twenty-four inches at the shoulder but very strongly made and well-muscled, so much so that he can be used for bear hunting. He is an enthusiastic and somewhat noisy hunter and will follow a track for hours with great persistence. He has a strong hard short coat which is slightly longer on the neck and tail, and he is black in colour with tan markings on head and feet. Like most of the hounds he is friendly with people.

Rastreador Brasileiro

This little-known breed was produced in Brazil by crossing the Foxhound with other breeds in order to produce a race of dogs capable of hunting the large wild cat of that country, the Jaguar. Leander J. McCormick describes in his stories of fishing round the world, published in 1937, a visit to an *estancia* where just such experimental breeding was going on. The rancher in this case was crossing the Foxhound with such breeds as the German Shepherd Dog, and was producing animals with the combined qualities of both breeds.

He is a big strong and rather coarse Foxhound with a short coat, great strength and courage and the pendant ears of his ancestors.

St Hubert Hound

The greatest of all patron saints of the chase was St Hubert who spent his youth hunting, even on Holy days. On one Good Friday when he was hunting in the forests of the Ardennes, he had a vision of a white stag with a crucifix between its horns. According to the legend Our Lord spoke to him and as a result he changed his ways, withdrawing to an abbey. Later he is said to have received a message instructing him to go to Rome and he finally became the bishop of Liege. The abbots in the Ardennes monastery developed the St Hubert Hound after their saint. The breed was renowned for its scenting and hunting qualities throughout the whole of Europe, and his fame spread to such an extent that assisted by the legend, a cult grew up around the dog. A mass known as the 'Mass of St Hubert' was celebrated, and as the dog became a legend, so the legend became a dog.

The St Hubert Hound is virtually the same dog as the Bloodhound, and there is no doubt that the breed now shown in most countries by that name is a direct

descendant of dogs imported into Britain from France. He is a dog that has proved his value as a hunter over centuries, being used in most parts of the world to track criminals, and slaves, and for competition work. His powers of tracking are very highly developed, and under ideal conditions has been known to follow a trail that is days old. In spite of his reputation in some quarters he is the kindest and most tractable animal imaginable.

Slovakian Hound (Slovensky Kopov)

This early breed of hound was evolved in Czecho-slovakia and is something of a national breed. There is a close and obvious relationship with the Polish Hound and the two breeds probably descended from the same stock. He is an excellent tracking dog, capable of following a trail for a considerable length of time and of picking up lost trails easily. He is smaller than the Polish Hound, standing only up to twenty inches at the shoulder but is capable of hunting the wild boar which still abounds in parts of his country. A number of devoted breeders are persevering with the breed, and his future is assured so long as boar hunting continues.

His coat is short, strong and thick with a dense undercoat, and in colour he is always black and tan, the tan markings occurring on the head, legs and feet and on the hindquarters. He is affectionate, gentle, and has well-developed guarding instincts. As dog shows increase in Czechoslovakia, his popularity in this, for him, new sphere, is almost certain.

Swedish Elkhound (Jämthund)

This is the largest and the strongest of the Elkhound types of dog native to Sweden. He can be up to twenty-five inches high at the shoulder and proportionately heavy. He is closely related to the well-known Norwegian Elkhound, but unlike that breed, he is hardly known outside Scandinavia. The hunting of the elk has been a pastime and indeed a necessity in Scandinavia for centuries, and the people of the Jämtland bred their own large version of the Elkhound which was recognised as a separate breed by the Svenska Kennelklub in 1946.

Since that time he has become a popular dog in Sweden being used as a guard as well as a hunting dog, and becoming quite popular as a show dog. He is seen in fairly large numbers at the major Swedish shows, where his admirers from overseas will undoubtedly eventually import examples into their own countries. He will make a spectacular addition to the show scene wherever he goes as he is the biggest dog of his type, has the same distinctive grey colour as his more popular and widely known cousin, and has the additional attraction of large cream marks on the jaws. He has proved a successful show dog in his own country, and is sufficiently positive in temperament to be steady and to stand with some defiance in the ring. He is in fact very friendly and intelligent with no vice and few handling problems.

FCI GROUP 6:
Hounds for hunting small game

Ariègeois

This is one of the smaller French hounds, comparable in size with the Harrier, up to twenty-four inches at the shoulder. He originated in the Ariège region of south-west France and was produced by crossing the Briquet with the Grand Gascon Saintongeous. He is a finely built and rather slender hound with long ears and a gaily carried tail. He is an ardent hunter and intelligent. His short coat is mostly white in colour with black patches or mottling and some tan markings. He is quiet and affectionate.

Austrian Hound (Carinthian Brandlbracke)

There are two very old native hound breeds in Austria which are descended from the once very widespread Black and Tan Hounds which were common to France and many other European countries. The Austrian Hound is one of them. He is a medium-sized dog standing up to twenty inches at the shoulder with a fairly long and deep chested body and pendant flat ears. He is smooth-coated, with a thick flat coat which is glossy and flexible, and is invariably black and tan in colour with some white markings on the chest. He is a good working dog, lively and active, and has an attractive quiet and calm temperament. He is not known outside his own country.

Balkan Hound (Balkanski Gonici)

The whole of the Eastern Mediterranean was for centuries an area in which empires rose and fell, nation conquered nation and new nations who spent their time either conquering other countries or opening up trade routes. As these trade routes spread into Europe and Asia, dogs, which were a form of merchandise also spread, with the result that the hounds which had been used for hunting in Egypt, found their way into many other countries. The Balkan states formed one of the routes through from the Mediterranean to eastern European countries and the hounds that traders took with them on their travels formed the basis for a number of indigenous types of hound in the Balkans.

The Balkanski Gonici is a typical example of the sort of hound that evolved from these early types, being a reliable hunter for a variety of game, hardy and a good tracker, and obedient and a hard worker. All these qualities were essential in a country in which hunting was as much a necessity as a sport. He is a medium-sized hound up to twenty-one inches in height, and is red with a black saddle and with black marks over his eyes. He is quiet and gentle and very obedient as well as being a hard worker. He is not known outside his own country.

Barbet

This is one of the most ancient of all the French breeds, reputed to have been the ancestor of the Bichon, the Poodle and some of the Sheepdogs. By the early part of the present century the breed had virtually disappeared, just a few specimens remaining in existence, and even those not definite in type. Efforts were made to preserve the breed, and in recent years they have again begun to appear in some numbers. He was originally one of the water dogs, if not even the Water Dog of Europe, and at the turn of the century is described as an excellent dog for waterfowlers, ap-

parently working happily in ice-covered water and being impervious to the worst weather. He was at that sime said to be identical with the old English Water Dog, and certainly Reinagle's engraving in the Sportsman's Repository bears this out.

He is a medium-sized dog, up to twenty-two inches at the shoulder, strong and well-boned with large round feet. His coat is long and woolly and with a tendency to cord. He is usually mixed in colour, white or grey predominating, with brown or black markings.

Basset Artésien Normand

This is probably the most popular of the short-legged hunting dogs from France, being seen regularly at both French shows and those of many other countries in Europe. A number of the ancient French hunting dogs were developed in the short-legged form in order to slow them down as the need arose for them to work in more restricted areas during the 18th century. The story that they were developed in order to allow the overweight members of the French court to follow them is probably a fallacy.

This particular little dog is a powerfully built long-bodied hound with the long folded ears of the St

Hubert Hound and the short smooth coat of so many of the pack hounds. He is not as heavy or as powerfully built as the Basset Hound proper which now has

world-wide acceptance and probably descended from him and the differences become very clear when they appear alongside one another in the show ring as they do from time to time. The Basset Artésien Normand is a much lighter built and more slender dog with a smaller head and muzzle and lighter bone. He is a friendly but rather wilful hound with strong hunting instincts.

Basset Bleu de Gascogne

This dog is probably somewhat misnamed as he did not originate in Gascogny, but is descended from the long-legged Petit Bleu de Gascon by a process of selective breeding to produce a short-legged and slower Hound which is more fitting for modern conditions. He is very like the Artésien Normand, but not so deep in the body, often shorter in the legs and more heavily boned. This gives him a more balanced outline. He has little in common with the Bassets of

centuries ago, which were more like short-legged Terriers, but is a rather elegant animal.

His distinctive feature, like that of his taller relatives, is his colour as he is white with blue and black marks and spotting and with distinctive tan markings on muzzle, head and feet. He has a short dense coat, and like the other Bassets has a well-developed hunting instinct allied with a friendly but somewhat stubborn nature. He is seen regularly in his own country, but remains virtually unknown in the rest of the world.

Basset Fauve de Bretagne

When the Bassets were first introduced into Britain from France, there were three main strains. This was around the late part of the 19th century. British enthusiasts had seen these varieties at the Paris show held in 1863 for the first time, and had decided which type was to be the one on which their own breeding experiments were to be based. The Basset Fauve de Bretagne was the one that did not enter into their plans, partly because of geography as he was centred in Brittany which was some way from the centre of affairs, and partly because of his very different appearance. He was certainly connected with the Basset Griffon Vendéen, but had none of the glamour of colour or coat of that or the other varieties.

He is a short-coated dog, but it is not the smooth coat of the Basset Bleu or the Artésien Normand. It is rather the hard rough coat of the Cardigan Corgi, indeed it has even been suggested that there was some early connection. He is self-coloured from wheaten to red and white marks are undesirable. He is a friendly and lively little dog, a good and enthusiastic hunter but remains practically unknown outside his own country.

Basset Griffon Vendéen

When the Basset was first introduced into Britain at about the middle of the 19th century, they were bred and shown as the one breed, but with either smooth or rough coats. They were known as Griffon Bassets but

were not considered a separate breed. When they were further imported in the middle of this century they were given their correct name, and achieved immediate popularity, appearing in the variety classes at most of the major shows in Britain. In France they vary in size to some extent, the larger dog being one of the biggest of the Bassets with a shoulder height of up to sixteen inches and corresponding weight.

He is mostly white in colour with markings of tan, grey or black, and has the typical Griffon hard stand-off coat with extra furnishing around the head and muzzle. His legs tend to be stronger and straighter than many of the other Bassets and he is remarkably active for his size and build. He is rather wilful as many of the Pack Hounds tend to be, but at the same time he is a very friendly and affectionate dog with great charm of manner and makes an excellent showdog and family pet.

Bavarian Schweisshund (Bayerischer Gebirgs-Schweisshund)

The Hanoverian Schweisshund proved too heavy and clumsy for the task of hunting the red deer in the mountains of Bavaria. This breed was therefore crossed with the old Bavarian Hound to produce a lighter and smaller dog. The Hanoverian was itself a cross between the heavy Leitbracke and the lighter Haidbracke, whilst the Bavarian was related to the much smaller and lighter Tyrolean Hound. The combination of all these foundation breeds produced a very agile and active Hound with excellent scenting powers.

He is a fairly small dog, up to twenty inches, with a rather light and long body and strong shortish legs. His coat is dense and hard and his colour varies from wheaten through fawn to red, red-grizzle or brindle. He is particularly suited to working in the mountains, either as a *limier* or free, is extremely adept at hunting down wounded game, and is owned almost exclusively by those who hunt deer. He is lively and responsive, but is unknown outside his own country.

Beagle Harrier

This small French Hunting dog fills the gap in size between the Beagle and the Harrier as his name suggests. He is normally between fifteen and seventeen inches in height at the shoulder. He was produced by selective breeding as a well-built and compact Hound which was at the same time energetic and active, for the hunting of hare, and it is interesting that for hundreds of years the Beagle and the Harrier were considered to be one breed. It could be that the French sportsmen in perpetuating this breed have gone full circle.

He is a distinctive dog, with certain elegance and yet substance. His head is typical of that of the larger Hounds and he has a lively and intelligent expression. His coat is fairly short and flat and he is generally tricoloured though greys are not frowned upon. He is not known outside France.

Berner Laufhund

In a small country such as Switzerland, in which there were a large number of different Hounds, many of which had developed along separate lines in different geographical locations, it would have been a simple matter for them all to have interbred until there were no individual types. Fortunately the Swiss Hound Club which was formed in 1931, has most carefully defined the different types of Hound in the country and has encouraged the breeding of the individual varieties.

The Bernese is a typical example of this individuality. He is very like the other Laufhunds in type, with a narrow head and pendant folded ears. His body is long and not heavy and his legs, though well-boned are not heavy. His coat in the smooth variety is dense, hard and close, and in the rough version is wiry and stand-off with a fairly long outer coat and a short dense and softer undercoat. In colour he is white with black patches and some ticking and some tan markings. He can also be tricolour. The medium version is around twenty inches at the shoulder and the short-legged version up to fifteen inches. He is gentle and affectionate.

Chien Courant de Bosnie à Poil Dur

This is a medium-sized hunting dog from Yugoslavia, and only recently recognised internationally although probably an old breed. He was previously known as the 'Chien Courant d'Illyria' or Illyrian Hound, and is used for hunting the hare, fox, and even wild boar. He is a medium-sized powerfully built running Hound with a strong body, pendant ears that reveal the part that the Celtic Hound played in his ancestry, and a rather long head. He stands up to twenty-two inches at the shoulder with the bitches slightly smaller.

His undercoat is soft and dense, and his outer coat long and stand-off with extra long guard hairs. In colour he is white, fawn or greyish with spots of other colours and some ticking, and tends to be paler under the throat, body and on the legs. He is an excellent hunting dog, a good tracker and has great stamina. His temperament is lively but friendly. He is not seen outside his own country.

Chien Courant de la Vallée de la Save

This is another of the smaller Hounds from Yugoslavia, used in the hunting of hare and small game. He was first registered in 1955 by the FCI under the name 'Chien Courant du Bassin du Kras'. He is a medium-sized strongly built dog around twenty-three inches in height at the shoulder and slightly long in the body. He is a strong working dog, with great stamina and a loud bell-like voice. His coat is short, up to an inch long and strong and dense with a little feathering on the legs and the tail. He is wheaten or reddish in colour with some white marks on the head and neck, the latter forming a collar. There are also white marks on his chest, stomach and lower part of his legs, but these must not cover the major part of the body. He is a lively dog with a good temperament, quiet and obedient when trained. He is not known outside his own country.

Chien d'Artois

This is one of the old forms of French hunting dogs, numbered along with the Vendéen, the Poitou and the Normand as one of the original types from which many of the others have descended. He himself originated in northern France as a descendant of the St. Hubert Hound, and at the beginning of this century there were still a number of packs of these Hounds being used for hare hunting. He is one of the smaller Hounds and more nearly approaches the Foxhound in general appearance and colour than many of the French Hounds. He is usually tricolour with a distinct saddle or large patches of fawn or grey, and his coat is smooth and dense. He is affectionate with people and courageous in the chase. He is not known outside his own country.

Drever

This little hunting dog, developed from the Dachsbracke of Westphalia, has become one of the more popular breeds in Sweden. He originated at the beginning of the present century and was used for the hunting of the fox, hare and wild boar. His mixture of blood from the hounds of Sweden and the hunting Dachshund type dog from Germany imprinted firmly on him the sheer hunting instinct as one of his more typical characteristics. He is a tracking and driving hound, particularly useful in hunting deer, which are nervous if driven too fast and break wildly. The slower moving Drever is more adept at keeping the game

moving gently towards the guns without exciting it too much.

He was recognised in Sweden in 1949, and since that time has become a popular show dog as well as a sporting hound, numbers of them appearing at most Swedish shows. He is a small dog and long in the body, but has many of the typical pack hound features, being very deep in the brisket and with a hound's head. Though it has ancestral connections with the Dachshund types in Germany it is not a great deal like a Dachshund, but has the lines of a lightly built short-legged Foxhound. The flashy white markings are a feature of the breed as they are said to make him more easily visible when hunting through the thick forests of Sweden, which are his normal environment.

Dunker

This is essentially a Norwegian dog, started by Wilhelm Dunker who crossed the Harlequin Hound from Russia with other hound types. He is a hunting dog used particularly to hunt the hare by scent rather than by sight, and though very much a tracking dog, can be used as a retriever. His one individual characteristic is his colour, as he is marbled black or blue on white, with brown patches, and in common with other dogs of this colour wall eyes are permitted. Herr Dunker started with one dog which happened not only to look like the breed that he was trying to develop, but also had the ability in the field which he as a hunting man desired. To that dog he mated others which were as near as possible to his foundation sire, in an attempt to fix the tracking ability and the distinctive appearance.

There was a later attempt to cross the breed with the Hygenhund, another Norwegian hunting dog developed from the Holsteiner Hound, and a notable scent hunting dog, but it was finally decided that in attempting to produce a hound that combined the best of two very good ones, some of the individual characteristics of both might be lost, and they remained two separate breeds. He is a strong dog and a typical

hunting hound in conformation, with deep chest and fairly long strong legs. He is rarely seen in the show ring, and is virtually unknown outside his own country. He is said to be affectionate, very trustworthy, and extremely confident.

Erz Mountains Dachsbracke

This breed, which looks rather like a cross between the Foxhound and the Dachshund, is in fact nothing of the kind, but is an entirely separate breed which originated in the Erz Mountains region of Bohemia. He was used for hare hunting and eventually spread

over a large area of Austria as his qualities became appreciated. Carinthia is now the area where the breed is most frequently met. He is distinguished from the German version, the Westphalian Dachsbracke by his colour as he is always either red, or black and tan.

He is a clever and versatile hound, useful in hunting hare and fox, and makes a good line dog or *limier*. He is affectionate and makes a good house pet, but is rarely seen at shows, and is virtually unknown outside his own country.

Finnish Hound (Finsk Stövare)

This is yet another of the fairly large number of hunting dogs from Scandinavia. It is a breed that has been developed from English Foxhounds, French and German Hounds and some of the Stövare types in Sweden. These dogs have been known for about the last hundred years and were originally shown in Finland in the late 1870s. Since that time, by further careful outcrosses the present type of hound has been fixed, appearance never being considered more important than hunting ability in a country in which that sport remains very popular. Consequently his numbers are now on the increase in Finland.

He is a big strong dog, taller than the other Scandinavian hounds, and about the size of the American Foxhound. He is very much the hunting dog, and has

most of the characteristics of that family, being friendly, and even affectionate, but with the streak of independence common to most of the scent hunting hounds. Like many of the bigger hounds, however, he is very generous and good-natured.

German Spaniel (Wachtelhund)

A type of Spaniel very like the Wachtelhund existed in Britain centuries ago, as it did in Europe, and was almost certainly the result of selective breeding from the old Water Dog from which so many of the European sporting dogs descended. Like the Wachtelhund of today he was a fairly small dog with typical spaniel features and a wavy coat. He disappeared, as did the miniature Trawler Spaniel, but played a large part in the evolution of the whole family of spaniels. He almost disappeared in Germany, but a group of enthusiastic spaniel breeders got together in 1897 with the aim of reviving the breed, which they did so successfully that he is now one of the popular German gun dogs.

He is noted for his working qualities, and German spaniel breeders maintain that he should not become a show dog for fear that he may lose some of his working abilities. He is especially useful in heavy woodland where his remarkable scenting powers make him a very good game hunter. He can also be trained as a retriever and is a good water dog. He is a strong dog half way in size between a Cocker and a Springer and has a fairly long slightly wavy coat which makes him attractive when well groomed. His temperament is excellent and he makes a very good companion in the country and a good house dog and guard.

Grand Griffon Nivernais

The race of dogs known as the Griffons are peculiar to France in the large hunting form. They should not be confused with the Griffon Bruxellois which is a toy and is probably not related. They more closely resemble the old Otter Hound of Britain than anything else, and they do the same sort of work. The Griffon

Vendéen is probably the best known of the group, but the Nivernais variety, which is on the whole darker in colour and longer in the body than the Vendéen, was at one time equally well-known. Packs of these hounds were kept for the rougher sort of hunting in the forests of the Nivernais province.

He was developed specifically for hunting the boar, and though not very tall, only up to twenty-four inches at the shoulder, he is courageous, active and strong, and is well-protected by his strong hard and shaggy coat. He is usually grey in colour of various shades, though he can be black and tan or fawn. He

is an affectionate and lively animal but is rarely seen outside his own country. A smaller version known as the Griffon Nivernais de Petit Taille also exists.

Greek Greyhound (Albanian Greyhound, Ellenikos Ichnilatis)

This is a large running dog from Greece, used extensively for coursing small game, particularly hare and small deer. In general appearance he is very like the Saluki, having a similar head and outline and roughly the same coat. He is a tall dog, up to twenty-seven inches at the shoulder with long slender well-muscled legs. He is a quick, lively dog with great stamina and is clearly related to the eastern Greyhound types. He works equally well in rocky mountainous country as on the plains.

He has the long head of the Saluki with similar soft pendant ears. His coat is short and close and a little hard and he is generally black and tan in colour though a white blaze on the chest is permissible. He hunts with a melodious voice, enjoys human company and the comforts of the home, and is an intelligent and pleasing companion.

Griffon Bleu de Gascogne de Petite Taille

This is one of the rough-coated hounds from France, similar in many ways to the Grand Bleu, but smaller, up to twenty inches at the shoulder only and distinguished by a rough hard coat. He has a rather slender neck which makes him more elegant than some of the other hounds, fairly long ears which lie flat and do not fold, and he is rather long-backed. His coat is harsh and flat-lying, is shorter on the head and ears but with prominent brow hair like the other Griffons, and rather wavy on the legs.

His colour is similar to the larger smooth-coated Grand Bleu, being a dark blue grey on white with small ticking in black to give an overall blue appearance. He has red marks on head and feet. He is an active friendly dog and affectionate with people. He is not seen outside his own country.

Griffon Fauve de Bretagne

This rough-coated hound was evolved in the Brittany area for the hunting of fox and wild boar and as a general purpose game hunting dog. He is medium-sized, up to twenty-two inches at the shoulder and is

strongly built with stout legs. His coat is his distinguishing feature, as it is very harsh but not overlong. He has a long tail covered with strong hair, and medium length supple ears hanging low on a fairly narrow head. His colour is always fawn of various shades from pale fawn to red, and black is not allowed.

He is a fairly strong-willed hound, not noted for his friendliness, but he is a great hunter as a pack hound, being very fast, tough and musical. He is virtually unknown outside France.

Haldenstövare

This hunting dog from Norway is named after the town of Halden in the South East corner of Norway near to the Swedish border, an area in which hunting has been a popular pastime for centuries. There are four recognised Stövare types and this is the largest of the family, standing around twenty-six inches at the shoulder. He was developed from the native hounds of the area by selective breeding and by crossing with imported hounds from Sweden, Germany and Russia, with possibly later crosses with French and British hounds. He is, however, very much a native hound, and is different from any other recognised type.

His most distinctive feature is his colour, as he is mostly white with large black patches often surrounded by brown shadings, and with brown markings on the head. Like the other Norwegian hounds he is not a pack dog, but hunts individually by his powers of scent. He is a big strong dog with deep chest and strong legs, possessed of great stamina to permit him to hunt through deep snow in the sometimes bleak winters of his native country. Like the other members of the family he is affectionate and completely trustworthy, and makes a very good family companion. He is not so frequently seen in the show rings of Scandinavia as some of the other hounds, and rarely outside his native country, though he clearly has visual qualities that would prove him popular.

Hamiltonstövare

This is a Swedish breed of general purpose hound, developed from the extinct Hölsteiner Hound and the Heiderbracke with the introduction of Curlandish Hound blood. He was developed by a Swedish sportsman named Hamilton who was interested more in the working quality of the breed than in its appearance. He did, however, manage to produce a very attractive dog that has made its mark in the show rings of Scandinavia. This is exemplified by the fact that since the turn of the century he has been the most popular of all the hound breeds of this type in Sweden, having classes of his own since 1886, and today frequently outnumbering the other scent hunting hounds at shows in his native country.

The breed is now appearing in other countries, and

after the first imports into Britain were mistakenly registered as Swedish Foxhounds, it was realised that there was a variety of such hounds in Sweden and the error has been corrected. He is not a pack dog, but hunts on his own through the deep snow-laden forests of Sweden, where he has proved popular as a show dog. He is a neat and stylish dog with attractive markings and colour, and a rather longer and more elegant head than some of the other scent hounds. He is very steady in the show ring, but an affectionate and cheerful character outside it, having a lively personality and being very active.

Hygenhound (Hygenstövare)

This is another of the Scandinavian hounds, separated one from the other almost entirely by size and colour, as in type they are very similar, and in many cases descended from the same basic stock. The Hygenhound originated in the middle of the 19th century in the kennel of the Norwegian breeder F. Hygen who crossed the old Hölsteiner Hounds with other Scandinavian breeds. For a time the breed was intermixed with the Dunker and was shown as one breed, but in 1934 they were divided and the Hygenhound was again recognised as a separate breed. The breed is not recognised by other kennel clubs, and is by no means one of the popular hounds at shows in its native country.

He is about the same size as the Dunker, and a good deal smaller than the Haldenstövare. He has a more pointed muzzle than the other Scandinavian hounds and a somewhat longer body, and he is mostly yellow in colour with white markings though other colours are permitted. He is a strong active dog with good bone and a deep chest, and makes a good individual hunting dog for smaller game. He is affectionate and very trustworthy, and like most of the type makes an excellent companion. In the ring he is steady and shows well, and his short, dense coat needs no preparation other than a good brush down.

Istrian Hound (Istarski Gonica)

This ancient breed of Yugoslavian hound exists in two forms, the short-coated or Kratkodiaki and the rough-coated or Resati, the latter undoubtedly playing a part in the ancestry of the Styrian Mountain Hound. He is used for hunting the hare and the fox, and is generally useful as a tracking dog. He is a medium-sized, twenty-inch dog with the long narrow head, prominent occiput and pendant ears of the French hounds. In the short-coated variety the coat is smooth and dense with a glossy finish whilst in the rough-coat it is long, hard and stand-off, with an abundance of protective hair on the body.

He is a white dog with yellow or orange markings on the body and rather heavier colouration on the head and ears. He is a tough and active hound with a good voice, and capable of long spells of work under strenuous conditions. In temperament he is friendly and lively but trainable. He is not seen outside his own country.

Italian Hound (Segugio)

This is the only remaining true Italian hound that is recognised as a separate breed. The breed descended from the ancient Celtic Hound, and more nearly approaches the description of the mythical black 'Dogs of Hell' than any of the other breeds. He has great endurance and will work either in a pack or as a single gundog, and exists in two varieties, smooth and rough. He is unusual in that he often occurs as a self-coloured dull black dog which must be one of the very old colour forms, unspoiled by crossing with other breeds. He also has the long fine pendant ears of the early hounds which fall into folds as do those of the St Hubert Hound. He can be brown or tricolour. The Segugio has the reputation of being quiet and gentle in his dealings with people and a good house dog.

Jura Laufhund

This hound from Switzerland differs from the other native hounds in that he is nearer in appearance to the St Hubert Hound. His head is larger and heavier with a broader skull and prominent occiput and his forehead is much more wrinkled than that of the other breeds. His ears are longer and heavier and very low-set, and he himself is heavier, longer and lower, a height of eighteen inches being ideal. He originates from the Jura mountains which Switzerland shares with France, and it was probably this close proximity which led to the French influence on the breed.

He is a very keen hound with an excellent nose and a resonant clear voice which he uses when on a trail. He exists in the one variety of coat only, a short, dense hard one, and in colour he is either tan with occasionally a black saddle, or black and tan, a white spot on the chest being permissible. The short-legged version is below fifteen inches at the shoulder and is a heavy, long-cast hound, reminiscent of the Basset Artésien Normand. Both types are used for hunting hare, fox and small deer.

Lundehund

This smaller member of the Spitz group has been bred for many years in Northern Norway for hunting the Puffin, the fat carcasses of which have been staple diet for centuries among the islanders. The breed originated in Vaerog, an island off the coast of Norway, and were trained to hunt on their own in the inaccessible rocky areas that are the habitual home of these little birds. The dogs caught the birds and carried them back to the hunters, and in season were trained to search for nests full of eggs.

He needed to be a small and very active dog with

the same manner of working as the Cairn or West Highland White Terrier of the Scottish islands. He needed to be capable of climbing like a cat, of forcing his way into narrow and confined spaces, and of doubling up as a retriever. The people of Vaerog produced such a dog in the Lundehund which proved very successful. Since that time he has been bred true, and is recognised by the Scandinavian countries though not elsewhere. He is quite small, only some nine to ten inches in height, and for his size is remarkably robust, having a strong deep body, well-boned legs and tough feet with double dew claws. He is intelligent, lively and boisterous, and the danger to

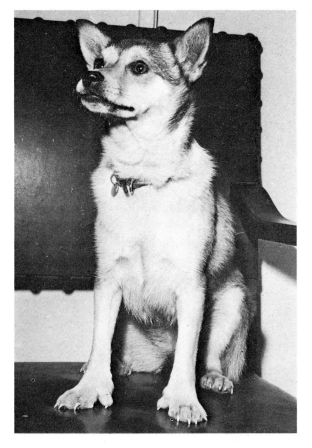

his future lies in the fact that if he becomes popular outside his native country he will be looked upon as a toy dog because of his lack of size.

Luzerner Laufhund

Hunting in Switzerland posed the dog breeder different problems from those that faced the sportsman whose country contained a greater proportion of flatter more heavily cultivated land. The result was a race of small fairly light hunting dogs divided into two sizes, the larger ones being only medium-sized animals and the shorter-legged versions developed by crossing with such breeds as the Dachsbracke or the Dachshund. The Luzerner Laufhund is a typical

example of the results of this careful selective interbreeding. He has the head qualities of the St. Hubert Hound, the colour of the Grand Bleu de Gascogne and the short legs in the Niederlaufhund version of the Teckel or Dachshund.

He is a lightly built, active and fast hound, not too heavily boned and with a fairly long body. His head is that of the St Hubert Hound with long folded ears and narrow skull. In the medium-sized hound a height of twenty inches is aimed at, and in the short-legged dogs a maximum of fifteen inches is allowed. Unlike the other two varieties, he is a short-coated dog only, with a dense hard and close coat, which is heavily ticked and marked with blue and black spots and patches on a white ground, with some tan marks. His temperament is like that of the other Swiss hounds, quiet and even affectionate.

Porçelaine

One of the most decorative and delightfully named of the French hounds, the Porçelaine is a very ancient

breed that has been bred true to type for centuries. He was used originally for the hunting of the hare and small deer and may have at one time been related to some of the Swiss breeds. He is one of the most elegant of hounds with long neck and finer bone than others, and looks more of the running dog. He is fairly tall, up to twenty-three inches at the shoulder, and is principally white with fairly round orange patches and small orange markings on the ears, which are fine, long and folded. He is not known outside France, which is perhaps unfortunate, as he could well become quite popular. He is friendly, very active and a good hunter.

Sabueso (Español de Monte)

This breed can be traced back to the old Celtic hound, though it is much more hound-like than many that have so descended. His name comes from some of the early inhabitants of France, though he is now essentially a Spanish dog. He exists in two sizes, but the smaller one, which is under twenty and a half inches in height is the one more frequently seen at the Spanish dog shows. He is a versatile dog, being very good in a pack, as a line or tracking hound and even as a police dog. He makes a good show dog and many excellent specimens are seen at the major Spanish shows.

He is a forceful hunter and not the easiest of dogs to train, being somewhat temperamental and wilful. For this reason he does not make the best of house-dogs or pets, but retains a considerable degree of popularity among sportsmen in a country devoted to the chase. He has a short, hard and dense coat, and is usually white with large orange or black patches.

Schillerstövare

This is yet another of the Scandinavian hunting dogs, and in this case a lighter-built and smaller hound, which whilst popular in some parts of Sweden as a hunting dog, does not rival the more popular Hamilton-stövare in the show ring. The breed descends from German, Austrian and Swiss hounds, and was perfected by a certain Mr Schiller who used his dogs for hunting his more open country. The breed was evolved earlier than the Hamiltonstövare and was breeding true before that breed appeared. He is used for hunting the snow hare and fox, and as a tracking dog, and is claimed by his admirers to be a much faster dog than the other Scandinavian hounds.

He is a short-bodied and long-legged hound with more of the look of the running dog about him than the stockier scent hounds. Scandinavian sportsmen prefer the lighter type of dog that will cover the ground more quickly in those areas which are not so heavily wooded. He makes a good show dog as most of the hounds do, being steady and obedient, and essentially willing. He is friendly and cheerful and makes a devoted companion, and his short dense smooth coat makes him a clean dog to have around the house as well as an easy dog to prepare for the show ring. It is doubtful whether he will ever become popular outside his own country as he is recognised by no other Kennel Club, and his admirers are quite happy with him as a hunting dog working in the field.

Schweizer Laufhund

This is one of the three principal types of hounds native to Switzerland, all of which exist in two forms, the long-legged and the short-legged version. They originated from the same sources as the ancient French hounds, but the terrain of Switzerland dictated that they should develop along different lines, and they are generally smaller and lighter than the surviving French hounds.

The Schweizer Laufhund is a medium-sized dog, up to twenty inches at the shoulder and has a fairly long head with a narrow skull on the lines of the Bloodhound but smaller. He is rather lightly built with a long body which is flexible and stands on long well-boned but not heavy legs. His coat is dense and short and close-fitting in the smooth variety, and a hard and stand-off outer coat with softer dense undercoat, in the rough-haired dogs. In colour he is white with varying sized pale to deep red patches and often a red mantle. He is a good hunter, and calm and quiet in behaviour when kept under domestic conditions. The Schweizer Niederlaufhund is similar to the larger version, but is below fifteen inches at the shoulder.

Sicilian Hound (Cirneco dell'Etna)

This breed of running dog from the island of Sicily would seem to be an ancient type of dog. It has a good

deal in common with the Pharaoh Hound and the Podenco, both of which probably had an older form of Mediterranean coursing dog as ancestor. In Sicily he has been bred true to type and with little influence from outside breeds and he is now accepted as a pure breed, being carefully preserved by a few enthusiasts. He is very active, finely built and extremely fast in the pursuit of rabbits which are his favourite quarry.

He is smooth-coated, red in colour with some white markings, and has a pleasing temperament, being friendly towards people and yet gay and forceful when hunting. He is virtually unknown outside Sicily.

Smalandsstövare

This is the oldest of the Stövare breeds of Scandinavia, originating in the dense forests of Smaland in southern Sweden. The breed differs from the others of the family in that some of them are born with a short tail, so that whilst docking is not permitted, many are seen with a tail that is unusually short for a hound. One of the earlier breeders, Baron von Essen had a preference for the short-tailed specimens, and it was his interest that preserved this characteristic despite the crossing with other of the stovares in order to improve the quality of the breed.

He is the smallest and the more heavily built of the family as might be expected in a dog bred to hunt the forests rather than the more open country. He is distinctive in colour, always black, with tan markings on muzzle and eyebrows and on the lower parts of the legs, with white flashes on tail end and feet, which makes him a very showy dog in the ring. His coat is particularly smooth and glossy and needs merely a good brushing and hand finish, as with the Whippet, to bring out the best in it. He was recognised by the Swedish Kennel Club in 1921, and is seen in fair numbers at most of the Swedish major shows. He is a quiet and steady dog with no vice, and makes a very affectionate and devoted companion.

Steinbracke

This medium-sized German running hunting hound is very like many of the other breeds used for the hunting of small game in Europe. He bears a close resemblance to some of the French hounds, and to the Swedish Stövare, in both shape and colour. There were at one time many different types of closely related hounds of this type in Germany, but in 1955 the German Hound Club issued a standard which was accepted by the FCI, in an effort to produce a line of dogs more easily recognised as a separate breed.

He is an excellent tracking dog, enthusiastic and with a very good nose and melodious voice, but is almost entirely in the hands of huntsmen and not seen at shows. He is elegant but with strong bone and the depth of brisket of the typical hound, and the long head of many of the French scent-hunting dogs. His

coat is short, hard and dense with some brush on the tail. His colour is always yellow to reddish-tan, with a black saddle and typical white markings on the head, chest, legs and tail tip. He is a friendly dog with a lively personality.

Styrian Mountain Hound (Peintinger)

This is a fairly modern breed of hound from the Austrian province of Styria. The breed was evolved towards the late 19th century by crossing some of the German hounds, the indigenous Austrian hounds and the rough-coated Istrian Hound. What was wanted was a hound which would work well in rough mountain country, with great stamina and a good voice, and the Styrian Mountain Hound was the result. He is a medium-sized hound up to twenty inches at the shoulder, rather long in the body and flexible. His head is typical of the hounds and his ears are medium-sized and flat.

He is a rough-coated hound to withstand extremes of weather, the coat being rough and hard, coarse but not as shaggy as some of the herding dogs, and with an inclination towards feathering on legs and chest. His colour varies from wheaten to red and a white patch on the chest is permissible. His hunting instinct is well-developed, so much so that he is not normally used for any other purpose, though he is quiet and becomes attached to his owner. He has a particularly loud and melodious voice.

Tyrolese Hound

This variety is very similar to the Austrian hound but differs in both size and colour, and can vary in coat. The breed is an ancient one, originating centuries ago with the old French hounds and the mountain hounds of Switzerland. His close resemblance to some of the Swedish hounds would also suggest the influence of some of the old German dogs. He is smaller than the

Austrian Hound, up to eighteen inches only, and a smaller version still, under fifteen inches also exists. He comes originally from the Tyrol and is used as a hunting dog, being used for both tracking and beating coverts.

He is black and tan or red, with some white marking on the chest, and his coat varies between the smooth, hard, and rough. In the rough variety there is some fringing and the tail is in the form of a brush. He is a vigorous and active hound with a good steady temperament.

Westphalian Dachsbracke

As distinct from the Erz Mountain Dachsbracke of Austria, which is an old and original breed, this dog was produced by crossing the Dachshund with the long-legged German hounds. German hunting men, looking for a dog which combined the best hunting qualities of the Dachshund and the greater speed of the Foxhound type, created this pack-hunting dog. He is taller than the Dachshund, being up to fourteen inches at the shoulder, which is the height of the small Shetland Sheepdog.

He is smooth coated and is usually hound-marked in any combination of hound colours with white. He has an attractive head and expression and a calm and obedient manner. As a hunting dog he is keen and has great persistence and stamina. He is not known outside his own country.

Yugoslavian Hound (Planinski Gonici)

This distinctive breed of running hound has descended from ancient indigenous Yugoslavian hounds. He is a medium-sized strong dog with a fairly broad head, low-slung medium-length ears and a muzzle which is slightly shorter than the length of the skull. He is used for hunting the hare, fox and other small game and is a persistent and enthusiastic scent hound. He has strong straight bone and feet which are a little longer than those of some of the hounds.

His coat is short and dense and very close-fitting but slightly longer on the throat and shorter on the head and ears. He is a black and tan hound with the classical markings of that colour, on the cheeks, over the eyes and on the feet, and a small white spot on the chest is not objected to. He is a quiet and affectionate dog that enjoys the company of people, but at the same time enjoys equally the work of the chase. The Yugoslavian Tricolour hound is a similar dog that differs principally in his colour.

FCI GROUP 7:
Gundogs, except the American and British gundogs. See page 457

Auvergne Pointer (Braque d'Auvergne)

This French pointer from the Auvergne, in the mountainous central part of the country, is one of the heavier early types of Pointer that shows less influence from English Pointer blood than most. He is said to have been brought originally from the south, and to have been crossed with pointers brought over later from Britain. At one time he existed in two forms, the Braque Bleu which is said to have had better proportions and more elegance, and the Grand Braque which was more of a heavy-weight.

He is an extremely good bird dog and an active worker with a good nose, slower than some of the other Pointers, but steady and certain. He has a short, hard glossy coat, and is mostly white, though with a great number of black speckles which gives him a somewhat grey overall appearance. The head has a good deal of black, which should be well-balanced around the eyes. He is very intelligent, quiet and easily trained, but is not known outside his own country.

Bourbonnais Pointer (Braque de Bourbonnais)

This is one of the older forms of French Pointer which shows less of the influence of the English Pointer blood. The breed became a separate one around the turn of the century in Bourbonnais in central France. He has never become very popular outside his home region, is not seen at shows and is unknown outside France. The indications are that he is on the decline and may well disappear. One of the reasons for this is that he is a rather unattractive looking dog, being cloddy, short and rather compact and lacking the elegance of many of the other Pointers. His muzzle is heavy and pendulous and his ears small and his back is humpy and rounded which gives him a clumsy outline. His tail is docked to around two inches in length.

He is however a very good working dog, much esteemed in his own area, and slow, careful and faultless when standing his game. He can in addition be taught to retrieve which makes him more useful to the one-dog man. He is a medium-sized dog, up to twenty-two inches at the shoulder. His coat is short, dense and waterproof, and he is always white with widespread ticking of fawn or pale brown. He is very docile and gentle.

Dupuy Pointer (Braque Dupuy)

The family of French Pointers have a good deal in common, they are all similar in size and conformation, and vary only in colour, length of tail and by their names, which are usually based on either the place where they were developed or the name of the person who did the early work on perfecting the variety. The Old Braque of France was a rather coarse animal with short neck and a head reminiscent of a hound rather than a gundog. The introduction of a great deal of English Pointer blood improved the appearance of the French Pointers and at the same time improved their speed of work, and to a certain extent their powers of scent.

The breed which shows the English influence more than most is the Braque Dupuy which was said at the beginning of this century to more nearly approach the English Pointer in appearance than any of the other Braques. He is a tall and elegant dog, so elegant in fact that the suggestion that he had Greyhound blood is not unreasonable. He has a long narrow and rather fine head, long ears that are rather thin and tend to hang in folds, and gentle expressive eyes. His short coat is hard and smooth and he is white with large patches of brown and some ticking. He is a good worker, useful in water, and is very much the sportsman's dog, rarely shown and unknown outside France.

French Pointer (Braque Français)

This breed of French Pointer is among the oldest of all the French breeds, having originated with the Spanish Pointer, described in detail in the Sportsman's Repository of 1826 and illustrated with a Reinagle engraving which looks remarkably like the present-day dog. He is described at that time as looking something like the old Southern Hound and having 'the tenderest nose and most exquisite scenting, joined with true game and steadiness in pursuit, and proportionate want of speed.' This, in a volume not much given to praise, is praise indeed. He has himself become the ancestor of many of the French gundogs, and it is somewhat surprising that he has survived so little changed.

He exists in two sizes, the Braque Français proper

which stands up to twenty-six inches at the shoulder, and the Braque Français Petite Taille, which does not exceed twenty-two. He is a tall looking dog as his body, whilst deep is not so far through as some of the other Pointers. His head is broader than the English Pointer, and in the smaller version differs in that the muzzle is shorter and that the ears are smaller and hang flat. He has a short dense coat and is invariably white with chestnut speckles and patches. The smaller version has more extensive chestnut marking. He is intelligent, easily trained and is kind and friendly.

Italian Pointer (Bracco Italiano)

This is one of the oldest Italian sporting dogs, based on the indigenous hounds, which were crossed with gundogs; the breed came into existence as a separate

one at the beginning of the 18th century. Since that time he has altered very little and remains one of the characteristic dogs of Italy. He is still both in appearance and temperament a mixture of the two types of dog, having the large heavy head of the early hounds but the body and limbs of a heavy-weight gundog. His temperament is also a mixture of typical houndlike independence and gundog enthusiasm.

He is fairly large, up to twenty-six inches in height which is about the same as a Pointer, but his tail is docked to roughly the same length as that of the German Short-haired Pointer. His coat is short, dense and glossy, which, allied with his striking white and orange or white and brown, makes him a very attractive looking dog. He is quiet, friendly and obedient, has remained fairly popular in his own country, but is rarely seen outside it.

St Germain Pointer (Braque Saint-Germain)

The French Pointers have existed for centuries in several different forms and it is probable that they, like

Dutch Partridge Dog (Drentse Patrijshond)

Although the name of this dog appears to indicate a degree of specialisation as far as work is concerned, he is famed in his country of origin as an all-purpose gun dog that will work well with any sort of game and is strong enough to retrieve pheasant or hare. He has been known in Holland for at least three hundred years and appears in old paintings, depicted almost exactly as he is today. The very fine head study by Henrick Goltzius (1558–1617) is a typical example. He originated in the province of Drenthe, in North East Holland bordering West Germany.

One of the more interesting things about the Drentse Patrijshond is that he represents the very early type of half Spaniel, half Setter that could well have been the ancestor of many of the modern gun dogs, and his origins could be much more ancient than the three hundred years with which he is normally

the English Pointer, owe their origin to the Spanish Pointer. The Braque St Germain is one of the older varieties and was evolved towards the early part of the 19th century by crossing the early Pointer with other old breeds of French gundogs. The breed was concentrated for a while in the area around St. Germain en Laye, which led to his name, and was used for hunting fairly large game.

He is a fine upstanding dog, rather more leggy than is fashionable with the English Pointer, and is invariably white with clear orange marking and spots, which result from his early ancestry which is known to have started from an orange and white bitch. His coat is short, soft and dense and he carries his full tail which is long and tapering. He is rather reserved with strangers, but gentle and quiet, and a willing worker.

Czechoslovakian Pointer (Cesky Fousek, Böhmisch Rauhbart)

This Czechoslovakian pointing dog which has an obvious resemblance to many of the old gundog breeds, is also fairly closely related to the German Rough-haired Pointer. During the period preceding the First World War he was one of the more popular of the rough-haired gundogs of Czechoslovakia, but during that war he almost disappeared. Between the wars the breed was resurrected by careful selection and encouragement and is now the second most popular gundog of his country.

He is a fairly tall dog with a distinctive coat which consists of a dense undercoat which disappears in the summer, and a fairly flat outer coat, itself overlaid with longer hairs up to about three inches in length. These tend to stick out from the coat giving the dog a rather shaggy or bristly appearance. He is either brown, or white with brown ticking, or with larger brown markings.

credited. He is a biggish strong dog with a fairly broad head full of character. He is very intelligent, easily trained, and an easy-going sort of dog. His popularity as a farmer's dog and as a pet has not declined although he has never become a particularly well-known show dog. As importations to other countries, particularly the United States of America and Britain are now taking place, this situation could well change.

Epagneul Français

This is one of the old French breeds of Spaniel, though, in common with other French breeds, it is longer in the leg than some people associate with the title, looking rather like a heavy-weight Setter. In fact, in the first few years of the present century it was said that he was actually a Setter in all essential respects, but that was at a time when English writers were stating that because of the success of British Setters in Europe, there was little point in encouraging the native breeds. The Epagneul Français in fact looks more like a

somewhat lanky English Springer than anything else, and is the same colour.

He is a fairly tall dog, up to twenty-five inches at the shoulder, and is strongly boned. He has the typical head of a Spaniel with long flat ears and a broad muzzle. His coat is thick, slightly wavy and he has some feathering on legs, ears and the tail, which is long. He is white with large brown patches and some speckles. There was a possibility at one time that the breed would disappear, partly because of the importation of British gundogs, and partly because of the increasing popularity of rival breeds of Spaniel. He has now, however, re-established himself in the favour of French sportsmen as he has proved himself to be very versatile. He is intelligent and obedient and very friendly.

Epagneul Pont Audemer

This breed originated towards the end of the 18th century as the result of crossing some of the old French

Spaniels with other gundog breeds. It was concentrated around the area of Pont-Audemer in Normandy but is now few in number. He is a fairly heavy medium-sized dog that looks rather like a woolly Springer Spaniel. He is adept at working in water and is used principally for wild duck and other marsh dwellers. His head, rather longer than that of the other Spaniels, is his distinguishing feature, being surmounted by a definite top-knot of longer hair. This crest together with the thick curly coat indicates the Water Dog or Irish Water Spaniel as one of his ancestors.

He is a medium-sized dog, twenty-three inches at the shoulder, with a sturdy body and strong legs. His coat is rather soft and curly and is either chestnut or grey with white markings, or self coloured chestnut. He is a very energetic worker, intelligent and easily trained, and makes an excellent companion. He is rarely seen in the show ring at the present time, and is unknown outside his own country.

German Long-haired Pointer (Deutscher Langhaar Vorstehhund)

There are three types of German Pointer, the Short-haired, the Wirehaired and the Longhaired, and whilst the first two are almost certainly closely related, the last is the product of crosses between other ancestors. He was used in earlier years for hawking and falconry and was produced by crossing the old Water Spaniel, a breed which has featured in the evolution of so many European breeds, with the Spaniels from France. As a result of these experiments a whole family of hunting pointing dogs with fairly long coat and many other characteristics in common, was produced. Since the early days, other blood has been introduced, including probably that of the Gordon Setter, and the resultant dog looks rather like a somewhat coarser version of the Irish Setter but liver, or liver and white in colour.

He is an excellent gundog, with a particular aptitude for working with feathered game, but versatile, useful in water and a very good dog in close coverts. He is a powerful dog with a feathered tail which may be shortened by docking. He is intelligent, very obedient and faithful, lively and a good companion. Unlike the Shorthaired version, he is virtually unknown outside his own country.

German Rough-haired Pointer (Deutscher Stichelhaar Vorstehhund)

This is one of the oldest of the German gundogs used for feathered game. He is very like the Pointing Griffon though less massive and with a smaller head. He has not achieved the popularity of the other varieties of German Pointer, but was revived in 1865 by a German breeder and saved from extinction. He is a tough rough-coated dog of about the same size and weight as the German Shorthaired Pointer, and is usually brown and white or a mixture of brown and grizzle with darker markings. He is obviously fairly closely related to the other rough pointers and to the French Griffons, but he is unknown outside his own country.

Griffon à Poil Laineux

This is the long-coated version of the Wire-haired Pointing Griffon of France, but has not achieved the international recognition of that breed. He is very like the Korthals Griffon, but was in fact developed by a M. Boulet in France at the beginning of the 19th century, probably by crossing the Wire-haired variety with the Barbet. He was known at one time as the Griffon Boulet after the gentleman who perfected the breed. He is fractionally smaller than the Korthals Griffon and differs from that breed in coat and colour.

His coat is long, soft and silky, lies fairly flat and is sometimes wavy but never curled. He is brown in colour with some small white markings at times, but never large areas of white. He is an intelligent and industrious gundog of considerable versatility, and is easily trained and quiet.

Old Danish Pointer (Gammal Dansk Honsehund)

This is a very old form of Danish gundog which was developed in the 17th century from the even older Spanish Pointer. He went into disfavour at one time and there was a risk of him becoming extinct, but a drive for revival took place and he was finally recognised by the Danish Kennel Club in 1962. In many ways he is as much like his Spanish ancestor as any of the other Pointers, having the same colouration and markings and the rather heavy and broad head of the Spanish dog. He is rather small for a Pointer, only twenty-two inches at the shoulder and is heavy around the neck. His coat is short and dense and in colour he is white with brown patches and some flecking. He is a good worker, easily trained and a general purpose

gundog suited to the flat terrain of his home country. He is quiet and intelligent but is rarely seen outside Denmark.

Perdigeiro Portugues

This is one of the native gundogs of Portugal, being related to early importations of gundogs from Spain as were most of the early Portuguese breeds. He is a bird dog, and indeed the name 'perdigueiro' means partridge. He is a smallish dog, around twenty-two inches in height, usually cream to red in colour with a dark mask and with or without white or black patches and with a short, rough coat. He is virtually unknown outside his own country, but in Portugal is a popular house dog as well as being used for hunting. He is friendly, easily trained, and a very lively companion.

Picardy Spaniel (Epagneul Picard, Epagneul Bleu de Picardie)

By the standards that have become accepted in most parts of the world, the Picardy Spaniels are not Spaniels at all, as in size, proportions and head qualities they are comparable with the Setters. The breed is an old

one, and has been popular in Picardy for many years where he has proved particularly suited to hunting the marshes and woodlands. His overall appearance recalls the engravings of early Springers and Setters, and is something like the early Gordon Setter.

He is a fairly tall dog, up to twenty-five inches at the shoulder and is strongly built on good legs and rather large feet. His coat is fairly long, rather dense and hard, but finer and longer on the ears and the tail. He exists in two colours, the Picardy proper being dark blue roan with flecks of red and some patches, and more red on the legs and feet. The Blue roan version without the red marking, but with red on head and feet is known as the Epagneul Bleu de Picardie. He is very intelligent, easily trained, and becomes attached to one owner.

Poodle Pointer (Pudel Pointer)

This dog completely gives the lie to those who say that the Poodle is a stupid beast not fit for anything but pampering and shows. He was produced by crossing the Pointer with the Poodle towards the end of the 19th century by those sportsmen who wanted all the excellent gun dog qualities of the Pointer with the dash and bright intelligence of the Poodle, and at the same time a dog that had the Poodle's protective coat. They remembered that the Poodle was itself descended from the old race of Water Dogs which were exceptional retrievers in water. It took some considerable time as there was a fair amount of divergence of type and it was not easy to fix, but well into this century it was accomplished and the Poodle Pointer became an established sporting dog in his native country.

In recent years he has been imported into the United States of America though he has not yet appeared in Britain, but in the former he is being found as superb a gun dog as his German originators originally intended him to be. He is a big strong dog with a hard and dense coat, and very little of the original Poodle about his appearance, looking very akin to the German Wirehaired Pointer apart from his colour, as he is always brown or the colour of dead leaves. He is an important sporting dog in Germany where he may only be entered into the stud book when he has succeeded in the field.

Rough-haired Vizsla (The Drótszörü Magyar Vizsla)

This variation on the normal smooth-coated and more popular Vizsla was obtained by crossing that breed with the Roughcoated German Pointer. The breed is of recent origin, being developed during the 1930s. The Vizsla himself is so outstanding a gundog that he has become accepted as something of a mascot by the sportsmen of Hungary who are extremely proud of their fine national dog. He has a great reputation, possessing a wonderful nose, fine ability as a tracker and can be trained to retrieve. The short-haired version had but one shortcoming, his very fine smooth coat was not entirely suitable for long hard days in the field under extreme conditions.

The Drótszörü version is said to have all the excellent qualities of his contemporary, and has in addition the ability to work under the most arduous conditions for considerable lengths of time. He is a great water dog, and will work in frozen marshland and icy water all day. In appearance he is almost exactly the same as the Vizsla proper, but he carries a rough hard coat of up to two inches in length with a soft undercoat. His tendency towards a beard and face whiskers is considered desirable. He is a very active and willing dog, easy-going and friendly.

Small Munsterlander (Kleiner Münsterländer)

This is yet another of the large number of sporting dogs descended from the old Spaniel types indigenous to Western Europe. They probably started life in Spain like the others, but variations resulted from crosses with other native dogs such as the Water Dog and the smaller rough-coated hounds popular in France centuries ago. With no natural boundaries a great deal of interbreeding would have taken place which resulted in numerous slightly different types. Bird dogs went out of fashion as the gun superseded the falcon, and smaller, slower breeds that would hunt and spring game became more popular. The Kleiner Münsterländer was developed in Westphalia in Germany from small gun dogs related to the Drentse Patrijshond and some of the French spaniels.

At the beginning of the present century he became quite popular as he proved to be a very hard-working all-round gun dog, but after a while he almost disappeared. Vigorous attempts to preserve the breed resulted in a revival after the First World War and the breed was eventually recognised by the German Kennel Club. He is now increasing in parts of Germany and is becoming known in other European countries though he has not yet been accepted outside Europe. He is smaller by about three inches than his larger cousin, and differs in that he is brown and white instead of black and white.

Spanish Pointer (Perdiguero Burgalés)

Pointers have existed in Spain for at least three hundred years, and although Alonzo de Espinar in his 'Arte de Ballesteria' mentions them in 1644, the Spanish Pointer as he is known today is a fairly modern breed. Espinar wrote that there were two types, the one that tracked and the one that hunted with the nose held high in the true Pointer fashion. The original dog was a fairly heavily built animal with little of the elegance and refinement of the British Pointer, but the introduction of blood from that breed has brought about changes.

He remains a larger dog, up to thirty inches at the shoulder and is more heavily built than his British counterpart, and is liver and white in colour with patches or ticking. He is an excellent gundog, being a good pointer, an eager worker and extremely active. Temperamently he is very quiet and trustworthy with the affection of the average gundog for his owner, and an easy-going nature which endears him to the family. He is often seen at the major championship shows in Spain where he is frequently placed high in the breeders and family groups as his well-matched size and colour make him very attractive. He is rarely seen outside his own country.

Spinone

This is one of the more popular native show dogs of Italy, appearing in fairly large numbers at the major Italian championship shows. He was produced by crossing a number of the ancient breeds of France, from where he is said to have originated. The Barbet,

the Griffon and some of the hounds may be among his ancestors. He is an ancient breed of dog, evolved as a hunter, and used successfully over the years, specialising in work through rough woodland and marshes. he bears some resemblance to the other native hunting dog of Italy, the Bracco, in that he has a heavy head and low-slung ears, which indicate the hound side of his ancestry.

He makes a very good show dog as he is calm and easily trained for exhibition purposes, is quiet in the ring and has a very attractive personality. His coat is his particularly distinguishing feature, being harsh and rugged like that of the French Griffons and he is mainly white with orange or chestnut patches and spots. He has the long eyebrow and jaw hair of the Griffon type which gives him a somewhat massive

appearance. He is a big friendly dog that can be trustworthy and staunch, and he makes a very good guard.

Stabyhoun

This small gun dog of the Spaniel type, originated in the Friesland province of Holland, where he is still seen though often in a bigger form than the standard requires. This confirms the conjecture that he was descended from the larger Drentse Patrijshond probably by crossing with the German or French Spaniels. He is a well-established breed that goes back many years and was developed as a gun dog to work in the flat country of Friesland where control and obedience are more important than speed or drive. It has never been a numerous breed, a dozen appearing at the Winner Show in Amsterdam in 1976, but its supporters are very faithful.

He is a first rate all-round gundog, makes an excellent retriever which is an important feature in Friesland where fairly small fields are divided by deep drainage ditches not easy for the sportsman to cross. He is good through water, and is strong, hardy and has great stamina.

He comes in four different colour patterns which makes a very attractive sight when several are running together, and he makes an excellent housedog and guard and is particularly patient with children.

Wetterhoun

This gun dog from the province of Friesland in Holland is one of the strongest of the Spaniel types of dog. He is very robust with a strong head, very short, broad and deep in the body and stands four square on stout legs. It is not surprising therefore to learn that he was developed largely for hunting the otter rather than as a normal gun dog. He was not used as part of a pack, but hunted singly, and is staunch enough

to face his courageous opponent. He has a good deal in common in appearance with the old Water Dog, having a curly coat, a curled tail and the same sort of pattern and colours, and it is likely that he is a fairly direct descendant of that now extinct breed.

In recent years the modern gundogs have become more fashionable and the Wetterhoun has been ousted from popularity as a wildfowling dog. He is however still used for the hunting of the otter, and will face up to a polecat. He is a popular guard and farm dog, remains an all-purpose gundog, and is impervious to the most severe weather conditions. He is intelligent and fairly easily trained though he has a streak of wilfulness and is a fairly tough character when aroused. Those who support the breed will admit that he needs a fairly firm hand, but when trained he makes an excellent watch dog. He is not seen a great deal at shows, rarely appears outside Holland and Germany, and has not yet reached the United States of America or Britain.

FCI GROUP 8:

American and British Gundogs.
See Sporting Dogs pages 25–92

FCI GROUP 9:

Companion dogs including the toy dogs

Bolognese

This is one of the family of Bichons, the small hairy dogs that have existed in Europe for centuries. The Bolognese is a small toy dog, under twelve inches in height and is covered with a mass of curls. There is an early example of the breed depicted in Kirchner's model of around 1730 for the Meissen factory, described oddly enough as a Bolognese Hound. He is probably related to the very early Shock Dog which was one of the European Water Dogs, and small enough to be developed as a lap dog.

He appears to have been in existence in Northern Italy in the 15th century and reached Britain via the Canary Islands some two hundred years ago. He is pure white in colour with often a few fawn or light yellow marks. His coat is very long and shaggy and consists of a mass of curls on most parts of the body with a shorter coat on the muzzle. He is still recognised in Italy, but is rarely seen outside that country.

Coton de Tulear

This little toy dog which is clearly related very closely to the Bichon family, originated in Southern Madagascar. His ancestors were probably brought into the country by the troops of the Indian Company who settled on the island of Bourbon from the year 1665. On the island of Reunion there is a very similar little dog known as the Chien Coton, and both this variety and the Coton de Tulear closely resemble the Maltese and the Teneriffe Dog. By successive cross-breeding over the past half century breeders in Madagascar have produced a delightful little dog, and by the later introduction of bloodlines from the Maltese, the breed has been strengthened and firmly established. A fairly large number of these little dogs were exported from the island, either to 'La Reunion' or to France as their owners finally left, and the breed is now thinly distributed throughout Madagascar.

He is a small dog, the males not more than twelve inches high, and the females considerably less, and weighing not more than nine pounds. His principal characteristic as his name suggests, is his coat, which is white, long and fluffy rather than silky. Some yellow markings are permitted. He has a lively and intelligent look underneath a dense crest of long white hair. His eyes are deep-seated and dark, and he makes an elegant and attractive pet.

German Spitz (Wolf Spitz)

The German Spitz has been in existence since around the beginning of the 17th century, and had two forms. The small white variety which was bred largely in Pomerania, and which, when exported to Britain, changed its colour, became smaller still and is known as the Pomeranian. The larger version, a dog with a minimum height of seventeen inches and closely resembling the Keeshond remained a German breed with his interests looked after by the German Spitz club formed in 1899 who issued standards for the

breed. There was a smaller black version which was bred in Württemberg to guard the vineyards.

The Wolf Spitz is a strongly made dog with a stand-off coat and a distinct mane, and from the colour of the coat, which is wolf grey, comes his name. Like many of the Spitz breeds he is an all-purpose dog, being sporting by nature, and yet an excellent guard and watchdog. The Small German Spitz is similar to the larger dog, but must be less than eleven inches in height, and varies considerably in colour. This leads to some confusion in shows in those countries that recognise both the British Pomeranian and the Small German Spitz, as the two are indistinguishable in the ring.

Harlequin Pinscher (Harlekinpinscher)

This is the most recent of the German Pinschers to be recognised, having been accepted as a separate breed by the FCI as recently as 1958. In size he comes between the Pinscher proper and the Miniature Pinscher and is the typical German short-haired terrier type of dog with short body and prick ears. His most distinctive feature, from which he gets his name is his colour, as he is patched with dark or black on a white ground. There was clearly at one time a basic form of dog in central Europe which had the harlequin colouration, as the Great Dane, and to a certain extent the Dalmatian, both of which emanated from Germany have a similar pattern.

He is a typical Terrier, a great hunter of vermin and small game, very sporting and full of fun, and is particularly suited to the duties of a guard and a house-dog. He is lively, attentive to humans, whose company he enjoys, and very faithful. He is very little seen outside his native country.

Japanese Small Size Dog (Shiba Inu)

This is the smallest of the ancient dogs of Japan. The breed has been traced through ancient remains to very primitive times, when it is believed that it was brought over from the Southern Seas. For a long time these little dogs have been used for hunting small wild animals in the mountains. At one time there was some confusion and he was included in with the larger version as one breed, but is now considered to be a separate variety under the name Shiba Inu which means 'small dog'.

He is a cheerful and active little dog, keen and rather highly strung, very watchful and both faithful and obedient. He has the typical head of the Spitz breeds, with broad skull, sharp muzzle and erect ears which are carried slightly forward. He is strong and very muscular for a small dog with straight bone and compact feet. His coat is hard and straight with a soft warm undercoat and some feathering on his tail. In colour he varies from white through red and brown to black with an occasional brindle. His height is

described in Japanese very picturesquely as '1 shaku 3 sun' which translates into thirty-nine centimetres or fifteen inches.

Japanese Spitz

Although the name Japanese Spitz has become accepted as almost the family name of the small group of dogs from Japan known as the Inu, and including the Akita, the Shiba and the Nippon, there is a small white Samoyed type of dog which has achieved some popularity in other countries than Japan which is known as the Japanese Spitz. They are seen in Ceylon, and one or two specimens have appeared in Britain though the breed is not recognised there. It could well be that this breed is a rather long-coated version of the family which is known sometimes by its familiar names of Japanese Large Size Dog, Japanese Middle Size Dog and Japanese Small Size Dog.

There is a possibility that the charming white dogs that are now seen in countries outside Japan have been produced from a cross between the Japanese dogs and the small white German Spitz that produced the Pomeranian. He is certainly a dog of considerable charm, makes a delightful show dog, being quite dramatic in appearance, smart in outline and repays grooming. He could easily become very popular in other countries as he is an excellent house dog and family pet.

Kromfohrländer

This is one of the newest breeds to be accepted by the German Kennel Club, being recognised in 1953, and is a typical example of an individual setting out to produce a new breed from an accidental mating and the resultant discovery of something attractive. Frau Schliefenbaum in the Krumme Furche area of Siegen in Germany owned a Wire-haired Terrier bitch and was presented with a nondescript little dog by some American troops at the end of the Second World War. These two when mated, produced a litter of puppies which so delighted Frau Schliefenbaum that she decided to attempt to fix the breed, an attempt which was successful when the German Kennel Club accepted it. Though the original sire is a matter of some conjecture, it is believed to have been a Griffon Fauve de Bretagne, a belief that is borne out by the similarity, apart from colour, between the two breeds.

He is a small dog, around sixteen to seventeen inches in height with the rough coat of his ancestors and a distinctive preferred white saddle. He is rapidly gaining in popularity in Germany, and since his acceptance by the FCI is becoming known in other countries. He is very intelligent, faithful and friendly, and makes an excellent watchdog.

Mexican Hairless Dog (Xoloizcuintli)

There are a number of hairless or partly hairless dogs, which are claimed by many experts to have originated in Africa and to have travelled by various means through China to America. It has been stated that the ancestors of the Chihuahua and the Mexican Hairless were brought to South America by traders as long ago as the 17th century, and there is an obvious similarity between this breed and the Chinese Crested Dog. They were imported into Britain during the early years of this century and created something of a sensation, though there was some confusion at that time as to whether they were actually Mexican Hairless or Chinese Crested.

Interest in the breed was maintained around the port of Acapulco and there is said to have been a con-

nection with an ancient religious cult, which led to the name. Despite his strange appearance, he is quite a sporting little dog, full of character and fun, and some of the early importations proved themselves adept at hunting rabbits and rats. He obviously is not suited to an outdoor life in a country subject to wintry conditions, but with care can adapt to a normal temperate climate. He has lost ground in popularity to the Chinese Crested Dog which is making some progress in Britain and other countries at present.

Volpino

The early history of the modern Pomeranian is often confused by those who claim that the small Spitz type of dog depicted on wall paintings, Roman drawings and carvings is in fact that breed. It is much more reasonable to suppose that it was in fact the Volpino that was being recorded, as this little dog has existed in Italy for as long as records have been kept. It could be of course that the Volpino went to Germany, from which country the Pomeranian originated, as many of the early Deutscher Kleinspitz were white. Further confusion is caused by the existence of a tiny white dog called the Seidenspitz in Germany at one time, and the continued existence of the Japanese Spitz which is merely a slightly larger version.

The Volpino is a small dog, no higher than eleven inches at the shoulder and not weighing more than nine pounds. The head is not so sharp and well-defined as the Kleinspitz. The coat, which is long and stand-off with a dense undercoat, is always white. Like so many of the smaller Spitz type, the noise that he can make is out of all proportion to his size, and he therefore makes an excellent watchdog.

FCI GROUP 10:
The coursing dogs

Magyar Agár

This is an ancient breed of Hungarian Greyhound, evidence on tombstones dating back to the conquest of Hungary in the 9th century pointing to the existence of a coursing dog very like the present day one at that time. In the 13th century Greyhounds were imported from other countries with the result that the modern dog looks very like the Greyhound proper of the United States and Britain. Between the two world wars the numbers of the older type of dog were much reduced and further importations took place. It is probable that the early Magyar dog was similar, and probably connected with the Sloughi and the other Eastern Greyhound types.

He is used as a coursing dog, principally for hare, though in earlier times he was used also for chasing and killing the fox. It is said in Hungary that he is

better hunting by sight and in not having a 'nose', and in fact this can be detrimental. He is extremely fast and clever, generations of coursing ancestors with no track-running blood having produced an animal more like the coursing Greyhound than the show dog. He is friendly, devoted to his owners, and is an excellent housedog and guard. He is not known outside his own country and is not seen at shows.

Sloughi

There has been considerable discussion about the claim of this breed to be distinct and separate, many experts stating that it is merely a smooth-coated Saluki which has degenerated in type by crossing with other running dogs. It is however recognised by the FCI and acknowledged as a separate breed by the Kennel Club in Britain. He originated basically in North Africa, though in an early form he was probably brought into that country from elsewhere. A type of Wolfhound existed in North Africa many centuries ago, and ancient drawings and carvings depict a strong running dog which could well have been one of the ancestors of the Sloughi. These dogs were probably brought back from places further east such as

Saudi Arabia, which leads to the suggestion by some authorities that they are descended from the ancient Eastern Greyhound from which came the Saluki and the Afghan Hound.

The name Sloughi appeared during the Middle Ages and followed the dog that we now know as the Saluki when that was first imported into Britain. At that time the name used was 'slughi' which led to even further confusion as they were undoubtedly not the Sloughi of Northern Africa which was well known at the same time. He is a strong fast running hound used for hunting hare and small deer, and has appeared at shows in Europe for a number of years. The early specimens that arrived in Britain were not completely typical and the European examples are better. He is a good watchdog, aloof with strangers but affectionate with those that he knows.

Spanish Greyhound (Galgo Español)

This breed is a typical Greyhound, though smaller than the one normally seen as the Greyhound in shows throughout the world. There has been considerable discussion concerning the position the breed occupies in relationship to the Ibizan Hound and the Greyhound proper, and whether in fact he descended from

the Pharaoh Hound. The fact that he is frequently fawn and white in colour lends credence to the latter theory. There has been some crossing with the British Greyhound, and there was an attempt to establish a breed known as the Anglo-Spanish Greyhound.

He is used as a coursing dog, frequently for hunting on horseback, and is an intelligent, fast and hardy running dog with excellent stamina. His coat varies, though for the most part it is short and strong. He is seen frequently at Spanish shows.

PART THREE:
Other Pedigree Breeds

GROUP A

Recognised in their native country, some at championship status

There are many breeds of dog which can be considered to be pedigree dogs, in that they exist as separate breeds, and have records of their breeding carefully kept, which are not recognised by any one of the major authorities. They are often, though not always, working dogs, and have been used for specific purposes in limited areas.

It is possible that in some cases the numbers are so small that the breed has almost ceased to exist, whilst in other cases, and the Jack Russell Terrier is a typical example, they exist in large numbers and have only failed to achieve recognition because their type remains unsettled. Many of them are shown at dog shows, as although they are not approved for the award of championship status, they are accepted as a distinct breed, whilst others appear at shows not under the authority of the Kennel Club concerned, as working dogs of one sort or another. They all, however, have their place in a book of this sort, the popular ones because they earn their place by virtue of that popularity, and the less common ones in the hope that their inclusion will draw attention to the need for preserving them.

Alano

This breed is a descendant of the old Celtic hound, which was crossed with the Mastiff to produce a powerful heavy-weight hunting dog. It was suggested at one time that it was the same breed as the so-called Spanish Bulldog which was imported into Britain at the turn of the century, but there is probably no basis in fact for this suggestion. He was said too at one time to have taken part in bullfights, but in fact he is more of a hunting than a fighting dog. He is used for the hunting of the wild boar, being used as a pack dog, cornering and holding the quarry at bay until the arrival of the huntsmen.

He is a massive dog with a large head, powerful body and a short harsh coat. He is red in colour with a dark mask, all of which gives him a Mastiff like appearance, though he is in fact a hunting dog. He is an ardent hunter, vigorous in the chase, but with the calm temperament of the larger hunting hounds.

American Toy Terrier (Amertoy)

Attempts have been made in recent years in the United States to produce a Toy Terrier. By selective breeding from small Smooth Fox Terriers a line of very small dogs which weigh only a few pounds has been developed and there have been moves to popularise them. The American Kennel Club has not recognised them as a separate breed. Earlier unsuccessful attempts were made in Britain to produce toy Bulldogs and Toy Bull Terriers, and they suffered from the normal disadvantages of poor bone quality and weak physique generally that accompanies such experiments. The Toy Terrier has the advantage of a foundation in an already fairly small dog which does from time to time produce an extra small specimen, and these experiments could well produce a tiny dog of great charm and all the Terrier characteristics.

Further crossing with the Chihuahua and the English Toy Terrier has resulted in a smooth-coated tiny dog with prick ears, a somewhat domed skull, generally white with some black and orange markings.

Anatolian Karabash

This Mastiff type herding dog from Turkey has a history which probably goes back to the time when animal husbandry first began there. The breed clearly has a close relationship with the rough-coated Mastiffs of Spain and Southern Europe, and was almost certainly at one time as important as a guard as it was as a herder of sheep. The climate in which it was developed and worked is not one that would be suitable for a lesser dog, and the flocks that it guarded, as they moved from one area to another needed protecting against wolves and other predators.

He does not herd in the normal way as they are fairly constantly moving slowly feeding as they go, and he normally patrols rather than herds. He works with his family in this duty and has evolved a technique of very effective ambush. He is an active, rather long-legged dog with great agility and stamina, and is hardy and capable of living under conditions which other dogs would find very trying. His coat is medium length, very dense, rather soft, and though pale colours such as fawn, with a black mask are most common, entirely black specimens do occur. In Turkey his ears are cropped and he wears a heavy spiked collar as extra protection.

Argentinian Mastiff (Dogue d'Argentine)

The origins of this dog are obscure, as although Mastiffs would certainly have been taken over to South America by the Spanish and Portuguese during the period of the exploitation of that country, they would hardly have been the type that is now accepted as the Dogue D'Argentine. The Spanish Mastiff is a large coloured dog with a fairly long coat whilst the Portuguese equivalent is also coloured and has longish hair. The Argentinian Mastiff, today, however, is an all-white dog with a short hard coat, and is little like the Fila Brasileiro which is descended from the early Mastiff types. The Argentine Mastiff is like a rather oversize white Boxer. He is used for hunting the puma and other big game and is a very strong and courageous animal with the loose skin around the neck of the fighting dogs. He is seen in other countries, but has not yet appeared in Britain.

Egyptian Sheepdog (Armant)

This is an ancient working dog used by Egyptian shepherds for hundreds of years. He is named after the village of Armant in Upper Egypt and is said to be descended from the French dogs which were taken there with the armies of Napoleon during the 18th century. Formerly he was purely a droving dog, but he later becme a guard and a fairly aggressive one. The breed first appeared in Europe when specimens were brought to Berlin by Professor Nachat Pascha whilst he was Ambassador. He is a medium sized dog somewhat smaller than a Collie, has a long, rough, shaggy coat, and is found in all shades of grey with a dark mask and some white marking, as well as in many other colours. He is somewhat suspicious of strangers, and makes an excellent guard. He is rarely seen outside his own country, and is not a show dog.

Artésien Normand

The old Norman Hound which appears to have been evolved during the time of Louis XIV was a heavy, strong dog, more along the lines of the Bloodhound than the Foxhound. He was developed to hunt many types of games in the French forests and is a fairly big and heavy dog. His head is rather like that of the Bloodhound, with loose skin on the cheeks, long in the skull and with a pronounced occiput, his ears are long and pendant with a definite twist. He has a longer body than some of the other hounds, and his general appearance lacks refinement. He is usually tricolour or white with darker patches and his coat is smooth and fine to the touch.

Australian Greyhound

Many of the dogs imported into Australia by the early settlers proved too slow to catch the faster game of that country, and the bone-hard and often extremely tough conditions under which they had to work did not suit the English Greyhound. A variety of Greyhound was produced, therefore, which was around the same size but very sturdy and stout in build with great musculation and very good feet. They were used for catching small game on the cattle and sheep stations. This type, smaller than the English show Greyhound, still appear at Australian dog shows, but the breed is not recognised by the Australian Kennel Council and is not mentioned in modern works on Australian dogs.

Barb

The two original dogs that produced all the present Kelpie bloodlines are known, they were a dog named Brutus and a bitch called Jennie. This was in 1870, and at around the same time, another line was being produced from a bitch named Sally which produced an outstanding working dog, named Barb after a well-known racehorse of the time. He was a black, prick-eared and a tremendous worker, and became so prepotent a stud force that a whole line of black dogs was produced which became known as Barbs. He was noted as a forceful worker with sheep and became expert at the special type of work required around the stockyards. The breed was shown with Kelpies though as recently as the 1940s classes as a separate variety were staged. The name now seems to have ceased though old herders will still refer to a black Kelpie as a Barb.

Basset d'Artois

This is the short-legged version of the Chien d'Artois, a hound that originated in the North of France from the St. Hubert Hound. He is described as one of the most beautiful of the Bassets, being powerful and vigorous rather than elegant, and having great length. It could well be that this particular variety of Basset played some part in the evolution of the Basset in Britain, as that too is on the whole a heavier and stronger dog than the popular forms of French Bassets.

The Basset d'Artois is what is known as a half-crook fronted dog with very strong bone and a large rib cage. His coat is short and dense, and he is usually tricolour, or, less frequently has orange or grey markings on a white or speckled ground. He is noted for his hunting ability and voice. He is not so well-known as some of the other French Bassets and is not seen outside his own country.

Belgian Pointer (Braque Belge)

Many of the gundogs of Northern Europe, like the hounds, differ from one another in very few details and frequently only in the matter of colour. The large family of pointers and hounds in France spread its influence into other neighbouring countries, and by the selection of the desired type in the first instance and by careful selective breeding, dogs were produced which bred true to type and were eventually accepted as a separate breed. The Braque Belge is typical of these. For the countryside over which he was to hunt, a fast showy dog was not required, but something that was steady and certain, and perhaps more thoughtful than some of the light Pointers.

He is most distinctive for his colour, as he is slate-grey with patches and spots of brown, a colour which probably came from a mixture of the Grand Bleu of France and the Old Danish Pointer. He is a fairly tall dog, standing around twenty-five inches at the shoulders, and is strongly built with good ribs and a broad loin. He is a smart dog, as his ears are rather small and his tail is normally docked. His coat is hard and dense, but close, and his head is rather broader, and with less stop than some of the traditional pointers. He is a good, steady and reliable worker, but is not a popular show dog and is practically unknown outside his own country.

Berger de Languedoc

This is a group of breeds rather than one variety of dog, originating in the area of Languedoc, in the country bordering the Golfe du Lion. There are five types, each taking its name from the district in which it evolved. They are the Camargue, the Grau, the Farou, the Carrigues and the Larzac. Although they differ in some details, in height for instance, where they vary between sixteen and twenty inches, and in coat, where they vary from smooth and short, to rough and long, they are all more or less the same colour. The colour ranges from fawn to reddish-fawn and black. They are all excellent working sheepdogs that have lived on the farms of the plains and flat lands of the Languedoc area, and have always doubled up as guards and farmyard dogs, protecting not only flocks and herds, but the property of their owners.

Border Collie

This breed is the most recent one to be recognised for show purposes in Britain, though it has been in exist-

ence for hundreds of years, and has been exhibited in other countries for some time. The breed was developed from a mixture of working sheepdogs which were carefully controlled and registered as such by the International Sheepdog Society whose registers pre-date those of the Kennel Club. The intelligence, and capacity for work and training, of the breed, is a legend wherever sheep are kept, and it is the top competitor in many countries where international sheepdog trials are held. Though its numbers do not at present warrant the status of championship competition in the show ring, there is little doubt that these will rapidly increase as the popularity of the breed is very high indeed.

He is a typical Collie type dog, strong, flexible and active with a keen head and expression, and though black and white is the most popular colour, many others are acceptable. He exists in two coat forms, the rough, which is a medium length tough but shiny outer coat, with thick undercoat, and the smooth which is sleek and glossy. He has been shown extensively in Australia where the standard for the breed was approved in 1963 and where individual states were issuing their own challenge certificates even earlier. He is rapidly becoming popular as a show dog in other countries and his remarkable obedience, loyalty and quiet temperament, suit him particularly well to beauty competition.

Braco Navarro (Braco Carlos VIII)

In the extreme South West of Spain there exists a variety of gundog known as the Braco Navarro, which is similar to some of the smaller and lighter gundogs of central France. Braques have been mentioned in works on dogs since the middle of the 17th century, and the Navarro is one of the older breeds. He is reported as having been exhibited before the First World War and to have been popular in the early part of the 19th century.

He is a medium-sized short-coated dog, powerfully built and is usually white with dark brown spots or ticking and often with tan markings. At one time he is said to have been seen sometimes with wall eyes which could indicate an early relationship with some of the herding dogs. He is, however, essentially a hunting dog and is used as such, not appearing in the show ring, and being virtually unknown outside his own country.

Bouvier des Ardennes

As with many other countries, the farmers of Belgium, where incidentally the farming of sheep has always been very successful, produced a variety of sheepdogs. For many years they remained somewhat mixed and unclassified, but recently they have been divided into their separated breeds, based largely upon the area in which they evolved. The wire-haired herder of the

Ardennes has been known for many years, and though not achieving the world-wide popularity of his contemporary the Bouvier des Flandres, he has always had a following in his own country.

He is a tall dog, some twenty-four inches in height at the shoulder, very strong, and with erect ears. His tail is docked very short and he is covered with a shaggy harsh coat of medium length, with pronounced whiskers and beard of slightly longer hair. He can be any colour, though at one time many of them were grizzle. He is a guard dog as well as a herder, and accustomed to defend his farm against intruders. The result is that he is suspicious and rather ill-tempered with those that he does not know, whilst at the same time he is obedient and easily trained by his owners. There may be small pockets of the breed still in existence, but according to the Société Royale Saint Hubert, of Belgium, the breed is now extinct.

Chinese Crested Dog

This breed, the Mexican Hairless and the African Hairless have a great deal in common, in fact at one time at the beginning of this century they were looked upon in Britain as all belonging to the same breed. At that time there were two distinct types in Britain, the one rather leggy and whippet-like and the other described as short and rather cloddy. It was the latter type which had hair between the toes, a distinct hairy mane, and a tuft on the tail, and this was undoubtedly the Chinese Crested as we know it today. They failed to become popular, and disappeared from the dog scene for a good many years.

Recently there have been a number of importations into Britain and the breed is achieving a degree of notoriety once more, if not popularity, as his strange appearance and distinctive characteristics have endeared him to the media. The breed is now seen in some numbers at British shows, and always creates something of a sensation, particularly among the less experienced. The number of registrations is approaching the hundred mark, and there is no doubt that they will eventually reach championship status. They are friendly and attractive little dogs, full of fun and very attached to their owners.

Chinese Hound

There existed at one time in China a breed of dog described as a hound, and carrying the name Ma-Chu-Gou. This could well have been the dog described at the turn of the century as the Phu-Quoc, specimens of which were brought to France but did not survive. He is described as having the appearance of a heavy Greyhound with pricked or semi-pricked ears, and is said to have descended from a long-coated dog native to Kashmir. He is a dark brown shaded dog with a very dense short coat, with a tendency towards a ridge in the fashion of the Rhodesian Ridgeback.

It is by no means certain that the breed still exists as it was said some fifty years ago to be disappearing. He is an excellent hunter with a very good nose and a high degree of intelligence. He is keen and persistent in the pursuit of game, strong enough to handle boar and deer, and hunts in packs to bay his quarry until the approach of the huntsmen.

Chortaj

This is one of the running dogs from Eastern Europe. He is a large hard-coated dog of the Greyhound type with long neck and arched body, but is more heavily built and coarser than the Greyhound that is seen in dog shows in most countries of the world. The Cynological Congress held in Moscow in 1952 accepted this breed as one of the pure Russian breeds and one to be preserved. He is an extremely keen hunting dog, is used exclusively for coursing and is not seen outside his native country.

German Sheep Pudel

Although the modern Poodle is thought by many people to have originated in France, the breed almost certainly began life in Germany as the Pudel, a breed which itself evolved from the Water Dog and the Barbet. Vero Shaw states 'There is also a "sheep" Poodle in Germany . . . presenting altogether a heavy and uncouth appearance'. The Schafpudel is still very much admired by German shepherds for his intelligence and working ability, and though he does not appear in the show ring, is still preserved as a separate variety. He is a fairly large dog, up to twenty-four inches at the shoulder, and is covered with a long, shaggy coat with a dense undercoat. His colour is white, with some coloured marks or shading allowed. He is intelligent and gentle, but an excellent guard.

Dutch Hound (Steenbrak)

In the 17th century there was a race of farm dogs mainly kept in the Brabant region of Holland, which were of the hound type. They were crossed with some of the other European hounds, particularly those from Germany, and a small hound, under eighteen inches, was produced which survives. He is very like the German hound, being lightly built, small and rather leggy and with long ears. He has a short thick and hard coat and in colour is typically hound-marked, white, yellow to red, and black patches principally over the saddle. He is a handsome little dog with white blaze and feet, and whilst still a hunting dog, is affectionate and friendly.

Estonian Hound

During the time of the Tzars, hunting was a favourite pastime in Russia and some fine breeds of hounds were developed there. The Borzoi is a typical example. There were, however, a number of scent hunting hounds which were used either as pack hounds, or singly by individual huntsmen. The Estonian Hound is one of the few that have remained since the Russian Revolution brought about the cessation of hunting as a fashionable pursuit, the others disappearing in the confusion that existed immediately after the upheaval. He is a medium-sized dog, twenty inches at the shoulder, and is rather long cast in body.

He has a short, hard and dense coat, the long folded ears of those dogs that have the St Hubert Hound in their ancestry, and a broad, deep and fairly rounded chest. His colour is the typical tricolour hound marking of yellow, white and black, the black sometimes covering almost the whole body and extending to the head. He is a fast hard-working hound with a good nose and excellent temperament.

Flemish Draught Dog (Vlaamsche Trekhond)

This large heavy-weight dog which descended from the old droving dogs of Belgium was used extensively as a draught dog to pull small carts for tradesmen. In the more remote areas he is still probably used to some extent for the purpose as he is capable of pulling quite heavy loads, is remarkably obedient and easily trained, and serves the double purpose of hauling as well as guarding property. He is a large dog up to thirty inches at the shoulder and tremendously strong. His coat is short, very hard and weather-resistant and he is usually ash-grey in colour with a dark mask.

German Hound (Deutsche Bracke)

In every respect other than size, this dog is very like many of the Foxhounds throughout the world. He is of the usual hound colours and markings, has the same type of head and is built along the same lines. In size he more nearly approaches the Harrier, however, and looks very like his geographical near neighbours, the Scandinavian Stövare. There were at one time many breeds of pack hounds in Germany, but they are now virtually extinct, and only the Deutsche Bracke remains as a separate breed. The standard was compiled by the Deutscher Bracken Club in 1955 in Olpe, with the result that he is sometimes known as the Olpe Hound.

He is a fine pack-hunting dog with a very good nose and an excellent voice, and like most of the scent hounds, is affectionate and friendly. He is not a show dog and is in the hands largely of huntsmen.

Glen of Imaal Terrier

As long as people in eastern Eire can remember there have been tough little dogs used for going to ground to badger. The centre of their activities has been in County Wicklow and especially in the Glen of Imaal. Primarily a hunting dog he developed such gameness that he was frequently used for staged dog fights, in which his toughness and protective coat gave him tremendous advantage.

He is not a common dog even in his native country, and was virtually ignored as a potential show dog until in 1933 the Irish Kennel Club staged classes for the breed. Since then he has gained a few supporters in other countries as well as his own, and is seen from time to time at the principal shows. He is a tough little dog, but with the delight in games that most of the Terriers have. He is a great hunter, likes nothing better than a walk in the country or a scramble over rough going, scenting out anything that smells catchable, and makes a wonderful companion.

Happa Dog

This is a little-known oriental breed from China, and in appearance is something like a Pekingese but without the long coat of that breed. The first were seen in England around 1907 when one was imported and exhibited by the Hon. Mrs Lancelot Carnegie at the first show of the Pekingese Club. To complete the oriental picture it was led into the ring by a Chinese lady in native costume. The dog was said to have looked rather like a very tiny miniature Bulldog and was black and tan. Little is known about the present state of the breed, and it is certainly not known outside China.

Havanese

This is another of the Bichon family, being the typical small woolly toy dog. His origin is said to have been in Cuba or the Philipines, both of which claim him as a native. He is undoubtedly descended from the other Bichons, and probably the Maltese, which found their way to those countries from the Mediterranean. At the turn of the century there were several exhibited at shows in France, but they seem to have disappeared from the scene in recent years.

He is a small dog, between eleven and thirteen inches at the shoulder, white, with large and small patches of biege, grey, or black, and can be solid chestnut. His coat is long, soft and curled and is silky rather than wiry. He is a gay little toy dog, very affectionate and an excellent house dog and pet.

Jack Russell Terrier

This breed originated as the result of many people deciding that the modern form of Fox Terrier had become far removed from the original English Terriers, and was a somewhat artificial animal bred solely for show purposes. They decided that a smaller, shorter-legged dog was more elemental, and proceeded to develop a Terrier along these lines. Considerable controversy resulted, and a number of unsuccessful attempts were made to persuade the Kennel Club in Britain to recognise the breed. These failed largely because of the number of different types that were being bred and sold as Jack Russell Terriers. The enormous popularity of these little dogs added to the problem, as they are not an obscure breed existing in small pockets in tiny numbers, but one of the most commonly seen breeds, not only in England, where they originated, but in many countries of the world.

They gain their name from a very famous Fox Terrier breeder, the Rev. John Russell, of Devonshire who had a great deal to do with the early development of the Fox Terrier. A model of one of his dogs is to be seen in the headquarters of the Kennel Club in London. A club has now been formed, and there is little doubt that when the breed has settled down it will achieve recognition. He is one of the spunkiest little dogs in the world, with tremendous spirit, a great hunter and one of the most persistent chasers of small game in the whole canine race.

Kangaroo Hound

In the early days, and indeed until quite recently the kangaroo was recognised as a pest in Australia, and its numbers needed to be reduced. Both the kangaroo and the wallaby are now however protected as part of Australia's policy of conservation, and the need to hunt them is reduced. For hunting, the Greyhound proved insufficiently tough, and a Greyhound/Deerhound cross was evolved which, by selection, has produced a very large and extremely tough running dog that can both catch and hold a kangaroo.

Although the need for such a dog has now ceased to exist, there are still some remote stations where he will be found. He is not shown, and is unknown outside his own country, and is probably now a dying breed.

Kerry Beagle

This hound, once fairly popular in Southern Ireland, but now limited to one pack, and a small number of individual animals, is one of the most attractive of the smaller hunting dogs. His history is obscure, but he is probably an offshoot of a much larger hound used at one time for deer hunting. The Scarteen pack was composed entirely of this type of hound in the second half of the 19th century and specimens can still be found in that part of the country. Though smaller than he was, he is still a much larger dog than the Beagle.

He is a dashing, close-coated hound, deeper in the muzzle and longer in the ears than the Foxhound, and is now mostly black and tan in colour. He is strong, melodious and spirited, and though essentially a pack hound, he obviously makes a reasonable companion, as specimens are still to be seen in that part of Ireland known as the Ring of Kerry. He is a handsome hound, with something of the French hounds about him, but the colour of the Swedish Hamiltonstövare. He is quiet and affectionate, and though he has the innate wilfulness of most of the pack-hunting hounds, he makes a friendly house pet.

Laika

The Laikas are really a family of dogs rather than an individual breed. Primarily a sporting dog he has been used for a number of purposes including herding and draught work. The members of the family were bird dogs and the name comes from the habit of giving tongue in the chase. The smallest is the one that comes from that area of Russia nearest to Finland, and is related to the Finnish Spitz. The European type is larger and stronger, is black, grey or fawn, but still a typical Spitz dog. The type that comes from Eastern Siberia is larger still, and tends to resemble the oriental breeds, but because of its weight and strength is used for sleigh work as well as sport. The dog that comes from the north of Russia varies considerably, but tends towards the Samoyed rather than to any other well-known breed. He is an intelligent dog, easily trained and used for military and guard duties. It was a Laika which was first used in Russian space experiments.

Lurcher

This breed, or really crossbreed, has been known of for centuries. It is the breed of the Romanies or Tinkers of Ireland, and has been produced by crossing the Greyhound with the Collie to produce a running hunting dog with particular characteristics. His history has been passed on by word of mouth from generation to generation of these wandering people. He has been produced for the purpose of poaching, and will run down rabbit or hare silently so as not to give away his presence, and will return to his master, game in mouth, as he is one of the best of retrievers.

He is trained to avoid humans whilst hunting, and will disappear from the scene if a stranger shows, only to continue the hunt when he has gone. If, on return to his owner, with or without game, a stranger is in conversation with him, the dog will remain hidden until the stranger disappears, even if they have moved a considerable distance. He is a tall dog, often rough-coated, and usually fawn or grey in colour, and is very quiet and affectionate. Attempts are now being made by a small number of enthusiasts to stabilise the breed and fix a type.

Macellaio Herding Dog (Cane di Macellaio)

This is a small to medium-sized herding dog peculiar to Sicily and differing from his Italian neighbour in that he has a short coat. He is usually around twenty inches in height, with a strong head on the lines of a

Rottweiler and a massive body, with deep chest and strong loins. His tail is normally cropped fairly short and his ears cropped to a neat erect appearance. His coat is hard and short and he is either black and tan, black, or fawn in colour though brindles also occur. He is active, forceful but obedient, and makes an excellent guard.

North Eastern Sleigh Dog

This sledge-hauling dog is fairly widespread throughout the regions of Manchuria and the far North East of Siberia. He is clearly related to the other arctic dog used for this work, and in appearance looks very like a smaller version of the Eskimo Dog. He is fairly large, standing twenty-three inches at the shoulder with a massive head, strong muzzle and erect ears. He has a very powerful robust body and long well-muscled legs, and large strong feet. His coat is fairly long, thick and stand-off, and he has a thick soft dense undercoat which makes him virtually weatherproof. He exists in several colours and mixtures of colours, is sometimes all white or black, but commonly black and white. He is a tough hard-working sleigh dog.

Nova Scotia Duck Tolling Retriever

This strangely named dog from Canada is at present enjoying something of a revival. He is something like a light Golden Retriever. He originated in the *Maritimes* where he was developed as a house pet and gundog. He is characterised by a quiet and apparently disinterested attitude, until such time as he is asked to work, when he becomes the alert and active sporting dog.

His head resembles that of the Golden Retriever and he is well-boned down to strong webbed feet. His coat is fairly long, sleek and soft and with a dense soft waterproof undercoat. He is red or fawn, rather lighter than the Irish Setter and with some lighter shading. White blazes are not objected to, though efforts are being made to eliminate them. He is a quiet dog, and easy to train. He is a swimmer with outstanding endurance, as well as an excellent house dog and guard. He is not known outside his own country at present.

Owtscharka

The Russian herding dogs exist as a family group of four. They are partly herders and partly guards, as there are still predators in the USSR where the sheep graze. The Transcaucasian is a large and shaggy dog of over twenty-five inches, usually with a docked tail. He is found in various colours and is a vigorous protector of herds. The North Caucasian is smaller and has a shorter coat. The Mid-Asiatic version is a big strong and rather coarser dog, with a strong coat of medium length and of any colour except self-black. The Owtscharka of Southern Russia is a smaller dog,

only around twenty inches, with some resemblance to the Gos d'Atura.

None of them is known outside Russia though there was an attempt to introduce them into Germany in the mid 1930s. The smaller southern variety has an attractive coat which repays grooming, and if any of the family are to make an impression on the Western show world, it could be this smaller variety. They are all said to be intelligent and to have a good temperament, and the variety from Southern Russia is said to be easily trained.

Rampur Hound

At the turn of the century a number of hounds were brought from North West India to Britain, and some were exhibited at Dublin. They were large, rather clumsy looking running dogs employed principally for hunting jackal, and were either mouse-grey or black. He has a roman nose and yellow eyes and his tail is carried slightly curled up at the end, in the fashion of many of the eastern running dogs. He is said to have been bred to withstand the hard ground better than the English Greyhound. He is of uncertain temper, being inclined to bite without warning, though friendly enough with those that he knows. There has been little record of this dog in recent years.

Rumanian Sheepdog

This is an indigenous breed of herding dog still found in Rumania, though not in large numbers. In the early years of this century there were a number of herding dogs in the country though there was no settled type. Since that time there has undoubtedly been some crossing with other sheep-herding dogs, such as the German Shepherd Dog.

He is a large, heavy, strong dog, and a very enthusiastic guard of both the herd and herders' encampment. He is by nature suspicious and curious, and does not take kindly to strangers. Herders need a dog that is easily distinguished from the wolf, and this breed is so by his colour which is usually pied or brown.

Russian Hound

Three types of hound are recognised in Russia, the Estonian Hound, the Russian Hound and the Black-and-fawn Russian Hound. Since the days of the revolution many of the distinctive hounds of Russia such as the Gontschaga Sobaka which were kept in large packs by the Czar and the Grand Dukes have disappeared and no longer exist as separate breeds. The Estonian Hound is a medium sized twenty inch dog which is very fast and is mostly black with some fawn markings. The Russian Hound is a larger version up to twenty-five inches and is red or grizzle and white. This dog is used for the hunting of hare, fox, and badger and usually hunts singly.

The Black-and-fawn Russian Hound is again one of the larger types, about the same size as the Russian Hound proper, but is always black and fawn in colour. He is sometimes known as the Drab Yellow version, and has been recognised as a separate breed for the past fifty years. All of them are good hunters, and none of them is known outside its own country.

Smoushond

This little hard-coated dog varies little from the Terriers of Britain, being about the size and weight of a Fox Terrier, and having the same sort of temperament. He is by tradition the stable-yard dog of the Dutch farm, and is much more the working dog than a house pet. The Dutch Smoushond Club which was founded in 1905, drew up a standard of points, which was based to some extent on the older form known as the Smous-bart, and ensured the preservation of the breed. The standard lays emphasis on the rough and hard quality of the coat, with its strong and often black beard, moustaches and eyebrows, and it is from these qualities that the name of the breed originates. He is a guard dog and vermin killer, being hardy and extremely quick in reaction. He is a lively companion, and a keen guard. Although they are certain of being preserved in their own country, they have rarely been seen outside Holland.

Staghound

As a separate breed the Staghound has probably now ceased to exist, but as the hunting of the stag still takes place, even though with packs of large Foxhounds, it is worth recalling that the breed did have a part to play in the sporting life of the country gentleman in quite recent years. There was an old line of Staghounds in the Royal kennels at Windsor in the early part of the 19th century, described as large thirty inch dogs mostly white in colour. The whole pack was purchased and transported to France, where they undoubtedly played a part in the production of the many varieties of large hounds now in existence in that country.

He was a very tall strong hound, fast and persistent, and had so selective a nose that he was capable of tracking one individual deer through a herd. He hunted as a pack, and had all the friendliness of the pack-hunting dogs.

Stumpy-tailed Cattle Dog

This breed still exists as a separate breed in Australia though its numbers are small. They descended from the same line as the Cattle Dog, being produced from a cross between the Smithfield Collie and the Dingo, and were a tail-less offshoot from that breeding. The originated with a drover named Timmins and became known as Timmins' Biters and occurred as both red and blue or blue mottled dogs. The bob tail became fixed by selective breeding and is natural. He looks very like the Cattle Dog, apart from the fact that he is squarer. He has great courage, is very loyal, and an invaluable worker. There are few breeders in Australia at present and the survival of the breed is largely due to the efforts of Mrs Heale of Brisbane.

Tahl-Tan Bear Dog

This breed of hunting dog was originally used by the Tahl-Tan Indians of Canada. To them he was a personal dog having become by centuries of breeding part of their tribal heritage. It was the custom of the Indians to make an annual hunting excursion into the hills and on these occasions the Bear Dog was an invaluable help in feeding the tribe. In hunting the bear the dogs cornered him and kept him busy, whilst the hunter approached virtually unnoticed and dispatched him. The decline in the demand for bearskin led to a reduction in the numbers of the Tahl-Tan Dog, and there was danger of extinction.

The breed was recognised by the Canadian Kennel Club in 1941. He is a surprisingly small dog for one used on such ferocious game as the bear, standing only up to sixteen inches at the shoulder. He is, however, remarkably agile and alert, darting in and nipping the quarry and getting out of the way before the bear can retaliate. He is usually patched in grey or black and white, and has a mostly black head. His expression is foxy with erect ears. He has a short to medium coat with a distinctive tail, usually black with a white tip, is extremely thick and carried erect. He is unknown outside his own country.

Tasy

This breed, also known as the Mid-Asiatic Greyhound is another of the Russian running dogs. He is rather like the coursing Greyhound though less graceful in build. The breed is an ancient one but in more recent times has been crossed with the Chortaj and has probably had an influx of western Greyhound blood as well. He is strong and fast and is used for hunting hare, small deer, and even wolves. He is independent in temperament and has great stamina. Another variety known as the Tajgan exists locally, but is not recognised as a separate breed. He is unknown outside Russia.

Tenerife Dog

The Bichons are a small family of tiny pet dogs which began life as descendants of the Barbet and the Water Dog. It is probable that the Bichon Frise is descended in a direct line from the Tenerife Dog, in fact it could well be the same dog. The breed first made its appearance in France in the 16th century, and became very popular as the toy dog of the courts of France, Italy and Spain.

The other forms that exist, the Havanese and the

Bolognese, may have had a little to do with the ancestry of the modern Bichon Frise, though the fourth member of the family, the Maltese is rather different. In earlier times the Havanese was frequently brown, which leaves the Bolognese and the Tenerife as possible contenders. In 1933 the standard of the Bichon was adopted in France under two names, but later the name Bichon Frise was adopted.

Trailhound

The pedigrees of this dog are carefully controlled by its own association, and in that respect it is a pedigree dog. The normal form of hunting with horses and packs of hounds, is not suitable in the country towards the western side of Cumberland, and the local farmers have developed a sport of their own racing fast scent hunting hounds against one another over a man-laid trail.

The trail layers race over a measured course up into the hills and by a round-about route back to the start. They lay a trail by dragging along a small container loaded with a liquid, usually aniseed, and at a given signal the hounds are loosed to race over the trail. He is a hound of the Foxhound type, but over the years by judicious introduction of other blood, a very fast long-legged running dog has been evolved. He is a handsome friendly dog that spends his days with the family, and at the same time intelligent and lively.

Working Sheepdog

These dogs are known throughout the world for their remarkable ability to herd sheep, and to be trained to a phenomenal degree of expertise in competition work, as well as for normal work around the farm. This has been largely due to the efforts of the International Sheepdog Society which has kept a register of the finest working bloodlines. They are of no particular breed, and vary considerably in type, but must be included in this book as their omission would pander to the idea that only national kennel authorities keep records and pedigrees. Special demonstrations by these dogs, held in London, have attracted as many as 150,000 spectators in one day, and the famous Longshaw trials have been held since 1894. The interest in sheepdog trials has spread and international championships are held annually.

The dogs used are collies, but not the collie of the show bench. They are frequently black and white, and from them has sprung the breed which is now fixed and recognised in many countries as the Border Collie, but other colours are found. There is in fact no restriction as to type, colour size, or indeed any other characteristic, placed on entry into the stud book of the ISDS, whose records are based purely on working ability.

GROUP B

Not recognised in their native country.

There are a great many breeds of dogs which exist, or which were known to exist until recently, about which information is restricted. Some are bred for very special purposes and whilst records are kept, these are used specifically for the preservation of the best bloodlines for that purpose and are not generally available. Others, whilst existing as separate breeds, do so in remote areas where records are not kept, and the type is preserved purely as a matter of preference and largely by chance. These latter are listed below in alphabetical order.

Austrian Pinschner. (Medium-sized terrier.) *Austria.*
Abyssinian Sand Terrier. (Small companion and hunting dog.) *Africa.*
Baganda Hunting Dog. (Medium-sized hunting dog.) *Africa.*
Bagirmi Dog. (Medium-sized watchdog.) *Africa.*
Bantu Dog. (Small hunting dog.) *Africa.*
Batak Spitz. (Medium-sized hunting and watchdog.) *Africa.*
Brazilian Greyhound. (Large coursing dog.) *Brazil.*
Cameroons Dog. (Medium-sized hunting dog.) *Africa.*
Chinese Greyhound. (Large and small coursing dog.) *China.*

Congo Pygmies' Bush Dog. (Medium-sized hunting dog.) *Africa.*
Dingo. (Wild dog.) *Australia.*
East African Dog. (Medium-sized hunting dog.) *Africa.*
Fila da Terceiro. (Medium-sized guard dog.) *Portugal.*
Greek Herder. (Medium-sized herding dog.) *Greece.*
Hutespitz. (Medium-sized sheepdog.) *Germany.*
Javanese Dingo. (Medium-sized native dog.) *Indonesia.*
Kabyle Dog. (Large guard and herding dog.) *Africa.*
Kaffir Dog. (Spitz type.) *Africa.*
Koikerhond. (Small spaniel.) *Holland.*
Kuri Dog. (Small guard dog.) *Africa.*
Labrit. (Medium-sized sheepdog.) *South of France.*
Liberian Dog. (Small terrier.) *West Africa.*
New Ireland Dog. (Medium-sized guard.) *New Guinea.*
Pachon de Vitoria. (Medium-sized gundog.) *Spain.*
Papuan Dog. (Small tribal dog.) *New Guinea.*
Poligar Hound. (Large coursing hound.) *India.*
Plott Hound. (Medium-sized hunting dog.) *United States.*
Pocket Beagle. (Very small beagle.) *United States/Britain.*

Pommerscher Hutehund. (Medium-sized sheepdog.) *Germany.*
Redbone Hound. (Medium-sized hunting dog.) *United States.*
Sealydale Terrier. (Large short-legged terrier.) *Africa.*
South Russian Greyhound. (Large coursing dog.) *Russia.*
Steenbrak. (Small farm dog.) *Holland.*
Tajgan (Variety of greyhound.) *Russia.*

Treeing Walker Hound. (Medium-sized hunting dog.) *United States.*
Trigg Hound. (Medium-sized hunting dog.) *United States.*
Walker Hound. (Medium-sized hunting dog.) *United States.*
Zanzibar Dog. (Medium-sized hunting dog.) *East Africa.*
Zulu Dog. (Small hunting and guard dog.) *Africa.*

PART FOUR:
Old and Extinct Breeds

There are many breeds of dogs which at one time enjoyed a certain popularity but which have now ceased to exist. Some of them disappeared because there was no longer any need for their retention as their use vanished as civilisation advanced. Others changed type as they were absorbed as other breeds were evolved, so that their ancestral form has disappeared, and with it the name. One or two have unfortunately become extinct in fairly recent years as fashion dictated changes with little thought for conservation. It is, however, important that their names at least should be preserved.

Alaunt. (Ancient mastiff.) *Britain.*
Albanian Wolfhound. (Large hunting dog.) *Greece.*
Ban Dog. (Ancient guard dog.) *Britain.*
Barukhzy Hound. (Early form of Afghan Hound.) *India.*
Black Spaniel. (Ancestral spaniel type.) *Britain.*
Blue Paul. (Ancient smooth terrier.) *Scotland.*
Blue and Tan Manchester Terrier. (Small terrier.) *England.*
Bruno. (Heavy hound.) *Switzerland.*
Carlin à Poil Longue. (Long-haired Pug.) *France.*
Charnique. (Large coursing dog.) *Spain.*
Clydesdale Terrier. (Medium terrier.) *Scotland.*
Congo Terrier. (Small hunting dog.) *Africa.*
Cowley Terrier. (Small terrier.) *England.*
Elterwater Terrier. (Small terrier.) *England.*
English Water Spaniel. (Medium spaniel.) *England.*
Epagneul Ecossais. (Small setter.) *France.*
Fox Collie. (Medium-sized sheepdog.) *Scotland.*
Hare Indian Dog. (Sledge dog.) *Canada.*
Indian Tailless Dog. (Medium companion dog.) *India.*
Kirghiz Greyhound. (Large coursing dog.) *Southern Siberia.*
Lancashire Heeler. (Small herding dog.) *England.*

Mackenzie River Dog. (Sledge dog.) *Canada.*
Manilla Spaniel. (Small toydog.) *Philippines.*
Medelan. (Bear-hunting dog.) *Russia.*
Mongolian Dog. (Small pet dog.) *France.*
Norfolk Retriever. (Medium retriever.) *England.*
Norman Hound. (Large hunting dog.) *France.*
Old Braque. (Large pointer.) *France.*
Old English White Terrier. (Small terrier.) *England.*
Persian Greyhound. (Ancestor of the Saluki.) *Persia.*
Phu Quoc Dog. (Guard dog.) *Indo-China.*
Pittenweem Terrier. (Small terrier.) *Scotland.*
Polish Water Dog. (Medium gundog.) *Poland.*
Potsdam Greyhound. (Small coursing dog.) *Italy.*
Roseneath Terrier. (Small terrier.) *Scotland.*
Rough Beagle. (Small hunting dog.) *England.*
Russian Retriever. (Large gundog.) *Russia.*
Rough Pintsch. (Medium terrier.) *Germany.*
Seidenspitz. (Small toydog.) *Germany.*
Shropshire Terrier. (Ancestral terrier.) *England.*
Smithfield Collie. (Medium-sized herding dog.) *England.*
Snap Dog. (Ancestor of Whippet and terriers.) *England.*
Southern Hound. (Large hunting dog.) *England.*
Sudan Greyhound. (Small coursing dog.) *Sudan.*
Talbot. (Large hunting dog.) *Britain.*
Tie Dog. (Ancient Mastiff.) *Britain.*
Toy Bulldog. (Small companion dog.) *Britain.*
Toy Bull Terrier. (Small pet dog.) *Britain.*
Trawler Spaniel. (Miniature spaniel.) *England.*
Truffle Dog. (Rough variety of poodle.) *France.*
Ulmer Dog. (Early form of Great Dane.) *Germany.*
Welsh Hound. (Large hunting dog.) *Wales.*
Welsh Setter. (Medium black and tan setter.) *Wales.*
Wire-Haired Black and Tan Terrier. (Small terrier.) *England.*
Wurtemburg Pointer. (Large heavy gundog.) *Germany.*

INDEX

Page numbers in **bold type** refer to the main descriptions of breeds.